THE WORKS
OF
NATHANIEL LEE

Edited with Introduction and Notes

by

Thomas B. Stroup
and Arthur L. Cooke

Professors of English,
University of Kentucky

Volume II

The Scarecrow Press
New Brunswick, N.J.   1955

CONTENTS

The Plays:

Occasional Poems:

iii

THE.
MASSACRE
OF
PARIS:
A
TRAGEDY.

As it is Acted at the

Theatre Royal

BY THEIR

MAJESTIES SERVANTS.

Written by *Nat. Lee*, Gent.

LONDON,

Printed for *R. Bentley* and *M. Magnes* at the the Poſt-Houſe
in *Ruſſel-ſtreet* in *Covent-Garden.* 1690.

Introduction

I Date and Stage History:

THE MASSACRE OF PARIS existed in manuscript before 18 July, 1682, for it was upon that date that THE DUKE OF GUISE was suppressed, and the author himself said (Dedication to THE PRINCESS OF CLEVE) that he had taken two scenes from THE MASSACRE OF PARIS for THE DUKE OF GUISE. Moreover, we know the play at the time of its composition did not reach the stage, since Dryden says in THE VINDICATION OF THE DUKE OF GUISE[1] that he had heard of the play but had never seen it. He goes on to say that it was prohibited at the request of the French ambassador; and the Epilogue to the play, written as a Prologue by Tom D'Urfey for the 1789 production, suggests that the French ambassador desired the suppression in order to protect the French Catholics in London. On the other hand, the play could hardly have been written before 18 October, 1678, the date of Godfrey's murder. THE MASSACRE OF PARIS is a document in the story of the Popish Plot and Titus Oates. It belongs with the numerous pamphlets, appearing in England during the years 1678-79, which drew the obvious parallel between this Plot and the Massacre of St. Bartholomew's Day.[2] Hence it was perhaps written in the spring of 1679 at the very height of the excitement raging over the Plot and the possibility of massacre. The reference to the Habeas Corpus act in the Epilogue seems, as Van Lennep suggests, to be without significance in dating the play, since the act was passed in May, 1679, ten years before the Epilogue was written.

No French Ambassador in the year 1689, however, was likely to secure the prohibition of a Protestant play in England under William and Mary; so on 7 November, 1689, permission being given, the play was produced by the United Companies at Drury Lane before the Queen and her ladies of honor. The cast was extraordinarily fine, with Mr. and Mrs. Betterton, Mountfort, Kynaston, Mrs. Barry, and Mrs. Jordan; and there was much weeping at the performance.[3] In fact, it should be noted that Louis XIV's persecution of the Huguenots was at the time being condemned throughout England. Indeed, the play became the stock offering of the London stage in times of anti-Protestant unrest: after the uprising of the "Old Pretender" in 1715 there were at least two separate revivals, one at Drury Lane on 9 August, 1716, when it ran for three nights, and one at the same theatre on 30 October, 1716;[4] it was revived again upon the occasion of the Scottish uprising under Charles the "Young Pretender", this time at Covent Garden, November 31, 1645, when it ran for as many as three performances.[5] These were its last recorded productions, however, for the play was apparently too bloody, especially in the final scenes, for the refined audience of the Age of Enlightenment.[6]

II Sources:

Although Langbaine says that Lee drew upon "Thuanus, Davila, Lib. 5, Pierre Matthieu, or (as some say) Monliard his Continuation of De Serres, Mezeray and other Historians in the Reign of Charles the IX," the basic source of his plot is Davila's HISTORIA DELLE GUERRE DI FRANCIA, translated by Cotterell and Aylesbury, 1647, reprinted in 1678. Professor Van Lennep has effectively shown how fully and in how much detail Lee depended upon this source.[7] Indeed, the play is a rather effective dramatization of this account of the Massacre of St. Bartholomew's day with little added to the plot from elsewhere. The love story of Guise and Marguerite, merely suggested by Davila, is developed effectively by Lee; and the clash between the Admiral and Guise in Act IV, not in Davila but derived in some measure from Bacon, is handled with excellent dramatic point. Outside of these two parts, the rest is almost wholly taken from Davila. Geiersbach's effort to show a relationship between Marlowe's MASSA-CRE OF PARIS and Lee's play seems futile.[8] As Van Lennep points out, it is quite unlikely that Lee ever saw Marlowe's play, since it was printed only once before Lee's time, and was not performed at all during the Restoration. Aside from two similarities, probably due to their common sources (namely, the impli-cation that the Queen Mother poisoned Charles to make way for Anjou and that she forced Charles against his better judgment to consent to the massacre), two tragedies dealing with the same material could hardly be more dissimilar.[9]

Some indication of Lee's heavy reliance upon his main source may be noted in the details. The idea of comparing Coligny to Cato Uticensis (Act II, sc. i, 118) is from Davila; the digression in Act III on how Ligneroles, favorite of An-jou, lost his life because he could not keep a secret is out of Davila; the details of how "Maurevell" shot the Admiral, taking off the forefinger of his right hand and wounding his left elbow, are from Davila; and the account of the Massacre itself follows exactly Davila's account. Even the spelling of the names in the Cotterell-Aylesbury translation is usually followed.

Bacon's essays, as mentioned, were perhaps the most important secondary source. William Oldys noted on his copy of Langbaine that Lee in this play had found Bacon's essays useful, especially in Act IV, ii, wherein the Admiral and the Duke of Guise come to their break.[10] Here Lee cleverly builds his dialogue out of Bacon's "Of the True Greatness of Kingdomes and Estates." And Pro-fessor Van Lennep shows that, out of the last thirty-two lines of this scene, some twenty-three derive from the essay. Similarly the King's last speech beginning, "The Angel's Words are true,..." derives from Bacon's "Of Unity in Religion;" and the Cardinal's cynical speeches on love in the opening scene of the play are paraphrased from Bacon's "Of Love". In this more than in any other of his plays Lee found use for his reading in Bacon. Aside from his debt to Davila and Bacon, however, Lee owed little to others for THE MASSACRE OF PARIS.

III Criticism:

The first of the critics of Lee, Langbaine, has given perhaps the best evalu-ation, assuredly the one most frequently heard and the one most generally agreed to, with regard to THE MASSACRE OF PARIS; for to him it "is written in a more simple and natural style than the generality of Lee's plays." The latest of the critics, Professor Van Lennep, only states this position more fully: "Of all the plays of Nathaniel Lee, THE MASSACRE OF PARIS most faithfully follows fact....the result is the swiftest moving and simplest of Lee's many plots. The scenes are packed with action."[11] He goes on to say that there are only a few long rhetorical passages and that the dialogue is unusually terse and animated.

Between these two, the criticism has varied relatively little. In his notes to Langbaine, Oldys suggested that the play did not hold the stage longer at its latest production because of the horror of the ending,[12] and THE BIOGRAPHIA DRAMATICA (1812) echoes his objection:

It has been truly observed, that without some interesting private story, the subject is too shocking for an audience. Mercier, in his BISHOP OF LI-SIEUX, has hit upon exactly the method to give it effect. He supposes a Protestant family protected by a Catholic Bishop, who risks his situation and his life for their succour; in consequence of which the soldiery revolt

from their inexorable duty, and a stop is put to the ravages of Charles IX.
and his profligate court. [13]

The comment here is most interesting in the light it throws upon the sentimental -- the need for the "private" or domestic subplot to appeal to the audience
of the early nineteenth century and the feeling of revulsion at the shocking bloodshed toward the end. A. W. Ward echoes Langbaine: "It is less disfigured by
rant than the generality of his plays, though this element is by no means absent;
and the action is both perspicuous in its management and spirited in its conduct."[14] He observes also that the "amorous intrigue" rather heightens the effect of the main plot than absorbs the whole interest. Roswell Ham says that the
play derived its immediate inspiration from Bishop Burnet's RELATION OF THE
BARBAROUS AND BLOODY MASSACRE (1678), a document calculated to point
the parallel between the events of this year and those of the massacre of St. Bartholomew's Day. Thus the play, in which the parallel between the events of the
year and those of the persecution of the Huguenots becomes more pointed, was
unwelcome to the London stage. Ham insists that it is a frenzied piece, lurid in
its presentation of the horrors of the massacre. Elwin considers it one of Lee's
weakest plays; [15] at the same time he thinks it derives from Marlowe's MASSA-
CRE OF PARIS. Such remarks seem to indicate a lack of familiarity with the
work and with the criticism.

Obviously, one must regard the play theatrically as among Lee's most lurid
and exciting; yet the sharp, rant-shorn dialogue and swift-moving plot distinguish
it among his plays. The quarrel between the Guise and the Admiral in Act IV,
scene ii, an episode which is not found in the source, is done with a skillful hand.
It is tense, effective drama. So is the opening scene, wherein the love of Guise
and Margaret is presented and the conflict within Guise between his love and his
ambition. In addition, the characters are more complex and convincing than most
of Lee's. Marguerite and the Queen Mother (though the latter is a Machiavellian
monster) are effectively done; and the King is a strange combination of weakness
and treachery. The Admiral, like Lucius Junius Brutus in his strength, is noble
without being priggish; his martyrdom is convincing. The revenge theme, the
excessive bloodshed at the end, the use of portents, the extreme cruelty of Lorrain, the Guise, and the Queen Mother, the intrigue and plotting -- all these remind one of the bloody revenge plays of the Jacobean period. Indeed, one must
conclude that Lee consciously followed the revenge-play tradition. The rather
direct, sharpened dialogue and swiftness of movement, the interesting and complex characters, and the abundance of action make it a surprisingly effective play
for the stage.

IV Text:
    Editions Compared:

Q_1	R. Bentley and M. Magnes,	1690
C_1	R. Wellington,	1713
C_2	M. P. & Sam. Chapman,	1722
C_3	W. Feales ...,	1734

As copy-text for this edition Q_1, 1690, [16] has been followed. Five copies
of this edition have been fully compared in order to determine possible corrections made while the book was being printed. Two are the copies in the University of Kentucky Library and three are copies in the Folger Shakespeare Library.
Variants among these are recorded in the footnotes to the text of this edition, the

copies being designated as follows: Q_1(KU 1), Q_1(KU 2), Q_1(DFo 1), Q_1(DFo 2), Q_1(DFo 3). [17]

The first and only known quarto of THE MASSACRE OF PARIS is dated 1690. The edition has the following collation:

4°; A2, B-H4; 30 leaves, pp. [4], 1-52, [4].

A1^r: title-page; A1^v: blank; A2^r: PROLOGUE; A2^v: Personae Dramatis SCENE PARIS.;B1^r: head-title THE / MASSACRE / OF / PARIS. / [rule] / ACT I. SCENE I. / [rule] / and text; B1^v-H2^v: text. Running title: The Massacre of PARIS.; H3^r-H3^v: EPILOGUE; H4^r-H4^v: A Catalogue of some Plays Printed for R. Bently and M. Magnes. (running title on H4^v: A Catalogue of Plays).

A comparison of five copies of this edition does not show that any corrections were made while it was going through the press. On G1^r(KU 1) a part of a line apparently failed to ink, so that we have the reading "Gun we" rather than "Gun went off!"; other copies read correctly. There are other similar instances of type slipping or failing to ink, [18] but no evidence of author's or compositor's corrections. In general, the quarto was carelessly printed. Numbers of obvious errors in the divisions of lines occur which have been corrected in later editions; spellings of names are irregular; the Dramatis Personae is far from complete; places for most scenes are not indicated; no letter of dedication appears; instances of very corrupt readings occur; and the staging of the last scene is not at all clear. Seemingly the play was printed from a theatre copy which was hurriedly and carelessly prepared for the printer perhaps by the author. Good evidence for this may be noted in the prompter's direction given on C1^v (Act II, Scene ii, line 55), as well as in the unusual number of directions for stage action. If Lee did prepare the copy for the press, it is rather difficult to believe that he saw it through the press: entirely too many errors appear in the finished product.

The later editions of the play make some corrections, though by no means all that are necessary to clear reading. Most of these involve only accidentals, corrections of line divisions, and an occasional rationalization. The readings of these later editions have been adopted by the present editors only when they are corrections of obvious errors in Q_1, in which case the reading of Q_1 is invariably given in the note.

C_1 was printed from a partially corrected copy of Q_1. This copy was corrected either by the author (and there is good evidence in favor of his correction) or by someone else who knew well the connection between this play and THE DUKE OF GUISE. It is possible that Wellington in preparing his collected edition had access to a copy of the play partially corrected by the author, though the alterations made do not require the hand of an author. C_2 was unmistakably printed from C_1, and C_3 was reprinted, line for line, from C_2.

It is interesting to note that in 1790 ten passages, marked as separate scenes, were translated into French and published as SCÈNES SINGULIÈRES, EXTRAITES D'UNE TRAGEDIE ANGLAISE, INTITULÉE LA SAINT-BARTHÉLEMI, OU LE MASSACRE DE PARIS, Par Nathaniel Lee, in a collection entitled PIÈCES IN-TÉRRESANTES E PEU CONNUES, POUR SERVIS À L'HISTOIRE E À LA LIT-TERATURE, Tome Septieme, Bruxelles, 1790. In 1790 one might have expected that the passages chosen from this play would contain political implications, but such does not seem to be the case. Mostly the passages are love scenes.

PROLOGUE

By Mr. Mountfort.

This day we shew you the most Bloody rage
That ever did Religious Fiends engage,
A Reconcilement, with a Wedding-Feast,
While Murther was the Treat for every Guest,
Which well may prove to Ages yet to come,   5
The Faith of France, the Charity of Rome,
France by the most detestable Perjury,
Enslav'd its Subjects who by Laws were free.
No Sacrament can this Great Hero bind,
Oaths are weak Shackles for his mighty Mind,   10
And worse than Heathens does he persecute.
His Priests want Sense and Learning to dispute;
But weak Divines by strong Dragoons confute:
And who-e're doubts of any Priestly Maggot,
The Heretick Dog must be convinc'd by Faggot.   15
With Rome's Religion and French Government,
What Slave so abject as to be content?
Now, idle Malecontent, what is't you'd have?
Would you be an Idolater or Slave?
What d'you murmur for, because you're free,   20
And this bless'd Isle enjoys its Liberty?
Cross but the Narrow Seas, and you will find
Slavery and Superstition to your mind.
Take with you all your Friends that grumble too,
The Land will happily be rid of You;   25
Then all as one with our Great Prince combin'd,
And his Allies by Sacred Union joyn'd;
Will such false Bloody Tyrants oppose,
Till none shall dare to own the Name of Foes?

---

6 Rome C_{2+}.
7 detested C_{2+}.
29 Foes. C_{1+}.

DRAMATIS PERSONAE

King Charles IX.	Mr. Mountfort.	
Duke of Guise.	Mr. Williams.	
Cardinal of Lorrain.	Mr. Kynaston.	
Duke of Anjou.	Mr. Pruet.	
Alberto Gondi.	Mr. Harris.	5
Lignoroles.	Mr. Bowen.	
Admiral of France.	Mr. Betterton.	
Cavagnes.	Mr. Freeman.	
Langoiran.	Mr. Alexander.	
Queen Mother.	Mrs. Betterton.	10
Marguerite.	Mrs. Barry.	
Queen of Navarre.	Mrs. Knight.	
Antramont Wife to the Admiral.	Mrs. Jorden.	
Genius.	Mr. Bowman.	
Prince of Navarre.		15
Prince of Conde.		
Colombier.		
Morvele.		
Aumale.		
Elbeuf.		20
Angolesme.		
Provost de Marchand.		
Sartabons.		
Besnie.		
Colonel D'O.		25

Commanders in the Admiral's Party: Count de Rochfaucalt, Marquis de
    Renel, Piles, Pluvialt, Pardillan, Lavardin.
Soldiers, Servants, Attendants, Gentlemen, etc.

15-28 Colombier...Gentlemen, etc.] om. Q_{1+}.

Act I. Scene I.

The Duke of Guise, Cardinal of Lorrain, Marguerite.

GUI. Just from your Arms, by this great Guardian rais'd,
Call'd to the Council of a wary King,
On whom depends the Fortune of Lorrain,
O, Marguerite, yet to drag at this,
After such full possession thus to languish: 5
If this be not to love thee, say what is!
Cease then the rolling Torrent of thy Tears,
Which when I strive to climb the Hill of Honour,
Washes my hold away, and drives me down
Beneath Man's Scorn, into the vale of Ruine.   10
MAR. Hear, hear him, O you Powers, because I love him
Above my Life, beyond all joys on Earth,
He says I am his Ruine; to my Face,
With a Court Metaphor, he Vows he loaths me.
For all Men hate their Ruine; nay, 'tis true,   15
I find your Falshood; 'tis the trick of great ones,
Like Beasts of Strength, to prey upon the Weakest.
GUI. I swear----
MAR.   O, do not, dear, Ambitious Guise;
For Perjury so necessary seems
To great Men's Oaths, thou must of course be damn'd: 20
Yet as I am, thus plung'd in this dishonour,
Like a fall'n Angel roll'd through all my Hells,
I cannot hate thee, Guise, but sighing far,
Far from the shining Clime where I was born,
I beg those cruel Fates that hurl'd me down   25
To pity thee, and keep thee from my ruine:
For I'm so curs'd, that I do not wish my Foe,
Much less the Man I love above the World.
GUI. As I love thee, and O be Witnesses
My Brain and Soul, there's not an Artery   30
That runs through all the Body of thy Guise,
But beats where e're it pass Marguerite;
Yet this is nothing: haste away, my Lord;
Go tell the King and Council I am sick;
For I'le to Bed again, or on a Couch   35
Sit gazing in her beauteous Eyes all day,
And let the business of a grave World pass.
MAR. No more, my Lord; you shall, you shall to Council:
I see 'tis necessary; but I find
My Soul presages Mischief, if not Murder;   40

---

27 curs'd, I do C_{1+}.

For if you should prove false, Crowns, Kingdoms, Empires,
Worlds should not save poor Marguerite from the Grave.
Ah, Guise, ah venerable Lorrain, view me,
Behold me on the Earth, I swear I love
As never Woman lov'd; I'm all a Brand,   45
With, or without you, I am ne're at rest:
Farewel; this Fever of my furious passion
Burns me to Madness, yet I say, farewel.
    GUI. Farewel. Yet why farewel, when e're the Evening
I shall again rush to eternal Sweets,   50
This bosom of the Spring!   [Marguerite going out.
    MAR. returning. What, no endearments at so sad a parting!
Alas, perhaps I ne're shall see you more.
You bow'd, you kiss'd, but did not press my hand;
You shou'd, like me, have stagger'd when you left me,   55
And eat your Marguerite with your hungry Eyes;
But you are cold and pall'd, a lukewarm Lover,
Must to the business of the cursed State,
Which will not let you think of dying Marguerite,
Who to her last gasp will remember you.   60
But see, I rave again, my Fits return:
Yet pity me, for oh, I burn, I burn.   [Exit.
    CAR. I think I never heard so fierce a Passion:
She's all Convulsion, and she gazes on you,
As you would do on him that kill'd your Father.   65
What have you done, my Lord, to make her thus?
    GUI. Causes are endless for a Woman's loving.
Perhaps she has seen me break a Lance on Horse-back,
Or, as my Custom is, all over Arm'd,
Plunge in the Seine or Loire; and where 'tis swiftest   70
Plow too my point against the headlong Stream.
Tis certain, were my Soul of that soft make
Which some believe, she has Charms, my Heav'nly Uncle,
Beyond the Art and Wit of Cleopatra:
Such was not she stretch'd in her Golden Barge,   75
As Marguerite was last Night in Bed,
Who, as she mourn'd at my unkind delay,
Hung all the Chambers round with Black; her Bed,
Her Coverings, nay, her Sarsnet Sheets were Black----
    CAR. Fy, fy, my Lord.
    GUI.   And for the Weathers heat   80
Were roll'd beneath the beauties of her Breasts,
Which with a White, more pure than new-fall'n Snow,
Would sure have tempted Hermits from their Orgies,
To nod and smile a little at the wonder.
    CAR. Come, come, my Lord, you anger me indeed,   85
Not for the Sin, that's as the Conscience makes it;
I had rather you should Whore a thousand Women,
Than love but one, tho' in a lawful way:
Shew me through all Memorials of Great Men,

Except the Partner of the Roman Empire,   90
Drooping Antonius, and the fam'd Decemvir,
One that e're bow'd before this little Idol!
    GUI. First know your Man, before your Application:
I love, 'tis true; but most for my Ambition;
Therefore I thought to marry Marguerite;   95
But, oh, that Cassiopeia in the Chair,
The Regent Mother, and that Dog Anjou;
Cross Constellations blast my Plots e're born:
The King too frowns upon me; for last night,
Hearing a Ball was promis'd by the Queen,   100
I came to help the Show; when at the Door
The King, who stood himself the Centry, stopt me,
And ask'd me what I came for? I reply'd,
To serve his Majesty: He, sharp and short,
Retorted thus; He did not need my Service.   105
    CAR. 'Tis plain, you must resolve, my Lord, to quit her;
For I am charg'd to tell you, she's design'd
To be the Wife of Henry of Navarre.
'Tis the main Beam in all that Mighty Engin
Which now begins to move so dreadfully   110
Against the Heads of the Rebellious Faction.
    GUI. I have it, and methinks it looks like D'Alva,
I see the very motion of his Beard,
His opening Nostrils, and his dropping Lids;
I hear him Croak too, to the King and Queen,   115
In Biscays Bay, at Bayonne,
Fish for the Great fish; take no care for Frogs:
Cut off the Poppy-heads: lay the Winds fast,
And streight the Waves (the People) will be still.
    CAR. Then you will leave her!
    GUI.   Hurl her to the Sea!   120
The Air, the Earth, or Elemental fire,
So I may see Chastillon in the Net.
Oh that Whale-Admiral: might I but view him,
After his thousand Fetches, Plots, and Plunges,
Struck on those Scouring Shallows which await him,   125
Furies and Hell, and I, stand by to gall him;
Were Marguerite all one World of Pleasure,
I'de sell her, and my Soul, for such Revenge.
    CAR. Speak lower.
    GUI.   What, upon my Father's Death!
O glorious Guise, be calm upon thy Murder!   130
No; I will hollow my Revenge so loud,
That his great Ghost shall hear me up to Heav'n.
In height of Honours, oh, to fall so basely,

---

123 Whale, Admiral! C_{2+}.
132 to Heav'n, C_{2+}.

When Orleance was blockt up, and Conquest Crown'd thee,
By damn'd Poltrot so villainously slain,   135
Poltrot, by Beza, and this curs'd Admiral,
Set on with hopes of Infinite Rewards
Here and hereafter, so to blast thy Glory!
O, I could pull my bursting Eye-balls forth,
But that they may one day prove Basilisks   140
To that detested Head of all these Broils,
Then Tortures, Racks and Death shall close thy wound,
Kill him in Riots, Pride, and Lust of Pleasures,
That I may add Damnation to the rest,
And foil his Soul and Body both together.   145
    CAR. Behold your Brother, and the Duke Delbeuf,
Mercour too comes; this outrage will undo us.
    GUI. No, not at all; for 'tis in general terms.
O my good Lords, what if the Admiral
Stood here before you; should he scape our Justice?   150
I see by each man's laying of his hand
Upon his Sword, you vow the like Revenge:
For me, I wish that both mine may rot off. ---
    CAR. No more; away, my Lords: the King calls for you.
    GUI. I go. That Vermin may devour my limbs,   155
That I may dy like the late puling King
Under the Barber's hands, Imposthumes choak me,
If while alive I cease to chew his ruin,
To hang him in Effigie, nay to tread,
Drag, stamp, and grind him, after he is dead.   [Exeunt.   160

Scene II.

The Cabinet Council.

Table with Lights on it.   A Chamber beyond it.

Queen Mother, Anjou asleep.

    Q. M. O my Anjou, the Wheels of this New Ruin
Go wrong, for want of one that knows to drive;
He sits too light upon the whirling Throne,
And totters, with the dismal prospect, down:
Young Charles, a smart suspicious doubtful Boy,   5
But, Charles, you must be rul'd in this dark Road,
Or with the Lightning of my Fatal Power,
Which never cracks nor claps, I'le melt thee down,
For ever lost amongst the Mass of Things,
That thou, the Darling of my doating Soul,   10

The Prince of my Eternal thought, may'st mount
Like Nero, tho' at Agrippina's Ruin.
But see the King with the new Count of Rhetz:
Let us withdraw; it may be worth our hearing.

        Enter King with Alberto Gondi.

  KING. Alberto Gondi.
  ALB.   Sir!
  KING.   I think thou lov'st me.   15
  ALB. More than my life.
  KING.   That's much; yet I believe thee.
My Mother has the Judgment of the World,
And all things move by that; but my Alberto,
She has a cruel Wit, and, let me tell thee,
Thus to destroy the Souldiers of the Kingdom;   20
Famous as ever fought for Rome or Greece,
Under a shadow of a thousand Oaths;
'Tis Barbarous, Alberto, is it not?
And seems to me unworthy of a King.
  ALB. The Provocation, Sir.
  KING.   I know it well.   25
But if thoud'st have my heart within thy hand,
I swear, Conspiracies of that foul Nature
For ever blot the Memory of Kings.
What Honours, Interest, with the World to buy him,
Shall make a brave Man smile and do a Murder?   30
Therefore I hate the Treachery of Brutus,
I mean the latter so cry'd up in Story:
Whom none but Cowards and White-Liver'd-Knaves
Would dare commend, lagging behind his Fellows,
His Dagger in his Bosom, Stab'd his Father.   35
This is a Blot, the Ciceronian Stile
Could ne're wipe off, tho' the mistaken Man
(Mistaken in his Love, for Brutus scorn'd him)
Makes bold to call those Traytors Men Divine.
  ALB. Tully was Wise, but wanted Constancy.   40
  KING. He did, Alberto. Heark, but one thing more,
For much I love thee, and would fain unburden
My Soul of half her Cares on such a Man,
So good.
  ALB. My ever Dear and Honour'd Master.

---

11 Prince] C_{1+}; Price Q_1.
19 has a cruel] C_{1+}; has cruel Q_1.
35 his Bosom,] C_{1+}; his ----- Q_1. See THE DUKE OF GUISE, II, i, line 62
    where this passage was inserted by Lee.
37 the mistaken Man] C_{1+}; the Man Q_1. See THE DUKE OF GUISE, II, i,
    line 64.

KING. No more of that. I'le tell thee then: last night,   45
As I lay tossing in a Feverish Dream,
I call'd for Drink; when streight my Mother brought it;
But as she reach'd it to my trembling Lips,
Methought her Eyes roll'd gastly upon me,
A Palsey shook her hand; yet I resolv'd,   50
Took off the Draught, when streight a fainting seiz'd me,
My Eyes wept Blood, my Ears, my Nose and Mouth
Pour'd forth whole Streams, and all my Sweat was Blood,
My Hair and Nails dropt off as Autumn Leaves,
When Tempests rise, fall from the wither'd Trees: 55
But, oh, the Fancy seems so much unnatural,
I'll think no more on't; yet I thought to tell thee,
Because she is a Woman whom no Art
Nor Wisdom of the World can ever fathom.
    ALB. O my Gracious Lord,   60
Judge not the Queen by Dreams, and vain Chimaera's;
Remember, Sir, how often in your Nonage
She manag'd with her Wit the weight of Empire,
Contending with th' Effects of blind Religion,
The Contumacy of Rebellious Subjects,   65
The deep dissimulation of the Court,
The want of Treasure, baffling with her Prudence
The utmost strength Ambition rais'd to gain her.
    KING. O Count of Rhetz, thou lead'st me through the Garden
Of every Grace, but darest not point her Weeds: 70
Is she not of a most deceitful Soul;
Perfidious even to violating Vows?
Is she not greedy too of Human Blood?
A Wit so wasteful in destroying Lives,
That she will turn a City to a Wild?   75
    Q. M. Good Morrow, Sir! 'Tis just the time you order'd,
I think the second Watch; and we are met
To wait on your Decrees.
    KING.   O Mother, Mother,
You have imbark'd me in a Sea of Blood;
And sure so damnable an Enterprise   80
Was never form'd by Man.
    Q. M.   If, Sir, you fear it,
Why give it o're, and let the Admiral Reign,
Call in the Hugonots, and drive your Friends,
Banish your Blood, and the Establish'd Peers,
Forget the long Succession of your Fathers,   85
The Throne of Kings; forget the Laws, Religion,
Cut off the Noble Spirits from your Council;
And from the Dregs of this Heretical Faction
Compose a Bastard Cabinet-Election,

---

74 Wit so wasteful] C$_1$+; Wit wasteful Q$_1$.

Let Knaves in Shops prescribe you how to Sway,   90
They read your Acts, and with their hardned Thumbs
Erase them out, or with their stinking Breath
Proclaim aloud they like not this or that;
Then in a drove come lowing to the Louvre,
And say, they'l have it mended, that they will,   95
Or you shall be no King.
    KING.   'Tis true the People
Ne're know a Mean when once they get the Power.
    Q. M. Did you not late dispatch by Lodowick
Thus to the Admiral, with Vows of Honour,
That young Navarre should streight Espouse your Sister,   100
So to root up all Seeds of least Suspicion;
And that those Nuptials should be solemniz'd
At Paris, to be bound with deepest Oaths?
    KING. Yet, Madam, I must fear; for, should it fail,
We should be less than our worst Foes could wish us,   105
The Poultron Court, the Scorn, the laughing Stock
Of all the Christian and the Barbarous World.
    Q. M. No, Sir, you cannot fear the sure Design,
But you're in fear of those that are about you:
You fear ev'n Me; but I have liv'd too long,   110
Since my own Bowels, nay, my very Heart–Strings,
(For so I alwaies lov'd and priz'd my Children)
Dare not confide in her that gave 'em Being.
    KING. Stay, Madam, stay, come back, forgive my fears,
Forgive my sifting Soul her narrow Searches,   115
Where all our Thoughts should creep like deepest Streams;
For know, I hate the Haughty Admiral,
And all his curst Accomplices to Death.
    Q. M. What brings the Cardinal of Lorrain from Rome?
    KING. That the new Pope is fully satisfy'd;   120
I sent the Legate too that Diamond Ring,
With this close Motto writ within the Gold:
By this, my solid Zeal I own;
And Blood can never melt it down.
    ANJ. A murd'ring Sentence for the Hugonots.   125
    KING. And which so clear'd the matter, that the Pope
Order'd a Dispensation for the Marriage.

      Enter the Duke of Guise, Cardinal of Lorrain. *

    Q. M. Behold the Duke of Guise, and Cardinal:
'Twere fit you send his Eminence to Rochel,
T'acquaint the Admiral of a War with Spain,   130

---

91 and with their hardned] C_{1+}; with hardened Q_1.
92 Erase them out,] C_{2+}; 'Em out, Q_1-C_1.
 * Enter the Duke of Guise, Cardinal of Lorrain]; <u>om.</u> Q_{1+}.

And that the Plot we form'd for the Low–Countries
Against the Catholick King, should streight be acted.
    KING. O Mother, oh, what's this that rends my heart,
That rides my Nights, and clouds my Days with horror?
Is it not Conscience? which sometimes appears   135
Like a She Wolf, in Jane of Albert's Shape,
And drags me on the Floor; now in the form
Of that old Lyon Admiral, it comes,
And grins, and roars, just gaping to devour me.
    Q. M. Why, let him: when his Throat is cut we'll trust him: 140
Clear up this furrow'd Brow. Believe me, Sir,
You'l see him shortly where you need not fear him;
For, should he stay behind the Queen and Princes,
Doubting the Marriage, fill'd with boding fears,
The War with Spain will so bewitch his Glory,   145
And lull his proud Ambition, that should Fate,
Which awes him now, leap up more terrible,
He'll follow with a speed shall make him foremost,
And scorn a Grave.   O, tis a dreadful Image;
    KING.
Yet when his brains are pash'd I shall be still,   150
The Morning rises, yet I cannot rest;
Like those eternal Lamps that wink above;
Methinks, O Mother, I could watch for ever.
Once more let me conjure you, all be hush'd,
Be secret on this horrid Consultation,   155
As Urns and Monuments, that never blab.
    GUI. Therefore let's lye like Furies on the watch,
As if it were an ambush for the World.
    KING. With Claws lock'd in, like Lions, couch to tear 'em,
Our Mother, thou so fierce upon the slaughter,   160
Direct thy Brood; we will not stir nor breath:
But when thou giv'st the Word, then start away,
Rush from the Shade, and make 'em all our prey.   [Exeunt.

End of ACT I.

---

143 Princes,]; Princess Q_{1+}
150 dash'd C_{2+}

Act II. Scene I.*

Admiral, Cavagnes, Langoiran.

ADM. Your Reasons are to all appearance fair;
Like Eden's Fruit, the Tempter hangs 'em forth,
But there's a canker-Queen within the Core,
That eats Colignie's firmest hopes away:
Like Paradise, she paves my spacious walk;   5
But oh, Cavagnes and Langoiran, look,
Do you not find her lurking in the Flowers?
With soft indented glides behold she comes;
I see the forked Tongue betwixt her Teeth,
Hissing us from the Stage of Life and Honour: 10
O, she's a Serpent equal to the first,
And has the will to damn another World;
Therefore I'm positive, till I'm convinc'd
The King foregoes her Counsel, I'le not stir:
I'le not to Court.
CAV.   Thus far I can make good,   15
She is believ'd, through all the Courts of Europe,
A most transcendent Wit, and absolute Woman.
ADM. That is an absolute Murderer and Dissembler;
Who that proceeds on such black principles,
That thinks there is no God above Ambition,   20
But may accomplish all that he intends:
Where's then the Art, the Reach, the Policy
Of this transcendent and most absolute Woman!
Is it not easie to Assassinate,
To Lie, and Swear you love the Man you hate,   25
Train him into the dark, and murder him?
I urge again, unless the King resolve
To rule alone, I will not come to Court.
LANG. Cavagnes is a Master in Court Secrets;
For me, I ruin'd the bus'ness of the War.   30
ADM. Perswade me while the Queen is at his Ear,
That if he were made up of Worlds of Mercy,
He ever would forgive me! pray look back
Into the former times, and see who sow'd
Those glowing grains which shot up to a War,   35
Who blew the coals of Calvin's kindled Doctrine,
And earth'd the little Sect at Hugo's Gate;
Was it not I that form'd 'em to a Body?

---

* The second act apparently has its setting at Rochelle.
21 intends? C_{1+}.

LANG. Stick to your self, Sir; follow your own methods.

ADM. Who therefore, while the pangs of Rage were on her,   40
Proclaim'd me in all Languages a Traytor,
Drag'd my Effigies through the streets of Paris,
Hung up my Statue on the common Gallows,
Set, by Court Officers, my Goods to sale,
My Houses raz'd, or burnt 'em to the ground.   45

CAV. I must confess that start of open vengeance,
Not common to the Nature of the Queen.

ADM. And why all this, not for a private grudge?
I judg'd 'twas time to view the ghastly flaws
Of that Religion that would rend the World;   50
That sticks not at the slaughter of whole States,
Blowing up Senates, nor at murdering Kings:
Driv'n with this thought, I push'd the War yet farther;
And, though we lost the Fight at Moncontour,
Yet speak, Cavagnes, did I fail in ought?   55

CAV. I was not there.

ADM.   Then give me leave to say,
I fought my self the Protestant Cause alone,
When in the head of our remaining Horse,
I met the Elder Rhinegrave hand to hand,
Shot him i'th'Face, and left him on the ground;   60
Then seeing all our Army quite defeated,
My Jaw-bone shatter'd, and my Voice quite spent,
I fled, with hopes to rise more terrible;
As it succeeded, to the astonishment
Of all the Christian World.   65

        Enter Colombier with a paper in his hand.

COL. My Lord the Cardinal of Lorrain's arriv'd,
To swear and sign the Articles of Peace;
The Queen at present holds him in discourse;
Mean time Commends this Paper to your view
Sent to her Majesty from the King of France.   70

ADM. reads.
"Madam, as you demanded, you have power o're all the County
"suddenly of Armagnac; Tell the great Admiral I seek his
"Friendship. Ask of Lorrain the rest, who knows my heart.

Perhaps, my Friends, it may be thus indeed,
That, quite tir'd out with infinite Distractions,   75
He may at last resolve to Rule alone,

----

55 Following this line in Q₁ appears the stage direction:
            [Q. of Navarre, P. of Navarre, P. of Conde.
    Apparently this was intended as a prompter's note in the manuscript
    to prepare for the entrance of these characters following line 83.

Come from his Page-ship, and put off the Mother;
Not lose his Youth, the pleasure of his Bloom
Among grey Senators, and withering Councils:
If it were so; but hold, there's something here   80
Forbids that thought; it rises like a Vapor,
A strange misgiving, such as Women swoon at,
And Men themselves may fear. But see, the Queen.

    Enter the Queen of Navarre, Prince of Navarre,
            and Prince of Conde.

    Q. NAV. I come, Sir, to forestall the Cardinal,
Who from the King offers these terms of Peace: 85
He adds to what Count Lodowick brought before,
His Mothers Policy shall sway no longer;
That He'll submit his Genius to your conduct,
Confirms your being Captain General
In that most glorius Enterprize on Spain,   90
Allows you fifty for your Person's Guard;
Therefore, for sealing this Eternal Bond,
And for the former weighty Consultations,
He begs you instantly to come to Court.
    ADM. What has your Majesty resolv'd to do?   95
    Q. NAV. To go with both the Princes streight to Paris,
And see the Nuptials of my young Navarre.
I know not what your Lordship does intend;
But I have sent already to the King
My Answer by Byron, and will attend him.   100
    ADM. Then 'tis too late to think of going back;
You have lanch'd me now indeed, and I must plunge
In this Abiss, tho' it be deep as Hell.
No, Madam, spite of all the Augurs here,
Since you are thus resolv'd, I'le go the foremost.   105
'Twas for your sake, and in the Prince's cause,
For Liberty of Conscience and Religion,
That I thus long did propagate the War;
And shall I now not follow where you lead me?
    LANG. Why should you, if it goes against your mind?   110
    ADM. Peace, peace, Langoiran; since the Main's produc'd,
I mean, the Resolution of the Queen,
My Fate cries out, we must, we must away:
Therefore, my Friend, go gather my Dependants,
Bid 'em prepare for Paris. Tell my Wife,   115
My dearest Martia, we must bid farewell;
Tell her, I'm forc'd to swim against the Stream;
Say, that her Cato's bound for Utica,

---

  96 Q. NAV.] C_{1+}; Q. M. Q_1.
 105 go the foremost.] C_{1+}; go to the foremost. Q_1.

From whence perhaps he never shall return.

                 Enter Cardinal of Lorrain.

      CAR. Conquest, prosperity, and smooth success   120
Be ever strow'd before our General's feet.
Thus, Sir, the King salutes you, with Commission
To turn the Torrent of your Arms on Spain.
      ADM. My Lord, I glory in the great Employ.
I hear beside, the King will rule alone;   125
For, Sir, what e're the Wit of Women be,
From War and Councils let 'em be remov'd.
I say again, with my old bluntness, Sir,
To have a Female finger in the State,
Is blasting to the Prince's Memory.   130
Let him but be sincere, and leave the Mother,
Old as I am, I will put on my Arms,
And with this hand, not wither'd yet in War,
Bear to th' Escurial his Imperial Standard.
      CAR. My Lord, for the sincerity of the King,   135
That he intends his Dear and Great Chastillon,
The very words that did express his love,
All Honours, Titles, Greatness, all Advancement,
Nay, to the curbing of his Mother's Will,
For the performance of each Article,   140
Without a pious catch, or trick of State;
Without the smallest Mental Reservation,
Equivocation, or the least Reserve;
In the King's Name, as I am Priest profess'd,
As I am sent from Heav'n, to teach Salvation,   145
I pawn the truth of my immortal Soul.
      ADM. He then, to whom our hearts are free and open,
Be judge betwixt his Majesty and me.
      CAR. O Sir, O Madam, oh, you make me weep,
Viewing by this the frailty of the World;   150
For if the Mind of Man be so suspicious
On such clear Demonstration of Affection,
How can you e're believe the Love Divine?
      Q. NAV. My Lord, you may return with our obedience,
And tell the King, the Admiral, the Princes,   155
My self, and all his humble faithful Subjects,
Will haste to throw our Bodies at his feet.
      ADM. My Lord, farewell; I must not doubt your Oaths,
But with implicite Faith believe the King,
At whose Tribunal I must shortly kneel,   160
For Pardon and Forgiveness.   [Exeunt. *

Admiral returns with Cavagnes.

ADM. Hark, my Cavagnes, write to Count Lodowick,
The Seirs de Genlis, and La-Nove, to haste,
And suddenly to make surprise of Mons.
    CAV. My Lord ---
    ADM.   Nay, write I say; I'le have it done,   165
On my Parisian entrance. I'm resolv'd
To see into the heart of this young Charles,
And force him thus upon a War with Spain;
For tho' this Cardinal Swear, and damn his Soul
As deep as Heaven's high, yet if his bowels   170
Be like the rest of that Blood-colour'd Robe,
And laughs at Ghosts, where's then the Admiral?
Caught by this perjur'd jugling man of God!
What, for the Cabinet Murderers to play with,
To toss Chastillon's Fate from one to t'other,   175
And grin my Life and Honor from the World?
But now for Paris. Call Colombier,
The Count la Rochfaucalt, Marquis de Renel,
Piles, Pluvialt, Pardillan, and Lavardin,
Bandine, and all my Gallants of the War: 180
For Paris bid 'em haste.

Enter Antramont, with Langoiran.

ANT.   Stay, stay, My Lord;
I charge you stay, for Martia does Arrest you.
And saies, you shall not go to Utica:
Martia resolves to hinder this Self-Murder.
    ADM. Self-Murder, Martia!
    ANT.   Yes; you turn the Sword   185
Upon your self, which Charles and that false Queen
Brandish against you, going thus to Court
Against your will; for so you sent me word.
Is not this running it in your own Bowels?
Is it not, Cato? but you shall not leave me: 190
You're now Betroth'd; and in this sad Condition,
Thus fraught with your clear Image, like a Bark
Too Richly laden, with an over Ballast,
Leave me not Gaspar, to a flood of Tears,
A Sea of Passion, and a Storm of Sorrow.   195
    ADM. Beg me not, Martia; 'tis impossible
To stay me now, my Honour is engag'd,
My Word is past.
    ANT.   Yet stay, Sir, stay so long
So long at least, as may preserve your Likeness;
For if I yield you now to those Court-Murderers,   200
My boding Fears will blast it e're 'tis Born;
For sure as Caesar's Butchery was perform'd

At Rome, your Murder is contriv'd at Paris:
Calphurnia's bloody Dream, and Scent of Slaughter,
Are nothing, Sir, to my Prophetick Spirit;   205
Which not by Visions, Fantoms of the Night,
But by day Arguments, and certain Reason,
Will give such Evidence for your undoing,
As you, your self being Judge, shall say are true.
    ADM. O, Antramont, away; why dost thou thus   210
Unman me with thy Tears? Tho' certain Death,
With all the Dagger'd Council stood to wait me,
Ev'n in my view, I swear I would among 'em.
    ANT. Then you are caught indeed; they hate you, Sir:
Your Wife, with this poor Innocent unborn,   215
With all your other Orphans, are undone:
The Glory of the Earth is laid along.
I see the Vine that spreads his Arms to Heav'n,
With all his Clusters rotting on the ground,
Blasted with Lightning from a clouded Council,   220
By her that is the Juno of your Fate,
That Murd'ring Sorceress, that dry Hag of Florence,
That Midnight Hecate of ten thousand forms,
That varies with all Shapes, that tryes all Spirits,
Selling her Soul to each, and all together,   225
To make your Fate inevitable sure.
    ADM. Give me your hand, and take this farewel Kiss:
If thou would'st have me think thou lov'st old Gaspar,
Reply no more, but leave me, and be dumb.
    ANT. I'm all Obedience; let me speak but once,   230
And whisper't in your Ear: By all my hopes
Of Earth and Heav'n, you shall not dye alone;
I'll gather all the Branches of your Body,
The little Arms, the Sprouts of him that was:
Yes, with that precious Fardel, bound together   235
By Cords of Hair, Cemented with my Tears,
And wreath'd about till Death with my Embraces,
I'll follow you to Court: I will, my Lord;
And since you'l have it so, we'll burn together.   [Exit.

Enter Commanders. *

    ADM. O, my brave Friends? my dear la Rochfaucalt,   240
Your hand; and yours, my rough Colombier;
My Gallant Piles; and thine, my plain Langoiran:
But say, how stand you to this Expedition,
This new Exploit, this dangerous Court Adventure?
    LANG. My Lord, I'll answer for 'em; there's not one   245

---

226 inevitably C_{1+}.
   * Enter Commanders.] C_{1+}; Enter Commander. Q_1.

But has resolv'd to follow; tho' they had rather
Run the most violent Shock of Glorious War,
Than stand one Complemental Death at Court.
    ADM.   Then our Opinions jump. But to the purpose;
Since 'tis resolv'd that we must go to Paris,   250
Because you're Strangers to the King and Queen,
I would instruct you in the Royal Tempers,
Draw the Queen Mother's Face in Minature,
For there the watch and ward of all our Caution
Must lye, if possible to wave the Ruin.   255
      LANG.   Fore-warn'd, fore-arm'd; fear not, we shall remember.
    ADM.   Imagin then the King, like Adam laid
Among the Sweets of Paradise to rest,
While to his listning Soul this Second Eve,
Full of the Devil, and design'd to damn us,   260
Thus breathes her Counsels fatal to the World:
What ever Paths you trod before your Reign,
'Tis Blood and Terror must your Throne maintain:
Scorn then thy Slaves; nor to thy Vassals bow;
Fix the Gold Circle to thy bended Brow,   265
By Murders, Massacres; no matter how.
For Conscience, and Heav'ns Fear, Religion's Rules,
They're all State-Bells, to toll in pious Fools.   [Exeunt.

        End of A C T II.

Act III. Scene. I.

Enter Queen Mother, and Marguerite.

MAR. Is Guise then false! or do you try me, Madam,
And search my Heart, to know how much I love him?
If it be so, I will resolve you quickly;
I'll swear to you by Heav'n, by all things Sacred,
By all that's great and lovely upon Earth,   5
By him, by Guise, by all the blessed Moments
Of that dear Life, which single I prefer
To Millions of my own, I love him more
Than you love Glory, Vengeance, and Ambition.
    Q. M. Then thou art lost, a Wretch, an out-cast Fool,   10
Not worthy of my Care, nor worth my seeking;
For, by my best Desires, I know he scorns thee,
And to my certain Knowledge, is betroth'd
To Catharine Cleve, the Prince of Porcien's Widow.
    MAR. 'Tis false; he's not, he shall not, nor he cannot: 15
You hate me, Madam, and you forge this Matter,
To make me dye, to kill your Marguerite;
For, if you did respect me as your Blood,
Why should you tear my Heart in thousand pieces?
Why should you make me rave with Jealousie?   20
For, oh, I love beyond all former Passion:
Dye for him! that's too little; I could burn
Piece-Meal away, or bleed to Death by drops,
Be flead alive, then broke upon the Wheel,
Yet with a Smile endure it all for Guise: 25
And when let loose from Torments, all one wound,
Run with my mangled Arms, and crush him dead.
    Q. M. Farewel; thou'rt mad indeed: I'le find the King,
And send him to convince you of the Truth.
    MAR. The Truth! O Heav'n! nay, stay, and I'le believe you. 30
But is he false? is't possible in Nature?
Is Guise then, like his Kindred Savages,
True Man, an Upright, Bold, and Hearty Villain?
    Q. M. I tell thee, as I love thy Life and Honour,
Tho' much I fear, the latter is past hope,   35
Their Marriage will be solemniz'd to morrow;
The Cardinal of Lorrain must joyn their hands.
    MAR. What, he that keeps the Tye, the sacred Contract,
I'll warrant too he'll be a Witness for him.
Why then, for ever throw off Modesty,   40
If thus Religion cheats us: let us haste,
With Messalina, to the common Stews,
Where Bauds are honester than Roman Church-men.

Q. M. Think no more on't, but with a generous Fury
Resolve to cast him from your Soul for ever.   45
Prepare your self for what the King commands,
Without delay, to wed the young Navarre.
    MAR. To wed my Tomb, to dwell in dust below,
Where we shall see no more deceitful Men,
Hear no more flattery, nor no damning Vows;   50
Where I shall never start from my cold Bed,
Nor walk with folded Arms about the Room,
With Eyes, like Rivers, ever running down;
While with my over-watching, I mistake
The rustling Wind, and every little noise   55
For Guise's coming; which not finding true,
I weep again, till all my face is drown'd,
And groan, as if there were no end of sorrow.
    Q. M. Then I must find some other Instruments,
That have the power to rule you: So farewel.   [Exit.   60
    MAR. Stay, Madam, stay. She's gone, and leaves me here,
To do a mischief on my Life. False Guise!
Perfideous Guise! but I will find thee out,
And wreck the Miseries of my Soul upon thee;
Nay, I'le alarm that Priest that makes thee wicked: 65
Priests, that like Devils, laugh at humane pains,
And Souls ne're reckon, so they count their gains.   [Exit.

Scene II.

Palace.

Duke of Guise, and Cardinal of Lorrain.

GUI. But are you sure he'll come?
CAR.   Most certain, Sir.
    GUI. Why then, I will not eat till I behold him.
O, I could pine my self into a Ghost,
So I at last might thrust my hungry Sword
In the curs'd Carcass of this Admiral,   5
And glut my greedy Vengeance with his Heart.
    CAR. The Queen too of Navarre, the Heretick Princes,
Gentlemen and Commanders, Knights, Barons, Counts,
With all the Combination of the Rebels,
Come to the Wedding of the young Bearnois.   10
    GUI. Why, what an Oglio will the Devil have?
A Feast for Hell, to cram it to the mouth,

---

64 reek the Miseries C_{2+}.
 7 Princes,]; Princess, Q_{1+}.

A Massacre of Souls: methinks I see
The glutton Death gorg'd with devouring Lives,
And stretching o're the City his swoln bulk,   15
As he would vomit up the Dead.
     CAR.   My Lord,
How brooks your Heart the Marriage of Navarre?
     GUI. Why, faith, Sir, as we must necessity:
The King resolves it; urging to my face,
The Man that dar'd to contradict his pleasure   20
Should make that opposition with his ruine:
On this I turn'd my Court to Porcien's Widow.
But O, Lorrain, Love mourn'd at the mistake,
As conscious of the cruel change he made.
Take then the prospect of a Summers Morn,   25
The gaudy Heav'n all streak'd with dappled Fires,
And fleck'd with Blushes like a rising Bride,
With sweets so pour'd from such a lavish Spring,
That it must begger all the years to come:
From this bright view, from Marguerite's form,   30
Now turn thy Eye upon the yellow Autumn,
On Porcien's Wife, the Widow of the Seasons.
     CAR. You speak, methinks, as if you lov'd the Princess.
     GUI. How e're I bragg'd before, I do confess it;
Spite of my Glory, spite of my Ambition,   35
And all the vow'd resolves of my Revenge,
Had she not poorly yielded to the Marriage,
I would have turn'd my Widow to the Common:
But I am satisfy'd; 'tis now the talk
Of the whole Court, how she in secret likes it;   40
Hears too, no doubt, of my design on Cleve,
Yet (Curses on that changeable Stuff her Soul)
Regards it not. But see, she comes: a Tempest

          Enter Marguerite.

Ruffles her Face! the Mother taught this cunning;
And she has catch'd the Plague of that Dissembler   45
So right, methinks I see the tokens on her.
     MAR. Look in my Face.
     GUI.   I do.
     MAR.   Nay, in my Eyes.
     GUI. I view 'em as I would the setting Sun,
Were I to dye at Midnight.
     MAR.   Come, you dare not.
     GUI. What, dare not dye?
     MAR.   Thou dar'st not one, nor t'other: 50
At least thou shouldst not, for thou art so wicked,

_____

42 Stuff] C_{2+}; Staff Q_1-C_1.

So gone in Sin, Damnation must attend thee.
    GUI. Why, then the Devil is sure of one great Man.
    MAR. Of one! of all; at Court he's no Retailer,
But deals in Gross, and takes you by the Lump.   55
In Country-Fields he's forc'd to sit all day,
With patience, angling down the guiltless Stream,
Yet rarely catches one for all his labour;
But when he comes to Court, the Sea of Pleasures,
He throws his Drag Net in from side to side,   60
Where none of all the Fry escape Perdition:
There may you see Whales plunging in the Meash,
Disgorging streams, like Drunkards on the ground;
The Sword-Fish, like the Souldier, fast in hold;
The floundring Priests, like Sharks, that gape for prey;   65
Fat Porcpise Bauds, the Mermaids too of Honour,
The Minim Pages, all the twinkling Host
So fill'd, the Snare of Hell must crack to hold you.
    GUI. No, there's another Cause for this fine Satyr,
Too well digested for a sudden thought,   70
An Argument at home, there in your heart,
Tho' you have learnt discretion thus to turn it.
    MAR. O Heav'ns! what means he?
    GUI.   D'ye seem amaz'd?
I say again, however you upbraid me,
You bear the Guilt, who bring the Accusation: 75
Yes, Marguerite, thou hast plaid me foul.
Nay, do not start, nor gaze, nor make false steps:
Come, Princess, these are tricks too stale for Guise,
Shew 'em your little Creatures; bid your Mother
Fetch something quainter from the Schools of Florence,   80
Where she has learnt the Art of Honest-dealing.
    MAR. O, all ye Pow'rs of Heav'n, of Earth, and Hell,
Where would he, whither, and when will he end?
    GUI. Madam, I've done already; but lest you should
Forget coherence, through your world of Passion,   85
I tell you, you are false; your Vows, your Tears,
Your Languishings, your very height of Pleasures,
Your grasping Joys are false; for even then
When you cry out, There can be nothing farther,
By all your perjuries, you wish 'em more.   90
    MAR. Furies and Devils! shall he bear it thus!
What with his Lip! his Eye! his every Scorn,
Walk thus before me, and defy me thus!
Ah Guise! disloyal, faithless, perjur'd wretch!
Thou art more damn'd, than any Fiend in Hell.   95
Impostor!
    GUI.   Woman.

---

96 Impostor!] C_{1+}; Imposture! Q_1.

MAR.   Traytor.
GUI.   Woman.
MAR.   Villain.
GUI. Woman still.
MAR. Hark Guise, hear Monster, hear and mark me:
While to thy Conscious Soul I sound the Name
Of Porcien.
GUI.   Of Navarre.
MAR.   Porcien I swear.   100
GUI. Navarre, Navarre.
MAR. Thou ly'st, thou ly'st: Porcien, the Widow --- Porcien.
O, I could cut my face! what, for a Widow!
Leave me for Porcien! O thou dull, dull Guise!
Wilt thou sit down to the refuse of Meals!   105
A Widow! what, the Monument of Man;
The Tomb Grave-Vault, the very Damp of Nature!
For this, I hate thee more than e're I lov'd thee;
And from my presence banish thee for ever.
GUI. No; I will banish this detested Guise   110
My self; you shall not buy him to your presence:
For, know, I hate more perfectly than you;
Yours is a gust, a puff of Woman's Fury;
But mine a manly, constant, setled hate,
Which, ever since you made your better choice,   115
Of young Navarre, took root within my heart.
MAR. 'Tis false, 'tis false, a Treason fetch'd from Hell,
But where! speak out; where was this Lye invented?
GUI. Thus then in short, and so farewell for ever:
The King and Queen, with all particulars   120
Avow'd it to me; and in general
The Court. You may perceive the Choice,
I made of Cleve, was more to be reveng'd
Than want of Constancy: but your's was weigh'd;
Navarre has youth, and may be King of France,   125
Tickling Variety for Love and Glory,
For the false appetite of Luxurious Woman,
Woman, damn'd Woman; but I waste breath to name her.
My Lord Lorrain, I charge you by your Friendship
Give me the Contract.
MAR.   Hold, my Lord. --- For what?   130
GUI. That I may tear it to as many pieces
As she has done her Vows. What, faith in Women!
The very fragments of the whole Creation,
Whose sever'd Souls, like many parted Mirrors,
Reflect the face of all Mankind at once,   135
Who with their weeping Smiles, and laughing Tears,

---

102 Divided as follows, Q_{1+}:
    MAR. Thou ly'st, thou ly'st: Porcien, the Widow ---
Porcien.

Were they allow'd a Heav'n, as sure they are not,
Would tempt the Angels to a second Fall.
But I grow wild; give me the Contract, Sir:
Nay, Madam, off; I swear you must unhand me.   140
    MAR. I will not. O my heart! Ah Guise, Guise, Guise!
You have got the Conquest, and you shall maintain it,
Tho' at th' expence of Marguerite's death.
'Tis true, my Mother mention'd such a Marriage;
But if I did not loath it, scorn, detest it,   145
O, if this be not true as thou art false,
(Forgive me, for I meant to say unkind)
Banish poor Marguerite from those Eyes
That feed her life, let me no more approach you;
But take, O take this Ponyard from my hand,   150
And stick it in my heart, that heart that loves you,
That when 'tis injur'd dares not stand before you,
But owns you for the Tyrant of my days.
    GUI. No, Marguerite, no;
You've found the way to temper me indeed,   155
Nay, turn it upon me, who am a Traytor,
Because I dar'd to counterfeit a Falshood
Against such perfect Love, to seem t'affect
The hated Porcien.
    MAR.   Did you then dissemble?
Did you not love her in your Heart, indeed?   160
    GUI. I swear by Heav'n.
    MAR.   O let me then embrace you.
Yet closer. O that I could get within you!
    GUI. My Life!
    MAR.   My Soul!
    GUI.   My Heart!
    CAR. My Lord, the Duke of Anjou moves this way.
    GUI. Farewel. And till I hear that thou art Marry'd,   165
The Heart of Guise is riveted to thine:
Which all the Hammers in thy Mother's Brain
Shall never loose.
    MAR.   They may compel my Body;
But till I hear thee say thy self, Thou'rt false,
Death shall not force my Soul to wed Navarre.   [Exit Marguerite.   170

      Enter Anjou, and Ligneroles.

    GUI. I'll stand the shock of this Imperious Duke,
This Anjou, that has got a Name in War,
I know not how, because his Horse was shot
At Moncontour: you see by what ensu'd,

---

145 if] C_{1+}; If Q_1.
146 if] C_{1+}; If Q_1.

Nature design'd him for a Reveller.   175
    ANJ. O Ligneroles, thou Partner of my Soul,
Be secret; for if once the King should know
What I have told thee through excess of Love,
The World could not redeem thee from the Grave.
Ha! Guise! But soft, my Soul. My Lord Lorrain,   180
'Tis said, the Admiral, and Hugonot Princes
Are scarce a League from Paris.
    CAR.   Yes, My Lord,
I hear so too: the Duke of Guise was going.
    ANJ. I hope he will not move for fear of me.
    GUI. You're right, my Lord; nor will not stay for love.   185
    ANJ. What, not a Woman's Love! Love of a Princess?
    GUI. No, nor a Boy's; your Sister may do much.
    ANJ. Haste Ligneroles, go bear the King this Packet.
My Lord of Guise, 'tis not impossible   [Exit Ligneroles.
But Anjou one day may be King of France;   190
Mark me, if then I find Valois dishonour'd,
I will not leave a Guise to gape at pow'r.   [Exit.
    GUI. 'Tis so: by all the Mysteries of Empire,
By the Eternal Fates, his Mother's Poison
Boils in the Brains of the young drooping King,   195
And speeds him to make way for curs'd Anjou.
Charles has Religion, which she wonders at,
And scarce believes him hers; laughs at his pity,
Calls his Remorse the Colick of the Mind;
His starts, and fears, the gripes and checks of Conscience.   200

       Enter King, Queen Mother, Ligneroles.

But see, the King? mark, mark, my dear Lorrain,
Mark how she tempers him betwixt her hands:
He has it in his Veins, the lingring draught
That moulders him away. Let's tell him of it:
By my Ambition, and my vow'd Revenge,   205
I'll do't.
    CAR. Away; you shall not: are you mad?
Where is your temper? Walk a little off,
And lay these Fumes.
    GUI.   Lead then the blind away;
Yet, if I meet him in the dark, I'le crush him.   [Ex. Car. and Gui.
    KING. Was ever such an Insolence? Read there.   210
My Brother has Intelligence from Rochel
The Admiral has order'd his Adherents
To seize on Mons, as he arrives at Paris,
So to assure the kindling of a War.

_____

197 has] C_{1+}; his Q_1.
201 King! C_{1+}.

O, Mother, now I feel thy flames inspire me;   215
Yes, by the injur'd Majesty of Kings,
I'le fetch this soaring Rebel from his height:
Traytor, Imperious, Saucy, Arrogant Slave!
    LIG. Why should your Majesty thus shock your Peace
With needless Fury, since the time draws on   220
When He, and all those Rebel Hugonots,
Shall never grieve you more?
    KING.   Your meaning, Sir.
    LIG. When, as your Royal Justice has decreed,
They shall be Massacred.
    KING.   A vain Surmise.
Go, Sir, and bid the Count of Rhetz attend me.   [Ex. Lig .   225
    Q. M. Well, Sir, what think you now?
    KING.   Death, and Destruction,
We're all undone; the Secret of the World,
Th'eternal Care of my contriving Soul,
Which has so many Moons, with constant watching,
Reduc'd me to this state, is blab'd by you,   230
Divulg'd, and made the Prattle of a Boy.
    Q. M. No, no, my Lord; I am not to be taught
By you, to keep a Secret: Look at home,
Collect, if in your late tempestuous Passion
You did not give suspicion of the truth.   235
    KING. Suspicion! no, 'tis more; we are betray'd:
He told me to my face he knew the matter,
How that the Admiral, and the Hugonots
Should streight be Massacred. O, I could rave!
Our hearts are Rebels to our Bosom-Councils.   240

       Enter Alberto Gondi.

But see, perhaps this Villain gave it Air.
Ah, Traitor! Ah perfidious false Alberto!   [Gondi kneels. *
Have I not rais'd thee from the dregs of baseness,
And lodg'd thee in the bosom of thy Master?
Nay, rise, and speak: where didst thou get the daring   245
T'unravel the close web of my sworn Councils,
And trust 'em to the giddy Ligneroles?
Confess; nay, hide not what thou hast reveal'd,
Or Racks, Blood, Blood and Fire, and lasting Torments
Shall force thee, speak.
    ALB.   Then let the Rack be brought: 250
Methinks I long to give a noble proof
How much I can endure in such a Cause.
    KING. I know not what to say, whom to accuse,
Or where to turn my self. Call hither Guise,

---

  * [Gondi kneels.] om. Q$_{1+}$.

And Cardinal of Lorrain. But see, my Brother.   255

        Enter Anjou.

It must be so: 'tis he, 'tis he, false man!
I had forgot! this Boy's his only Minion,
The very turn-key of his Cabinet-thoughts.
But speak, Anjou; how didst thou dare to trust
So strong a Secret, such important Counsels,   260
That from the Book of Fate must wipe for ever
A hundred thousand Lives, or quash the Throne?
O, I'm not able to contain the Transport!
Why did'st thou trust a business of such weight
To Ligneroies?

      Enter Cardinal and Guise.

   ANJ.   'Tis true, my Lord, I did;   265
But I'le ingage my life he'll ne're divulge it.
    KING. No, Sir; I pass my word he never shall.
    ANJ. My Lord, I beg ---
    KING.   Speak not, stir not hence.
My Lord of Guise, I must engage your Service.
    Q. M. Think no more of him, lest the violent King,   270
Whom yet I never saw so strangely mov'd,
Should turn his rage on you.
    GUI.   My Lord, 'tis done.
Two of my Train there are that bear him grudge.
    KING. When he's dispatch'd, let your Friends go to Prison,
To put a little varnish on his blood;   275
Then you, or some that have the seeming Power,
Beg for their Pardon, and it shall be sign'd.

      Enter Alberto.

   ALB. My Lord, the Admiral's arriv'd.
    KING.   O, Madam,
Give me your hand, and yours and yours to prop me;
Now we must shew a Master-piece indeed,   280
To meet the Man whom we would make an end of,
Ev'n at that time when mortal Wars within,
When the blood boils and flushes to be at him,
Yet then to shew the signs of heartiest Love,
To cringe, to fawn, to smile, to weep, and swear,   285
Are Masks for women, not for men to wear.   [Exeunt.

---

   279 Divided as follows Q_1-C_1:
       Give me your hand, and yours and yours
       To prop me;

Scene III.

Enter Admiral, Queen of Navarre, the Princes, Commanders,
Gentlemen, &c.

ADM. Cavagnes, would'st thou think it possible,
I scarce have breath to tell thee I'm not well?
  CAV. Why should you fear?
  ADM.   Because it goes against me.
Upon the way, my sad presaging heart
At the first view of Paris sunk within me,   5
I stopt, and started, and answer'd without thought,
Like one that breaks his sleep with his own brawl,
As if my Genius shock'd me with a question,
And ask'd me, whither I was bound for Death?
But it must be, Cavagnes: nay, what's more   10
Than Death it self, confess my self a Traytor,
Ev'n in the Theater of all the Kingdom
Do Penance for the glorious Wars I made,
In view of those that have so bravely back'd me.

Enter the King, Queen Mother, Anjou, Alberto Gondi, Cardinal of
Lorrain. All the Hugonots kneel.

KING. Madam, you're welcome; this the Prince your Son   15
Most welcome; this the Prince of Conde, welcome;
Welcome to Paris, welcome to the Court:
The heart of Charles bids welcome to you all.
Who's that upon the Earth! the great Chastillon,
The glorious Admiral, the fam'd Coligni,   20
The scourge of Kingdoms! O, my Father, rise;
Or, by the Majesty of Age, the Reverence
Due to these hairs, the King himself shall kneel.
  ADM. O Sir, is't possible! can this be real!
Can you forgive this Out-law; this Offender;   25
Who has so often turn'd your Subjects Arms
Against their Lawful Soveraign; made whole wilds
Of populous Towns, and brav'd the Lions fury!
Now you have drawn me quite unarm'd to Court,
Can you so far be Master of your temper   30
As not to hew me in a thousand pieces?
  KING. Can you, who had the power to make me tremble,
Can you, my awful Subject, be so good
To kneel before my feet, and ask my Pardon,

---

6 started,] C_{2+}; start, Q_1-C_1.

And shall I be so barbarous to refuse it!   35
No, mighty Warrior, in the heat of Broils,
When thou so terribly becam'st the Field
Had'st thou thus sought me, by those Saints we worship,
I had receiv'd thee with a breast of Mercy.
    ADM. Forgive me, Sir; my heart so rises in me,   40
I cannot speak.
    KING.   Let then the World be witness,
All that is Honest, Sacred, Good, and Just,
Be witnesses the powers of Heav'n and Earth,
With this embrace I pardon thee thy Errors,
I bid thee welcome, as my better Angel,   45
Thou shalt direct in all my bosom Councils;
My Genius; O! and while I hold thee thus,
Methinks I press my Father in my Arms.
    ADM. O! Sir, what have you done you've burst the heart
Of your old Gasper, with this Flood of Goodness: 50
And see, it gushes from my Aged Eyes.
    KING. No more.
    ADM.   I must, I must make way, my Lord,
For this dear Load that makes me sore within:
But haste, employ my Arm; Let Fortune raise
Some Fo that's worthy of Chastillon's Sword: 55
Nay, I shall quarrel with the Fates themselves
Unless they rouze me up some brave occasion,
To signalize my Loyalty, my Conduct
And constant Zeal for your Immortal Glory.
    KING. Your Friendship to the Queen, who courts it too,   60
Will more oblige me than your Wars abroad.
    ADM. For all past Faults thus low I ask her Pardon.
    Q. M. Rise, rise, my Lord: let us forgive each other.
May I, when dying, miss the Throne of Mercy,
If, when I saw the King and you embrace,   65
My wounded heart did not weep blood for joy.
    KING. Come, come, my Lord, since you're so fierce to serve me,
I'll find your Sword Employment. Rest a while,
And then for Flanders, where the Duke of Alva
Will hold you to't.
    ADM.   I long, my Lord, to try him: 70
He who so curses the Reform'd Religion.
I wish that, with some thousands I could raise
Of those poor Protestants whom he disdains,
I could but face him on the dusty Plain,

---

  44 Errors,] C_{1+}; Er Q_1.
  67 <u>Divided</u> <u>as</u> <u>follows</u> <u>in</u> Q_1:
      KING. Come, come, my Lord, since you're so fierce to
   Serve me,
   <u>Printed</u> <u>as</u> <u>one</u> <u>line</u> <u>in</u> C_{1+}.

Tho' to his Aid he call'd his Catholick Master,   75
With thousand Arms held up to thousand Saints;
Ev'n with this handful of my old Commanders
Heading the well truss'd Body of our Men,
We'd on, to make the Mytred Armies yield,
And drive the trembling Crosiers from the Field.   [Exeunt.   80

End of A C T III.

Act IV. Scene. I.

The Scene draws; the King, the Queen Mother, the Duke of Anjou,
    Duke of Guise, Cardinal of Lorrain: The Body of Ligneroles
    held up all bloody.

ANJ. Ah Traytor Guise! but I will have thy life---
GUI. Let go your hand; or by the Majesty
That Governs here, I'll send you to your Boy.
    KING. Tear 'em asunder.
    ANJ.   I'le have Satisfaction.
    KING. Remove the Body. You my Lord of Guise,   5
Say how this murder hapned.
    GUI.   Thus, my Lord.
Charles Count of Mansfeild, and the Count of Guerchy,
When with this Mornings hunt, the Hills, and Groves,
The Skies and Fountains seem'd one mutual cry,
Riding in company, with this bold Spirit,   10
On fiery Coursers, chanc'd to discompose him:
He frown'd, they laugh'd, and so the beaten road
Of Quarrels, hot words rose, then Blows and Thrusts,
The Youth betwixt 'em fell, I know not how;
And there's an end of him.
    ANJ.   Traytor, thou ly'st: 15
Thou know'st the cause.
    KING.   No, Sir, it was my Order.
Now, as you have respect to your own Safety,
No more of this. Had you not blush'd in Blood,
In the Heart-blood of him you dearest lov'd;
By my dead Father's Soul, by my Revenge,   20
You should your self have mourn'd so gross a failing.
    Q. M. Sir, he repents.
    KING.   He does but what he ought.
Now to the Business.
Since then the Cloud that holds our horrid Vengeance
Comes nearer racking o're the Hugonots heads;   25

---

7 Divided as follows in Q_1:
        Charles Count of Mansfeild, and the Count
        of Guerchy,
    Divided as above in C_{1+}.
15-16 Divided as follows in Q_1-C_1:
        And there's an end of him.
            ANJ. Traytor thou ly'st; Thou know'st the cause.
            KING. No, Sir, it was my Order.
        Divided as above in C_{2+}.

Let's help the fall, and stir not from this place
Till we have fixt the Plat-form of their Ruine:
First, for the Queen, Jane Albert of Navarre,
Because a Woman, and of Royal Blood,
My Mother judg'd that she should dye by Poison.   30
    Q. M. Dispatch'd with Sweets. Pass to the rest; she's dead.
    KING. Yet not without suspicion of the Princes,
Who therefore, by my Order, were desir'd
To see her Body open'd; which was done
Before the chief of all the Hugonots;   35
Only her Head was spar'd, as I appointed,
Out of a seeming Reverence; but indeed,
Lest that the Poison, tho' it pass'd unseen,
Like a close Murderer, through the Lanes of Life,
Might yet at last be taken where it lodg'd.   40
With this, in part, I satisfy'd their Murmurs.
    Q. M. Therefore you must confer more favours still
Upon the Admiral, lull him with Honours;
Strike him but in the throat of his Ambition,
You have him sure: yet let him play a while,   45
And roll at random down the stream of Glory.
My Lord of Guise you have not yet convers'd him;
Therefore, while this suspicion on the death
Of the late Queen flies warm about his ears,
Visit him, as commanded by the King;   50
But so as if enforc'd: and by degrees,
Proceed to half a Quarrel, that the King,
Being made the Judge, as coming there by chance,
May give it quite against you in appearance,
And force you to submit your self for Pardon.   55
    GUI. It shall be so: And fear not, I'le provoke him;
'Twill ease my Heart a little, with keen words,
To right my Father's wrongs, and shed the Venom
That swells me all within.
    KING.   On this proceed
To the intended Marriage of Navarre;   60
Which once perform'd, as if that were the Lightning
To the sure Peal of Horrour that must follow,
Begin our Vengeance with the Admiral's Death.
    ANJ. First, Sir, it would be known how Guise approves
The Marriage of Navarre with Marguerite.   65
    KING. I know the Duke approves what I resolve;
And on so great a push, would forfeit both
A Ligneroles and Marguerite too.
    Q. M. Come, come it's monstrous but to make a Scruple,
To stand on Pets, Intrigues, and foolish Passions,   70
When such a Fate is now upon the Bolt,
As ne're perhaps yet Thunder'd with Success,
Since first the World began.
    GUI.   My Lord, I yield;

And take Prince Porcien's Widow for my Wife.
    KING.   I sent the Count of Rhetz to bring her hither.   75
My Lord Lorrain, pray let me view the Contract.
This, by the hand of Guise, must first be torn,
And then presented her.
    GUI.   Excuse me, Sir.
    KING.   If Prayers or threats can bend her, Sir, you shall not;
But, if those fail, my Lord, without more words,   80
I charge you for your Honour, and my own,
To act as I command: or, by my blood,
Nor you, nor I shall ever see her more.
    GUI.   That's a home thrust indeed: Sir, I obey,
And wait your farther order.
    KING.   My Lord Lorrain,   85
Attend the Duke while I examine Marguerite,
Wait till I stamp, and when thy trouble's over
Make to the Admiral; and I will follow.   [Car. and Guise retire
                                          to rear of Stage. *

      Enter Alberto with Marguerite.

How, Marguerite, weeping? all in tears!
Sure then the Count of Rhetz mistook the Message.   90
I sent to give thee Joy, to tell my Sister
She must be marry'd.
    MAR.   And I come, my Lord,
To shew my heart before your Majesty,
To beg your favour, mercy, and your pardon;   [Kneels. **
For O, my Lord, I cannot, if I would,   95
Be marry'd to Navarre.
    KING.   You cannot? Rise,
And tell me why: I'le hear you out with patience.
    MAR.   Ah, Sir, how shall I speak your Sister's Frailty?
How shall I, but thus drown'd with tears and blushes,
Confess the fault of Duty? I am marry'd,   100
Betroth'd, my Lord.
    KING.   To whom?
    MAR.   Alas, you're angry;
But I must own the truth, tho' on your brow
A thousand deaths sat menacing my Soul:
Yes, Sir, I'm marry'd to the Duke of Guise.
    KING.   Not marry'd, Marguerite; but contracted: 105
And so far I'le forgive thy heedless Youth;

---

  * [Car. and Guise retire to rear of Stage.] ; om. Q$_1$+.
 90 Divided as follows in Q$_1$:
      Sure then the Count of Rhetz mistook the
      Message.
      Divided as above in C$_1$+.
 ** [Kneels.] ; om. Q$_1$+.

But on condition that, without more noise,
Thou raze the haughty Guise from thy remembrance;
Or, by the violation of our Name,
I will not spare to drain thy tainted blood,   110
Till I have mounted thee by death a Victim
To the great memory of the wrong'd Valois.
    MAR. Call then, my Lord, call forth your fierce Tormentors,
Propose to Marguerite flames and wounds,
And all the cruel Arts of thoughtful Fury,   115
See your poor Sister's Spirit parch'd away
By lingring fires, to make my death more dreadful;
Yet, Sir, with my last breath I must avow
My Love to Guise, and hatred to Navarre.
    KING. No; I have thought on't better; I'll proclaim thee,   120
A Prostitute; thou shalt no more be Royal:
Poor, and abandon'd, with thy shame upon thee,
I'll turn thee forth a Beggar to the World,
    MAR. Do, do, my Lord, rather than wed Navarre,
And make it death for any to relieve me,   125
Set the mad multitude like Dogs upon me,
To tear, to worry me like common flesh,
To drag me to a Ditch, and leave me gasping;
Yet with my last sighs I will groan to Heav'n,
'Tis easier this, than to be false to Guise.   130
    KING. But, Marguerite, was there ever Love
Without brave Revenge on Provocation?
Yet, Wretch, thou lov'st without being lov'd again:
Since in my presence Guise now past his word
To leave thee, and to wed the Widow Porcien.   135
    MAR. No, no, my Lord; that Art was us'd before;
Yet, Sir, you make me tremble; for methinks
There's something more resolv'd, more stern in you,
Than in my Mother; yet my heart's confirm'd
Not to believe ev'n you; O therefore cease,   140
Or rather execute your former rage,
And give me up to those Tormentors hands
That wait your Call.
    KING.   But if I bring the Duke
Before thy face, that Contract in his hand,
Which past betwixt you, and he tears it here   145
Openly, in the presence of us all;
Wilt thou then quit him, with resolv'd revenge,
And wed Navarre?
    MAR.   Why should you ask me, Sir?
Prove me but half as much, but half that falshood,
That Impudence, that Treason to the Throne   150

---

129 Yet will I groan with my last sighs to Heav'n, C_{2+}.
132 Without a brave C_{2+}.

Of our crown'd Loves, and I will wed a Slave:
There's not a thing so loath'd upon the Earth,
But you shall bind me to it for my life,
To Age, Deformity, to all that's hateful,
                    [King stamps foot; Guise tears Contract. *
Blasting, and deadly. ---Ha! what's this he tears?   155
The Contract? O, it is the cursed Contract!
Then I'll tear too. Death, Furies, Hell, and Devils!
                            [Exeunt. Card. and Guise. **
But call him, Sir, call back the perjur'd Traytor;
Let your Guards hold him; you shall see, my Lord,
How well I hate him: Give me but a Dagger,   160
And I will gore his heart with thousand wounds;
Nay, if 'twere possible, I'de stab his Soul,
Fill it so full, brimful of Womans Gall,
That, tho' he were an Angel, it should damn him;
But he's a Devil, Devil, Devil, Devil.   165
   KING. Give me your hand; you shall along with me
To a young King, that will be proud to serve you.
   MAR. O, Sir, I know not what to say, or do,
But fling this load of misery at your feet:
You have my promise; but with all my blood   170
I would retrieve it; for since Guise is false,
Whom I believ'd the worthiest of the World,
Since he has prov'd himself so damn'd a Villain,
O, give me leave, Sir, give me leave to shun,
To hate, to loath, to curse all Humane Kind.   175
   KING. I'le have no more delay; I claim your Promise:
Come then; or, by my Crown, I'le have thee drag'd:
What hoa? without there.

               Enter Attendants.

   MAR.   Mother, pity me.
Have patience, Sir, a little time, my Lord,
To vent these bursting sighs, and I will go;   180
Let me but dry my Eyes, and I will go;
This remnant of a wretched Royal woman,
This stain to all your Blood, O cruel Heav'n!
This curs'd, forlorn, unhappy Bride shall go
Thus to the Altar where my Fate's decreed;   185
But like a Victim that is doom'd to bleed.
                                        [Exeunt.

———————————

   * [King stamps foot; Guise tears Contract.] ; om. Q$_{1+}$. See line
      87 above.
  ** [Exeunt Card. and Guise.] ; om. Q$_{1+}$.
 186 doom'd] C$_{2+}$; doom Q$_1$-C$_1$.

Scene II.

Admiral, Antramont, Cavagnes, Langoiran.

ANT. Poison'd; the Royal dead Navarre was poison'd?
'Tis the first Thunder-clap of that vast Storm
That seems already breaking o're your head:
Why are you senseless then, and deaf to warning;
When, wheresoe're you cast your Eyes, the storm   5
Looks blacker yet? Why stays the Duke of Guise?
Why does he summon all his Blood to Court,
With Barons, Knights, that hold the Catholick Party,
With Foreign Gentry living on his Pensions,
And therefore ready upon all occasion,   10
With hazard of their lives to act his pleasure.
    ADM. Peace, Antramont.
    ANT.   Alas, my Lord, I cannot.
Why should the Visdam Chartres, Count Mongomery,
Resolve to lodge themselves beyond the Sein,
Unless their minds presage some dreadful mischief!   15
'Tis coming; O, with deeper Policies
The King and Queen delude your easie Soul
With fatal Praises, and undoing Honours:
O, they have caught you! my Prophetick Soul
Sees the red Tempest thunder down in blood,   20
In blood of you, of me, of all about you.
    ADM. O, Antramont, you foil me now indeed;
Yet I shall answer, if your Passion please:
First, for the Queen, I saw her Body open'd,
The parts whereof were sound, untouch'd by Poison,   25
And by our own Physicians 'twas concluded
She dy'd a natural Death. Then for the Guises,
Some little satisfaction must be given,
As to permit their Presence at the Marriage;
But, for the management of State-affairs,   30
Or Favour from the King, they're lost for ever:
Nor shall it keep my dauntless Powers awake,
Tho' Chartres and Mongomery will not come.
But, to forbear the Subject, leave me here
With my Cavagnes.
    ANT.   I am commanded, Sir;   35
Yet, for the safety of your innocent Babes,
Beware, my Lord, be cautious, O prevent.   [Exit Antramont.
    ADM. Fear not; Farewel; be gone; I will beware,
Why should I fear, Cavagnes, when the King
Inclines his heart to the Reform'd Religion;   40
When the whole management of Home-affairs,

With all Confederacies made abroad,
Are left to me, as Judge and Arbitrator,
The Genius and the Oracle of France?
But, if the Will of Heav'n has set it down,   45
That all this trust is deep dissimulation,
That there's no Faith nor Credit to be given
To the inviolable Royal Word;
O, my Cavagnes, if 'tis possible,
If this be so, I yield, I yield to die: 50
I am contented for the Protestant Faith
Here to be hewn into a thousand pieces,
And made the Martyr of so good a Cause.
    LANG. My Lord, I take my leave; and am resolv'd
To leave the Court.
    ADM.   Cavagnes, prethee speak,   55
It is not worth our smile: But why, Langoiran,
Why dost thou leave the Maker of thy Fortune?
Is it not worth the hazard?
    LANG.   No, my Lord.
I'm sorry, Sir, to see you made so much of:
And so Farewel. For my part, I'm content   60
To save my self with Fools; rather than perish
With those that are too wise.   [Exit.

                Enter a Servant.

    SERV. My Lord the Duke of Guise.

        Enter Guise.   [Exeunt Cavag. and Serv.*

    GUI. The King, my Lord, commanded me to wait you,
And bid you welcome to the Court.
    ADM.   The King   65
Still loads me with new Honours; but none greater
Than this, the last.
    GUI.   There is one greater yet,
Your high Commission for the War with Spain:
I, and my Family, are charg'd to serve you;
And 'twill be glorious work.
    ADM   If you are there,   70
There must be Action.
    GUI.   O, your pardon, Sir;
I'm but a Stripling in the Trade of War:
But you, whose life is one continu'd Battel,
What will not your Triumphant Arms accomplish?
Who, as your self confess'd, or Fame is false,   75

---

   * [Exeunt Cavag. and Serv.] C_{2+}; [Exeunt Cavag. Serv. and all. Q_1-C_1.
64-75 Quoted with very little change in THE DUKE OF GUISE, II, ii.

Have quite out-gone the memory of the Ancients,
Of Alexander, and of Julius Caesar,
For they in all their Actions had success;
But you, in spite of your malicious Fortune,
After the loss of four most signal Battels,   80
Still rose more fierce and dreadful to your Foes:
And last, when all men thought you had no way
To save your life, but wander through the World;
You forc'd the King to grant your own Conditions,
More proper for a Conquerour than one   85
That was o'recome.
    ADM.   No more of that, my Lord.
    GUI. But, Sir, since I must make a little one
In this great Business, let me understand
What 'tis you mean; and why you put the King
Upon so dangerous an Expedition.   90
    ADM. Know, I intend the Greatness of the King,
The Greatness of all France, whom it imports
To make their Arms their Aim and Occupation:
Since then the Genius of the Kingdom's rouz'd,
I'll turn the Fever of those Civil Broils   95
To wholesom Exercise, to war with Strangers.
    GUI. Stor'd Arsenals, and Armories, and Fields of Horse,
Ordnance, Ammunition, and the Nerve of War,
Sound Infantry; not harrass'd and diseas'd,
To meet a Veteran Army, should be thought of;   100
Nor ought you to rely on Protestants,
Those Mercenaries that must come: for he
Who, thus resolv'd, depends on such, shall spread
His Feathers now; but mew 'em all to morrow.
    ADM. I find; my Lord, the Argument grows warm,   105
Therefore thus much, and I have done. The King
Intends to send an Army into Flanders,
A powerful one, and under my Command:
First then, altho' the Wars of later Ages
Are, in respect of former, made i'th' dark,   110
Chastillon will not steal a Victory.
    GUI. The Phrase of Alexander at Arbela!
    ADM. No place of Honour, Office, or Command
Through the whole Series of this glorious War,
For Profit, Favour, or for Interest,   115
Not of the greatest shall be bought or sold:
Whereas too, for th' incouragement of Fighters,
There are degrees promiscuously conferr'd
On Souldiers, and no Souldiers, this man Knighted,
Because he charg'd a Troop before his dinner,   120
And sculk'd behind a hedge in th' afternoon;

---

109 latter Ages C_{1+}.

I will have strict Examination made
Betwixt the meritorious and the base;
And, since I am entrusted as I wish,
I'll spoil the Traffick of this Brandy Court,   125
And vye Rewards for Merit with old Rome.
    GUI. You will, my good Lord Admiral?
    ADM.   Sir I will.
Upon the very Spot of Victory
For Gallant Men---
Erect their Tropies, Funeral Laudatives,   130
And Monuments for those that dy'd in War,
Crowns of distinction, Garland Personal,
All but the Stile of Emperour, which the King
Of the whole Universe did after borrow;
That for my Master: and perhaps for me   135
The Triumph of their Generals on return.
    GUI. You have mouth'd it bravely; and there is no doubt
Your deeds would answer well such haughty words:
Yet, let me tell you, Sir, there was a man
(Curse on the hand that sped him) that would better,   140
Better than you, or all the bragging Generals,
That when he shone in Arms and sun'd the Field,
That better would become the great Battallion,
Mov'd, spoke, and fought, and was himself a War.
    ADM. The Noble Guise, your Father, Sir, you mean;   145
But yet, my Lord---
    GUI.   No yet, my Lord; no yet:
By Arms, I bar you that;
For never was his like, nor shall again,
Till murder'd by Poltrot; curs'd, damn'd Poltrot,
Whose Soul now gluts the Maw of Lucifer.   150
    ADM. Speak with more Charity.
    GUI.   Ha! Charity!
Damnation on the Soul that harbours it.
Were I in Heav'n, and saw him scorch'd in Flames,
I would not spit my Indignation down,
Lest I should cool his Tongue. For Beza too,   155
That set him on, with the Rewards of Heav'n,
To act so black, so deep, so damn'd a Murder.
O why will Charles thus sheath the Sword of Justice
Till he has rooted up this Sect of Villains,
And collar'd to the Stake that canting Slave   160
That preach'd my God-like Father from the World?
    ADM. Come, come, my Lord, hear with a little patience,
And you shall find 'tis not the Protestant way
To stab, and beat the Brains out in the dark:
Look home, my Lord, go to the Vatican;   165

---

132 Garlands C$_{2+}$.

See, if in all those Politick Discourses,
There be not one Red-letter'd Page for killing.
    GUI. Ha, Admiral! then dur'st thou justify
The Villain, whom my Vengeance marks for death?
    ADM. My Lord, I will not justify a Villain   170
More than your self: But if you thus proceed,
If that a great Man's breath can puff away
On every Pet the Lives of Free-born People;
What need that awful General Convocation,
Th' Assembly of the States? nay, let me urge,   175
If thus you threat the Venerable Beza,
What may the rest expect?
    GUI.   What if I could,
They should be certain of; whole Piles of Fire.
    ADM. 'Tis very well, my Lord, I know your mind
Which, without fear or flatt'ry to your Person,   180
I'll tell the King; and then, with his Permission,
Proclaim it for a Warning to our People.
    GUI. Come, you're a Murd'rer, your self.
    ADM.   Away.
    GUI. You were Complotter with that Villain Beza,
The black Abetter of my Father's Murder.   185
    ADM. This wou'd sound well, my Lord, in Front-Battle,
But here upon a Visit from the King
It looks not like the Guise.
    GUI.   My Father's Murder?
Bid me not stand on points when that's remember'd!
But track me to the Forest with thy Sword,   190
Thus Man to Man, back'd with all thy People,
Follow me, or I will proclaim thee Traytor, Coward.
    ADM. O King, King, King! still let me sound thy Name,
Lest this Fool-hardy-Boy, this knotty Trifler,
This Spawn of Words, this Urchin of the War,   195
Should raise my Anger past the pulling down.

    Enter King, Queen Mother, Alberto, Anjou, and Morvele.

But see, He's here, I scorn to ruine thee:
Therefore go tell him, tell him thy own Story.
    KING. What now, my Lord of Guise? Is this your Visit?
I charge you on your life, without reserve,   200

---

186 Front of Battle C_{2+}.
188-89 Divided as follows in Q_1-C_1:
          It looks not like the Guise.
              GUI. My Father's Murder? bid me not stand on points
          When that's remember'd!
          Divided as above in C_{2+}.
191 back'd] C_{2+}; bark'd Q_1-C_1.

Tell me the truth; how hapned this disorder?
Those rufled hands, red looks, and port of Fury?
   GUI. I told him, Sir, since you resolve to have it,
He was the Murderer of my Noble Father;
Therefore a Traytor, Villain, and a Coward.   205
   KING. Is't possible?
   ADM.   No matter, Sir, no matter;
The Old Man rouz'd, and shook himself, my Lord;
A few hot words; no more, upon my life:
So, if your Majesty will do me Honour,
I do beseech you, let the business dye.   210
   KING. Guise, go, submit your self, and ask his pardon.
   GUI. My Lord, I cannot speak.   •
   KING.   Where are our Guards?
   ADM. Hold there. Come, Sir, I will interpret for you.
My Lord, this close embrace makes up the breach:
We will be sorry, Sir, for one another.   215
   GUI. You have out-done me, Sir; but you'l excuse me,
'Twas a great Rack that screw'd me to this Folly.
   ADM. More than enough, we're riveted the faster.
   KING. My Lord of Guise.
   Q. M.   My good Lord Admiral,
Now use your Power, and quite oblige the Court: 220
Villandry has provok'd the King at Play,
In such a nature, that he's doom'd to die;
My Son refus'd my Intercession for him;
Therefore, when he has done his Check to Guise,
For your affront; pray, my good Lord, intreat him.   225
   KING. The Marriage stays within; which past, resolve
His Execution sudden as you can.   [Aside to Guise. *
   GUI. Morvele.
   MOR. My Lord?
   GUI. I by the King's Commission, have Command   230
To take the Admiral's life.
   MOR.   I'le shoot him.
   GUI.   Right:
As he returns from Court.
   MOR.   From some Out-Lodging
I'le watch him till I execute your Order.
   ADM. I am a Suitor to your Majesty
For poor Villandry's life.
   KING.   Haste, bring him forth.   235
I think, my Lord, if you should ask my heart,
My yielding breast would open to your hand.
But, Father, let's away; the Cardinal
Stays for Navarre.
   ADM.   We'll wait your Majesty.   [Exit King with the Court.

---

   * [Aside to Guise.] ; <u>om</u>. Q₁+.

O, my Cavagnes, where's Langoiran now?   240
Where's Antramont? but haste, and tell her all;
Tell her th' extravagant kindness of the King,
Tell her, but stay; why such repeated Oaths?
That's to be thought on: Hollow was his aspect,
Graves in his smiles; Death in his bloodless hands.   245
O, Antramont! I'le haste to meet thy Eyes:
The Face of Beauty on these rising horrours,
Looks like the Midnight-Moon upon a Murder:
It drives the Shades that thicken from the State,
And gilds the dark design that's ripe for Fate. [Exeunt. 250

     End of ACT IV.

240 There is no stage direction in any edition for the reentrance of
    Cavagnes. He may come in with the King's party.

Act V. Scene I.

The King rises from a Couch.

KING. From Amber shrouds I see the morning rise
Her Rosy hand begins to paint the Skies;
And now the City Emets leave their Hive,
And rouzing Hinds to chearful labour drive;
High Cliffs, and Rocks are pleasing objects now,   5
And Nature smiles upon the Mountains brow;
The Joyful Birds salute the Sun's approach;
The Sun too laughs, and mounts his gaudy Coach,
While from his Car the dropping Gems distil,
And all the Earth, and all the Heaven does smile: 10
But Charles, still wrapt in Shades, like Night appears,
His sighs the Vapors, and the Dews his Tears.
Yet, O Just Power, with pity, O behold
The wretch, whose fault is in your Book inroll'd:
Behold these streams, with which his Soul aspires   15
To slake your wrath, and quench your angry fires.

Enter Genius.

GEN. Thy Genius, lo, from his sweet Bed of rest,
Adorn'd with Jassamin, and with Roses drest,
The Pow'r Divine has rais'd to stop thy Fate;
A true Repentance never comes too late: 20
So soon as born, she made her self a Shroud,
The weeping Mantle of a Fleecy Cloud,
And swift as thought, her Airy Journy took,
Her hand Heav'ns Azure Gate with trembling strook;
The Stars did with amazement on her look;   25
She told thy Story in so sad a Tone,
The Angels start from Bliss, and gave a groan.
But Charles beware, oh dally not with Heav'n,
For after this no Pardon shall be giv'n.   [Exit.

Enter the Queen Mother, Cardinal of
Lorrain, Anjou, Alberto Gondi.

CAR. The King upon the Earth? O rise, my Lord.   30
Q. M. He has of late been troubled with such Faintings,
And see he bleeds at Mouth.
KING.   Stand from me all.

---

1 KING.]; <u>om.</u> Q$_{1+}$.

O, Mother, Mother! Whither will you lead me?
Through what a Vault of Monuments, and Sculls,
And dead Men's Bones? And you, my Lord Lorrain,   35
Must I still journey through this Vale of Death,
And never reach the Paradise you promis'd?
I must not let the Massacre go forward:
I'm warn'd from Heav'n, I swear I think from Heav'n.
   Q. M. Some Scar-crow of a Dream? So far from Sin,   40
Or ought that's damnable, is our Design;
That my Lord Cardinal will tell you, Sir,
'Tis meritorious: and when e're we strike,
The Church shall bless it, as a blow from Heav'n.
   CAR. Therefore, my Lord, I wish you to suspect   45
Whatever thwarts you in your holy purpose;
However veil'd, tho' in an Angel's form,
Conclude it the suggestion of the Devil.
   Q. M. So; now, I hope, these Qualms are at an end,
And we may close pursue the main intention.   50
Suppose the Admiral kill'd: on this, the Hugonots
Fall on the House of Guise; the City rises
And cuts 'em all to pieces: now imagine
Which I am apt to think the Hereticks
Are more discreet, and only sue for Justice,   55
Without a Tumult; shall the business stand?
   CAR. No. If we find they do not run to Uproar,
(Our only hope to colour o're their ruine)
Proceed to instant Slaughter; or they'l find
Some means for flight, and kindle up the War   60
More dreadfully than ever.
   ANJ.   Is't determin'd
That, with the rest, the Princes too shall bleed?
   Q. M. My Judgment is most positive in this:
Let not one Soul of all be left alive;
For 'tis ridiculous, in such Extreams,   65
Ith' mid'st of Slaughter, Ruine, Blood, and Death,
To think of ever being prais'd for Mercy.
Nor can a mean be us'd; the Duke of Guise
Meddles not in it, if a man escape:
And says, in such a desperate Purge of Humours,   70
If any Relick of the great Distemper

---

39 Divided as follows in Q_1:
    I'm warn'd from Heav'n, I swear I think from
    Heav'n.
  Divided as above in C_{1+}.
51 Suppose] C_{1+}; Supposed Q_1.
53 imagine, C_{1+}.
54 think, C_{1+}.
62 bleed?] C_{1+}; bleed, Q_1.

Be left behind, it runs to a Relapse
More dangerous than before.
    KING.   As I remember,
Madam, it has been oft your Oracle,
In these late Civil Wars, to avoid a Battel,   75
That limbs, tho' ne're so foul, should not be lopt
Without the utmost, last Necessity;
Because the Body feels too great defect,
Sharp Pains, and almost irrecoverable Weakness:
And will you now cut the great Arteries,   80
The Princes of the Blood? Most horrid thought!
    Q. M. Compose your self; Navarre and Conde live.
Come, come, you must put off this Melancholy;
'Twill breed Suspicion, Sir, let me intreat you
To go upon the Instant streight to Tennis,   85
While Morvele does his business.
    KING.   O my heart!
If you would have me fixt, you must not leave me,
You must talk out to my distracted Soul,
Lest Conscience drown the Voice of Policy.   [Exeunt all but Car.
    CAR. This 'tis to have a Conscience? --- Here comes one   90

                    Enter Guise.

Sear'd as my self, of my own Family.
Is he dispatch'd!
    GUI.   Not yet; but Morvele waits him,
His Fuzee cock'd, and planted at the Window:
All, all is fitted.
    CAR.   What, your Marguerite,
Said she was sick, and would not bed the Prince   95
Last night?
    GUI.   I know not that; but here I stay
To take her as she passes to the Gardens.
How fares the King?
    CAR.   A little bound in Conscience:
He pukes at Dreams; and as I hear of late,
Spits Blood.
    GUI.   A Fit, a fit, my Lord, o'th' Mother: 100
I told you so. But see: the furious Princess?
Away: I'le clap my Prow upon the Storm;
And, if a Wrack must follow, let it come.

               Enter Marguerite.

    MAR. Ha! Villain? Traytor? Devil? Hence, be gone;
Or I must get into my Grave to hide me: 105

---

75 these] C_{1+}; this Q_1.

I've sworn, I've sworn to fly thee like a Fury,
And I am Damn'd if e're I see thee more.
    GUI. I will obey you. And indeed the Fates
Of these sad Souls that must to day be dol'd
Require my haste: I beg you but to hear me: 110
Grant me but this, By Hell, and Hell's worst Horrors,
And all the Murders of this bloody day;
You ne're shall see me more.
    MAR.   What can'st thou say?
For see, I know not how, thou'st charm'd my rage.
    GUI. Know then, the lives of every Hugonot   115
This moment now are sentenc'd to the Grave
A Massacre of all.
    MAR.   A Massacre!
    GUI. Madam, I've done. But hark! a Gun went off!
My leaping heart cries out, It is the Admiral.
The Marriage of Navarre was for this end   120
Design'd, to bring the Princes to the Court:
And, on so great an Enterprise, the King
Compell'd me to the tearing of the Contract,
Or threatned the destruction of my House,
And which was worse, your death before my eyes.   125
What, hoa! Morvele! He pass'd the Anti-chamber.

Enter Morvele.

Permit me to consult him. Ha! speak out;
Say, is the Admiral ---
    MOR.   Not dead, my Lord.
I think I saw some of his Fingers fly,
And part of his left Arm: I'm sure I hit him.   130
    GUI. Here, take this Key; fly to my Closet, haste;
Thou art pursu'd: Farewell.
    MOR.   I'm gone, my Lord.   [Exit.
    GUI. 'Twas in this manner just, my noble Father
Was palted from the Fame of all the World
By such another Villain: and my Soul   135
Leaps with Revenge, that this proud Admiral
Should, like an Eagle, in his utmost flight
Be topled from the Clouds of all his Glory.
Madam, farewel: I hope you will excuse
What I, enforc'd, did act: I love you still;   140
And, on this sad affair, in which perhaps
Your Guise may perish, it would warm my heart
To hear you do not hate me.
    MAR.   Death and Horrour!
Infamy, Vengeance, Murder, Massacre!

---

118 Gun we Q_1(KU 1); Gun went off! Q_1(KU 2), Q_1(DFo 1, 2, 3), C_{1+}.

GUI. Now by the life and heart of our design   145
'Tis well dissembled; stood thy Lord in view,
I thus wou'd charge thee; bear thee in my arms,
From the proud hurry of a clashing World:
To Mahomet's Paradise, to Beds of Pleasure,
Where we shall spin the silken Joys for ever,   150
Without a break: lengthening the twinkling moment
To an Eternity of deathless Pleasure.
    MAR. Touch me not for thy life, thou Traytor! Murderer!
Ravisher! Oh thou titled Villany!
In Purple dipt to give a gloss to mischief!   155
Follow the bloody bark of thy Ambition,
And never see me more ---
    GUI.   It cannot be,
Unless you chain me, drag me in Sunless Caves:
You are my Earthly goodness, all my hope
Of Comfort here: nor wish I more hereafter.   160
    MAR. Hold, hold, Prophaner, thou hast dishonour'd me,
But this is little to the Crimes that follow,
Thou hast betray'd me, after all my Vows,
To marry one I hate; for thy Ambition
Mak'st me the Cause of this most horrid Vengeance.   165
At which the Earth shall sicken, Saints be sad,
And none but Furies like your self ---
    GUI. Did not your Mother form the whole design?
    MAR. Whoever form'd or helpt in such contriving,
Hell and Damnation waste 'em; but for thee,   170
Sear'd as thou art, with Cruelty, Revenge,
I pity thee, O Guise! because I lov'd thee,
And beg thee view those Fiends that gape to seize thee:
Allow at least a possibility;
An unknown Country, after you are dead,   175
As well as there was one e're you were born.
    GUI. Admit me then once more to share your Breast,
To taste those Secrets from those lovely Lips,
And I in time may be a Proselyte.
    MAR. Here look your last! for from the time I leave you   180
Ne're hope to see lost Marguerite more.
    GUI. I am a Rebel, and have sworn to see you:
By all our former Dearness, and I will
By Heav'n: I will, in spite of your resolve,
I'le gaze upon you till these Crystals run.   185
    MAR. You have broke my heart a thousand several ways,
And now against my will this parting melts me.
    GUI. Speak not of parting: by those Eyes I beg,
Nor melting hearts: The blood runs down from mine.

---

154 titled Villain! C_{1+}.
156 bloody mark C_{2+}.

MAR. For all the wrongs you have done me, my Dishonour,   190
For all your delays, your slights, your thousand Oaths,
Your most considerate Pride in falling out,
That I might court you to be Friends again.
    GUI. Stop yet: and Oh eternal Love shall crown thee.
    MAR. For all my Midnight groans.
    GUI.   Hold, Marguerite.   195
    MAR. My Tears, my Watchings,
The bleeding tokens of the fondest Love.
    GUI. Take this, and strike it to my heart;   [Offers a Dagger.
But speak your griefs no more.
    MAR.   By all I've said,
I beg you, Sir, to spare my Husband's life.   200
    GUI. What, Marguerite? ha! Navarre agen?
This was too much.
    MAR.   Save him, if possible,
And so farewel, thou Ruine of my Glory:
Farewel, thou strong Seducer of my Youth;
Yet I will Eye thee hungerly at last: 205
Nay, take this sigh too that thus splits my heart,
My Husband's life. In all that I implore,
To save Navarre, and never see me more.   [Exit Mar.
    GUI. She's gone, for ever gone: why, let her go.
Henceforth pronounce all Woman-kind thy Foe;   210
Or if thy feeble Soul to Love return,
Do not, like Anthony, for life time burn:
But as a Lion, eager of his prey,
Compell'd by thirst, turns from his purpos'd way;
And in some silver Fountain slacks his rage,   215
Then runs more fiercely on his Foes t'ingage;
So having quench'd thy fires with Beauties Charms,
Forget the Pleasures, and rush to Arms.   [Exit.

    Enter King, Q. Mother, Anjou, Lorrain, Alb. Gondi.

    KING. Command that all the City-Gates be shut,
Except but two, for bringing in Provisions;   220
And these my Lord of Rhetz, see strictly Guarded,
Lest that the Murderer escape.
    Q. M.   You bear it bravely!
Now to the wounded Admiral: be there
As you are now, seem soft and pitiful,
Fond him with tears, cry out with your impatience   225
To be reveng'd upon the Murderer.
    KING. You that are made of Artifice instruct me.   [Exeunt.

---

190 Dishonour,] C$_{1+}$; Dishonou Q$_1$.
218 rush on to Arms. C$_{2+}$.

Scene II.

The Admiral Dressing, with all the Hugonots about him.

ADM.   A finger and an arm? what all this noise
About the shattering of a Limb? Away.
And in a Cause so great, so glorious too?
Nay, let 'em burn the other to the shoulder,
Or let that Badger Queen grind every Bone   5
Betwixt her teeth, and grin to hear 'em crack.
CAV.   Let's instantly resolve to bear him forth.
ADM.   No: with this mangled flesh held to Heav'n,
This horrid mash of Blood, and Bone, and Marrow,
Upon my knees I beg the Power Divine   10
T'establish thus the Protestant Religion,
To plant it in the Blood of lost Coligni,
If that, Alas, may satisfy their Fury.
CAV.   Take heart, Sir; hope one day for full Revenge.

Enter Antramont.

ANT.   'Tis well, my Lord! 'tis well, my Cato! well!   15
You call'd this Paris Utica at first:
The Stars of Great men have a cast Divine,
And when they mould with second thought, the Spirit,
The Air, the Life, the Golden Vapour's gone.
Langoiran! O Langoiran!
ADM.   Fate, my Martia;   20
There is a Providence that over-rules:
Therefore submit; haste, for thy life, away;
I beg thee fly, my Martia, to Geneva:
My little ones shall, with Teligny, follow.
ANT.   What, Sir, is't possible!   25
Is a planck in this great Vessel rived?
Is't necessary that a Wreck should follow?
ADM.   O, Antramont, there is no going forth;
If the King be not in th' Assassination,
Fear not; I shall have Justice: If he be,   30
Farewel for ever, I'll ne're see thee more.
ANT.   You shall, you shall: why burst you not away?
There are at least ten thousand, your Adherents,
Will clear your passage to Chastillon:
Why do you drag then, when your Fate cryes on?   35
ADM.   Once more I say, my Fate is in the King;

8 held up to C_{2+}.

Therefore away: If things go right, you come
To me again; if not, there's one preserv'd
T'embalm my Bowels. O my Antramont,
I mean my Babes, that thus have force to thaw me.   40
That Power, whose most unsearchable Decree
Thus dooms our parting, give thee strength to bear it;
To bear my Death; perhaps thou'lt hear it shortly:
Yet thou shalt hear nothing unworthy me,
Nothing that's faint and flagging at the Goal,   45
But my last Gasp like my first start of Glory.
    ANT. What, leave thee, Gaspar, e're I kiss thy wound?
O, let me touch the Batt'ry of his Arm!
Forgive me; thus far I will be a Roman:
There's Virtue here, in this most Sacred Relict,   50
I swear I think there is, to save a Soul.
    ADM. Be gone, I say; I cannot bear thy Kindness:
Force her away, and bear her to St. Germain.
    ANT. I go. For thee, this Prayer I leave behind me:
When-e're thou dy'st, the Arms of Angels waft thee   55
To those smooth Joys that have no gritty moments.
For her that brought thee to this barbarous end,
The Whips of Conscience drive her to Despair;
Conscience! Sh' has none: why then the stings of Pleasure,
Sores and Diseases, Disappointments plague her;   60
May all her Life be one continu'd Torment,
And that more Racking than a Mother's labour:
In meeting Death, may her least trouble be
As great, as now my parting is with thee.   [Exit.

       Enter Alberto Gondi.

    ALB. My Lord, his Majesty, the Queen, his Mother,   65
Approach, to mourn your Chance, and give you Justice.

     Enter King, Queen, Anjou, Lorrain.

    KING. My Lord, I come to pour the Balm of Tears
Into your Wound; I come to threaten death
To that bold Villain who durst act this outrage:
And by my Soul I swear, my Father shall   70
Have such Revenge, as if a King were kill'd.
    ADM. I thank your Majesty, and humbly crave
Your leave, Sir, to retire home to Chastillon;
Where, from these tumultuous Parisians,
I may, my Lord, recover this Misfortune.   75
    Q. M. What, take a Journey, Sir, in this condition?
Your Death must follow: but, alas, I fear,

---

48 me] C_{1+}; we Q_1.

I fear the truth, with tears I must avow it,
My Lord, you dare not trust the King and Me.
    ADM. O, do not tax me with the least Suspicion: 80
I must believe the Royal Majesty;
But all my fear is for my dear Companions,
And these lov'd Princes, whom the Heav'ns defend.
    KING. Therefore my Brother streight shall draw the Guards
Within the City, while for present Safety   85
I order Monsieur Cosen's Company
To keep your Quarters from all fear of Tumult.
O, Father, Father, do not wound my Soul
By a distrust unworthy of us both.
    Q. M. Ah, my Lord Admiral, can you imagine   90
That we are past all fear, or hope of Mercy,
That there's no Conscience, no regard of Vows,
No Grace, no Reverence, fear of Heav'n, nor Hell,
Nor common Care of Fame, ev'n in this World?
    KING. To Bed, to Bed; let me intreat you rest.   95
    Q. M. Nay, you shall go, my Lord, supported thus
Betwixt your Bosom-Friends: believe me, Sir,
This is not feign'd; there are not two alive
That love you more, than those that now sustain you.
    ADM. Is't possible? Why, if it were dissembled,   100
The very Counterfeit of such a Friendship
Were worth a dying for. Alas, my Lord?
O, Madam! Why, why must this trouble be?
But lead me, lead your poor old Admiral,
Blind with his Tears, and faint with his Blood: 105
If I do well again, I'll thank you, Sir,
I'll thank you in the Field; O, grant it, Heav'n,
That I may end where no Assassins are,
And fall a Victim in the Glorious War.   [Exeunt.

Scene III.

Guise, Aumale, Elbeuf, Angolesme, with Parisians.

    GUI. Look you, my Lords, this is the Royal Order;
The Dukes of Nevers and Monpensier
Must wait to guard the Person of the King,
With all the Royal Regiment in Arms:
Haste, for the day begins to wear apace.   5
    ANG. ELB. We obey.   [Exeunt ambo.
    GUI. President Charton, Provost de Marchand,
The Head of the Parisians.

---

105 with loss of Blood: C_{2+}.
  1 this is the] C_{1+}; this is, this is the Q_1.

PROV.   Here, my Lord.
GUI.   Provide two thousand men compleatly arm'd;
Let each particular man, on his left arm   10
Wear a Shirt-sleeve, and a white Cross in's Hat,
That, upon notice given, all may be ready
To execute his Majesty's Commands:
The Eschevins of every several Ward
See in just order and precisely set,   15
That upon ringing the Palace-bell,
Lights may be put directly on the instant
In every Window all throughout the Town.
PROV.   It shall be done.   [Exit.
GUI.   My Lord Grand Prior,
With what Commanders we can rise, be ready   20
To take the Admiral's life. But see the Queen?

Enter Queen Mother, Cardinal, Anjou.

Q. M.   Come, come, my Lords, let's lose no longer time;
The Hugonots proceed not to a Tumult,
But only vent their Fury in high words:
Therefore away. My Lord of Guise, your Father,   25
Looks from the Clouds, and cryes, Revenge, Revenge.
I think 'twere better too, while you kill the Admiral,
The King's Grand Provost should pursue his Wife.
GUI.   The old gray Sire, the Dam, and little Babes,
I'le take 'em all together in the Nest,   30
And pash 'em till they Sprawl. You and the Cardinal
Haste to the Louvre; when the Gates are shut,
Call the Chief Hugonots down, and cut their Throats.
My Lord, the Duke of Anjou, to your Care
The King commits the City: So Farewell;   35
There wants no more but ringing of the Bell.   [Exeunt Severally.

Scene IV.   The City.

Lights in the Windows. The President Marches his Men over the Stage:
the Bell of the Palace rings out.

Enter Admiral in his Night-Gown.

ADM.   The Palace Bell rings out, loud Cries of Murder,
Guns fir'd, and groans of dying men below;
The King has giv'n his Warrant for my last;
His Vows, his Oaths, and Altar-Obligations
Are lost: the Wax of all those Sacred Bonds   5

---

20 raise C_{1+}.

Runs at the Queens Revenge, the Fire that melts 'em.
They are no more: the Admiral's no more.

              Enter Cavagnes bleeding.

    CAV. My Lord, God calls us; Death is in the Court:
Fate, in the shape of Guise, all over Blood.
I saw your Son in Law Teligny dye;   10
Roura, the Son of Baron des Atrets,
With Colonel Montaumar, Gallant Guerchy,
Wrapping his Cloak about his Arm, fought on
Till he was all one wound, and so Expir'd:
But hark, they come!
    ADM.   Why, let 'em, let 'em come;   15
We shall e're long, my Friend, be worth their Envy:
To dye thus for Religion, O, Cavagnes,
It puts the Soul in everlasting Tune,
And sounds already in the Ears of Angels!
And, O, what cause had ever such Foundation!   20
I tell thee that the Root shall reach the Center,
Spread to the Poles, and with her top touch Heav'n.
But see, they come: stand fixt, and look on Death
With such Contempt, so Masterly an Eye,
As if he were thy Slave.   25

        Enter Besnie, Sartabons, 4 Souldiers.

    BESN. See where he stands! ha, Slaves, what makes you pause.
1 SOULD. Kill him your self, for my part I'le not touch him.
2 SOULD. Nor I: for my part I am sorry for what is done already.
    ADM. Cowards indeed! thus to be terrified
Ev'n with the shadow of th' Admiral.   30
    BESN. It goes against me; yet I must obey:
Sheath all your Daggers in the Traytor's Breast.
    ADM. Young Man, thou oughtest to reverence these gray hairs;
But I command thee, do as thou art order'd,
Thou'lt cut but little from the Line of Life.   35
    BESN. Dye then, dye both: now for his Wife and Children.
                        [Stabs both, and Exeunt.
    ADM. Heard'st thou, Cavagnes? said they not my Children.
    CAV. I know not what you say; the stroak of Death
Has stun'd my sense of Hearing.
    ADM.   Yet let's crawl
With all our Wounds into each others Arms,   40
And hand in hand go Martyr'd thus to Heaven.
    CAV. I am gone, farewel.   [Dyes.
    ADM.   Why dost thou shudder thus,
And gasp upon my Bosom? 'Twas his last;

---

    37 my Children? C_{1+}.

My Soul so likes her house, she's loth to part;
But, O what Builder can repair the ruines?   45
The Lights are choak'd, the Windows are damn'd up,
The main Beams crack, and the Foundation sinks;
Besides, the Lordly Owner warns me forth:
I come, great Master of the World and me,
And, O revenge, revenge thy Peoples blood.   50
A hundred thousand Souls for Justice call;
Let not the guiltless without Vengeance fall.   [Dyes.

        Enter the Duke of Guise and Souldiers.

    GUI. So fling him down, down with him to the Court,
Expose his Carcass to the Peoples mercy,
Drag him away, and hurl him from the Window: 55
See all his Bastards strangled on the spot;
There's Orders for't. The Hostel de Chastillon
Be raz'd for ever: his Posterity
Be made incapable of bearing Office,
Or being Noble; burn his Statue, haste: 60
There's a Commission granted for the deed;
Nay, kill, as if 'twere Sport to see 'em bleed.   [Exeunt.

Scene V.

The Louvre. *

Queen Mother, Cardinal, Duke of Anjou, Colonel D'O.

    Q. M. Here Colonel bring forth your Prisoners,
And let me see these Leaders of the Faction.

        The Scene draws, showing the Commanders standing with their
        hands ty'd behind 'em betwixt the Souldiers in a rank.

        The Count de Rochfaucalt, Marquis de Renel, Piles,
            Pluvialt, Pardillan, and Lavardin.

Give the Word Colonel.
    D'O.   Fire on 'em all.   [Shoot.

---

    * The scene is marked thus in all editions, though its handling is some-
    what confusing. Apparently the Queen Mother is standing above in a
    window of the Louvre, and orders the Colonel with the firing squad be-
    low to fire upon the Huguenots. The body of the Admiral is shown at
    the back of the stage.

The Scene draws, and shews the Admiral's Body burning.

GUI. I saw the Master Villain dragg'd along
To Execution, by the Common People,   5
Who from the Shoulders tore the mangled Head,
Cut off his Hands, and at Mountfaucon hung him,
Half burning, by one Leg upon the Gallows.

Enter King, Princes, Alberto Gondi.

KING. O horror! horror! O thou cruel Guise!
O Mother! Brother! and thou Murd'ring Priest!   10
Dost thou not blush to sail in Seas of ruin,
To hang the Flag of a Damn'd Pyrat forth,
Yet call thy bloody Bark the Christian Church?
Or, tell me, Canst thou lay the Furies here,
Pale Hugonots that haunt me up and down   15
Through Chambers, into Closets, Beds, and Couches?
Or dar'st thou shield me, when the Admiral's Ghost
Claps to my Heart the Dagger of my Word?
      Q. M. Why are you thus?
      KING.   The Angel's words are true,
And Charles is near his end. O Mother! Mother!   20
Hear my last words, and take my dying Counsel,
Stop the vast Murder that you have begun;
For know, all Churches by Decree and Doctrine,
Kings by their Sword and Balance of their Justice,
All Learning, Christian, Moral, and Prophane,   25
Shall by the virtue of their Mercury Rod
For ever damn to Hell those curs'd Designs
That with Religion's Face to ruin tend,
And go by Heav'n to reach the blackest end.   [Exeunt Omnes.

FINIS.

EPILOGUE*

By Mr. Powell.

How Wise are they, that can with patience bear,
And just Reflections moderately hear,
Unmov'd by Passion, as unsway'd by Fear.
To them we Dedicate this Play to night,
That having long been Banish'd from the Light,   5
Hush'd and Imprison'd close, as in the Tow'r,
Half prest to Death by a Dispensing Pow'r;
To take a lawful Tryal for each Fact,
Is just come out by th' Habeas Corpus Act.
Rome's Friends, no doubt, suppos'd there might be shown   10
Just such an Entertainment of their own,
The Plot, the Protestants, the Stage, the Town.
But no such fear our Hugonots allarm'd,
True English Hearts are always better arm'd.
For if the Valliant in a little Town,   15
Batter'd and Starving, their brave Cause durst own;
If Peasants scorning Death, can Guard our Walls,
And the mild Priesthood turn to Generals,
Britains stand firm, and in short time you'l see,
Your own, and Neighbouring Realms serene and free,   20
Clear'd from the choaking Fogs of Popery.
No Massacres, nor Revolutions fear,
Affairs are strangely alter'd since last year,
Infallibility himself does run,
The Garden's weeded, and the Moles are gone.   25
Not Gold to Lawyers, to th' Ambitious Power,
Not lusty Switzer to a lustful Whore,
To Gamesters luck, to Beauty length of days,
Nor to a wrinkled wither'd Widdow praise,
Can give such Joy, as to behold once more,   30
An English Army on the Gallick Shore.
That this will be, the Poets Prophesie,

---

* This Epilogue seems to have been taken from A PROLOGUE TO THE
MASSACRE OF PARIS: FOR MR. BETTERTON, which appears in
the SONGS COMPLETE of Tom D'Urfey, 1719, pp. 351-352. D'Urfey
wrote what he thought was to be the prologue for Lee's play. It turned
out to be the epilogue. The version here given in the 1690 edition of
Lee's play is far from what appears to have been the original version,
that is, the version D'Urfey printed in his SONGS COMPLETE. The
two versions are so different, indeed, that it seems wise to give the
text of the 1719 edition following the 1690 version.

The Poets all were Prophets formerly.
T'inspire 'em then, give ours, to night his due,
His Tale is somewhat bloody, but 'tis true.   35
A Tragick Truth shown to an Honest end,
And can the Good or Wise of neither Sect offend.
Fancy and Stile, far as the rest excel,
In our Deliv'rance-Year, let no Tongue tell,
Poets the only curst on whom no Manna fell.   40
Plead that they may by Caesar's Influence breathe,
And mix a Lawrel with his Oaken Wreath.
Then shall his Glory Flourish to the height,
Then every Pen shall Panegyrick write.
This, this was He, who blest by Sacred Pow'r,   45
To England its Religion did restore,
So firm, that Rome cou'd never hurt it more.

FINIS.

EPILOGUE — 1719 VERSION

BRAVE is that Poet that dares draw his Pen,
To expose the nauseous Crimes of guilty Men:
As once did our Immortal Patron, Ben.
And Wise are they that can with Patience bear,
And just Reflections moderately hear,   5
Unmov'd by Passion, as unsway'd by Fear:
These we present a Tragick piece to Night,
That has some Years been banish'd from the Light;
Hush'd and imprison'd close, as in the Tower,
Half press'd to Death by a dispensing Power: 10
Rome's Friend, no doubt, suppos'd there might be shown,
Just such an Entertainment of their own,
The Plot, the Protestants, the Stage, the Town:
But no such Fear our Hugenots alarm'd,
True English Hearts are always better Arm'd: 15
For if the Valiant in a little Town,
Batter'd and starving their brave Cause, durst own,
And now to take a Tryal for it's fact,
Is just come out by th' Habeas Corpus Act.
If Peasants scorning Death can guard their Walls,   20
And the mild Priesthood, turn to Generals;
Britains look up, and this blest Country see,
In spite of byass'd Law serene and free,
Cleer'd from it's choaking Foggs of Popery.
No Massacres or Revolutions fear,   25
Affairs are strangely alter'd in one Year:
Lord what a Hurry was there here one Night,
The Irish come, they Burn, they're now in sight;

A city Taylor swore, with Fear grown Wild,
He saw a huge Tall Teague devour a Child; 30
We have no Nuncio in our Councils now,
Nor pamper'd Jesuites with our Heifers Plough:
Infallibility himself does run,
The Garden's Weeded, and the Moles are gone;
The barbarous French too that Thuanus quotes, 35
Of old so diligent in cutting Throats:
Which as Example to Posterity,
To Night you'll here this dreadful Mirrour see,
Must be remember'd in their Progeny:
A spurious Race now on our Seas are steering, 40
And beat us by the way of Buccaneering;
Not Gold to Lawyers, to th' Ambitious Power,
Not Lusty Switzer to a lustful Whore:
To Gamesters Luck, to Beauty length of Days,
Nor to a wrincled wither'd Widow Praise; 45
Could give such Joy as to our Country-men,
To see great Orange sieze his own again:
This glorious Chace, no doubt, you'll all pursue,
Mean while our Author begs a Favour too;
You that his Merit and Distress have known, 50
To guard him from the Criticks of the Town:
That this will be the Poet's Prophecy,
The Poets all were Voters formerly;
To incourage then give ours to Night his due,
His Tale is somewhat Bloody, but 'tis true, 55
A moral Truth shown to an honest End,
And can the Good or Wise of neither Sect offend:
Fancy and Stile far as the rest excel,
In our deliverance Year let no Tongue tell,
Poets the only Curst, on whom no Manna fell. 60
Plead therefore that they may by Caesar's influence breath,
And mix a Lawrel with his Oaken Wreath;
So shall his Glory flourish to the height,
Then every Pen in leaves of Brass shall write:
This, this was he, that blest by sacred Power, 65
To England its Religion did Restore,
So firm, that Rome could never hurt it more. *

---

65 [This, this]; This this LC. Spacing in LC copy indicates that the comma had fallen out.
* The copy-text for this "Prologue" is that in the Library of Congress, indicated as LC.

Cæsar Borgia;

SON OF

Pope Alexander

THE

S I X T H:

A

TRAGEDY

Acted at the

Duke's Theatre

BY

Their Royal Highnesses Servants.

Written by *NAT. LEE.*

LONDON:

Printed by *R. E.* for *R. Bentley*, and *M. Magnes*, in *Russel-*
Street in *Covent-Garden*, near the *Piazza*. 1680.

CAESAR BORGIA

Introduction

I Date and Stage History:

Genest gives the date of the first performance of CAESAR BORGIA as 1680; Ward gives the same date. Nicoll, on the other hand, says that it was produced about September, 1679, and Ham agrees with this as the approximate date. However, if the reference in the Epilogue to burning "the Pope's Effigies" is an allusion to the pope-burning procession of November 17, 1679, then the play must have been produced after that date, possibly in the last part of 1679 or the beginning of 1680. Apparently, after permission to produce THE MASSACRE OF PARIS was refused in 1679, Lee hurriedly wrote CAESAR BORGIA in order to capitalize upon the current anti-Catholic feeling stirred up by the Popish Plot. A remark in the anonymous comedy ROMES FOLLIES; OR, THE AMOROUS FRYARS (1682) implies that Lee had considerable difficulty in getting permission to produce his tragedy.[1] It appeared at Dorset Garden, with Betterton in the title role, and Mrs. Lee as Bellamira. An enigmatic comment by Downes seems to indicate that it succeeded "but indifferently."[2] Certainly Charles himself could not have looked with favor on a play which attacked the Catholics so violently; and Lee, in his Dedication, complains that he had "been so harshly handl'd" by the critics that his "courage quite fail'd." Apparently the play was not a success, and Genest lists only two revivals of it: Haymarket, Aug. 19, 1707, and Drury Lane, Jan. 3, 1719. There is no record of any later production.

II Sources:

The chief sources of the plot of CAESAR BORGIA were three Italian works:
(1) Guicciardini's HISTORIA d'ITALIA (1561), translated by Geffrey Fenton, 1568, with later editions in 1577 and 1618.
(2) Tomaso Tomasi's VITA DEL DUCA VALENTINO (1655), translated into French in 1671.
(3) Machiavelli's SINIGALLIA TRACT, or DESCRIPTION OF THE METHODS ADOPTED BY THE DUKE VALENTINO WHEN MURDERING VITELLOZZO VITELLI, OLIVEROTTO DA FERMO, etc. (1502).

From these sources Lee drew the historical facts concerning Caesar Borgia's murder of his brother, the Duke of Gandia, and of the Orsini; but Lee altered and adapted these materials considerably in order to suit his dramatic purposes. For instance, Tomasi says that Borgia and his brother were in love with the same woman, and that Borgia murdered his brother because the woman preferred his brother; but in Tomasi's account, this woman is their sister Lucretia. Lee mentions the rivalry of the two brothers over Lucretia, but in his love plot, he substitutes a fictitious character, Bellamira, for Lucretia. This fictitious character also plays a part in the affair between Borgia and the Orsini. Historically, Borgia was determined upon the death of the Orsini because of their opposition to his power; Machiavelli relates that Borgia enticed them with false promises and then murdered them, but there was no question of any love affair between a daughter of Paul Orsini and Borgia. By making Bellamira the daughter of old Paul, Lee connected the Orsini affair with his love plot and thereby gave his play greater dramatic unity.

Lee also drew upon these sources for many minor historical details in his play, such as Borgia's unsuccessful love affair with Charlotta, his raping of the Venetian Lady, the ceremony of the Rose, and the accidental death of the Pope

by poisoning. These details are pointed out specifically in the explanatory notes
to the play.

The part which Machiavelli plays in the drama was largely fabricated by
Lee. According to historical accounts Machiavelli was sent by the Florentines
to aid Borgia against the Orsini, but he played no part in the rivalry between
Borgia and his brother. Lee portrays his character according to the Renaissance
misconception of the man rather than according to history, making him a Jacobean
villain similar in many ways to Iago, Edmund, De Flores, and Bosola. A number
of passages in the play, expressing Machiavelli's philosophy, are drawn directly
from THE PRINCE, but often with a misinterpretation of Machiavelli's real principles.

Lee was also considerably indebted to Shakespeare for certain dramatic
situations. The influence of OTHELLO is especially notable. Machiavelli arouses Borgia's jealousy in the same diabolical fashion that Iago arouses Othello's
jealousy, and with the same result -- the murder of his wife. In each play the
wife and her supposed accomplice are innocent; and in each instance the ambition
of the villain is the chief motivating force. Unlike Iago, however, Machiavelli is
sincerely attached to Borgia and does not wish to gain any revenge, either upon
him or upon Gandia. Bellamira, unlike Desdemona, moreover, is actually in
love with another man and not with her husband.

Further indebtedness to Shakespeare can be found in certain other parts of
the tragedy. The character of Stephano, invented by Lee, bears a close resemblance to that of Prince Arthur in KING JOHN. Ascanio's account of how the
common people took the news of Gandia's murder (Act V, iii) is very similar to
Hubert's account of how the common people reacted to the death of Arthur (KING
JOHN, IV, ii). And the whole scene in which Borgia and Machiavelli vie with
each other in cursing Gandia and Bellamira (Act IV, i) is merely a paraphrase
of a similar scene in HENRY VI, Part II (III, ii). Frequently, also, particular
lines throughout the play bear a marked resemblance to lines in Shakespeare,
as is pointed out in the explanatory notes.

III Criticism:

In the Dedication to this play, Lee complained that he had been "harshly
handl'd" by the critics of the time. This contemporary criticism apparently was
verbal, for it has not survived in print to the present time; but many later critics
have handled CAESAR BORGIA with similar harshness. A. W. Ward bitterly de-
nounced it: "The play forms one of the most outrageous attempts of Restoration
tragedy to revive the worst horrors of the Elisabethan drama in the days of its
crudity and in those of its decay; and the language is frequently as outrageous as
the theme...."[4] R. G. Ham describes it as "a mélange of atrocity culled by
the playwright from Guicciardini and from Dacres' translation of Machiavelli,
and then concocted after an Elizabethan recipe."[5] It is, he says, "altogether
Jacobean in its joy of poisoned gloves and sudden strangulation." Nettleton,
also, speaks of it disparagingly: "CAESAR BORGIA proceeds to its grim conclusion with the strangling of the heroine on the stage, and with the poisoning of
the rest of the chief characters."[6]

On the other hand, Genest commented: " -- this is on the whole a good play,
with little bombast."[7] And Allardyce Nicoll felt that it had good as well as bad
elements:

Externally it is but a gruesome murder drama, filled with the true "heroic" exclamations, with little to stay our attention. Bellamira, the innocent victim of this hotbed of lust and of bloodthirstiness, we somehow cannot feel for: she is too weak and ephemeral. In Caesar, however, Lee has evidently tried to present what is rarely seen in Restoration tragedies -- a complex character. In him we see, not the nauseous struggle of love and honour, but of manliness and vicious influence, of conscience warring against the pernicious atmosphere in which he has been bred. This complexity in places is not badly worked out, particularly in the second act, where the action and the dialogue, from the scene between Orsino and Bellamira to that between Caesar and Machiavel, rise to very near poetic heights. [8]

Dobrée, likewise, feels that certain passages, such as Gandia's farewell to and renunciation of Bellamira, deserve praise, despite the dominant fury and extravagance of the play as a whole. And he says of Lee's Machiavelli, that he is "surely the most machiavellian Machiavelli ever drawn."[9]

Van Lennep agrees with Nicoll that the character of Borgia is a complex one, and he points out that it shows a development or rather degeneracy throughout the play, until at the last Borgia has become a completely hardened villain. But the most important aspect of the play, he feels, is its reflection of Renaissance influence:

> CAESAR BORGIA displays how completely he had renounced the heroic drama and turned to the Elizabethans, especially Shakespeare, for inspiration. The play is a tragedy of blood in direct line with THE SPANISH TRAGEDY, HAMLET, and the works of Webster and Tourneur. [10]

It is not, in Van Lennep's opinion, a really good imitation of Jacobean tragedy, since it has "too little sanity and too much blood and thunder"; also it is "marred by hastiness of composition and wildness of expression." Lee could not rival the great Jacobean dramatists; yet Van Lennep believes he deserves credit for making the attempt:

> Lee had neither Webster's genius for this type of tragedy nor Webster's insight into character. Yet the play is powerfully written and indicates that, of all the Restoration dramatists, Lee alone had capability of following in the footsteps of Webster. [11]

Van Lennep's judgment on the play is a sound one. Certainly we do not find in CAESAR BORGIA the dark genius which inspires THE DUCHESS OF MALFI. There is too much extravagance, too much horror for the sake of horror; and in the final act Lee seems to take a fiendish delight in the piling up of atrocities. Still, the play does have a powerful fascination, even though it may be the fascination of horror; the plot moves irresistibly onward, through the evil genius and designs of Machiavelli, just as that of OTHELLO does through the stratagems of Iago; and the denouement, although it may involve too much of abhorrence, is not entirely lacking in the Aristotelian elements of pity and fear.

IV Texts:

Editions compared:

Q₁	R. Bentley and M. Magnes	1680
Q₂	R. Bentley	1696
Q₃	Rich. Wellington	1711
C₁	R. Wellington	1713
C₂	M. P. & Sam. Chapman	1722
C₃	W. Feales...	1734

As copy-text for this edition, the first quarto, 1680, has been followed. Five copies of this quarto have been compared in order to determine what stop-press corrections may have been made. One of these is the copy in the University of Kentucky Library; two copies are in the Folger Shakespeare Library; and two are in the Library of the University of Texas. Variants among these copies are recorded in the textual footnotes, and the copies are designated as follows: Q_1(KU), Q_1(DFo 1), Q_1(DFo 2), Q_1(TxU 1), Q_1(TxU 2).[12]

The edition has the following collation:

4°; A-K^4, 40 leaves, pp. [8], 1-70, pp. [2].

[A1^r]: title-page; [A1^V]: blank; A2^r: Epistle Dedicatory To the Right Honourable PHILIP, / Earl of PEMBROKE, and / MONGOMERY, &c. / ; A2^V-3^V: running title The Epistle Dedicatory.; A4^r: PROLOGUE; A4^V: Dramatis Personae., The Scene ROME.; B1^r: head title Caesar Borgia. / [rule] / ACT I. SCENE I. / [rule] / and text; B1^V-K3^V: text. Running title CAESAR BORGIA.; K4^r: [double rule] EPILOGUE.; K4^V: Epilogue.

A comparison of the five copies of Q_1 reveals two variations. One is a printer's error in outer forme K(TxU 1), corrected in other copies. The other, and the only significant change made while the quarto was going through the press, was the alteration in the Epistle Dedicatory which appears in Q_1(DFo 2), involving both outer and inner formes A, details of which are given in a textual footnote to the Epistle.

The first quarto of CAESAR BORGIA, although brought out by Lee's regular publishers, Bentley and Magnes, is not so carefully printed as the first quartos of most of his other plays. In the matter of accidentals, there is a tendency to use a question mark where a period, colon, or some other mark would be expected. The later editions usually correct this punctuation. The present editors have, nevertheless, followed the later editions in only those instances where Q_1 departs sharply from the printing practices found in the first quartos of Lee's other plays. Also, in the matter of substantive readings the first quarto presents some problems. A few passages do not seem to be intelligible, nor are these passages amended in the later editions. In one or two cases, the probable meaning can be gathered from the context, and in such instances the present editors have made the proper correction, footnoting the original reading. Lastly, a number of passages in Q_1 have obviously irregular lining; this irregularity appears also in the later editions. In a few instances, where the regular line division is obvious, the present editors have substituted this for the original, footnoting the change. In some cases, where the division is not so unquestionable, the original lining has been left, and a probable re-lining has been suggested in the footnotes. With the exceptions noted above, the present edition follows the first quarto both in substantive readings and in accidentals.

The later editions show few changes, aside from an occasional attempt to regularize the accidentals of the text or to rationalize the substantive reading. The changes have been adopted only rarely in the present text. Wherever the present editors adopt a later reading, the original reading of Q_1 is noted in the footnotes; but variations in the later editions not adopted into the text have been recorded in the footnotes only when such variations are of interest as corrections which an author might approve, or as alterations which reflect the publisher's "improvements" and "clarifications." It should be noted here that Q_2 is printed from Q_1, Q_3 from Q_2, C_1 from Q_3, C_2 from C_1, and C_3 from C_2. In no case did a later edition go back to Q_1 for its text.

To the Right Honourable PHILIP,

Earl of PEMBROKE, and

MONTGOMERY*, &c.

My Lord;
  When an Universal Consternation spreads through the Kingdom, and the
peace which every man enjoys becomes dreadful to him; when mens minds
in this dead calm of State are as busie, as 'tis fear'd, the hands of some
wou'd be in the Tempest of a Battel, to see a Poet plotting in his Chamber
quite another way, painting fast as vigorous Fancy can inspire him, draw-   5
ing the past World, the present, and to come, in a narrow space, is an
Image not unworthy a grave man's Contemplation. It is the business of
poor Poets to be the diversion of mankind; pleasure is their being. I think
I may call 'em the Mistresses of the World; which if granted, I am sure 'tis
easie to prove their Gallants very brutish, for they generally loath them as   10
soon as they are enjoy'd: The best of 'em come under the severest lash of
the greatest men; nay, the least will be shooting their Bolts, and when the
Mastiffs worry 'em, the little Curs will be barking; the whole World censures, and ev'ry daring Poet that comes forth, must expect to be like the
Almanack Hero, all over wounds. For my own part, I have been so harshly   15
handl'd by some of 'em, that my courage quite fail'd me; nor wou'd I now
appear in print, but under the Protection and Patronage of your Lordship.
Your Illustrious Forefathers, and indeed all your Eminent Relations, have
always been of the First-rate Nobility, Patrons of Wit and Arms, magnif-
icently brave, true old-stampt Brittons, and ever foremost in the Race of   20
Glory. Not to unravel half your Honourable Records, I challenge all the
men of Fame to show an Equal to the Immortal Sidney, ev'n when so many
contemporary Worthies flourish'd, I mean Sir Philip, the name still of your
Lordship, true Rival of your Honour, one that cou'd match your Spirit, so
most extravagantly great, that he refus'd to be a King. He was at once a   25
Caesar and a Virgil, the leading Souldier, and the foremost Poet, all after
this must fail: I have paid just Veneration to his Name, and methinks the
Spirit of Shakespear push'd the commendation.
  That there are in your Lordship all these Excellent Grains which made
this Perfect Man, I think my self bound by reason to tell the World, which   30

---

* MONTGOMERY,] Q$_{2+}$; MONGOMERY Q$_1$.
29 ff. One copy of the 1680 edition (Q$_1$) of this play, and the only one that
    Fredson Bowers has found in his examination of twenty copies of this
    quarto, is described in the Folger catalogue thus:
        "Another issue. Apparently varies only in alterations in the ded-
        ication, including the insertion of a slightly revised version of
        Shakespeare's epitaph, sig. A2^V."
    It seems that this issue involved the change of two formes while it was
    being printed, in that it goes from A2^V to A3^V. It further appears that

to my particular observation and certain knowledge has done you wrong. I
must acknowledg, that your boiling Youth has made great Salleys; and so
did Alexander, and our Great Fifth Henry: Your Spirit complains, as Alexander's did, for Action, who grudg'd his Fathers Conquests, as if his Soul
was pent, and wanted Elbow-room, resolv'd to go abroad o're Walls, if not   35
through Doors; and men of Sense laugh at your precise Fellow, your Cyn-
ick in a Tub, who thwarts the course of Nature, and is never pleas'd, but
when he sees grey Hairs upon a young Head. If to be truly Valiant, ev'n in
cold Blood, Magnificent as the old Nobility, infinitely Charitable, modest as
Humility it self, the fastest Friend upon Earth, where your Lordship is   40
pleas'd to fix the Honour; if these Ingredients can compound one admirable
Man, then may your Lordship stand forth a Monument of lasting Honour.
Perhaps for this I shall incur the notion of a Flatterer; Flattery indeed is a
Catholick ill, it passes through the World, and suits with all Complexions:
'Tis an insinuating Poyson, a Jesuit's Powder, which seems to intend the   45
Cure of the Disease it promotes: I am confident, all those who have the
honour of your Lordships acquaintance, will tell me I have said too little.
Let it suffice, that I imitate the best of Poets in a short but hearty acknowl-
edgment of my Obligations to your Lordship.

----

this version of the dedication is perhaps an earlier printing than that
appearing in other copies of the quarto, though it would perhaps be
difficult to determine for sure whether it was first or last.

    The change is as follows: A2^V, line 23 ff., adds this:
        ..."let Shakespear then, who made his own, give him his epi-
    taph.

            Reader, for Jesus sake forbear,
            To stir the Dust inclosed here:
            Blest be the man that spares these Stones,
            And curst be he that moves my Bones.

    That there are in your Lordship all these Excellent Grains
    which made this Perfect Man, I think my self bound by rea-
    son to tell the World, which on my Conscience, and with all
    the Asseverations that an honest man should make, has done
    you wrong."

Then the text follows the other Q$_1$'s down to "Disease it promotes."
Thereafter it varies thus:
        "But if ought I have said, of so good a Subject as your Lord-
    ship, be false, may all my Writings be despis'd, and vile to
    view, as common Whores in Boxes, or damn'd Actors in a
    good Play. Your Lordships Great Uncle shone upon the
    mighty Ben. with a full Favour, though my best Merits are
    not the ten thousand part of his smallest labours; yet I doubt
    but your Lordships infinite goodness will accept of my honest
    intentions, which to your Lordships service shall ever be
    humbly offer'd,
                        By my Lord,
                Your Lordships most Humble and
                    Obedient Servant,
                        Nat. Lee"

Therefore I hope, as your Lordships Great Uncle shone upon the mighty   50
Ben. with a full Favour, (though my best Merits are not the ten thousand
part of his smallest labours) your Lordships infinite goodness will accept
of my honest intentions, which to your Lordships service shall ever be humbly offer'd,

By my Lord,

Your Lordships most Humble and

Obedient Servant,

NAT. LEE.

PROLOGUE, Written by Mr. Dryden.

Th' unhappy man, who once has trail'd a Pen,
Lives not to please himself but other men:
Is always drudging, wasts his Life and Blood,
Yet only eats and drinks what you think good:
What praise soe're the Poetry deserve,   5
Yet every Fool can bid the Poet starve:
That fumbling Lecher to revenge is bent,
Because he thinks himself or Whore is meant:
Name but a Cuckold, all the City swarms,
From Leaden-hall to Ludgate is in Arms.   10
Were there no fear of Antichrist or France,
In the best times poor Poets live by chance.
Either you come not here, or as you grace
Some old acquaintance, drop into the place,
Careless and qualmish with a yawning Face.   15
You sleep o're Wit, and by my troth you may,
Most of your Talents lye another way.
You love to hear of some prodigious Tale,
The Bell that toll'd alone, or Irish Whale.
News is your Food, and you enough provide,   20
Both for your selves and all the World beside.
One Theatre there is of vast resort,
Which whilome of Requests was call'd the Court.
But now the great Exchange of News 'tis hight,
And full of hum and buzz from Noon till Night: 25
Up Stairs and down you run as for a Race,
And each man wears three Nations in his Face.
So big you look, tho' Claret you retrench,
That arm'd with bottled Ale, you huff the French:
But all your Entertainment still is fed   30
By Villains, in our own dull Island bred:
Would you return to us, we dare engage
To show you better Rogues upon the Stage:
You know no Poison but plain Rats-bane here,
Death's more refind, and better bred elsewhere.   35
They have a civil way in Italy
By smelling a perfume to make you dye,
A Trick would make you lay your Snuff-box by.
Murder's a Trade --- so known and practis'd there,
That 'tis Infallible as is the Chair ---   40
But mark their Feasts, you shall behold such Pranks,
The Pope says Grace, but 'tis the Devil gives Thanks.

---

12 blest times Q_3-C_1, C_3; blest time C_2.

DRAMATIS PERSONAE.

Caesar Borgia,	} Sons of Alexander the Sixth	Mr. Betterton.
Palante, Duke of Gandia.		Mr. Williams.
Machiavel,	Secretary of Florence	Mr. Smith.
Paul Orsino,	Head of the Factions against Borgia	Mr. Gillow.
Ascanio Sforza,	A Buffoon Cardinal.	Mr. Lee. 5
Vitellozzo,	Chief of the Vitelli.	Mr. Peircifull.
Enna,		
Ange,		
Alonzo,		
Don Michael,		10
Adrian,		
Oliverotto,		
Duke of Gravina,		
Seraphino, son of Caesar Borgia,		
Cardinals, &c.		15
Bellamira,	Daughter of Orsino.	Mrs. Lee.
Adorna,	Her Kinswoman and Confident.	Mrs. Price.
Attendants, &c.		

The Scene R O M E .

---

6 Mr. Percival. Q_{2+}.
9-11 Alonzo, Don Michael, Adrian,] C_{2+}; om. Q_1-C_1.
12-14 Oliverotto, Duke of Gravina, Seraphino, son of Caesar Borgia,];
om. Q_{1+}.

Act I. Scene I.

Scene is a Chamber of State, at distance are discovered little
American Boys with Boxes of Jewels in their hands; on each side of
the Stage, from the flat Scene to the Chamber, long Indian Screnes
are spread at their full length.

Enter Alonzo, and Don Michael.

D. MICH. Are these the Presents, say'st thou, of the late
New Cardinal Ascanio Sforza?
ALON. They are; he offers thus to Machiavel,
And thinks that Gold may bribe him to betray
The Duke Valentinois. But, Michael, tell me   5
What does the World report of this Creation,
Does it not rail, and grin, and bite the Pope?
D. MICH. Has it not Reason? For, betwixt our selves,
Would any man in his high Dignity
So vilely sell the Glories of the Church?   10
Twelve Cardinals at once created!
Ascanio first, because he bids him most:
A fine effeminate Villain, bred in Brothels,
Senseless, illiterate, the Jear of Rome,
A blot to the whole See! One fitter far   15
For Hospitals, that paints and patches up
A wretched Carkass worried in the Stews.
But, see! the gaudy Pageant moves this way:
How spruce he looks! and with a Pocket-Glass
Surveys the gloating Image.
ALON.   All Luxury: 20
I heard, the night succeeding his Creation,
That he got drunk, and kiss'd the Prelates round
For joy --- But, see he comes; retire and leave me. [Ex. D. Mich.

Enter Ascanio Sforza.

ASCA. Well, Borgia, well! if I am not reveng'd!
Was there none else in Rome, but Bellamira?   25
Ah Bella, Bella, Bella, Bella, Bellamira!
I saw her first at Mass, as I remember;
Cherubin and Seraphin were nothing to her:
Oh such a skin full of alluring flesh!
Ah, such a ruddy, moist, and pouting Lip;   30
Such Dimples, and such Eyes! such melting Eyes,
Blacker than Sloes, and yet they sparkl'd fire,
Then such a way she had to roul 'em round;
As thus, and thus --- a thousand amorous ways;
And wink and gloat, and turn 'em to the corners ---   35

ALON. My Noble Lord!
ASCA.   My dear, my dear Alonzo!
Nay, let me greet thee: 'twas the Fathers Custom.
But tell me, lovely, dear Alonzo, tell me:
Thou hast the softest fine Complexion for
A Lover; best take heed of walking late: 40
Tell me I say, or I will pinch thy Cheek?
Moves he this way, or does he teem alone
With some state Birth? if so, I'll wait agen.
ALON. Whom does your Eminence intend?
ASCA.   Thy Lord:
Whom should I mean, intend, or think of else?   45
Thy Lord and mine. Well he's an Oracle! intend!
Why man I dream of nothing else!
ALON.   But Wenches.
ASCA. O, Machiavel! there, there's a word, a sound,
An Air, a blast, a Thunder-clap of wit,
To rowse our Foggy thick scul'd Cardinals: 50
I'll say no more; Would he were Pope,
Head of the Christian world, and I his Engine,
His particular member, to bring, to cast,
To throw, disperse, convey the warmest
Sprinklings of his benediction.   55
ALON. My Lord I humbly offer'd your Address,
While with an eye, swift as the Sun and piercing,
He ran your Letter o're: and sure it stirr'd him;
For strait he turn'd, and darting me, he ask'd
If the great Cardinal, meaning you, my Lord,   60
Which shews the deep respect he bears your person,
Knew not that Borgia was his best of Friends.
Borgia, he cry'd again, to whom the Lords
Of Florence sent me their Ambassadour
With promis'd aid against the Rebel Orsins.   65
ASCA. Has he receiv'd --- stay, I say, has he? here,
Open thy Fist, now gripe me fast, and tell me.
ALON. I durst not name your Presents;
But, bowing, soon retir'd, and plac'd 'em here,
That as he follows, he may view at once   70
All your Magnificence --- if ought of Earth
His temper holds, this lightning will dissolve it:
But see! He comes; be pleas'd, Sir, to retire,
And you shall hear the Zeal with which I serve you.

----

36 dear Alonz! Q_2-C_1.
37 thy Father's C_{2+}.
41 Cheek, C_{2+}.
56 Lord, Q_{2+}.
65 Rebel Orsino. Q_{3+}.

Enter Machiavel.

MACH. Thus have I drawn the platform of their Fates;   75
As oft I have beheld, by Masters hands,
A Tale in painting admirably told;
Here a soft Dido stabb'd into the brest,
A Hero there thrown headlong from a Window,
To meet her Lover wrack'd upon the Shore: 80
So have I form'd in more than Brass or Marble,
The Deaths of those whom I intend to hush.
O, Caesar Borgia! such a Name and Nature!
That is my second self; a Machiavel!
A Prince! who, by the vigor of this brain,   85
Shall rise to the old height of Roman Tyrants.
ALON. He deeply thinks; nor dare I interrupt him,
Till he comes forward.
ASCA. Peace, and give him way --- Oh such a Head-piece!
MACH. In all my strict enquiries, all the humors   90
Which I have drain'd with more then Chymists pains,
I have not found a temper so compleat
To finish forth a greatness as my Caesar's.
First; he's a Bastard, got in a fit of Nature!
She shook him from her Nerves in a Convulsion;   95
His Father stampt the Bullion in a heat,
And taking from the Mint the fiery ore,
His Image blest, and cry'd, it is my own.
Yet more, a Priest begot him, and 'tis thought
That Earth is more oblig'd to Priests for Bodies,   100
Than Heav'n for Souls! nay, and a young Priest too,
Perhaps in the Embraces of a Nun,
Who ventur'd life to clasp the lusty joy.
ASCA. Oh, if a man could but hear him now! Brain, all brain;
Alas, Alonzo, we are stuff to him ---   105
Meer Entrails, but the Guts of Government,
Nothing to him -- hark --- he goes on ---
MACH. Why, what a start of Nature is this man
Whom by Ambition, not by Love I'll raise?
Therefore Ascanio's new golden World,   110
I gravely take, for ruine to the Bride,
To her old doting Father, Brothers, Uncles,
And the whole race of Orsin and Vitelli
Is fixt by Fate and me: No more! the fleeting Air
May catch the sounds, and walls themselves have ears.   115
ALON. My Lord! the Cardinal Ascanio [coming forward and bowing.
Is planted to your order.
MACH.   Let him hear us ---
Urge me no more, --- for 'tis impossible!

---

112 To tell her C₃.

ALON. My Lord, he thinks not so:
He sayes your voice is as the mouth of Heav'n,   120
Stiles you a God, and in the extravagance
Of his unbounded admiration, swears
Nothing to you can be impossible.
  MACH. Extravagance indeed!
Yet such extravagance expresses love,   125
And merits all my thanks; and had he mention'd
Ought but the ruine of my best of Friends,
I would with all the Wings of expedition
Have shot through 1000 bars to do him service.
  ALON. My Lord! he does not hint at Borgia's ruine.   130
  MACH. Does he not wish that I should break the Nuptials?
'Tis sure the marriage I at first dislik'd;
I pierc'd the Charmer with a narrow eye,
And found how Wit and beauty threatn'd in her,
With all the subtlest graces, that might lull   135
Stubborn ambition to inglorious rest:
But love already had perform'd his part,
And laid the Warring Borgia at her Feet,
How then should I oppose his first Enjoyment,
Who was his Legate and sollicited   140
The Parents of the beauteous Bellamira.
  ALON. At least, Sir, for the future, lay some block
That may disturb the progress of their loves;
And since you have alledg'd 'tis for his glory
This marriage were undone: since it is done,   145
Let it be hurtful in the consequence.
  MACH. Thus I should prove indeed a Friend to Florence,
Who hate Orsino's Race: Nay, I should Act
The truest Part of Friendship to my Borgia,
Snatching this Soft'ner from his War-like Bosom,   150
And turning him new bent, for Arms and Glory. ---
Ha! What new Scene of Gallantry is this?
Whence, and from whom comes this Magnificence?
And wherefore kneel these Offerers at my Feet?
  ALON. They are the Children of the new-found World,   155
The Forms of Zemes, call'd the Indian Gods.
  MACH. Away with 'em, and bid 'em tell their Lord,
Machiavel's Virtue never shall be brib'd;
And for their service give 'em twenty Crowns:
But if thou darest to rob 'em of a Spangle,   160
You know my humour, --- never see me more.
  ALON. Doubt not, my Lord, but I'll observe your humour. ---
Come in, my Lord. --- I told you he would melt.

---

129 one thousand Q$_3$, C$_3$; a thousand C$_{1-2}$.
141 Bellamira? C$_{2+}$.

Sir, the great Cardinal. So, --- now they cringe;   [Aside. *
What, and embrace too! Oh thou damn'd, damn'd World!   165
These will be heard, and make your States-man smile,
When Orphans, Widows, and the crippled Souldiers
Are Elbow'd off, and thrust away in frowns.   [Exit, with the Boys.
    MACH. My Lord, you make me wonder! Sure you've been
In love your self with old Orsino's Daughter!   170
    ASCA. Lov'd her, my Lord! witness these falling tears!
Why do you thaw my Nature with your Questions?
Witness bright Stars! witness you golden Planets!
And all ye Woods, and all ye purling Streams;
And Birds and Flocks, and Grots, and Rocks, and Flow'rs!   175
Nay Sir, I tell you, she was mine betroth'd,
If I could cast my Coat, which had been done,
For nothing tickles the present Pope like Gold,
Dazles him that he weeps Indulgences,
Forgives, absolves, all for Omnipotent Gold;   180
Dispenses Pardons sometimes in a fury,
He sends his Bulls abroad that roar like Thunder:
When strait a golden Calm
Comes o're their backs, and then they're still as Lambs;
Why should I hold you long amongst the rest,   185
That saw her Borgia, that unlucky Bastard,
Beheld and lov'd her. --- I, my Lord, was ruin'd.
    MACH. My Lord, I wish the Mariage may not prosper:
He's bent to enjoy her, and in that I sooth him:
For subtly offering once to bring him off,   190
I found pale anger in his Face like Death,
Whereon I feign'd compliance, and have wrought
The business to a head --- But let time work,
And rest assur'd, that what so mean a man
As Machiavel with honour can performe,   195
To pay you perfect service shall be done.
    ASCA. My Lord! farewel --- when I protest and swear,
Ev'n by the Altar of fair Bellamira,
My life is yours: Believe I am your Servant,
Not a step further by my Robe! your Captive,   200
Your Eminence most humble Creature, Servant, Slave. [Ex. Ascanio.
    MACH. I am ty'd for ever.   [Walking.
No dull Buffoon! thou walking lump of Lust;
Not to revenge thy ungorg'd appetite
Shall Borgia kill her; But for his own Renown: 205
He is my Champion-prince, Italian Tyrant,
Not form'd to languish in a Womans arms.
Oh --- 'tis a fault, were I so fram'd for greatness,

---

    * [Aside.]; <u>om</u>. Q_{1+}.
166 Statesmen Q_{3+}.
187 her-- C_1; her? C_{2+}.

E're I would amble in a Female Court,
And cringe, and skip, and play the Ladies Cripple,   210
I would be Gibbetted i'th' Common-way,
For Crows and Daws to peck my Carrion Limbs.
But I must rouze him, and I'll do't by Death,
Ev'n by the bloody Death of her he doats on.

         Enter Adorna.

Here's one Ingredient I must mix to make   215
The potion Death --- The Wretch is deep in Love
With Borgia's Brother, the young Duke of Gandia,
That way I make her sure!
    ADOR.   My Lord.
    MACH.   My dear Adorna,
How goes the marriage forward? and how treats
The gallant Borgia, great Valentinois,   220
Romania's Duke his fair and Virgin Bride?
    ADOR. The Rites are to be solemniz'd this morning;
Tho' Bellamira quite abhors the Marriage,
Who still when Borgia humbly sues for Love;
Answers him with her Tears, and pays his Vows   225
With Ominous weeping.
    MACH.   And how takes he that?
    ADOR. He walks and muses deeply, speaks to no man,
But Paul Orsino, whose most watchful wit
I fear descries where she has lockt her heart;
With a bent brow he eyes the Duke of Gandia,   230
Salutes him not of late: He came this morning
Into her Chamber; dreadful was his action,
Unworthy of my blood, he thundred out;
But if the generous Borgia is refus'd;
Think not of Gandia, but of blood and death.   235
    MACH. What inauspicious Chance discovered to him
A secret, which I thought conceal'd from all,
But thee and me, and those unhappy Lovers?
    ADOR. I cannot guess; he paus'd a while, then sigh'd,
And starting up in fury charg'd her rise: 240
Receive, he cry'd, receive him as a Husband
Whom the selected vertues of thy Sex
Can ne're deserve, adorn thee like a Bride,
And meet him, tho' thy Treacherous heart is Mortgag'd;
Meet him at least with well dissembled Love,   245
Or by my hopes, I'll wreke my anger on thee,
With all the Torments that Italian Fury
Could e're invent for an Adulterous Wretch:
He cry'd I will, and after make thee nothing.

----

225 with Tears Q$_{3+}$.

MACH. Haste thee away! charm with thy utmost skill   250
The mourning Bellamira, to obey him:
The knot once ty'd, Gandia will soon despair.
Leave me to work him then: Millions to one
But I shall make him thine.
    ADOR. But did the Duke of Gandia once protest?   255
    MACH. Protest! He did protest, and swear, and vow.
Go go, and haste! for the day grows upon us.   [Ex. Adorna.
His Brother too! this Duke of Gandia bleeds;
For he is grown of late the Romans darling,
Warm'd in the very Bosom of the Pope,   260
And dearer than my Borgia to his Sister,
The famous Lucrece, who can charm her Father
In all the heat of Excommunications,
When he throws Bulls, like Thunderbolts about him;
She like a Venus to this angry Jove   265
Moves with incestuous Fires, folds her white arm
About his chafing Neck, strokes his black Beard,
And smooths his furrow'd Cheeks to dimpled smiles;
The Brothers too enjoy'd her. O Heav'n, and Earth!
Not the first day, after such infinite time   270
That Motion had th' irregular matter rowl'd,
When all the wandering Atoms hit at last
Into this beauteous form, even when our Sires
First mingled, was there such a loose of Nature,
Such a triumvirate of Lawless Lovers,   275
Such Rivals as out-do even Lucian's Gods!
Ha! the Orsini here! and the Vitelli!
They move this way in murmuring Cabals;
Methinks Death darkens every Visage there.
'Tis so --- They are no more --- Or this is true,   280
Or Machiavel knows nothing of Man-kind.   [Ex. Mach.

      Enter Orsino, Vitellozzo, Ascanio, Adrian, Enna,
      Ange, three Cardinals. Oliverotto, Gravina.

    VITEL. I say agen, I do not like the Marriage;
Were Bellamira mine, I'd sell her off
For Gold, I'd merchandize her tender beauty
With Infidels, and send her to the Turk,   285
Like an Andromada, to gorge the Monster,
Rather than wed her to perfidious Borgia.
    ORSI. You are too violent.
    VITEL.   I think not so:
A drowning man will grasp at any thing,
Nay, sink his Friend that leap'd among the Waves   290

---

255 did the Duke] C_{2+}; did Duke Q_1-C_1.
265 his angry Q_2-C_1; her angry C_{2+}.

To give him life: but you tho in the gulph,
Ride on to ruine, tho your Friends call out.
    ANGE. Nay, though they point the Whirle-pool just before you,
That would devour us all.
    ADRI.   Besides 'tis Impious,
Against all Right of Nature, Law of Reason,   295
To act the Tyrant o're a Daughters will.
    ASCA. She knows the Cruelties of Caesar Borgia,
Has heard his Rapes and Murders! mercy on me!
How did he use the poor Venetian Lady?
He forc'd her in a Wood, nay in a Ditch,   300
As I am credibly inform'd by those
That heard her squeak, in a Dry-Ditch deflowr'd her!
Add yet to this, my Lords; How, when the French,
At sacking of a Town, broke open Nunneries,
He truss'd at least 40 the pretty'st Rogues,   305
The tenderst quaking things! never broke up!
All spotless Maids, like Buds ne're blown upon,
Nor touch'd even with the tip of any Finger,
And kept 'em for his Letchery.
    ORSI. Methinks my Lord Ascanio! my Lord of Millain,   310
Or my Lord Cardinal, more moderation
Would better fit a man of your profession?
I would not come to the old Argument,
For then we clash: Borgia is now my Son;
Therefore I pray once more forbear to tax him;   315
The Theme is great and worthy that we mention,
Romania's Duke and Nephew to the Pope.
    ASCA. Prithee, old Paul: Prithee now ben't so hot:
Good Reverend Gray-beard: if you'l name his Greatness,
Pronounce him right, ev'n as his Holiness   320
Has own'd him to the World without a blush,
His natural Son, his Nephew, or his By blow,
That is, in short, old Paul, his down right Bastard.
    ORSI. Without a blush: should I stand up the Champion
Of absent Borgia, and unravel thee,   325
I tell thee, Priest; thou scandal to the Altar,
Thy Front, thy Eyes, thy Lips, each part of thee
Would blush with Scarlet deeper than thy Robe.
    ASCA. Peace Dotard, peace:
I say old stuttering Paul, thou'lt ha' the worst on't: 330
Therefore peace, peace Dotard.
    ORSI.   Ha!
    VITEL. Forbear: my Lord, Remember!

---

312 Profession. C_{2+}.
322-23 Divided as follows in Q_{1+}:
       His natural Son, his Nephew, or his By blow, that is,
       In short, old Paul, his down right Bastard.

ORSI. How dares he thus provoke me?
Who knows, yet urges me, knows in his heart
How I have pierc'd into his deepest thoughts,   335
Have had intelligence of all his Vices,
Ev'n of his closest, darkest Deeds of Lust,
And dar'st thou call me Dotard? Saucy Churchman!
Thou that gav'st Whores Indulgences for Sin;
So rank, that he frequents the Common Stews;   340
For a new Face would give his Scarlet Coat
To make the Strumpet fine.
    OLIV. My Lord, Consider where, to whom, of whom,
And what it is you utter?
    ORSI.   Place me, some Power,
Upon Saint Peter's Vane, the very Ball,   345
And turn my Voice to Thunder, that I may
Lay open to the World the Hellish Acts
Of this Contagious Prelate.
    ASCA. Spit, spit thy Venom; nay, nay, let him out with't ---
Mark how he shakes now; by my Holy-Dame   350
I have nettled him: Poor Paul --- I pity the old Fool ---
    ORSI. Then Priest, let me demand thee,
Is not the Cupping-glass that burns thy Lust,
And draws thy rising Gall to such a Blister,
My Daughter's scorn, and loathing of thy person?   355
Ha! is't not that? I think I've stung you, Cardinal!
Worse than the Neapolitan Pox you gave
Our Roman Harlots ---
    ASCA. Why how now, Paul, what dost thou grow foul
Mouth'd now? by my Holy-Dame, had I a Sword   360
I'd firk thee, Orsin --- I'd so whip thee, Paul,
So flawg and scourge thee, thou should'st eat thy words.
The Pox! why, how now? ha! the Pox i'faith!
The Pox to me! let me come at him --- hah!
    ORSI. Ha! wilt thou fight?   365
So forward Priest! by Heav'n I'll shave your Crown;
Stand back and let me mow this Poppy off;
This rank red Weed that spoils the Churches Corn.
    VITEL. Did ever fury run to such a height!
Why, my Lord Cardinal, know you this place,   370
And how 'tis priviledg'd?
    ASCA.   My Lord, I am silenc'd.
An easie Man, made up of patience, I!
No Gall in me! give me thy hand, Old Paul:
Henceforth w'are Friends, and as a Friend I'll tell thee,
Ev'n from my Heart, I'll tell thee what I think: 375
Thou are bewitch't, Old Paul, besotted, fool'd ---
This Son-in-Law of thine has seal'd thine Eyes,
And shortly I shall see thee walk the Streets
With a Dog and a Bell --- nay -- prithee be not angry,
For 'tis in love: I'll tell thee of a Dotage,   380

And so your Servant noble Vitellozzo,
Ange and Enna yours -- Farewell, my Lord,
And lastly thine whose Neck is in the Noose,
Old Woodcock, Orsin.   [Exit Cardinal.
    D. GRAVIN.   I am not us'd to fear,
But yet methought Ascanio's last words   385
Were dreadful to my Ears.
    ORSI.   I have engag'd
My Daughter, Life and Honour, and all my Fortunes,
For the Duke's Faith, and the security
Of every person here; why should we doubt him?
Have we not seen his Labour in this matter?   390
Four thousand Duckets, given us down in hand,
With an assurance of our former pay;
Nay more, he binds himself not to constrain
Any one of us to appear in person
Before him, but who pleases of himself: 395
Therefore let me intreat you clear your Brains,
Meet all this day together at the Marriage,
And pay him, as he merits, faithful homage.
    VITEL. There's something here fore-bodes, in spite of
The Musick that he makes, a harsh Conclusion.   400
    ORSI. For shame no more! the very fears of Children,
Because he gives our Friends allowances,
And honours them with Charges, Governments,
Beyond their Qualities, we dread his Dealing,
And swear he means to draw our Faction from us.   405
    VITEL. Henceforth say what you will, do what you please,
Since to your Interests I am link'd by Fate:
I will no more oppose your specious Reasons,
But instantly go wait upon the Duke.   [Trumpets.
    ORSI. This day to add new Honours to the Marriage,   410
Our Son-in-law, the Duke Valentinois,
Receives the Rose before the Consistory,
A Grace which seldom is vouchsafed to Kings;
Indeed the greatest which the Sacred Head
Of the whole Christian World can give to Man,   415
The very highest Round of Humane Glory.

      Scene draws, and shews the Consistory: Borgia comes forward,
          with the Rose carri'd before him in great Pomp. His Son
        Seraphino led by Alonzo, Machiavel, Attendants, Ascanio,
                 and five Cardinals, & c.

    BORG. O Machiavel! was ever Pomp like this?
The Morning dawns with an unwonted Crimson;
The Flow'rs more od'rous seem, the Garden Birds

---

399 spite of all C$_3$.

Sing louder, and the laughing Sun ascends   420
The gaudy Earth with an unusual brightness ---
All Nature smiles, and the whole world is pleas'd,
Even all the World, but thy unhappy Borgia.
    MACH. And why should he, whom every man concludes
The Darling of the Times, whom bounteous Heav'n   425
Has Crown'd with Glory in successful Wars,
Whom it now doubly Crowns with Beauty too,
The brightest of her Sex, why should he thwart
The whole Worlds Vogue, and think himself unhappy?
    BORG. Yes Machiavel! thou worthi'st of Mankind,   430
To thee I'll strip my Heart, that secret Bed,
With Vices, Vertues, every naked thought,
And shew thee all the mixture of a Man.
We are observ'd --- Think me not over-frail
Because I love: were Bellamira dearer,   435
Her Father bleeds, and all the Rebel-Race;
I'll first insnare the Fools: then preach Fate to 'em.
    MACH. And let 'em know, just as the Cords are drawing,
None ought to offend his Prince, and after trust him.
    BORG. My Lord Orsino! O forgive me, Heav'n!   440
Who have thus grosly fail'd to pay the Reverence
I owe the best of Fathers, best of Friends:
This day, this glorious day, for ever blest,
And never to be lost in Times dark Legend,
Crowns me your Son. Thus then I bend my knees,   445
Which are not us'd to kneel but at the Altar:
And O! permit me thus to kiss your Hand,
And pay the Eternal Vows of my Obedience.
    ORSI. O rise, my Lord, all Duty is out-done
With but one single bare Acknowledgment;   450
Yet for a satisfaction to this Company,
Say, do you love my Daughter Bellamira?
    BORG. Ha! what says my Father? do I live?
O Heav'n! why do you wound me with the Question?
Does the poor suff'ring Fair One Vertue love,   455
Who drinks the Brook, and eats what Nature yields,
Rather than feast in Courts with loss of Honour?
Do those, who on the Rack for Heav'n expire,
Love Angels, and Eternal brightness there?
'Tis sure they do: And oh --- 'tis full as sure,   460
That Caesar Borgia dies for Bellamira.
    ORSI. No more; you honour her and me too much:
Therefore this day I give her to your Arms
With all the pleasure of a proud old Father,
O'rejoy'd to see his Daughter match'd above him: 465
By Heav'n, my eyes grow full; here all our Discord
For ever end, all Jars betwixt the Orsins,
Vitelli, and the Duke of Valentinois,
Be buri'd ever in this strict Imbrace.

BORG. Since you will have it so, forgive my Duty;   470
Let me grow bold, and as a Friend imbrace you---
    ORSI. See here, my Lord, for scarce can I distinguish,
Through the bright joy that dazles my weak sight,
Oliverotto, and the Duke Gravina,
With Vitellozzo come to grace your Nuptials: 475
All on their Knees acknowledge you their Prince.
    BORG. My Equals all: Nor shall this Homage be,
I swear it shall not: Rise my Lords; your Arms:
Let me imbrace you round: by all things sacred,
I swear that none of you have been too blame.   480
Were you Confederates against my Arms?
You were: but Borgia's infinite Ambition
Forc'd you against your wills to let him know,
His head-strong Youth, like a young fiery Horse,
Unless you kindly stopt him in his speed,   485
Would hurl him from some Precipice to ruine.
    ORSI. See Vitellozzo! how he takes our Crimes
Upon himself.
    BORG.   Behold this Child, my Son!
I know not any thing the World calls precious,
Which in the dearness of my heart can match him,   490
But Bellamira. Take him Vitellozzo,
Take the dear blood that trickles from my heart,
The very strings that wind about my life,
And let him for my part be Surety,
As beauteous Bellamira is for yours.   495
    ORSI. Farewel, my Lord: with these Attendants here
I go to haste the Bride; and let my life
Be answer for the little Seraphino.   [Ex. Orsin. Vitelli.
    ASCA. He has her now, that delicate bit of Beauty
Which I reserv'd for my own Letchery,   500
He drills her from her old deluded Sire:
Hell! and she melts; she melts into his mouth:
But by my Holy-Dame I'll be reveng'd
On every part of him: His little Bastard,
Because he doats on him, shall strait be mangled ---   505
I'll do't I say: Yes by my Holy-Dame,
I will revenge my loss of Letchery ---
Ha! what a jerk was that? it grates my bones;
Pray Heav'n it ben't a Spice, a little Tang
Of the Neapolitan Itch, O my Holy-Dame.   [Ex. with Cardinals.   510
    BORG. Now Machiavel, prepare to hear my Soul,
Hear to what softness and effeminate mourning
All my dear Victories at last are melted:
For I will tell thee, though thou'lt scarce believe,

---

475 With] ; When Q$_{1+}$.
480 to blame. Q$_{3+}$.

Since first I saw the Charming Bellamira,   515
The very Image of Charlotta's scorn,
I have not had one hour of free repose;
Ev'n when at last I have resolv'd to joyn
Our hands, and trust her with my tender glory,
I've started from my Bed, at midnight rose,   520
And wander'd by the Moon: Then laid me down
Upon some dewy bank, and slept till morn.
 MACH. Therefore there must be some strange Circumstance
That first induc'd those fears, some dang'rous hint
For your suspitions ---
 BORG.   Yes, Machiavel,   525
There is, there is a cause for my suspitions.
 MACH. Are you sure of it?
 BORG.   Most sure I am;
Sure as reserv'dness does imply aversion:
Yet I, as if my flames were fire in Frost,
The more she cools, scorch, rage, and burn the more ---   530
 MACH. I guess your meaning; like Charlotta, she
Has pawn'd her heart---but 'tis confess'd you know him---
 BORG. Ha! did I know the name of him I dread?
What God in Arms should save him from my Sword?
Here thou hast rouz'd the Lion in my heart,   535
Italian spite, revenge and blasting fury
Devours my Soul! all mildness sleeps like Death:
I boil like Drunkards Veins---Death! Hell and Vengeance!
 MACH. Suppress this Fury---
Come! come! my Lord---I find you are better skil'd   540
In Camps than Courts, and know not yet Loves World.
She is reserv'd you say, when you approach her;
Why, let her weep too: was it ever known
A subtle Bride laugh'd on her Wedding Day,
Or clasp'd her Lover in the eye o'th world?   545
I find you are unlearn'd! Sir---'tis their Trade,
The very Nature, Soul, and Life-blood of 'em---
To whine, and cry, and turn their heads away,
When their hearts dote on what they seem to scorn!
 BORG. If it were so!
 MACH.   Why it was always so,   550
Is so, and will be so to the worlds end!
Give me your hand, and take her on my word;
I have been bred in Courts; sounded the humours
Even of all Woman-kind: Therefore advise you
Repair immediately to old Orsino,   555
Who with his Beauteous Daughter waits your Coming.
 BORG. Could she be truly mine! the wings of Winds
Would be too slow to waft me to her arms!

---

554 Women-kind: Q_{2+}.

    MACH. Once more I say, she is and shall be yours,
Truly, religiously, devoutly yours ---   560
Why all this thought and groundless Jealousy?
Let manly Confidence and Roman Vertue
Master this Gothick Fury in your blood.
    BORG. By arms! by all the glories I have won!
Thou hast awak'd my Love, and Charm'd my fears.   565
Charlotta! O the very figure of her;
But sure the beauteous Lines are softer here:
And now I find 'tis ruine to forgo her ---
    MACH. No more my Lord. 'Tis I that thus embark you,
And if some starting Plank should flaw the Vessel,   570
To your destruction --- I am ruin'd too ---
Since all I have, or am, or ever would be,
Is to be yours; your sworn, unbyass'd friend.
    BORG. Thou best of men:
Thou art my Oracle, my Heav'n, my Genius,   575
And, as some God, shalt guide me through the World.
Let's go to Conquest, tho through Death we go;
Marriage and Death both new Experiments.
Methinks I see the Taper in the Window,
The Busie Nurse unveils the weeping Maid,   580
And I must naked pass through Seas to reach her.
O fatal Marriage! O thou dismal Gulph!
Which like the Hellespont do'st rore between
Me and my Joys: Is there no other way?
None, none, the Winds and the dash'd Rocks reply: 585
Why let 'em roar; and let the Billows swell;
Till the rack't Orbs be with the Deluge drown'd.
'Tis fixt; I'll plunge, or perish, or enjoy her---
    MACH. Justly resolv'd; nor let a few false Tears
Melt you again to an untimely mildness.   590
Charlotta thus deluded you in France,
Which render'd all your Court ridiculous:
Remember that, and lest the like disgrace
Should happen now, drag her if she refuses!
    BORG. I will, my Machiavel, --- O Arms! O Glory!   595
What an Eternal Rust would smear your Luster,
Did not this Spirit of Ambition fire me!
I'll tell her that the lives of all her race
Are now within my power.
    MACH.   Nay, threaten her!
    BORG. I will do more than threaten;   600
Think not the dreadful Caesar will be rows'd
To threaten only; that's a sleeping Borgia,
A loving, dreaming, Conscientious Borgia;
But when I wake there's always Execution---
    MACH. It has been so.
    BORG.   And shall I swear again;   605
No, Machiavel; she must be mine or dye;

Should she for refuge to the Temple flie!
I'd after her; there, if she scorns my flame,
To the dumb Saints I will my Vows proclaim;
And in their view resolve the glorious game: 610
   Upon the Golden Shrines I'll lay her head,
   And ev'n the Altar make my Bridal Bed---

                [Ex. Ambo.

        End of A C T I.

Act II. Scene I.

Enter Orsino and Bellamira in Mourning.

ORSI. Where didst thou get the daring thus to move me?
By thy dead Mothers shrowd, not the first Night,
When in my Youthful arms I grasp'd her to me,
Was I so hot with Love as now with rage,
Thou Young and Virgin Witch, thou new-found Fury?   5
BELL. Ah, Sir! for I am afraid to call you Father,
Give me my Death: give to these trembling breasts
A thousand wounds; or cut me Limb from Limb;
But do not look so dreadfully upon me ---
Nor blast me with such sounds. Oh pity me!   10
There's not one fatal sentence, one dread Word,
But runs like Iron through my freezing blood.
What have I done? Ah, what is my offence?
And tell me how, which way I shall atone you?
ORSI. O, thou vile wretch! what is thy offence?   15
Dost thou not know it? Exquisite dissembler!
Thou leading Sorc'ress! Hecat of thy Sex!
Subtlest of all thy kind, that ever rowld
Their false deluding eyes, and in their Glasses
Conjur'd for looks to cheat the simple world!   20
But to take all evasion from thy guilt,
Did I not charge thee, as thou fear'st my curse,
This very Morning to adorn thy self
As one, whom the great Duke intends to honour
By making thee his Bride?   25
BELL.   Alas! you did;
And I am come, Oh Heaven! and all you Powers
That pity womans weakness, I am come
My Lord as you commanded; and have vow'd,
Tho Death attends my Nuptials, to obey you.
ORSI. Thou ly'st even in thy heart, thou know'st thou ly'st,   30
Thou hast maliciously, most grosly fail'd
In this obedience: Say, declare, haste, answer,
Thou most ungrateful wretch; Ah, how unlike
Thy meek, thy Perfect bright and blessed Mother,
Is this a habit for a glorious Bride?   35
Dost thou thus meet the generous Borgia?
I know thy awkard Heart; thou meanst by this
To tell the World, thou dost not like thy Husband,
And dash him at the Altar: but by Heav'n,

---

34 Mother! C_{2+}.

Whither thou, Murdress, now art sending me,   40
This shall not serve thy purpose: In this dress
That blasts my eyes, and strikes my Soul with sadness,
I'll see the Priest for ever make you one.
    BELL. Ah! how have I deserv'd this cruel usage?
Did ever Daughter yet obey like me?   45
Not she who in the Dungeon fed her Father
With her own Milk, and by her Piety
Sav'd him from Death, can match my rigorous Vertue;
For I have done much more: torn off my Breasts,
My Breasts, my very Heart, and flung it from me,   50
To feed the Tyrant Duty with my blood.
    ORSI. Call'st thou the lawful Imposition of
A careful Father, that intends thee honour,
Tyrannical and bloody? Rage resume me;
Here, seest thou this? O would the gallant Borgia   55
Could fling thee from his Soul, as I from mine,
For 'tis respect to him that saves thy life;
Else by the Feaver that quite burns me up,
I'd ponyard thee till all thy Robes were Crimson:
Yet since thou hast the Impudence to brave me,   60
And call thy Father Tyrant to his face,
I that have foster'd thee even from the Womb,
And bred thee in my Bosom, hear and tremble;
For I will curse thee till thy frighted Soul
Runs mad with horrour, till thy Mother starts   65
From her cold Monument, to beg me cease,
Though all in vain.
    BELL.   I cast me at your feet;
I'm all Obedience: See, Sir, --- see me here
Grovelling upon the Earth.
    ORSI.   Curs'd be the Night,
Ten thousand Curses on that fatal hour,   70
When my great Spirit trifled with thy Mother
For the Production of so false a Joy!
    BELL. O horrid blasting breath!
    ORSI.   When I am dead,
My troubled Ghost shall nightly haunt thy Dreams.
    BELL. Ah, hold --- I kiss your feet, and hug your knees.   75
    ORSI. Though in thy Husbands Arms, I'll draw the Curtains,
And stare thee into Frenzy; and thy Lord
I'll Charm so fast, thy shrieks shall not awake him.
    BELL. Yet Sir, forbear; tread on me, trample me.
    ORSI. And all the day, when other Spirits sleep,   80
I'll follow thee with groans, and curse thee still:
Nay, when thou seek'st for company to scape me,
I'll make thee scream. See there his Spirit stands.
    BELL. Hear him not Heav'n!
    ORSI.   After thy first imbrace,
May thy Lord loath thee; swear thou art no Virgin,   85

And cast thee off as a most leud Adulteress.

 BELL. If there be Saints or Angels: Oh I charge you ---

 ORSI. Or if thy Husband should by chance retain thee,

Heart-burnings, Jealousies incite him still

To plague thee with a thousand Hells on Earth,   90

And after end thee in some horrid manner.

 BELL. Ponyard me as you promis'd Sir! Oh stab me!

 ORSI. Eternal Barrenness shut up thy Womb;

If ought that's humane chance to raise thy hopes,

May it be monstrous at the curst Production,   95

An after-birth, or some abhorr'd Conception.

    Enter Duke of Gandia in Mourning.

 BELL. Y'have said enough! my heart, my spirits fail me,

And I have now my wish without a Dagger.

 ORSI. What now? another Mourner? Hell and Furies!

They both have plotted to undo my Honour.   100

Well --- Duke of Gandia --- but I'll call the Bridegroom.

 GAND. Ha! how's this? the beauteous Bellamira

Upon the Earth. Help, help --- my Lord, she's cold,

Your Daughter Swoons. ---

 ORSI.   I care not, let her perish;

And thou, who hast seduc'd her, perish with her: 105

Swoon with her, sink with her: Die both, and both be damn'd.

                [Ex. Orsino.

 GAND. Wake Bellamira from this sleep of Death:

Life of Palante's life! give me a word;

See thou art safe, clasp'd in thy Gandia's arms,

Palante holds thee. Say, what Murderer   110

Offer'd this cruelty, and I'll revenge thee!

 BELL. Where am I? ha! loose, loose me from your arms;

Stand off; fly from me; fly, Palante, fly!

For we must never, never meet agen:

The Poles may sooner joyn: O I am lost,   115

By an inexorable Father ruin'd;

Cursed, blasted; and for thee, unhappy Prince,

Thou hast undone me, though not by thy will;

For sure thou lov'st the wretched Bellamira:

Yet by the consequence of this affection,   120

Thou hast destroy'd my peace of mind for ever:

Thou hast been ruinous and mortal to me!

As Robbers, Ravishers, or Murderers!

Therefore be gone! fly from my eyes for ever,

And never let me see Palante more.   125

 GAND. I go for ever from you, as you charge me,

------

 92 promis'd! Oh stab me! Q_{3+}.

 101 thee Bridegroom. Q_{3+}.

And for that purpose I did hither come;
But little thought that you would drive me thus:
I hop'd, at least, that when I parted from you,
And bid you everlastingly farewel,   130
I hop'd; but oh those flattering hopes were vain!
That gentle Bellamira would have sigh'd,
Or dropt a tear, when I should take my leave,
And never see her more.
    BELL.   O Cruelty!
You rend the Plaister from a bleeding wound.   135
    GAND.   An Elder Brother calls you to his Bed,
And you perhaps will not be ravish'd thither:
O Bellamira! I had once those Vows
Which thy frail heart does now resign to Borgia.
But I have staid too long: Farewel for ever;   140
When I am gone, and thou for many years
Enjoy'st the Change thy Father forc'd thee to,
(For sure I cannot think it all thy doing!)
If happy Caesar Borgia chance to fold thee
More closely in his arms than was his Custom;   145
Say to thy heart with a relenting thought,
Thus, if our Fates had pleas'd, the wretched Gandia
Would thus have lov'd me. But no more, farewel.
You're pleas'd to banish me --- and --- I'll obey.   [Exiturus.*
    BELL. Come back! come back! you shall not leave me thus: 150
Let Fathers Curse, and Jealous Husbands Rage,
Love has a force that can surmount the World.

        Enter Borgia [unobserved]**

If then 'tis destin'd that you must be gone,
And leave me to the Arms of Cruel Borgia ---
    BORG. Ha! but observe: there may be more in this.   155
    BELL. If we two Lovers, whom for tenderness
The World can never match, must part for ever ---
    GAND. O, that for ever!
    BORG.   It's Apparition all;
By Heav'n, a Dream; I swear, a very Dream.
    BELL. Yet take, O take this dying farewel with thee: 160
And whomsoe're thy passion shall Espouse,
Remember! O remember this, and leave me:
No Man was ever so by Woman lov'd,
As thou Palante art by Bellamira.
    GAND. Stop there; for to go on will give me Death.   165

---

132 should have Q_{2+}.
133 I would take Q_{2+}.
  * [Exiturus.] C_{2+}; [Exiturns. Q_{1-3}.
 ** [unobserved]; <u>om.</u> Q_{1+}.

O! thou hast utter'd Sounds of such a strain
As Nature cannot bear: like utmost Musick,
Which while it charms the Sense, makes chill the Blood.
No more! for by my glimmering joys, I fear
Thou'lt sing my Soul to Everlasting Sleep!   170
  BORG. Then let me wake you.
  BELL.   O Heav'ns! we are undone!
  BORG. Start not, nor weep not! beauteous Bellamira!
For there is nothing toward you, but well;
Fortune her self now smiles on your design,
And Heav'n and Earth conspire to make you happy: 175
These Mourning Habits on your Wedding Day,
Had chance not guided me to hear your Loves,
Would have betray'd the secret ---
  GAND. O Brother! what must I expect? I know not
Whether I ought to hope or fear.
  BORG.   Hope all: 180
For curst is he that parts whom Heav'n has joyn'd:
I stand convinc'd that Love has made you one;
And may those Chaster Fires that warm your hearts,
Vie with the Stars for Immortality ---
  GAND. Speak it again, again confirm this goodness,   185
For one so Noble sure this World contains not:
O! 'tis too little but to name him Noble,
For such a Soul aspires above the Clouds;
So great, Ethereal, and so God-like fram'd,
He must look down on Kings: such vast compassion,   190
Such an unheard magnificence of Mercy
As we must both adore: Kneel, Bellamira,
For 'tis a God we talk with.
  BORG.   O you must not.
Methinks fair Bellamira, who still answers
With the accustom'd Language of her Tears,   195
Methinks you should have told me all this while,
Your Beauties were not doom'd for Caesar Borgia.
'Tis true, I often fear'd by your reserv'dness,
Your Heart must be ingag'd --- Or thou, Palante,
Had'st thou but told me when I woo'd her first,   200
How many sighs and sorrows hadst thou sav'd me!
I would not then have launch'd, but yielded up
The Noble Fraight, this more than Indian Treasure,
And given thee all my interest in her Father.
  GAND. Alas! I fear'd!
  BORG.   I hold you Sir excus'd: 205
May you be happy as your Souls can wish;
But I must beg you from this place retire
For your own Interest; Orsino here

---

173 nothing meant toward C_{2+}.

Entreated me to wait him, and 'tis now
Upon this day, allotted for my Marriage,   210
Unfit to break the business of your Loves.
Yet doubt not, O most happy lovely Pair,
But Care and Time shall perfect all your Wishes.
    GAND. Give me your Arms: I had design'd this Morning,
Made desperate with my griefs, t'acquaint your ear   215
With all the progress of my ruin'd passion:
I thought that you would storm, and use me ill,
And had design'd I know not what to forfeit
My life, rather than lose my Bellamira:
But you have so prevented me ---
    BORG.   No more.   220
How, fairest Bellamira! not one word?
Am I ordain'd the Proxy of your Love,
Without the Breath of thanks?
    BELL.   The bounteous Heav'ns
Rain on your head whole Deluges of mercies,
For this great goodness! Hear me, oh ye Powers,   225
Hear me upon my knees; where-e're he goes,
Guard him with blessings! give him his own wishes:
If to the Wars he pass, Renown attend him,
And growing Conquest dwell upon his Arms;
Let him attain by a long course of Valour,   230
And gallant acts, to the old Roman Greatness;
And when at last in Triumph he returns,
May all the sighing Virgins strow his way,
And with new Garlands Crown his coming Glory.   [Ex. with Gandia.

       Enter Machiavel.

    MACH. Something's discover'd, and I guess the business!   235
My Lord, you're wanted, and the beauteous Bride.
    BORG. I charge thee name her not upon thy life.
Here, tear, tear off these unbecoming Garments,
Get me my Horse, and bid my Arms be ready;
Yes, Machiavel, with to morrows dawn,   240
Thou shalt behold me in another Dress,
Breathing Defiance to these softer Wars.
    MACH. But why, Sir! why? how comes this sudden change?
Why have you charg'd me that I should not speak
Of Bellamira?
    BORG.   Cruel Machiavel!   245
Why dost thou bring the fatal Charmer back,
Whom I would drive for ever from my Soul?
    MACH. This wondrous alteration of your humour,
Must sure arise from some as wondrous cause.
Have you discover'd ought?
    BORG.   All, all's discover'd;   250
And such an over-sight in thee: but where,

Where now is thy profound Sagacity?
Where all thy Depositions, Promises,
Warrants, Ingagements that she should be mine;
Chastly, religiously, devoutly mine?   255
    MACH.　And is she not?
    BORG.　　　　　　By Heav'n quite opposite:
All that my boding heart presag'd to thee
Before, has happen'd; happen'd in such manner,
As quite out-went my own Imagination.
    MACH.　Who-e're he is that has supplanted you,   260
By your just rage he was a secret Villain,
The closest Traytor that e're plotted mischief,
And justly has deserv'd the stab you gave him.
    BORG.　How, Machiavel? ha, didst thou talk of stabbing?
    MACH.　I neither think, nor know what's your intention,   265
But that's your Countries Custom in such cases:
Besides, Sir, when I did discourse you last,
You fell into Convulsions of Despair,
With mentioning the very name of Rival,
And thunder'd out whole Volleys of revenge.   270
    BORG.　True Machiavel: but could not think my Rival
Should prove my Brother.
    MACH.　　　　　　Ha!
    BORG.　　　　　　　　Raise, raise me Heav'n,
Some other man that dares to take her from me,
To snatch the only Beauty I can love,
And at the Altar too, from my imbraces;   275
If I not end him, though he were Imperial,
Ev'n in the middle of his Guards ---
    MACH.　　　　　　　Your Brother!
And have you Confirmation that she loves him?
    BORG.　Why dost thou wonder? I both saw and heard;
Heard all his Vows, and her most passionate Answers: 280
She loves him: Yes, these cursed Remembrancers,
These eyes have seen it. O! she dotes on him,
Feeds on his looks --- eyes him, as pregnant Women
Gaze at the precious thing their Souls are set on.
    MACH.　And you perhaps will bear it from a Brother   285
With all the meekness of an Anchorite,
A man of quite another World! you'd best
Go to the Wars, be shot, and leave this Brother
The Heir of all, sole Darling of the Pope.
    BORG.　'Tis certain, that I seem'd to all appearance   290
Mild and relenting; begg'd 'em leave me here,
That I might think ---
    MACH.　　　　　Think! by your Holy Father,
You have no blood, no soul, nor spirit left!
The Genius of your house must blush at this;
A Brother! why, so much the more a Villain.   295
    BORG.　O Machiavel!

MACH.   O Conscientious Borgia!
By all that's great, it is in him flat Incest;
There's for your Conscience, if you will have Conscience,
She was betroth'd yours by her Fathers will,
Publish'd to the World, and what else makes a Marriage?   300
And for a Brother thus to undermine you,
And carry it too? Are you Italian born?
Begot by one? O, make it not a doubt,
I grieve, I groan, I am mad to see you thus!
What, to be made the talk, the jeer of Rome,   305
As once you were at Paris by Charlotta:
No --- I'll revenge thee! cold as thou art and dead!
And may this Steel be sheath'd in Machiavel,
If that the treacherous Duke of Gandia scape me.   [Exiturus. *
    BORG. Come back, I say; for what is to be done,   310
I'll act my self. Where was I? or where am I?
No Machiavel, thou know'st 'tis not my Conscience
That lets the Villain live: I think thou hast heard
The fatal Jars w'have had about my Sister:
For I remember, being in her Bath,   315
And by her Women told we were at words,
She ran in haste half naked to the Pope,
Who came to part the fray; and swore in fury,
With horrid Imprecations, who-e're fell
By th' others hand, he never would have mercy   320
On the Survivor. This, my Machiavel,
Is Borgia's Conscience --- For to do a murder,
And not be safe, is Drunkards policy.
    MACH. What then is your intent?
    BORG.   To follow Nature;
For so do Flames that burn, and Seas that drown;   325
Yes, Machiavel, and care not what comes on't:
So when security, and black occasion
Point me to death, I will be rough as those,
And blood him, till he changes to a Ghost:
Yet since my Fathers threats bar present murder,   330
I'll find a way to rack him.
    MACH.   Ha! you mean ---
To take again your beauteous Prize; that is,
The lovely Bellamira still retains
Some holds about your heart.
    BORG.   O, 'tis confess'd;
And howsoe're my Tongue has plaid the Braggart,   335
She Reigns more fully in my Soul than ever:
She Garrisons my Breast, and Mans against me
Even my own Rebel thoughts, with thousand Graces,
Ten thousand Charms, and new discover'd Beauties.
O! hadst thou seen her when she lately blest me,   340

---

    * [Exiturus.] C$_{2+}$; [Exiturns. Q$_1$-C$_1$.
331 you mend --- Q$_{3+}$.

What tears, what looks, and languishings she darted;
Love bath'd himself in the distilling Balm:
And oh the subtle God has made his entrance
Quite through my heart: he shouts and triumphs too,
And all his Cry is Death, or Bellamira.   345
    MACH. Why! this is like the Spirit of your Father.
You bring his graceful vigour just before me,
Just, just as first he wore the triple Crown,
Just so he walk'd, just with that fiery Movement;
So sparkled too his eyes! so glow'd his Cheeks.   350
Nor fear Palante, when she's in your Arms,
When she perceives the fervour of your passion
Panting upon her naked Breasts for Mercy.
    BORG. Sighing, as if my very Soul would burst;
And gasping, Machiavel, as if Deaths pangs were on me.   355
    MACH. Now stealing to her Lips, dissolv'd in Tears,
And pressing close, but softly to her side;
Whispering, O why, why, gentle Bellamira?
Then with a sudden start let loose your love;
Grasp her as if you could no longer bear it;   360
Clasp her all night, and stifle her with Kisses:
O, there are thousand ways!
    BORG.   Ten thousand thousand;
Millions, and infinite, yet add to those,
I'll try 'em all: nor shall a drop of mercy
Fall from my eyes, though I beheld Palante   365
Dead at her door. O expectation burns me!
O Bellamira! heart! how she does inflame me?
    MACH. Then there's no need of warlike preparations?
    BORG. Talk no more of War, for now my Theme's all Love:
The War like Winter vanishes; 'tis gone,   370
And Bellamira with eternal Spring,
Drest in blew Heav'ns, and breathing Vernal sweets,
Drops like a Cherubin in smiles before me.
    MACH. Oh, that the World could but behold you thus!
That Bellamira saw you in this height   375
Of dazling Passion, and becoming Fury!
    BORG. Thus, to a glorious Coast, through Tempests hurl'd,
We sail like him who sought the Indian World.
'Tis more; 'tis Paradise I go to prove,
And Bellamira is the Land of Love: 380
I have her in my view; and hark, she talks,
And see, about, like the first Maid she walks:
Fair as the Day when first the World began;
And I am doom'd to be the happy man.   [Exeunt.

End of ACT II.

---

355 grasping, Machiavel, Q$_{3+}$.
367 she inflames C$_{2+}$.

ACT III. Scene I.

Enter Ascanio and Alonzo.

ALON. My Lord, this is an Act so newly horrid,
So ghastly a contrivance of Revenge,
That Fiends themselves would start at the Proposal.
I to do this; I, who have bred him up!
Oh Seraphino! Nurs'd thee in my Bosom,   5
To gash thy Cheeks, and tear out both thy Eyes!
ASCA. The sums of Gold are order'd to be paid;
Half on your bare consent: on Execution
The whole. Alonzo! thou hast no compassion
When Interest comes in play: Don't I know,   10
At the Command of Machiavel, or Borgia,
Thou would'st not stick to poyson ev'n the Pope ?
Come, come, dissemble not thy Occupation,
Murder's thy Trade, and Death thy Livelihood;
Therefore perform this act of spritely Vengeance,   15
And I'll Create thee Noble ---
ALON. 'Tis sure, e're long, when I have serv'd their turn;
That they will end me too, for fear of talking;
Therefore, my Lord, how-e're my Conscience stings me,
For 'tis most true, I love the Innocent Boy;   20
Send home the Gold. ---
ASCA.   Thou shalt along with me;
I will not send, but pay it thee in hand,
Full twenty thousand Crowns --- Why, what a sum is that?
Full twenty thousand Crowns!
Why, I will tell thee, there are Rogues in Orders,   25
Monks, Fryers, Jesuits, that would kill their Fathers,
Ravish their Mothers, eat their Brothers and Sisters,
For half the sum: what, twenty thousand Crowns!
Away, away! Come, come, pull out his eyes,
And make a Cupid of the little Bastard.   30
I swear thou shalt; what, twenty thousand Crowns!
ALON. My Lord, I am Charm'd.

Enter Machiavel and Adorna.

ASCA. My good Lord Machiavel.
MACH.   My Noble Lord,
The humblest of your Servants. ---   [Ex. Ascanio and Alonzo. *

---

18 They will Q_2.
 * [Ex. Ascanio and Alonzo.] C_{1+}; [Ex. Q_1-3.

Now, my Adorna, now the time is coming,   35
When thou shalt Rival ev'n the Queen of Love;
For, by my life, a Bridegroom like Palante
Might match an Empress --- But he's thine; no more.
I've sworn he's thine: This day, that gives his Brother
Thy beauteous Cousin, is the blest Fore-runner   40
Of my Adorna's certain happiness.
    ADOR. Heav'n only knows the issue of my Fate;
But did not love and languishing desire
Transport me from my self, I should endeavour
To help the poor despairing Bellamira.   45
Not many hours ago she ran upon me
With Extasies, even crying out for joy,
In spite of Fate, Palante shall be mine;
Then told me all that you discourst but now:
When on that minute cruel Borgia enter'd   50
With old Orsino, who commanded her,
I'th' midst of pray'rs and tears, and shrieking sorrows,
Strait to attend her Husband to the Temple.
    MACH. Excellent! And how bears Palante this?
    ADOR. So much the worse, because quite unexpected.   55
And while I told it in most moving terms,
He struck his Breast, and cast his eyes to Heav'n,
Enquir'd for you; then talkt of blood, and vanish'd.
    MACH. I have been ever since I came to Rome
A Confident to both: I like the Method,   60
The Machine moves exactly to my mind,
Sails like a Ship well ballast through the Air,
And ploughs the rising mischiefs clear before me.
I've heard thee often talk of pretty Letters
That past between Palante and thy Cousin.   65
    ADOR. I have 'em all in keeping, by her order.
    MACH. Let me peruse 'em.
    ADOR.   Will you be secret then?
    MACH. Away, and fear not, they shall make thy Fortune:
Soon as the Marriage Rites are past, we'll meet.   [Ex. Adorna.
But lo, they come! the Duke of Gandia frowns;   70
I fear my Caesar, and must watch their clashing.

> Scene draws, and discovers the Progress of a stately
> Marriage; Ascanio, Adrian, Enna, Cardinals, going
> before, Orsino following: Bellamira supported by two
> Virgins in White: Borgia follow'd by Vitellozzo,
> Alonzo, &c.

    GAND. Sir, I must speak with you.
    BORG.   'Tis inconvenient.
    GAND. 'Tis not our first of Jars. Remember Lucrece,
Our Sister Lucrece, and be then perswaded
Necessity requires your ear.

BORG.   For what?   75
GAND.   If you dare walk aside with me, I'll tell you.
BORG.   After the Priest. ---
GAND.   No Sir---before the Priest---
Fate hovers near us; you shall give me hearing.
BORG.   What Boy! how say'st thou? Shall!---
GAND.   Yes Sir, you shall.
BORG.   No more; for fear we should be over-heard: 80
I'll instantly return upon my Honour:
Let me but wait Orsino to the Gate,
And I'll attend thee; on my word I will---
The Priest shall wait till thou hast satisfaction.

                        [Ex. all but Mach. and Gand.

MACH.   What have you said, my Lord?
GAND.   Forbear to know;   85
I think thou lov'st me, yet a proof were well;
And since occasion now demands a tryal,
Refuse not what my Friendship shall enjoyn thee.
MACH.   'Tis granted, though the consequence be death.
GAND.   Be gone, this moment leave me to my self.   90
MACH.   I apprehend: Let me imbrace you.
Why shall I leave you? but my word's ingag'd;
Call all those pow'rful provocations up,
Your wrongs, your most ignoble injuries,
To steel your arm, and dye your Victory   95
In blood: I go -- because you grow impatient.
No more, but Conquest, Death, or Bellamira ---
Yet I must watch you hereabouts: For Borgia,   [Aside. *
Though skill'd and gallant, yet may meet his Death,
And that I must prevent, for I'll allow   100
No stroke to Chance, though my undaunted Hero
Dares all that Man can dare ---   [Ex. Mach.
GAND.   Why comes he not?
I know he's brave, Renown'd in Forreign Wars,
And to his skill in Arms has such a Courage,
As makes a rash man run upon his ruine: 105
Yet in his height of fury I can dare him,
My blood defies him mortally to death.
Yes Machiavel, I'll take thy fatal counsel;
The word is Conquest, Death, or Bellamira.

---

84   thou have Q_{2+}.
  *   [Aside.]; <u>om</u>. Q_{1+}.
100-102 <u>Divided thus in</u> Q_{1+}:
                And that I must prevent, for I'll allow no stroke
                To Chance, though my undaunted Hero dares all
                That Man can dare---

Enter Borgia.

BORG. So Sir, you see I have obey'd your Summons;   110
You must be satisfi'd, though Beauty stays,
Though the Bride stays, though Bellamira stays:
That is, tho Heav'n with all its waiting glories
Stops at your call, and stands to give you hearing.
    GAND. Y'have us'd me basely.
    BORG.   No.
    GAND.   I say you have,   115
Without a provocation.
    BORG.   That were base
Indeed: when unprovok'd I do a wrong,
May I, when justly urg'd, want due revenge.
    GAND. Y'have falsifi'd your word, betray'd me basely,
Betray'd a Brother: O my Stars, a Brother!   120
That would have burst through all the bars of death,
And yielded all things to you, but his Love.
O, foolish eyes! but these are your last tears,
And I must mend your course with blood.
    BORG.   He weeps!
Was ever seen Hypocrisie like this?   [Aside.   125
O thou young impudent and blooming lyar,
Who, like our Curtezans, art early practis'd,
And in their Nonage taught the Arts of Vice.
But I forego my temper--- Is this all?
You know I am in haste, and cannot brook   130
A longer Conference.
    GAND.   I know you cannot,
But I shall force you: yes, thou Tyrant Brother,
Thou that art fallen from all thy height of glory,
To the low practice of the worst of Slaves,
I will revenge the honour thou hast lost: 135
Nor shalt thou pass to Bellamira's Arms,
Till through my heart thou cutt'st thy horrid way.
Draw then --
    BORG.   I will not.
    GAND.   By Revenge and Fury
Thou shalt not pass, but on my Rapiers point.
    BORG. Think not, thou young Practitioner in Arms,   140
That all thy force, though levell'd at me naked,
Should stop me, if I once resolv'd my way:
But I am calm; and wish thee, for thy safety,
To let me pass. Thou talk'st awhile ago
Of Lucrece --- but no more of that --- my Father,   145
O, fear'd I not his Thunder which so oft

─────────────

141 thou levell'd Q$_{2-3}$.

Has menac'd me if e're I rose against thee,
Long, long e're this, had'st thou been dust; even now
For that abuse which late thou gav'st my ear,
For that abhorr'd Conception of my Sister,   150
For that damn'd mention, by the lowest Hell,
And by the burning Fiends, thou should'st be Ashes.
    GAND. Blush not, nor purse thy threatning Brow, but draw;
And dare not to despise the weakest arm
That strikes with Justice. Yes, upon thy breast   155
Elate, and haughty as thou carri'st it,
I doubt not but my Sword shall write thee Traytor.
    BORG. No more: O that I had
Some one Renown'd, and winter'd as my self,
T'encounter like an Oak the rooting Storm!   160
But thou art weak, and to the Earth wilt bend,
With my least blast thy Head of Blossoms down:
If by thy hand I fall (as who e're div'd
So deep in Fate, but sometimes was deceiv'd?)
I do bequeath thee more than all my Dukedoms,   165
Far more indeed than Worlds, my beauteous Bride;
But if I conquer thee, and shew thee mercy,
Never love more; nor after I am marri'd,
Dare for thy Soul to speak of Bellamira.
    GAND. I thank thee, and accept the terms with joy,   170
Which blood must ratifie: And here I swear,
If vanquish'd by thy Arm (though Death, I hope,
Will, more than Oath, confirm the fatal bargain)
For ever to renounce all Claim, and yield
By my Eternal Absence Bellamira.   175
    BORG. Come on then: And let Love and Glory steel
Thy unflesh'd arm: think on this moment hangs
Thy whole lifes Joy, or worse than Death, Despair;
I would not win such Beauty without blood:
But as the brave Gonsalvo, being shot,   180
Mov'd not at all, nor chang'd his mighty Look;
As if the Gallantry of such demeanour
Could charm coy Victory to raise the Siege:
So would I with my blood distilling down,
Answering her tears, lead Bellamira on,   185
And woo her at the Altar with my wounds.
    GAND. No more.
    BORG.   Agreed. The word is Bellamira. -- [Fight, Gandia
                                                        is wounded.
Hold, hold Palante, for thou bleed'st.
    GAND.   A scratch.
    BORG. My Father crys out, save him on thy life. [Fight again, Borgia
    GAND. Guard well thy life.   is wounded on the arm,
                                                      but disarms Gandia.

Enter Machiavel.

MACH.   What means this noyse of Arms?   190
Why these Swords drawn? what now, my Lords,
Both wounded?   [Borgia throws
                                                          Gandia his Sword.
By Heav'n, I swear, you shall proceed no further.
    BORG.   'Tis now too late to tell thee how we quarrell'd,
Look to his wound: soon as the Cure's perform'd,   195
I'll serve the Duke of Gandia with my Fortune,
But far from Rome; for he has agreed
Never to see my Bellamira more.
For me -- I'll to the Temple.
    MACH.   My Lord, you bleed.
    BORG.   The skin's but rac'd: 200
Would it were deep in the most mortal part,
So Bellamira, when the blood gush'd forth,
Would sink upon my breast, and swear she lov'd me.
But that's too much to hope; what e're is doom'd,
I swear this night to grasp the conquer'd Prize: 205
Yes, yes, Palante, hear, and fly for ever;
All the White World of Bellamira's Beauty
This night I'll travel o're, to feast my Love;
The Little Glutton shall be gorg'd with Revels,
He shall be drunk with spirits of delight;   210
With all that amorous wishes can inspire,
And all the Liberties of loose desire.   [Exit.
    GAND.   I'll after him, and at the Altar end him.
Was't not enough to wound and vanquish me,
But he must triumph too? I rave and talk   215
I know not what; for he is generous,
And nobly merits what his valour won:
Yes, happy Borgia, I will keep my word;
And, since thus lost to all that I held dear,
Abandon this loath'd world.
    MACH.   You must retire.   220
    GAND.   I will devote the sad remains of life
To the blest company of holy men:
Learn Contemplation, and the dregs of life
Purg'd off, taste clearer and more sprightly joys,
Partake their transports in the brightest Visions,   225
See opening Heav'ns, and the descending Gods:
Then as I view the dazling tracks of Angels,
Sigh to my heart, and cry, see there, and there,
In full perfection thousand Bellamira's.
    MACH.   My Lord, your wound bleeds fast.
    GAND.   O Machiavel!   230

———————

200 rais'd: C_{2+}.

When I am shut for ever from the world,
Thou tenderst-hearted, gentlest, best of Friends,
Wilt visit me sometimes: I know thou wilt.
    MACH. Why do you droop thus? lean upon my arm:
All shall be well. Yes, I will find a way,   235
In spite of Fortune, yet to heal your sorrows,
And pour the Balm of Bellamira's tears
Upon your wound.
    GAND.   Could I but see her once
Before I die!
    MACH.   Once, twice, a hundred times;
Doubt not, you shall; but haste to your Apartment. [Ex. Gandia.   240
Methinks if mischief had but this to vaunt,
That, like a God, none knows her but her self,
It were enough to mount her o're the World.
I love my self; and for my self, I love
Borgia my Prince: Who does not love himself?   245
Self-love's the Universal Beam of Nature,
The Axle-tree that darts through all its Frame:
And he's a Child in thought, who fears the sting
Of Conscience; and will rather lose himself,
Than make his Fortune by anothers ruine!   250
Conscience, the Bug-bears roar, the Nurses howl,
Our Infant lash and whip of Education.

                Enter Adorna.

My Genius, my Love, my little Angel,
Hast thou the Letters?
    ADOR.   First, my Lord,
If I have breath to utter, let me tell you,   255
Never was Marriage solemniz'd like this.
    MACH. Go on.
    ADOR.   The Bride in Mourning Robes was led,
Or rather born like a pale Course along;
I saw her when she first approach'd the Temple,
How, rushing from the arms of those that held her,   260
She threw her body on the Marble steps,
When strait the Bridegroom with a kindled face
Drew near, and blushing stretcht his bloody arm,
Wrapt in a Scarf, and gave it to the Bride:
Then, bowing, wish'd the Priest perform his Duty.   265
    MACH. What follow'd?
    ADOR.   Urg'd, or rather brib'd before,
The Priest, at Old Orsino's Intercession,
Soon joyn'd their hands: all from the Temple haste,
Orsino and his Son in deep discourse,
And Bellamira blind with weeping, led   270

---

258 Coarse C_{1-2}; Corse C_3.

This way.
    MACH. I am glad on't, for I wait to speak with her.
Prithee produce the Letters: Come, I know
Thou hast 'em: nay, 'tis thy own interest.
    ADOR. See Bellamira enters: stay some time,   275
And I'll discover to your own desire.   [Exit. *

Enter Bellamira.

    MACH. Madam, I would entreat a word in private.
    BELL. Can misery, like mine, be worth discourse?
    MACH. The dead are only happy, and the dying:
The dead are still, and lasting slumbers hold 'em;   280
He, who is near his death, but turns about,
Shuffles awhile to make his Pillow easie,
Then slips into his Shroud, and rests for ever.
    BELL. My mind presages, by the bloody hand
That seiz'd me at the Altar. ---
    MACH.   In their Nonage   285
A sympathy unusual joyn'd their loves;
They pair'd like Turtles, still together drank,
Together eat, nor quarrell'd for the choice:
Like Twining-streams both from one Fountain fell,
And as they ran, still mingled smiles and tears: 290
But oh, when Time had swell'd their Currents high,
This boundless World, this. Ocean did divide 'em,
And now for ever they have lost each other.
    BELL. For ever! Oh the horrour that invades me!
Thou seem'st to intimate some horrid act: 295
I charge thee speak, how fares the Duke of Gandia?
Not answer me! why dost thou shake thy head,
And cross thy arms, and turn thy eyes away?
Has there been ought betwixt my Lord and him?
    MACH. There has, they fought.
    BELL.   The Cause, the cursed Cause   300
Stands here, before thy eyes she stands to blast thee:
I know 'tis thus; Borgia for me was wounded;
And, oh my fears! by his relentless hand,
Perhaps that poor despairing lost Palante
Is miserably slain: If it be so,   305
Spite of my Father, I'll renounce my Vows,
Forgo, forswear all comforts in this life,
And fly the world.
    MACH.   Would I were out on't;
Nothing but fraud and cruelties reign here.
He is not slain: but, as his Surgeons bode,   310
I fear him much. Oh would you be so kind

---

    * [Exit.]; om. Q$_{1+}$.

To see the wounds he suffers for your sake,
And charm his pains but with one parting view
Before your Lord return. ---
    BELL.   Alas! I dare not!
    MACH. He graspt me by the wrist, and weeping, vow'd   315
'Twould be a Heav'n, a Lightning in his Grave,
Where else he must for ever lye unpiti'd.
Now, on my Soul, you must, you ought to see him,
Who ballancing the Scales of doubtful life,
Lies in your way: a glance, one grain of favour   320
Turns him from Death. Come, come, you must have mercy:
Madam, I'll wait and intercept your Lord.
    BELL. A Visit! just upon our Marriage too---
But 'tis the last that he shall e're receive;
Therefore I'll go; Nature, Compassion, Fate;   325
And Love, far more tyrannical than those,
Forces me on: I feel him here; he throbs,
And beats a Mournful March.
    MACH.   Fear not, away:
I'll guard the passage: look not back, but haste. [Ex. Bellamira.
If I remember story well, old Rome   330
Was free from all this weakness of the mind;
For Women! oh how slightly were they thought of,
When the great Cato gave his Friend his Wife,
To breed him his Heirs, because she was a Teemer;
And after he was dead, again receiv'd her.   335
This was before the Vandals made us Slaves,
Who mingling with our Wives, begot a Race
That nothing holds of the old Lyon, Glory.

          Enter Borgia.

But hush, more work, and now I am compos'd.
    BORG. Welcom, my best of Friends, my Machiavel!   340
Let me unlade on thee my fraught of joy;
For Bellamira's mine, her Vows are mine;
Her Father gave her, and the Holy man
Has link'd our hands: Fortune perhaps, e're long,
May joyn our hearts: However, dearly bought,   345
I say, she's mine.
    MACH.   However, dearly bought!
    BORG. True Machiavel, most dearly; but alas,
He that would reach the Mine, must burst the Quarry,
And labour to the Center---Ha---thou'rt cold;
Start from this Lethargy, and tell me why,   350
Why dost thou shake my joys with that stern look?
Speak, for to me thy face is as the Heav'ns,
And, when thou smil'st, I cannot fear a Storm:
But now thy gather'd brows prognosticate
Ill weather: Lightning sparkles from thy eyes;   355

Speak too, though thunder follow.
  MACH. On what conditions had the Prince his life?
  BORG. It was agreed betwixt us solemnly,
And bound by Oath, that he who was subdu'd
Should never speak to Bellamira more.   360
  MACH. I am satisfi'd. ---
  BORG.   O Machiavel! is this friendly,
To hide the Cause of thy disorder from me?
Thou said'st, I am satisfied; but at that moment
I saw two Furies leap from thy red Eyes,
That said thou'rt not, thou art not satisfi'd.   365
This coldness of thy Carriage! this dead stillness
Makes me more apprehend than all the noise
That mad-men raise: Speak then, but do not blast me:
Speak by degrees, let the Truth break away
In oblique sounds; for if it come directly,   370
I fall at once, split, ruin'd, dash'd for ever,
So little am I Master of my Passion.
  MACH. Therefore I dare not tell you.
  BORG.   Therefore 'tis horrid, ha!
Monstrous! 'tis so; therefore thou dar'st not tell me:
But speak; though trembling thus from head to foot,   375
I will be calm, press down the rising sighs,
And stifle all the swellings in my heart:
I will be Master far as Nature can.
  MACH. If that you knew such Fire was in your temper,
And thus would burn you up, why would you marry?   380
  BORG. Because resistless Love! resistless Beauty
Hurry'd me on. But speak, thou stav'st me off.
If thou hast sense of Honour, tell me, Machiavel!
Speak, I conjure thee, as thou art my Friend.
  MACH. The fault's not great, and you may pardon it; 385
Yet 'twas a fault, I think: Where did you leave
Your Bride?
  BORG. Why dost thou ask? I know not where:
This way they led her; and as I perswaded,
Orsino, though unwilling, judg'd it fit
She should retire again to her Apartment,   390
That her full griefs might have a time to waste.
  MACH. She is retir'd, my Lord.
  BORG.   Ha! whither? speak:
She is retir'd where she should not retire!
'Tis true, most plain, most undeniable,
I know it by the fashion of thy Wit,   395
Thy accent swears it; mouth thy Tale no more,
But say distinctly whither she's retir'd:
I charge thee, pray thee, and conjure thee, speak,
For what, with whom, and on what new occasion?
  MACH. You have a Brother.
  BORG.   O the perjur'd Traytor!   400

I have! what then?
  MACH.   She's with him now.
  BORG.   With whom?
  MACH. Why with the Duke of Gandia; with your Brother
Palante, Son, or Nephew to the Pope.
  BORG. What Bellamira with him? Ponyards! Daggers!
  MACH. This way, but now, I saw her come in haste;   405
Whether she guess'd the matter by your Wound,
I know not, but with faultring speech she ask'd
How far'd Palante, if he were in being?
Whereon I nothing mus'd, but in plain terms,
With moderation, told her what I knew;   410
But had you seen the starts and stops she made!
  BORG. No doubt she did; Ten thousand Curses, oh---
Go on; for yet I am a fangless Lyon.
  MACH. Had you but heard when first his Wound I mention'd,
How she shriek'd out; how oft she forced me swear,   415
And swear, and swear again, it was not mortal!
  BORG. Undone for ever! O destruction seize her!
  MACH. But when I told your hurt, she seem'd scarce griev'd,
And lessening sorrow yielded to attention;
I do not say she flatly did rejoice,   420
But sure I am she smil'd, and touch'd my hand,
And begg'd me, if you came this way, to hold you
In talk, while to the sick she made a visit.
  BORG. Thy Bosom be my Grave; bear me a while
Or I shall burst. O Bellamira! Oh!   425
  MACH. Raise, raise your self. Ha, Prince! is this the Fire
We fear'd but now, that most transporting fury?
  BORG. No more; 'tis gone: O Marriage! now I find thee;
Thou costly Feast, on which with fear we feed,
As if each Golden dish we taste were poison'd;   430
Where, by the fatal Tyranny of Custom,
Our Honour, like a Sword just pointing o're us,
Hangs by a Hair. Ha! but it comes, 'tis faln!
Like a forked Arrow stuck into my Skull.
No more: I am deaf as Adders, and as deadly: 435
Mercy! no more! thy Voice is quite uncharm'd;
All pity thus be dry'd from my weak Eyes;
Here will I look my Mothers softness off,
And gaze till Southern Fury steels my Soul,
Till I am all my Father; till his Form,   440
All bloody o're from Head to Foot with slaughter,
Skims o're my pollish'd Blade, in frowns to haste me.
  MACH. What mean you, Sir?
  BORG.   I know not what my self!
Off from my Arms; away. I've oftentimes heard
At Princes Murders, Monstrous Births forbode;   445
The Heavens themselves rain Blood: Why, let it rain!
If my Heart holds her purpose, with this hand

I'll swell the Purple Deluge. Vengeance! Death and Vengeance. [Exit.
    MACH. No, my brave Warrior! 'tis not gone so far:
These starts are but the hasty Harbingers   450
To the slow Murder that comes dragging on:
The Mischief's yet but young, an Infant Fury;
'Tis the first brawl of new-born Jealousie:
But I have Machiavellian Magick here
Shall nurse this Brood of Hell to such perfection   455
As shall e're long become the Devil's Manhood:
But hark! the Noise approaches, and the Time
Put's me in mind of Bellamira's Letters---   [Exit.

      Enter Borgia, Bellamira, Gandia.

    BORG.   Furies and Hell! yet e're thou dy'st, proud Villain,
Let me demand thee how thou dar'st abuse   460
My Mercy thus?
    GAND.   I give thee back the Title;
And have a heart so well assur'd of Death,
That I disdain to answer.
    BORG.   Dye then, Traytor!
    BELL.   Hold, Borgia, hold! Hear Bellamira speak.
    BORG.   Confusion! off: and play not thus with Thunder,   465
Lest it should blast thee too; Hence, off, I say:
Tho thou deserv'st a Fate as sharp and sudden,
I will take leisure in thy death. Be gone.
    BELL.   Behold, I grasp the Dagger, draw it through
And gash my Veins, and tear my Arteries;   470
I'll fix my hand thus to the wounding Blade
While life will let me hold, and force thee hear me.
    BORG.   Say'st, ha! wilt thou? dar'st thou brave me thus?
Thus guilty too; once more forego my Ponyard.
    BELL.   No: draw it, Cruel; let thy Bloody Deeds   475
Be swifter than thy Threats: I fear thee not;
But thus will wound my self, or quite disarm thee.
Now you shall hear me.
    BORG.   Is this possible?
Ha! Borgia! where! where is thy Fury now?
Where thy Revenge? O Woman in perfection!   480
Thou dazling Mixture of ten thousand Circe's
In one bright heap cast by some hudling God,
How dar'st thou venture thus? how dar'st thou do this?
Yet heave thy Breasts, pant, breathe, and think on mercy?
    BELL.   My Acts have shown the care indeed I take   485
To save my life: No, Prince, not for my own
I would be heard, but for your innocent Brother's,
Palante.
    BORG.   Ha! Palante! Yes, I know thee,
There hangs thy Joy, thy Pulse, thy Breath and Motion,
Blood, life and Soul, thy Darling-Blessing's here,   490

And more than all the joyes of Heaven hereafter.
O World of Horrour! O Contagion, on
The Day when first I saw thee.
     BELL.   Would you but hear---
     BORG. Come, off, I say! tear my scarf'd Wound, tear't up,
With these distilling drops; come glut thy Eyes,   495
Glut 'em with Blood; for Borgia's Blood's thy Joy;
For say--- When at the Altar I stood bleeding,
Speak, Tygress, barbarous Wretch, thou she Palante,
Did'st thou once ask the occasion of my Wound?
No--- I remember thy uneasie Carriage,   500
How often thou look'st back with longing Eyes!
How oft in secret thou didst curse the Priest,
The tedious length of whose slow Ceremonies
Kept thee from flying to Palante's Arms.
     GAND. Farewel, my Lord; think Bellamira guiltless,   505
And you shall never see Palante more.
     BORG. Stay, Sir; come back, I know your Wound's a trouble;
But the reward I mean is worth your waiting.
Here, take him, Bellamira; clasp him;
I give him thee, as our Physicians do   510
Prescribe last Remedies, to save thy life?
I give him thee to save thy gasping Soul,
Which would be damn'd without him; yet observe
There is a Deed that must, that shall be done
Before you laugh and kiss. See here, my Bosom,   515
Strike, and strike deep, deep as Palante burns thee;
For in thy Heart, hot in thy inmost Veins,
I know the curs'd, the too lov'd Traytor lies.
     GAND. I do renounce the name, and to the Giver
Retort it with an equal Indignation!   520
     BORG. Retort it! what?
     GAND.   The name of Traytor.
     BORG.   Ha!
Provoke me not, lest as I am, unarm'd,
I crush thee with my Hands, and dash thee Dead.
     BELL. Hold off, and hear me; noble Borgia, hear me!
Hear me, my Lord, my Husband, hear me kneeling;   525
Thou, whom the Heavens have destin'd to my Arms,
The constant Partner of my nicest thoughts,
Doom'd to my Bed, whom I must learn to love,
And will, unless you turn my Heart to Stone.
     BORG. Ha!   530

---

494 my]; thy Q_{1+}.
501 look'dst C_2.
511 life! Q_3-C_1; life: C_{2+}.
523 I crush] Q_{2+}; crush Q_1. I, catch-word on p. 38, Q_1, has clearly fallen
    out of the forme at top of p. 39, line 1.

O! such sweet words ne're fell from that fair Mouth
Before, nor can I trust 'em now!
    BELL.   If you call back
The Vengeance which your impious Vows let slip,
I swear, thus sinking on your Feet, I swear
Never from this sad hour, never to see,   535
Nor speak, no, nor (if possible) to think
Of poor Palante more.
    BORG. Go on; go on; I swear the Wind is turn'd,
And all those furious and outragious passions
Now bend another way.
    BELL.   I will hereafter,   540
With strictest duty, serve you as my Lord,
And give you signs of such most faithful love,
That it shall seem as if we languish'd long,
As if we had been us'd to mingle sighs,
And from our Cradles interchang'd our Souls;   545
As if no breach had ever been betwixt us;
As if no cruel Father forc'd the Marriage;
I so resigning as if always yours,
And you so mild as if no other proof
But my dishonour e're could make you angry.   550
    BORG. O my heart's joy! Rise, Bellamira, rise!
There's nothing left, nothing of rage to fright thee;
Thou hast new tun'd me, and the trembling strings
Of my touch'd heart dance to the Inspiration,
As if no harshness, nor no jars had been: 555
Had these sweet sounds but met my entrance here,
My ghastly fears and cloven jealousies,
With all the Monsters that made sick my Brain,
Had fled (so soft and artful are thy strains,)
Like sullen Fiends before the Prophets Charms.   560
    BELL. I came, 'tis true, my Lord, to see Palante,
But thought him on his Death-bed.
    BORG.   O, no more!
I do intreat thee mention that no more;
All's well; and we have mutually forgiven!
I love thee, Bellamira; therefore pass   565
This Errour by; yes, for thy self I love thee!
To glut my fancy with thy endless Charms,
And snatch the pleasures of all Woman-kind:
Thy fair Repentance, and thy graceful Vows,
Have turn'd the eagerness of sworn revenge   570
To furious Wishes for the promis'd Joy.

Enter Orsino.

    GAND. O blasting sight! O death to all my hopes!
Life, thou art vile, and I will wait no longer.
    ORSI. Ha! Traytor Prince! -- why, Borgia, does he live,

Who has himself broke all the tyes of blood?   575
Where is the leud Adult'ress too, my Daughter?
For I will stab 'em in each others Arms.
    BORG. Hold! hold Orsino! for revenge is now
No more; Thy Daughter is most innocent,
And melts into my Arms. O happy Night!   580
Not to the weary Pilgrim half so welcome,
When after many a weary bleeding step
With joyful looks he spies his long'd-for Home.
See, see, my Lord, the effects of our Vexation!
Thus comes to the despairing Wretch, the glad   585
Reprieve: 'Tis Mercy, Mercy at the Block:
Thus the toss'd Seaman, after boisterous Storms,
Lands on his Country's Breast; thus stands, and gazes,
And runs it o're with many a greedy look;
Then shouts for joy, as I should do, and makes   590
The Ecchoing Hills and all the Shoars resound.
    ORSI. Now Blessings on thy Heart; more Blessings on thee,
Than, on thy Disobedience, Curses. Take him, Girl,
And lay him to thy heart; the warmest Gift
That Nature, or thy Father, can bestow!---   595
    GAND. Farewell, thrice happy Lover! never shall
This Wretch again disturb you. Bellamira,
O Bellamira---   [Exit.
    BELL.   O farewell, for ever!
    BORG. Why dost thou weep? and pour into my Wounds
New Oyl to make 'em blaze?
    BELL.   I've done, my Lord;   600
Let me but dry my Eyes, and I will wait you,
To Death or to your Bed---
    BORG.   O ill compar'd!
Be constant Bellamira to thy Vows,
So shall we shine, as in the in-most Heav'n;
The fixt and brightest Stars with silent glory,   605
Where never Storm, nor Lightnings flash, nor stroak
Of Thunder comes: but if thou fail in ought,
Then shall we fall like the cast Angels down,
Never to rise again: Therefore I warn thee---
    BELL. Fear not, my Lord.
    BORG.   O! I must fear my temper;   610
But I will purge it off with resolution,
And with a confidence thou wilt be mine:
For shouldst thou not: Hence Gorgon Jealousie!
Cam'st thou uncall'd to set me on the Rack?
Be gone, I say, she's chaste, and I defie thee.   615
O plague me, Heaven! plague me with all the woes
That man can suffer: root up my possessions,

---

578 Hold! Orsino! Q_2-C_1; Hold, dear Orsino! C_{2+}.

Shipwrack my far-sought Ballast in the Haven;
Fire all my Cities, burn my Dukedoms down,
Let midnight Wolves howl in my Desart Chambers: 620
May the Earth yawn; shatter the frame of Nature;
Let the rack'd Orbs in Whirlwinds round me move,
But save me from the rage of jealous Love.   [Exeunt.

End of A C T   III.

Act IV. Scene I.

Soft Musick, with an Epithalamium to Borgia and Bellamira.

1.

Blush not redder than the Morning,
Though the Virgins gave you warning;
Sigh not at the chance befel ye,
Though they smile, and dare not tell ye.

2.

Maids, like Turtles, love the Cooing,   5
Bill and murmur in their Wooing.
Thus, like you, they start and tremble,
And their troubl'd joys dissemble.

3.

Grasp the pleasure while 'tis coming,
Though your Beauties now are blooming;   10
Time at last your joys will sever,
And they'l part, they'l part for ever.

Enter Machiavel and Adorna.

MACH. Say'st thou, so loving?
ADOR.   O! he has got ground
Beyond all expectation: Had you seen
His graceful manner, when the sighing Bride   15
Was last night by our Arms given to his Bed;
When after she was laid, quite drown'd in tears,
How, aw'd with trembling, he the Curtains drew,
And kneeling by her Bed-side, took her fair hand,
With which she strove to hide her Blushes from him,   20
And sighing, swore upon't,--- if so she pleas'd,
If her cold heart refus'd him utterly,
He would forgo his joys, though death ensu'd.
You muse, my Lord.
MACH.   This day attend my Motion:
Soon as my purpose hits, which you must watch,   25
I'll train the Bridegroom near Palantes Lodging;
Whence, as you were before by me instructed,
You with this Letter (which from all the Pacquets
I chose, and notably suits our design)
Shall issue forth, and act as I inspir'd ---   30
ADOR. I fear this business,
Lest he should kill me: in this height of fury,
Murder his Brother, or his Innocent Lady.

    MACH. I tell thee, though a Whirlwind drove him on,
I'll make him calm. The consequence of this   35
Is thine: He drives Palante from the Palace,
Who else may linger after Bellamira;
And then thou know'st ---
    ADOR.   I will about it streight.
If I get clear of this, use me no more,
For I have sworn to cease ---
    MACH.   Prithee, be gone ---   [Ex. Adorna.   40
Use me no more: For she has sworn to cease,
To dip her Lady-finger in new mischief:
Yes -- thou shalt cease to live when I have us'd thee,
Poor useless thing. -- But see the Bridegrooms here.

          Enter Borgia.

My Lord, I give you joy: your motion gives it   45
Your wondrous gallantry, and sprightly action.
But has she wholly yielded to your wishes,
Without the least reserve?
    BORG.   Oh!
I cannot tell thee ought but this, I am happy
Above expression, blest beyond all hope;   50
And sure such perfect joy cannot last long,
Lest we be Gods. O thou great Chymist, Nature,
Who drawst one spirit so sublimely perfect,
Thou mak'st a Dreg of all the World beside.
    MACH. Why, this at first I told you, but you fear'd,   55
And push'd the blessing from you with both hands.
I grant you that she lov'd your Brother first;
I know he's young, and handsom, has a Wit
Most suitable to Womans inclination,
A subtle Genius, soft and voluble,   60
That winds with their discourse, and hits the Vein:
'Tis true, you are not of this subtle Mould;
But if you have enjoy'd her, 'tis all one,
My life she loves you: so the Act's resolv'd,
Leave them to manage. O ye know 'em not: 65
Those subtle Creatures, when necessity
Forces compliance, in a case like yours,
Will make the best on't.
    BORG. How Machiavel, the best on't! Ha! how mean'st thou?
    MACH. Why thus; she may, ev'n Bellamira may,   70
Spite of her Fathers will, her Vows in Marriage,
And all her after-Oaths, even in your Arms
Bestow her self upon the Duke of Gandia.
    BORG. Ha!

---

    44 Bridegroom's C_{1+}.

MACH. I say not (pardon me!) she does, or will;   75
But to make good my former argument,
Affirm they may, they can, they will do thus.
As for example: though your Bellamira,
Compell'd as all Rome knows to this late Marriage,
Admits you to her Bed; you cannot think,   80
But her Palante had been much more welcom.
    BORG. Heav'n.
    MACH. 'Tis likely too her Fancy workt that way
I urg'd before, she took you for Palante:
'Tis dark, she sees you not; you are his Brother,   85
Form'd in one Womb, of the same flesh and blood
Therefore she yields as to foreknown Embraces:
And as you gently draw with trembling arms
Her nicer Beauties to your heaving Breasts;
She shuts her eyes with languishing delight,   90
And whispers to her heart, it is Palante.
    BORG. Cease, Machiavel; hold, as thou lov'st my life,
I charge thee hold: O, 'tis most true I swear!
Thou know'st the very depth of Woman-kind;
They are what thy Imagination paints 'em,   95
Charmers and Sorceresses. O, I'll tell thee,
When I the chastest, as I thought her then,
I am sure the sweetest of the Earth, imbrac'd ---
'Twas with complainings, Machiavel; such tremblings,
I could have sworn her cold as Winter streams,   100
But oh the horrours thou hast conjur'd up!
Soon as soft sleep had seal'd her melting eyes,
I heard her sigh; for till the morn I wak'd,
Palante. Oh --- what have we done, Palante?
    MACH. By Heav'n, that was too much.
    BORG.   O much, --- much more.   105
For stealing nearer me; her glowing arm,
Cast o're my Cheek, thrice prest me to her Breast;
Ev'n that coy arm, so nicely strange before,
Familiar grew, and circled in my Neck,
With all the freedom of acquainted Love: 110
And I too piti'd her, and thought that Nature
Work'd her imperfectly; but now I know,
I find, I see, it was her hearts design,
The black contrivance of her blotted Fancy:
Blood, Blood and Death; thus has she set me down,   115
Through the whole course of her polluted nights,
To be her Bawd, her most industrious Groom,
The Drudge of her damn'd Lust --- Palante's stale ---
    MACH. Are you incens'd indeed? or do you, Sir,
Put on this jealous Fit to make you sport?   120

─────────────

86 blood; Q_{2+}.

For if so small a Spark thus makes you glow,
A little more will blow you into Flame:
Therefore be serious in your Answer.
    BORG.   Ha!
Thou know'st before my Marriage how I fear'd,
How when my Honour was ingag'd by Vows,   125
Like Flax my jealous temper caught the Flame,
And scarce could all her melting sorrows quench me.
    MACH. I do remember well.
    BORG. But now I have enjoy'd her; mark me, Machiavel,
If I was Flax before, I am Powder now,   130
And will fly up in general Conflagration:
For I would chuse to scramble at a Door,
Make my loath'd Meals out of the common Basket,
With Dungeon Villains, wallow in the Stews,
And get my Bread by poysoning my firm Limbs,   135
E're pass an hour with her I have Espous'd,
If but in thought consenting with another.
    MACH. I am glad to find the Genius of your Climate
Inflames you thus; my Lord, give me your Hand:
Prepare your Soul, gather your Nobler Spirits,   140
And bid 'em stand to Arms, like Towns besieg'd,
That must receive no Quarter.
    BORG.   Let me go:
So deep thou threaten'st, that I fear ev'n thee;
And from this moment, like the fearful Plant,
Shrink Back my arms from every humane touch: 145
But speak, I charge thee, slip the strugling Thunder,
And foil my Soul.
    MACH. This Morning, just before you enter'd here,
I saw in haste Adorna cross the Garden,
And as she ran, a Note dropt from her Bosom,   150
Which I took up, and in it read these words;
<u>Mourn</u> <u>not</u>, <u>my dear</u> <u>Palante</u>, <u>for the time</u>
<u>Draws on</u>, <u>when spite of this inhumane Borgia</u>
<u>We will be happy</u>.
    BORG.   Yes, she shall, she shall;
I'll joyn 'em Breast to Bosom, stab 'em through,   155
And clinch my Dagger on the other side.
    MACH. This, as I oft perus'd in great amazement,
I saw her who had miss'd the Note come back,
And briefly let her know that I had read it;
With Menaces, unless she told me all,   160
Immediately to carry you the Letter.
Why should I rack you longer? your Chaste Wife
Has with the help of this her Kinswoman
Concluded, on the date of your first absence,
To admit your Brother.
    BORG.   'Tis impossible!   165
'Tis mountainous to Faith; I'll not believe it:

For Hell it self ne're teem'd with such a falshood.

Enter Adorna.

MACH. Ha -- as I live, just from Palante now,
The private way from his Apartment, see
Their Emissary comes.
    BORG.   O thou vile Bawd!   170
Thou Midnight Hag; thou most Contagious Blast,
Which Bellamira with a Strumpets breath
Blows to Palante, and he back to her:
Whence com'st thou? speak! what bear'st thou? Ha, produce it,
Or I will tear thee Limb from Limb.
    ADOR.   O Heav'ns!   175
I am betray'd, undone, for ever ruin'd;
And I shall lose my life.
    BORG.   Thou shalt be safe,
I swear thou shalt, if thou confess the truth:
But if thou hide ought from me, I will rack thee,
Till with thy horrid Groans thou wake the Dead.   180
    ADOR. O, my Lord!
I do confess that Bellamira sent me;
But sure no harm was in the Letter.
    BORG.   None,
None at all; Hell knows her Innocence:
But speak ---
    ADOR.   I have, my Lord, confess'd already   185
All that I know, to my Lord Machiavel.
    BORG. Thou ly'st, damn'd Wretch! look here, and dare not urge me!
Show me the Answer to the Morning Message,
Or I will cut thee to Anatomy,
And search through all thy Veins to find it out.   190
    ADOR. O, save my life! behold, my Lord, this Paper:
What it contains, I know not.
    BORG.   'Tis his hand.
    MACH. Be gone; and on thy life no talk of this. ---   [Ex. Adorna.
    BORG. reads. Palante waits upon your motion. Death and Devils!
And when you call, he comes; or the long sleep   195
Shall hush him ever.
Daggers! Poyson! Fire.   [Tears the Letter.
Woe, and ten thousand horrours on their Souls.
    MACH. What now, my Lord?
    BORG.   Off --- or I'll stab thee through!
Stab --- I could mangle, tear up my own Breast,   200
Drag forth my heart that holds her bleeding Image,

176-78 Printed in Q_{1+} thus:
    I am betray'd, undone, for ever ruin'd; and I shall lose my life.
        BORG. Thou shalt be safe, I swear thou shalt, if thou confess the truth:

And dash it in her face.
    MACH. Talk no more on't; but do, Sir, do.
    BORG. Yes, Machiavel, I will -- I will do deeds
Grain'd as my wrongs: I will, I will be bloody   205
As Pyrrhus, daub'd in Murder at the Altar;
As Tullia, driving through her Fathers Bowels;
As Caesars Butchers in the Capital;
As Nero bathing in his Mothers Womb;
With all succeeding Tyrants down to ours.   210
Lords of the Inquisition, black Contrivers
Of Princes Deaths, and Heads of Massacres;
Orsino, Vitellozzo, Duke Gravina,
Oliverotto too; all, all at once,
Even the whole Race, a Hecatomb to Vengeance.   215
    MACH. Hear me one word.
    BORG. Bid the Sea listen, when the weeping Merchant,
To gorge its ravenous Jaws, hurls all his Wealth,
And stands himself upon the splitting Deck,
For the last plunge. No more! let's rush together;   220
For Death rides Post.
    MACH.   Though Death should meet me,
More horrid than you Name, I'd cross this fury,
This blind, ungovern'd rage: Sir, you shall hear me.
    BORG. Barr'st thou my Vengeance?
    MACH.   No --- I'll further it:
You shall have proof so plain, the World shall say,   225
The Pope himself, dear as he loves your Brother,
Shall say the stroke was just. This Night I'll bring you
Into her Chamber, if with some pretence
You seem t' absent your self: my Lord, I'll bring you
With a false Key into the Bridal Lodging;   230
Where you shall see, even with those eyes behold,
And gaze upon their curst incestuous Loves.
    BORG. Just reeking from my arms! O thou Adult'ress!
Whose Name to mention, sure would rot my Lungs,
And blister up my Tongue; Insatiate Scylla!   235
Bark'st thou for more? then let the Furies seize thee,
Whose burning Lust damns to the lowest Hell,
Smoaks to the Heav'ns, and sullies all the Stars.
    MACH. Compose your looks, smooth down that starting hair,
And dry your eyes, which spite of this distraction,   240
I see are full, brim-full of gushing tears.
    BORG. Had she not fall'n thus, O ten thousand Worlds
Could not have balanc'd her, for Heav'n is in her,
And joys which I must never dream of more;
I weep, 'tis true: But, Machiavel, I swear,   245
They're Tears of Vengeance, drops of liquid fire:
So Marble weeps when Flames surround the Quarry,
And the pil'd Oaks spout forth such scalding Bubbles
Before the general blaze; for that she dies,

Though clinging to the Altar; Guardian Gods,   250
Though starting from their Shrines, shall not redeem her.
    MACH. Pretend to night, nor is it bare pretence;
For, as I hear, the Sinigallian Victors
Come on to wait you here: Pretend to her,
To Bellamira, you can scarce return   255
In forty hours.
    BORG.   I will do what I may.
    MACH. Away then.
    BORG.   Ha! methinks thou dost not share
In my resentment, Machiavel, as thou ought'st:
If thou art my Friend, and art indeed concern'd,
Relieve my weari'd fury, bate my Vengeance,   260
Call up a friendly rage, and curse 'em, Machiavel,
Curse these Triumphers o're thy Borgia's ruine.
    MACH. Diseases wait 'em: Wherefore should I curse 'em?
If that my Breath were sulph'rous as the Lightning
That murders with a blast; or like the Vapours,   265
The choaking stench, which those that die of Plagues
Send with their parting groans, then I would curse 'em
With Accents that should poyson from my Tongue,
Deliver'd strongly through my gnashing Teeth;
More harsh, more horrible, and more outragious,   270
Than Envy in her Cave, or Mad-men in their Dens.
    BORG. Excellent, Machiavel! more, more, to lull me.
    MACH. My Tongue should stammer in my earnest words;
My eyes should sparkle like the beaten Flint.
    BORG. This hoary Hair should start, and stand an end,   275
And all thy shaking joynts should seem to curse 'em.
    MACH. Nay, since you urge me, Sir, my heart will break,
Unless I curse 'em! Poyson be their drink.
    BORG. Gall, Gall and Wormwood! Hemlock! Hemlock! quench 'em.
    MACH. Their sweetest Shade, a Dell of duskish Adders.   280
    BORG. Their fairest Prospect, Fields of Basilisks;
Their softest touch, as smart as Vipers Teeth.
    MACH. Their Musick horrid as the hiss of Dragons,
All the foul terrours of dark-seated Hell.
    BORG. No more; thou art one piece with me my self: 285
And now I take a pride in my revenge.
    MACH. You bid me ban, and will you bid me cease?
Now, by your wrongs that turn my heart to steel,
Well could I curse away a Winters night,
Though standing naked on a Mountains top,   290
And think it but a minute spent in sport.
    BORG. Thou best of Friends! come to my Arms, my Brother:
But the time calls, and Vengeance bids us part;

---

260 beat Q_{2+}.
280 a Dale C_{2+}.

Henceforth, be thou the Mistress of my Heart.   [Ex.
    MACH. Now it grows ripe; the Orsins, and Vitelli,   295
Are buri'd by my Wit without a noise.
O! 'tis the safer course, for threats are dang'rous,
But there's no danger in the Execution;
For he that's dead, ne're thinks upon revenge.
What, hoa --- Alonzo!

                Enter Alonzo.

    ALON.   Here, my Lord.   300
    MACH. Are the Gloves brought I sent to the Perfumers?
    ALON. They are.
    MACH.   Where is Adorna?
    ALON.   She waits without.
    MACH. As you see her enter,
Bring me the Gloves: 'T were easie strangling her,
But this is quainter. --- O my bright Adorna!   305

                Enter Adorna.

With confidence I swear the Duke is thine.
    ADOR. May I believe it?
    MACH. Be judge, thy self, whether I have been idle!
These were a Present from the King of Spain,
To the Popes Niece; of whom the fond young Duke   310
Begg'd 'em for thee.
    ADOR. Is't possible?
    MACH.   Stay Madam --- we must change
One Present for another. Lend me the Key
To Bellamira's Chamber.
    ADOR.   For what?
    MACH. Nay, if we barter words.
    ADOR.   Here, here, my Lord.   315
Now give me the dear Present.
See, see, my Lord, they are emboss'd with Jewels,
And cast so rich an odour, they o're come me. ---
Help me --- my Lord --- O help me --- lend your Arm ---
The Earth turns round with me! O mercy, Heaven ---   [Dies.   320
    MACH. Remove the Body ---
Then haste, and find the Duke of Gandia out,
E're he removes, as he intends to night;
Having Commission from the Pope to lead
Th' Italian Armies: earnestly entreat him,   325
To honour me by making one last Visit,
Which equally imports him as his life.

          Enter Borgia and Bellamira.

    BORG. Upon the instant, Fairest, I must leave you;

The Lord of Firmo, with the Duke your Uncle,
Have taken Sinigallia by surprize: 330
What else, but meeting thy Victorious Kinsmen,
Should draw me from thy Arms? yet thus divided
But for a day or two, methinks I part,
As Souls are sever'd from their warmer Mansions,
To wander in the bleak and desart Air.   335
O Bellamira!
    BELL.   Why do you sigh, my Lord?
If 'tis your pleasure, let 'em wait you here;
Or if my Presence can dispel these Clouds
That make you sad, I will attend you thither;
For while life lasts I will be all obedience.   340
    BORG. Could'st thou hold there, how might we laugh at Fate!
So kindled both by Love, and by Ambition,
How would I sweep, like Tempests, with a waste
Over all Italy, and Crown thee Empress
Here in the Heart of Rome --- my bright Augusta,   345
But 'tis impossible.
    BELL. Then you conclude, my Lord, I am not true.
    BORG. Why, art thou? Is there such a thing in Nature
As a true Wife? No, Bellamira, no ---
Thou would'st be monstrous then, ev'n to derision: 350
For the whole Flock of common Wives would whoot thee,
And drive thee, like a Bird, without one Feather
Of thy own kind.
    BELL.   Once more upon my knees,
In view of all the Hierarchy of Heav'n,
I here attest my spotless Innocence.   355
    BORG. Still Machiavel, still let us keep to death
Our Principle, that we are dust when dead;
For, were there any Hell, or any Devil
But hot enough to make an Exhalation,
Would he not fetch her now? would he not dam her?   360
I do believe thee guiltless: Therefore rise;
But since thou art so confidently clear,
Swear Bellamira, if I prove thee false,
What e're I threat, nay, though I put in act
Those Menaces, thou wilt not call me Tyrant.   365
    BELL. I swear by Heav'n I will submit my life
To the severest stroke of your revenge.
    BORG. If then I prove thee false, O Bellamira!
Not that Celestial Copy, ev'n thy Face,
Shall scape; but I will race the Draught, as if   370
It ne're had been the pattern of the Gods.
    BELL. Act what you please; but speak no more, my Lord,

---

345 Augusta,] Q_{3+}; Angusta, Q_{1-2}.
370 raze the Draught, C_3.

For every word's a bolt, and strikes me dead.
    BORG. If thou art false, and if I prove thee so,
That skin of thine, that matchless Weft of Heav'n,   375
Which some more curious Angel cast about thee,
Will I tear off, though cleaving to the Shrine.
    BELL. Speak to him, Machiavel! O fatal Marriage!
    BORG. If thou dost play me false, think not of mercy;
Thy Father shall be burnt before thy eyes.   380
    BELL. O horrid thought!
    BORG.   Thy Uncles, Brothers, Sisters,
All that have any relish of thy blood,
I'll rack to death, and throw their Limbs before thee:
Therefore look to 't; beware, if thou art false,
I'll take thee unprepar'd, and sink thy Soul: 385
Therefore, I say again, beware! I've warn'd thee;
Body and Soul, ev'n everlasting ruine;
For so may Heav'n have mercy upon mine
At my last gasp, as I'll have none on thine. ---   [Exit.
    BELL. O 'tis too plain! I am lost, undone for ever.   390
What, but one Night, ev'n the first Nuptial Night,
So sought, so courted, and so hardly won;
And the next day, nay, the succeeding Morn
To be us'd thus --- Let me go, let me go,
For I'll proclaim him through the streets of Rome   395
The Traytor, Monster --- O, I could shake the world
With thundring forth my wrongs; Hollow his name
To the resounding Hills? Borgia! Traytor Borgia!
Methinks that word, that spell, that horrid sound,
That groan of Air should cleave the neighbouring Rocks,   400
And scare the babling Ecchoes from their Dens.
    MACH. Perhaps some busie Slave has whisper'd him
I know not what, that chafes his melancholy
Against your Honour.
    BELL.   That's impossible!
And I deni'd to admit him to my Bed,   405
Some seeming cause, some reason for distrust
Might then be given: but the bright Heav'ns know
I had resolv'd to take him for my Lord,
And love him too, or force my inclination,
So subtly had he wrought by deep dissembling   410
Upon my plain and undiscerning weakness:
But now he's gorg'd, the Monster shews himself,
Appears all Beast, and I must die, he cries.
Ah Cruelty! and all my wretched Race.
    MACH. Madam, you know how near a Friendship grows   415
Betwixt the Duke of Gandia, and my self:

---

398 Hills! C_{1+}.
405 Had I deny'd C_{1+}.

After this night you'll never see him more:
Yet, e're he goes, as he to night is order'd,
He will unfold, if you permit him leave,
The only means to save your Fathers life!   420
Nay, and the lives of all your Family.
    BELL. O Machiavel! now, where is thy advice?
Had I not reason for my dreadful fears?
My Father dies; and by whose hand but Borgia's?
What shall I do? where shall I go? and whither shall I run?   425
Ten thousand horrours! O, instruct me, Machiavel,
For I grow desperate!
    MACH.   Admit the Duke of Gandia,
This night, for one last conference: your Husband
Cannot return, unless he ride the Wind
In forty hours ---
    BELL.   Here I am lost again: 430
Should he return, and find Palante with me,
Whom I have sworn never to see, discourse,
Never to hear of, scarce to think of more,
What Mountains then should hide me from his fury?
Yet if I see him not, my poor old Father,   435
With all his Children, Brothers, and Relations,
Top, Root and Branches, all must be cut down;
Hear, Heav'n, hear! I must kneel to thee for succour;
O aid my Vertue, and support my weakness:
Methinks I am inspir'd; some Guardian-Spirit   440
Whispers me, save, O save thy Fathers life!
Bring him then, Machiavel, bring the Duke of Gandia:
Yet stay! methinks I see the Tyrant there!
My bloody Husband, with his Ponyard drawn,
Just at the Door: Stop, stop, the Duke of Gandia,   445
He shall not come: Why, then thy Father dies;
O horrid state! weep eyes, and bleed, O heart!
Let Nature burst with these unheard of suff'rings!
Forbid him, Machiavel; or let him come,
All have their Fate, and I'll expect my Doom. ---   [Ex. severally.   450

        End of A C T   IV.

---

435 Yet if I] C_{1+}; Yet I Q_{1-3}.

Act V. Scene I.

Enter Machiavel, and Alonzo.

ALON. My Lord, I have been diligent.
MACH. And always wer't my subtle Emissary;
My glance of Death, and Lanthorn to my mischiefs.
ALON. I met the Duke of Gandia at the Head
Of his new Forces, and acquainted him   5
As you directed; and he'll streight attend you:
But as I whisper'd him, Duke Valentine
With a vast Train came up to take his leave,
Being call'd (as Fame reports) to Sinigallia:
But had you seen the Embraces, heard the Vows   10
Which Borgia swore should be inviolable,
And ratifi'd 'em with a parting kiss.
MACH. 'Tis my own Borgia; a very Limb of me;
And when he dies, thou'lt see me halt, Alonzo.

Enter Gandia.

My Lord, most welcom! Alonzo---hence---O Prince!--- [Ex. Alon.   15
Was ever Slave so careful for his Lord,
That watch'd his Nod, as I have been for you?
GAND. I must with shame to Death acknowledge it.
But did'st thou know, or could'st thou guess, how near
The loss of Bellamira touches me,   20
Thou would'st forgive me.
MACH.   I have excus'd you, Sir:
And for a Witness of my faster Friendship,
This night have sent the Duke to Sinigallia,
That you might take your last farewel of Love,
And Bellamira.   25
GAND. And has the Cruel Fair consented to it?
MACH. She has consented, rather by constraint,
Than her own will: I was forc'd to tell her,
How you had signifi'd to me, her Father
Was in great hazard: but if she vouchsaf'd   30
A Visit, you would satisfie her better.

Enter Alonzo.

GAND. Ha! what's this? a sudden fall of Spirits---
ALON. My Lord, he's in's Litter muffled up,   [Aside to Mach.

_____

33 [Aside to Mach.]; om. Q₁₊.

In a dark Avenue behind the Palace;
And bid me fly to tell you, Tarquins Poppies   35
Are bound up all together in one Sheaf.
    MACH. Haste thee, and make my answer thus--The Time
Calls for their Heads. [To Gandia] This Key, my Lord, admits you---
    GAND. 'Tis now no time for thanks; but if I live---   [Exit.
    MACH. Why, this is true Italian! turning thus   40
A Key with Machiavellian slight of hand,
Two Families of the best Southern Blood,
With the first Prince in Rome, are quite extinct:
What foggy Northern Brain would dream of this?

        Borgia muffled in a Cloak.

    BORG. My Machiavel!
    MACH.   My Prince, my God-like Borgia!   45
    BORG. Tell me my Bosom-sin; am I awake?
Alive? and may I credit this thy Summons?
    MACH. No sooner were you gone, but your Chast Wife,
Whom I imagin'd dead with what you utter'd:
I say, this Wife, this heavenly Wife of yours,   50
Rearing her Head, and wiping her dry Eyes,
Dropping her Chin to make her smile more scornful,
Cry'd out, Lord Machiavel, you see, you see,
What Things these Husbands are, and left the Room.
    BORG. Racks, racks, and fire; Caldrons of molten Lead,   55
How shall I torture her?
    MACH.   Streight, by her walking Pacquet,
She signifi'd her pleasure to the Duke,
Who soon approach'd, and with a matchless boldness
Desir'd my friendship in this private business:
I smil'd, and promis'd that I would not see,   60
Though I beheld Adorna let him in;
Whom since I poyson'd, lest she should betray
The secret of your coming.
    BORG.   By Death and Vengeance
I could turn Cannibal, and with my teeth
Tear her alive. But let us talk no more.   65

        Enter D. Michael.

What Hoa, Don Michael! when I stamp my foot
Against the ground, bring forth the Prisoners,
And execute as I shall order.   [Ex. Michael.
    MACH. Pass the back way, my Lord; this Door is lock'd,
If that be shut too, force it open, while   70

---

38 [To Gandia]; om. Q_{1+}.

I set a Guard on this: Millions to one,
But when she hears your voice, she'll hide the Duke,
And then deny him boldly to your face.
'Tis like those subtle Creatures.
    BORG.   Dam 'em, Serpents!
What needs this aggravation? Revenge! away---   [Exit.   75
    MACH. Now like a Grey-hound barking in the slips,
Death struggles for a loose; I must be gone,
And lurk in Shadows till the Murder's done.
Hark, 'tis doing, the Doors are thunder'd down!
O! for an Earth-quake now to swallow all,   80
All that oppose my Tyrant, to the Center.---   [Exit.

      Scene draws: Borgia, Bellamira, Duke of Gandia
                disarm'd: D. Michael, &c.

    BORG. Slave, run you down, and bar the Palace Gates;
Let not a Souldier stir on pain of death,
Till I appoint. What's he you have disarm'd?
Haste, drag him forth, and put the Tapers near him: 85
Lightning and Thunder! Ha! the Duke of Gandia!
Rage burn me up; it is not possible:
Woman, O Woman!
    BELL.   O Heav'ns! O all ye Powers!
Is there not one, one Door for Mercy left?
    BORG. Pull off his Robes, and bind him to a Chair;   90
Ply him with Fire and Wounds---Yes, Bellamira,
There is a Flood-gate---but it is of Blood;
A Gate for Mercy wide, as thou hast shown
For Honour, Chastity, and Bridal Vertue.
See here the Sluce I draw, through doors of wounds;   95
Thy Vows; this sulphurous stench thy Kisses.
    BELL. Hold, hold, Tormentors!
    BORG.   Seize the Furies Arms,
And execute my Orders.
    GAND.   O unmerciful!
O Borgia: when, when shall my Torments end?
    BELL. Ha! is it doing? Wretches, Villains, Dogs,   100
Miscreants, Sons of Hell, and Broods of Darkness!
    GAND. Humanity can bear no more. My heart, strike there.
    BELL. 'Tis done; O the dark deed is done!
O let me gather all the rage of Woman,
And tell this Tyrant to his Teeth, he is a Villain.   105
    GAND. Mercy, gentle Borgia, mercy!
    BELL. He gentle; then the Devils themselves have mercy,
O Monster, rocky Villain, Tyger, Hell-hound,
Seize him you Fiends, and Furies dam him, dam him,
May Hell have infinite stories, and this Devil   110
Be damn'd beneath the bottomless Foundation.

    BORG. By Heav'n she weeps: here, dip her Handkerchief,
Dip't in his blood, and bid her dry her eyes.
    BELL. O thou Eternal Mover of the Heav'ns,
Where are thy Bolts ?
    GAND.   I go, O Bellamira!   115
Think'st thou, alas, that we shall know each other
In the bright World; I fear we shall not---Oh!
Borgia farewel: Thy Bride is Innocent;
Let Bellamira live, and I forgive thee. ----   [Dies.
    BELL. He's gone; to Heav'n he's gone, as sure as thou   120
Shalt sink to Hell, thou Tyrant, double damn'd:
Nay, thou would'st have me rage, and I will rage,
And weep, and rage, and show thee to the World,
Thou Priest, Archbishop, Cardinal, and Duke,
Thou that hast run through all Religious Orders,   125
And with a form of Vertue cloak'd thy horrors!
Thou proper Son of that old cursed Serpent,
Who daubs the holy Chair with blood and Murders:
But sure the Everlasting has a Chain
To bind your Charms, and link you both together;   130
Hells Vicar, and his first begotten Devil,
Hotter than Lucifer in all his Flames.

Enter Alonzo.

    BORG. What, hoa, Alonzo! strangle the prisoners,
Orsino! Vitellozzo: haste, I say,
Without reply. ----
    BELL.   O spare him! spare my Father!   135
And I'll unsay, forswear all that I have said:
O, I have play'd the Woman now indeed,
A lying, foolish, vext, outragious Woman!
To set your Wrath against the Innocent;
There was a seeming cause for the Dukes Death   140
And mine; But, Oh! what has Orsino done ?
Orsino loves you: Oh, that good old man!
Your Father--- For so a thousand times
I've heard you call him, seen you kiss, embrace him!
Therefore he must not, cannot dye!   145
    BORG. Alonzo!
    ALON.   My Lord!
    BORG.   Slave, I'll strangle thee [Strikes him.
With my own hands! if thou delay'st my Vengeance:
Say, Villain, what, not dead ?
    ALON.   My Lord, they are:
And, if I live, you shall repent this blow---   [Aside.

---

136 all I C_{2+}.

    BORG. Go, draw the Curtain; glut her eyes with Death,   150
And strangle her: my Veins are all on Fire,
And I could wade up to the eyes in blood.
Draw, draw the Curtain.

     [Orsin. Vitelloz. D. Gravina, Oliverotto, appear disguised.

    BELL.   Gorgon, Medusa, Horror;
Yet I will shoot through Daggers, rush through flames
To clasp him in my armes, O wretched Paul,   155
O noble Orsin, what quite cold? pale, dead?
And you, dear Images, will you not give
One gasp of breath, one groan, one last farewell?
Horror! Confusion! and eternal shame
Light on thee for this deed: I tell thee, Borgia,   160
I see thee on thy Death-bed, all on Fire,
As if some Hellish poison had inflam'd thee;
I see thee thrown ten Fathom in a Well,
Yet still come up, like Aetna belching Flames.
    BORG. I hope thou wilt go mad, and prophesie!   165
    BELL. Yes, Tyrant, thus, thus to thy face I brave thee,
And tell thee in despite of Threats, e're long
Thou and thy holy Father shall be seiz'd,
And carry'd to the Everlasting Goal;
From whence not all your Spanish Cardinals,   170
Your Bayliffs in red Liveries, shall redeem you---
    BORG. Dy in thy prophesie; Alonzo end her---
    BELL. Thus, on my knees then---And for terror to thee,
Hear my last prayer, and mark my dying words.
If I in thought, in word, in private act   175
Have yielded up this Body to the Armes
Of ought that's Mortal, but inhumane Borgia!
Oh thou impartial and most awful Judge!
Shut, shut thy gates of bliss against my Soul;
But if my tortur'd vertue merits glory,   180
Pardon my frailties, see with what joy
I leave this life, and bring me to perfection.   [She is strangled.
    BORG. What, at her Death! she that believ'd a Heav'n,
And fear'd a Hell, yet to depart a Lyar:
But how know I that she believ'd a Heav'n?   185
Or why with hopes that in the pangs of Death
I would reprieve her, might she not deny
Her Whoredom to the last? But that's unnatural!
What wouldst thou then? I will no more of this;
It clouds my brain: Hence, Alonzo, bear,   190
Bear the Duke of Gandia's Body to the Tiber

----

169 Jail; C_{2+}.

In some close Chair, tye at his neck a Weight,
And plunge him to the Bottom.
     ALON.   My Lord 'tis done.   [Ex. Executioners
                                                  with the Body.
     BORG. I swear I have been cruel to my self,
For that I lov'd her, is as true, as she   195
Is past the sense on't: she is cold already---

               Enter Machiavel.

     MACH. Ha! this is stately Mischief! what, my four Foes
Of Florence? But they are dumb. Ha! gazing there,
I like not that---
     BORG.   Her lips are lovely still;
The Buds, tho gather'd, keep their Damask Colour: 200
Yes, and their odour too! haste, Machiavel,
Rush to my aid: I grow in Love with death.
She shall not dye! Run Slaves! fetch hither Spirits,
I will recover her again!
     MACH.   Again to plague?
To meet again another Duke of Gandia?   205
     BORG. Death on that thought: no, let her dye, and rot;
The damn'd Adultress! perish the thoughts of her.
Ha, tell me, come: I will no more of her.
How shall the bodies be dispos'd? I sent
My Brother to the Tyber.
     MACH.   That's a trouble,   210
I'll find an easier way for these, and her
That sleeps within my Closet. Go, Don Michael,
Bury 'em all together in quick Lime;
In some few hours the flesh will be consum'd:
Then burn the bones, and all is dust and ashes.   215
                          [Draw here the Curtains on 'em.
     BORG. I swear this body shall not be consum'd;
I'll have't embalm'd to last a thousand years.
O Machiavel! I swear, I know not why,
But with a world of horror on my soul,
With tremblings here, Convulsions of the heart;   220
As if I heard some God thus whisper to me,
Thou ought'st to grieve for Bellamira's Death.
     MACH. My Lord, a very fond and foolish Fancy.
     BORG. I say, my Lord, your policy is out:
Furies and Hell! how should you judge of Love,   225
That never lov'd? Thou hast no taste of Love,
No sense; no rellish---why did I trust thee then?

---

217 to stay a Q_{2-3}.
219 horror to Q_{2-3}.

Had any softness dwelt in that lean bosom,
My Bellamira now had been alive:
Tho I had cause to kill her, thou hadst none;   230
To set me on, but honour; jealous honour!
Oh the last night! I tell thee, Pollititian!
When I run o're the vast delight, I curse thee,
And curse my self; nay wish I had been found
Dead in her Armes; But take her, bear her hence: 235
And thou lov'st me, drive her from my Memory.   [They remove her.
Tell me my Brothers Murder is discover'd;
That the four Ghosts are up again in arms:
Say any thing to make me mad, and lose
This Melancholly, which will else destroy me.   240
    MACH. I hear the Pope has sent to Sinigallia
To call you back.
    BORG.   By Heav'n, I had forgot,
And thou most opportunely has remembred:
You know twelve Cardinals were then created,
That solemn Morn that I receiv'd the Rose;   245
And I will tell thee, half those Fools to morrow,
That bought so high, shall veil their Caps for ever.
    MACH. He mends apace; 'tis but another shrug,
And then this Love, this Ague Fit is lost.
    BORG. I swear--I'll to the Wars, and ne're return   250
To Rome, till I have brav'd this haughty French-man,
That menac'd so of late.
    MACH.   Why, this is Borgia.
Come, come, you must not droop; look up, my Lord;
Methinks I see you Crown'd Rome's Emperour.
No doubt, Sir, but among your glorious Plunder,   255
You'll find some Woman---
    BORG.   Ha! no more, I charge thee.
I swear I was at ease, and had forgot her:
Why did'st thou wake me then, to turn me wild,
And rouze the slumbering Orders of my Soul?
To my charm'd Ears no more of Woman tell;   260
Name not a Woman, and I shall be well.
Like a poor Lunatick that makes his moan,
And for a time beguiles the lookers on;
He reasons well; his eyes their wildness lose,
And vows the Keepers his wrong'd sense abuse: 265
But if you hit the Cause that hurt his Brain,
Then his teeth gnash, he foams, he shakes his Chain,
His Eye-balls rowl, and he is mad again.   [Exeunt.

_____

236 And if thou C_{1+}.
243 hast C_{1+}.

Scene II. The Bank of the Tiber.*

Enter one Executioner with a dark Lanthorn, follow'd by another
at a distance; they part often, look up and down, and
hem to the rest.

1. EXEC. The Coast is clear, and all the Guards are gone.
2. EXEC. Hark, hark; what noise was that?
1. EXEC.   The Clock struck three.
2. EXEC. See, the Moon shines; haste, and call our Fellows.
Hem to 'em; that's the Sign.
   1. EXEC.   They come, they come.

Enter four Executioners more; two carry the Body of the Duke
of Gandia in a Chair; the others follow, and scout behind.

3. EXEC. So---set him down, and let 'em bear their part,   5
For I am weary---
4. EXEC. And so am I: I sweat; but 'tis with fear.
1. EXEC. Make no more words on't; take him from the Chair.
2. EXEC. A ghastly sight. The Weight about his Neck
Has bent him almost double: I'll not touch him---   10
3. EXEC. Cowardly Villain---Come, my Princely Master,
The Fishes want their Break-fast.
4. EXEC.   Joyn all together,
And hurl him o're this Wall into the Tyber.
2. EXEC. Fly, fly---I hear a noise: The Guards, the Guards.
3. EXEC. He lies, he lies; the Coynage of his fears: 15
Once more, I say, joyn all your hands together.
Remember the Reward, two thousand Crowns
A Man: but for that Milk-sop, I suspect him;
Therefore let's watch our time, decoy him on;
And when this business is a little o're,   20
Strangle him in some Corner, lest he prate
Of what is done. Now, now's the time, away---

They joyn all together; take him by the Legs and Arms, and
hurl him over the Wall into the Tyber: A noise is heard,
as of a Body falling into the Water---They look about
once more, then start, take up the Chair, and run out---
Scene shuts.

_____

  * There is no new scene marked at this point in any edition,
although the scene obviously changes from Bellamira's apartment
to the bank of the Tiber.

Scene III.

Enter Borgia and Machiavel.

MACH.   Though Orsini, the Vitelli, and Colonni
Are hush'd; the Spaniard, and the French, no doubt,
Would buy your Friendship at the dearest rate.
Nay, more; I yield you Lord of Tuscany,
And Master of such Forces as might march   5
Against the haughtiest Power of Christendom:
But Prince, forgive me, if I am too free,
Do you remember whence this glory comes,
And how this Golden Fortune is deriv'd?
The Pope---from that rich source these Currents rowl;   10
And when another Pope succeeds, who knows
But he may strip you bare of all those Honours
Which this has given, and turn you to the World.
    BORG.   No, Machiavel, I am prepar'd for Fate,
Though Alexander should expire to night.   15
First, who is left of all the Families
I have defac'd, if a new Pope were made,
To say I wrong'd 'em; none that I remember:
'Tis not my way to lop; for then the Tree
May sprout again; but root him, and he lies   20
Never to bluster.   But I will tell thee,
Quite to unhinge that hold, no Pope shall e're
Be fixt in Rome, while Borgia is alive,
But by this hand.   The Gentry are all mine
For ever, gain'd by Presents and Preferments: 25
The Spanish Cardinals are mine devoted,
With all that are conspicuous in the College:
What then can Fortune do?   I laugh at her;
Spurn all those Shrines and Altars, which weak Wretches,
Hero's and Fools, devoutly raise to gain her.   30
    MACH.   Yet hear me, Borgia, hear the oddest story
That ever Melancholly told the World:
This morning, being early in the Vatican,
Far in the Library, at the upper end,
Methought I saw two stately Humane Forms,   35
Lying at distance, wrapt in Linen Shrouds:
Approaching nearer with a stedfast gaze,
As now I look upon the Prince I honour,
I saw the Figure of the Pope your Father

---

16 the Families] Q$_{2+}$; the the Families Q$_1$.
21 bluster more. C$_{2+}$.

Stretcht on the Floor, pale, ghastly, cold, and dead;   40
And by his side, with horrour upon horrour,
And double tremblings, saw my Lord, your self,
My very Caesar, like a new-laid Ghost,
Swoln black, and bloated, while your inclos'd eyes,
All blood-shot, fixt on mine their dreadful beams.   45
    BORG. Fumes, fumes, my Machiavel, the effects of phlegm;
Gross humors, fumes, which from thy thicker blood
Stream up like vapours from a foggy pool.
    MACH. I am apt to think it but a leap of fancy,
A jading of the mind, which, quite tired out   50
With thoughts eternal toil, strikes from the road:
Yet, as you prize your life, let me conjure you,
Beware Ascanio, his long red Coat
Hides a most mortal and inveterate Foe.
    BORG. I know him Machiavel, and sooth him on,   55
As he would me. But Borgia does assure thee,
That he, that scarlet poisonous Luxury,
With his adherent Brothers, shall this night,
Even in the midst of kisses, Oaths, Embraces,
Burst in the Vatican, and shed their Venom.   60
    MACH. Your Father is a Master of his breast,
The occasion gives new life, fresh vigour to him,
Even at the very verge of bottomless death,
He stands and smiles as careless and undaunted,
As wanton swimmers on a Rivers brink   65
Laugh at the rapid stream.
    BORG.   Therefore my Friend,
Let us despise this Torrent of the world,
Fortune, I mean, and dam her up with fences,
Banks, bulworks, all the Fortresses, which Vertue,
Resolv'd and man'd like ours, can raise against her;   70
That if she does ore-flow, she may at least
Bring but half Ruine to our great designs:
That being at last asham'd of her own weakness,
Like a low-bated flood, she may retire
To her own bounds, and we with pride ore-look her.   75

Enter Don Michael, and the Butler.

    D. MICH. My Lord, your Servant waits as you appointed.
    BORG. Are my Provisions come?
    BUTL.   They are, my Lord.
    BORG. Do you remember what I gave in charge?
    BUTL. That none should touch the gilded flask of wine.
    BORG. I charge thee none, but such as I shall order.   80
Don Michael, is my Father yet arriv'd?
    D. MICH. He is, my Lord, and gone.
    BORG.   Say'st thou?
    D. MICH. When first he enter'd, quite o're-come with heat;

Thirsting, and faint with the hot seasons rage,
He call'd for wine, and tho disswaded from it,   85
Drank largely, mingled with the Cardinals,
And walk'd, and laugh'd, play'd with Columbus Boyes,
Heard their rude Musick, and beheld 'em dance;
When on a sudden starting up, he ask'd
For you, my Lord; bow'd, as his custom is,   90
With deep humility to all, desir'd 'em
To sit, and so went out---but with a promise
Of a most quick return---

    Scene draws, and discovers a Chair of state under a Canopy, a
       large Table, with a rich Banquet---and many Candles on't.

      Enter Ascanio, Adrian, Enna, Ange, two Cardinals more.

    ASCA. My Lord, the Vatican Society,
Who were oblig'd to sacrifice this night,   95
As every looser Genius should inspire,
To Air, and Wine, and warmer Conversation,
Grow dull for want of you: His Holiness
Himself's retir'd---Therefore let us entreat you---
    BORG. O my good Lord Ascanio, I am born   100
To be at your Command---My Lords, I wait you.
Sirrah, remember him---I charge thee fill
Of the gilt Flask to him---
    BUTL.   My Lord---I shall.
This Wine is sure the richest of the World,
Because he charges me so strictly of it: 105
That Cardinal's a Friend, and he must taste it.
    ASCA. Lord Machiavel, you have been charitable,
I thank your love; nay, with my life, I thank you----
    MACH. My Lord---I wish you would explain your self.
    ASCA. It needs not, Sir, for this the meanest know, 110
The Rabble, base Mechanicks talk of murders:
I saw a sweating Weaver in his Shirt,
Ran puffing with his Shuttle in his hand,
To ask a Neighbour Butcher of the news,
Who with his Knife in's mouth abruptly tells   115
Orsino's death; yes, and his Daughters too:
Then comes a Taylor with his hair tuck'd back,
Behind his ears, on tiptoes, in his Slippers,
And crys in haste, the Duke of Gandia's murder'd:
Then spits upon his Iron, casts up his eyes,   120
Threads through the company, as 'twere a Needle,

107-08 In Q$_{1+}$ divided thus:
      ASC. Lord Machiavel, you have been charitable, I thank your love;
      Nay, with my life, I thank you---

And vanishes; no more, my Lord, I thank you.
Nay, by my life, but for the Company,
I'd kiss the bottom of your Robe; your Lordships ever:
Your Highness servant: My Lords, let's drink a Health to   125
His Holiness--But in my heart, I say, the Devil take him.
    BORG. Lord Machiavel, you are my Guest to night:
Were the Society made up of Gods,
As sure it is of Saints, Spirits above
The common Elevation; yet this man,   130
I say, my Lords, this Humane Prodigy,
Would not be set to wait, but fixt among 'em,
To dazle with the brightest being here.
Wine there! ---My Lord Ascanio Sforza,
Health to all here, and to the general joy--- [Drinks.   135
    ASCA. Fine work, my Lords, fine work, I say, look to't,
The Duke of Gandia's murder'd.
    ADRI.   'Tis the common rumour.
    ENNA. The Pope this morning in the Consistory,
When first he heard the News, leapt from his Throne,
Crossing his Breast, and looking up to Heav'n,   140
He vow'd hereafter most severe amendment,
As from this time to fast for forty hours,
And all his life wear next his humble flesh,
A Shirt of Hair.
    ASCA. A Shirt of Hair! bating Lucretian nights: 145
She'll not endur't; look you, her skin's too tender:
A Shirt of Hair, a very prickling Penance.
Now, by my Holy-dame, meer Letchery:
Don't I know him? Slave, more Wine, I say;
Fill up my Glass: Come, come, my Lords, 'tis time   150
To look about us, and reform the Church---   [Drinks.
Prune it, I say; or else like Babylon,
Like Babels Whore, 'twill run up all to seed.
Hark you, Lord Ange.
    ANGE.   My Lord.
    ASCA. My Lord of Enna too; we four are   155
As one Soul: This Pope's a very leud
And wicked Head;---he's never well, but
When he's plotting Murders. Why, look you, Sirs,
If a man cannot speak his mind of
State Affairs,---but he must streight be   160
Dogg'd by Hell-hounds, Blood-suckers, Decoyers,
Rascals, that watch to throttle him in some
By-corner, then quoit him like a Cat into
The River, 'tis very fine: Now, by my Holy-dame,
It may be our turn next---by the Mass it may;   165
I say, my Lord, it may. ---   [The Indian Boys dance.

155-73 The irregularity of these lines may be intentional, designed to show
      Ascanio's increasing intoxication or the effects of the poison.

Ha, my Lords, how do you
Like the motion? Very pretty, very fine.
O brave Columbus! More Wine there; a bigger
Glass; I'll drink Columbus's health---Now, by my   170
Holy-dame, I am frolicksome, and will be active.
Ha, my Lords, ha, I learnt at Paris, when I was
A Stripling; yet these are pretty Children, very fine Boys. ---

                        Enter D. Michael.

   D. MICH. My Lord, I grieve to bring you Mortal News,
Which were I silent, yet in some few minutes   175
Must wound your ears; your Father's dead.
   BORG.   Hence, Raven,
Thou Boder of the blackest deed of Death!
My Lords, this Villain says the Pope's dead;
Went he not hence but now, sound, firm, and healthful,
And promis'd to return?
   D. MICH.   My Lord, he did: 180
But 'tis most certain, e're he went from hence,
As all our best Physitians give on Oath,
He was by some pernicious Traytor poyson'd.
   BORG. O Machiavel, where is our forecast now?
My heart misgives me, and my bosom's hot.   185
Who ministred? who gave my Father Wine?
   D. MICH. Your Servant: for when first your Father enter'd,
His own Provisions were not come.
   BORG.   O Confusion!
Answer me, Villain! ha! fill'd you his Wine?
   BUTL. My Lord, I did.   190
   BORG. What, from the gilded Flask? why dost thou tremble?
Horrour consume thee, gnaw thee, burn thy Entrails,
Wilt thou not speak?
   BUTL.   My Lord, by your strict Charge,
That none should taste those Flasks but whom you order'd,
I judg'd the Wine most Excellent, and gave   195
Part of it to your Father. ---
   BORG.   O damn'd Dolt!
Curst, sensless Dog! Now, Machiavel, where are we?
Ha! by the Furies that invade my Breast,
And crumble all my Bowels into dust,
I am caught my self! Speak, tell me, horrid Villain,   200
Or I will have thee dragg'd in thousand pieces;
Torn by mad Horses like the flesh of Dogs:
Thou gav'st me Wine too from the gilded Flasks! ha, Traytor!

----

182 an Oath, Q_{2-3}.

Come, double damn thy self, and swear thou did'st not.
    BUTL. My Lord--I must confess I gave the same   205
To you, that was directed for your Friend,
My Lord Ascanio.
    BORG. Take thy reward then, which the Devil thou pour'st
Into my Breast, thus gives thee back again!   [Stabs him.*
O Machiavel, O do not look upon me;   210
I am below thy scorn, thus vile caught,
O basely, basely sold by my own Wile.
    ASCA. Oh, oh, oh---I have my share on't too, the Devil
Thank you---Fire, fire, fire! oh my Guts--brimstone
And fire---haste there---fly for Antidotes.   215
    BORG. None, none on Earth,
I tell thee, Priest, can save thy rotten Carkass;
No Cardinal, lye down, lye down, and roar,
Think on thy Scarlet sins, and fear damnation.
    ASCA. Legions of Furies here, Hell is broke loose,   220
And all the Devils are quarter'd in my Bowels.
Run Slave! and for a last revenge, produce
His mangled Bastard---that's some pleasure yet.
    BORG. O Machiavel, thy hand, I am all flames;
Yet thou shalt hear no noise: sit down, my Friend,   225
Upon the Earth---for there's my Mansion now,
Dust, and no more---and yet methinks 'twas hard
That this Elaborate Scheme of mighty man,
This Parchment, where the Lines of Roman greatness
By thee so well were drawn, should by the hand   230
Of scribling Chance be blotted thus for ever.
    ASCA. I burn, I burn, I toste, I roste, and my Guts fry,
They blaze, they snap, they bounce like Squibs
And Crackers: I am all fire---
    MACH. Is't possible that you can bear the pangs   235
Of violent poyson, thus unmov'd?
    BORG.   'Tis little
To one resolv'd: No, let the Coward States-man,
Women, and Priests, whine at the thoughts of death;
For me, whose mind was ever fierce and active,
Death is unwelcom, only for this reason,   240
Because 'tis an Eternal laziness---

      Enter Alonzo, leading in Seraphino, with his Eyes
             out, and Face cut.

    MACH. I must confess my mind, by what I saw
This morning, and by what has happen'd since,

---

    * [Stabs him.]; om. Q_{1+}.
211 vilely C_{1+}.
212 Wile.] C_{1+}; wild. Q_{1-3}.

Is deeply shockt, even from her own Foundation.

    ASCA. Bear the blind Bastard to his Father, go,   245
And bid him laugh---oh!

    MACH.   Horrour! new horrour!
My Lord, your Son, by that most bloody Cardinal,
Mangled and blind.

    BORG.   Why dost thou wonder at it?
'Tis all the work of Chance, and trick of Fortune?
Yet this methinks is horrible indeed.   250
Come hither Boy---

    SERA.   Alas, I hear your voice,
And cannot find the way;
But am like one benighted in a Wood.

    BORG. A Wood indeed;
But oh the Brambles there have us'd thee vilely.   255

    SERA. O Father, you are arm'd, and have a Sword;
Will you not, for your Seraphino's sake,
Cut down those Thorns that prick'd out both my eyes?
I know you will; for you were always kind
And tender of me: oft-times have you held me   260
Fast in your Arms, and smil'd, and plaid with me;
Though you're a Prince, a very busie Prince,
And call'd me little Eyes, little indeed,
For now they're out, and all my Face is cut:
Nay, they have starv'd me too.

    BORG.   Death and horrour!   265

    SERA. Why do you press me thus between your Arms,
As if you lov'd me still? I am sure you cannot.
Pray let me hide my face within your Bosom;
For if you look upon me I shall fright you.
O! I've a pain here just about my heart!   270
When you, my Lord, a long time after me
Shall dye, will you not lay my little Bones
By yours? Alas! my pain encreases---Oh, ---   [Dies.

    BORG. Revenge thee, Boy! I ask but that from Fate:
And see 'tis given me: Through a thousand wounds,   275
Thus, horrid Priest! purge out thy lustful blood, [Stabs Ascan.
And Vomit thy black Soul---

    ASCA.   Oh! Devil! Devil! Devil ---   [Dies.

    BORG. No, Machiavel, 'tis now fit time to rave;
For I am now enrag'd to that degree,
That I will live even in despight of Fortune,   280
Stars! Fates! and all the Juggles of a Heaven.
Hence, bear me, Slaves, and plunge me into Tyber,
Deep as I sunk the Duke of Gandia down!

---

249 Fortune: C_{1+}.
269 shali Q_1(TxU).
271 When you,] C_{1+}; When, you Q_{1-3}.

Till I have quench't this Hell within my bowels;
Then flay me an Oxe hide and swadle me,   285
Like Hercules in the Nemean-skin.
'Till all my poison'd flesh like bark peels off,
And my bare Trunck stands every brushing wind!
    ENNA. Where are our Guards? My Lords, I judg it fit
That Machiavel and Borgia should be seiz'd.   290
      BORG. Seize me! what sawcy Priest durst start that motion?
Am I not Tyrant here? The Lord of Rome?
Does not France dread my Frown? and Spain adore me?
Who then dares talk of seizing me? what, he?
This wag-tail Priest, with the black picked Beard,   295
That scowrs the Country round for freckled Wenches?
Or was it you my Lord of Enna? Ha!
Death, where's my Majesty? or vail your Caps,
Or I will trample you beneath my Feet?
You, Ange! that could prostitute your Sister   300
To gain a Hat? lye there Lord of St. Peter:
You Cardinal ad Vincula, you pack of Hell hounds,
That trace me by the blood. On, on I say,
On to the brink of Hell: Thence plunge together,
Where, on his Throne, behold the Master Devil   305
With a great pair of glowing horns red hot
To gore you for your lives incontinence,
You Ravishers, you Virgin pioners,
You Cuckold-makers of the forked World.
    ANGE. Where are our Guards?
      BORG.   Hark, I hear 'em coming: 310
Or is it Dooms-day? Ha--by Hell it is:
And see, the Heav'ns, and Earth, and Air are all
On fire: the very Seas, like Moulten-glass,
Rowl their bright Waves, and from the smoky deep
Cast up the glaring Dead: The Trumpet sounds,   315
And the swift Angels skim about the Globe
To summon all Mankind. Rome, Rome is call'd?
Work, work for Hell. Hoa, Satan! Belzebub!
Belial, and Baal---Whence this Thunderclap?
They've blown us up with Wild fire in the Air;   320
And look how the ball'd Fryers in Russet-gowns
Croak like old Vultures, how the flutt'ring Jesuits,
In black and white, chatter about the Heav'ns!
Capuchins, Monks, with the whole Tribe of Knaves!
Then let me burst my spleen! Look how the Tassels,   325
Caps, Hats and Cardinals Coats, and Cowls and Hoods

------

287 peels] C_{1+}; pills Q_{1-3}.
299 Feet; C_{1-2}; Feet. C_3.
308 Pioneers, Q_{3+}.
317 call'd. Q_2; call'd! C_1; call'd, C_{2+}.

Are tost about---the sport the sport of winds---
Indulgences, Dispences, Pardons, Bulls, see yonder!
Priest, they fly---they're whirld aloft. They fly,
They fly or'e the backside o'th' world,   330
Into a Limbo large, and broad, since call'd the Paradise
Of Fools.
    ENNA. 'Tis just we give him way! this fit of rage
Has wasted him to Death, see he breaths short,
The Taper's spent, and this is his last Blaze.   335
    BORG. Ha! Breath I short? Prelate, thou ly'st: my pulse
Beats with a constant fire and spritely motion;
The strings of my tough heart as strong as ever:
No---I will live; in spight of Fate I'll live
To be the scourge of Rome: I'll live to act   340
New mischiefs, and create new wicked Popes,
To ponyard Heretick Princes that refuse
To lay their Necks beneath the holy Slipper.
Murder successively two Kings of France;
Brittain attempt, though her most watchful Angel   345
Saves the Lov'd Monarch of that happy Isle,
And turns upon our selves the plotted Wound,
That sinks me to the Earth: yet still wee'll on,
And hatch new deeds of darkness; O Hell, and Furies!
Why should we not, since the great Head himself   350
Will back my Plots, joyn me in blood and horror,
And after give me Bond for my Salvation:
I swear I will---I'll have it---nay, Sir, you shall---
Or I will thunder to your Holiness:
But hark he whispers, what a little Gold---   355
With all my heart: thus Devils buy souls for trash---
I'll fee your itching palm for Absolution.
Gold for my pardon, hey---'tis seal'd and given!
And for a Ducat thus I purchase Heav'n---   [Dies.
    MACH. The mighty soul there forc'd her furious passage,   360
And plunges now in deep Eternity---
I see, my Lords, you have resolv'd to guard me,
And I submit to strict Examination:
By you to be acquitted or condemned?
Yet this I must avow before you all,   365
Though you should cast me to the Inquisition,
Skill'd as I am in all Affairs of Earth,
Known both to Popes and Kings, and often honor'd
With Cabinet Councils of Imperial Heads;
I here resolve on this, as my last Judgment;   370
    No Power is safe, nor no Religion good,
    Whose Principles of growth are laid in Blood.

End of A C T V

---

364 condemned. C1+.

EPILOGUE.

Well, then be you his Judges; what pretence
Made them roar out, this Play would give offence?
Had he the Pope's Effigies meant to burn,
And kept for sport his Ashes in an Urn?
To try if Reliques would perform at home   5
But half those Miracles they do at Rome:
More could not have been said, nor more been done,
To damn this Play about the Court and Town;
Not if he had shown their Philters, Charms and Rage,
Nay conjur'd up Pope Jone to please the Age,   10
And had her Breeches search'd upon the Stage.
First, then he brings a scandal on the Gown,
And makes a Priest both Leacher and Buffoon:
Why, was no Fool, yet ever made a Flamen,
But dulness quite entail'd upon the Lay-men;   15
Or was it ever heard in Rome before,
That any Priest was question'd for his Whore?
Yet more, the horrid Chair the Mid-night show---
He says 'twas done two hundred years ago:
He only points their ways of murdering then;   20
If you must damn, spare the Historian's Pen,
And damn those Rogues that act 'em o're again.
But Dominicks, Franciscans, Hermits, Fryars,
Shall breed no more a Race of zealous Lyars;
Villains, who for Religion's Propagation,   25
Come here disguis'd in ev'ry mean Vocation,
And sit in Stalls to spy upon the Nation.
Old Emissaries shall their Trade forbear,
Spread no more Savoy Reliques, Bones and Hair,
Shall sell no more like Baubles in a Fair: 30
Monks under ground shall cease to Earth like Moles,
And Father Lewis leave his lurking-holes;
Get no more Thirty Pounds for a blind Story,
Of freeing a Welch Soul from Purgatory,
Jesuits in Rome shall quite forswear their Function,   35
And not for Gold give Whores the Extreme Unction:
High English Whores, that have all Vices past,
Shall cease to turn true Catholicks at last,
When Poets write, tho by exactest Rules,
And are not judg'd by Knaves, and damn'd by Fools.   40

FINIS.

---

4 Urn; C_{1+}.
17 any] Q_{2+}; any, Q_1.

THE
PRINCESS
OF
CLEVE,

As it was Acted

AT THE

Queens Theatre

IN

DORSET-GARDEN.

By *Nat. Lee*, Gent.

Tuque, dum procedis, Io Triumphe,
Non semel dicemus: Io Triumphe,
Civitas omnis, dabimusque thvis
------*Thura benignis.* Horat.

LONDON, Printed in the Year, 1689.

THE PRINCESS OF CLEVE

Introduction

I Date and Stage History:

THE PRINCESS OF CLEVE was presented at Dorset Garden some time before the union of the two companies in 1682, but the exact date of its first performance is questionable. Dryden wrote a prologue and epilogue for it,[1] and in the prologue he referred to Shaftesbury as Achitophel; this made some scholars conclude that the play must have been produced after the appearance of Dryden's ABSOLOM AND ACHITOPHEL in 1681. However, since it has been shown that Shaftesbury was often referred to as Achitophel before Dryden's poem appeared, this is no certain evidence as to the date. Probably the best evidence is the reference to the death of Rochester in Act I, as being of recent occurrence. Rochester died July 26, 1680, and it seems likely that the play was produced shortly after this, probably in August or September, 1680. According to Downes, it was "well Acted, but succeeded not so well as the others."[2] Apparently, Lee's satirical attack on the immorality of the times did not appeal to the Restoration audience. At all events, the play was never revived, and it was not printed until 1689.

II Sources:

The serious plot of this "Farce, Comedy, Tragedy or meer Play", as Lee called it in his Dedication, was taken from the Countess de La Fayette's novel LA PRINCESS DE CLÈVES, which had been published in Paris in 1678, and had been translated into English in 1679. Lee used the translation, as can be seen from his following its error in putting "Cleve" in its running title instead of "Clèves". So far as the events of the plot are concerned, Lee followed the novel quite closely. He departed from it in only two particulars: (1) in the play, the letter which is dropped in the tennis court belongs to Nemours, whereas in the novel it belongs to the Vidam; (2) in the novel, there is no duel between Nemours and the Prince of Clève, as there is in the play. In all other particulars, Lee adhered to the plot of the novel. But he departed from the novel widely in his depiction of the characters. As he himself states in the Dedication, "when they expected the most polish'd Hero in Nemours, I gave 'em a Ruffian reeking from Whetstone's-Park." In the novel, Nemours is a sincere lover and an honorable man; in the play he has been turned into an exaggeration of the typical Restoration rake and debauchee, whose main interest in life is the seduction of as many women as possible, and whose honor is no more than a word. This change in Nemours' character alters the whole tone of the story. It is true that the characters of the Princess and the Prince of Cleve remain much as they were in the novel, but the degradation of Nemours' personality transforms the Countess de La Fayette's tender and delicate love story into a tale of sordid lust which ends on a final note of triumphant licentiousness when Nemours boasts that despite the intention of the Princess never to see him again, he will "Bed her eighteen months three weeks hence, at half an hour past two in the Morning."

For the comic subplot of Poltrot, St. Andre, and their wives, there appears to be no source, and it is presumably original with Lee.

III Criticism:

Genest commented briefly on THE PRINCESS OF CLEVE that the main plot was "serious, and somewhat dull---the comic part is very good;" and he found

Nemours "a spirited character."[3] Most later critics have been far more acid-
ulous in their comments upon the play. A. W. Ward states that "it envelopes a
more than hazardous sentimental situation in ribald comedy of almost unequalled
grossness."[4] Nettleton denounces it as a "coarse offspring of Madame de La
Fayette's French romance."[5] Roswell Ham is of much the same opinion:

> As a play it need not detain us, for all the acute analysis of sentiment and
> character evaporated from Mme de La Fayette's novel once it was turned
> to the purposes of Restoration comedy. It was a production comparable to
> Otway's FRIENDSHIP IN FASHION, irreligious and cynical, but lacking the
> power of the latter. Nemours lays about him, as Lee remarked, "like the
> Gladiator in the Park," and Margaret, introduced from the MASSACRE--
> where she was a figure of all nobility -- enters here in company with a bawd
> and a cuckold. Only the Princess of Cleve herself retained that gentle trag-
> edy which Lee might have been expected to take over from the original.[6]

Nicoll is even more vitriolic, condemning the play as "ineffectual and worthless."
He feels that the plot "is chaotic and the atmosphere corrupt," and he ends by
likening the play to "a rotting dung-heap."[7]

Van Lennep agrees with a number of these criticisms. He denounces the
degradation of the character of Nemours; he finds the subplot outrageous and exclaims: "its licentiousness is equalled by the obscenity of the language in which
it is clothed." He notes that the satire of the play is somewhat similar to that of
Wycherley, but goes on to add: "whereas Wycherley's wit cloaks the vulgarity
of THE COUNTRY WIFE, Lee's wit is insufficient to hide the coarseness of THE
PRINCESS OF CLEVE, which is one of the most offensive plays in Restoration
comedy."[8] Yet Van Lennep does find some points to praise. At some times,
he feels, "there is a sprightliness and verve to Lee's prose which makes the comic plot entertaining reading." He also feels that the satire is effective, and that
there are some redeeming aspects even to Nemours' character: "Like Manly,
the Plain Dealer, Nemours displays a hate of hypocrisy in morals."[9]

Certainly THE PRINCESS OF CLEVE is not a masterpiece of comedy. Its
main plot makes a travesty out of Madame de La Fayette's novel, and its subplot
is excessively coarse, even for Restoration times. The fact that this coarseness
was an intentional satire upon the immorality of the day does not entirely justify
it, but serves at least to excuse it from being regarded as mere bawdry for bawdry's sake. Actually the play belongs in the same category as THE COUNTRY
WIFE and THE PLAIN DEALER; it is a trenchant and sardonic attack upon the
profligacy and viciousness of the times. As such, it is an interesting piece of
social comment upon the Restoration period. In addition, the play has some historical significance in the development of the drama because of its sentimental
tendencies.[10] The characters of the Princess and the Prince of Cleve are distinctly sentimental, and the final determination of Nemours to reform at the end
of the play strikes one of the distinctive themes of sentimental comedy -- the ref-
ormation of the rake. Lee's one attempt at comedy can not be called a success;
it was in no way a great piece of dramatic work; but it may be regarded, none the
less, as an interesting experiment in sex, satire, and sentimentalism.

IV Texts:

Editions compared:

Q_1	A. Roper,	1689
Q_2	J. O. for R. Wellington,	1697
C_1	R. Wellington,	1713
C_2	M. P. & Sam. Chapman,	1722
C_3	W. Feales ... ,	1734

As copy-text for this edition the first quarto, 1689, has been followed. Five copies of this quarto have been compared in order that stop-press corrections might
be determined. One of these copies is that in the Library of the University of
Kentucky; one is in the Folger Shakespeare Library; one in the Newberry Library;
one in the Library of the University of Chicago; and one in the Library of the University of Texas. The one variant among these copies is recorded in a textual
footnote. The copies are designated as follows: Q_1(KU), Q_1(DFo), Q_1(ICN),
Q_1(ICU), and Q_1(TxU).[11] The variant mentioned involves the cancellation of D1.

The edition has the following collation:

4°: A-C^4 D^4(-D^1) E-K^4; 39 leaves, pp. [8], 1-16, 19-71, [1].

[A1^r]: title-page; [A1^v]: blank; A2: [triple rule] Epistle Dedicatory TO THE /
Right Honourable Charles Earl of Dorset and / Middlesex, Lord Chamberlain of
His Majesties Household, and one of His Majesties / most Honourable Privy-
Council, & c.; / A3^r: Song to be inserted in Act V. Scene III; A3^v: blank; A4^r:
THE PROLOGUE.; A4^v: The Names of the Actors. Scene Paris.; B1^r: [double
rule] THE / Princess of Cleve. / [rule] / ACT I. SCENE I. / [rule] and text;
B1^v-C4^v, D2^r-K4^r: text. Running title The Princess of Cleve. K4^v: THE EPI-
LOGUE.

A comparison of the five copies reveals no variations except for the cancellation of D1. This leaf appears in the DFo, TxU, and ICN copies, but does
not appear in the KU and the ICU copies. For a discussion of this cancellation,
see the textual note to II, i, 30-37.

The text of the first quarto, printed carelessly and, except for the cancel,
giving no indication of authorial corrections as it went through the press, presents a few particular problems. This quarto was not printed until nine years
after the play had been produced, and Lee tells us in his Dedication that he had
cut out certain scenes which he had originally borrowed from THE MASSACRE
OF PARIS. It is possible that at the same time he made other alterations in the
original version. The first quarto unmistakably bears marks of hurried cutting
and mending. It was very probably printed from the author's rough copy, hurriedly and carelessly marked for the printer, rather than from the finished copy
which was prepared for the theatre in 1680. The stage directions are often faulty:
sometimes there is no entrance marked for a character; sometimes there is no
exit; sometimes an entrance comes at the wrong place; and sometimes the action
intended upon the stage is not at all clear. In addition, speeches are not infre-
quently assigned to the wrong character, and now and then the wording of the text
is obviously faulty. Line divisions of the poetry are at times garbled. Moreover,
the later editions make little effort to correct these faults. Q_2, printed from Q_1,
shows some attempt on the compositor's part to correct incidentals, but as many
careless errors creep into his work as he corrects. C_1 was printed from Q_2;
C_2, though it makes numbers of alterations, follows C_1; and C_3 follows C_2 carefully.

As a consequence of the condition of the texts, the present editors have found it necessary to make their own emendations of this play more frequently than has been usual in the case of others. These emendations, however, have been made as sparingly as possible; they have been based on a careful study of the context; and in all instances the reading of the first quarto has been given in the textual notes. As has been customary with the other plays, the variant readings of the later editions have been recorded in the notes when such readings are of interest as corrections which an author might approve, or as alterations which reflect the publisher's "improvements" and "clarifications."

To The Right Honourable
Charles Earl of Dorset and Middlesex, Lord Chamberlain
of His Majesties Houshold, and one of His Majesties most
Honourable Privy-Council, & c.

May it please your Lordship,

This Play, when it was Acted, in the Character of the Princess of Jainville, had a resemblance of Marguerite in the Massacre of Paris, Sister
to Charles the Ninth, and Wife to Henry the Fourth King of Navar: That
fatal Marriage which cost the Blood of so many Thousand Men, and the
Lives of the best Commanders. What was borrowed in the Action is left   5
out in the Print, and quite obliterated in the minds of Men. But the Duke
of Guise, who was Notorious for a bolder Fault, has wrested two whole
Scenes from the Original, which after the Vacation he will be forc'd to
pay. I was, I confess, through Indignation, forc'd to limb my own Child,
which Time, the true Cure for all Maladies, and Injustice has set togeth-   10
er again. The Play cost me much pains, the Story is true, and I hope the
Object will display Treachery in its own Colours. But this Farce, Comedy,
Tragedy or meer Play, was a Revenge for the Refusal of the other; for
when they expected the most polish'd Hero in Nemours, I gave 'em a Ruffian reeking from Whetstone's-Park. The fourth and fifth Acts of the   15
Chances, where Don John is pulling down; Marriage Alamode, where
they are bare to the Waste; the Libertine, and Epsom-Wells, are
but Copies of his Villany. He lays about him like the Gladiator in the
Park; they may walk by, and take no notice. I beg your Lordship to excuse
this account, for indeed 'tis all to introduce the Massacre of Paris to   20
your Favour, and approve it to be play'd in its first Figure.

Your Lordships

Humble and Obedient Servant,

Nat. Lee.

The PROLOGUE.

Trust was the Glory of the foremost Age,
When Truth and Love with Friendship did engage;
When Man to Man cou'd walk with Arms entwin'd,
And vent their Griefs in spaces of the Wind;
Express their minds, and speak their thoughts as clear,   5
As Eastern Mornings op'ning to the year.
But since that Law and Treachery came in,
And open Honesty was made a Sin,
Men wait for Men as Dogs for Foxes prey,
And Women wait the closing of the day.   10
There's scarce a man that ventures to be good,
For Truth by Knaves was never understood;
For there's the Curse, when Vice o'er Vertue rules,
That all the World are Knaves or downright Fools.
So they may make advantage of th' Allay,   15
They'll take the Dross and through the Gold away.
Women turn Usurers with their own affright,
And Want's the Hag that rides 'em all the night.
The little Mob, the City Wastcoateer,
Will pinch the Back to make the Buttock bare,   20
And drain the last poor Guinea from her Dear.
Thus Times are turn'd upon a private end,
There's scarce a Man that's generous to his Friend.
But there's a Monarch on a Throne sublime,
That makes Truth Law, and gives the Poets Rhime;   25
Be his the bus'ness of our little Fates,
Our mean Contentions, and their high Debates.
By Sea and Land our most Imperial Lord,
With all the Praises Blest that Hearts afford,
With Lawrels Crown'd, unconquer'd by the Sword: 30
William the Sovereign of our whole Affairs,
Our Guide in Peace, and Council in the Wars.

---

16   throw the Gold Q_{2+}.

DRAMATIS PERSONAE

Prince of Cleve	Mr. Williams.	
Duke Nemours	Mr. Betterton.	
Bellamore	Mr.	
Jaques	Mr.	
St. Andre	Mr. Lee.	5
Vidam of Chartres	Mr. Gillo.	
Poltrot	Mr. Nokes.	
Pedro		
Boy		

Women.

Princess of Cleve	Mrs. Barry.	10
Tournon	Mrs. Lee.	
Marguerite	Lady Slingsby.	
Elianor	Mrs. Betterton.	
Celia	Mrs.	
Irene	Mrs.	15
La March	Mrs.	

Scene Paris.

---

8 Pedro] ; <u>om</u>. Q₁+.
9 Boy] ; <u>om</u>. Q₁+.

Act I. Scene I.

Nemours, Bellamore. Fiddles Playing.

NEM. Hold there you Monsieur Devol; prithe leave off playing fine in
Consort, and stick to Time and Tune --- So now the Song, call in the Eu-
nuch; come my pretty Stallion, Hem and begin.

SONG.

All other Blessings are but Toyes
To his that in his sleep enjoyes,   5
Who in his Fancy can possess
The object of his Happiness;
The Pleasure's purer for he spares
The Pains, Expenses, and the Cares.

II.

Thus when Adonis got the stone,   10
To Love the Boy still made his moan;
Venus the Queen of Fancy came,
And as he slept she cool'd his flame;
The Fancy charm'd him as he lay,
And Fancy brought the Stone away.   15

NEM. Sirrah, stick to clean Pleasures, deep Sleep, moderate
Wine, sincere Whores, and thou art happy; Now by this damask
Cheek I love thee; keep but this gracious Form of thine in
health, and I'll put thee in the way of living like a man --- What
I have trusted thee with --- My Love to the Princess of Cleve,   20
Treasure it as thy Life, nor let the Vidam of Chartres know it; for
however I seem to cherish him, because he has the knack of telling a
Story maliciously, and is a great pretender to Nature, I cast him
off here --- 'Tis too much for him: Besides he is her Uncle, and
has a sort of affected Honour, that wou'd make him grin to see   25
me leap her --- Hey Jaques --- When Madam Tournon comes, bring
her in; and hark you Sir, whoever comes to speak with me,
while she is with me ---
JAQ. What if the Dauphin comes?
NEM. What if his Father comes, Dog -- Slave -- Fool! What if   30
Paris were a fire, the President and Council of sixteen at the door!
I'm sick, I'm not within --- I'm a hundred mile off -- My bosom
Dear --- So young, and yet I trust thee too --- But away, to the
Princess of Cleve, thou art acquainted with her Women, watch
her Motions, my sweet-fac'd Pimp, and bring me word of her rising.   35

26 No edition gives an entrance for Jaques at this point; presumably he is on the stage at the opening of the scene.

BELL. She is a prize, my Lord, and oh what a night of pleasure
has Cleve had with her -- the first too!

NEM. Any thing but what makes such a pleasure, wou'd I give
for such another --- But be gone, and no more of this provoking
discourse, lest Ravishing shou'd follow thee at the heels, and   40
spoil my sober design.   [Exeunt severally.

Enter Tournon, La March.

JAQ. Madam, my Lord was just now asking for you.

TOUR. Go tell him I'm coming -- Is he dress'd?

JAQ. Yes -- But your Ladiship knows that's all one to him ---

TOUR. Honest Jaques, 'tis pity such Honesty should not be encourag'd -- 45

JAQ. This comes of Pimping, which she calls Honesty.   [Exit. Jaq.

TOUR. Thus thou mayst see the method of the Queen --- We are
the lucky Sieves, where fond men trust their Hearts, and so she
sifts 'em through us ---

LA M. What of Nemours, whom you thus early visit?   50

TOUR. The Queen designs to rob him of a Mistress, Marguerite
the Princess of Jainville, whom he keeps from the knowledge of
the Court; and if the Queen be a Judge, is contracted to her ---
The Dauphin loves her too, whereon the Queen,
Who works the Court quite round by Womankind,   55
And thinks this way to mould his supple Soul,
Resolves, if possible, to gain her for him.

LA M. But how is't possible to work the Princess from the
Duke Nemours, who loves him as the Queen affects Ambition?

TOUR. Why thus she knows Nemours his Soul is bent   60
Upon variety, therefore to gain her ends
She has made me Sacrifice my Honour, nay
I'm become his Bawd, and ply him ev'ry day
With some new face, to wean his heart
From Marguerite's Form, nor must you longer be   65
Without your part.

LA M. Employ me, for you know the Queen commands me.

TOUR. There was a Letter dropt in the Tennis-Court
Out of Nemours his Pocket, as I'm told,
And read last night in the presence --- 'Tis your Task   70
Slily to insinuate with Marguerite.
This Note which came from some abandon'd Mistress,
Is certainly the Dukes ---

LA M. Then Jealousie's the ground on which you build.

TOUR. Right, we must make 'em jealous of each other; Jeal-   75
ousie breeds disdain in haughty minds, and so from the extreams
of violent Love, proceeds to fiercest hate. But see
the gay, the brisk, the topping Gallant St. Andre

---

59 Ambition?] Q_{2+}; Ambition. Q_1.

Enter St. A. and Boy. *

here, Couzen to Poltrot, who arrived from England
with a pretty Wife last week, and Lodges in the Palace of this 80
his related Fool --- St. Andre has a Wife too of my acquaintance ---
Both for the Duke my Dear; but haste I'm call'd ---   [Exit La March.
     JAQ. Madam ---
     TOUR. I go.   [Exit Tournon.
     ST. A. Monsieur Jaques, your most obliged faithful humble Ser- 85
vant. What, his Grace continues the old Trade I see, by the Flux
of Bawds and Whores that choak up his Avenues, and I must
confess, excepting my self, there's no man so built for Whoring
as his Grace, black sanguine Brawny --- a Roman Nose --- long Foot
and a stiff --- calf of a Leg.   90
     JAQ. Your Lordship has all these in Perfection.
     ST. A. Sir your most faithful obliged humble Servant. Boy ---
     BOY. My Lord ---
     ST. A. How many Bottles last night?
     BOY. Five my Lord.   95
     ST. A. Boy.
     BOY. My Lord.
     ST. A. How many Whores?
     BOY. Six my Lord.
     ST. A. Boy ---   100
     BOY. My Lord.
     ST. A. What Quarrels, how many did I kill?
     BOY. Not one my Lord --- But the night before you Hamstrung a
Beadle, and run a Link-man in the Back ---
     ST. A. What, and no Blood nor Blows last night?   105
     BOY. O yes my Lord, now I remen.ber me, you drew upon
a Gentleman that knock'd you down with a Bottle.
     ST. A. Not so loud you Urchin, lest I twist your neck round --
Monsieur Jaques is his Grace stirring?
     JAQ. My Lord, he's at Council ---   110
     ST. A. Od I beg his Pardon, pray give my duty to him, and
tell him, if he pleased to hear a languishing Air or two, I am at
the Princess of Cleve's with a Serenade --- Go Raskal, go to Monsieur Poltrot --- tell him he'll be too late --- Black airy shape --- but
then Madam Cleve is Vertuous, Chast, Cold --- Gad I'll write to 115
her, and then she's mine directly, for 'tis but reason of course,
that he that has been Yoak'd to so many Dutchesses, should at
last back a Princess: Sir, your most obliged faithful and very
humble Servant Sir.
                              [Exeunt.

---

* and Boy.]; om. Q$_{1+}$.

Scene II.

Nemours, Tournon.

TOUR. Undone, undone! will your sinful Grace never give over,
will you never leave Ruining of Bodies and Damning of
Souls --- cou'd you imagine that I came for this? What have you
done?

NEM. No harm, pretty Rogue, no harm, nay, prithee leave blubbering.   5

TOUR. 'Tis blubbering now, plain blubbering, but before you
had your will 'twas another tone; why Madam do you wast
those precious Tears, each falling drop shines like an Orient Pearl,
and sets a Gaity on a Face of Sorrow.

NEM. Thou art certainly the pleasantest of Womankind, and I   10
the happiest of Men; dear delightful Rogue, let's have another
Main like a winning Gamester, I long to make it t'other hundred
Pound.

TOUR. Inconsiderate horrid Peer, will you Damn your Soul
deeper and deeper, can you be thus insensible of your Crime?   15

NEM. Why there's it, I was as a man may be, very dry, and
thou kind Soul, gav'st me a good draught of Drink; now 'tis
strange to me, if a man must be Damn'd for quenching his thirst.

TOUR. Ha, Ha --- Well, I'll swear you are such another man ---
who wou'd have thought you cou'd delude a Woman thus, and   20
a Woman of Honour too, that resolv'd so much against it; Ah
my Lord! your Grace has a cunning Tongue.

NEM. No cunning Tournon, my way is downright, leaving Body,
State and Spirit, all for a pretty Woman, and when gray Hairs,
Gout and Impotence come, no more but this, drink away pain,   25
and be gathered to my Fathers.

TOUR. Oh thou dissembler, give me your hand, this soft, this
faithless violating hand, Heaven knows what this hand has to
answer for.

NEM. And for this hand, with these long, white, round, pretty   30
Bobbins, t'has the kindest gripe, and I so love it, now Gad's
Blessing on't, that's all I say --- But come tell me, what no new
Game, for thou knowest I dye directly without variety.

TOUR. Certainly never Woman lov'd like me, who am not satisfied
with sacrificing my own Honour, unless I rob my delights   35
by undoing others ---

NEM. Come, come, out with it, I see thou art big with some
new Intrigue, and it labours for a vent.

TOUR. What think you of St. Andre's Lady?

NEM. That I'm in Bed with her, because thou darst befriend me.   40

TOUR. Nay, there's more -- Monsieur Poltrot lodges in his
House, with a young English Wife of the true breed, and the prettier
of the two.

NEM. Excellent Creature, but command me something extra-
vagant, as thy kindness, State, Life and Honour.   45
    TOUR. Yet all this will be lost when you are married to Marguerite.
    NEM. Never, by Heaven I'm thine, with all the heat and vigorous
Inspiration of an unflesh'd Lover --- and so will be while
young Limbs and Lechery hold together, and that's a Bond methinks shou'd last till Doomsday.   50
    TOUR. But do you believe if Marguerite shou'd know ---
    NEM. The question's too grave --- when and where shall I see
the Gems thou hast in store?
    TOUR. By Noon or thereabouts; take a turn in Luxemburgh Gar-
den, and one, if not both, shall meet you.   55
    NEM. And thou'lt appear in Person?
    TOUR. With Colours flying, a Handkerchief held out; and yet
methinks it goes against my Conscience.
    NEM. Away, that serious look has made thee old:
Conscience and Consideration in a young Woman too?   60
It makes a Bawd of thee before thy time.
Nay, now thou put'st me in Poetick Rapture,
And I must quote Ronsard to punish thee:
Call all your Wives to Council, and prepare
To Tempt, Dissemble, Flatter, Lye and Swear;   65
To make her mine, use all your utmost skill,
Vertue! An ill-bred crosness in the will;
Honour a Notion, Piety a Cheat,
Prove but successful Bawds and you are great.
Come, thou wilt meet me.   70
    TOUR. 'Tis resolv'd I will, till which time, thou dear Man ---
    NEM. Thou pretty Woman.
    TOUR. Thou very dear Man.
    NEM. Thou very pretty Woman one Kiss.
    TOUR. Hey Ho ---   75
    NEM. Now all the Gods go with thee ---
    TOUR. A word my Lord, you are acquainted with these Fops;
set 'em in the modish way of abusing their Wives, they are turning
already, and that will certainly bring 'em about.
    NEM. Bellamore shall do't with less suspicion: farewell --- [Exit Tour.80
Hey Jaques ---

                    Enter Jaques with the Vidam. *

Ha! my grave Lord of Chartres, welcome as Health, as Wine,
and taking Whores --- and tell me now the bus'ness of the Court.

---

54 Luxemburgh] C_{1+}; Lunemburg Q_{1-2}.
77 A word from my Lord, Q_{2+}.
 * This stage direction lacking in Q_{2+}. Note that Jaques apparently
     retires, for he reenters line 108.
82-83 This speech, attributed to Jaques in Q_{1+}, obviously belongs to
     Nemours.

VID. Hold it Nemours for ever at defiance,
Fogs of ill humour, damps of Melancholy,   85
Old Maids of fifty choak'd with eternal Vapours,
Stuff it with fulsome Honour --- dozing Vertue,
And everlasting dullness husk it round,
Since he that was the Life, the Soul of Pleasure,
Count Rosidore, is dead.
     NEM.   Then we may say   90
Wit was and Satyr is a Carcass now.
I thought his last Debauch wou'd be his Death ---
But is it certain?
     VID.   Yes I saw him dust.
I saw the mighty thing a nothing made,
Huddled with Worms, and swept to that cold Den,   95
Where Kings lye crumbled just like other Men.
     NEM. Nay then let's Rave and Elegize together,
Where Rosidore is now but common clay,
Whom every wiser Emmet bears away,
And lays him up against a Winters day.   100
He was the Spirit of Wit --- and had such an art in guilding his
Failures, that it was hard not to love his Faults: He never spoke
a Witty thing twice, tho to different Persons; his Imperfections
were catching, and his Genius was so Luxuriant, that he was
forc'd to tame it with a Hesitation in his Speech to keep it in   105
view --- But oh how awkard, how insipid, how poor and wretchedly
dull is the imitation of those that have all the affectation of his
Verse and none of his Wit.

Enter Jaques.

     JAQ. My Lord, Monsieur Poltrot desires to kiss your Grace's hand.
     NEM. Let's have him to drive away our Melancholy ---   110
     VID. I wonder what pleasure you can take in such dull Dogs,
Asses, Fools.
     NEM. But this is a particular Fool Man, Fate's own Fool, and
perhaps it will never hit the like again, he's ever the same thing,
yet always pleasing; in short, he's a finish'd Fool, and has a fine   115
Wife; add to this his late leaving the Court of France, and going
to England to learn breeding.

Enter Poltrot.

     POL. My Lord Duke, your Grace's most obedient humble Servant,
My Lord of Chartres and Monsieur Jaques, yours Monsieur; St. Andre
desires your Grace's presence at a Serenade of mine and his together --- 120
And I must tell your Grace by the way, he is a great Master,
and the fondest thing of my Labours ---
     NEM. And the greatest Oaf in the World.
     POL. How my Lord ---
     VID. The whole Court wonders you will keep him company.   125

NEM. Such a passive Raskal, he had his Shins broke last night
in the Presence, and were it not fear'd you wou'd second him, he
wou'd be kick'd out of all Society.

POL. I Second him my Lord, I'll see him Damn'd e'er I'll be
Second to any Fool in Christendom --- For to tell your Grace the   130
truth, I keep him company and lye at his House, because I intend
to lye with his Wife; a trick I learnt since I went into England,
where o' my Conscience Cuckoldom is the Destiny of above half
the Nation.

NEM. Indeed!   135

POL. O there's not such another Drinking, Scowring, Roaring,
Whoreing Nation in the World --- And for little London, to my
knowledge, if a Bill were taken of the weekly Cuckolds, it wou'd
amount to more than the Number of Christnings and Burials put
together.   140

VID. What, and were you acquainted with the Wits?

POL. O Lord Sir, I liv'd in the City a whole year together, my
Lord Mayor and I, and the Common-Council were sworn Brothers ---
I cou'd sing you twenty Catches and Drolls that I made for
their Feast-days, but at present I'll only hint you one or two ---   145

NEM. Pray do us the Favour Sir.

POL. Why look you Sir, this is one of my chief ones, and I'll
assure your Grace, 'twas much Sung at Court too.

        O to Bed to me --- to Bed to me --- &c.

NEM. Excellent, incomparable.   150

POL. Why is it not my Lord? This is no Kickshaw, there's substance
in the Air, and weight in the words; nay, I'll give your Grace a
taste of another, the Tune is, let me see --- Ay, Ay ---

        Give me the Lass that is true Country bred ---

But I'll present your Grace with some words of my own, that I   155
made on my Wife before I married her, as she sate singing one
day in a low Parlour and playing on the Virginals.

NEM. For Heavens sake oblige us dear pleasant Creature ---

POL. I'll swear I'm so ticklish you'll put me out my Lord, for I
am as wanton as any little Bartholomew Bore-Pig ---   160

VID. Dear soft delicate Rogue sing.

POL. Nay, I protest my Lord, I vow and swear, but you'll
make me run to a Whore --- Lord Sir, what do you mean?

NEM. Come then begin ---   [Poltrot Sings.

        Phillis is soft, Phillis is plump,   165
        And Beauty made up this delicate lump:
        Like a Rose bud she looks, like a Lilly she smells,
        And her Voice is a Note above sweet Philomel's.

Now a little Smutty my Lord is the fashion ---

II.

Her Breasts are two Hillocks where Hearts lye and pant,   170
In the Herbage so soft, for a thing that they want;
But Mum Sir for that, tho a notable Jest,
For if I shou'd name it you'd call me a Beast.

Enter St. Andre without his Hat and Wig.

ST. A. My Lord, the Serenade is just begun, and if you don't
come just in the nick --- I beg your Grace's Pardon for interrupting   175
you --- But if you have a mind to hear the sweetest Airs in the
World ---
NEM. With all my heart Sir ---
POL. Nay, since your Grace has put my hand in, I'll sing you
my Lord, before you go, the softest thing --- compos'd in the   180
Nonage of my Muse; yet such a one as our best Authors borrow
from. Nay, I'll be judg'd by your Grace, if they do not steal
their Dying from my Killing ---
ST. A. Nay prithee Poltrot thou art so impertinent.
POL. No more impertinent than your self Sir, nor do I doubt   185
Sir, but my Character shall be drawn by the Poets for a Man of
Wit and Sense Sir, as well as your self Sir ---
VID. Ay I'll be sworn shall it ---
POL. For I know how to Repartee with the best, to Rally my
Wife, to kick her too if I please Sir, to make Similes as fast as   190
Hops Sir, tho I lay a dying slap dash Sir, quickly off and quickly
on Sir, and as round as a Hoop Sir ---
ST. A. I grant you Dear Bully all this, but let's have your Song
another time, because mine are begun.
POL. Nay, look you Dear Rogue, mine is but a Prologue to   195
your Play, and by your leave his Grace has a mind to hear it, and
he shall hear it Sir ---
NEM. Ay and will hear it Sir, tho the Great Turk were at
St. Dennis's Gate; come along my Orpheus, and then Sir we'll
follow you to the Prince of Cleve's ---   200

Ballad --- When Phoebus had fetch'd, &c.   [Exeunt Singing.

Scene III.
The Prince of Cleve's Palace.   Musick.

Song.
In a Room for Delight, the Landskip of Love,
Like a shady old Lawn
With the Curtains half drawn,
My Love and I lay, in the cool of the day,
Till our Joyes did remove.   5

---

190 make Smiles Q_{2+}.

II.

So fierce was our Fight, and so smart e'ry stroak,
    That Love the little Scout
    Was put to the Rout;
His Bow was unbent, e'ry Arrow was spent,
    And his Quiver all broke.   10

Enter Vidam, Nemours.

NEM. I have lost my Letter, and by your Description
It must be that which the Queen read at Court.
But are you sure the Princess of Cleve has seen it?
    VID. Why are you so concern'd, does your wild Love
Turn that way too? -- She is too Grave.   15
    NEM. Too Grave, as if I cou'd not laugh with this, and try
with that, and veer with every gust of Passion --- But has she seen it?
    VID. She has the Letter, the Queen Dauphin sent it her.
    NEM. Then you must own it on occasion, and whatever else I
shall put upon your Person ---   20
    VID. Why?
    NEM. Lest it shou'd reach the Ears of Marguerite,
For, Oh my Vidam! 'tis such a ranting Devil,
If she believes this Letter mine, when next
We meet, beware my Locks and Eyes --- No more,   25
But this remember that, you own it.   [Exit.

Enter St. Andre and Poltrot.

ST. A. His Bow was unbent, &c.   [Singing with Poltrot.
Come, my Lord, we'll have all over agen.

Enter the Prince of Cleve.

VID. See, we have rais'd the Prince of Cleve:
My Lord, good Morrow ---   30
    PRINCE C. Good morrow my good Lord --- Save you my dear Nemours!
    POL. Give you Joy my Lord: What a little blew under the Eyes,
Ha, Ha ---
    ST. A. Give you Joy my Lord: Ha, my Lord, Ha. [Holds up 3 Fingers.
    POL. Ha, my Lord, Ha ---   [Holding up five Fingers.   35
    PRINCE C. You are merry Gentlemen --- I am not in the vein,
Therefore, Dear Chartres, take these Fingers hence.
    ST. A. My Lord, you look a little heavy, shall we Dance, Sing,
Fence, take the Air, Ride ---

---

14 concern'd? C_{1+}.
15 too? --] C_{1+}; too -- Q_{1-2}.
26 remember, that] Q_{2+}; remember that, Q_1.
31 <u>Thus in Q_{1+}, although Nemours has left the stage, line 26.</u>

VID. Come away Sir, the Prince is indispos'd.   40
ST. A. Gad I remember now I talk of riding, at the Tournament
of Mete, as I was riding the great Horse ---
VID. Leave off your Lying, and come along.
ST. A. With three pushes of Pike, and six hits of Sword, I
wounded the Duke of Ferrara, Duke of Millain, Duke of Parma,   45
Prince of Cleve ---
PRINCE C. My Lord, I was not there ---
ST. A. My Lord --- I beg your Lordships pardon, I meant the
Vidam of Chartres.
VID. You Lye, I was then at Rome.   50
ST. A. My Lord ---
POL. Ha, Ha --- Lord, Lord, how this World is given to Lying!
Ha --- Come, come,you're damnably out, come away.
ST. A. My Lord, I beg your pardon, I see you are indispos'd,
besides the Queen oblig'd me this Morning to let 'em choose   55
Colours for my Complexion ---
VID. Heark you, will you go or shall I --- [Pulling him off by the Nose.
ST. A. My Friend, my Lord you see, is a little Familiar, but I
am ever your Highness's most humble faithful obedient Servant. [Exeunt.

Manet Prince of Cleve.

PRINCE C. Full of himself, the happy Man is gone;   60
Why was not I too cast in such a Mould?
To think like him, or not to think at all.

Enter the Princess of Cleve.

Had he a Bride like me, Earth wou'd not bear him:
But Oh I wish that it might cover me!
Since Chartres cannot love me: Oh I found it!   65
Last night I found it in her cold Embraces;
Her Lips too cold --- Cold as the Dew of Death:
And still whene'er I prest her in my arms,
I found my Bosom all afloat with Tears.
PRINCESS C. He weeps, O Heaven! my Lord -- the Prince of Cleve.   70
PRINCE C. My Life, my Dearest part!
PRINCESS C.   Why Sighs my Lord?
What have I done Sir, thus to discompose you?
PRINCE C. Nothing.
PRINCESS C.   Ah Sir, there is a Grief within,
And you wou'd hide it from me.
PRINCE C. Nothing my Chartres, nothing here but Love.   75
PRINCESS C. Alas, my Lord, you hide that Secret from me,
Which I must know or think you never lov'd me.

---

42 Metz, C_{1+}.
60 PRINCE C.]; om. Q_{1+}.

PRINCE C. Ah Princess! that you lov'd but half so well!

PRINCESS C. I have it then, you think me Criminal,
And tax my Honour ---

PRINCE C.   Oh forbid it Heaven ---   80
But since you press me Madam, let me ask you,
Why when the Princess led you to the Altar,
Why cak'd the Tears upon your Bloodless Face?
Why sigh'd you when your hand was clasp'd with mine?
As if your Heart, your Heart refus'd to joyn.   85

PRINCESS C. Ah Sir ---

PRINCE C.   Behold, you're dash'd with the remembrance;
Why when my Hopes were fierce, and Joys grew strong,
Why were you carri'd like a Coarse along?
When like a Victim by my side you lay,
Why did you Gasp, why did you Swoon away?   90
O speak ---
You have a Soul so open and so clear,
That if there be a Fault it must appear.

PRINCESS C. Alas you are not skill'd in Beauties cares,
For Oh! when once the god his Wrath declares;   95
And Stygian Oaths have wing'd the bloody Dart,
To make its passage thro the Virgins Heart:
She hides her Wound, and hasting to the Grove,
Scarce whisp'ring to the Winds her conscious Love.
The touch of him she loves she'll not endure,   100
But Weeps and Bleeds, and strives against the Cure:
So judge of me when any Grief appears,
Believe my Sighs are kind, and trust my Tears.

PRINCE C. Vanish my Doubts, and Jealousies be gon ---
On thy lov'd Bosom let me break my Joy,   105
O only Sweets that Fill, but never Cloy:
And was it, was it only Virgins fear?
But speak for ever and I'll ever hear.
Repeat, and let the Ecchoes deal it round,
While list'ning Angels bend to catch the Sound;   110
Nay, Sigh and Weep, drain all thy precious Store,
Be kind, as now, and I'll complain no more.   [Exit.

PRINCESS C. Was ever Man so worthy to be lov'd,
So good, so gentle, soft a Disposition,
As if no Gaul had mixt with his Creation: 115
So tender and so fearful to displease,
No barbarous Heart but thine wou'd stop his entrance;
But thou Inhumane banisht him from his own.
And while the Lordly Master lyes without,

Enter Irene.

---

99 Love, C_{2+}.

Thou Trait'ress, Riotests with a Thief within.   120
    IREN. Ah Madam, what new Grief!
    PRINCESS C.   Alass Irene,
Thou Treasurer of my thoughts ---
What shall I do? how shall I chase Nemours,
That Robber, Ravisher of my Repose?
    IREN. For the great care you wish, may I enquire   125
Whether you think the Duke insensible,
Indifferent to the rest of Woman-kind?
    PRINCESS C. I must confess I did not think him so
Tho now I do --- But wou'd give half my Blood
To think him otherwise ---
    IREN.   Without the Expense,   130
There take your wish, --- a Letter which he dropt
In the Tennis-court, given the Queen Dauphin
By her Page, and sent to you to read
For your Diversion.
    PRINCESS C.   Alas! Irene ---
Why trembles thus my Hand, why beats my Heart?   135
But let us Read ---

Reads ---

Your affection has been divided betwixt me and another, you
are False --- a Traytor to the truest Love --- never see me more ---
    PRINCESS C. Ah 'tis too plain, I thought as much before; but Oh!
we are too apt to excuse the faults of those we love, and fond of   140
our own undoing.
Support me Oh to bear this dreadful pang,
This stab to all my gather'd Resolution.
    IREN. Read it agen, and call Revenge to aid you.
    PRINCESS C. Perhaps he makes his boast too of the Conquest,   145
For Oh! my Heart he knows too well, my Passion ---
But as thou hast inspir'd me, I'll revenge
The Affront, and cast him from my Poyson'd Breast,
To make him room that merits all my thoughts.

Enter the Prince of Cleve with Nemours.

    PRINCE C. Madam there is a Letter fall'n by accident into your   150
hands --- my Friend comes in behalf of the Vidam of Chartres to
retrieve it, when I am dismiss'd from the King my Lord, I'll wait
you here again.

---

120 riot'st C_{2+}.
134 Q_{1+} print "For your Diversion" as a part of line 133.
138 truest Lover C_{2+}.
139 The speech tag here, given in Q_{1+}, marks the end of the letter.
139-141 Q_{1+} print these lines as prose, though the author may have
      intended them as blank verse.

NEM. My Lord ---
PRINCE C. Not a step further.   [Exit Prince C.   155
NEM. Madam, I come most humbly to enquire, whether the
Dauphin Queen sent you a Letter which the Vidam lost?
    PRINCESS C. Sir, you had better
Find the Queen Dauphin out, tell her the truth,
For she's inform'd the Letter is your own.   160
    NEM. Ah Madam! I have nothing to confess
In this Affair --- or if I had, believe me,
Believe these Sighs that will not be kept in,
I shou'd not tell it to the Dauphin Queen.
But to the purpose; Know my Lord of Chartres   165
Receiv'd the Note you saw, from Madam Tournon,
A former Mistress --- But the Secret's this ---
The Sister of our Henry long has lov'd him.
    PRINCESS C. I thought the King intended her for Savoy.
    NEM. True Madam, but the Vidam is belov'd;   170
In short, he dropt the Letter, and desir'd,
For fear of her he loves, that I wou'd own it;
I promis'd too to trace the Business for him,
And if 'twere possible, regain the Letter.
    PRINCESS C. The Vidam then has shewn but small Discretion, 175
Being engag'd so high ---
Why did he not burn the Letter?
    NEM. But Madam, shall I dare presume to say,
'Tis hard to be in Love and to be wise?
Oh did you know like him --- like him! Like me,   180
What 'tis to languish in those restless Fires.
    PRINCESS C. Irene, Irene, restore the Duke his Letter.

Enter Iren.

    NEM. Madam, You've bound me ever to your Service,
But I'll retire and study to repay,
If ought but death can quit the Obligation.   [Exit.   185
    PRINCESS C. O 'tis too much, I'm lost, I'm lost agen ---
The Duke has clear'd himself, to the confusion
Of all my settl'd Rage, and vow'd Revenge;
And now he shews more lovely than before:
He comes agen to wake my sleeping Passion,   190
To rouze me into Torture; O the Racks
Of hopeless Love! it shoots, it glows, it burns,
And thou alas! shalt shortly close my Eyes.
    IREN. Alas! you're pale already.
    PRINCESS C.   Oh Irene ---
Methinks I see Fate set two Bowls before me,   195
Poyson and Health, a Husband and Nemours;

---

163 Believe me these Q_{2+}.

But see with what a whirl my Passions move,
I loath the Cordial of my Husband's Love;
But when Nemours my Fancy does recal,
The Bane's so sweet that I cou'd drink it all.   200

End of A C T   I.

Act II. Scene I.

Tournon, La March.

TOUR. It works, my Dear, it works beyond belief,
The Letter which he lost has sprung a Mine
That shatters all the Court, each Jealous Dutchess
Concludes her Man concern'd, and strait employs
A Confident to find the Mystery out.   5
But that which takes the Queen, and makes me dye
With Pleasure, is, that Marguerite thinks
Spite of the Imprecations of Nemours,
The Letter sent to him---
    LA M. I see 'em move this way.   10
    TOUR. Hast to St. Andre's Palace, watch their Wives, till I appear---
I have promis'd Nemours an Afternoon Assignation with 'em in
Luxemburg Garden, but I will antedate the bus'ness as he is waiting,
and set Marguerite upon him just as he meets 'em, which will
heighten the design; be gone while I attend the bus'ness here---   15
                       [Exit La March.

Enter Marguerite, Nemours.

MARG. Away, you have combin'd to ruine me,   [The Vidam. *
You have conspir'd the Death of her you hate;
But tell me, Oh! confess and I'll forgive thee;
Say it was thine, nay, look not on the Vidam,
There is Discourse in Eyes, Consent, Denial,   20
All understood by looks, say it was thine,
Confess, and lay this Tempest with a word.
Not yet? why then I'll have it in despite
Of thee and him, I'll sell my Soul to Hell,
If Woman can be worth the Devil's purchase,   25
After she has been blown upon by Man;
That I may tell thee, as I sink for ever,
Thou hast been False.
    NEM.   You have heard me more than once
Affirm, the Vidam (if you'll give him leave)
Will own it to your Face.

---

  * In Q_{1+} the words "The Vidam" are set off with a bracket at
    the margin of line 16, as above, apparently to indicate that
    he stays to one side of the stage.

MARG.   Hear, hear him Heav'n;   30
By all Extreams thou art False, therefore be gone,
For if I look upon thee in this Rage,
I shall do mischief; speak not, but away----

                    [Nemours beckons the Vidam, they steal off.

       Tournon comes forward.*

TOUR.   Madam, the Duke has taken you at your word, and is gone with the
Vidam; I made bold to over-hear part of your Discourse, because I have   35
more of his Infidelity to tell you ---- Betwixt one and two in Luxemburg
Garden he has appointed some Ladies ----
MARG. Furies and Hell! ---
TOUR.   Have Patience for an hour, I'll bring you to the place, where,
if you please, you may flesh your Fingers in the Blood of those young   40
Women, whom he meets to enjoy.
MARG.   No, no, I have a better Cast, if I can conquer this rising
Spleen --- How long will it be e'er you call me?
TOUR.   An hour or thereabouts---
MARG.   And by that time I'll put on a Disguise; fail not---   45
TOUR.   But what do you intend?
MARG.   I know not yet my self; Revenge---
TOUR.   You had a Lover once, Francis the Dauphin---

30-37 This passage appears in some copies of Q_1 (such as Folger,
       Chapin, and Newberry), and does not appear in others, be-
       cause of a faulty cancellation of D1. See Fredson Bowers,
       "A Crux in the Text of Lee's PRINCESS OF CLEVE (1689)",
       HARVARD LIBRARY BULLETIN, IV, No. 3(1950), 409-411,
       for a full discussion of the question. In those copies which
       have the cancelled D1, $D1^r$ merely repeats $C4^r$; then on $D1^v$
       following the entrance of Nemours and Marguerite, Margue-
       rite's long speech is omitted and the passage ls. 30-37 is
       printed at the bottom of the page. In those copies which lack
       this cancelled leaf, there is no D1, and the text jumps from
       Nemours' speech l. 30 directly to Marguerite's speech l. 38,
       which is printed at the top of $D2^r$; thus these copies have
       no direction for the exit of Nemours and the Vidam. Van
       Lennep believes that this is where Lee cut out one of the
       scenes which he had borrowed from THE MASSACRE OF
       PARIS. Q_2-C_3 follow the cancelled text.
 * In the copies of Q_1 which contain this passage, this stage direc-
       tion reads: Enter Tournon. However, Tournon has never left
       the stage; at the exit of La March(l. 15) she apparently retires
       back stage to over-hear the conversation of Nemours and Mar-
       guerite, as she confesses in l. 35.
43 you] Q_{2+}; your Q_1.

MARG. Be that then the last Card --- I know not what;
The Dauphin shall--- I'll do't, and openly affront him---   50
And as the little Worshippers adore me,
Spy the Duke out, and leaning on the Prince,
Enquire who's that: It shall be so, I will---
Revenge, Revenge, and shew thy self true Woman.
Down then, proud Heart, down Woman, down, I'll try,   55
I'll do't, I've sworn, to curb my Will or dye.   [Exeunt.

Scene II.

St. Andre, Poltrot, Bellamore.

BELL. Well, Gentlemen, good Morrow, and remember my Counsel.
POL. What, to bear our selves like Men of Wit and Sense,
Snub our Wives, Rally 'em, and be as Witty as the Devil?
ST. A. With all my heart, 'tis not my time of Assignation yet with my
Dutchesses, and this is very Fashionable.   5
BELL. I've put you in the way--And so good Morrow.   [Exit.
POL. They come, they come,

Enter Elianor and Celia.

Walk by 'em, take no notice, and Repeat Verses.
Phillis did in so strange a Posture lye
Panting and Breathless, languishing her Eye,   10
She seem'd to live, and yet she seem'd to Dye.
ST. A. I grow sick of the Wife--Prithe Poltrot let 's go.
POL. Whither thou wilt, so we get rid of 'em---Z'life I am as weary
of mine, as a Modish Lady of her old Cloaths---
CEL. What does the Maggot bite, you must be jogging from this place   15
of little Ease? yet I am resolv'd to know some reason, why a Wife may
not be as good Company as a Wench.
POL. Prithe Spouse---do not provoke me, for I'm in the Witty Vein,
and shall Repartee thee to the Devil.
ELI. Pray, St. Andre, leave trising your Curls, your affected Nods,   20
Grimaces, taking of Snuff, and answer me----Why are we not as pleasing
as formerly?
ST. A. Why, Nell---Gad 'tis special---This Amarum is very pungent---
Why, Nell, I can give no more reason for my change of humour, than for
the turning of a Weather-cock; only this, I love Whoring, because   25
I love Whoring.
POL. Nay, since you provoke us, know I can give a reason; we run

---

20 trying your Curls, C_{2+}.
23 pugnant Q_{2+}.

after Whores, because you bar us from 'em--- As some take pleasure
to go a Deer-steeling that have fine Parks of their own--- Gad, and
there I was with her--- This itch of the Blood, Spouse, is nothing but   30
a Spice of the first great Jilt your Grand-mother Eve; we long for the
Fruit, because it is forbidden.

    ST. A. Nay, that's not all, for Misses are really more pleasant than a
Wife can be, Probatum est. A Wife dares not assume the Liberty of
pleasing like a Miss, for fear of being thought one. A Wife may pretend   35
to dutiful affection, and bustle below, but must be still at night.
'Tis Miss alone may be allow'd Flame and Rapture, and all that---

    CEL. Yet how do you know, but a Wife may have Flame and Rapture,
and all that---

    POL. 'Tis impossible, 'tis the Nature of a Wife to be as cold as a   40
Stone---There's Slap Dash for you---

    CEL. Yet out of a Stone a Man of Sense wou'd strike Fire: There's
Slap Dash for you---

    ELI. Will you be Constant to us, if we make it appear by your own
Confession, that we can please as well as the subtl'st She that ever   45
charm'd you?

    ST. A. Till which Miracle come to pass, since 'twas your own Propo-
sition, I St. Andre and thou Elianor come not between a pair of Sheets---

    ELI. How shou'd they know then?

    POL. Nor I Antony with thee Celia.   50

    ELI. But we hope you are not in earnest, you cannot be so Inhumane.

    CEL. 'Tis a Curse beyond all Curses, to have a Man that can and will
not; 'tis worse than teaching a Fool, or leading the Blind.

    ELI. To Marry and live thus, is to be like Fish in Frosty Weather,
have Water, but pine for want of Air.   55

    CEL. Yet, who knows but Heav'n may send some Kind Good Man,
that in meer pity may break the Ice, and give us a Breathing?

    ELI. Can you be so hard-hearted?

    POL. Come Bully, let's away, for fear we shou'd melt; look ye Spouses
of ours, if our Wenches prove ill-humour'd, we'll come back to you.   60

    ST. A. Agreed, rather than grow Rusty let our Wives File us---
But I thank Heav'n 'tis not come to that yet--There's no such want,
I'll have you to know Nell, there's no Woman can resist me if she wou'd,
no Dutchess scapes me, if I make it my bus'ness to compass her.

    POL. Any Man of Wit and Sense like us, Charms all Women, as   65
one Key unlocks all Doors at Court--- Nay, I'll say a bold word for
my self, Turn me to the sharpest Shrow that ever Bit or Scratch'd, if I
do not make her feed out of my hand like a tame Pidgeon, may I be
condemn'd to lye with my Wife.

    ELI. Flesh and Blood can endure no longer, you are the vainest lying   70
Fellows that ever liv'd, you compass a Dutchess--- There's not a Foot-
man but wou'd shame you.

    ST. A. Z'Death and Fury, if they shou'd try---

---

67 Shrew C_{2+}.

CEL. You pitiful, sneaking, rascally Cuckolds, countenanc'd Scoundrels,
that dare Bespatter Ladies of Honour thus---For Heaven sake what   75
are you, how do you live, and where do you spend your time? in Tennis-
Courts, Taverns, Eating-houses, Bawdy-houses, where you quarrel
in Drink for your Trulls, who while you Manfully Fight their Cause,
they run away with your Hats and Belts---

ELI. Then you come home, and swear you'll be reveng'd on this Lord,   80
or that Duke, that assaulted you single, with all his Foot men.

CEL. And, says my Gentleman, if I had not been the most Skillful
Person alive, my Body had been by this time like an Old-fashion'd Suit,
Pink'd all over, and full of Ilet-holes.

ELI. But did he not disarm my Lord at last?   85

CEL. By all means, and made him beg his Life.

ELI. When indeed he compounded with the Constable for his own
Liberty.

CEL. You Persons of Quality--- What Person of Honour wou'd keep
company with such Debauches? Z'life Madam, an Orange-wench is above   90
their Ambition.

ELI. An Orange-wench! If they can but run in her debt, and the poor
Creature come dunning 'em to their Lodgings, they'll Swear they lay
with her, when they dare not be known that they are within.

CEL. Sometimes lye Lolling upon a long Scarf in the Play-house, talking   95
loud and affectedly, and Swear at night they had the prettiest thing
just come out of the Country.

ELI. And wish themselves Damn'd if she did not smell of the Grass.

CEL. When in truth 'twas some disguis'd Bawd, that met 'em there
according to Assignation.   100

POL. Hark you Potiphar's Wife of mine, by Pharaoh's lean Kine thou
shalt starve for this.

ST. A. And for thee Nell---Mark me, thou shalt Dream and be tormented with Imagination, like one that having drunk hard is thirsty in
the Night, dreams of Vessels brim-full, and drinks and drinks, yet never   105
is satisfied.

POL. For my part, I'll serve my Damn'd Wife as Tantalus was punish'd,
the Fruit shall bob at her Lips, which she shall never enjoy.

[Exeunt St. A., Pol.

ELI. Very well, the World's come to a fine pass; if this be Marrying,
wou'd I were a Maid agen. Men take Wives now as they snatch up a   110
Gazette, look it over and then fling it by.

CEL. They forget us in a day or two, or if they read us over agen, 'tis
only to rub up Remembrance, and commonly they fall asleep so.

ELI. What's to be done Child? for rather than live thus---

CEL. Rather than live thus let's do any thing.   115

ELI. Any thing Rogue, why Cuckolds are things.

CEL. Perhaps they think we have no such thing as Flesh and Blood

---

74 Cuckolds] C_{2+}; Cuckold Q_1-C_1.
80 and then swear Q_{2+}.
107 punish'd,] Q_2; punish'd Q_1; punish'd; C_{1+}.

about us, but we'll make 'em know, a young Woman in the flour of
her Age, is not like painted Fruit in a Glass, only to be look'd on---
Perhaps you are a more Contemplative Person, and will go farther about.   120

 ELI. What, Dear Rogue, dost think I will leave thee ? by this Kiss
not I.

 CEL. Thus then we'll slip on long Scarfs, and black Gowns, put on Masks,
and ramble about.

 ELI. Rare Rogue, let me Kiss thee agen---Certainly Intrigueing is   125
the pleasantest part of Life; to meet a Gallant abroad in a Summers
Evening, and Laugh away an hour or two in a Garden Bower, where
no body sees nor no body knows, methinks 'tis so pretty and harmless,
Lord, how it works in my Fancy---

 CEL. We must tell Madam Tournon by all means---   130

 ELI. I believe her Secret, and know her very good Natur'd; but for
all that, methinks she has the Cant of a refin'd Florence Bawd---

Enter Tournon.

 CEL. The better for our purpose, she comes as wish'd.

 TOUR. Dear Precious Rosebuds your Servant, now for all the World
you look as you were New-blown; and how do ye my pretty Primroses ?   135
'tis a whole day since I saw ye.

 CEL. Oh Madam! we have a Suit to your Ladiship.

 TOUR. I grant it whate'er it be; speak my Hyacinth.

 ELI. Our Husbands are worse than ever.

 CEL. They use us as if we had neither Beauty nor Portion.   140

 TOUR. What's this I hear ? O Ingrate and Ignoble! Revenge your selves
Sweetings---'Tis time to pule and put Finger in Eye, when you are
past Propagation. But my Lady-birds you are in your Prime, let me
touch your delicate Hands---Well, and do not these humid Palms
claim a Man---Nay, and your Breasts, Lord! Lord! how swoll'n   145
and hard they are, how they heave and pant now, by Cynthia, as if they
were ready to burst? look to't, have a care of a Cancer, draw 'em down,
draw 'em down, for let me tell you Jewels, it may be dangerous for you
to go thus long without Cultivation---

 ELI. What wou'd you have us do Madam?   150

 TOUR. Do Violet? why do as all the World does beside, lose no Time,
catch him by the Forelock, get a Man to your mind---I'll acquaint
you with one that's as true as the day, that will Fight like a Lion, and
Love like a Sparrow---He has Eyes as black as Slows, you can hardly
look on 'em, and a Skin so white---and soft as Sattin with the Grain: 155
And for thee Tulip---

 CEL. For me Madam!

 TOUR. For thee Hony-Suckle, such a Man, well, I shall never forget
him, such a strait bole of a Body, such a Trunk, such a shape, such a
quick strength, he will over any thing he can lay his hand on, and Vaults   160
to Admiration.

---

147 burst! C_{1+}.

ELI. But Madam, will you provide us Lodgings on occasion---

TOUR. The Richest in the Town, the costliest Hangings, great Glasses,
China Dishes, Silver Tables, Silver Stands, and Silver Urinals--And
then these Gallants are the closest Lovers, so good at keeping a Secret--   165
Well, give me your Man that says nothing, but minds the bus'ness in
hand--For a Secret Lover's like a Gun charg'd with White Powder, does
Execution but makes no noise.

CEL. Well, and let me tell you that's the Point, Madam---

TOUR. Ay, and 'tis a Precious Point, a Feeling Point, and a Pleasing   170
Point; you shall know him, you must know him, I shall dye if you don't
know him---He has the fling of a Gentleman.

ELI. Pray Madam, how's that?

TOUR. Why thus Apricock---Into your Arms, then stops your Mouth
with a double-tongu'd English Kiss, that you can't be angry with him for   175
your Blood.

CEL. I know 'tis my filthy Country way---But I'll assure you if he
should serve me so, my Blood would rise at him.

TOUR. But then you'd repent and fall before him, for he has the most
particular obliging way, and she whom he particularly loves, is so oblig'd   180
with his Particular---Well, for my part, my Twins of Beauty, I set
an infinite Value on their Charesses, Distresses and Addresses; nay, I
cou'd refuse a Quilt Imperial, to be oblig'd by them, tho on the bare
Boards, or the cold Stones.

ELI. But, Madam, are they in being---   185

TOUR. They are my Blossoms---Then they Kiss beyond Imagination,
just for all the World as when you cut a pure Juicy China Orange, the
Goodness runs over---Lord! now it comes in my Cogitation, I'm just
now going to take a View of 'em in Luxemburg Garden, where, if you
please to walk, they shall Sun themselves in your Smiles---Come my   190
Carnations, nay, I protest I will not go before ye.

CEL. But, Madam, we're at home.

TOUR. O Lord, Beauties! I know not the way.

ELI. Indeed Madam you must---or we shall use Violence---

TOUR. Well Ladies, since 'tis your command, I dare not but obey.   195

[Exeunt.

Scene III.

Nemours, Bellamore.

NEM. Thou Dear Soft Rogue, my Spouse, my Hephestion, my Ganymed,
nay, if I dye to night my Dukedom's thine---But art thou sure the
Princess of Cleve withdraws here after Dinner---

BELL. One of her Women whom I have Debauch'd, tells me 'tis her

---

2 the Dukedom's Q$_{2}$+.

Custom; you may slip into the Closet and over-hear all, and yet me-   5
thinks 'tis hard, because the Prince of Cleve loves you as his Life.

NEM. I sav'd his Life, Sweet-heart, when he was assaulted by a mistake
in the dark, and shall he grudge me a little Fooling with his Wife,
for so serious an Obligation?

Enter the Vidam---

A Pox upon him, here comes the Vidam with his sowre Morals---   10

VID. 'Tis certain I like her---She's very pretty, and Tournon shall
help me to her---

NEM. In Love, by my Lechery--Ay, and she shall help thee to her--
But who, but who is't my Man of Principles---

VID. To tell your Grace, I am sure were to be a Man of none for my   15
self---You that are the Whores Ingrosser---Let me see---There's
Tournon your Ubiquitary Whore, your Bawd, your Bawd Barber or
Bawd Surgeon, for you're ever under her hands, and she Plaisters you
every day with new Wenches---Then there's your Domestick Termagants--
Elianor and Celia, with something new in Chase---Why you outdo   20
Cesar himself in your way, and dictate to more Whores at once
than he did to Knaves---Believe me Sir, in a little time you'll be nick'd
the Town-Bull.

NEM. Why there's the difference betwixt my Sense and yours; wou'd
I were, and your Darklin Mistress the first shou'd come in my way,   25
Jove and Europa, I'd leap her in thy Face---Why, how now Vidam,
what Devil has turn'd thee Grave, the Devil of Love, or the Devil of
Envy?

VID. Friendship, mere Friendship and care of your Soul; I thought it
but just, to tell you the whole Town takes notice of your way.   30

NEM. Why then the whole Town does me wrong, because I take no
notice of theirs; thus t'other night I was in company with two or three
well-bred Fops, that found fault with my Obscenity, and protested
'twas such a way--- Why 'tis the way of ye all, only you sneak with
it under your Cloaks like Taylors and Barbers; and I, as a Gentleman   35
shou'd do, walk with it in my hand. For prithee observe, does not
your Priest the same thing? did not I see Father Patrick declaiming
against Flesh in Lent, strip up to the Elbow; and telling the Congre-
gation he had eat nothing but Fish these twenty years, yet protest to the
Ladies, that Fat Arm of his, which was a chopping one, was the least   40
Member about him?

BELL. Faith, and it may be so too.

NEM. Does not your Politician, your little great Man of bus'ness, that
sets the World together by the Ears, after all his Plotting, Drudging
and Sweating at Lying, retire to some little Punk and untap at Night?   45

VID. I submit to the weight of your Reasons, and confess the whole

-----

19 Termagants] C_{2+}; Termagant Q_1-C_1.
45 sweating and lying, C_{2+}.

World does you Injustice, wherefore I judge it fit that they bring your
Grace their Wives and Daughters to make you amends.

NEM. Why now thou talk'st like an honest Fellow, for never let
bus'ness Flatter thee Frank into Nonsense: Women are the sole Pleasure   50
of the World; nay, I had rather part with my whole Estate, Health
and Sense, than lose an Inch of my Love---I was t'other day at a pretty
Entertainment, where two or three Grave Politick Rogues were wond'ring,
why Women shou'd be brought into Plays; I as gravely reply'd,
the World was not made without 'em; he full Pop upon me---But   55
Sir, it had been better if it had---

VID. And then no doubt a gloomy Smile arose---

NEM. These are your Rogues, Frank, that wou'd be thought Criticks,
that are never pleas'd but with something new, as they call it, just,
proper, and never as men speak; you're out of the way men, that hate   60
us Rogues with a way---

BELL. But after all this they'll run you down, and say your Grace is no
Scholar---

NEM. Why, Faith, nor wou'd be, if Learning must wrench a Man's
Head quite round; I understand my Mother-tongue well enough, and   65
some others just as I do Women, not to be married to 'em, but to serve
my turn; what's good in 'em never scapes me, but as for Points and
Tags, for which those solemn Fops are to be valued, I slight 'em, nor
wou'd remember 'em if I cou'd; for he that once listens to Jingling, ten
to one if ever he gets it out of his head while he lives---But prithee   70
be gone, and leave me to my Musing; find Tournon out, my Vidam, and
bid her remember the Handkercher--Away, thou art concern'd in the
bus'ness, therefore away.   [Exeunt Vidam, Bellamore.

Enter the Princess of Cleve, Irene.

NEM. She comes, ye Gods, with what a pompous State;
The Stars and all Heav'ns Glories on her wait.   75
That's out of the way too---But now for my Closet.   [Exit.

PRINCESS C. No, no, I charge thee pity me no longer,
But on the Earth let us consult our Woes:
For Earth I shall be shortly; sit and hear me,
While on thy Faithful Bosom thus I lean   80
My akeing Head, and breath my cruel Sorrows.

IREN. Speak Madam, speak, they'll strangle if contain'd---

PRINCESS C. As late I lay upon a flow'ry Bank,
My Head a little heav'd beyond the Verge,
To look my Troubles in the Rockless Stream,   85
I slept, and dreamt I saw
The bosom of the Flood unfold;
I saw the Naked Nymphs ten Fathom down,
With all the Crystal Thrones in their Green Courts below,

---

47 Justice, C_{1+}.
60 way men,] C_{1+}; way, men Q_{1-2}.

Where in their busie Arms Nemours appear'd: 90
His Head reclin'd, and swoll'n as he were drown'd,
While each kind Goddess dew'd his Senseless Face
With Nectars drops to bring back Life in vain:
When on a sudden the whole Synod rose
And laid him to my Lips---Oh my Irene!   95
Forgive me Honour, Duty--Love forgive me,
I found a Pleasure I ne'er felt before,
Dissolving Pains, and Swimming shuddering Joys,
To which my Bridal Night with Cleve was dull---

     Enter the Prince of Cleve.

    IREN. Behold him, Madam.
    PRINCE C.   Ha! my Chartres---How---   100
Why on the Earth?
    PRINCESS C.   Because, my Lord, it suits
The humble posture of my sad Condition.
    PRINCE C.   These Starts agen; but why thy sad Condition?
O rise and tell me why this Melancholy!
Why fall those Tears? Why heaves this Bosom thus?   105
Nay, I must then constrain thee with my Arms.   [Rise. *
Is't possible? does then thy load of Grief
Oppress thee so, thou canst not speak for Sighing---
Ah Chartres, Chartres! then thou didst but sooth me,
There is some cause, too frightful to be told,   110
And thou hast learnt the art too to dissemble.
    PRINCESS C.   O Heavens! dissemble when I strip my Soul,
Shew it all bear, and trembling to your view;
Can you suspect me Sir, for a Dissembler?
    PRINCE C.   By all my Hopes, Doubts, Jealousies and Fears, 115
I know not what to think, I think thou show'st
Thy inmost thought, and now I think thou dost not.
I think there is a Bosom secret still,
And have a dawn of it through all thy Folds
That hide it from my view: O trust me Cleve!   120
Trust me whate'er it be; I love thee more
Than thou lov'st help for that which thus inthrauls thee.
Trust thy Dear Husband, O let loose the pain
That makes thee droop, though it shou'd be my death!
By thy dear self I'll welcome it to ease thee.   125
    PRINCESS C.   Thou best of all thy Kind, why shou'd you rack me,
Who dare not, cannot speak--No more but this,
Take me from Paris from the Court.
    PRINCE C.   Ha, Chartres, how!
What from the Court of Paris, why?

----

   * [Rises. C$_{2+}$.

PRINCESS C.   Because--
My Mothers Death-bed Counsel so advised me,   130
Because the Court has Charms, because I love
A Grotto best, because 'tis best for you
And me, and all the World.
    PRINCE C.   Because, O Heaven!
Because there is some cursed Charm at Court,
Which you love better than me and all the World.   135
The Reason's plain, for which you wou'd remove,
To lose the Mem'ry of some lawless Love.
    PRINCESS C. Why then am I detain'd, if that's your fear?
    PRINCE C. It is, it ought, and shall, and Oh! you must
Confess this horrid Falshood to my Face.   140
    PRINCESS C. Never, my Lord, never confess a Lye,
By Heav'ns I love your Life above my own.
    PRINCE C. Not that, not that, speak home and fly not wide,
Swear by thy self, thou dearly purchas'd Pleasure,
Swear by those Chaster Sweets thy Mother left thee;   145
Swear that thy Soul, which cannot hide a Treason,
Prefers me ev'n to all the World; Hold Precious,
Swear that thou lov'st him more---And only lov'st him,
And in such Sense as not to love another.
    PRINCESS C. Ah, Sir! why will you sink me to your Feet, 150
Where I must lye and groan my Life away?
    PRINCE C. Speak Chartres, Speak, nor let the name of Husband
Sound Terror to thy Soul; for by my hopes
Of Paradice, howe'er thou usest me,
I am thy Creature, still to make and mould me   155
Thy cringing crawling Slave, and will adore
The hand that kills me---
    PRINCESS C.   O you are too good!
And I must never hope for Pardon--Yet
I cou'd excuse it; but my Lord I will not.
Know then--I cannot speak.
    PRINCE C.   Nor I by Heav'n.   160
    PRINCESS C. I Love.
    PRINCE C.   Go on.
    PRINCESS C.   I love you as my Soul.
    PRINCE C. Ha---But the rest.
    PRINCESS C.   Alas, alas, I dare not---
    PRINCE C. Why then farewel for ever---
    PRINCESS C.   Stay and take it---
Take the extreamest Pang of tortur'd Vertue,
Take all, I love, I love thee Cleve as Life;   165
But Oh! I love, I love another more---
    PRINCE C. Oh Chartres! Oh---
    PRINCESS C.   Why did you rack me then?

---

130 Q$_{1+}$ print "Because--" as part of line 130.

You were resolv'd, and now you have it all.
    PRINCE C. All Chartres! All! Why, can there then be more?
But rise, and know I by this Kiss forgive thee.   170
Thou hast made me wretched by the clearest proof
Of perfect Honour that e'er flow'd from Woman.
But crown the misery which you have begun,
And let me know who 'tis you wou'd avoid,
Who is the happy man that had the power   175
To burn that Heart which I cou'd never warm.
    PRINCESS C. Forgive me Sir, in this Prudence commands
Eternal silence---
    PRINCE C.   Ha! if silent now,
Why didst thou speak at all? If here thou stop'st
I shall conclude that which I thought thy vertue,   180
A start of passion which thou cou'dst not hide,
And now Vexation gnaws thy guilty Soul
With a too late Repentance for confessing
His name---
    PRINCESS C.   You shall not know it---Yes my Lord,
Now a too late Repentance tears my Soul,   185
And tells me I have done amiss to trust you;
Yet by my hopes of ease at last by Death,
I swear my Love has never yet appear'd
To any Man but you---
    PRINCE C. Weep not my Chartres, for howe'er my Tongue   190
Upbraid thy Fame, my Heart still worships thee,
And by the Blood that chills me round--I swear
From this sad Moment, I'll ne'er urge thee more;
All that I beg of thee, is not to hate me.
    PRINCESS C. The study of my Life shall be to love you.   195
    PRINCE C. Never, Oh never! I were mad to hope it,
Yet thou shalt give me leave to fold thy hand,
To press it with my Lips, to sigh upon it,
And wash it with my Tears---
    PRINCESS C. I cannot bear this kindness without dying.   200
    PRINCE C. Nay, we will walk and talk sometimes together,
Like Age we'll call to mind the Pleasures past;
Pleasures like theirs, which never shall return,
For Oh! my Chartres, since thy Heart's estrang'd,
The pleasure of thy Beauty is no more,   205
Yet I each night will see thee softly laid,
Kneel by thy side, and when thy Vows are paid,
Take one last kiss, e'er I to Death retire,
Wish that the Heav'ns had giv'n us equal fire;
Then sigh, it cannot be, and so expire.   [Exeunt.   210

----

183 confessing. C3.

Enter Nemours.

NEM. She Loves, she Loves, and I'm the happy Man,
She has avow'd it, past all president,
Before her Husbands Face---
Ha! but from Love like hers such daring virtue,
That like a bleeding Quarry lately chas'd,   215
Plunges among the Waves, or turns at Bay,
What is there to expect--But--let it come
The worst can happ'n, yet 'tis glorious still.
To bring to such Extreams so chast a mind,
And charm to love the wisest of her Kind.   220

Enter Vidam.

Ah Vidam! I cou'd tell thee such a Story of such a Friend of mine,
the oddest, prettiest, out of the way of bus'ness, but thou art so flippant
there's no trusting thee.
     VID. Tournon says the Flag's held out---
     NEM. Tournon be Damn'd---Know then, but be secret, there is a   225
Friend of mine belov'd----But by a Soul so Vertuous,
     VID. That was too much---
     NEM. That quite from the method of all Womankind, she told it to
her Husband.
     VID. That's strange indeed: And how did her Husband like it?   230
     NEM. Why, after a tedious passionate Discourse, approved her car-
riage, and swore he lov'd her more than ever; so they cry'd and kiss'd,
and went away most lovingly together.
     VID. Why then she Cuckolds him to rights, nor can he take the Law
of her; and I'll be judge by any Bawd in Christendom---And so my   235
Lord farewell, I have bus'ness of my own, and Tournon waits you---
     NEM. But heark you, Frank, I have occasion for you, and must press
thee, I hope, to no unwellcome Office--only a Second---
     VID. With all my heart, my Lord, the time and place.
     NEM. Just now in Luxemburg Garden, betwixt one and two, a Challenge 240
from a couple, the smartest, briskest, prettiest Tilting Ladies---
     VID. Your Servant Sir, and as you thrive, let me hear from your Grace,
and so Fate speed your Plow.   [Exit.

Enter Tournon with Marguerite, Masked. *

NEM. And so Fate speed your Plow, and you go to that, and I shall
tell you Sir, 'twas not handsomly done, to leave me thus to the Mercy of 245
two unreasonable Women at once.

---

211 NEM.] ; om. Q_{1+}.
218 still: C_{2+}.
   * Masked.] ; om. Q_{1+}.
244 go that, Q_2-C_1; go that way; C_{2+}.

TOUR. You have him now in view, and so I leave you. [Exit. Tour.

MARG. Stand Sir.

NEM. To a Lady, while I have breath.

MARG. Wou'd you not fall to a Lady too, if she shou'd ask the Favour?   250

NEM. Ay, Gad, any pretty Woman may bring me upon my Knees at her plea.sure.

MARG. O Devil---

NEM. Prithee my dear soft warm Rogue, let thee and I be kind---

MARG. And Kiss, you were going to say.   255

NEM. Z' Life, how pat she hits me, why thou and I were made for one another--Let's try how our Lips fit.

MARG. Is that your fitting?

NEM. 'Fore Heaven she's wond'rous quick; Nay, my Dear, and you go to that, I can fit you every way---   260

MARG. You are a notorious talker.

NEM. And a better doer; prithee try.

MARG. As if that were to do now.

NEM. Nay then I'm sure of thee, for never was a Woman mine once, but was mine always.   265

MARG. Know then you are a heavy sluggish Fellow; but I see there is no more Faith in Man than Woman, Cork and Feathers.

NEM. Make a Shittlecork that's Woman, let me, if you please, be Battledoor, and by Gad for a day and a night I'll keep up with any Fellow in Christendom.   270

MARG. Come away then and I'll keep count I warrant you--Monster--Villain---

NEM. Now is the Devil and I as great as ever---I come my Dear--But then what becomes of my other Dears---For whom I was Prim'd and Charg'd---   275

MARG. Why dont you come my Dear?

NEM. There with that sweet word she cock'd me---

MARG. Lord! how you tremble---

NEM. There the Pan flash'd---

MARG. I'll set my Teeth in you.   280

NEM. Now I go off---O Man! O Woman! O Flesh! O Devil!

End of AC T II.

---

268 Shittlecock, Q$_{2}$+.

Act III. Scene I.

The Vidam, Tournon.

TOUR. A Woman in Love with another, and confess it to her Husband ---
What wou'd I give to know her --- Without all question Nemours is the
Person belov'd.

VID. That's plain by his eagerness in the Discovery, he forc'd me to
hear him whether I wou'a or no; yet what I so admire in his Temper,   5
is, that for all the former Heat, I no sooner mentioned you, but he flew
from it, and run upon another Scent, as if the first had never been.

TOUR. Where did you find him?

VID. At the Princess of Cleve's, and my Heart tells me that's the Lady
that acquainted her Husband how she was determin'd to make him a   10
Cuckold -- If he pleas'd to give his consent ---

TOUR. My Judgment, which is most Sagacious in these Matters, is most
positive in your opinion, for by his whitely cast, the Prince of Cleve
must be the Man fork'd in the Book of Fate ---

VID. And yet 'tis odd, that Nemours of all Men, shou'd have such luck   15
at this Lottery.

TOUR. O to choose, my Lord! because she's nice and precise; your
demure Ladies that are so Squob in company, are Devils in a corner;
they are a sort of melancholy Birds, that ne'er peep abroad by day, but
they to whit, to whou it at night; nay, to my particular knowledge,   20
all grave Women love wild Men, and if they can but appear civil at
first, they certainly snap 'em; for mark their Language, the Man is a
handsom Man, if he had but Grace; the Man has Wit, Parts and excellent Gifts, if he wou'd but make a right use of 'em; why all these
If's are but civil Pimps to a most Bawdy conclusion --- But see, I descry   25
him with a Mask yonder ---

VID. You'll remember St. Andre's Lady for this Discovery.

TOUR. If she be not yours to night, never acquaint me with a Mystery
agen ---

VID. Not a word to the Duke --- My Gravity gets me a hank over   30
him --- Therefore if you tell him of any Love Matters of mine, you must
never hope for more Secrets ---

TOUR. Trouble not your head, but away.   [Exit. Vid.
So this gets me a Diamond from the Queen, an Embassadors Merit at least.
Confess to her Husband, alas poor Princess -- See, they come; but that   35
which startles me, is how a Woman of Marguerite's Sex can contain all
this while as she seems to do; but perhaps she designs to pump him --
Or has some further end, which I must learn.

---

30 hanker over C_{2+}.
34 at last. Q_{2+}.

Enter Nemours and Marguerite, Masked. *

MARG. But did you never promise thus before?

NEM. Never --- But why these Doubts --- Thou hast all the Wit   40
in the World --- Thou know'st I love thee without Protestations, why
then this delay?

MARG. I have not convers'd with you an hour, and you are for running
over me: No Sir, but if you can have patience till the Ball --- Oh I
shall burst ---   45

NEM. Patience, I must; but if it were not for the clog of thy Modesty,
we might have been in the third Heav'n by this, and have danc'd at the
Ball beside --- Ha! you faint --- Take off your Mask ---

MARG. Unhand me, or --- But pray, e'er we part, let me ask you
a serious question; what if you shou'd have pick'd up a Devil Incarnate?   50

NEM. Why, by your loving to go in the dark thus, I make me begin
to suspect you --- But be a Devil and thou wilt, if we must be Damn'd
together, who can help it ---

MARG. I shall not hold ---

NEM. Yet, now I think on't, thou canst be no Devil, thou art so fraid   55
of a Sinner; for you refus'd me just now, when I profer'd to sell my
self, and seal the Bargain with the best of my Blood.

MARG. But if I shou'd permit you, cou'd you find in your heart to in-
gender with a damn'd Spirit?

NEM. Yes marry cou'd I, for all you ask the question so seriously: For   60
know, thou bewitching Creature, I have long'd any time this seven years
to be the Father of a Succubus ---

MARG. Fiend, and no Man ---

NEM. Besides, Madam, don't you think a feat Devil of yours and
my begetting, wou'd be a prettier sight in a House, than a Monkey or   65
a Squirrel? Gad I'd hang Bells about his neck, and make my Valet
spruce up his Brush Tail ev'ry Morning as duly as he comb'd my head.

MARG. But is it possible (for I know you have a Mistress, a Convenience
as you call her,) that you cou'd leave her for me, who may be Ugly, Diseas'd,
or a Devil indeed for ought you know?   70

NEM. Why, since you tax me with truth, I must answer like a Man
of Honour; I cou'd leave her for thee or any else of your Tribe, so
they were all like you ---

MARG. But in the name of Reason, what is there in us Runners at All,
that a Wife, or a Mistress of that nature, may not possess with more   75
advantage?

NEM. Why, the freedom Wit and Roguery, and all sort of acting, as
well as Conversation. In a Domestick she, there's no Gaity, no Chat,
no Discourse, but of the Cares of this World and its Inconveniencies;
what we do we do, but so dully; by Gad, my Thing ask'd me once,   80
when my Breeches were down, what the Stuff cost a Yard --- Ha! what

---

* Masked.]; <u>om</u>. Q_{1+}.

51 thus, makes me Q_{2+}.

72 or else any Q_2-C_2; or any C_3.

now, upon the Gog agen? nay, then have with you at all Adventures,
at least to put you in mind of the Ball ---   [Exeunt.

Enter Tournon.

   TOUR. Ha! yonder she lost him --- see, what can she intend by keeping
her self so close --- But see La March has seiz'd her, and now the Mystery 85
will open of it self.

Re-enter Marguerite with La March.

   LA M. But have you found him false?
   MARG.   Curses, Damnation,
The Racks of Womens Wits, when her Soul
Is bawk'd of Vengeance, wait on his desires.
   LA M. Why did you leave him so upon the sudden?   90
   MARG. Because I found my Passion move too strongly,
My foolish Heart wou'd not obey my Will;
I found my Eyes grow full, my Sighs had choak'd me,
And I was dying in his Arms ---
   LA M.   But now
You have got Breath, what is your purpose Madam?   95
   MARG. To meet him as I promis'd, to enjoy him
With the last Pang of a revengeful Pleasure;
And let him know ---
Then make him Damn himself with thousand Oaths,
That he'll ne'er see forsak'n Marguerite more,   100
The curst fond, foolish, doting Marguerite;
For thus with an extorted Gallantry,
I'll force him to revile me to my face;
Then throw the Mask away, and vent my Rage;
Tell him he is a Fiend, Devil, Devil, Devil,   105
Or what is worse, a Man ---
And leave him to the Horror of his Soul.   [Exit.
   TOUR. I've heard her Rave, and must applaud thy Conduct;
To the next task, then when she has satisfied
This odd Figary of Revenge and Pleasure,   110
Take her in the height of her disdain
And ply her with the Dauphin; then tell Nemours
Of her resolve to cast him further off,
Millions to one we carry the design.
But hast and scout, while I attend the Duke,   115
That harps upon the loss of his new Mistress.   [Exit La M.*

---

  86 open it self. Q_{2+}.
  87 MARG.]; TOUR. Q_{1+}.
  88 Woman's C_{2+}.
  96 MARG.] Q_{2+}; NEM. Q_1.
108 Conduct;] C_{1+}; Conduct Q_{1-2}.
  * [Exit La M.]; <u>om</u>. Q_{1+}.

Enter Nemours.

NEM. Death and the Devil --- We went talking along so pleasantly,
when of a sudden whisp'ring, she wou'd not fail me at the Ball, she
sprung from me at yon dark corner and vanish'd. Well if she be a Devil,
Hell by her shou'd be a merry place, or perhaps she has not been there   120
yet, but fell this Morning and took Earth in her way; my Comfort is,
I shall make a new discovery if she keeps her word, and she has too much
wit to break it before she tryes me.
TOUR. And where are you to make this new discovery?
NEM. At the Ball in Masquerade --- Thus wou'd I have Time rowl still   125
all in these lovely Extreams, the Corruption of Reason being the Generation of Wit; and the Spirit of Wit lying in the Extravagance of Pleasure: Nay, the two nearest ways to enter the Closet of the Gods, and
lye even with the Fates themselves, are Fury and Sleep --- Therefore the
Fury of Wine and Fury of Women possess me waking and sleeping; let   130
me Dream of nothing but dimpl'd Cheeks, and laughing Lips, and flowing Bowls, Venus be my Star, and Whoring my House, and Death I
defie thee. Thus sung Rosidore in the Urn --- But where and when, with
my Fops Wives, be quick, thou know'st my appointment with this
unknown, and the Minute's precious.   135
TOUR. Why, I have contriv'd you the sweetest Wight in the World, if
you dare.
NEM. Dare, and in a Woman's Cause! why, I have no drop of Blood
about me, but must out in their service, and what matter is't which way?
TOUR. Know Poltrot's Lady has inform'd me, how St. Andre walks in   140
his sleep, and that her Husband last night attempted to Cuckold him,
that she watch'd and overheard the whole matter, but Poltrot cou'd not
find the door before St. Andre return'd; she doubts not but he will try
agen to night --- Now if you can nick the time when Poltrot rises, and
steal to her, ten to one but she'll be glad to be reveng'd ---   145
NEM. Or she wou'd not have told thee the bus'ness --- There wants but
speaking with her, taking her by the hand, and 'tis a bargain ---

Enter Celia, Elianor Mask'd. Poltrot, St. Andre following.

TOUR. Step, step aside, they are upon the hunt for you, and their Hus-
bands have 'em in the wind; stand by a while to observe, and I'll turn
you loose upon 'em ---   *[Exeunt Tournon, Nemours.* *   150
ST. A. Ha, Tournon! by my Honour a Prize, let's board 'em.
POL. Be not too desperate my little Frigat, for I am, that I am, a
Furious Man of Honour.
CEL. Now Heav'n defend us, what will you give us a Broad-side?
ELI. Lord! how I dread the Guns of the lower Tire.   155

----

136 sweetest Night C_{2-3}.
 *   [Exeunt Tournon, Nemours.]; om. Q_{1+}. The words "stand by a
     while to observe" may indicate that Tournon and Nemours retire
     backstage, but the later direction (lines 214-15) implies that Ne-
     mours leaves.

ST. A. Such notable Marks-men too, we never miss hitting between Wind and Water.

CEL. I'll warrant they carry Chain-shot; Pray Heav'n they do not split us Sister!

POL. Yield then, yield quickly, or no Mercy, we have been so shatter'd to day already by two she Pirates, that we are grown desperate. 160

ELI. But what alas have we done, that you shou'd turn your Revenge upon us poor harmless Innocents, that never wrong'd you, never saw you before?

CEL. If you shou'd deal unkindly with us, 'twou'd break our Hearts, 165 for we are the gentlest things.

ST. A. And we will use you so gently, so kindly, like little Birds, you shall never repent the loss of your Liberty.

ELI. I'll warrant Sister they'll put us in a Cage, or tye us by the Legs.

POL. No, upon the word of a Man of Honour, your Legs shall be at 170 liberty.

CEL. What will you Pinnion our Wings then, and let us hop up and down the House?

ST. A. Not in the House where we live, pretty Soul, for there's two ravenous Sow-Cats will Eat you. 175

ELI. Your Wives you mean.

POL. Something like, two Melancholy things that sit purring in the Chimney-corner, and to exercise their spite, kill Crickets.

CEL. Oh! for God-sake keep us from your Wives.

ST. A. I'll warrant thee little Rosamond, safe from my jealous Elianor --- 180

POL. And if any Wife in Europe dares but touch a hair of thee, I say not much, but that Wife were better be a Widow.

ELI. But are your Wives handsome and well qualited? for whatever you say to us, when you have had your will you'll home at night, and for my part I cry All or none. 185

POL. And All thou shalt have dear Rogue, never fear my Wife's Beauty or good Nature, they are things to her like Saints and Angels, which she believes never were nor never will be --- She's a Bason of Water against Lechery, and looks so sharp whenever I see her, like Vinegar she makes me sweat. 190

ST. A. And mine's so fulsome, that a Goat with the help of Cantharides wou'd not touch her.

CEL. But then for their Qualities ---

ST. A. Such Scolds, like Thunder they turn all the Drink in the Cellar.

POL. Such Niggards, they eat Kitchin-stuff and Candles ends --- Once 195 indeed raving mad my Wife seem'd Prodigal, for a Rat having eat his way through an old Cheese, she baited a Trap for him with a piece of pareing --- But having caught him, by the Lord she eat him up without mercy tail and all.

ELI. Are they not ev'n with us Sister? 200

ST. A. 'Tis hop'd tho, the Hangman will take 'em off of our hands, for they are shroadly suspected for Witches, mine noints her self ev'ry

---

186 Wife's] C_{2-3}; Wive's Q_1-C_1.
202 shrewdly Q_{2+}.

Night, sets a Broom-staff in the Chimny, and op'ns the Window, for
what purpose but to fly?

POL. Gad, and my Wife has Tets in the wrong place, she's warted all   205
over like a pumpl'd Orange.

CEL. Yet sure, Gentlemen, you told these Hags another story once,
and made as deep Protestations to them as you do to us?

ST. A. Never by this hand, the Salt Souls fell in Lust with us, and
haul'd us to Matrimony like Bears to the Stake.   210

POL. Where they set a long black thing upon us, that cry'd Have and
Hold.

ELI. Put the question they had been Handsome, brought you great
Portions, were Pleasant and Airy and willing to humour you.

Enter Nemours with the Vidam.

NEM. Nay then I can hold no longer: Z'death, there's it Madam,   215
Willing! That Willingness spoils all my Dear, my Hony, my Jewel,
it Palls the Appetite like Sack at Meals --- Give me the smart disdainful
she, that like brisk Champaign or spritely Burgundy, makes me smack
my Lips after she's down, and long for t'other Glass.

ST. A. Nay if your Grace come in there's no dallying, I'll make sure   220
of one.

POL. Nay, and for my part I am resolv'd to secure another; come
Madam no striving, for I am like a Lion, when I lay hold, if the Body
come not willingly, I pull a whole Limb away ---

NEM. Yes Madam, he speaks truth, take it on my word who am a   225
rational Creature, he is a great furious wild Beast.

CEL. Pray Heav'n he be not a horned Beast, is the Monster married?

VID. Yes Ladies, they are both married.

ELI. Married! For Heav'n sake, Gentlemen, save us from the Cattle.

POL. Why, what is the Breeze in your Tails? Z'death Ladies we'll not   230
eat you.

CEL. Say you so? But we'll not trust you, I am sure you both look
hungrily.

VID. It may be their Wives use 'em unkindly.

ELI. And the poor good-natur'd things take it to heart.   235

CEL. I swear 'tis pity, they have both promising looks.

NEM. Proceed, sweet Souls, we'll defend you to death, spare 'em not.

ELI. Or it may be we mistake all this while, and their pitiful looks are
caused by loving too much.

VID. Right Madam, a little too Uxorious; Ha, Ha!   240

ST. A. Now have not I one word to say, but stand to endure all Jerks
like a School-boy with my Shirt up.

POL. I'll have one fling at 'em tho' I dye for't; why Ladies you'll over-
shoot your selves at this rate --- Must we only be the Butts to bear all
your Railery? methinks you might spend one Arrow at random, and   245
take off that Daw that Chatters so near you --- Gad, and I think I paid
'em there ---

CEL. Butts and Daw! Let me never Laugh agen, if they be not Witty
too --- Why, you pleasant Rogues, Z'life I cou'd Kiss 'em if they did not

stink of Matrimony.   250

    ST. A. Mum, Mum, Mum. Did not I tell you 'twas a madness to
speak to 'em?

    ELI. They envy my Friend too here, this pleasant Companion.

    CEL. This dear agreeable Person.

    NEM. Ay, Damme Madam, the Rogues envy us ---   255

    ELI. What a gentle Aspect?

    CEL. How proper and Airy?

    ELI. See, here's Blood in this Face.

    VID. Pure Blood, Madam, at your Service.

    CEL. Will you walk dear Sir? give me your hand ---   260

    ELI. And me yours ---

    NEM. Come you dear ravishing Rogues --- Your Servant Mr. Butts ---

    VID. Gentle Mr. Butts ---

    ELI. Adieu sweet Mr. Butts.

    CEL. Witty Mr. Butts, Ha, Ha, Ha!   [Exeunt Nem. Vid. Cel. Eli.   265

    ST. A. Well, I'll to a Dutchess.

    POL. Lord! thou art always so high-flown --- Hast thou never a cast
Countess for me ---

    ST. A. Come along to the Ball and thou shalt see, the Duke of Nemours
is the Gallant to night --- and Treats at his Palace, because 'tis the King's 270
Birth-day --- Let me see, what new Fancy for the Masquerade? Oh! I
have it --- Because the Town is much taken with Fortune-telling, I'll act
the Dumb Man, the Highlander that made such a noise, and thou shalt
be my Interpreter --- Come along, and as we go I'll instruct thee in the
Signs.   275

    POL. Dear Rogue, let's practise a little before we stir --- As what sign
for Lechery, because we may Nick our Wives.

    ST. A. Why thus, that's a glanting squeez'd Eye -- or thus -- for a
moist Hand, or thus, for a Whore in a corner, or thus for downright
Cuckolding.   280

    POL. Well, I swear this will be rare sport, and so my damn'd Spouse,
I am resolv'd to tickle her with a squeez'd Eye and a moist Hand; and a
Whore in a corner till she confess her self guilty of downright
Cuckoldom; then in revenge for her last Impudence, Sue for a Divorce:

          And holding to her Face the flying Label,   285
          Call her in open Court the Whore of Babel.   [Exeunt.

Scene II.

The Prince and Princess of Cleve.

    PRINCE C. Madam, the King commands me to attend
His Daughter into Spain, and further adds,
Because no Princess Rivals you in Fame,
You will oblige the Court in going with me.

PRINCESS C. My Lord, I am prepar'd, and leave the Court   5
With such a Joy as wou'd admit no bounds ---
 PRINCE C. As wou'd admit no bounds! and why? because
It takes you from the Charms which you wou'd shun:
This is a Vertue of such height indeed,
As none but you can boast nor I deplore.   10
But Madam, Rumor says the King intends
To joyn another with me.
 PRINCESS C.   Who my Lord?
 PRINCE C. 'Twas thought at first the Chevalier de Guise.
 PRINCESS C. He is your Friend, nor cou'd the King choose better.
 PRINCE C. I say at first 'twas thought the Duke of Guise ---   15
But I was since instructed by the Queen,
That Honour's fixt upon the Duke Nemours.
 PRINCESS C. Nemours my Lord?
 PRINCE C.   Most certain.
 PRINCESS C.   For what reason?
 PRINCE C. Because I mov'd the Dauphin Queen to gain him.
 PRINCESS C. 'Twas rashly done, against your Interest mov'd.   20
 PRINCE C. Perhaps 'tis not too late yet to supplant him.
 PRINCESS C. Do't then, be quick, Nemours will share your Honours,
Eclipse your Glory ---
 PRINCE C. Ha -- I must confess
The Soldiers love him, and he bears the Palm
Already from the Marshals of the Field.   25
 PRINCESS C. And in the Court he's call'd the Rising Star:
You see each night at every Entertainment
Where he moves, what Troops of Beauties follow;
How the Queens praise him, and all Eyes admire him ---
 PRINCE C. Ha! Chartres ---
 PRINCESS C.   Ah! my Lord -- what have I done?   30
 PRINCE C. Nothing, my Chartres, but admire Nemours!
O Heaven and Earth! and if I had but Patience
To hear you out, how had you lost your self
On that Eternal Object of your Love?
No Madam, no, 'tis false, 'tis not Nemours: 35
'Twas my invention to find out the truth,
Your trouble has convinc'd me 'tis Nemours:
Which curst Discovery in another Woman,
I shou'd have made by her too eager Joy.
Why speak you Not? you're shock'd with your own Vertue,   40
The resolution of your Justice aws you,
Which cannot, dares not give it self the Lye.
 PRINCESS C. My Lord, my Love, my Life; Alas my Cleve! [Kneels.*
O pity me! I know not what to answer,
I'm mortally asham'd, I'm on the Rack;   45

---

35 'tis not]; 'tis no Q_{1+}.
 * [Kneels.]; <u>om</u>. Q_{1+}.

But spare this humble Passion --- Take me with you,
Where I may never see a Man again.
    PRINCE C. O Rise my Chartres! Rise if possible;
I'll force thee to be mine in spite of Fate:
My constant Martyrdom and deathless Kindness,   50
My more than Mortal Patience in these Sufferings,
Shall poize his noblest Qualities, O Heav'n!
No fear, my Chartres, tho these Sorrows fall,
That I suspect thy Glory; thou hast strength
To curb this Passion in, that else may end us.   55
All that I ask thee, is to bend thy Heart.
    PRINCESS C. I'll break it.
    PRINCE C.   Turn it from Nemours, Nemours ---
But Oh! that name presents thy danger greater,
Look to thy Honour then, and look to mine;
I ask it as thy Lover and thy Husband;   60
I beg it as a Man whose Life depends
Upon thy Breath, that offers thee a Heart
All bleeding with the Wounds of Mortal Love,
All hack'd and gash'd, and stab'd and mangled o'er;
And yet a Heart so true, in spite of pain,   65
As ne'er yet lov'd, nor ever shall again.   [Exit Prince C.

                   Enter Irene.

    IREN. Ha! Madam, speak, how is it with your Heart?
    PRINCESS C. As with a timorous Slave, condemn'd to Torments,
That still cries out, he cannot, will not bear it,
And yet bears on.
    IREN.   Ah, Madam! I wou'd speak,   70
If you cou'd bear the dreadful News I bring.
    PRINCESS C. Alas! thou canst not add to grief like mine.
    IREN. May I demand then, if you have not told
The Secret to your Husband?
    PRINCESS C.   Ha! Irene ---
Why dost thou ask?   75
    IREN. Because but now --- Tournon, a Lady of the Queens,
Told me 'tis blaz'd at Court --- Nemours confessed
He is belov'd by one of such nice Virtue,
That fearing --- lest the Passion might betray her,
She own'd, confess'd, and told it to her Husband.   80
    PRINCESS C. Death and Despair --- But does Nemours avow it?
    IREN. He own'd it to the Vidam, who agen
Told it to Madam Tournon --- she to others;
'Tis true, Nemours told not the Ladies name,
Nor wou'd confess himself to be the Party,   85

---

48 Q_{1+} use punctuation as above. It is possible that the author
    intended the following: Rise; if possible /I'll ...

But yet the Court in general does believe it.

    PRINCESS C. I am undone -- my Fame is lost for ever,
And death, Irene, must be my remedy;
'Tis true, indeed, I laid my Bosom op'n,
I shew'd my Heart to that ungrateful Cleve,   90
Who since in dangerous search of him I love,
To the eternal ruine of my Honour,
Has trusted a third Person --- But away
I hear his tread, and am resolv'd to tax him.

Enter Prince C. *

Ah! Sir, what have you done? if you must kill me,   95
Are there not Daggers Pois'n --- But the Jealous
Are Cruel still, and thoughtful in Revenge;
And single Death's too little; must your will
Of knowing Names, my duty durst not tell you,
Oblige you to betray me to another;   100
So to divulge the Secret of my Soul,
That the whole Court must know it?
    PRINCE C.   Ha! know what?
Know my Dishonour, have you told it then?
    PRINCESS C. No 'tis your self, 'tis you reveal'd it Sir,
To gain a Confident for more Discovery,   105
A Lady of the Queen's just now declar'd it,
To your eternal Shame you have divulg'd it,
She had it from the Vidam, Sir, of Chartres,
And he from the Duke Nemours ---
    PRINCE C.   Nemours ---
How, Madam, said you -- What Nemours -- Nemours!   110
Does Nemours know you love him? Hell and Furies!
And that I know it too, and not revenge it!
    PRINCESS C. That's yet to seek, he will not own himself
To be concern'd, he offers not at names,
But yet 'tis found, 'tis known, believ'd by all,   115
He cannot hold it, 'twill be shortly posted,
That Cleve your Wife's that curst dishonour'd She
You told him of ---
    PRINCE C.   Is't possible I told him?
Peace, Peace, and if it lyes in Humane Power
To reason calmly, tell me Murd'ress, tell me,   120
Compose that Face of flush'd Hypocrisie,
And answer to a truth --- Was it my Interest
To speak of this? was I not rather ty'd
To wish it buried in the Grave in Hell!
Whence it might never rise to blot my Honour ---   125
But you have seen him, by my hopes of Heaven,

---

    * Prince] Q$_{2+}$; Princess Q$_1$.

You have met and interchang'd your secret Souls;
On that Complotted; since I bore so tamely
Your first Confession, I shou'd bear the latter.
    PRINCESS C. Believe it if you please ---
    PRINCE C.   I must believe it ---   130
This last Proceeding has unmask'd your Soul,
He sees you ev'ry hour, and knows you love him:
Nay, for your greater freedom, you have joyn'd
To make this loath'd detested Cleve your Stale.
Ha --- I believ'd you might o'ercome this passion,   135
So well you knew to Charm me with the show
Of seeming Vertue, 'till I lost my Reason.
    PRINCESS C. 'Tis likely Sir, it was but seeming Vertue,
And you did ill to judge so kindly of me ---
I was mistaken too in that Confession,   140
Because I thought that you wou'd do me Justice:
    PRINCE C. You were mistaken when you thought I wou'd,
Sure you forgot that I was desperate,
Sentenc'd and doom'd by Fate, or rather damn'd
To love you to my Grave -- And cou'd I bear   145
A Rival, what and when I was your Husband,
And when you own'd your passion to my face,
Confess'd you lov'd me much -- But lov'd him more:
Ha -- Is not this enough to make me mad?
    PRINCESS C. You have the power to set all right agen,   150
Why do you not end me?
    PRINCE C.   No, I'll end my self,
My Thoughts are grown too violent for my Reason.
By this last usage, Oh! Thou hast undone me;
I know not what -- This ought not to be thine ---
I have offended and wou'd Sue for pardon;   155
But yet I blush, the Treason is too gross;
After that most unnatural Confession,
I wonder now that I have liv'd so long:
Confess and then divulge, make me your Bawd ---
It Scents too far, the God of Love flies wide,   160
He gets the Wind, and stops the Nose at this;
No more -- Farewel -- False Chartres, False Nemours,
False World, False All, since Chartres is not true!
But you your Wish with lov'd Nemours shall have,
And shortly see your Husband in the Grave.   [Exit.   165

    PRINCESS C. <u>Sola.</u>
False World, False Cleve, False Chartres, False Nemours,
Farewel to all, a long and last Farewel:
From all Converse, to Deserts let me fly,
And in some gloomy Cave forgotten lye.

----

152 Thoughts] Q_{2+}; Toughts Q_1.

My Bower at Noon the shade of some old Trees   170
With whistl'ing Winds t'endulge my pomp of ease,
And lulling Murmurs rowl'd from neighb'ring Seas.
Where I may sometimes hasten to the Shore,
And to the Rocks and Waves my Loss deplore:
Where when I feel my hour of Fate draws on,   175
Lest the false World shou'd claim a parting groan;
My Mothers Ghost may rise to fix my mind,
And leave no thought of tenderness behind.

      End of A C T   III.

Act IV. Scene I.

Musick, Songs, Maskers, &c.

Nemours with Musick, Celia*.

NEM. He has confess'd to me he intends to Cuckold St. Andre
when he walks in his sleep---Therefore if Love shou'd inspire
me to nick the opportunity, I hope you will not bar the door which your
Husband op'ns---
    CEL. Ingrateful Monster--- 5
    NEM. Ingrateful, that's certain, and it lyes in your power to make
him a Monster.
    CEL. I dare not.
    NEM. What?
    CEL. Trust you. 10
    NEM. Nay then I am sure thou wilt, let me but in to shew the power
you have over me.
    CEL. As how my Lord?
    NEM. Why, when I have thee in my Arms, by Heav'n I'll quit my
Joys at thy desire--- 15
    CEL. That will indeed be a perfect tryal of your love; come then
through the Garden back-stairs, and when you see the Candle put out,
thrust op'n the door.
    NEM. By Heav'n I'll eat thy hand---Thou dear sweet Seducer, how
it fires my Fancy to steal into a Garden, to rustle through the Trees, 20
to stumble up a narrow pair of back stairs, to whisper through the
hole of the door, to kiss it open, and fall into thy Arms with a flood
of Joy---
    CEL. Farewel, the company comes, I must leave you a while, to
engage with my Husband, you'll fall asleep before the hour--- 25
    NEM. If I do, the very transport of Imagination shall carry me in my
sleep to thy Bed, and I'll wake in the Act.   [Exit Celia.
So there's one in the Fernbrake, and if she stir till Morning I have lost
my aim; but now, why what have we here? a Hugonot Whore by this
light---Have I? For the forward brisk she that promis'd me the Ball 30
Assignation, that said, there was nothing like slipping out of the crowd
into a corner, breathing short an Ejaculation, and returning as if we
came from Church---Let me see, I'll put on my Mask, fling my
Cloak over my shoulder, and view 'em as they pass, not thou nor thou---

---

   * Celia] ; Lady Poltrot Q_{1+}. <u>Changed</u> <u>to</u> Celia <u>and</u> Cel. <u>in</u>
<u>following</u> <u>speech</u> <u>tags</u> <u>for</u> <u>regularization.</u>
  30 brisk] Q_2; brisk, Q_1, C_{1-3}.

Enter Tournon in the Habit of a Hugonot. *

TOUR. Ah thou unclean Person, have I hunted thee there like a Hart   35
from the Mountains to the Vallies, and thou would'st not be found;
verily thou hast been amongst the Daughters of the Philistines--Nay, if
you are Innocent, stand before me, and reply to the words of my mouth---
NEM. I shall truly---
TOUR. Say then---Hast thou not defil'd thy self with any Dalilah,   40
since last you felt upon my Neck and loved much?
NEM. Nay verily---
TOUR. Have you not overheated your Body with adulterate Wines?
have you not been at a Play, nor touch'd Fruit after the leud Orange
Women?   45
NEM. I am unpolluted.
TOUR. And yet methinks there is not the same colour in your cheeks,
nor does the Spirit dance in your Eye as formerly, why do you not
approach me?   [Unmasking.
NEM. Tournon turn'd Heretick! why thou dear Raskal, this is such a   50
new Frolick, that though I am engag'd as deep as Damnation to another,
thou shalt not 'scape me.   [Marg. claps him on the shoulder.
MARG. I love a Man that keeps the Commandment of his word.
NEM. And I a Woman that breaks hers with her Husband, yet loves
her Neighbour as her self---I wou'd fain be in private with you.   55
MARG. And I with you, because I am resolv'd never to see you more.
NEM. Never to see me more? the reason?
MARG. Because I hate you.
NEM. And yet I believe you love me too, because you are precise to
the Minute.   60
MARG. True, yet I hate you justly, heartily and maliciously---
NEM. By Gad, and I'll love the as heartily, justly and maliciously,
as thou canst love me for thy blood; come away Riddle, and I'll unfold
thee.   [Exeunt.

Poltrot, St. Andre disguis'd with Elianor, Celia, ** coming
up to 'em ---

ELI. But is it true indeed, that your Friend can tell all the actions   65
of our Life past, present, and to come, yet cannot speak one word?
POL. O he's infallible! why what did you never hear of your second-

---

41 fell upon my neck C_3.
 * Nemours sees Tournon before she enters. See line 29.
45 Orange-Woman? Q_{2+}.
52 In Q_{1+} no provision for Marguerite's entrance is made; she
    apparently comes forward with the maskers at this point.
56, 58, 61 MARG.]; CEL. Q_{1+}.
57 reason?] C_{1+}; reason. Q_{1-2}.
** Celia]; Lady Poltrot Q_{1+}. Changed for regularization.
65 But it is true Q_2.

sight men, your Dumb High-landers that tell Fortunes? why you wou'd
think the Devil in Hell were in him, he speaks so exactly.

    ELI. I thought you had said he was Dumb?   70

    POL. Right, but I am his Interpreter, and when the fit comes on him,
he blows through me like a Trunk, and strait I become his speaking
Trumpet.

    CEL. Pray, Sir, may not I have my Fortune told me too?

    POL. Ay--and there were a thousand of you, he will run you 'em over   75
like the Chriss cross-row, and never miss a tittle; he shall tell ye his
name that cry'd God bless you when you sneez'd last, tell you when you
wink'd last, when and where you scratch'd last, and where you sate o'
Saturday---

    ELI. Pray let him tell us then, for we are Sisters, our Tempers and   80
Conditions, whither married or unmarried, with all the Impertinences
thereunto belonging---

    POL. I'll speak to him--Son of the Sun, and Emperor of the Stars---

    ST. A. Ha, Ha---

    POL. Look ye, look ye, he's pleas'd to tell you, but you must go near   85
him, for he must look in your hand, touch your Face, Breasts, and
where-ever else he pleases.

                [St. A. Makes Horns with both his hands,
                puts his Finger in his Mouth and Laughs*.

    POL. In nomine domine Bomine. I protest I am confounded; well
Ladies, I cou'd not have thought it had been in you, but 'tis certainly
true, and I must out with it; first he says, you are both married, you   90
are both Libidinous beyond example, and your Husbands are the greatest
Cornutors in Christendom---

    ELI. ⎫
    CEL. ⎭ Indeed.

    POL. Ay indeed, indeed and indeed---He says you are a couple of
Messalina's, and the Stews cannot satisfie you; he says your thoughts are   95
swell'd with a Carnosity; nay, you have the Green Sickness of the
Soul, which runs upon nothing but neighing Stallions, churning Boars,
and bellowing Bulls---

    CEL. O! I confess, I confess---But for Heav'n sake, dear Sir---
Let it not take Air, for then we are both undone.   100

    ELI. O! Undone, undone Sir, if our Husbands shou'd know it, for
they are a couple of the Jealousest, troublesome, impertinent Cuckolds
alive.

    POL. Alack! Alack -- O Jezabel! but I will have my Eunuchs fling her
from the Window, and the Dogs shall eat her.   105

    CEL. But, pray Sir, ask him how many times---

    POL. What, how many times you have Cuckolded 'em?

---

69 so exactly.] Q$_{2+}$; exactly. Q$_1$.

* <u>Printed in</u> Q$_1$ <u>as a speech of</u> St. A.; <u>corrected</u> Q$_{2+}$.

97 neighing] C$_3$; weighing Q$_1$-C$_2$.

ELI. Spare our Modesty, you make the Blood so flush in our Faces.

POL. But by Jove I'll let it out, I'll hold her by the Muzzle, and stick
her like a Pig--- 110

CEL. Will you speak to him Sir?

POL. See, he understands you without it, he says your Iniquities are
innumerable, your Fornications like the hairs of your head, and your
Adulteries like the Sands on the Sea shore; that you are all Fish downward; that Lot's Wife is fresh to you, and that when you were little 115
Girls of Seven, you were so wanton, your Mothers ty'd your hands behind
you---

ELI. All this we confess to be true, but we confess too, if Fate had
found out any sort of Tools, but those leaden Rogues our Husbands.

CEL. Whose Wits are as dull as their Appetites--- 120

ELI. Mine such a Utensil, as is not fit to wedge a Block.

CEL. Nor mine the Beetle to drive him---

ST. A. Nay then 'tis time to uncase and be reveng'd.

POL. Heark you Strumpet---

ELI. ⎱ Ha, Ha, Ha, are you not fitted finely, 125
CEL. ⎰ ---You must turn Fortune-tellers, must you?

ELI. And think we cou'd not know you?

CEL. Well Gentlemen, shall homely Beck go down with you at last?

POL. But didst thou know me then indeed?

CEL. As if that sweet Voice of yours cou'd be disguis'd in any shape. 130

POL. Nay, I confess I have a whirl in my Voice, a warble that is parti-
cular---

ELI. And what say you Sir, shall musty Wife come into Grace agen?

ST. A. She shall, and, here's my hand on't, all Friends Nell, and when
I leave thee agen, may I be Cuckold in earnest. 135

POL. Certain as I live, all this proceeded from his Lady, my dreaming
Cuckold Wife cou'd never think on't; well, I am resolv'd this very night,
when he Rambles in his sleep, to watch him, slip to his Wife and say nothing. Hey! Come, come, where are these Dancers, a little Diversion
and then for Bed. 140

Dance.

TOUR. <u>to Eli.</u> I have lock'd the Vidam in your Closet, who will be
sure to watch your Husbands rising, therefore be not surpriz'd---
[Exit Tournon.

ST. A. Come, well let's away to bed.

ELI. And what then?

ST. A. Nay, Gad that I can't tell, for what with Dancing, Singing, 145
Fencing, and my last Dutchess, I am very Drowzy.

POL. And so am I, perhaps our Wives have giv'n us Opium, lest we
shou'd disturb 'em in the night.

ELI. Don't these Men deserve to be fitted?

CEL. They do, and Fortune grant they may--Hear us, O! hear us 150

---

124 POL.]; L. P. Q$_{1+}$.

good Heav'n, for we pray heartily.

                      [Exeunt as Nemours and Marguerite enter.

    NEM. Was ever Man so blest with such possession,
Thou Ebbing, Flowing, Ravishing, Racking Joy;
A Skin so white and soft, and yielding Mould
Lets not the Fingers stay upon the dint,   155
But from the beauteous Dimples slips 'em down
To pleasures that must be without a name.
Yet Hands, and Arms, and Breasts we may remember,
And that which I so love, no smelling Art,
But sweet by nature, as just peeping Violets,   160
Or op'ning Buds.
    MARG.   Than you do love me ?
    NEM. O! I cou'd dye methinks this very hour,
But for the luscious hopes of thousand more,
And all like these, yet when I must go out,
Let it be thus, with beauty laughing by me,   165
Songs, Lutes and Canopeis, while I Sacrifice
To thee the last dear ebbing drop of Love.
But show me now that face.
    MARG. No, you dissemble, you say the same thing to every one you
meet; I thought once indeed to have fixt my Heart upon you, but I'm   170
off agen, and am resolv'd you shall never see me.
    NEM. You dally, come, by all the kindness past.
    MARG. Swear then.
    NEM. What ?
    MARG. Never to touch your dear Domestick she,   175
That lives in Shades to all the World but me.
Do you guess I know you now ?
    NEM. I do, and swear, but are these equal Terms, that you shall never
touch a Man but me ?
    MARG. I will--But how can you convince me ? Oaths with you   180
Libertines of Honour are to little purpose.
    NEM. But this must satisfie thee, there is more pleasure in thee after
Enjoyment, than in her and all Womankind before it; thou hast Inspiration,
Extasie, and Transport, all these bewitching Joys that make men mad---
    MARG. Unmasking] And thou Villany, Treachery, Perjury, all those   185
Monstrous, Diabolical Arts, that seduce Young Virgins from their Innocent
homes, to set 'em on the High-way to Hell and Damnation.
    NEM. Ha! Ha! my Marguerite, is't possible ?
    MARG. Call me not yours, nor think of me agen,
I am convinc'd you're Traytors all alike,   190
And from this hour renounce you---
Not but Ill be reveng'd,

  159-161 Q2+ as follows:
          And that which I love, no smelling Art,
          But sweet nature, as just peeping Violets, or op'ning Buds.
  191-92 Printed as one line in Q2+.

Yes, I will try the Joys of Life like you,
But not with Men of Quality, you Devils of Honour;
No, I will satisfie   195
My Pride, Disdain, Rage and Revenge more safely,
By all the Powers of Heav'n and Earth I will;
I'll change my loving lying Tinsel Lord,
For an obedient wholsome drudging Fool.
  NEM. Why this will make the matter easie to both,   200
Take you your Ramble Madam, and I'll take mine.
But is't possible for one of your nice tast
To Bed a Fool?
  MARG. To choose, to choose my Lord
A Fool, now by my Will and pride of Heart,
There's Freedom, Fancy and Creation in't,   205
He truckles to the Frown, and cries forgive me;
Besides the moulding of him without blushing;
And what wou'd Woman more, now view the other
Your Man of Sense, that vaunts despotick Pow'r,
That reels precisely home at break of day,   210
Thunders the House, brains half the Family,
Cries, where's my Whore, what will she Stew till Doomsday?
When she appears, and kindly goes to help him,
Roars out a Shop, a walking-shop of Scents,
Flavours of Physick, and the clammy Bath,   215
The stench of Orange-flow'rs, the Devil Pulvilio;
These, these, he cries, are the Blest Husband's Joys!
  NEM. I swear most natural and unaffected--Ha! Ha---
  MARG. But if he chance to use her civilly,
Take heed, there's covert malice in his Smiles,   220
Millions to one the Villain has been Whoreing,
And comes to try Experiments on her,
Besides a thousand under Plots and Crosses,
Prescribing silence still where-e'er he comes,
No chat, he cries, of Colours Points or Fashions.   225
  NEM. Preach on Divine, Ha, Ha---
  MARG. Let me not hear you ask my sickly Lady,
Whither she found Obstructions at the Waters.
  NEM. Fye, that's Obscene---
  MARG. Thus Damns the Affectation of our Prattle,   230
And Swears he'll Gag the Clack, or what is worse.
  NEM. Nay, hold---
  MARG.   Send for the new found Lock---
  NEM.   What Mad---
  MARG. Do Villain, Traytor---
Contrive this Mischief, if thou canst, for me,

195-96 <u>Printed</u> <u>as</u> <u>one</u> <u>line</u> <u>in</u> Q$_{2+}$.
202-03 <u>Printed</u> <u>as</u> <u>one</u> <u>line</u> <u>in</u> Q$_{2+}$.
 214 Roars out, Q$_{2+}$

Send thou the Padlock, but I'll find the Key.   [Exit.   235
   NEM. Whir goes the Partridge on the purring Wing--
Yet when I see my time I must recall her,
For she has admirable things in her, such as if I gain not, the Princess
of Cleve may fix me to her, without nauseating the Vice of Constancy--
Ha! Bellamore.   240

Enter Bellamore.

What News, my Dear, Ha--Hast thou found her? Speak.
   BELL. I have.
   NEM.   Where, how, when and by what means?
   BELL. After I had enquir'd after the Prince's Health,
I ask'd a Woman of his Lady, who told me,
She was retir'd into the great Bower in the Garden.   245
   NEM. The very place where first I saw and lov'd her,
When after I had sav'd the Prince's Life,
He brought me late one ev'ning to the view,
There Love and Friendship first began;
My Love remains and Friendship, as   250
Much as Man can have for his Cuckold.
Nay, I know not that Man upon Earth I love so well, or cou'd take so
much from, as this hopeful Prince of Cleve---Didst thou see her in
the Garden---
   BELL. My Lord, I did, where she appear'd like her that gave Acteon   255
Horns, with all her Nimphs about her, busie in tyeing Knots which she
took from Baskets of Ribbons that they brought her; and methought she
ti'd and unti'd 'em so prettily, as if she had been at Cross Questions, or
knew not what she did, her Face, her Neck, and Arms quite bare---
   NEM. No more, if I live I'll see her to night, for the Heroick Vein   260
comes upon me--Death and the Devil, what shall become of the back-stair
Lady then---Heark thee Bellamore, take this Key, dost thou hear Rogue?
go to St. Andre's House, through the Garden up the back-stairs,
push open the door and be blest. Hell! can't I be in two places at once?
Heark thee, give her this, and this, and this, and when thou bitest her   265
with a parting blow, sigh out Nemours.
   BELL. I'll do't---

Enter the Prince of Cleve.

   NEM. Go to Tournon for the rest, she'll instruct thee in the Manage-
ment: Away.   [Exit Bell.
Ha! he comes up but slowly, yet he sees me,   270
Perhaps he's Jealous, why then I'm jealous too;
Hypocrisie and Softness, with all the Arts of Woman,
Tip my Tongue.
   PRINCE C. I come, my Lord, to ask you if you love me.

272-73 <u>Printed</u> <u>as</u> <u>one</u> <u>line</u> <u>in</u> Q2.

NEM.   Love thee, my Cleve, by Heav'n, e'er yet I saw thee,   275
Thus were my Prayers still offer'd to the Fates,
If I must choose a Friend, grant me ye Powers
The Man I love may seize my Heart at once;
Guide him the perfect temper of your selves,
With ev'ry manly Grace and shining Vertue;   280
Add yet the bloom of Beauty to his Youth,
That I may make a Mistress of him too.
    PRINCE C.   O Heav'n!
    NEM.   That at first view our Souls may kindle,
And like two Tapers kindly mix their Beams;
I knelt and pray'd, and wept for such a Blessing,   285
And they return'd me more than I cou'd ask,
All that was Good or Great or Just in thee.
    PRINCE C.   You say you love me, I must make the proof,
For you have brought it to a doubt---
    NEM.   In what?
    PRINCE C.   In this, you have not giv'n me all your Heart,   290
You Muse of late, ev'n on my Bridal day,
I saw you sit with a too thoughtful brow,
You sigh'd and hung your Head upon your Hand:
Nay in the midst of Laughter---
You started, blush'd and cry'd 'twas wond'rous well,   295
And yet you knew not what--Speak like a Friend,
What is the cause my Lord?
    NEM. Shall I deal plainly with you? I'm not well.
    PRINCE C. I do believe it, how hap'ned the Distemper?
    NEM. It is too deep to search, nor can I tell you.   300
    PRINCE C.   Then you're no Friend.
Shou'd Cleve thus answer to Nemours, I cannot:
Say rather that you will not trust a Man
You do not love.
    NEM.   By Heav'n I do.
    PRINCE C.   By Heav'n you do? Yet 'tis too deep to search   305
For such a shallow Friend.
    NEM.   Of all Mankind
You ought not---
    PRINCE C.   Nay, the rest.
    NEM.   It is not fit,
Be satisfied, I'll bear it to my Grave
Whate'er it be.
    PRINCE C.   You are in Love my Lord,
And if you do not Swear--But where's the need?   310

282-83 In Q$_2$ "O Heav'n!" is printed as part of line 282.
300 Printed as two lines in Q$_1$.
308-09 These lines appear as follows in Q$_{2+}$:
      Be satisfied I'll bear it to my Grave whate'er it be.
      PRINCE C. You are in Love my Lord,

You start, you change, you are another Man,
You blush, you're all constraint, you turn away.
    NEM. Why take it then; 'tis true, I am in Love,
In Torture, Racks, in all the Hells of Love,
Of hopeless, restless and eternal Love.   315
    PRINCE C. Her name my Lord.
    NEM.   Her name my Lord to you?
    PRINCE C. To me Confusion, Plagues and Death upon me,
Why not to me? And wherefore did you say,
Of all Mankind I ought not--There you stopt,
But wou'd have said--To pry into this business---   320
Yet speak to ease the Troubles of my Soul,
By all our Friendship, by the Life thou gav'st me,
I do conjure thee, thunder in my Ears,
'Tis Chartres that thou lov'st, Chartres my Wife.
    NEM. Your Wife, my Lord?   325
    PRINCE C. My Wife, my Lord, and I must have you own it.
    NEM. I will not tell you Sir, who 'tis I love,
Yet think me not so base, were it your Wife,
That all the subtlest Wit of Earth or Hell
Shou'd make me vent a Secret of that nature   330
To any Man on Earth, much less to you.
    PRINCE C. Yet you cou'd basely tell it to the Vidam,
And he to all the Court---But I waste time,
By all the boiling Venom of my Passion,
I'll make you own it e'er we part---Dispatch,   335
Say thou hast Whor'd my Wife, Damnation on me,
Pronounce me Cuckold.
    NEM. But then I give my self the Lye,
Who told you just before, I wou'd not speak,
Tho I had done it---Which I swear I have not---   340
Beside, I fear you are going Mad.
    PRINCE C. Draw then and make it up,
For if thou dost not own what I demand,
What you both know and have complotted on me,
Tho neither will confess, I swear agen,   345
That one of us must fall.
    NEM.   Then take my Life.
    PRINCE C. I will, by Heav'n, if thou refuse me Justice;
Draw then, for if thou dost not I will kill thee,
And tell my Wife thou basely didst confess
Thy Guilt at last, in hopes to save thy Life.   350
    NEM. That is a blast indeed, that Honour shrinks at,
Therefore I draw, but Oh! be witness Heav'n,
With such a trembling Hand and bleeding Heart,
As if I were to fight against my Father.
Therefore I beg thee by the name of Friend,   355
Which once with half this Suit wou'd have dissolv'd thee;
I beg thee, gentle Cleve, to hold thy hand.
    PRINCE C. I'm Deaf as Death, that calls for one or both.

[Cleve is disarm'd, Nemours gives him his Sword agen.

    NEM.   Then give it me, I arm thy hand agen,
Against my Heart, against this Heart that loves thee;   360
Thrust then, for by the Blood that bears my Life,
Thou shalt not know the name of her I love;
Not but I swear upon the point of Death,
Your Wife's as clear from me, as Heav'n first made her.
    PRINCE C. No more my Lord, you've giv'n me twice my Life.   365
    NEM. Are you not hurt ?
    PRINCE C.   Alass, 'tis not so well,
I have no Wound but that which Honour makes,
And yet there's something cold upon my Heart,
I hope 'tis Death, and I shall shortly pay you,
With Chartres love, for you deserve her better.   370
    NEM. No Sir, you shall not, you shall live my Lord,
And long enjoy your beauteous vertuoқs Bride;
You shall, Dear Prince, why are you then so cold?
    PRINCE C. I cannot speak---
But thus, and thus, there's something rises here.   375
    NEM. I'll wait you home, nay, shake these drops away,
And hang upon my arm---
    PRINCE C.   I will do any thing,
So you will promise never to upbraid me.
    NEM. I swear I will not.
    PRINCE C.   But will you love me too
As formerly?
    NEM.   I swear far more than ever.   380
    PRINCE C. Thou know'st my Nature soft, yet Oh such Love!
Such Love as mine, and injur'd as I thought,
Wou'd spleen the Gaul-less Turtle, wou'd it not?
    NEM. It wou'd by Heav'n--You make a Woman of me.   [Weeping.
    PRINCE C. Why, any thing thou sayst to humour me,   385
Yet it is kind, and I must love these Tears,
I hope my Heart will break, and then we're ev'n;
Yet if this cruel Love thy Cleve shou'd kill,
Remember after Death thou lov'st me still.   [Exeunt.

374-375 <u>Printed as one line in</u> Q$_{2+}$.
379-380 <u>These lines are printed as follows in</u> Q$_{2+}$:
        NEM. I swear I will not.
        PRINCE C. But will you love me too as formerly?
        NEM. I swear far more than ever.

Scene II.

Enter Tournon with the Vidam.

TOUR. So let that corner be your Post, and as soon as ever you see
St. Andre come stalking in his Dream, slip to his Lady, and when you
have agreed upon the Writings, I'll be ready to bring you off with a
Witness---

VID. Thou Dear obliging---   5

TOUR. No more o' that; away, mark but how easily those that are
gifted with Discretion bring things about; in the name of Goodness let
Men and Women have their Risks, but still be careful of the Main--
Here's a hot-headed Lord goes mad for a prating Girl, Treats her, Presents her, Flames for her, Dies for her, till the Fool complies for pure   10
Love, and when the bus'ness fails, is forc'd to live at last by the love
of his Footmen; but she that makes a firm Bargain, is commonly thought
a great Soul, for my Lord having consider'd on't, thinks her a Person of
depth, and so resolves to have it out of her---But why do I talk so
my self, when there's something to do, certainly I shou'd have made a   15
rare Speaker in a Parliament of Women, or a notable Head to a Female
Jury, when his Lordship gravely puts the question, whither it be Satis
or Non Satis or Nunquam Satis, and we bring it in Ignoramus---
Ha! but who comes here? I must attend for Bellamore.

Enter Poltrot, Celia over-hearing.

POL. My Wife and I went to Bed together, and I'll warrant full she   20
was of Expectation, so white and clean, and much inclin'd to laugh, and
lay at her full length, as who wou'd say come eat me.

CEL. Said she so sweet Sir?

POL. Not a bit by the Lord, not I, not I---

CEL. Alas! nice Gentleman.   25

POL. A Farmer wou'd say this was barbarously done, because he loves
Beef---But I have Plover in reserve---Ha! St. Andre, heark, I
hear him bustle, O Lord! how my heart goes pit a pat! nay, I dreamt
last night I was Gelt---

Enter St. Andre in his sleep.

'Tis he, 'tis he, by the twilight I see him-- [The Vidam goes in---   30
Ay, now the politick head goes, it shall be branch'd by and by--What
was that stop for, there's neither Gate nor Stile in your way; now by
that sudden stretch, he seems as if he wou'd take a jump, or practice on
the High rope; O your humble Servant Sir, I'll but do a little bus'ness

31 shall branch Q$_2$+.

for you, and be with you agen. Nay, look you Sir, I have as many   35
Bobs as Democritus when he cry'd Poor Jack--There's more Pride in a
Puritans Band, short Hair, and Cap pinch'd, than under a Kings Crown.
Poor Jack, Citizens, Citizens, look to your Wives, the Courtiers
come, look to 'em, they'll do 'em, look to 'em, they'll do 'em, Poor
Jack---   [Exit. *   40
    ST. A. Ha! Ha! You'll tickle me to death---Nay, prithee Pen--
Your Mistress will hear us--Thou art the wantonest Rogue---

                    Enter Tournon with Bellamore.

    TOUR. Madam.
    CEL. Here's.
    TOUR. Here's a Thief I took in your Chamber---   45
    BELL. Ah Madam! retire for a moment, and I'll make you the whole
Confession.
    CEL. Confess and you know what follows, however I am resolv'd to
hear what you can say for your self.   [Exeunt.
    ST. A. Nay Pish, nay Fie sweet heart---   50
But I'll kiss you if I can;
I did not take you for to be
Such a kind of a Man.

                    Re-enter Poltrot.

But I'll go call my Mother as loud as I can cry,
Why Mother, Mother, Mother, out upon you, Fye.   55
    POL. O Lord! O Lord! I had like to have trod upon a Serpent that
wou'd have bit me to death. I went to take up the Cloths as gently as
I cou'd for my Life, when a great huge hoarse Voice flew in my face,
with Damme you Son of a Whore, I'll cut your Throat; you may guess
I withdrew, for o' my Conscience the Fright had almost made me un-   60
clean; but I'll to my own Spouse, and if the Lord be pleas'd to bring
me off safe this bout, I'll never, never go a Cuckold-making agen while
my eyes are open.   [Exit.
    ST. A. Heark, my Wife's coming up Stairs---Help up with my
Breeches; so, so smooth the Bed---What damn'd Luck's this---   65
So, fall a rubbing the Room agen---Heark you Wife, Celia has been
upon the hunt for you all this day, she's below in the Garden, go, go,
we'll kiss when you come back---Now Sirrah, now you Rogue, she's
gone, come, come, lose not your opportunity, I'll keep on my Breeches
for fear---Ay? No, no, not upon the Bed, Pish, against the back of   70
this Chair--Won't it--How can you tell--Try--I'll buy thee a new
Gown, and a Fan, and a lac'd Petticoat, and pay thee double Wages;
O! thou dear pretty soft sweet wriggling Rogue, what wou'dst thou

---

    * [Exit.] ; <u>om</u>. Q$_{1+}$.
    41 prithee Pen-- <u>om</u>. Q$_{2+}$.
    50-3 <u>Printed</u> <u>as</u> <u>two</u> <u>lines</u> <u>in</u> Q$_{2+}$.

dodge me, Gad but I'll have thee, Gad but I'll catch thee; Ay, and
have at thee agen and agen.   [Exit. Re-enter Poltrot.   75
  POL. Was ever Man of Honour thus unfortunately met with? I went
into my Chamber and trod as softly as a half-starv'd Mouse, for fear of
waking my Cat, when coming close to my Bed-side, methought it rock'd
to and fro like a great Cradle, and the Cloaths heav'd as if some Beast
lay blowing there---But the Beast was by the Bed-side it seems--Yes, I   80
am, and who can help it, as very a Cornuto as e'er was grafted---
I heard my beloved Wife too--The Plagues of Egypt on her---Speak
so lovingly and angrily together---Nay, Prithee my Dear--Nay, now
you are tiresome--I shall be asham'd to look you in the face agen! Why,
how will she look upon me then? O Lord--O Lord--What shall I do?   85
shall I stand thus like a Cuckoldly Son of a Whore, with my Horns in
my Pocket and not be reveng'd---

                    Enter St. Andre.

But here comes as very a Cuckold as my self, I am resolv'd to wake
him, and we'll fall upon 'em together---Allo, St. Andre, St. Andre.
  ST. A. Ti--ti 'tis im--im--im--possible I-I-I shou'd be the Man,   90
Fo-Fo-For I cannot speak a plain word.
  POL. You're a Cuckold, a Cuckold, a Cuckold.
  ST. A. Why lo-lo-look you, I said it co-co-cou'd not be me, for Sir,
I all the World knows I am no Cu-Cu-Cu-ckold.
  POL. Wake, wake, I say, or I'll shake the bones out of your Body,   95
your Horns are a growing, your Bed is a going, your Heifer's a Plowing.
  ST. A. Why, let her Plo-Plo-Plow on, if the Se-Se-Seed be well
Sown, we shall have a good Cro-Crop---
  POL. Worse and worse, why then I will roar out directly and raise the
Neighbours--Help! Ho, Help! Murder! Murder! Fire! Fire! Fire!   100
Cuckoldom! Cuckoldom! Thieves! Murder! Rapes! Cuckoldom!

           Enter the Vidam and Bellamore. The Vidam comes up
        to Poltrot, shoots off a Pistol, St. Andre and Poltrot fall down
      together--Tournon enters with the Ladies---Tournon leads off the Vidam
                          and Bellamore.

  CEL. Thieves! Thieves! Ho! Jaques! Pedro--Thoma--
  ELI. Thieves! Thieves---Wake! wake! my Lord.
  ST. A. Waking] Why, what a Devil's the matter? where am I?
  ELI. O! you'll never leave this ill habit of walking in your sleep--   105
'Tis a mercy we had not all been Murder'd---You went down in your
Shirt Sir, open'd the door, and let in Rogues that had like to have cut
all our Throats--But for the future I am resolv'd to tye you to me with
the Bed-cord, rather than endure this---
  ST. A. Where's Poltrot?   110
  CEL. Murder'd Sir, here! here! here! one of the Villains discharg'd
a Pistol just in his Belly---
  ST. A. Shot in the Guts! Lord bless us! here Thom. a light! light!
light! shot in the Guts say you---

POL. Oh! Oh--Lower, lower, lower--Feel, feel, search me, lower,   115
lower---

ST. A. Cold hereabouts--Let's bear him to his Bed, and send for a
Surgeon---

POL. Softly! softly! softly--Come not near me Crocodil; Oh! Oh---

ST. A. Unhappy Chance, no where but just in the Guts?   120

POL. Yes, yes, yes, in the Head too, in the Head Man, in the Head:
Nay, and let me tell you, you had best search your own, but bear me off
or I shall Swoon, I feel something trickle, trickle in my Breeches;
Oh! Oh! Oh!   [Exeunt.

Scene III.

Enter Nemours, Pedro list'ning.

NEM. Alass! Poor Prince, I protest the Violence of his Passion has
cast him in a Fever, he dies of it---And how then? shall I Marry the
Princess of Cleve, or stick to Marguerite as we are? for 'tis most
certain she has rare things in her, which I found by my last Experiment,
and I love her more than ever, almost to Jealousie; besides Tournon   5
tells me, the Dauphin begins to buz about her agen, and who knows
but in this heat of hers, as she says, she will hang her self out to
sale, but he may nick the time and buy her---I like not that---
No, I'll throw boldly, clear the Table if I can, if not, 'tis but at
last forswearing Play, shake off my new acquaintance, and be easie with   10
my reserve---Heark, I am just upon the Bower Musick---

PED. I have hitherto obey'd my Master's order, but I'm resolv'd to
dog him till he's lodg'd---

NEM. Now do I know the Precise will call me damn'd Rogue for wrong-
ing my Friend, especially such a soft sweet natur'd Friend as this gentle   15
Prince---Verily I say they lye in their Throats, were the gravest of
'em in my condition, and thought it shou'd never be known, they wou'd
rouze up the Spirit, cast the dapper Cloak, leave off their humming and
haing, and fall too like a Man of Honour.   [Exit.

PED. I'll face him till he enters the Bower, and then call my   20
Lord.   [Exit.

Scene the Bower, Lights, Song.*

The Princess of Cleve, Irene.

Song.
Lovely Selina, Innocent and Free

---

* Apparently the scene draws so as to reveal the bower in the back
of the stage.

From all the dangerous Arts of Love,
Thus in a Melancholy Grove
Enjoy'd the sweetness of her Privacy,   25
Till th'envious Gods designing to undo her,
Dispatcht the Swain, not unlike them, to wo her:
It was not long e'er the design did take,
A gentle Youth born to perswade,
Deceiv'd the too too easie Maid;   30
Her Scrip and Garlands soon she did forsake,
And rashly told the Secrets of her Heart,
Which the fond Man would ever more impart.
False Florimel, Joy of my Heart, said she,
'Tis hard to Love and Love in vain,   35
To Love and not be Lov'd again,
And why shou'd Love and Prudence disagree?
Pity ye Powers that sit at ease above:
If e'er you knew what 'tis to be in Love.
   PRINCESS C. Alas! Irene, I do believe Nemours   40
The Man thou represents him; yet, Oh! Heav'n,
And Oh my Heart! in spite of my resolves,
Spite of those matchless Virtues of my Husband,
I love the Man my reason bids me hate:
Yet grant me some few hours ye Saints to live,   45
That I may try what Innocence so arm'd
As mine, with vows can do in such a cause!
The War's begun, the War of Love and Vertue,
And I am fixt to conquer or to dye.
   IREN. Your Fate is hard, and since you honour'd me   50
With the important Secret of your Life,
I've labour'd for the Remedy of Love.
   PRINCESS C. I must to Death own thee my better Angel,
Thou know'st the struglings of my wounded Soul,
Hast seen me strive against this lawless Passion,   55
Till I have lain like Slaves upon the Rack,
My Veins half burst, my weary Eye-balls fixt,
My Brows all cover'd with big drops of Sweat,
Which strangling Grief wrung from my tortur'd Brain.
   IREN. Alass I weep to see you thus agen.   60
   PRINCESS C. Thou hast heard me curse the hour, when first I saw
The fatal charming Face of lov'd Nemours,
Hast heard the Death-bed Counsel of my Mother.
Yet what can this avail, spite of my Soul
The Nightly Warnings from her dreadful Shroud?   65
I love Nemours, I languish for Nemours,
And when I think to banish him my Breast,
My Heart rebels, I feel a gorgeing pain
That choaks me up, tremblings from Head to Foot;
A shog of Blood and Spirits, Mad-mens Fears,   70
Convulsions, gnawing Griefs and angry Tears.

Enter Nemours.

Ha! but behold--My Lord---
    NEM.   O! Pardon me,
Spare me a minute's space and I am gone.
    PRINCESS C. Is this a time Sir?
    NEM.   O! I must speak or dye.
    PRINCESS C. Dye then, e'er thus presume to violate   75
The Honour of your Friend, your own and mine---
    NEM. Yet hear me, and I swear by all things Sacred,
Never to see you more.
    PRINCESS C. Speak then---And keep your word.
    PRINCE C. [at a window]   Horrour and Death!
    NEM. Did you but know what 'tis to love like me,   80
Without a dawn of Bliss to dream all day,
To pass the night in broken sleeps away,
Toss'd in the restless tides of Hopes and Fears,
With Eyes for ever running o'er with Tears;
To leave my Couch, and fly to beds of Flow'rs,   85
T'invoke the Stars, to curse the dragging hours,
To talk like Mad-men to the Groves and Bow'rs.
Cou'd you know this, yet blame my tortur'd Love,
If thus it throws my Body at your Feet:
Oh! fly not hence;   90
Vouchsafe but just to view me in despair,
I ask not Love, but Pity from the Fair.
    PRINCESS C. O Heavens! inspire my Heart.
    NEM.   The Heavenly Powers
Accept the poorest Sacrifice we bring,
A Slave to them's as welcome as a King.   95
Behold a Slave that Glories in your Chains,
Ah! with some shew of Mercy view my Pains;
Your piercing Eyes have made their splendid way,
Where Lightning cou'd not pass---
Even through my Soul their pointed Lustre goes,   100
And Sacred Smart upon my Spirit throws;
Yet I your Wounds with as much Zeal desire,
As Sinners that wou'd pass to Bliss through Fire.
Yes, Madam, I must love you to my Death,
I'll sigh your name with my last gasp of Breath.   105

72-3 These lines are printed as follows in Q$_{2+}$:
    Ha! but behold-- My Lord--
    NEM. O Pardon me, spare me a minute's space and I am gone.
  79 In Q$_1$-C$_1$ this line is given to Prince C. without any stage direction.
    He is not on the stage, but presumably at a window, watching and
    overhearing. In C$_{2-3}$ this line is assigned to Princess C.
89-90 Printed as one line in Q$_{2+}$.

    PRINCESS C. No more, I have heard you Sir, as you desir'd,

            Enter the Prince of Cleve, Pedro. *

Reply not, but withdraw, if possible;
Fix to your word, and let us trust our Fates,
Be gon I charge you, speak not, but retire.   [Exit. Nem.
    PRINCE C. Excellent Woman, and Oh! matchless Friend,   110
Love, Friendship, Honour, Poison, Daggers, Death.   [Falls.
    PRINCESS C. O Heaven! Irene, help! help the Prince my Lord.
My Dearest Cleve, wake from this dream of Death,
And hear me speak---
    PRINCE C.   Curse on my Disposition,
That thus permits me bear the Wounds of Honour!   115
And Oh! thou foolish, gentle, love-sick Heart,
Why didst thou let my hand from stabbing both?
    PRINCESS C. Behold, 'tis yet my Lord within your Power
To give me Death---
    PRINCE C.   I do entreat thee leave me,
I'm bound for Death my self, and I wou'd make   120
My passage easie, if you wou'd permit me:
All that I ask thee for the Heart I gave thee;
And for the Life I love in thy behalf,
Is, that thou'dst leave me to my self a while,
And this poor honest Friend---
    PRINCESS C.   I wou'd obey you,   125
But cannot stir---I know, I know my Lord,
You think that I design'd to meet Nemours
This night, but by the Powers above I Swear.
    PRINCE C. O! do not Swear, for Chartres credit me,
There is a Power that can and will revenge;   130
Therefore dear Soul, for I must love thee still,
If thou wilt speak, confess, repent thy fault,
And thou, perhaps, may'st find a door of Mercy:
For me, by all my hopes of Heav'n, I swear
I freely now forgive thee---Oh! my Heart---   135
Pedro, thy arm, let me to bed---
    PRINCESS C. And do you then refuse my help?
    PRINCE C. In Honour Chartres, after such a Fall,
I ought not to permit that thou shou'dst touch me---
    PRINCESS C. But Sir, I will, your arm? I'll hold you all   140
Thus in the closest strictest dearest Clasps;
Nor shall you dye believing my Dishonor,

---

106 desir'd C_{1+}.
  * Pedro.]; <u>om.</u> Q_{1+}.
137 <u>Printed as one line in</u> Q_{2+}; <u>as follows in</u> Q_1:
    PRINCESS C. And do you then refuse
    My help?

I swear I knew not of Nemours his coming,
Nor had I spoke those words which yet were guiltless,
Had he not vow'd never to see me more: 145
By our first Meeting, by our Nuptial Joys,
By my dead Mother's Ghost, by your own Spirit;
Which Oh! I fear is taking leave for ever,
I swear that this is true ---
     PRINCE C.   I do believe thee;
Thou hast such Power, such Charms in those dear Lips,   150
As might perswade me that I am not dying.
Off Pedro, by my most untimely Fate
I swear -- I'm reconcil'd; and heark thee Cleve,
If thou dost Marry, Ha! I cannot speak,
Away to Bed, yet love my Memory ---   155
     PRINCESS C. To Bed, and must we part then?
     PRINCE C.   O! we must ---
Were I to live I shou'd not see thee more ---
But since I am dying, by this Kiss I beg thee,
Nay, I command thee part, be gone and leave me.
     PRINCESS C. I go, and leave this Farewel Prayer behind me.   160
For me, if all I've said be not most true,
True as thou think'st me False, all Curses on me!
The Whips of Conscience, and the Stings of Pleasure,
Soars and Distempers, Disappointments plague me;
May all my Life be one continu'd Torment,   165
And that more Racking than a Woman's Labour;
In meeting Death may my least Trouble be
As great as now my parting is with thee.   [Exeunt severally.

End of A C T IV.

---

160 leave thee this Q₂₊.

Act V. Scene I.

Poltrot, Bellamore.

BELL. Come, come, take her into Grace agen, 'twas but a slip.

POL. Take her into Grace agen? -- Why sure you wou'd have her bring me to that pass she did in England, when my Lord Hairbrain us'd to keep me in awe, stand biting my Lips, twisting my Hat, playing with my Thumbs while they were at it, and I durst not look behind me. 5

BELL. Meer Jealousie; you say your self you saw nothing.

POL. No Sir, I thank you, I had more care of my Throat; neither is this the first Fault; for once upon a time, a little while after we were Married, at London -- a Pox o' that Cuckolding Trojan Race; she was talking to me one day out of her Window more pleasantly than ordinary -- 10 And acted with her Head and Body wond'rous prettily -- Butting at me like a little Goat, while I butted at her agen. I being glad to find her in so good humour, what did I Sir, but stole away, and came softly up the back-stairs, thinking to cry Bo -- But Oh! Lord -- How was I Thunder-struck, to find my Lord Hairbrain there all in a Sweat --- 15 Kissing and Smacking, Puffing and Blowing so hard, you wou'd have sworn they had been at Hot-cockles ---

BELL. A little Familiar perhaps, things of Custom ---

POL. Ay Sir, Kiss my Wife and welcome, but for that Zeal in her shogging and Butting -- Noli me tangere I cry -- I am sure it ran so in 20 my Imagination, I have been Horn-mad ever since -- Therefore spare your pains, for I am resolute.

Enter Celia.

BELL. See where she comes my Lord -- But you are resolv'd you say -- However, let me advise you, have a care of making her desperate. [Exit.

POL. Desperate -- Damn her, Polluter of my Sheets -- Damn her. 25

CEL. Seek, not to shun me, for where'er you fly,
I'll follow -- hang upon thy knees and dye.
Poltrot, behold --- Ah! canst thou see me kneel,
And yet no Bowels of Compassion feel?
Why dost thou bluster by me like a Storm, 30
And ruffle into Frowns that Godlike Form?
Why dost thou turn away those Eyes of thine,
In which Love's Glory and his Conquests shine?

POL. What is this thing call'd Woman? she is worse
Than all Ingredients ram'd into a Curse. 35
Were she a Witch, a Bawd, a Noseless Whore,

---

26 CEL. Seek,]; Seek, Celia, Q_{1+}.
34-9 <u>Attributed</u> <u>to</u> <u>Celia</u> <u>in</u> Q_{2+}.

I cou'd forgive her, so she were no more:
But she's far worse, and will in time Forestall
The Devil, and be the Damning of us all.

CEL. Yet Honour bids you sink with her you call   40
So foul, whose Frailties you too sharply nam'd;
Like Adam you shou'd choose with her to fall,
And in meer Generosity be Damn'd.

POL. No, by thy self, and all alone be curst,
And by the Winds thy Venom dust be hurl'd;   45
For thou'rt a Serpent equal to the first,
And hast the will to Damn another World.

CEL. But am I not thy Wife? Let that attone ---

POL. My Dear Damn'd Wife, I do confess thou art
Flesh of my Flesh, and Bone too of my Bone,   50
Wou'd mine had all been broke when first thou wert.

CEL. Why then I'll cringe no longer, heark you Sir, leave off your
Swelling and Frowning, and awkward ambling, and tell me in fine,
whether you'll be reconcil'd or no, for I am resolv'd to stoop no longer
to an ungrateful Person.   55

POL. To your Husband, to your Head, to your Lord and Master, you
will not Goodey Bathsheba, but you cou'd stoop your Swines Flesh last
night you cou'd, to your Rank Bravado, that wou'd have struck his
Tusks in my Guts; he had you with a Beck, a Snort, nay, o' my Conscience thou wou'dst not give him time to speak, but hunch'd him on   60
the side like a full Acorn'd Boar, cry'd Oh! and mounted ---

CEL. Are you resolv'd then, never to take me into Grace agen for
one Slip?

POL. No, I'm the Son of a Carted Bawd if I do; a Slip do you call
it? what, when I heard the Bed crack with the Violence of my Cuckoldom! 65
No, I will ascend the Judge of my own Cause, proceed to Condemnation,
and banish thee for ever the Confines of our Benevolence ---

CEL. What here, before the Vidam here?

POL. Yes, Impudence, before the Vidam and the Duke Nemours; nay,
to thy eternal Confusion, I will post thee in the Market-place; but   70
first I'll find out St. Andre, and tell him the whole matter, that he
may know too, what a Ram his blessed Ewe has made him, and then ---

CEL. And then I'll have your Throat cut.

POL. Ha! Tygress, cut my Throat! why thou Shee Bear! thou Dam of
Lyons Whelps, thou Cormorant of Cormorants, why what wilt thou   75
devour me Horns and all?

CEL. He that miss'd your Guts in the dark, shall take better aim at
your Gullet by day-light; nay, to thy Terror of Heart be it known, thou
Monster of ill nature, if I wou'd have consented last night to have run his
Fortune, which is no small one, he wou'd have murder'd thee in thy Bed,   80
for I heard him speak these very words, Let him lye, In Mortuis -- & in
limbo Patrum -- Where I must have pray'd for that unthankful Soul, or
thou wou'dst have been Damn'd to all Eternity, dying suddenly and without
Repentance ---

POL. O Lord! O Lord! In Mortuis, & in limbo Patrum; what, to   85
be toss'd on burning Pitchforks for my Sins, why, what a Bloody-minded
Son of Belial is this?

CEL. In fine, since you will have the truth, he has long had a design
upon both our Bodies, to Ravish mine, and rip open yours.

POL. Why then he's a Cannibal; Lord! Lord! Lord! Lord! why   90
what pleasure can it be to any Man to rip me open? to Ravish thee
indeed, there's some Sense in that -- But there's none in ripping me open;
why this is such a brutish Cruelty ---

CEL. Rogue, and so I told him -- Therefore when he found that nothing
cou'd make me consent to your Murder, he Swore, and caught me by   95
the hair, if I stir'd, or made the least noise, he wou'd Murder us all,
set the House o' Fire, and so leave us to our selves ---

POL. And so thou wert forc'd to consent; why then by this Kiss, I
Swear from my Soul, which might have been Damn'd as thou sayst, but
for thee, I forgive thee -- And what was he that Cuckolded St. Andre,   100
such another Mephostophilus as this too?

CEL. O! my Dear, there are not such a pair of Fiends upon Earth
agen --- Why, they look upon't as a Favour to our Sex if they Ravish
a Woman, for you must know they were formerly Heads of the Banditti ---

POL. Well, and I must praise thy Discretion in Sacrificing thy Body,   105
for o' my Conscience, if they had seen this Smock-face of mine, I had
gone to pot too before my Execution.

CEL. They sent their Pages this Morning to know whether it was our
pleasure to have your Throats cut: But we answered 'em all was well,
and desir'd 'em as ever they hop'd to see us agen, to stir no further in   110
the matter.

POL. Mum, Mum, dear sweet Soul, secure my Life and thou shalt
command me for the future with as full a swing as thou canst desire,
only like those that use that exercise, let it be too and fro, sometimes
at home and sometimes abroad, and we'll be as merry as the day is long.   115

CEL. Be thou but true to me, and like the Indian Wives, I'll not
out-live thee ---

POL. And I'll Swear now, that was kindly said, as I hope for mercy,
but it makes me weep, what burn for me -- And shall I not return, I
will, I will, I will return when thou dost burn;   120

Enter St. Andre, Elianor.

Nay, when thy Body in the Fire appears,
My Ghost shall rise and quench it with his Tears.

ST. A. All Flesh is Grass, that's certain, we're all Mortal, the Court's
in Mourning for the Prince of Cleve, the Vidam of Chartres is extreamly
griev'd --- Heark you Poltrot, sure as I am alive he dy'd of Jealousie.   125
Well Nelle, for this last care of thine, I Swear to be constant to thy
Sheets, and as thou sayst, I think it will not be amiss to tye me to
thee now and then for fear of the worst -- Ha! Poltrot ---

POL. Ha! Bully, I heard your kind Expressions to your Nelle, and I'll
Swear I'll vie thee with who shall love most, for I'll Swear these daily   130
Examples make my hair stand an end --- Cut my Throat, and rip me open,
he shall Cuckold me all over first, like the Man in the Almanack, nay,

he shall Ravish her while I hold the door to my own deflow'ring.

[Exeunt. *

Scene II.

Tournon, Nemours.

NEM. Resolv'd never to see me more, and give up her Honour to
the Dauphin, that puling sniveling Prince, that looks as if he suck'd
still, or were always in a Milk Diet for the Sins of his Florentine
Mother.

TOUR. Bless me! you are jealous.   5

NEM. I confess it --- The last time I had her in Disguise, she made
such Discoveries as I shall never forget: Lose her I must not, no, I'll
lose a Limb first, therefore go tell her, tell her the Prince of Cleve's
Death has wrought my Conversion, I grow weary of my wild Courses,
repent of my Sins, am resolv'd to leave off Whoreing and marry his   10
Wife ---

TOUR. So the Town talks indeed.

NEM. The Town is as it always was and will be, a Talk, a Hum, a
Buz, and a great Lye --- Do as I bid thee, and tell her, just as you left
me, I was going to make my Court to the Princess upon her Husband's   15
Tomb, which is true too, I mean a Visit by the way of Consolation,
not but I knew it the only opportunity to catch a Woman in the undress
of her Soul; nay, I wou'd choose such a time for my life, and 'tis like
the rest of those starts, and one of the Secrets of their Nature --- Why
they melt, nay, in Plagues, Fire, Famine, War, or any great Calamity --   20
Mark it -- Let a man stand but right before 'em, and like hunted Hares
they run into his lap.

TOUR. But who's the Instrument to bring you to her?

NEM. Her Uncle the Vidam, she lies at his House immur'd in a dark
room, with her Husband's Image in her view, and so resolves, he says,   25
for Death. However I'll sound her in the ebb of her Soul, if my Boat
run aground 'tis but calling for Marguerite, and she'll weep a Tide that
shall set me afloat agen --- As thus, I'll lay the Dauphin in her dish,
nose her in the Tiptoe of her Pride, Railing, Lying, Laming, Hanging,
Drowning, Dying, and she comes about agen.   [Exit.   30

TOUR. Go thy ways Petronius, nay, if he were dying too, with his
Veins cut, he wou'd call for Wine, Fiddles and Whores, and laugh himself into the other World.

Enter La March.

Where's Marguerite?

---

* [Exeunt.]; <u>om.</u> Q₁₊.

LA M. She follows like a Wind, with swollen Cheeks, ruffled Hair,   35
and glareing Eyes, the Princess of Cleve has found her Fury, nor will she
yet believe it.

Scene III.

The Princess of Cleve, Irene in Mourning, Song,* as the
Princess kneels at the State.

I.

Weep all ye Nymphs, your Floods unbind,
    For Strephon's now no more;
Your Tresses spread before the Wind,
    And leave the hated Shore:
See, see, upon the craggy Rocks,   5
    Each Goddess stripp'd appears;
They beat their Breasts, and rend their Locks,
    And swell the Sea with Tears.

II.

The God of Love that fatal hour,
    When this poor Youth was born,   10
Had sworn by Styx to show his Power,
    He'd kill a Man e'er Morn':
For Strephon's Breast he arm'd his Dart,
    And watch'd him as he came;
He cry'd, and shot him through the Heart,   15
    Thy Blood shall quench my Flame.

III.

On Stella's Lap he laid his Head,
    And looking in her Eyes,
He cry'd, Remember when I'm dead,
    That I deserve the Prize: 20
Then down his Tears like Rivers ran,
    He sigh'd, You Love, 'tis true;
You love perhaps a better Man,
    But Ah! he loves not you.

Chorus.

Why should all things bow to Love,   25
Men below, and Gods above?
Why should all things bow to Love?

---

* This Song is printed on A3^r in Q$_1$, but is inserted at the proper place
in later editions.

> Death and Fate more awful move,
> Death below, and Fate above,
> Death below, and Fate above.   30
> Mortals, Mortals, try your skill,
> Seeking Good, or shunning Ill,
> Fate will be the burden still,
> Will be the burden still,
> Fate will be the burden still,   35
> Fate will be the burden still.

    PRINCESS C. Dead thou dear Lord -- Yet from thy Throne of Bliss,
If any thing on Earth be worth thy view,
Look down and hear me, hear my Sighs and Vows,
Till Death has made me cold, and Wax like thee: 40
Water shall be my Drink and Herbs my Food,
The Marble of my Chappel be my Bed;
The Altars Steps my Pillows, while all night
Stretch'd out, I groaning lye, upon the Floor,
Beat my swoll'n Breasts, and thy dear loss deplore.   45
    IREN. Ah! Madam, what a Life have you propos'd?
    PRINCESS C. Too little all for an Offence like mine;
Yet Death will shortly purge my dross away,
For Oh! Irene, where's the Joy? I find it here,
Yes, I shall dye without those violent means   50
That might have hazarded my Soul -- O Heaven ---
O thou that seest my Heart, and know'st my Terrors,
Wilt thou forgive those Crimes I cou'd not help,
And wou'd not hide?
    IREN.   Doubt not but your Account
Shall stand as fair in his Eternal Book,   55
As any Saints above ---
    PRINCESS C.   Take, take me then
From this bad World, quench these Rebellious thoughts;
For Oh! I have a pang, a longing wish
To see the Luckless Face of lov'd Nemours,
To gaze a while, and take one last Farewel,   60
Like one that is too loose a Limb -- 'Tis gone --
It was corrupt, a Gangreen to my Honour,
Yet I methinks wou'd view the bleeding part,
Shudder a little -- Weep -- and grudge at parting.
But by the Soul of my triumphant Saint,   65
I swear this longing is without a guilt,
Nor shall it ever be by my appointment.

----

48 Yet Death has made me cold, and wax like thee. Q_{2+}; obviously a
    repetition of line 40.
49 Joy?] Q_{2+}; Joy Q_1.
61 to lose Q_{2+}.

Enter Nemours.

IREN. But if he shou'd attempt this cruel visit,
How wou'd your Heart receive him?
PRINCESS C.   With such Temper,
So clear and calm in height of my Misfortune,   70
As thou thy self perhaps wou'dst wonder at.
IREN. Ha! but he's here ---
PRINCESS C.   Is't possible my Lord?
Has then my Uncle thus betray'd my Honour?
NEM. Start not, nor wonder Madam, but forgive
The Vidam who has thus entrap'd your Virtue,   75
To end a ling'ring Wretch -- That dies for Love ---
PRINCESS C. For Love, my Lord, is this a time for Love,
In Tears and Blacks, the Livery of Death?
But what's your hope, if I shou'd stay to hear you?
Ah! What can you expect from rigorous Vertue,   80
From Chastity as cold as Cleve himself?
You that are made, my Lord, for other Pleasures ---
NEM. Is this then the reward of all my Passion?
As if there cou'd be any Happiness
For this disconsolate despairing Wretch,   85
But in your Love alone?
PRINCESS C.   You're pleas'd my Lord
That I shou'd entertain you, and I will,
Before this dear Remembrancer of Cleve;
We'll talk of murder'd Love -- And you shall hear
From this abandon'd part of him that was,   90
How much you have been lov'd.
NEM.   Ha! Madam ---
PRINCESS C.   Yes,
Sighing I speak it Sir, you have inspir'd me
With something which I never felt before,
That pleas'd and pain'd the quicknings of first Love;
Nor fear'd him then, when with his Infant Beams,   95
He dawn'd upon my chill and senseless Blood.
But Oh! when he had reach'd his fierce Meridian,
How different was his form! that Angel Face,
With his short Rayes, shot to a glaring God.
I grew inflam'd, burnt inward, and the Breath   100
Of the grown Tyrant, parch'd my Heart to Ashes.
Nor need I blush to make you this Confession,
Because, my Lord, 'tis done without a Crime.
NEM. Because for this most blest discovery,
I am resolv'd to kneel an Age before you.   105
PRINCESS C. Rise, I conjure you, rise, I've told you nothing

---

91 "Yes" is printed as the first word of line 92 in Q_{2+}.
104 Because of Q_{2+}.

But what you knew, my Lord, too well before:
Not but I always vow'd to keep those Rules
My Duty shou'd prescribe.
    NEM.   Strike me not dead
With Duty's name, by Heav'n I Swear you're free   110
As Air, as Waters, Winds or open Wilds,
There is no Form of Obligation now;
Nay, let me say, for Duty: O forgive me,
'Tis utmost Duty now to keep that Love
You have confess'd for me.
    PRINCESS C.   'Tis Duty's Charge,   115
The voice of Honour and the cry of Love,
That I shou'd fly from Paris as a Pest,
That I shou'd wear these Rags of Life away
In Sunless Caves, in Dungeons of Despair,
Where I shou'd never think of Man agen.   120
But more particularly that of you,
For Reasons yet unknown.
    NEM.   Unknown they are,
And wou'd to Heav'n they might be ever so,
Since 'tis impossible they shou'd be just;
Nay, Madam, let me say the Ghost of Cleve ---   125
    PRINCESS C. Ah! Sir, how dare you mention that dear name,
That drains my Eyes, and cries to Heav'n for Blood.
Name it no more without the Consequence,
For 'tis but too too true, you were the Cause
Of Cleve's untimely Death, I Swear I think   130
No less than if you had stabb'd him through the Heart.
    NEM. O! Cruel Princess, but why shou'd I answer,
When thus you raise the shadow of a reason
To ruin me for ever? Is it a fault
To Love? Then blame not me; No, Madam, no,   135
But blame your self, who told it to your Husband;
But Oh! you wou'd not argue thus against me
If ever you had lov'd ---
You have deceiv'd your self and flatter'd me;
Why am I thrown else from the Glorious Height,   140
Snatch'd in a moment from my blissful State,
And hurl'd like Lightning by the hand of Fate?
    PRINCESS C. Be satisfi'd, my Lord, you are not flatter'd,
I have such Love for you, that Duties bar,
Wou'd prove too weak to hinder our Engagement.   145
But there is more.
    NEM.   More Fancy, more Chimera!
But let it come, I'll stand the stalking Nothing,
And when the bladder'd Air wou'd turn the Ballance,
I'll cast in Love substantial, pondrous Love,
Eternal Love, and hurl him to the Beam.   150
But speak, and if a Hell of Separation
Must part my Soul and Body, do not Rack me,

But let the Poyson steal into my Veins,
And Damn me mildly, Madam, as you can.
    PRINCESS C. Hear then, my bosom thought -- 'Tis the last time   155
I e'er shall see you, and 'tis a poor reward
For such a Love, yet, Sir, 'tis all I have,
And you must ask no more.
    NEM.   Be Witness, Heav'n,
Of my Obedience, I will ask her nothing.
    PRINCESS C. Know then, my Lord, you're free, and I am so   160
Free from the eternal Bond of Marriage ---
My Heart too is inclin'd by Love like yours,
Nor can I fear the censuring World shou'd blame us.
But now, my Lord, What Power on Earth can give
Security that Bond shall prove Eternal?   165
    NEM. Ha! Madam.
    PRINCESS C.   Silence, silence I command you;
No, no, Nemours. I know the World too well,
You have a Sense too nice for long Enjoyment,
Cleve was the Man that only cou'd love long:
Nor can I think his passion wou'd have lasted,   170
But that he found I cou'd have none for him.
'Tis Obstacle, Ascent, and Lets and Bars,
That whet the Appetite of Love and Glory;
These are the fuel for that fiery Passion,
But when the flashy stubble we remove,   175
The God goes out and there's an end of Love.
    NEM. Ah Madam! I'm not able to contain,
But must perforce break your commands to answer,
Once to be yours, is to be for ever yours,
Yours only, without thought of other Woman.   180
    PRINCESS C. Why this sounds well and natural till you're cloid,
But Oh! when once satiety has pall'd you,
You sicken at each view, and ev'ry glance
Betrays your guilty Soul, and says you loath her.
I know it, Sir, you have the well-bred cast   185
Of Gallantry and Parts to gain success;
And do but think when various Forms have charm'd you,
How I shou'd bear the cross returns of Love?
    NEM. Ah Madam! now I find you're prejudic'd
To blast my hopes.
    PRINCESS C.   'Tis Reason, all calm Reason;   190
Nature affirms no violent thing can last,
I know't, I see't, ev'ry new Face that came
Wou'd charm you from me -- Ha! and cou'd I Live

---

161 from] Q_{2+}; for Q_1.
182 once]; one Q_{1+}.
190 "To blast my hopes" printed as a part of line 189 in Q_{2+}.
193 Live]; Love Q_{1+}.

To see that Fatal day, and see you scorn me,
To hear the Ghost of Cleve each hour upbraid me;   195
No, 'tis impossible, with all my Passion,
Not to submit to these Almighty Reasons;
For this I brave your noblest Qualities,
I'll keep your Form at distance, curb my Soul,
Despair of Smiles and Tears, and Prayers and Oaths,   200
And all the Blandishments of Perjur'd Love:
I will, I must, I shall, nay, now I can,
Defie to Death the lovely Traytor Man.
    NEM. No. Madam, think not you shall carry't thus,
'Tis not allowable, 'tis past example,   205
'Tis most unnatural, unjust and monstrous;
And were the rest of Women thus resolv'd,
You wou'd destroy the purpose of Creation.
What, when I have the happiness to please,
When Heav'n and Earth combine to make us happy,   210
Will you defeat the aim of Destiny,
By most unparallel'd extreams of Vertue,
Which therefore take away its very Being?
    PRINCESS C. Away, I must not answer, but conjure you
Never to seek occasion more to see me;   215
Farewel --- 'Tis past.
    NEM.   I cannot let you go;
I'll follow on my Knees, and hold your Robe,
Till you have promis'd me that I shall see you,
To shew you how each day by slow degrees
I dye away: This you shall grant by Heav'n,   220
Or you shall see my Blood let out before you.
    PRINCESS C. Alas! Nemours, O Heav'n! why must it be,
That I shou'd charge you with the death of Cleve?
Alas! why met we not e'er I engag'd
To my dead Lord? And why did Fate divide us?   225
    NEM. Fate does not, No ---
'Tis you that cross both Fortune, Heav'n and Fate;
'Tis you obstruct my Bliss, 'tis you impose
Such Laws as neither Sense nor Vertue warrant.
    PRINCESS C. 'Tis true, my Lord, I offer much to duty,   230
Which but subsists in thought, therefore have patience,
Expect what time, with such a love as mine,
May work in your behalf; my Husband's death
So bleeding, fresh I see him in the Pangs;
Nay, look, methinks I see his Image rise.   235
And point an everlasting Separation;
Yet Oh! it shall not be without a Tear.
    NEM. O! stay.

---

202 nay, I can, Q_{2+}.
235 rise, C_{1+}.

PRINCESS C.   Let go, believe no other Man
Cou'd thus have wrought me, but your self, to Love ---
   NEM. Stay then.
   PRINCESS C.   I dare not -- Think I love you still ---   240
   NEM. I do -- But stay and speak it o'er agen ---
   PRINCESS C. Believe that I shall love you to my death.
   NEM. I will. But live and love me.
   PRINCESS C.   Off, I charge you.
Believe this parting wounds me like the Fate
Of Cleve or worse: Believe, but Oh! farewel ---   245
   NEM. Believe, but what? That last thought I implore.
   PRINCESS C. Believe that you shall never see me more.   [Exit.

Enter the Vidam.

   VID. Well, and how goes the Game? What, on the Knee, a gather'd
Brow, and a large dew upon it? Nay, than you are a looser.
   NEM. Didst thou see her pass?   250
   VID. I did -- she wrung me by the hand and sigh'd,
Then look'd back twice,
And totter'd on the threshold at the door.
   NEM. Believe that you shall never see me more -- she Lyes, I'll Wager
my State, I Bed her eighteen months three weeks hence, at half an hour   255
past two in the Morning.
   VID. Why Faith, and that's as exact as e'er an Astrologer of 'em all.
   NEM. Give me thy hand, Vidam, I know the Souls of
Women better than they know themselves;
I know the Ingredients just that make 'em up,   260
All to loose Grains, the subtlest volatile Atoms,
With the whole Mish-mash of their Composition.
Heark there without, the voice of Marguerite,
Now thou shalt see a Battle worth the gazing,
Mark but how easily my reason flings her,   265
And yet at last I'll swing into Friendship
Because I love her ---

Enter Bellamore.

   BELL. The Princess --- shall I stop her?
   NEM.   No, let her come,
With flying Colours, and with beat of Drum ---
Like the Fanatick, I'll but rub me down,   270
And then have at her, Vidam, stay you here ---
By Heav'n I'm jealous of this changeable Stuff,

---

238 "NEM. O! stay." <u>printed as part of line</u> 237 <u>in</u> Q$_1$.
249 You're a looser Q$_{2+}$.
251-53 <u>Printed as prose in</u> Q$_{2+}$.
266 swing her into Friendship C$_{2-3}$.

Therefore the hits will be the livelier o' both sides,
The Dauphin, but no more -- she comes, she comes.

Enter Marguerite pushing Bellamore.

MARG. Be gon, Villain, Devil, Fury, Monster of a Man.   275
NEM. But hear me but six words in private.

Enter Poltrot, Celia, St. Andre, Elianor.*

POL. And I swear by this lascivious bit of Beauty, I will cleave to
my Celia for Better for Worse, in Searge, Grogrum or Crape, though a
Queen shou'd come in my way in Beaten Gold ---
NEM. What then, Gentlemen, I perceive there have been Wars at home --- 280
POL. Not a Battle, my Lord, only a Charge, a Charge sounded or so.
NEM. What was it a Trumpet, or through a Horn Sir?
POL. A Horn Sir, a Horn Sir, no Sir, 'twas not a Horn Sir -- Only my
Celia was a little disdainful, but we are Friends agen Sir, and what then
Sir?   285
NEM. Come, come, all Friends, were Tournon here I wou'd forgive her,
a little Scorn in a Pretty Woman, so it be not too much affected, is a
Charm to new Friendship; therefore let each Man take his Fair one by
the hand, thus lay it to his Lips, and Swear a whole Life's Constancy ---
ST. A. As I will to my Nelle, though I haule Cats at Sea, or cry Small-   290
coal; and for him that upbraids her, I'll have more Bobs, than Democritus
when he cry'd Poor-Jack. There's more Pride in Diogenes, or under a
Puritan's Cap, than in a King's Crown.
NEM. For my part, the Death of the Prince of Cleve, upon second
thoughts, has so truly wrought a change in me, as nothing else but a   295
Miracle cou'd -- For first I see, and loath my Debaucheries -- Next, while I
am in Health, I am resolv'd to give satisfaction to all I have wrong'd;
and first to this Lady, whom I will make my Wife before all this Company e'er we part -- This, I hope, whenever I dye, will convince the
World of the Ingenuity of my Repentance, because I had the power to   300
go on.

He well Repents that will not Sin, yet can,
But Death-bed Sorrow rarely shews the Man.

End of ACT V.

---

    * St. Andre, Elianor.]; <u>om</u>. Q$_{1+}$.
282 thro' a Trumpet, or a Horn Sir? C$_{2-3}$.

THE EPILOGUE.

What is this Wit which Cowley cou'd not name?
The rare Inducement to a perfect Fame,
The Art of Nature curious in a Frame.
Is it a Whig, a Trimmer, or a Tory,
Or an Old Fop forgotten in the Story? 5
'Tis Honour veil'd in Honesty's Disguise,
Or Cesar like a Fencer in a Prize;
'Tis Pindar's Ramble, Nature in Misrule,
A Politician acted by a Fool.
'Tis all Variety that Arts can give, 10
The Danaid's filling of a Leakey Sieve:
The Valleys Sweets, and the distilling Spring,
The brimming Bacchus that the Muses bring,
To drink the Health of England's Glorious King.
A Statesman thoughtful for a Clown revil'd, 15
A Pestle and a Mortar for a Child.
'Tis a true Principle, but hardly shown,
An Artificial Sigh, a Virgins Groan,
When the first night her Lover layes her on.
'Tis like a Lass that Gads to gather May, 20
'Tis like the Comedy you have to day,
A Bulling Gallant in a wanton Play.

FINIS.

THEODOSIUS:

O R,

The Force of Love,

A

T R A G E D Y.

A C T E D   B Y

Their ROYAL HIGHNESSES Servants,

A T   T H E

Duke's Theatre.

Written by *N AT. LE E.*

W I T H   T H E
MUSICK betwixt the ACTS.

————*Nec minus periculum ex magna
Fama quam ex mala.* Tacit.

L O N D O N,
Printed for *R. Bentley* and *M. Magnes,* in *Ruſſel-ſtreet,*
near *Covent-garden.* 1 6 8 o.

THEODOSIUS: OR, THE FORCE OF LOVE, A TRAGEDY.

Introduction.

I Date and Stage History:

The exact date of the first presentation of THEODOSIUS is somewhat uncertain. Since the first quarto appeared in 1680, it seems likely that the play was produced in that year, and Nicoll gives the approximate date of September, 1680, for the first production, a date with which Van Lennep concurs. If, however, THE PRINCESS OF CLEVE was produced in August or September, 1680, this would make the two plays almost coincide; and if the production of the scurrilous PRINCESS OF CLEVE had only shortly preceded that of THEODOSIUS, Lee would hardly have remarked in his Dedication of the latter to the Duchess of Richmond: "All I can promise, Madam, and be able to perform, is That Your Grace shall never see a Play of mine that shall give offence to Modesty and Vertue." The date of September, 1680, therefore, is open to some question. It is possible that the play appeared earlier in that year.

Whatever the exact date may have been, the first production was a great success. Downes remarks:

All the Parts in't being perfectly perform'd, with several Entertainments of Singing; Compos'd by the Famous Master Mr. Henry Purcell, (being the first he e'er Compos'd for the Stage) made it a living and Gainful Play to the Company: The Court; especially the Ladies, by their daily charming presence, gave it great Encouragement. [1]

Lee himself remarks in his Dedication that the reception accorded to his latest drama was "more than I could well hope from so Censorious an Age." And he gallantly attributes its popularity with the court party to the influence of the Duchess of Richmond.

This popularity apparently continued. Charles Gildon included it among four plays of Lee which he said had "gain'd the several actors that have succeeded each other not less than fifty thousand pounds, and yet the author scarce got one hundred pounds a piece for his labour." [2] Throughout the eighteenth century it was a favorite stock piece, as can be seen from the following list of performances: L.I.F., March 11, 1717; D.L., April 23, 1722; C.G., March 16, 1738; D.L., Dec. 15, 1746, April 27, 1768, Oct. 25, 1770, Dec. 30, 1772, Dec. 3, 1773; C.G., April 22, 1775, Nov. 24, 1780, Feb. 23, 1786; D.L., Jan. 20, 1797. Its popularity extended even to America, and Odell records two performances of it in New York: Feb. 4, 1762, and May 24, 1773. [3] It was apparently produced at Williamsburg, Virginia, in 1752, [3a] and in Charleston, South Carolina, on March 29, 1764, and again on Feb. 19, 1774. Since plays normally ran three times a week in Charleston, each of these records probably indicates at least three performances. [3b]

II Sources:

Both the main plot and the subplot of THEODOSIUS are drawn from La Calprenède's PHARAMOND (1661) which had recently been translated into English by John Phillips in 1677. [4] The main plot of Varanes, Athenais, and Theodosius is founded on "The History of Varanez Prince of Persia" in Part I of PHARAMOND, and Lee follows his source fairly closely, with the exception of some five or six differences which were made either for dramatic unity or dramatic effect. For example, in PHARAMOND, Varanes' refusal to marry Athenais occurs in Athens, and it is after this refusal that she and her father come to Constantinople,

where they are converted to Christianity; Lee has the refusal occur in Constantinople for the sake of dramatic unity. Lee also differs from La Calprenède in
making Theodosius and Varanes old friends; in the romance they meet for the
first time when Varanes comes to Constantinople. Likewise Lee has Theodosius
first see Athenais in Persia, when she is bathing; here he falls in love with her,
though he does not know who she is. In the romance he meets her for the first
time in the apartments of his sister Pulcheria. The denouement of the play is
also different from that of the romance. In PHARAMOND, in the last scene between Athenais and Varanes, she does not show any affection for him; she willingly
marries Theodosius, and Varanes goes off after another lady named Rosamond;
when she also disdains him, he finally marries Princess Sydemiris. Naturally
Lee changed this outcome in order to turn the story into a tragedy and gain the
maximum emotional effect by having Athenais really in love with Varanes, and
making the play come to an end with the death of the two lovers.

The subplot of Marcian and Pulcheria is taken from "The History of Martian"
in Part II of PHARAMOND, but here Lee followed his source far less closely.
In the romance, Martian, a general, loves the Princess Pulcheria; she looks with
some favor upon his love in its early stages; but when he becomes more ardent,
she becomes more conscious of the difference between their social positions, and
banishes him from the court. Lee ennobles the character of Pulcheria, who banishes Marcian only as a test of his love, and never really carries the banishment
into effect. Lee also ennobles the character of Marcian, making him into another
Clytus, a stern example of old Roman virtue in contrast to the effeminacy of the
court.

Lee drew almost nothing from actual history. Historically, Athenais was
the daughter of an Athenian philosopher Leontius. After his death, the avarice
of her brothers drove her to Constantinople, where she sought refuge with the
Princess Pulcheria. The latter took her into favor, and decided to marry her to
Theodosius. She was baptized as Eudocia, was married to the emperor, and
lived happily thereafter. Her love affair with Varanes is mere fiction, and the
latter is a creation of La Calprenède. Marcian also appears in history; he did
marry Pulcheria, and proved a good ruler after the death of Theodosius; but the
marriage was largely a matter of state convenience, and the account of their love
affair as given by Lee is fictional. The only important detail that Lee drew from
history was the signing of Athenais' death warrant by the emperor; this incident
appears in Tillement's MEMOIRES ECCLESIASTIQUE, where, however, the warrant is for her enslavement, not her death.

Two plays on this same theme had appeared before Lee's time: Massinger's
tragi-comedy, THE EMPEROR OF THE EAST (1631) and Mairet's L'ATHENAIS
(1642). But Lee does not seem to have been indebted to either of these, or to
Corneille's PULCHERIE (1672), which deals with events after the death of Theodosius. It seems probable, however, that the scene in which Marcian upbraids
Theodosius (Act IV, ii) was suggested to Lee by a similar scene in Fletcher's
VALENTINIAN, in which Aëcius upbraids Valentinian. Langbaine's remark that
Lee followed Eusebius' HISTORIA ECCLESIASTICA is, as Resa remarks, with-
out foundation.

III Criticism:

Most critics have looked rather favorably upon Lee's THEODOSIUS. Genest
remarked: "...it is very unequally written, but with all its faults it is preferable

to the more correct and cold productions of modern authors ... in Theodosius Lee has very happily blended history with fiction."[5]   THE BIOGRAPHIA DRA-MATICA was far more enthusiastic: "It is Lee's master-piece. The passions are very finely touched in it, and the language is in many parts extremely beautiful"; the main plot is "uniform, noble and affecting"; but the minor plot is "trifling, and unconnected and unnecessary to the main plot of the play."[6] H. M. Sanders regarded THEODOSIUS as a play of pure pity worthy to rank with Otway's ORPHAN or with Ford's BROKEN HEART.[7] Van Lennep reflects very much the same opinion. He, too, condemns the subplot as "unconvincingly treated", and says that "it appears cold and artificial" in contrast to the "warmth and sincerity" of the main plot; but the play as a whole he regards as "one of Lee's finest tragedies and clearly superior to THE RIVAL QUEENS, its only rival in point of popularity."[8] The subplot has been praised, however, by Malcolm Elwin, who claims that "the parts played by Pulcheria, one of the finest portraits in Lee's gallery of women, and Marcian, are worthy of the plaudits of praise which were lavished upon the play for more than a century."[9] And Nicoll also found Pulcheria "one of the few really artistically-drawn women figures of Restoration tragedy, a character that inestimably raises in our eyes the worth of Lee as a dramatic poet."[10]

Probably the most notable characteristic of THEODOSIUS, in contrast to Lee's other plays, is its marked restraint: both in the use of language and the use of violence or bloodshed. Lee himself was apparently conscious of this quality in his play; for in his Dedication he speaks deprecatingly of the extravagance found in his earlier works: "It has been often observed against me, That I abound in ungovern'd Fancy; but I hope the World will pardon the Sallies of Youth." Certainly we do not find in THEODOSIUS the ranting which characterizes NERO and THE RIVAL QUEENS; nor do we find the violence and Jacobean delight in bloodshed which so strongly mark THE MASSACRE OF PARIS and CAESAR BORGIA. As Van Lennep has remarked, the dominant quality of THEODOSIUS is a "general tone of softness... which distinguishes it from all of Lee's other plays."[11] It was this softness and restraint which made the play so popular with the ladies at its first appearance and insured its continued popularity during the following century.

It is true that the play has some weakness of structure: especially in the poor connection between the main plot and the subplot. Yet, if the two plots are badly joined, they are well developed. Lee vastly improved upon La Calprenède in his handling of the story of Athenais. By making her actually in love with Varanes, and making Varanes and Theodosius boyhood friends, he gave the main plot a depth, intensity and emotional appeal which were lacking in the romance. All three of the main characters are well drawn, and display conflicting emotions. Athenais is not merely the beautiful, pale heroine of conventional heroic drama; nor are Varanes and Theodosius the conventional, boastful heroes. There may not be any great depth to these characters, but they are not without complexity and skillful shading.

The subplot, too, deserves the praise of Nicoll and Elwin. Marcian is a successful recreation of the old Roman warrior, similar to Ventidius and to Clytus; nor is he made "a whining, amorous slave", as Rochester complained that Lee had made Hannibal. Pulcheria also is an appealing character, showing that strength which appears so frequently in Lee's heroines.

Addison once remarked: "Among our modern English poets, there is none who was better turned for tragedy than Lee; if, instead of favouring the impetuosity of his genius, he had restrained it, and kept it within its proper bounds."[12] THEODOSIUS illustrates the justice of Addison's remark. The play may lack the strength of some of Lee's other dramas; but it also lacks the extravagance, the violence and the occasional repulsiveness; and it possesses a tenderness, warmth, and emotional appeal which is not found in his other plays. THEODOSIUS may not be the greatest of Lee's plays, but it is in many ways the most charming.

IV Text:

Editions compared:

Q_1	R. Bentley and M. Magnes,	1680
Q_2	R. Bentley and S. Magnes,	1684
Q_3	T. Chapman,	1692
Q_4	R. Bentley,	1697
Q_5	Rich. Wellington,	1708
C_1	R. Wellington,	1713
C_2	M. P. & Sam. Chapman,	1722
C_3	W. Feales ...,	1734
Resa	The Resa Edition, Berlin, 1904 (in LITTERAR-HISTORISCHE FORSCHUNGEN),	1904

As copy-text for this edition, the first quarto, 1680, has been followed. Five copies have been compared so as to determine what stop-press corrections were made. One of these copies is in the University of Kentucky Library, one is in the William Andrews Clark Library, one is in the Huntington Library, and two are in the Folger Shakespeare Library. Variants among these copies are recorded in the footnotes. The copies are designated in order as follows: Q_1(KU), Q_1(CLUC), Q_1(CSmH), Q_1(DFo 1), Q_1(DFo 2).[13]

The edition has the following collation:

4°; A-I^4 [K-L^1], 41 leaves, pp. [8] 1-62, [12].

[A1^r]: title-page; [A1^v] blank; A2^r: Epistle Dedicatory TO / HER GRACE / THE / DUTCHESS / OF / RICHMOND. / A2^v-3^v: running-title The Epistle Dedicatory.; A4^r: The PERSONS. The SCENE CONSTANTINOPLE.; A4^v: PROLOGUE.; B1^r: [double rule] head-title THEODOSIUS: / OR, THE / Force of Love. / [rule] / ACT I. SCENE I. and text; B1^v-I3^v: text. Running-title: THEODOSIUS; Or, The Force of Love.; I4^r: Epilogue.; I4^v: A Catalogue of some Plays Printed for R. Bentley / and M. Magnes, in Russel-street, near Co- / vent-Garden.[14]; [K1]: SONG after the First ACT.; [K2-3]: SONG after the Second ACT.; [K4] SONG after the Third ACT.; [L1] SONG after the Fourth ACT.

The first quarto was printed from a prompter's copy, as is evidenced by the prompter's directions left in the text. These directions were retained in all later quartos. Q_2 was obviously printed from Q_1, the text following it line for line; Q_3 was derived from Q_2, with some alteration of the punctuation; Q_4 follows Q_3; and Q_5 is a page for page, line for line reprint of Q_4.

A comparison of the five copies of Q_1 reveals no stop-press corrections, unless it be in outer forme C, where KU reads "depl re t y"; but where all other copies read correctly "deplore thy." The faulty reading here in the Kentucky quarto may be due to a failure of the type to ink properly or to the falling out of type. Apparently the collected editions follow Q_4 or Q_5, as is indicated by their repeating such an error as that in Act III, ii, 207. By and large the first quarto is well printed and presents few textual problems.

NATHANIEL LEES TRAUERSPIEL THEODOSIUS OR THE FORCE OF LOVE, edited by Fritz Resa (Berlin und Leipzig, 1904) and appearing in LITERARHIS-TORISCHE FORSCHUNGEN, is the only modern edition. It attempts to modernize the capitalization, but otherwise to retain the incidentals (with a few exceptions in punctuation) of the earlier editions. The effort is unfortunately not satisfactory. Punctuation is frequently changed for the worse. The notes record many variants in incidentals and yet fail to record substantive variants that would be of use in the reading. The song at the end of the third act is included; the songs for the ends of acts one and two are omitted. Obvious errors in stage directions, such as one in Act IV, ii, 316, are neither noted nor corrected. Yet the editor declares, p. 109, that he has based his text on that of the first quarto. In some instances, he appears to follow more closely later quartos. The edition is without explanatory notes. Altogether, the text is far from satisfactory.

TO HER GRACE

THE DUTCHESS OF

RICHMOND.

Madam,

The Reputation that this Play received on the Stage, some few Errors
excepted, was more than I could well hope from so Censorious an Age,
from whom I ask but so much necessary Praise as will serve, once or
twice a Year at most, to gain their good Company, and just keep me
alive.   5

> There is not now that Mankind that was then,
> When as the Sun and Man did seem to strive
> (Joynt-Tenants of the World) who should survive:
> When if a slow-pac'd Star had stol'n away
> From the Observers marking, he might stay   10
> Two or three hundred years to see't agen,
> And then make up his Observation plain.   Dr. Donn.

For, 'tis impossible in our limited Time (and I bring his Opinion
to back my own, who is without comparison the best Writer of the Age) to
present our Judges a Poem half so perfect as we cou'd make it. I must   15
acknowledge, Madam, with all humility, I ought to have taken more time
and more pains in this Tragedy, because it is dedicated to Your Grace,
who being the best Judge, (and therefore can when You please make us
tremble) yet with exceeding Mercy have pardon'd the defects of THEODO-
SIUS, and given it Your entire Approbation. My Genius, Madam, was   20
Your Favourite when the Poet was unknown, and openly receiv'd Your
Smiles before I had the Honour to pay Your Grace the most submissive
Gratitude for so illustrious and advantageous a Protection. To let the
World too know that You do not think it beneath You to be officiously Good,
even from extremest Heights to discern the lowest Creatures, and give them 25
all the Noblest Influence You can, You brought Her Royal Highness just
at the exigent Time, whose single Presence on the Poet's day is a Subsis-
tence for him all the Year after. Ah, Madam, If all the short-liv'd Happiness that miserable Poets can enjoy, consist in Commendation onely; nay,
if the most part are content with Popular Breath, and even for that are   30
thankfull: how shall I express my self to Your Grace, who by a particular
Goodness, and innate Sweetness, meerly for the sake of doing well, have
thus rais'd me above my self. To have Your Graces Favour, is, in a word,
to have the Applause of the whole Court, who are its Noblest Ornament, magnificent and eternal Praise. Something there is in Your Meen so much   35
above that we vulgarly call Charming, that to me it seems Adorable, and
Your Presence almost Divine, whose dazling and Majestick Form is a proper

---

13 Opinion] Q_{2+}; Opinion: Q_1.
33 self? C_{2-3}.

Mansion for the most elevated Soul: And let me tell the World, nay, sighing
speak it to a Barbarous Age (I cannot help calling it so, when I think of Rome
and Greece) Your extraordinary Love for Heroick Poetry is not the least   40
Argument to shew the Greatness of Your Mind, and fulness of Perfection.
To hear You speak with that infinite Sweetness and Chearfulness of Spirit
that is natural to Your Grace, is, methinks to hear our Tutelar Angels;
'Tis to bemoan the present malicious Times, and remember the Golden Age:
But to behold you too, is to make Prophets quite forget their Heaven, and   45
bind the Poets with eternal Rapture.

> Her pure and eloquent Blood
> Spoke in her Cheeks, and so distinctly wrought,
> That one might almost say, her Body thought.

> You for whose Body God made better Clay,   50
> Or took Souls Stuff such as shall late decay,
> Or such as needs small change at the last day. Dr. Donn.

Ziphares and Semandra were first Your Graces Favourites; and though I
ought not, Madam, to praise Your Wit by Your Judgment of my Painting, yet
I must say, Such Characters every Dawber cannot draw. It has been often   55
observed against me, That I abound in ungovern'd Fancy; but I hope the
World will pardon the Sallies of Youth: Age, Despondence, and Dulness
come too fast of themselves. I discommend no Man for keeping the beaten
Road; but I am sure the Noble Hunters that follow the Game, must leap
Hedges and Ditches sometimes, and run at all, or never come in to the fall   60
of the Quarry. My comfort is, I cannot be so ridiculous a Creature to any
Man as I am to my self: for, who should know the House so well as the Good
Man at home? who when his Neighbours come to see him, still sets the best
Rooms to view; and if he be not a wilful Ass, keeps the Rubbish and Lumber
in some dark Hole, where no body comes but himself, to mortifie at melan-   65
choly Hours. But how then, Madam, in this unsuitable condition, how shall
I answer the infinite Honours and Obligations Your Grace has laid upon me?
Your Grace, who is the most beautiful Idea of Love and Glory; who, to that
Divine Composition, have the noblest and best-natur'd Wit in the World?
All I can promise, Madam, and be able to perform, is, That Your Grace   70
shall never see a Play of mine that shall give offence to Modesty and Vertue;
and what I humbly offer to the World, shall be of use at least, and I hope
deserve Imitation: which is, or ought to be, I am sure, the Design of all
Tragedies and Comedies both Ancient and Modern. I should presume to
promise my self too some Success in things of this nature, if Your Grace   75
(in whom the Charms of Beauty, Wit, and Goodness seem reconcil'd) at
a leisure Hour would condescend to correct with Your excellent Judgment,
the Errors of,

MADAM,

Your Graces most humble,
most obedient, and
devoted Servant,

NAT. LEE.

PROLOGUE.

Wit long opprest, and fill'd at last with rage,
Thus in a sullen mood rebukes the Age.
What loads of Fame do modern Hero's bear,
For an inglorious, long, and lazy War?
Who for some Skirmish or a safe Retreat,   5
(Not to be dragg'd to Battle) are call'd Great.
But oh, what do ambitious States men gain!
Who into private Chests whole Nations drain?
What sums of Gold they hoard is dayly known,
To all mens cost, and sometimes to their own.   10
Your Lawyer too, that like an O Yes bawls,
That drowns the Market-Higler in the Stalls,
That seems begot, conceiv'd, and born in brawls;
Yet thrives: He and his crowd get what they please,
Swarming all Term-time thro' the Strand like Bees,   15
They buz at Westminster, and lye for Fees.
The godly too their ways of getting have;
But none so much as your Phanatick Knave:
Wisely the wealthiest Livings they refuse,
Who by the fattest Bishopricks wou'd loose;   20
Who with short hair, large Ears, and small blue Band,
True Rogues, their own, not Gods Elect, command.
Let Pigs then be profane; but Broths allow'd,
Possets and Christian Caudles may be good,
Meet helps to reinforce a Brothers blood;   25
Therefore each Female Saint he does advise,
With groans, and hums, and ha's, and gogling eyes,
To rub him down, and make the Spirit rise.
While with his zeal transported, from the ground
He mounts, and sanctifies the Sisters round.   30
On Poets onely no kind Star e're smill'd;
Curst Fate has damn'd 'em every Mothers Child:
Therefore he warns his Brothers of the Stage
To write no more to an ingrateful age.
Think what penurious Masters you have serv'd;   35
Tasso ran mad, and noble Spencer starv'd:
Turn then, who e're thou art that canst write well,
Thy Ink to Gaul, and in Lampoons excell.
Forswear all honesty, traduce the Great,
Grow impudent, and rail against the State;   40
Bursting with spleen, abroad thy Pasquils send,
And chuse some Libel-spreader for thy Friend:
The Wit and Want of Timon point thy mind,
And for thy Satyr-subject chuse Mankind.

DRAMATIS PERSONAE

Theodosius.	Mr. Williams.	
Varanes.	Mr. Betterton.	
Marcian.	Mr. Smith.	
Lucius.	Mr. Wiltshire.	
Atticus, Chief Priest.	Mr. Bowman.	5
Leontine.	Mr. Leitherfull.	
Aranthes.		
Chorus.		

Pulcheria.	Mrs. Betterton.	
Athenais.	Mrs. Barry.	10
Julia.		
Delia.		
Marina.		
Flavilla.		
Attendants, Singers.		15

The SCENE

CONSTANTINOPLE.

---

7 Aranthes] ; <u>om</u>. Q_{1+}.
13-14 Marina. Flavilla.] ; <u>om</u>. Q_1-C_2.

THEODOSIUS:
OR, THE
FORCE OF LOVE.

Act I. Scene I.

A stately Temple, which represents the Christian Religion, as in its
first Magnificence: Being but lately* establisht at Rome and Constantinople. The side Scenes shew the horrid Tortures with which the Roman
Tyrants persecuted the Church; and the flat Scene, which is the limit
of the prospect, discovers an Altar richly adorn'd, before it Constantine, suppos'd kneels, with Commanders about him, gazing at a bloody
Cross in the Aire, which being incompass'd with many Angels, offers it
self to view; with these words distinctly written, (In hoc signo vinces!)
Instruments are heard, and many Attendants; The Ministers at Divine
Service, walk busily up and down. Till Atticus the chief of all the
Priests, and successor of St. Chrysostom, in rich Robes, comes forward
with the Philosopher Leontine. The Waiters in ranks bowing all the way
before him.

A Chorus heard at distance.

> Prepare, prepare! the Rites begin,
> Let none unhallow'd enter in;
> The Temple with new Glory shines,
> Adorn the Altars, wash the Shrines,
> And purge the place from Sin.   5

ATTIC. O Leontine! was ever Morn like this,
Since the Celestial Incarnation dawn'd?
I think no Day since that, such Glory gave
To Christian Altars, as this morning brings.
    LEONT. Great Successor of holy Chrysostom,   10
Who now Triumphs above a Saint of Honour,
Next in degree to those bright Sons of Heav'n;
Who never fell, nor stain'd their Orient Beams:
What shall I answer? How shall I approach you
Since my Conversion, which your breath inspir'd?   15
    ATTIC. To see this Day, th' Emperour of the East,
Leave all the pleasures that the Earth can yield,
That Nature can bestow, or Art invent;
In his Life's spring, and bloom of gawdy years,
To undergo the penance of a Cloyster,   20
Confin'd to narrow Rooms, and gloomy walks,
Fastings, and Exercises of Devotion,
Which from his bed at midnight must awake him,
Methinks, O Leontine! is something more,
Than yet Philosophy could ever reach.   25
    LEONT. True, Atticus; you have amaz'd my reason.

---

* lately] Q₂+; latey Q₁.

    ATTIC. Yet more, to our Religions lasting honour:
Marina and Flavilla, two young Virgins,
Imperial born, cast in the fairest mould
That e're the hands of beauty form'd for Woman;   30
The Mirors of our Court, where Chastity
And Innocence might Copy spotless Luster;
To Day with Theodosius leave the World.
    LEONT. Methinks at such a glorious resignation,
The Angellick Orders should at once descend,   35
In all the Paint and Drapery of Heav'n;
With Charming Voices, and with lulling strings,
To give full grace to such Triumphant Zeal.
    ATTIC. No, Leontine; I fear there is a fault:
For when I last confest th' Emperour,   40
Whether disgust and melancholly bloud,
From restless Passions, urg'd not this Divorce:
He only answer'd me with sighs and blushes;
'Tis sure his Soul is of the tenderest make:
Therefore, I'll tax him strictly; but my Friend,   45
Why should I give his Character to you,
Who, when his Father sent him into Persia,
Were by that mighty Monarch then appointed
To breed him with his Son, the Prince Varanes.
    LEONT. And what will raise your Admiration, is,   50
That two such different Tempers should agree:
You know that Theodosius is compos'd
Of all the softness that should make a Woman,
Judgment almost like Fear fore-runs his Actions;
And he will poise an injury so long,   55
As if he had rather pardon than revenge it:
But the Young Persian Prince quite opposite,
So Fiery fierce, that those who view him nearly
May see his haughty Soul still mounting in his Face;
Yet did I study these so different Tempers,   60
Till I at last had form'd a perfect Union,
As if two Souls did but inform one body,
A friendship that may challenge all the World;
And at the proof be matchless.
    ATTIC.   I long to read
This Gallant Prince, who, as you have inform'd me,   65
Comes from his Fathers Court to see our Emperor.
    LEON. So he intended till he came to Athens;
And at my homely board beheld my Daughter;
Where, as Fate ordered, she who never saw
The Glories of a Court, bred up to Books   70
In Closets like a Sybill. She, I say,
(Long since from Persia brought by me to Athens!)

------

42 Divorce? Q_2-C_1; Divorce; C_2+.

Unskill'd in Charms, but those which Nature gave her,
Wounded this scornful Prince: In short, he forc'd me
To wait him hither, with deep protestations   75
That Moment that bereft him of the sight
Of Athenais, gave him certain Death.

   Enter Varanes, and Athenais.

But see my Daughter honoured with his presence.
  VARA. 'Tis strange! O Athenais! wondrous, all
Wondrous the Shrines, and wonderful the Altars!   80
The Martyrs, though but drawn in painted Flames,
Amaze me with the Image of their suff'rings:
Saints Canoniz'd that dar'd the Roman Tyrants.
Hermits that liv'd in Caves, and fed with Angels.
By Oromasdes, it is wondrous all;   85
That bloody Cross, in yonder Azure Sky,
Above the Head of kneeling Constantine;
Inscrib'd about with Golden Characters:
Thou shalt or'e-come in this. If it be true,
I say again, by Heav'n 'tis wond'rous strange.   90
  ATHEN. O Prince! if thus Immagination stirs you,
A fancy rais'd from Figures in dead Walls,
How would the Sacred breath of Atticus
Inspire your Breast, purge all your dross away,
And drive this Athenais from your Soul,   95
To make a Virgin room, whom yet the mould
Of your rude Fancy cannot comprehend.
  VARA. What says my Fair? Drive Athenais from me:
Start me not into Frenzy, lest I rail
At all Religion, and fall out with Heav'n: 100
And what is she! alas! that should supplant thee?
Were she the Mistress of the World, as fair
As Winter Stars, or Summer setting Suns,
And thou set by in Nature's plainest Dress,
With that chast modest look when first I saw thee,   105
The Heiress of a poor Philosopher,   [Recorders ready
I swear by all I wish, by all I love,   to flourish. *
Glory and Thee, I would not lose a thought,
Nor cast an Eye that way, but rush to thee,

---

75 thither Q_{2+}.
78-79 Resa inserts a stage direction between these two lines:
  Exeunt Leontine and Atticus. This direction he found
  written in a copy of Q_5 in the British Museum. Such
  direction is in error, for both Atticus and Leontine have
  remained upon the stage. See lines 158, 204.
85 Oromasdes,] Resa; Orosmades, Q_1–C_3.
 * This direction shows the text to be printed from a prompter's copy.

To these lov'd arms, and lose my self for ever.   110
   ATHEN. Forbear, my Lord.
   VARA.   O cruel Athenais!
Why dost thou put me off, who pine to death?
And thrust me from thee when I would approach thee?
Can there be ought in this? Curse then thy birth-right,
Thy glorious Titles and ill-suited Greatness,   115
Since Athenais scorns thee: Take again
Your ill-tim'd Honours; take 'em, take 'em Gods!
And change me to some humble Villager,
If so at least for toils at scorching Noon,
In mowing Meadows, or in reaping Fields,   120
At night she will but crown me with a smile,
Or reach the bounty of her hand to bless me.
   ATHEN. When Princes speak, their Subjects should be silent,
Yet with humility I would demand
Wherein appears my scorn, or my aversion?   125
Have I not for your sake abandon'd home,
Where I had vow'd to spend my calmer days?
But you perhaps imagine it but little
For a poor Maid to follow you abroad,
Especially the Daughter of old Leontine,   130
Yet I must tell you Prince---
   VARA.   I cannot bear
Those Frowns: I have offended, but forgive me.
For who, Athenais, that is toss'd
With such tempestuous tydes of love as I
Can steer a steady course? Retire, my Fair.   [Recorders flourish.   135
Hark! the Solemnities are now beginning,
And Theodosius comes: Hide, hide thy Charms,
If to his clouded Eyes such Day should break,
The Royal Youth who dotes to Death for Love,
I fear would forfeit all his Vows to Heav'n,   140
And fix upon thy World, thy World of Beauty.   [Exeunt.

     Enter Theodosius leading Marina and Flavilla (all three
       drest in white) followed by Pulcheria.

   THEO. Farewell, Pulcheria! and I pray no more:
For all thy kind Complaints are lost upon me.
Have I not sworn the world and I must part?
Fate has proclaim'd it, therefore weep no more,   145
Wound not the tenderest part of Theodosius,
My yielding Soul, that would expire in Calms!
Wound me not with thy tears, and I will tell thee,
Yet e're I take my last farewell for ever,
The Cause of all my sufferings: O, my Sister!   150

---

135 course?] Q₃₊; course. Q₁₋₂.

A bleeding heart, the stings of pointed Love,
What Constitution soft as mine can bear?
    PULCH. My Lord, my Emp'rour, my dearest Brother,
Why all this while did you conceal it from me?
    THEO. Because I was asham'd to own my weakness,   155
I knew thy sharper wit, and stricter Wisdom,
Would dart Reproofs, which I could not endure.
Draw near, O, Atticus! and mark me well,
For never yet did my complaining Spirit
Unlaid this weighty Secret upon him,   160
Nor groan a syllable of her Oppression.
    ATTIC. Concealment was a fault, but speak at large,
Make bare the Wound, and I will pour in Balm.
    THEO. 'Tis Folly all, and fondness---O, Remembrance!
Why dost thou open thus my Wound again,   165
And from my heart call down those warmer drops
That make me dye with shame? Hear then, Pulcheria!
Some few preceding days before I left
The Persian Court, hunting one morning early,
I lost my self and all the Company: 170
Still wandring on as Fortune would direct me,
I past a Rivulet, and alighted in
The sweetest Solitude I ever saw;
When streight, as if enchantment had been there,
Two charming Voices drew me 'till I came   175
Where divers Arbours over-lookt the River.
Upon the Osier Bank two Women sate,
Who when their Song was ended talkt to one,
Who bathing stood far in the Crystal stream.
But oh what thought can paint that fair perfection,   180
Or give a glimps of such a Naked Glory!
Not Sea-born Venus, in the Courts beneath,
When the green Nymphs first kiss'd her Coral lips,
All polisht, fair, and washt with Orient Beauty,
Could in my dazling Fancy match her brightness.   185
    ATTIC. Think where you are?
    THEO.   O! Sir, you must forgive me,
The chast Enthusiastick Form appears,
As when I saw her; yet I swear Pulcheria,
Had cold Diana been a looker on,
She must have prais'd the Virtues of the Virgin,   190
The Satyrs could not grin, for she was vail'd:
Nothing Immodest, from her naked bosom
Down to her knees the Nymph was wrapt in Lawn:
But oh for me! for me, that was too much!
Her legs, her Arms, her Hands, her Neck, her Breasts,   195
So nicely shap'd, so matchless in their Luster!

---

187 appears,] Q3+; appears. Q1-2.

Such all-perfection, that I took whole draughts
Of killing Love, and ever since have languisht
With lingring surfeits of her Fatal Beauty!
Alas! too fatal sure! Oh Atticus!   200
Forgive me, for my story now is done,
The Nymph was drest, and with her two Companions,
Having descry'd me, shriekt and fled away,
Leaving me motionless, till Leontine,
Th' Instructer of my Youth, by chance came in,   205
And wak'd me from the wonder that entranc'd me.
    ATTIC. Behold, my Lord, the man whom you have nam'd,
The Harbinger of Prince Varanes here.
    THEO. O Leontine! ten thousand Welcomes meet thee;
Thou Foster Father of my tender Youth,   210
Who rear'd the Plant, and prun'd it with such care
How shall I look upon Thee, who am fallen
From all the Principles of manlier Reason
By thee infus'd to more than womans weakness?
Now by the Majesty Divine that aws   215
This sacred place, I swear you must not Kneel:
And tell me, for I have a thousand things
To ask thee; where, where is my God-like Friend?
Is he arriv'd, and shall I see his face
Before I am Cloister'd from the World for ever?   220
    LEONT. He comes, my Lord, with all the expecting joys
Of a young promis'd Lover, from his Eyes
Big hopes look forth, and boiling fancy forms
Nothing but Theodosius still before him;
His thought, his every word, is Theodosius.   225
    THEO. Yet, Leontine, yet answer me once more.
With tremblings I demand thee.
Say---hast thou seen? Oh, has that Heav'nly form
Appear'd to thee again? Behold he's dumb:
Proceed then to the Solemn last farewell;   230
Never was man so willing, and prepar'd.

        Enter Varanes, Aranthes, Attendants.

    VARA. Where is my Friend! oh where is my belov'd,
My Theodosius! point him out ye Gods,
That I may press him dead betwixt my Arms;
Devour him thus with over-hasty Joyes,   235
That Languish at his Breast, quite out of breath,
And cannot utter more.
    THEO.   Thou mightiest pleasure!
And greatest blessing that kind Heav'n could send,
To glad my parting Soul, a thousand welcomes!

---

206 entranc'd] Q3+; extranc'd Q1-2.

O when I look on thee, new starts of Glory   240
Spring in my breast, and with a backward bound
I run the Race of lusty Youth again.
  VARA. By Heav'n it joyes me too, when I remember
Our thousand pastimes, when we borrow'd Names;
Alcides, I, and thou my dearest Theseus,   245
When through the Woods, we chac'd the foaming Boar,
With Hounds that open'd like Thessalian Bulls,
Like Tygers flu'd, and sanded as the shore,
With Ears, and Chests, that dasht the morning Dew:
Driv'n with the sport, as ships are tost in storms,   250
We ran like Winds, and matchless was our Course;
Now sweeping o're the limit of a Hill!
Now with a full Career come thund'ring down
The precipice! and sweat along the Vale.
  THEO. O glorious time! and when the gathering Clouds   255
Have call'd us home; say, did we rest my Brother?
When on the Stage to the admiring Court
We strove to represent Alcides fury,
In all that raging heat, and pomp of madness,
With which the stately Seneca adorn'd him;   260
So lively drawn, and painted with such horror,
That we were forc'd to give it o're, so lowd
The Virgins shriek'd, so fast they dy'd away.
  VARA. My Theodosius still; 'tis my lov'd Brother;
And by the Gods wee'l see those times agen;   265
Why then has rumour wrong'd thee, that reported
Christian Enthusiasm had charm'd thee from us;
That drawn by Priests, and work'd by Melancholly,
Thou hadst laid the golden Reins of Empire down,
And sworn thy self a Votary for ever?   270
  THEO. 'Tis almost true; and had not you arriv'd,
The solemn business had by this been ended.
This I have made the Empress of the East,
My elder Sister: These with me retire,
Devoted to the Pow'r whom we adore.   275
  VARA. What Pow'r is that that merits such Oblations?
I thought the Sun more great and glorious,
Than any that e're mingled with the Gods;
Yet even to him my Father never offer'd
More than a Hecatomb of Bulls and Horses: 280
Now by those golden Beams, that glad the World,
I swear it is too much: For one of these,
But half so bright, our God would drive no more,
He'd leave the darkn'd Globe, and in some Cave
Injoy such Charms for ever.
  ATTIC.   My Lord, forbear!   285

---

269 laid down the golden Reins of Empire, C₃.

Such Language does not suit with our Devotion:
Nothing prophane must dare to murmur here,
Nor stain the hallow'd Beauties of the place;
Yet thus far we must yield: The Emperor
Is not enough prepar'd to leave the World.   290
    VARA.   Thus low, most Reverend of this sacred place,
I kneel for pardon, and am half Converted,
By your permission that my Theodosius
Return to my Embraces. O my Brother!
Why dost thou droop, there will be time enough   295
For Pray'r and Fasting, and Religious Vows;
Let us enjoy, while yet thou art my own,
All the Magnificence of Eastern Courts;
I hate to walk a lazy life away:
Let's run the Race which Fate has set before us,   300
And post to the Dark Goal.
    THEO.   Cruel Destiny!
Why am not I thus too? O my Varanes!
Why are these costly Dishes set before me?
Why do these sounds of pleasure strike my Ears?
Why are these Joys brought to my sick remembrance;   305
Who have no appetite; but am to sense,
From Head to Foot, all a dead palsie o're?
    VARA.   Fear not, my Friend! all shall be well again;
For I have thousand ways, and thousand stories
To raise thee up to pleasure, we'll unlock   310
Our fastest secrets, shed upon each other
Our tenderest Cares, and quite unbar those doors,
Which shall be shut to all Mankind beside.
    ATTIC.   Silence and Reverence are the Temples dues:
Therefore while we pursue the Sacred Rites   315
Be these observ'd, or quit the awful place.
Imperial Sisters, now twin-stars of Heav'n,
Answer the Successor of Chrysostom,
Without least Reservation answer me,
By those harmonious Rules I charg'd ye learn.   320

        Atticus Sings.

ATTIC.   Canst thou, Marina, leave the World,
        The World that is Devotions bane;
        Where Crowns are tost, and Scepters hurld,
        Where Lust and proud Ambition Reign?

2 PRIEST.   Can you your costly Robes forbear,   325
        To live with us in poor attire,
        Can you from Courts to Cells repair,
        To sing at midnight in our Quire?

3 PRIEST.   Can you forget your golden Beds,
        Where you might sleep beyond the morn,   330

On Matts to lay your Royal heads,
And have your beautious Tresses shorn?

ATTIC.   Can you resolve to fast all day,
And weep and groan to be forgiv'n,
Can you in broken slumbers pray,   335
And by affliction merit Heav'n?

CHOR.   Say, Votaries, can this be done,
While we the grace Divine implore,
The world has lost, the battel's won,
And sin shall never charm ye more?   340

MARINA   The gate to bliss does open stand,
Sings.   And all my pennance is in view;
The world upon the other hand
Cries out, O do not bid adieu!

Yet, Sacred Sir, in these extreams,   345
Where Pomp and Pride their glories tell;
Where Youth and Beauty are the Themes,
And plead their moving Cause so well.

If ought that's vain my thoughts possess,
Or any Passions govern here,   350
But what divinity may bless:
O may I never enter there!

FLAVILLA
Sings.   What! what can Pomp or Glory do;
Or what can humane Charms persuade,
That mind that has a Heav'n in view,   355
How can it be by Earth betray'd!

No Monarch full of Youth and Fame,
The Joy of Eyes, and Natures Pride,
Should once my thoughts from Heaven Reclaim;
Though now he woo'd me for his Bride.   360

Haste then, Oh haste! and take us in,
For ever lock Religion's Door,
Secure us from the Charms of sin,
And let us see the World no more.

ATTIC.   Hark! hark! behold the Heavenly Quire,   365
Sings.   They cleave the Air in bright attire,
And see his Lute each Angel brings,
And hark Divinely thus he Sings!
To the Pow'rs Divine, all glory be given,
By men upon Earth, and Angels in Heaven.   370

Scene shuts, and all the Priests with Marina, and Flav. disappear.

PULCH. For ever gone! for ever parted from me!
O Theodosius, till this cruel moment
I never knew how tenderly I lov'd 'em;
But on this everlasting separation
Methinks my Soul has left me, and my Time,   375
Of dissolution points me to the Grave.
THEO. O my Varanes, does not now thy temper
Bate something of it's Fire? dost thou not melt
In meer Compassion of my Sisters Fate,
And cool thy self with one relenting thought?   380
VARA. Yes, my dar'd Soul rowls inward, melancholly
Which I ne're felt before, now comes upon me;
And I begin to loathe all human greatness.
Oh! sigh not then, nor thy hard Fate deplore;
For 'tis resolv'd, we will be Kings no more: 385
We'll fly all Courts, and Love shall be our guide,
Love, that's more worth than all the world beside.
Princes are barr'd the Liberty to Roam,
The fetter'd mind still languishes at home;
In golden bands she treads the thoughtful round,   390
Business and Cares eternally abound.
    "And when for Air the Goddess would unbind,
    "She's clogg'd with Scepters, and to Crowns confin'd.   [Exeunt.

End of ACT I.

---

380 thought?] Q_{3+}; thought. Q_{1-2}.

SONG after the First ACT.*

Now, now the Fight's done, and the great God of War
    Lies sleeping in shades, and unravels his ears;
Love laughs at his rest, and the Soldiers allarms;
    He Drums and he Trumpets, and struts in his Arms;
He rides on his Lance, and the Bushes he bangs,   5
    And his broad bloody Sword on the Willow-tree hangs.

Love smiles when he feels the sharp point of his Dart,
    And he wings it to hit the grim God in the heart,
Who leaves his Steel Bed, and Bolsters of Brass,
    For Pillows of Roses, and Couches of Grass.   10
His Courser of Lightning is now grown so slow,
    That a Cupid ith' Saddle sits bending his Bow.

Love, Love is the cry; Love and Kisses go round,
    Till Phillis and Damon lie clasp'd on the ground.
The Shepheard too quick does her pleasure destroy,   15
    'Tis abortive, she cries, and he murders my Joy:
But he rallies again by the force of her Charms,
    And Kisses, Embraces, and dies in her Arms.

FINIS

---

*   In Q₁ these songs between the acts are printed at the end of
the play with the music by Purcell; they are not printed in
the later editions. Even Resa omits them.

ACT. II. SCENE I.

Enter Pulcheria, Julia, Attendants.

PULCH. These Packets for the Emperour Honorius,
Be swift, let the Agent haste to Rome ---
I hear, my Julia, that our General
Is from the Goths return'd with Conquest home.
    JUL. He is; to day I saw him in the presence,   5
Sharp to the Courtiers, as he ever was:
Because they went not with him to the Wars.
To you he bows and sues to kiss your hand.
    PULCH. He shall, my dearest Julia; oft I have told thee
The secret of my Soul; if e're I marry,   10
Marcian's my Husband, he is a man, my Julia,
Whom I have study'd long, and found him perfect:
Old Rome at ev'ry glance looks through his eyes,
And kindles the beholders: Some sharp Atomes
Run through his Frame, which I could wish were out.   15
He sickens at the softness of the Emperour,
And speaks too freely of our Female Court;
Then sighs, comparing it with what Rome was.

Enter Marcian, with sword drawn, and Lucius. *

    PULCH. Ha! Who are these that dare prophane this place,
With more than barb'rous insolence?
    MARC.   At your Feet,   20
Behold I cast the scourge of these Offenders,
And kneel to kiss your Hand.
    PULCH.   Put up your Sword,
And e're I bid you welcome from the Wars,
Be sure you clear your Honour of this rudeness;
Or Marcian leave the Court.
    MARC.   Thus then, Madam,   25
The Emperour receiv'd me with affection,
Embrac'd me for my Conquests, and retir'd;
When on a sudden all the Guilded Flies
That buz about the Court came flutt'ring round me:
This with affected Cringes, and minc'd Words,   30
Begs me to tell my Tale of Victories;
Which done he thanks me, slips behind his fellow,
Whispers him in the Ear, then smiles and listens,
While I relate my Story once again:

---

  * with sword drawn,]; <u>om.</u> Q_{1+}; <u>but see line 22.</u>

A third comes in and asks me the same favour;   35
Whereon they laugh, while I still ignorant
Go on; but one behind, more impudent,
Strikes on my shoulder; then they laught out-right,
But then I guessing the abuse too late,
Return'd my Knight behind a box o'th' Ear;   40
Then drew, and briefly told 'em they were Rascals.
They laughing still cry'd out the General's musty,
Whereon I drove 'em, Madam, as you saw:
This is in short the Truth, I leave the Judgment
To your own Justice, if I have done ill,   45
Sentence me and I'll leave the Court for ever.
    PULCH. First you are welcome, Marcian, from the Wars;
And still when e're occasion calls for Arms,
Heav'n send th' Emperor a General
Renown'd as Marcian; as to what is past   50
I think the World will rather praise than censure
Pulcheria, when she pardons you the action.
    MARC. Gods! Gods! and thou great Founder of old Rome!
What is become of all that mighty Spirit,
That rais'd our Empire to a pitch so high?   55
Where is it pent? What but Almighty Power
Could thus confine it, that but some few Atoms
Now run through all the East and Occident?
    PULCH. Speak calmly, Marcian. ---
    MARC.   Who can be temperate,
That thinks as I do, Madam? Why here's a fellow,   60
I have seen him fight against a Troop of Vandals
In your defence, as if he lov'd to bleed:
Come to my arms, my Dear! Thou canst not talk,
But hast a Soul above the proudest of 'em.
O Madam! when he has been all over blood,   65
And hackt with wounds that seem'd to mouth his praises,
I have seen him smile still as he pusht death from him,
And with his actions rally distant Fate.
    PULCH. He has a noble Form.
    MARC.   Yet ev'n this man,
That fought so bravely in his Countries Cause,   70
This excellent man, this Morning in the presence
Did I see wrong'd before the Emperor,
Scorn'd and despis'd because he could not Cringe,
Nor plant his feet as some of them could do.
One said his Cloaths were not well made, and damn'd   75
His Taylor --- Another said he look'd
As if he had not lost his Maiden-head.
If things are suffer'd to be thus, down all
Authority, Preeminence, Degree and Vertue.
Let Rome be never mention'd, no, in the Name   80
Of all the Gods, be she forgotten ever.
Effeminate Persians, and the Lydian softness,

Make all your Fights, Marcian shall out no more;
For by my Arms it makes a Woman of me;
And my swoln eyes run o're to think this worth,   85
This fuller Honour than the whole Court holds,
Should be ridiculous to Knaves and Fools;
Should starve for want of what is necessary
To Life's Convenience. When luxurious Bawds
Are so o're-grown with Fat, and Cram'd with Riot,   90
That they can hardly walk without an Engine.
    PULCH. Why did you not inform the Emperor?
    MARC. Because he will not hear me: Alas, good man!
He flies from this bad World, and still when Wars
And dangers come, he runs to his Devotions,   95
To your new thing, I know not what you call it,
Which Constantine began.
    PULCH. How, Marcian! are not you of that
Religion which the Emperour owns?
    MARC. No, Madam, if you'll see my naked thought,   100
I am not of their Principle that take
A wrong; so far from bearing with a Foe
I would strike first, like old Rome; I wou'd forth,
Elbow the neighbouring Nations round about,
Invade, enlarge my Empire to the bounds   105
Of the too narrow Universe. Yes, I own
That I despise your holy Innovations.
I am for the Roman-Gods, for Funerall Piles,
For mounting Eagles, and the fancied greatness
Of our Fore-Fathers. Methinks my heated Spirit   110
Cou'd utter things worth losing of my Head.
    PULCH. Speak freely, Marcian, for I know thee honest.
    MARC. O, madam! long, long, may the Emperour live;
But I must say his gentle disposition
Suits not: Alas! the Oriental sway: 115
Bid him but look on Pharamond; O Gods!
Awake him with the Image of that Spirit,
Which like a Pyramid reverst is grown,
Ev'n from a point to the most dreadful greatness;
His very name already shakes the World;   120
And still in person heading his fierce Squadrons,
Like the first Caesar o're the hardy Gauls,
He seems another Thunderbolt of War.
    PULCH. I oft have blam'd my Brother most for this,
That to my hand he leaves the State-affairs,   125
And how that sounds you know ---
    MARC.   Forgive me, Madam;
I think that all the greatness of your Sex,
Rome's Clelia, and the fam'd Semiramis,

---

121 first Squadrons Q$_{2+}$.

With all th' Amazonian valour too
Meet in Pulcheria; yet I say forgive me,   130
If with reluctance I behold a Woman
Sit at the Empires Helm, and steer the World.
  PULCH. I stand Rebuk'd ---
  MARC.   Mark but the growing French,
The most auspicious Omen of their greatness,
That I can guess, is their late Salique Law,   135
Blest by their Priests, the Salij, and pronounc'd
To stand for ever; which excludes all Women
From the Imperial Crown: But, oh! I speak
The least of all those infinite grievances,
Which make the Subjects murmur: In the Army,   140
Tho' I proceeded still like Hannibal,
And punisht ev'ry Mutineer with death;
Yet, oh! it stabb'd me through and through the Soul
To pass the Wretches Doom, because I knew
With Justice they complain'd; for hard they fought,   145
And with their blood earn'd that forbidden Bread,
Which some at Court, and great ones, though un-nam'd,
Cast to their Hounds, while the poor Souldier's starv'd ---
  PULCH. Your pity too in mournful fellowship,
No doubt might sooth their murmurs.
  MARC.   Yes, it did,   150
That I might put 'em once again in heart.
I said 'twas true, the Emperour was to blame,
Who dealt too coldly with his faithful Servants ,
And paid their great Arrears by second hands:
I promis'd too, when we return'd to Court,   155
Things should be mended ---
But how! oh Gods! forgive my blood this Transport !
To the Eternal shame of Female Councils!
And to the blast of Theodosius Name,
Whom never Warlike Chronicle shall mention!   160
O let me speak it with a Roman Spirit,
We were receiv'd like undone Prodigals,
By curst ungrateful Stewards, with cold looks;
Who yet got all by those poor wretches ruin.
Like Malefactors at the hands of Justice.   165
I blush, I almost weep with bursting rage:
If thus receiv'd, how paid our long Arrears?
Why as intrusted Misers pay the Rights
Of helpless Widdows or the Orphans tears.
O Souldier, for to thee, to thee I speak it,   170
Baw'ds for the drudgery of Citizens Wives,

---

151 heart, Q_{4+}.
164 ruin; C_{2-3}.
165 Justice, Q_3-C_1.

Would better pay debilitated Stallions.
Madam, I have said perhaps too much; if so,
It matters not, for he who lyes like me
On the hard ground, is sure to fall no further.   175
    PULCH. I have given you patient hearing, honest Marcian!
And far as I can see into your temper,
I speak my serious Judgment in cold blood,
With strictest Consultation on the matter;
I think this seeming plain and honest Marcian,   180
An exquisite and most notorious Traytor.
    MARC. Ha! Traytor!
    PULCH.   Yes, a most notorious Traytor.
    MARC. Your Grand Father, whose Frown could awe the World,
Would not have call'd me so --- or if he had ---
    PULCH. You would have taken it --- But to the business,   185
Was't not enough! Oh Heaven! Thou know'st, too much!
At first to own your self an Infidel,
A bold Contemner, even to Blasphemy,
Of that Religion which we all profess,
For which your hearts best blood can ne're suffice: 190
But you must dare with a seditious Army,
Thus to conspire against the Emperour;
I mention not your Impudence to me,
Taxing the folly of my Government
Ev'n to my Face: Such an irreverence,   195
As sure no barb'rous Vandal would have urg'd,
Beside your libelling all the Court, as if
You had engrost the whole Worlds honesty:
And Flatterers, Fools, Sycophants, Knaves,
Such was your language, did inhabit here.   200
    MARC. You wrest my honest meaning, by the Gods
You do, and if you thus go on, I feel
My struggling spirit will no longer bear it.
    PULCH. I thought the meaning of all rational men
Should still be gather'd out of their Discourse,   205
Nor are you so imprudent without thinking
To vent such words, tho' now you fain would hide it;
You find the guilt and bawk the accusation:
But think not you shall scape so easily!
Once more I do confront you as a Traytor;   210
And as I am entrusted with full pow'r,
Divest you, in the Name of Theodosius,
Of all your Offices, Commissions, Honours,
Command you leave the Court within three Days,
Loyal, plain-dealing, honest Marcian.   215
    MARC. Gods! Gods!

---

177 And, as far Q_{2+}.
199 Fools, and Sycophants, and Knaves, C_3.

    PULCH.   What now! ha! does the Traytor murmur?
If in three days! mark me; 'tis I that doom thee!
Rash inconsiderable man, a Wretch beneath
The Torments I cou'd execute upon thee!
If after three Days space thour't found in Court,   220
Thou dy'st! thy head, thy head shall pay the forfeit.
Farewell: Now rage! now rail and Curse the Court;
Sawcily dare to abuse the best of Princes,
And let thy lawless Tongue lash all it can;
Do, like a madman rave! deplore thy Fortune,   225
While Pages laugh at thee. Then haste to the Army,
Grow popular, and lead the multitude:
Preach up thy wrongs, and drive the giddy Beast
To kick at Caesar. [Aside.] Nay, if thou weep'st I am gone,
O Julia! if I stay, I shall weep too.   230
    Yet 'tis but just that I the heart should see
    Of him who once must Lord it over me.   [Ex. Pulcheria, &c.
    LUC. Why do you droop, Sir --- Come no more o' this,
You are and shall be still our General:
Say but the Word, I'll fill the Hyppodrome   235
With Squadrons that shall make the Emp'ror tremble;
We'll fire the Court about his Ears.
Methinks like Junius Brutus I have watcht
An Opportunity, and now it comes!
Few words and I are friends; but, noble Marcian,   240
If yet thou art not more than General,
E're dead of Night, say Lucius is a Coward.
    MARC. I charge thee, in the name of all the Gods,
Come back. I charm thee by the name of Friend,
All's well, and I rejoyce I am no General.   245
But hush! within three days we must begon,
And then, my Friend, farewell to Ceremony.
We'll fly to some far distant lonely Village,
Forget our former state, and breed with slaves.
Sweat in the Eye of day, and when night comes,   250
With bodies coursely fill'd and vacant Souls,
Sleep like the laboured Hinds, and never think;
For if I think again I shall go mad.

    Enter Leontine and Athenais, &c.

Therefore no thought. But see, we are interrupted!
O Court! O Emperor! yet let Death Threaten,   • 255
I'll find a time. Till then be still my Soul ---
No General now! A member of thy Country,
But most corrupt, therefore to be cut off,

---

225 depl re t y Fortune, Q$_1$(KU).
229 [Aside.]; om. Q$_{1+}$.

Loyal, plain-dealing, honest Marcian!
A Slave, a Traytor! O ye Eternal Gods ---   [Exeunt.   260
    LEONT. So, Athenais! now our Complement
To the young Persian Prince is at an end,
What then remains but that we take our leave,
And bid him everlastingly Farewell?
    ATHEN. My Lord!
    LEONT.   I say that decency requires   265
We should begon, nor can you stay with Honour.
    ATHEN. Most true, my Lord.
    LEONT.   The Court is now at peace,
The Emperors Sisters are retired for ever,
And he himself compos'd, what hinders then,
But that we bid adieu to prince Varanes?   270
    ATHEN. Ah, Sir, why will you break my heart?
    LEONT.   I would not;
Thou art the only comfort of my age;
Like an old Tree I stand among the storms,
Thou art the only Limb that I have left me: [She Kneels.
My dear green branch, and how I prize thee, Child,   275
Heaven only knows; why dost thou kneel and weep?
    ATHEN. Because you are so good, and will I hope
Forgive my fault, who first occasion'd it.
    LEONT. I charg'd thee to receive and hear the Prince.
    ATHEN. You did, and Oh, my Lord! I heard too much!   280
Too much I fear for my eternal quiet.
    LEONT. Rise, Athenais! Credit him who bears
More years than thou: Varanes has deceiv'd thee.
    ATHEN. How do we differ then? You judge the Prince
Impious and base; while I take Heaven to witness,   285
I think him the most Vertuous of men:
Therefore take heed, my Lord, how you accuse him
Before you make the Tryal: Alas, Varanes,
If thou art false, there's no such thing on Earth
As solid goodness, or substantial Honour.   290
A thousand times, My Lord, he has sworn to give me
(And I believe his Oaths) his Crown and Empire;
That day I make him Master of my Heart.
    LEONT. That day he'll make thee Mistress of his power,
Which carries a foul name among the Vulgar.   295
No, Athenais! let me see thee dead,
Born a pale Corps, and gently laid in Earth,
So I may say she's chast, and dy'd a Virgin,
Rather than view thee with these wounded eyes
Seated upon the Throne of Isdigerdes,   300
The blast of Common Tongues, the Nobles scorn,
Thy Fathers Curse; that is the Prince's Whore.
    ATHEN. O horrid supposition! how I detest it!
Be witness Heav'n, that sees my secret thoughts!
Have I for this, my Lord, been taught by you   305

The nicest Justice and severest vertue,
To fear no death to know the end of Life,
And with a long search discern the highest good?
No, Athenais! when the day beholds thee
So scandalously rais'd, pride cast thee down,   310
The scorn of honour, and the people's prey!
No, cruel Leontine, not to reedeem
That aged head from the descending Axe,
Not tho' I saw thy trembling Body rackt,
Thy wrinckles about thee fill'd with blood,   315
Would I for Empire to the man I love
Be made the Object of unlawful pleasure.
    LEONT. O greatly said, and by the blood which warms me,
Which runs as rich as any Athens holds,
It would improve the vertue of the World,   320
If every day a thousand Votaries,
And thousand Virgins came from far to hear thee!
    ATHEN. Look down ye pow'rs, take notice we obey
The rigid principles ye have infus'd;
Yet, oh my noble Father! to convince you,   325
Since you will have it so, propose a Marriage;
Tho' with the thought I am covered o're with blushes,
Not that I doubt the Prince, that were to doubt
The Heav'ns themselves. I know he is all truth:
But modesty ---   330
The Virgins troublesome and constant guest,
That, that alone forbids ---
    LEONT.   I wish to Heav'n
There prove no greater bar to my belief:
Behold the Prince, I will retire a while,
And when occasion calls come to thy aid.   [Ex. Leont.   335

      Enter Varanes, and Aranthes.

    VARA. To fix her on the Throne to me seems little,
Were I a God, yet would I raise her higher.
This is the nature of thy Prince: But oh!
As to the World thy judgment soars above me,
And I am dar'd with this Gigantick honour,   340
Glory forbids her prospect to a Crown,
Nor must she gaze that way; my haughty soul,
That day when she ascends the Throne of Cyrus,
Will leave my body pale, and to the stars
Retire in blushes, lost, quite lost for ever.   345
    ARAN. What do you purpose then?
    VARA.   I know not what,
But see she comes, the glory of my arms,
The only business of my instant thought,
My souls best Joy, and all my true repose.
I swear I cannot bear these strange desires,   350

These strong impulses which will shortly leave me
Dead at thy Feet ---
    ATHEN.   What have you found, my Lord,
In me so harsh or Cruel, that you fear
To speak your griefs?
    VARA.   First let me kneel and swear,
And on thy hand seal my Religious Vow,   355
Streight let the breath of Gods blow me from Earth,
Swept from the Book of Fame, forgotten ever,
If I prefer thee not, O Athenais!
To all the Persian greatness.
    ATHEN.   I believe you!
For I have heard you swear as much before.   360
    VARA. Hast Thou? O why then did I swear again?
But that my Love knew nothing worthier of thee,
And could no better way express my passion.
    ATHEN. O rise, my Lord ---
    VARA.   I will do every thing
Which Athenais bids: if there be more   365
In Nature to convince thee of my Love,
Whisper it oh some God into my Ear!
And on her breasts thus to her listning Soul
I'll breath th' Inspiration! Wilt thou not speak?
What but one sigh, no more! Can that suffice   370
For all my vast expence of Prodigal Love?
O Athenais! what shall I say or do,
To gain the thing I wish?
    ATHEN.   What's that my Lord?
    VARA. Thus to approach thee still! thus to behold thee ---
Yet there is more ---
    ATHEN.   My Lord, I dare not hear you.   375
    VARA. Why dost thou frown at what thou dost not know?
'Tis an imagination which ne're pierc'd thee;
Yet as 'tis ravishing, 'tis full of Honour.
    ATHEN. I must not doubt you, Sir: but oh I tremble
To think if Isdigerdes should behold you,   380
Should hear you thus protesting to a maid
Of no degree, but vertue, in the World. ---
    VARA. No more of this, no more; for I disdain
All Pomp, when thou art by; far be the noise
Of Kings and Courts from us, whose gentle Souls   385
Our kinder stars have steer'd another way.
Free as the forrest Birds, we'll pair together,
Without remembring who our Fathers were;
Fly to the Arbors, Grots, and Flow'ry Meads,
And in soft murmurs interchange our Souls,   390
Together drink the Christal of the stream,
Or taste the yellow Fruit which Atumn yields,

---

392 Autumn Q_{2+}.

And when the golden evening calls us home,
Wing to our Downy Nest, and sleep till morn.
    ATHEN. Ah Prince! no more!   395
Forbear, forbear to charm me,
Since I am doom'd to leave you, Sir, for ever.
    VARA. Hold Athenais ---
    ATHEN.   I know your Royal temper,
And that high honour reigns within your Breast,
Which would disdain to waste so many hours   400
With one of humble blood compar'd to you;
Unless strong passion swaid your thoughts to love her,
Therefore receive, oh Prince! and take it kindly,
For none on Earth but you could win it from me,
Receive the guift of my Eternal Love.   405
'Tis all I can bestow, nor is it little,
For sure a heart so coldly chaste as mine,
No Charms but yours, my Lord, could e're have warm'd?
    VARA. Well have you made amends by this last comfort,
For the cold dart you shot at me before,   410
For this last goodness! (Oh my Athenais!)
(For now methinks I ought to call you mine!)
I empty all my soul in thanks before you:
Yet oh! one Fear remains, like Death it chills me;
Why my relenting Love did talk of parting!   415
    ATHEN. Look there, and cease your wonder, I have sworn
To obey my Father, and he calls me hence ---

Enter Leontine.

    VARA. Ha, Leontine! by which of all my Actions
Have I so deeply injur'd thee, to merit
The smartest wound revenge could form to end me?   420
    LEONT. Answer me now, O Prince! for vertue prompts me,
And honesty will dally now no longer,
What can the end of all this passion be,
Glory requires this strict accompt, and asks
What you intend at last to Athenais?   425
    VARA. How, Leontine!
    LEONT. You saw her, Sir, at Athen's, said you lov'd her,
I charg'd her humbly to receive the Honour,
And hear your passion: Has she not, Sir, obey'd me?
    VARA. She has, I thank the Gods! but whither would'st thou?   430
    LEONT. Having resolv'd to visit Theodosius,

395-396 These would obviously make only one full line, but are printed
    as two lines in all editions. The division might have been intended
    to indicate a long pause at the end of line 395.
408 warm'd! Q_{3+}.
427 Athens, Q_{2+}.

You swore you would not go without my Daughter,
Whereon I gave command that she should follow.
    VARA. Yes, Leontine, my old Remembrancer,
Most learn'd of all Philosophers, you did.   435
    LEONT. Thus long she has attended, you have seen her,
Sounded her Vertues and her Imperfections;
Therefore, Dread Sir, forgive this bolder Charge,
Which Honour sounds, and now let me demand you ---
    VARA. Now help, Aranthes, or I am dasht for ever.   440
    ARAN. Whatever happens, Sir, disdain the marriage.
    LEONT. Can your high thoughts so far forget themselves,
To admit this humble Virgin for your Bride?
    VARA. Ha!
    ATHEN. He blushes, Gods! and stammers at the question.   445
    LEONT. Why do you walk, and chafe your self, my Lord?
The business is not much.
    VARA.   How, Leontine!
Not much, I know that she deserves a Crown;
Yet 'tis to reason much, tho' not to Love;
And sure the World would blush to see the Daughter   450
Of a Philosopher on the Throne of Cyrus.
    ATHEN. Undone for ever!
    LEONT.   Is this your answer, Sir?
    VARA. Why dost thou urge me thus, and push me to
The very brink of Glory? where, alas!
I look and tremble at the vast descent: 455
Yet even there to the vast bottom down
My rash Adventurer Love would have me leap,
And grasp my Athenais with my Ruin.
    LEONT. 'Tis well, my Lord. ---
    VARA.   Why dost thou thus provoke me,
I thought that Persia's Court had store of honour   460
To satisfie the height of thy Ambition.
Besides, old man, my Love is too well grown,
To want a Tutor for his good behaviour,
What he will do, he will do of himself,
And not be taught by you ---
    LEONT.   I know he will not!   465
Fond Tears away, I know, I know he will not;
But he would buy with his old mans preferment,
My Daughter for your Whore.
    VARA. Away, I say, my Soul disdains the motion!
    LEONT. The Motion of a Marriage, yes, I see it;   470
Your angry looks and haughty words betray it.
I found it at the first; I thank you Sir,
You have at last rewarded your old Tutor
For all his Cares, his Watchings, Services;

---

459 me? C$_{2-3}$.

Yet let me tell you, Sir, this humble Maid,   475
This Daughter of a poor Philosopher,
Shall if she please be seated on a Throne
As high as that of th' Immortal Cyrus.
    VARA. I think that age and deep Philosophy
Have crackt thy brain: Farewel, Old Leontine,   480
Retire to Rest, and when this brawling humour
Is rockt asleep, I'll meet my Athenais,
And clear the accounts of Love, which thou hast blotted.   [Exit.
    LEONT. Old Leontine! perhaps I am mad indeed.
But hold my heart, and let that solid vertue,   485
Which I so long ador'd, still keep the Reins.
O Athenais! But I will not chide thee,
Fate is in all our Actions, and methinks
At least a Father Judges so, it has
Rebuk'd thee smartly for thy Easiness;   490
There is a kind of mournful Eloquence,
In thy dumb grief which shames all clamorous sorrow.
    ATHEN. Alas! my Breast is full of Death; Methinks
I fear ev'n you ---
    LEONT.   Why shouldest thou fear thy Father?
    ATHEN. Because you have the Figure of a man!   495
Is there, O speak, a possibility
To be forgiven?
    LEONT.   Thy Father does forgive thee,
And Honour will, but on this hard Condition,
Never to see him more ---
    ATHEN.   See him! Oh Heavens!
    LEONT. Unless it be, my Daughter, to upbraid him.   500
Not tho' he should repent and streight return,
Nay proffer thee his Crown --- No more of that.
Honour too cries revenge, revenge thy wrongs,
Revenge thy self; revenge thy injur'd Father.
For 'tis revenge so wise so glorious too,   505
As all the world shall praise ---
    ATHEN.   O give me leave,
For yet I am all tenderness, the woman,
The weak, the mild, the fond, the Coward Woman;
Dares not look forth; but runs about my Breast,
And visits all the warmer Mansions there,   510
Where she so oft has harbour'd false Varanes.
Cruel Varanes! false, forsworn Varanes!
    LEONT. Is this forgetting him? is this the Course
Which honour bids thee take?
    ATHEN.   Ah, Sir, allow
A little time for Love to make his way;   515
Hardly he won the place, and many sighs
And many tears, and thousand Oaths it cost him.
And oh I find he will not be dislodged
Without a groan at parting hence for ever.

No, no! he vows he will not yet be raz'd   520
Without whole floods of grief at his farewell,
Which thus I sacrifice! And oh I swear,
Had he proved true, I would as easily
Have empty'd all my blood, and dy'd to serve him,
As now I shed these drops or vent these sighs,   525
To shew how well, how perfectly I lov'd him.
    LEONT. No Woman sure, but thou, so low in Fortune,
Therefore the nobler is thy fair Example,
Would thus have griev'd, because a Prince ador'd her:
Nor will it be believ'd in after-times,   530
That there was ever such a Maid in being;
Yet do as I advise, preserve thy vertue;
And since he does disdain thee for his Bride,
Scorn thou to be ---
    ATHEN.   Hold, Sir, oh hold, forbear;
For my Nice Soul abhors the very sound;   535
Yet with the shame of that, and the desire
Of an immortal name, I am inspir'd!
All kinder thoughts are fled for ever from me,
All tenderness, as if I ne're had lov'd,
Has left my Bosom colder than the Grave.   540
    LEONT. On, Athenais! on, 'tis bright before thee,
Pursue the track, and thou shalt be a star.
    ATHEN. O, Leontine, I swear, my noble Father,
That I will starve e're once forgo my Vertue;
And thus let's joyn to contradict the World,   545
That Empire could not tempt a poor old man
To sell his Prince the Honour of his Daughter;
And she too match'd the Spirit of her Father;
Tho' humbly born, and yet more humbly bred;
She for her Fame refus'd a Royal bed;   550
Who, tho' she lov'd, yet did put off the hour,
Nor could her Vertue be betray'd by Pow'r.
"Patterns like these will guilty Courts improve,
"And teach the fair to blush at conscious love;
    "Then let all Maids for Honour come in view,   555
    "If any Maid can more for Glory do.   [Exeunt.

End of A C T   II.

SONG after the Second ACT.

Sad as Death at dead of night
    The fair complaining Caelia sat,
But one poor Lamp was all her light,
    While thus she reason'd with her Fate;

Why should Man such Triumphs gain,   5
    And purchace Joys that gives us pain.
Ah! what Glory; ah what Glory can ensue;
    A helpless Virgin to undo.

Curse the Night then, Curse the Hour
    When first he drew thee to his arms,   10
When virtue was betray'd by power,
    And yielded to unlawful Charms,

When Love approach'd with all his Fires
    Arm'd with hopes and strong desires,
Sighs and tears, & ev'ry wile   15
    With which the Men the Maids beguile,

    Dream no more of Pleasures past,
Since all thy torments are to come;
    The secret is made known at last,
And endless shame is now thy Doom;   20
    The false forsworn alas is gone,
And left thee to despair alone.
Who that hears of Caelia's pain,
    Will ever trust a Man again.

Act. III. Scene I.

Enter Varanes and Aranthes.

VARA. Come to my Arms, my Faithful, Dear Aranthes,
Soft Counsellor, Companion of my Youth;
If I had longer been alone, most sure,
With the distraction that surrounds my heart,
My hand would have rebell'd against his Master,   5
And done a Murder here.
  ARAN.   The Gods forbid.
  VARA. I swear, I press thee with as hearty joy,
As ever fearful Bride embrac'd her man,
When from a Dream of Death she wak'd and found
Her Lover safe and sleeping by her side.   10
  ARAN. The Cause, my Lord?
  VARA. Early thou know'st last Night I went to rest;
But long, my Friend, e're slumber clos'd my eyes;
Long was the Combat fought, 'twixt Love and Glory;
The Fever of my Passion burnt me up,   15
My pangs grew stronger, and my Rack was doubled,
My bed was all a-float with the cold drops
That mortal pain wrang from my lab'ring Limbs;
My groans more deep than others dying gasps:
Therefore, I charge thee, haste to her Apartment;   20
I do conjure thee tell her, tell her all
My fears can urge, or fondness can invent:
Tell her how I repent, say any thing;
For any thing I'll do to quench my Fires:
Say I will marry her now on the Instant;   25
Say all that I would say; yet in the End
My Love shall make it more than Gods can utter.
  ARAN. My Lord! both Leontine and she are gone
From their Apartment. ---
  VARA.   Ha! gone, sayst thou! whither?
  ARAN. That was my whole Employment all this day: 30
But, Sir, I grieve to speak it, they have left
No track behind for care to find 'em out;
Nor is it possible---
  VARA. It is, it shall;
I'll struggle with impossibilities,
To find my Athenais: Not the Walls   35
Of Athens, nor of Thebes, shall hide her from me:
I'll bring the force of all my Fathers Arms,
And lay 'em waste, but I'll redeem my Love.
O, Leontine! morose old Leontine,
Thou meer Philosopher! O cruel Sage,   40

Who for one hasty word, one Chollerick doubt,
Has turn'd the Scale; though in the sacred Ballance
My Life, my Glory, and my Empire hung.
    ARAN. Most sure, my Lord, they are retir'd to Athens,
I will send Post to Night---
    VARA.   No, no, Aranthes;   45
Prepare my Chariots, for I'll go in Person;
I swear till now, till I began to fear
Some other might enjoy my Athenais,
I swear, I did not know how much I lov'd her;
But let's away, I'll to th' Emperour,   50
Thou to the hasty management of my business;
Prepare! to day I'll go, to day I'll find her:
No more; I'll take my leave of Theodosius,
And meet thee on the Hypodrome: away,
Let the wild hurry of thy Masters Love,   55
Make quick thy apprehension: Haste, and leave me.   [Exeunt.

Scene II.

    Pulcheria, Atticus, Leontine, Votaries leading Athenais in
        procession after her Baptism, to be confirm'd.

Atticus Sings.

      O, Chrysostom! look down and see,
      An Off'ring worthy Heav'n and thee!
      So rich the Victim, bright and fair,
      That she on Earth appears a Star:
CHOR.   Eudosia is the Virgins Name,   5
      And after-times shall sing her Fame.
ATTICUS
Sings.   Lead Her Votaries, lead her in,
      Her holy Birth does now begin.
1 VOTARY. In humble weeds, but clean array,
      Your hours shall sweetly pass away: 10
      And when the Rites Divine are past,
      To pleasant Gardens you shall haste.

2 VOTARY. Where many a flowry bed we have,
      That Emblem still to each a Grave:
      And when within the stream we look,   15
      With tears we use to swell the Brook:
      But Oh, when in the liquid glass,

```
                    Our Heav'n appears, we sigh to pass?
       CHOR.        For Heav'n alone we are design'd,
                    And all things bring our Heav'n to mind.                20
       ATHEN.   O Princess!  O most worthy of the World,     [Kneels.
That is submitted by it's Emperour,
To your most wise and providential sway:
What Greek, or Roman Eloquence, can paint
The Rapture and Devotion of my Soul!                                      25
I am adopted yours; you are my Goddess,
That have new-form'd, new-moulded my Conceptions,
And by the plat-form of a Work Divine,
New-fram'd, new-built me to your own desires;
Thrown all the Lumber of my Passions out,                                30
And made my heart a Mansion of perfection;
Clean as an Anchorites Grot, or Votaries Cell,
And spotless as the glories of his steps
Whom we far off adore!
       PULCH.             Rise, Eudosia,
And let me fold my Christian in my Arms.                                  35
With this dear pledge of an Eternal Love
I Seal thee, O Eudosia!  mine for ever.
Accept, blest Charge, the vows of my affection;
For, by the sacred Friendship that I give thee,
I think that Heav'n by Miracle did send thee,                            40
To ease my Cares, to help me in my Councils,
To be my Sister, partner in my bed;
And equally, through my whole Course of Life,
To be the better part of thy Pulcheria,
And share my Griefs and Joys.
       ATHEN.                 No, Madam, no;                               45
Excuse the Cares that this sad Wretch must bring you.
O rather let me leave the World for ever;
Or if I must partake your Royal Secrets,
If you resolve to load me with such Honour,
Let it be far from Cities, far from Courts,                               50
Where I may fly all humane Conversation;
Where I may never see, nor hear, nor name,
Nor think, nor dream, O Heav'n!  if possible,
Of Mankind more.
       PULCH.        What now, in Tears, Eudosia?
       ATHEN.   Far from the guilt of Pallaces!  O send me.               55
Drive me!  O Drive me from the Traytor man:
So I might 'scape that Monster, let me dwell
In Lyons haunts, or in some Tygers Den;
Place me on some steep, craggy, ruin'd Rock,
That bellies out, just dropping in the Ocean;                            60
Bury me in the hollow of it's Womb;
```

----

18 pass! Q3+.

Where, starving on my cold and flinty bed,
I may from far, with giddy apprehension,
See infinite Fathoms down the rumbling deep!
Yet not ev'n there, in that vast whirle of Death,   65
Can there be found so terrible a ruine,
As Man: false Man, smiling destructive Man.
    PULCH. Then thou hast lov'd, Eudosia; or my Sister;
Still nearer to my heart, so much the dearer;
Because our Fates are like, and hand in hand   70
Our Fortunes lead us through the Maze of Life:
I am glad that thou hast Lov'd; nay, Lov'd with danger,
Since thou hast 'scapt the ruin. ---Methinks it lightens
The weight of my Calamities, that thou
(In all things else so perfect and Divine,)   75
Art yet a-kin to my Infirmity,
And bear'st thy part in Loves melodious ill:
Love that like bane perfum'd infects the mind,
That sad delight that Charms all Woman-kind.
    ATHEN. Yes, Madam, I confess, that Love has charm'd me,   80
But never shall agen. No, I renounce him;
Inspire me all the wrongs of abus'd Women,
All you that have been Cozen'd by false Men:
See what a strict Example I will make;
But for the perjuries of one I will revenge ye   85
For all that's past, that's present, and to come.
    PULCH. O thou far more than the most Masculine Vertue!
Where our Astraea; where, O drowning brightness,
Where hast thou been so long? Let me again
Protest my admiration and my Love;   90
Let me declare aloud, while thou art here,
While such clear Vertue shines within our Circle,
Vice shall no more appear within the Pallace,
But hide her dazled eyes, and this be call'd
The holy Court: But loe, the Emperour comes.   95

    Enter Theodosius, and Attendants.

Beauty like thine may drive that Form away
That has so long entranc'd his Soul---My Lord---
    THEO. If yet, alas! I might but hope to see her;
But, oh forgive me Heav'n! this wilder start,
That thus would reach impossibility: 100
No, no, I never must behold her more,
As well my Atticus might raise the Dead,
As Leontine should charm that Form in view.
    PULCH. My Lord, I come to give your grief a Cure,
With purer Flames to draw that cruel Fire   105

----

89 hast thou] Q_{2+}; has thou Q_1.

That tortur'd you so long---Behold this Virgin---
The Daughter of your Tutor Leontine.
    THEO. Ha!
    PULCH. She is your Sisters Charge, and made a Christian,
And Athenais is Eudosia now;   110
But sure a fairer never grac'd Religion,
And for her Vertue she transcends Example.
    THEO. O all ye blest above, how can this be?
Am I awake, or is this possible?   [Athen. Kneels.
    PULCH. She kneels, my Lord, will you not go and raise her?   115
    THEO. Nay, do thou raise her, for I am rooted here;
Yet if laborious Love and melancholly
Have not o'recome me, and quite turn'd me mad,
It must be she! that naked dazling sweetness:
The very figure of that morning Star,   120
That dropping Pearls, and shedding dewy Beams,
Fled from the greedy Waves when I approach'd:
Answer me, Leontine, am I distracted?
Or is this true? by thee in all incounters
I will be rul'd, in Temperance and wildness,   125
When Reason clashes with extravagance;
But speak---
    LEONT. 'Tis true, my Lord, this is my Daughter,
Whom I conceal'd in Persia from all Eyes
But yours, when chance directed you that way.
    THEO. He says, 'tis true: Why then this heartless Carriage?   130
O! were I proof against the Darts of Love,
And cold to Beauty as the Marble-Lover
That lies without a thought upon his Tomb;
Would not this glorious dawn of Life run through me,
And waken Death it self---Why am I slow then?   135
What hinders now, but that in spite of Rules
I burst through all the bands of Death that hold me,   [He Kneels.
And fly with such a haste to that appearance,
As bury'd Saints shall make at the last Summons?
    ATHEN. The Emperour at my Feet! O Sir! forgive me,   140
Drown me not thus with everlasting shame;
Both Heav'n and Earth, must blush at such a view;
Nor can I bear it longer. ---
    LEONT. My Lord, she is unworthy---
    THEO. Ha! what say'st thou, Leontine!   145
Unworthy! O thou Atheist to perfection!
All that the blooming Earth could send forth fair;
All that the gawdy Heav'ns could drop down glorious!
Unworthy, say'st thou! Wert thou not her Father,
I swear I would revenge---But haste, and tell me,   150

---

111 Be sure Q4+.

For love like mine will bear no second thought.
Can all the Honours of the Orient,
Thus sacrific'd with the most pure affection,
With spotless thoughts and languishing desires,
Obtain, O Leontine, (the Crown at last)   155
To thee I speak, thy Daughter for my Bride?
   LEONT. My Lord, the Honour bears such estimation,
It calls the blood into my aged Cheeks,
And quite ore-whelms my Daughter with Confusion;
Who with her Body prostrate on the Earth   160
Ought to adore you for the proffer'd Glory.
   THEO. Let me embrace, and thank thee: O, kind Heav'n!
O, Atticus! Pulcheria! O, my Father!
Was ever change like mine? Run through the Streets;
Who waits there? Run, and lowd as Fame can speak,   165
With Trumpet-sounds proclaim your Emperours joy:
And, as of old, on the great Festival
Of her they call the Mother of the Gods,
Let all work cease, at least an Oaken Garland
Crown each Plebeian head; let spritely Bowls   170
Be dol'd about, and the toss'd Cimbals sound:
Tell 'em their much lamented Theodosius
By Miracle is brought from death to life:
His Melancholly's gone, and now once more
He shall appear at the State's Helm again;   175
Nor fear a Wrack while this bright Star directs us;
For while she shines no Sands, no cowring Rocks,
Shall lye unseen, but I will cut my way
Secure as Neptune through the highest stream,
And to the Port in safety steer the World.   180
   ATHEN. Alas, my Lord, consider my Extraction,
With all my other wants---
   THEO.   Peace, Empress, peace!
No more the Daughter of old Leontine,
A Christian now, and Partner of the East.
   ATHEN. My Father has dispos'd me, you command me;   185
What can I answer then but my Obedience?
   THEO. Attend her, dear Pulcheria; and, oh tell her,
To Morrow, if she please, I will be happy.   [Ex. Pulc. and Athen.
O why so long should I my Joys delay?
Time imp thy Wings, let not the Minutes stay,   190
But to a moment change the tedious day.
The day! 'twill be an Age before to Morrow:
An Age, a Death, a vast Eternity,
Where we shall cold, and past Enjoyment lye.

----

151 thought, Q_{2+}.
156 to my Bride? Q_{2+}.
190 thy minutes Q_{4+}.

Enter Varanes and Aranthes.

VARA. O, Theodosius!
THEO.   Ha! my Brother here!   195
Why dost thou come to make my bliss run o're?
What is there more to wish? Fortune can find
No flaw in such a glut of happiness,
To let one Misery in---O, my Varanes!
Thou that of late didst seem to walk on Clouds,   200
Now give a loose, let go the slacken'd Reins,
Let us drive down the Precipice of Joy,
As if that all the Winds of Heav'n were for us.
VARA. My Lord, I am glad to find the Gale is turn'd,
And give you joy of this auspicious Fortune.   205
Plough on your way, with all your Streamers out:
With all your glorious Flags and Garlands ride
Triumphant on---And leave me to the Waves,
The Sands, the Winds, the Rocks, the sure destruction
And ready Gulphs that gape to swallow me.   210
THEO. It was thy hand that drew me from the Grave,
Who had been dead by this time to Ambition,
To Crowns, to Titles, and my slighted Greatness.
But still as if each work of thine deserv'd
The smile of Heav'n---thy Theodosius met   215
With something dearer than his Diadem,
With all that's worth a wish, that's worth a life;
I met with that which made me leave the world.
VARA. And I, O turn of Chance! O cursed Fortune!
Have lost at once all that could make me happy.   220
O ye too partial Powers! But now no more.
The Gods, my dear, my most lov'd Theodosius,
Double all those joys that thou hast met upon thee;
For sure thou art most worthy, worthy more
Than Jove in all his prodigality   225
Can e're bestow in blessings on Mankind!
And oh methinks my Soul is strangely mov'd,
Takes it the more unkindly of her Stars,
That thou and I cannot be blest together:
For I must leave thee, Friend! this night must leave thee, 230
To go in doubtful search of what perhaps
I ne're shall find; if so my cruel Fate
Has order'd it: Why then farewell for ever,
For I shall never, never see thee more.
THEO. How sensible my tender soul is grown   235
Of what you utter! O my Gallant Friend!
O Brother! O Varanes! Do not judge
By what I speak! for sighs will interrupt me;

---

207 Flags and Streamers Q4+.

Judge by my Tears, Judge by these strict embraces,
And by my last Resolve: Tho' I have met   240
With what in silence I so long ador'd,
Tho' in the rapture of protesting joyes;
I had set down to morrow for my Nuptials;
And Atticus to night prepares the Temple;
Yet, my Varanes, I will Rob my Soul   245
Of all her health, of my Imperial Bride,
And wander with thee in the search of that
On which thy life depends---
    VARA.   If this I suffer,
Conclude me then begotten of a Hind,
And bred in Wilds: No, Theodosius, no;   250
I charge thee by our Friendship, and conjure thee
By all the Gods, to mention this no more:
Perhaps, dear Friend, I shall be sooner here
Than you expect, or I my self imagine:
What most I grieve is that I cannot wait   255
To see your Nuptials: Yet my Soul is with you,
And all my adorations to your Bride.
    THEO. What, my Varanes, will you be so cruel
As not to see my Bride before you go?
Or are you angry at your Rivals Charms,   260
Who has already ravisht half my heart,
That once was all your own?
    VARA. You know I am disorder'd!
My melancholly will not suit her blest Condition.   [Ex. Theo.
And the Gods know, since thou, my Athenais,   265
Art fled from these sick Eyes, all other Women
To my pall'd Soul seem like the Ghosts of Beauty,
And haunt my memory with the loss of thee.

    Enter Athenais, Theodosius leading her.

    THEO. Behold, my Lord, the occasion of my Joy.
    VARA. O ye immortal Gods! Aranthes! oh!   270
Look there, and wonder: Ha! is't possible?
    ATHEN. My Lord, the Emperour says you are his Friend,
He charges me to use my interest,
And beg of you to stay, at least so long
As our Espousals will be solemnizing;   275
I told him I was honour'd once to know you;
But that so slightly, as I could not warrant
The grant of any thing that I should ask you---
    VARA. O Heaven! and Earth! O Athenais! why,
Why dost thou use me thus? had I the World   280
Thou know'st it should be thine.
    ATHEN.   I know not that---
But yet, to make sure work, one half of it
Is mine already, Sir, without your giving.

My Lord, the Prince is obstinate, his glory
Scorns to be mov'd by the weak breath of Woman;   285
He is all Heroe, bent for higher game;
Therefore, 'tis nobler, Sir, to let him go:
If not for him, my Lord, yet for my self
I must intreat the Favour to retire.   [Ex. Athen. &c.
    VARA. Death! and despair! Confusion! Hell and Furies.   290
    THEO. Heav'n guard thy health, and still preserve thy Vertue.
What should this mean? I fear the Consequence,   [Aside. *
For 'tis too plain they know each other well.
    VARA. Undone! Aranthes! lost, undone for ever.
I see my doom, I read it with broad eyes,   295
As plain as if I saw the Book of Fate:
Yet I will muster all my Spirits up,
Digest my griefs, swallow the rising passions.
Yes, I will stand this shock of all the Gods
Well as I can, and struggle for my life.   300
    THEO. You muse, my Lord: and if you'l give me leave
To judge your thoughts; they seem employ'd at present
About my Bride: I guess you know her too.
    VARA. His Bride! O, Gods! give me a moments patience! [Aside. *
I must confess the sight of Athenais,   305
Where I so little did expect to see her,
So grac'd, and so adorn'd, did raise my wonder.
But what exceeds all admiration is
That you should talk of making her your Bride;
'Tis such a blind effect of monstrous Fortune,   310
That tho' I well remember you affirm'd it,
I cannot yet believe---
    THEO.   Then now believe me,
By all the pow'rs divine, I will espouse her.
    VARA. Ha! I shall leap the bounds. Come, come, my Lord,
By all those pow'rs you nam'd, I say you must not.   315
    THEO. I say, I will; and who shall bar my pleasure?
Yet more, I speak the Judgment of my Soul,
Weigh but with Fortune merit in the Ballance,
And Athenais loses by the Marriage.
    VARA. Relentless Fates! malicious cruel Pow'rs!   320
O for what Crime do you thus rack your Creature?
Sir, I must tell you this unkingly meanness
Suits the Profession of an Anchorite well.
But in an Oriental Emperour
It gives offence; nor can you without scandal,   325
Without the notion of a groveling Spirit,
Espouse the Daughter of old Leontine,
Whose utmost Glory is to have been my Tutor.
    THEO. He has so well acquitted that Employment,

---

* [Aside.]; om. Q1+.

Breeding you up to such a gallant height   330
Of full perfection, and imperial greatness,
That ev'n for this respect, if for no other,
I will esteem him worthy while I live.
    VARA. My Lord, you'l pardon me a little Freedom;
For I must boldly urge in such a Cause,   335
Who-ever flatters you, tho' ne're so near
Related to your blood, should be suspected.
    THEO. If Friendship would admit a cold suspition,
After what I have heard, and seen to day,
Of all Mankind I should suspect Varanes.   340
    VARA. He has stung me to the heart; my groans will choke me, [Aside. *
Unless my struggling passion gets a vent.
Out with it then---I can no more dissemble---
Yes, yes, my Lord, since you reduce me to
The last necessity, I must confess it;   345
I must avow my Flame for Athenais.
I am all Fire! my passion eats me up,
It grows incorporate with my flesh and blood!
My pangs redouble, now they cleave my heart!
O Athenais! O Eudosia---oh---   350
Though plain as day I see my own destruction,
Yet to my death, and oh let all the Gods
Bear Witness! I swear I will adore thee.
    THEO. Alas! Varanes. Which of us two the Heav'ns
Have mark'd for Death, is yet above the stars;   355
But while we live let us preserve our Friendship
Sacred and just, as we have ever done.
This onely Mean in two such hard Extreams
Remains for both: To morrow you shall see her,
With all advantage in her own Apartment;   360
Take your own time, say all you can to gain her;
If you can win her, lead her into Persia;
If not, consent that I espouse her here.
    VARA. Still worse and worse! O Theodosius! oh,
I cannot speak for sighs, my death is seal'd   365
By this last sweetness; had you been less good,
I might have hop'd; but now my doom's at hand.
Go then, and take her, take her to the Temple:
The Gods too give you joy. O Athenais!
Why does thy Image mock my Foolish sorrow?   370
O Theodosius, do not see my Tears:
Away, and leave me! leave me to the Grave.
    THEO. Farewel; lets leave the issue to the Heav'ns.
I will prepare your way with all that Honour
Can urge in your behalf, tho' to my Ruine.   [Ex. Theo.   375
    VARA. O, I could tear my Limbs, and eat my Flesh;

---

   * [Aside.]; om. $Q_{1}+$.

Fool that I was, fond, proud, vain-glorious fool!
Damn'd be all Courts, and treble damn'd Ambition:
Blasted be thy remembrance! Curses on thee.
And plagues on plagues fall on those Fools that seek thee.   380
    ARAN. Have comfort, Sir---
    VARA.   Away, and leave me, Villain;
Traytor, who wrought me first to my destruction---
Yet stay and help me, help me to curse my pride,
Help me to wish that I had ne're been Royal,
That I had never heard the name of Cyrus,   385
That my first Brawl in Court had been my last.
Oh that I had been born some happy Swain,
And never known a life so great, so vain!
Where I extreams might not be forc'd to choose,
And blest with some mean Wife, no Crown could lose: 390
    Where the dear Partner of my little state,
    With all her smiling Off-spring at the Gate,
    Blessing my labours, might my coming wait.
    Where in our humble Beds all safe might ly,
    And not in cursed Courts for glory dy. ---   [Exeunt.   395

SONG.*

1.

    Hail to the Mirtle Shade,
    All hail to the Nymphs of the Fields;
    Kings would not here invade
    Those pleasures that vertue yields.
CHOR.   Beauty here opens her Arms,   5
    To soften the languishing mind;
    And Phillis unlocks her Charms;
    Ah Phillis! ah why so kind?

2.

    Phillis, thou Soul of Love,
    Thou joy of the neighb'ring Swains;   10
    Phillis that Crowns the Grove,
    And Phillis that gilds the Plains.
CHOR.   Phillis, that ne're had the skill,
    To paint and to patch and be fine;
    Yet Phillis, whose eyes can kill,   15
    Whom Nature had made Divine.

3.

    Phillis, whose charming Song,
    Makes Labour and pains a delight
    Phillis that makes the day young,
    And shortens the live-long night.   20
CHOR.   Phillis, whose lips like May,

---

* In Q1 this song appears here at the end of Act III and at the back
with the music.

Still laughs at the sweets that they bring;
Where Love never knows decay,
But sets with Eternal Spring.

End of **ACT III.**

ACT. IV. SCENE I.

Enter Marcian, and Lucius at a distance.

MARC. The General of the Oriental Armies,
Was a Commission large as Fate could give:
'Tis gone: why what care I: O Fortune, Fortune!
Thou laughing Empress of this busie world,
Marcian defies thee now ---   5
Why what a thing is a discarded Favourite?
He who but now, tho' longing to retire,
Cou'd not for busie Waiters be alone,
Throng'd in his Chamber, haunted to his Closet
With a full Crowd, and an Eternal Court;   10
When once the favour of his Prince is turn'd,
Shun'd as a Ghost, the Clouded man appears;
And all the gawdy worshippers forsake him;
So fares it now with me where-e're I come,
As if I were another Cataline.   15
The Courtiers rise, and no man will sit near me,
As if the Plague were on me all men fly me:
O Lucius! Lucius! if thou leav'st me too,
I think, I swear I think I cou'd not bear it;
But like a Slave, my Spirit broke with suffering,   20
Should on these Coward knees fall down and beg,
Once to be great again ---
     LUC.   Forbid it, Heav'n!
That e're the noble Marcian condescend
To ask of any, but the immortal Gods;
Nay, I avow, if yet your Spirit dare,   25
Spite of the Court, you shall be great as Caesar.
     MARC. No, Lucius, no; the Gods repel that humour.
Yet since we are alone, and must e're long
Leave this bad Court; let us like Vetterans
Speak out --- Thou say'st, alas! as great as Caesar: 30
But where's his greatness? Where is his Ambition?
If any sparks of Vertue yet remain
In this poor Figure of the Roman Glory;
I say, if any be, how dim they shine,
Compar'd with what his great Fore-Fathers were;   35
How should he lighten then, or awe the World,
Whose Soul in Courts is but a Lambent-Fire,
And scarce, O Rome! a Glow-worm in the Field:
Soft, young, Religous, God-like qualities,
For one that should recover the lost Empire;   40

---

39 Religous, Q$_{2+}$.

And wade through Seas of blood, and walk o're Mountains
Of slaughter'd Bodies to immortal Honour.
    LUC. Poor heart! he pin'd a while ago for Love.
    MARC. And for his Mistress vow'd to leave the World;
But some new chance, it seems, has chang'd his mind.   45
A Marriage! but to whom, or whence she came,
None knows: but yet a Marriage is proclaim'd,
Pageants prepar'd; the Arches are adorn'd;
The Statues Crown'd; the Hyppodrome does groan
Beneath the Burden of the mounted Warriors;   50
The Theater is open'd too, where he
And the hot Persian mean to act their Follies.
Gods! Gods! Is this the Image of our Caesars?
Is this the model of our Romulus?
O why so poorly have you stampt Rome's glory!   55
Not Romes, but yours! Is this Man fit to bear it?
This waxen Portraicture of Majesty!
Which every warmer passion does melt down,
And makes him fonder than a Woman's longing.
    LUC. Thus much I know, to the eternal shame   60
Of the Imperial blood; this upstart Empress,
This fine new Queen is sprung from abject Parents;
Nay, basely born! but that's all one to him,
He likes and loves, and therefore marries her.
    MARC. Shall I not speak? Shall I not tell him of it?   65
I feel this big swollen throbbing Roman Spirit
Will burst, unless I utter what I ought.

    Enter Pulcheria with a Paper in her hand, and Julia.

    MARC. Pulcheria here! why she's the scourge of Marcian:
I tremble too when ever she approaches;
And my heart dances an unusual measure,   70
Spite of my self I blush and cannot stir
While she is here --- What, Lucius, can this mean?
'Tis said Calphurnia had the heart of Caesar:
Augustus doted on the subtle Livia:
Why then should I not worship that fair Anger?   75
Oh didst thou mark her when her fury lightned,
She seem'd all Goddess; nay, her frowns became her;
There was a beauty in her very wildness.
Were I a man born great as our first Founder,
Sprung from the blood divine: But I am cast   80
Beyond all possibility of hope.
    PULCH. Come hither, Marcian! read this Paper o're,
And mark the strange neglect of Theodosius:
He signes what-e're I bring; perhaps you have heard
To morrow he intends to Wed a Maid of Athens   85
New made a Christian, and new nam'd Eudosia;
Whom he more dearly prizes than his Empire:
Yet in this Paper he has set his hand,

And seal'd it too with th' Imperial Signet,
That she shall lose her head to morrow morning.   90
  MARC. 'Tis not for me to Judge; yet this seems strange ---
  PULCH. I know he rather would commit a murder,
On his own person, than permit a vein
Of her to bleed; yet, Marcian, what might follow,
If I were envious of this Virgins honour,   95
By his rash passing whatsoever I offer ---
Without a view -- ha, but I had forgot!
Julia, let's haste from this infectious person ---
I had forgot that Marcian was a Traytor;
Yet by the powr's divine, I swear''tis pity,   100
That one so form'd by Nature for all honour,
All Titles, Greatness, Dignities Imperial,
The noblest Person, and the bravest courage,
Should not be honest: Julia, is't not pity? ---
O Marcian, Marcian! I could weep to think   105
Vertue should lose it self as thine has done.
Repent, rash man, if yet 'tis not too late,
And mend thy errors; so farewell for ever. [Ex. Pulch. Jul.
  MARC. Farewell for ever! no Madam, e're I go,
I am resolv'd to speak, and you shall hear me: 110
Then if you please, take off this Traytors head;
End my Commission and my life together.
  LUC. Perhaps you'l laugh at what I am going to say;
But by your life, my Lord, I think 'tis true:
Pulcheria loves this Traytour! did you mark her?   115
At first she had forgot your banishment;
Makes you her Counsellour, and tells her secrets,
As to a Friend; nay, leaves 'em in your hand,
And says, 'tis pity that you are not honest,
With such Description of your gallantry   120
As none but Love cou'd make: Then taking leave,
Through the dark lashes of her darting eyes,
Methought she shot her Soul at every glance;
Still looking back, as if she had a mind
That you should know she left her heart behind her.   125
  MARC. Alas! thou dost not know her, nor do I!
Nor can the Wit of all man-kind conceive her;
But let's away. This Paper is of use.
  LUC. I guess your purpose;
He is a Boy, and as a Boy you'l use him;   130
There is no other way.
  MARC.   Yes, if he be not
Quite dead with sleep, for ever lost to honour:
Marcian with this shall rouze him. O, my Lucius!
Methinks the Ghosts of the great Theodosius,
And thundring Constantine appear before me: 135
They charge me as a Souldier to chastise him,
To lash him with keen words from lazy Love,
And shew him how they trod the paths of honour. [Exeunt.

SCENE II.

Theodosius lying on a Couch, with two Boys drest like Cupids
singing to him as he sleeps.

SONG.
Happy day! ah happy day!
That Caesar's Beams did first display,
So peaceful was the happy day.
The Gods themselves did all look down,
The Royal Infant's Birth to Crown,   5
So pleas'd they scarce did on the guilty frown.

Happy day! ah happy day!
And oh thrice happy hour!
That made such Goodness Master of such Pow'r:
For thus the Gods declare to men,   10
No day like this shall ever come agen.

Enter Marcian with an Order.

THEO. Ha! what rash thing art thou, who set'st so small
A value on thy life thus to presume
Against the fatal Orders I have given,
Thus to entrench on Caesar's solitude,   15
And urge me to thy ruine?
    MARC.   Mighty Caesar,
I have transgrest, and for my Pardon bow
To thee, as to the Gods when I offend:
Nor can I doubt your Mercy when you know
The nature of my Crime. I am Commission'd   20
From all the Earth to give thee thanks and praises,
Thou Darling of Mankind! whose Conqu'ring Arms
Already drown the Glory of great Julius,
Whose deeper reach in Laws and Policy
Makes wise Augustus envy thee in Heav'n;   25
What mean the Fates by such prodigious Vertue?
When scarce the manly Down yet shades thy Face,
With Conquest thus to over-run the World;
And make Barbarians tremble? O, ye Gods!
Should Destiny now end thee in thy Bloom,   30
Methinks I see thee mourn'd above the loss
Of lov'd Germanicus, thy Funerals
Like his are solemniz'd with tears, and blood.
    THEO. How, Marcian!
    MARC.   Yes, the raging multitude,
Like torrents, set no bound to their mad grief;   35

Shave their Wives heads, and tear off their own hair,
With wild despair they bring their Infants out
To brawl their Parents sorrow in the Streets:
Trade is no more, all Courts of Justice stopt;
With stones they dash the Windows of their Temples,   40
Pull down their Altars, break their house-hold Gods;
And still the Universal groan is this,
Constantinople's lost, our Empire's ruin'd:
Since he is gone, that Father of his Country;
Since he is dead, O life, where is thy pleasure?   45
O Rome! Oh conquer'd World, where is thy Glory?
    THEO. I know thee well, thy Custom and thy manners;
Thou dost upbraid me; but no more of this,
Not for thy Life ---
    MARC.   What's life without my Honour?
Could you transform your self into a Gorgon,   50
Or make that beardless Face like Jupiter's,
I would be heard in spight of all your Thunder:
O pow'r of Guilt, you fear to stand the Test
Which Vertue brings; like Sores your Vices shake
Before this Roman-healer: But, by the Gods,   55
Before I go I'll rip the Malady,
And let the Venom flow before your eyes.
This is a debt to the great Theodosius,
The Grandfather of your illustrious blood:
And then farewell for ever.
    THEO.   Presuming Marcian!   60
What canst thou urge against my innocence?
Through the whole Course of all my harmless youth,
Ev'n to this hour, I cannot call to mind
One wicked act which I have done to shame me.
    MARC. This may be true: yet if you give the sway   65
To other hands; and your poor subjects suffer,
Your negligence to them is as the Cause.
O Theodosius credit me, who know
The world, and hear how Souldiers censure Kings;
In after-times, if thus you shou'd go on,   70
Your memory by Warriors will be scorn'd,
As much as Nero or Caligula loath'd,
They will dispise your sloth, and backward ease,
More than they hate the others cruelty.
And what a thing, ye Gods! is scorn or pity?   75
Heap on me, Heav'n, the hate of all mankind;
Load me with Malice, envy, detestation:
Let me be horrid to all apprehension,
And the world shun me, so I escape but scorn.
    THEO. Prithee no more!   80
    MARC. Nay, when the Legions make Comparisons;
And say, thus cruel Nero once resolv'd
On Galba's Insurrection, for revenge,

To give all France as plunder to the Arms,
To poison the whole Senate at a Feast;   85
To burn the City, turn the wild beasts out;
Bears, Lions, Tygers, on the Multitude;
That so obstructing those that quench'd the Fire,
He might at once destroy Rebellious Rome.
    THEO. O cruelty! why tell'st thou me of this?   90
Am I of such a barb'rous bloudy temper?
    MARC. Yet some will say; this shew'd he had a spirit,
However fierce, avenging, and pernicious,
That savour'd of a Roman; but for you,
What can your partial Sycophants invent,   95
To make you Room among the Emperors?
Whose utmost is the smallest part of Nero;
A pretty Player, one that can act a Heroe,
And never be one. O ye immortal Gods!
Is this the old Caesarian Majesty?   100
Now in the name of our great Romulus,
Why sing you not, and fiddle too as he did?
Why have you not like Nero a Phenascus?
One to take care of your celestial Voice?
Ly on your back, my Lord, and on your stomach   105
Lay a thin plate of Lead, abstain from fruits;
And when the business of the Stage is done,
Retire with your loose Friends, to costly Banquets,
While the lean Army groans upon the ground.
    THEO. Leave me, I say; lest I chastise thee: 110
Hence, begon, I say ---
    MARC. Not till you have heard me out ---
Build too like him a Pallace lin'd with gold,
As long and large as that to the Esquiline:
Inclose a pool too in it like the Sea,   115
And at the Empires cost let Navies meet:
Adorn your starry Chambers too with Gems,
Contrive the plated Ceilings to turn round,
With Pipes to cast Ambrosian Oyles upon you:
Consume with his prodigious Vanity,   120
In meer perfumes, and Odorous distillations,
Of Sisterces at once 400 Millions,
Let naked Virgins wait you at your Table,
And wanton Cupids dance and clap their Wings;
No matter what becomes of the poor Souldier;   125
So they perform the drudgery they are fit for;
Why let 'em starve for want of their Arrears,
Drop as they go, and lye like Dogs in Ditches.
    THEO. Come, you are a Traytor!

---

125 Soldiers; C_{2-3}.

MARC.   Go too, you are a Boy ---
Or by the Gods ---
    THEO.   If arrogance like this,   130
And to the Emp'ror's face, should scape unpunish'd,
I'll write my self a Coward; dye then Villain,
A death too glorious for so bad a man,
By Theodosius hand.   [Marcian disarms him, but
                                  is wounded.

    MARC.   Now Sir, where are you?
What in the name of all our Roman Spirits   135
Now charmes my hand from giving thee thy Fate?
Has he not cut me off from all my honours?
Torn my Commissions, sham'd me to the Earth,
Banisht the Court, a vagabond for ever?
Does not the Souldier hourly ask it from me?   140
Sigh their own wrongs, and beg me to revenge 'em?
What hinders now, but that I mount the Throne?
And make to that this purple Youth my Footstool?
The Armies Court me, and my Countryes Cause:
The injuries of Rome and Greece perswade me.   145
Shew but this Roman blood which he has drawn,
They'll make me Emperor whether I will or no:
Did not for less than this the latter Brutus,
Because he thought Rome wrong'd, in person head
Against his Friend a black Conspiracy?   150
And stab the Majesty of all the World?
    THEO. Act as you please, I am within your Power.
    MARC. Did not the former Brutus for the Crime
Of Sextus drive old Tarquin from his Kingdom?
And shall this Prince too, by permiting others   155
To act their wicked Wills and lawless pleasures,
Ravish from the Empire it's dear health,
Well being, happiness, and ancient glory,
Go on in this dishonourable rest?
Shall he, I say, dream on, while the starv'd Troops,   160
Lye cold and waking in the Winter Camp;
And like pin'd Birds for want of sustenance
Feed on the Haws and Berries of the Fields?
O temper! temper me! ye gracious Gods!
Give to my hand forbearance; to my heart   165
Its constant Loyalty! I would but shake him,
Rouze him a little from this death of Honour,
And shew him what he should be.
    THEO.   You accuse me,
As if I were some Monster, most unheard of:
First, as the Ruin of the Army; then   170

---

129 are a Boy ---] Q_{3+}; are Boy --- Q_{1-2}.
143 make besides this C_3
159 rest?] Q_{2+}; rest. Q_1.

Of taking your Commission: But, by Heav'n
I swear, O Marcian! this I never did;
Nor e're intended it: Nor say I this
To alter thy stern usage; for with what
Thou hast said, and done, and brought to my remembrance,   175
I grow already weary of my life.
    MARC. My Lord, I take your word: you do not know
The wounds which rage within your Countries Bowels:
The horrid usage of the suff'ring Souldier:
But why will not our Theodosius know,   180
If you intrust the Government to others
That act these Crimes: Who but your self's to blame?
Be witness, ye Gods! of my plain-dealing,
Of Marcian's honesty, how-e're degraded:
I thank you for my banishment! but, alas!   185
My loss is little to what soon will follow;
Reflect but on your self and your own joys:
Let not this Lethargy for ever hold you:
'Twas rumor'd through the City that you lov'd:
That your Espousals should be solemniz'd;   190
When on a sudden here you send your Orders:
That this bright Favourite, the lov'd Eudosia,
Should lose her head.
    THEO.   O Heav'n, and Earth! What say'st thou,
That I have seal'd the death of my Eudosia?
    MARC. 'Tis your own hand and Signet: Yet I swear,   195
Tho' you have given to Female hands your sway,
And therefore I as well as the whole Army
For ever ought to Curse all Woman-kind,
Yet when the Virgin came, as she was doom'd,
And on the Scaffold, for that purpose rais'd,   200
Without the Walls appear'd before the Army!
    THEO. What, on a Scaffold! ha, before, the Army!
    MARC. How quickly was the tide of Fury turn'd
To soft compassion and relenting tears: But when the Axe
Sever'd the brightest beauty of the Earth   205
From that fair body, had you heard the groan,
Which like a peal of distant Thunder ran
Through all the Armed Host, you would have thought,
By the immediate darkness that fell round us,
Whole Nature was concern'd at such a suff'ring,   210
And all the Gods were angry.
    THEO.   O, Pulcheria!
Cruel ambitious Sister, this must be
Thy doing. O support me, noble Marcian!
Now, now's the time, if thou darst strike; behold
I offer thee my Breast, with my last breath   215

---

183 O ye Gods! C$_{2-3}$.

I'll thank thee too, if now thou drawst my blood.
Were I to live, thy Counsel should direct me;
But 'tis too late ---   [He swoons.
    MARC.   He faints! what, hoa there, Lucius!   [Enter Lucius.
My Lord, the Emperour, Eudosia lives;
She's here, or will be in a minute, moment,   220
Quick as a thought she calls you to the Temple.
O Lucius, help --- I have gone too far; but see,
He breathes again --- Eudosia has awak'd him.
    THEO. Did you not name Eudosia?
    MARC.   Yes, she lives;
I did but feign the story of her Death,   225
To find how near you plac'd her to your heart:
And may the Gods rain all their plagues upon me,
If ever I rebuke you thus again:
Yet 'tis most certain that you sign'd her Death,
Not knowing what the wise Pulcheria offer'd,   230
Who left it in my hand to startle you:
But, by my Life and Fame, I did not think
It would have toucht your life. O pardon me,
Dear Prince, my Lord, my Emp'ror! Royal Master!
Droop not because I utter'd some rash words,   235
And was a Mad man --- by th' immortal Gods!
I love you as my Soul: what-e're I said,
My thoughts were otherwise; believe these tears
Which do not use to flow; all shall be well:
I swear that there are seeds in that sweet temper,   240
To attone for all the Crimes in this bad age.
    THEO. I thank thee. First for my Eudosias life.
What but my Love could have call'd back that life
Which thou hast made me hate, and oh methought
'Twas hard, dear Marcian, very hard from thee,   245
From him I ever reverenc'd as my Father,
To hear so harsh a Message --- but no more:
We are Friends: Thy hand; Nay, if thou wilt not rise,
And let me fold my Armes about thy Neck,
I'll not believe thy Love! In this forgive me.   250
First let me wed Eudosia, and we'll out;
We will my General, and make amends
For all that's past: Glory and Armes ye call,
And Marcian leads me on ---
    MARC.   Let her not rest then,
Espouse her streight; I'll strike you at a heat;   255
May this great humour get large growth within you,
And be encourag'd by the emboldening Gods:
O what a sight will this be to the Souldier;
To see me bring you drest in shining Armour,
To head the shouting Squadrons --- O ye Gods!   260

---

244 hate? But Q_{4+}.

Methinks I hear the ecchoing Cries of Joy;
The sound of Trumpets, and the beat of Drums.
I see each starving Souldier bound from Earth,
As if some God by miracle had rais'd him,
And with beholding you grow fat again: 265
Nothing but gazing eyes, and opening mouths;
Cheeks red with joy, and lifted hands about you:
Some wiping the glad tears that trickle down
With broken Io's, and with sobbing raptures,
Crying to Arms: He's come! our Emp'ror's come   270
To win the World. Why, is not this far better
Than lolling in a Ladies lap, and sleeping,
Fasting, or praying? Come, come, you shall be merry.
And for Eudosia, she is yours already:
Marcian has said it, Sir, she shall be yours.   275
    THEO. O Marcian! oh my Brother! Father! all:
Thou best of Friends, most faithful Counsellor,
I'll find a match for thee too e're I rest,
To make thee Love me. For when thou art with me,
I'm strong and well: But when thou art gone, I am nothing.   280

    Enter Athenais, meeting Theodosius.

    THEO. Alas, Eudosia, tell me what to say;
For my full heart can scarce bring forth a word,
Of that which I have sworn to see perform'd.
    ATHEN. I am perfectly obedient to your pleasure.
    THEO. Well then I come to tell thee that Varanes   285
Of all man-kind is nearest to my heart;
I love him, dear Eudosia, and to prove
That love on trial all my blood's too little;
Ev'n thee, if I were sure to dy this moment,
(As Heav'n alone can tell how far my Fate   290
Is off!) O thou my Soul's most tender joy,
With my last breath I would bequeath him thee.
    ATHEN. Then you are pleas'd, my Lord, to yield me to him.
    THEO. No, my Eudosia; no, I will not yield thee
While I have life; for Worlds I will not yield thee: 295
Yet, thus far I am engag'd to let thee know,
He loves thee Athenais more than ever.
He languishes, despairs, and dies like me;
And I have past my word that he shall see thee.
    ATHEN. Ah, Sir, what have you done against your self,   300
And me? Why have you past your fatal word?
Why will you trust me, who am now affraid
To trust my self? Why do you leave me naked
To an assault, who had made proof my Vertue,
With this sure guard never to see him more.   305
For, oh with trembling Agonies I speak it,
I cannot see a Prince, whom once I lov'd,

Bath'd in his grief, and gasping at my Feet,
In all the violent trances of despair,
Without a sorrow that perhaps may end me.   310
    THEO. O ye severer Pow'rs! too cruel Fate!
Did ever Love tread such a maze before?
Yet, Athenais, still I trust thy Vertue;
But if thy bleeding Heart cannot refrain,
Give, give thy self away; yet still remember,   315
That moment Theodosius is no more ---
                         [Ex. Theo. with Marc. Luc.*
    ATHEN. Now glory! now, if ever thou didst work
In Womans mind, assist me --- Oh my heart!
Why dost thou throb, as if thou wer't a breaking?
Down, down, I say, think on thy Injuries,   320
Thy wrongs! thy wrongs. 'Tis well my Eyes are drye,
And all within my Bosom now is still.

        Enter Varanes, leaning on Aranthes.

Ha! is this he! or is't Varanes Ghost:
He looks as if he had bespoke his Grave,
Trembling and pale; I must not dare to view him;   325
For oh I feel his melancholly here,
And fear I shall too soon partake his sickness!
    VARA. Thus to the angry Gods offending Mortals,
Made sensible by some severe affliction,
How all their Crimes are registred in Heav'n,   330
In that nice Court, how no rash word escapes,
But ev'n extravagant thoughts are all set down:
Thus the poor Penitents with fear approach
The reverend Shrines, and thus for mercy bow,   [Kneels.
Thus melting too, they wash the hallowed Earth,   335
And groan to be forgiven ---
O Empress! O Eudosia! such you are now,
These are your Titles, and I must not dare
Ever to call you Athenais more.
    ATHEN. Rise, rise, my Lord, let me intreat you rise,   340
I will not hear you in that humble posture:
Rise, or I must with-draw --- The World would blush
For you and me, should it behold a Prince,
Sprung from immortal Cyrus, on his knees
Before the Daughter of a poor Philosopher.   345
    VARA. 'Tis just, you righteous Gods! my doom is just;
Nor will I strive to deprecate her anger.
If possible I'll aggravate my Crimes,

---

   * [Ex. Theo. with Marc. Luc.]; [Ex. Theo. with Attic. Pulc. Leon.
  Q_{1+}. Since Atticus, Pulcheria, and Leontine are not on the stage,
this direction is an error.

That she may rage till she has broke my heart:
For all I now desire, and let the Gods,   350
Those cruel Gods that joyn to my undoing,
Be witnesses to this unnatural wish,
Is to fall dead without a wound before her.
    ATHEN. O ye known sounds! But I must steel my soul.
Methinks these Robes, my Delia, are too heavy.   355
    VARA. Not worth a word, a look, nor one regard!
Is then the Nature of my fault so hainous,
That when I come to take my eternal leave,
You'll not vouchsafe to view me? This is scorn
Which the fair soul of gentle Athenais   360
Would ne're have harbour'd ---
O, for the sake of him, whom you e're-long
Shall hold as fast as now you'r wishes form him,
Give me a patient hearing; for how-ever
I talk of death, and seem to loath my life,   365
I would deliberate with my Fate a while
With snatching glances eye thee to the last,
Pause o're a loss like that of Athenais,
And parly with my ruine.
    ATHEN.   Speak, my Lord,
To hear you is the Emperor's command;   370
And for that Cause I readily obey.
    VARA. The Emperor, the Emperor's command;
And for that cause she readily obeys,
I thank you Madam that on any terms
You condescend to hear me ---   375
Know then, Eudosia. Ah, rather let me call thee
By the Lov'd name of Athenais still;
That name that I so often have invok'd!
And which was once Auspitious to my Vows;
So oft at Midnight sigh'd amongst the Groves: 380
The Rivers murmur and the Eccho's burden,
Which every Bird could sing and wind did bear!
By that dear Name, I make this protestation,
By all that's good on Earth, or blest in Heav'n:
I swear I love thee more, far more than ever,   385
With conscious blushes too! Here, help me Gods,
Help me to tell her, tho' to my Confusion,
And everlasting shame; yet I must tell her,
I lay the Persian Crown before her Feet.
    ATHEN. My Lord, I thank you, and to express those thanks,   390
As nobly as you offer 'em I return
The guift you make, nor will I now upbraid you
With the Example of the Emp'ror;

---

375 condescend] Q_{2+}; codescend Q_1.
385 thee] Q_{2+}; the Q_1.

Not but I know 'tis that that draws you on,
Thus to descend beneath your Majesty;   395
And swell the Daughter of a poor Philosopher
With hopes of being great.
     VARA. Ah, Madam! Ah you wrong me, by the Gods
I had repented e're I knew the Emp'ror ---
     ATHEN. You find perhaps too late that Athenais,   400
How'ever slighted for her birth and Fortune,
Has something in her Person, and her vertue,
Worth the Regard of Emperors themselves.
And to return the Complement you gave
My Father, Leontine, that poor Philosopher,   405
Whose utmost glory is to have been your Tutor:
I here protest, by vertue, and by Glory,
I swear by Heav'n and all the Pow'rs Divine,
The abandoned Daughter of that poor old man
Shall ne're be seated on the Throne of Cyrus.   410
     VARA. O death to all my hopes! what hast thou sworn?
To turn me wild! Ah cursed Throne of Cyrus!
Would thou hadst been o're-turn'd and laid in dust,
His Crown too thunder-strook. My Father, all
The Persian Race, like poor Darius ruin'd,   415
Blotted, and swept for ever from the world;
When first Ambition blasted thy Remembrance ---
     ATHEN. O Heav'n! I had forgot the base affront
Offer'd by this proud man! a wrong so great,
It is remov'd beyond all hope of mercy: 420
He had design'd to bribe my Fathers vertue,
And by unlawful means ---
Fly from my sight, lest I become a Fury ---
And break those rules of temp'rance I propos'd,
Fly, fly, Varanes! fly this sacred place   425
Where Vertue and Religion are profess'd:
This City will not harbour Infidels,
Traytors to Chastity, Licentious Princes:
Begon, I say, thou can'st not here be safe,
Fly to Imperial Libertines abroad;   430
In forreign Courts thou'lt find a thousand Beauties
That will comply for gold, for gold they'll weep,
For gold be fond as Athenais was;
And charm thee still as if they lov'd indeed.
Thou'lt find enow Companions too for riot;   435
Luxuriant all, and Royal as thy self;
Tho' thy loud Vices should resound to heav'n.
Art thou not gone yet?
     VARA.   No, I am charm'd to hear you:

-----

401 However Q_{2+}.
412 me] Q_{2+}; we Q_1.

O from my Soul I do confess my self
The very blot of Honour; I am more black   440
Than thou, in all thy heat of just revenge
With all thy glorious Eloquence, canst make me.
   ATHEN. Away, Varanes.
   VARA.   Yes, Madam, I am going ---
Nay, by the Gods, I do not ask thee pardon;
Nor while I live will I implore thy mercy.   445
But when I am dead, if as thou dost return,
With happy Theodosius from the Temple,
If as thou go'st in Triumph through the streets,
Thou chance to meet the cold Varanes there,
Born by his Friends to his Eternal home;   450
Stop then, O Athenais! and behold me;
Say as thou hang'st about the Emp'ror's Neck,
Alas! my Lord, this sight is worth our pity;
If to those pitying words, thou add a tear,
Or give one parting groan --- If possible,   455
If the good Gods will grant my Soul the freedom,
I'll leave my shrow'd, and wake from Death to thank thee.
   ATHEN. He shakes my resolution from the bottom:
My bleeding Heart too speaks in his behalf,
And says my Vertue has been too severe.   460
   VARA. Farewell! O Empress: No Athenais, now;
I will not call thee by that tender Name;
Since cold despair begins to freeze my Bosom;
And all my Pow'rs are now resolv'd on Death.
'Tis said, that from my Youth I have been rash,   465
Chollerick, and hot; but let the Gods now Judge
By my last wish, if ever patient man
Did calmly bear so great a loss as mine;
Since 'tis so doom'd by Fate you must be wedded,
For your own peace, when I am laid in Earth,   470
Forget that e're Varanes had a being;
Turn all your Soul to Theodosius bosom:
Continue Gods their Days, and make 'em long:
Lucina wait upon their fruitful Hymen,
And many Children, beautious as the Mother,   475
And pious as the Father, make 'em smile.
   ATHEN. O Heav'ns!
   VARA.   Farewell --- I'll trouble you no more:
The malady that's lodg'd within grows stronger;
I feel the shock of my approaching Fate:
My heart too trembles at his distant march;   480
Nor can I utter more, if you shou'd ask me.
Thy arm, Aranthes! O farewell for ever ---
   ATHEN. Varanes, stay, and e're you go for ever,

---

457 Shrowd, Q_{2+}.

Let me unfold my heart.
     VARA.   O, Athenais!
What further cruelty hast thou in store   485
To add to what I suffer?
     ATHEN.   Since it is doom'd
That we must part, let's part as Lovers shou'd,
As those that have lov'd long and Lov'd well.
     VARA. Art thou so good! O Athenais, oh!
     ATHEN. First from my Soul I pity and forgive you;   490
I pardon you that hasty little Error,
Which yet has been the cause of both our ruines.
And let this sorrow witness for my heart,
How eagerly I wish it had not been,
And since I cannot keep it, take it all.   495
Take all the Love, O Prince, I ever bore you;
Or if 'tis possible, I'll give you more;
Your noble carriage forces this Confession:
I rage! I burn! I bleed! I dye for Love:
I am distracted with this world of passion.   500
     VARA. Gods! cruel Gods! take notice I forgive you.
     ATHEN. Alas! my Lord! my weaker tender Sex
Has not your manly patience; cannot curb
This Fury in; therefore I let it loose;
Spite of my rigid duty, I will speak   505
With all the dearness of a dying Lover,
Farewell most lovely, and most lov'd of men;
Why comes this dying paleness o're thy Face?
Why wander thus thy eyes? Why dost thou bend
As if the fatal weight of Death were on thee?   510
     VARA. Speak yet a little more; For by the Gods;
And as I prize those blessed happy moments,
I swear, O Athenais! all is well!
O never better!
     ATHEN.   I doubt thee, dear Varanes;
Yet, if thou dy'st I shall not long be from thee.   515
Once more farewell and take these last embraces.
Oh! I could crush him to my heart! Farewell,
And as a dying pledge of my last Love,
Take this, which all thy Pray'rs could never Charm; [Kisses him.*
What have I done? oh lead me, lead me, Delia!   520
Ah, Prince farewell! Angels protect and guard thee.
     VARA. Turn back! O Athenais! and behold me!
Hear my last words, and then farewell for ever:
Thou hast undone me more by this confession:
You say, you swear you love me more than ever: 525
Yet, I must see you marry'd to another,

---

511 the Gods! Q$_{2+}$.
   * [Kisses him.]; <u>om</u>. Q$_{1+}$.

Can there be any plague or hell like this?
O Athenais! Whither shall I turn me?
You have brought me back to life: but oh what life?
To a life more terrible than a thousand Deaths;   530
Like one that had been buried in a Trance,
With racking starts, he wakes and gazes round,
Forc'd by dispair his whirling Limbs to Wound,
And bellow like a Spirit under-ground.
    Still urg'd by Fate, to turn, to toss, and rave,   535
    Tormented, dash'd and broken in the Grave.
                                        [Exeunt.

            End of A C T   I V .

Act V. Scene I.

Athenais drest in Imperial Robes, and Crown'd, a Table
with a bowl of Poison, Delia. *

ATHEN. A Midnight Marriage! must I to the Temple,
Thus at the Murderers hour? 'Tis wond'rous strange;
But so thou say'st my Father has commanded;
And that's Almighty reason.
    DELIA. Th' Emperor in compassion to the Prince,   5
Who would perhaps fly to extravagance,
If he in Publick should resolve to espouse you,
Contriv'd by this close Marriage to deceive him.
    ATHEN. Go fetch thy Lute, and sing those lines I gave thee: [Exit Delia. **
So, now I am alone; yet my Soul shakes;   10
For where this dreadful draught may carry me,
The Heav'ns can onely tell; yet I am resolved
To drink it off in spite of Consequence,
Whisper him, O some Angel! what I am doing;
By sympathy of Soul let him too tremble,   15
To hear my wondrous Faith, my wondrous Love,
Whose Spirit not content with an Ovation
Of lingring Fate, with Triumph thus resolv'd:
Thus in the rapid Chariot of the Soul;
To mount and dare as never Woman dar'd: [Drinks. ***   20
'Tis done, haste, Delia, haste! come bring thy Lute,
And sing my waftage to immortal Joys,

Enter Delia. ****

Methinks I cannot but smile at my own bravery,
Thus from my lowest Fortune rais'd to Empire,
Crown'd and adorn'd! worshipt by half the Earth,   25
While a young Monarch dyes for my embraces:
Yet now to Wave the glories of the World:
O my Varanes! tho' my Birth's unequal:
My vertue sure has richly recompenc'd;
And quite out-gone Example!   30

---

   * Delia.]; om. Q_{1+}.
  ** [Exit Delia.]; om. Q_{1+}.
 *** This direction comes at the end of line 21 in Q_{1-5}; at the end of
    line 20 in C_{1-3}.
**** Enter Delia.]; om. Q_{1+}. Though it is barely possible that Delia
    enters with the lute at line 30, it seems more probable that she
    enters here.

SONG.

Ah Cruel bloody Fate,
What canst thou now do more?
Alas, 'tis all too late,
Philander to restore:
Why should the Heavenly Powers perswade   35
   Poor Mortals to believe,
    That they guard us here,
    And reward us there,
Yet all our Joys deceive.
       2.

Her Poinyard then she took,   40
And held it in her hand;
   And with a dying look,
    Cry'd, thus I Fate command:
Philander! ah my Love I come,
   To meet thy shade below;   45
    Ah, I come, she Cry'd,
    With a wound so Wide,
There needs no second blow.
       3.

In Purple Waves her blood
Ran streaming down the Floor;   50
   Unmov'd she saw the flood,
    And blest her dying hour:
Philander! ah, Philander! still
   The bleeding Phillis cry'd,
    She wept a while,   55
    And she forc'd a smile;
Then clos'd her eyes and dy'd.

Enter Pulcheria.

PULCH.   How fares my dear Eudosia? ha, thou look'st,
Or else the Tapers cheat my sight, like one
That's fitter for thy Tomb than Caesar's Bed: 60
A Fatal sorrow dims thy shaded eyes,
And in despight of All thy Ornaments,
Thou seem'st to me the Ghost of Athenais.
   ATHEN.   And what's the punishment, my dear Pulcheria;
What Torments are alloted those sad Spirits,   65
Who groaning with the burden of despair;
No longer will endure the Cares of Life,
But boldly set themselves at liberty,
Through the dark Caves of Death to wander on,

31ff. SONG. In Q₁ printed both in the text of the play and at the end
     with the music, where it is erroneously designated as the song
     "after the Fourth Act."

Like wilded Travellers without a Guide,   70
Eternal Rovers in the gloomy Maze,
Where scarce the Twilight of an Infant Moon,
By a faint glimmer checkering through the Trees,
Reflects to dismal view the walking Ghosts,
And never hope to reach the blessed Fields?   75
   PULCH. No more o' that; Atticus shall resolve Thee,
But see, he waits thee from the Emperour;
Thy Father too attends.

      Enter Leontine, Atticus, &c.

   LEONT. Come, Athenais! Ha, what now in tears?
O fall of honour, but no more I charge thee,   80
I charge thee, as thou ever hop'st my blessing,
Or fear'st my Curse, to banish from thy Soul
All thoughts, if possible the memory,
Of that ungrateful Prince that has undone thee.
Attend me to the Temple on this instant,   85
To make the Emperour thine, this night to wed him,
And lye within his Arms.
   ATHEN.   Yes, Sir, I'le go---
Let me but dry my Eyes, and I will go,
Eudosia, this unhappy Bride shall go,
Thus like a Victim crown'd and doom'd to bleed,   90
I'le wait you to the Altar, wed the Emperour,
And if he pleases, lye within his Arms.
   LEONT. Thou art my Child agen.
   ATHEN. But do not, Sir, imagine that any Charms,
Or threatnings shall compell me   95
Never to think of poor Varanes more:
No my Varanes: No---
While I have breath, I will remember thee.
To thee alone, I will my thoughts confine,
And all my Meditations shall be thine,   100
The Image of thy Woes my Soul shall fill,
Fate and my end, and thy remembrance still,
As in some Pop'lar shade the Nightingale
With piercing moans does her lost young bewail,
Which the rough Hind, observing as they lay   105
Warm in their Downy-Nest, had stolen away,
But she in mournful sounds does still complain,
Sings all the night, tho' all her Songs are vain,
And still renews her miserable strain:
So my Varanes till my death comes on   110
Shall sad Eudosia thy dear loss bemoan.   [Exeunt. *

----

   70 wildred C_{2-3}.
    * [Exeunt.] ; [Ex. Athenais, Atticus. Q_{1+}.

Scene II.

Enter Varanes.

VARA. 'Tis Night, dead night, and weary Nature lies
So fast as if she never were to rise:
No breath of Wind now whispers through the Trees;
No noise at Land, nor murmur in the Seas;
Lean Wolves forget to howl at Nights pale Noon;   5
No wakeful Dogs bark at the silent Moon:
Nor bay the Ghosts that glide with horror by,
To view the Cavernes where their bodies lye:
The Ravens perch, and no presages give;
Nor to the Windows of the dying cleave.   10
The Owls forget to scream, no midnight sound
Calls drowsie ecchoe from the hollow ground,
In vaults the walking Fires extinguisht lye,
The stars Heav'ns centry wink and seem to dye.
Such Universal silence spreads below,   15
Through the vast shades where I am doom'd to go
Nor shall I need a violence to wound:
The storm is here that drives me on the ground;
Sure means to make the Soul and Body part,
A burning Feaver and a broken heart.   20
What hoa, Aranthes!   [Enter Aranthes.
I sent thee to the Apartment of Athenais!
I sent thee, did I not, to be admitted?
    ARAN. You did my Lord; but oh
I fear to give you an account.
    VARA.   Alas!   25
Aranthes, I am got on the other side
Of this bad World; and now am past all fear.
O ye avenging Gods is there a plague
Among your hoorded Bolts and heaps of Vengeance
Beyond the mighty loss of Athenais,   30
'Tis contradiction, speak, then speak Aranthes,
For all misfortunes if compar'd with that,
Will make Varanes smile---
    ARAN.   My Lord, the Empress,
Crown'd and adorn'd with the Imperial Robes,
At this dead time of Night with silent pomp,   35

---

14 Heav'ns] Q_{3+}; Heav'n Q_{1-2}.
22-23 Divided <u>as</u> <u>follows</u> Q_{1+}:
         I sent thee to the Apartment of
         Athenais! I sent thee, did I not, to be admitted?

As they design'd from all to keep it secret,
But chiefly sure from you; I say the Empress
Is now conducted by the General,
Atticus and her Father to the Temple,
There to espouse th' Emperor, Theodosius.   40
  VARA. Sayst thou? is't certain! hah.
  ARAN. Most certain, Sir, I saw 'em in procession.
  VARA. Give me thy Sword, Malicious Fate! O Fortune!
O giddy chance! O turn of Love and greatness!
Marry'd! she has kept her promise now indeed;   45
And oh her pointed fame, and nice revenge,
Have reacht their end. No Aranthes! no!
I will not stay the Lazy execution
Of a slow Feaver, Give me thy hand, and swear
By all the Love and Duty that thou ow'st me   50
To observe the last Commands that I shall give thee;
Stir not against my purpose, as thou fearst
My anger and disdain; Nor dare to oppose me
With troublesome unnecessary formal reasons;
For what my thought has doom'd my hand shall seal.   55
I charge thee hold it stedfast to my heart,
Fixt as the Fate that throws me on the point.
Tho' I have liv'd a Persian, I will fall
As fair, as fearless, and as full resolv'd
As any Greek or Roman of 'em all.   60
  ARAN. What you command is terrible but sacred,
And to attone for this too cruel duty,
My Lord, I'll follow you---
  VARA.   I charge thee not!
But when I am dead take the attending slaves,
And bear me with my blood distilling down   65
Straight to the Temple, lay me! O Aranthes!
Lay my cold Coarse at Athenais Feet,
And say, O why, why do my eyes run o're!
Say with my latest gasp I groan'd for pardon;
Just here my Friend, hold fast, and fix the Sword;   70
I feel the Artery, where the life blood lies;
It heaves against the Point---Now o' ye Gods;
If for the greatly wretched you have Room,
Prepare my place for dauntless loe I come!
  The force of Love thus makes the Mortal wound,   75
  And Athenais sends me to the ground. [Kills himself.

---

38 General,] C_{1+}; General. Q_{1-5}.

Scene III. The outward part of the Temple.

Enter Pulcheria and Julia at one door, Marcian and Lucius at another.

PULCH. Look Julia, see the pensive Marcian comes;
'Tis to my wish, I must no longer lose him;
Lest he should leave the Court indeed: he looks
As if some mighty secret work'd within him,
And labour'd for a vent, inspire me Woman,   5
That what my Soul desires above the world,
May seem impos'd and forc'd on my affections---
   LUC. I say she loves you, and she stays to hear it
From your own Mouth: now in the name of all
The Gods at once, my Lord, why are you silent?   10
Take heed, Sir, mark your opportunity;
For if the Woman lays it in your way,
And you over-see it: She is lost for ever.
   MARC. Madam, I come to take my eternal leave,
Your doom has banisht me, and I obey: 15
The Court and I shake hands, and now we part,
Never to see each other more; the Court
Where I was born, and bred a Gentleman;
No more, till your illustrious bounty rais'd me,
And drew the Earth-born vapour to the Clouds: 20
But as the Gods ordain'd it I have lost,
I know not how through ignorance, your Grace:
And now the Exhalation of my glory
Is quite consum'd and vanisht into Air.
   PULCH. Proceed, Sir---   25
   MARC. Yet let those Gods that doom'd me to displease you,
Be witnesses how much I honour you---
Thus worshipping I swear by your bright self,
I leave this Infamous Court with more content,
Than Fools and Flatterers seek it. But, oh Heaven!   30
I cannot go if still your hate pursues me,
Yes, I declare it is impossible,
To go to banishment without your pardon.
   PULCH. You have it; Marcian, is there ought beside,
That you would speak, for I am free to hear.   35
   MARC. Since I shall never see you more, what hinders,
But my last words should here protest the truth,
Know then Imperial Princess, matchless woman,
Since first you cast your eyes upon my meanness,

35 hear? Q3+.

Ev'n till you rais'd me to my envy'd height,   40
I have in secret lov'd you---
  PULCH.   Is this, Marcian?
  MARC. You frown; but I am still prepar'd for all;
I say I lov'd you and I love you still,
More than my life, and equal to my Glory;
Methinks the Warring Spirit that inspires   45
This Frame, the very Genius of old Rome!
That makes me talk without the Fear of Death,
And drives my daring soul to acts of honour,
Flames in your eyes! our thoughts too are a-kin,
Ambitious, fierce, and burn alike for glory: 50
Now, by the Gods! I lov'd you in your Fury,
In all the thunder that quite riv'd my hopes,
i lov'd you most ev'n when you did destroy me.
Madam, I've spoke my heart, and cou'd say more;
But that I see it grieves you, your high blood   55
Frets at the arrogance and sawcy pride
Of this bold Vagabond: may the Gods forgive me:
Farewell; a worthier General may succeed me;
But none more faithful to the Emperors interest,
Than him you are pleas'd to call the Traytor, Marcian.   60
  PULCH. Come back, you have subtilly play'd your part indeed;
For first, th' Emperor, whom you lately school'd,
Restores you your Commission; next commands you,
As you're a Subject not to leave the Court.
Next, but oh Heav'n! which way shall I express   65
His cruel pleasure, he that is so mild
In all things else, yet obstinate in this,
Spite of my tears, my Birth, and my Disdain,
Commands me, as I dread his high displeasure,
O Marcian! to receive you as my Husband.   70
  MARC. Ha, Lucius! what, what does my Fate intend?
  LUC. Pursue her, Sir, 'tis as I said, she yields,
And rages that you follow her no faster.
  PULCH. Is then at last my great Authority,
And my intrusted pow'r declin'd to this?   75
Yet oh my Fate, what way can I avoid it!
He charg'd me streight to wait him to the Temple;
And there resolve! O Marcian! on this Marriage.
Now genrous Souldier as you're truly noble;
O help me forth, lost in this Labyrinth;   80
Help me to loose this more than Gordian Knot,
And make me and your self for ever happy.
  MARC. Madam, I'll speak as briefly as I can,
And as a Souldier ought the onely way
To help this knot is yet to tye it faster.   85
Since then the Emperor has resolv'd you mine,
For which I will for ever thank the Gods,
And make this Holiday throughout my life,

I take him at his word, and claim his promise;
The Empire of the World shall not redeem you.   90
Nay, weep not Madam, though my outside's rough,
Yet by those eyes your souldier has a heart
Compassionate and tender as a Virgins,
Ev'n now it bleeds to see those falling sorrows,
Perhaps this grief may move th' Emperour   95
To a Repentance! Come then to the Tryal;
For by my Arms, my Life, and dearer honour,
If you go back when given me by his hand,
  In distant Warrs my Fate I will deplore,
  And Marcian's Name shall ne're be heard of more.   [Exeunt.   100

Scene IV. The Temple.

Theodosius, Athenais, Atticus joyning their hands --- Marcian,
    Pulcheria, Lucius, Julia, Delia, &c. Leontine.

ATTIC.   The more then Gordian knot is ty'd,
            Which Deaths strong Arm shall ne're divide,
            For when to bliss ye wafted are,
            Your Spirits shall be Wedded there,
            Waters are lost, and Fires will dye,   5
            But Love alone can Fate defie.

Enter Aranthes with the Body of Varanes.

ARAN.   Where is the Empress? where shall I find Eudosia?
By Fate I am sent to tell that cruel Beauty,
She has robb'd the World of Fame; her eyes have giv'n
A blast to the big blossom of the War;   10
Behold him there nipt in his Flowry Morn,
Compell'd to break his promise of a day;
A day that conquest would have made her boast,
Behold her Lawrel wither'd to the Root
Canker'd and kill'd by Athenais scorn.   15
    ATHEN. Dead! dead, Varanes!
    THEO.   O ye Eternal Pow'rs
That guid the World! why do you shock our Reason,
With acts like these that lay our thoughts in dust?
Forgive me Heav'n this start, or elevate
Imagination more, and make it nothing.   20
Alas! alas, Varanes! But speak, Aranthes,
The manner of his Fate: Groans choak my words;
But speak, and we will Answer thee with Tears.
    ARAN. His Feaver would no doubt by this have done
What some few minutes past his Sword perform'd,   25

He heard from me your progress to the Temple,
How you design'd at midnight to deceive him,
By a Clandestine Marriage: But, my Lord,
Had you beheld his Racks at my Relation;
Or had your Empress seen him in those Torments,   30
When from his dying Eyes swoln to the brim
The big round drops rowl'd down his manly Face;
When from his hollow Breast a murmuring Crowd
Of groans rush'd forth, and eccho'd, all is well:
Then had you seen him! O ye cruel Gods!   35
Rush on the Sword I held against his Breast,
And dye it to the Hilts with these last words---
Bear me to Athenais---
    ATHEN.   Give me way, my Lord,
I have most strictly kept my promise with you,
I am your Bride, and you can ask no more,   40
Or if you did, I am past the power to give:
But here! oh here! on his cold bloody Breast,
Thus let me breath my last.
    THEO. O Empress, what, what can this transport mean?
Are these our Nuptials! these my promis'd Joys.   45
    ATHEN. Forgive me, Sir, this last respect I pay
These sad remains---And oh thou mighty Spirit,
If yet thou art not mingled with the stars,
Look down and hear the wretched Athenais,
When thou shalt know before I gave consent   50
To this indecent Marriage, I had taken
Into my Veins a cold and deadly draught,
Which soon would render me, alas, unfit
For the warm Joys of an Imperial Lover,
And make me ever thine! yet keep my word   55
With Theodosius: Wilt thou not forgive me?
    THEO. Poison'd to free thee from the Emperor!
Oh, Athenais! thou hast done a deed
That tears my heart! what have I done against thee
That thou shou'dst brand me thus with Infamy   60
And everlasting shame! Thou mightest have made
Thy choice without this cruel act of Death.
I left thee to thy will, and in requital
Thou hast murder'd all my Fame---
    ATHEN.   O pardon me!
I lay my dying body at your Feet,   65
And beg, my Lord, with my last sighs intreat you
To impute the fault, if 'tis a fault, to love;
And the ingratitude of Athenais,

---

37 Hilt C_{2-3}.
45 Joys? Q_{2+}.
50 shalt] Q_{2+}; shall Q_1.

To her too cruel Stars; Remember too,
I beg'd you would not let me see the Prince,   70
Presaging what has happen'd; yet my word,
As to our Nuptials was inviolable!
    THEO. Ha! she is going! see her languishing eyes
Draw in their Beams, the sleep of Death is on her.
    ATHEN. Farewell, my Lord! alas! alas, Varanes!   75
To embrace thee now is not immodesty;
Or if it were, I think my bleeding heart,
Would make me criminal in Death to clasp thee,
Break all the tender nicities of honour,
To fold thee thus and warm thee into life,   80
For oh what man like him cou'd woman move!
O Prince belov'd! O Spirit most divine!
Thus by my death, I give thee all my Love,
And seal my Soul and Body ever thine---   [Dies.
    THEO. O Marcian! O Pulcheria! did not the Pow'r   85
Whom we adore plant all his Thunder-bolts
Against self-Murderers, I would perish too:
But as I am I swear to leave the Empire:
To thee my Sister I bequeath the World;
And yet a gift more great the gallant Marcian!   90
On then, my Friend, now shew thy Roman Spirit:
As to her Sex, fair Athenais was,
Be thou to thine a pattern of true honour,
Thus we'll attone for all the present Crimes,
That yet it may be said in after-times;   95
    No age with such Examples cou'd compare,
    So great, so good, so vertuous, and so fair.
                               [Ex. Omnes.

End of ACT V.

EPILOGUE.

Thrice happy they that never writ before;
How pleas'd and bold they quit the safer shore:
Like some new Captain of the City Bands,
That with big looks in Finsbury Commands,
Swell'd, with huge Ale he cries, beat, beat a Drum,   5
Pox o' the French-King, uds bud let him come:
Give me ten thousand Redcoats, and alloo,
We'll firk his Crequi and his Conde too.
Thus the young Scriblers, Mankinds sense disdain;
For ignorance is sure to make 'em vain,   10
But far from Vanity, or dang'rous pride;
Our cautious Poet courts you to his side:
For why should you be scorn'd, to whom are due,
All the good days that ever Authors knew.
If ever gay 'tis you that make 'em fine;   15
The Pit and Boxes make the Poet dine,
And he scarce drinks but of the Criticks Wine.
Old Writers should not for vain glory strive
But like old Mistresses think how to thrive,
Be fond of ev'ry thing their Keepers say,   20
At least till they can live without a Play.
Like one that knows the Trade, and has been bit;
She doats and fawns upon her wealthy Cit;
And swears she loves him meerly for his Wit.
Another more untaught than a Walloon,   25
Antick and ugly, like an old Baboon;
She swears is an accomplisht Beau-garson,
Turns with all winds, and sails with all desires;
All hearts in City, Town, and Court, she fires,
Young callow Lords, lean Knights, and driv'ling Squires.   30
She in resistless flattery finds her ends,
Gives thanks for Fools, and makes ye all her Friends,
So should wise Poets sooth an awkard Age,
For they are Prostitutes upon the Stage:
To stand on points were foolish and ill-bred,   35
As for a Lady to be nice in Bed:
Your wills alone must their performance measure,
And you may turn 'em ev'ry way for pleasure.

FINIS.

SONG after the First ACT.

Now, now the Fight's done, and the great God of War lies

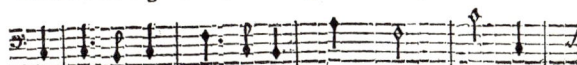

sleep--ing in shades, and un--ra--vels his ears; Love laughs at his

rest, and the Soldiers al--larms; he Drums and be Trum-pets, and

struts in his Arms; he rides on his Lance, and the Bush-es he

[ ]

bangs, and his broad bloo--dy Sword on the Wil-low-tree bangs.

2.

Love smiles when he feels the sharp point of his Dart,
  And he wings it to hit the grim God in the heart,
Who leaves his Steel Bed, and Bolsters of Brass,
  For Pillows of Roses, and Couches of Grass.
His Courser of Lightning is now grown so slow,
  That a Cupid ith'Saddle sits bending his Bow.

3.

Love, Love is the cry ; Love and Kisses go round,
  Till Phillis and Damon lie clasp'd on the ground.
The Shepheard too quick does her pleasure destroy,
  'Tis abortive, she cries, and he murders my Joy :
But he rallies again by the force of her Charms,
  And Kisses, Embraces, and dies in her Arms.

FINIS.

SONG after the Second ACT.

Sad as Death at dead of night the fair complaining Cælia sat, but

one poor Lamp was all her light, while thus she rea-son'd

with her Fate; Why should Man such Tri umphs gain, and

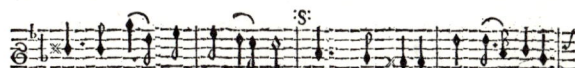

purchace Joys that gives us pain. Ah! what Glory; ah what Glory

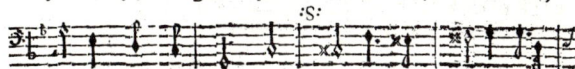

can en——sue; a help—less Vir—gin to un——do.

Chorso

[ ]

Curse the Night then, Curse the Hour when first he drew thee

to his arms, when vir--tue was be- tray'd by pow-er, and

yield--ed to un-- law---ful Charms, when Love approach'd with

all his Fires arm'd with hopes and strong de-sires, sighs and tears, &

ev'ry wile with which the Men, with which the Men the Maids be-

guile, with which the Men, with which the Men the Maids beguile.

Dream

SONG after the Second ACT.

Dream no more of Plea-sures past, since all thy tor-ments are to

come; the se--cret is made known at last, and end-less shame is

now thy Doom; The false for--sworn a--las is gone, and

left thee to de-spair a--lone. Who that hears of Cælia's pain, will

e — ver trust, will e — ver trust a Man a---gain.

Chorus.

Chorus.

The false for-sworn a ——— las is gone, and left thee to de-

The false for-sworn a ——— las is gone, and left thee to de-

spair a ——lone. Who that hears of Cælia's pain, will e --ver

spair a —lone. Who that hears of Cælia's pain, will e—ver

trust, will e ——— ver trust a Man a———gain.

trust, will e ——— ver trust a Man a———gain.

SONG after the Third ACT.

Hail to the Myrtle shade, all Hail to the Nymphs of the Fields,

Kings will not her in—vade, tho Vir-tue all free-dom yields.

Beauty here opens her arms to soften the languishing mind, and

Phillis un—locks her Charms, ah Phillis! ah! why so kind?

[ ]

Chorus:

Beauty here opens her Arms to soften the languishing mind, and

Beauty here opens her Arms to soften the languishing mind, and

soft.

Phillis un_locks her Charms; ah! Phillis! ah! why so kind? ah
soft:

Phillis un_locks her Charms; ah Phillis! ah! why so kind? ah
soft.

Phil_lis! ah! why so kind?

Phil_lis! ah! why so kind?

SONG after the Fourth ACT.

Ah Cru-el Bloo—dy Fate, what cauſt thou now do more? A-las

'tis now too late Philander to re-ſtore. Why ſhould the Heav'nly

Powers perſwade poor Mortals to believe that they guard us here, or re-

ward us there, yet all our Joys deceive.

Fer

[ ]

2.

Her Ponyard then she took,
And held it in her Hand,
And with a dying look,
Cry'd, thus I Fate command.
Philander! *Ah my Love, I come*
To meet thy Shade below!
Ah! I come, she cry'd,
With a Wound so wide,
There needs no second blow.

3.

In Purple Waves her Blood,
Ran streaming down the Floor,
Unmov'd she saw the Flood,
And blest the Dying Hour.
Philander! *Ah* Philander! *still*
The bleeding Phillis *cry'd;*
She wept a while,
And she forc'd a smile,
Then clos'd her Eyes, and dy'd.

F I N I S.

LUCIUS JUNIUS BRUTUS;

FATHER of his COUNTRY.

A

TRAGEDY.

Acted at the Duke's Theater, by their Royal
Highnesses Servants.

Written by *Nat. Lee.*

——cæloque invectus aperto
Flectit equos, curruque volans dat lora Secunda, Virg. lib. 4.

LONDON,

Printed for *Richard Tonson*, and *Jacob Tonson,*
at *Grays-Inn* Gate, and at the Judges-Head
in *Chancery-Lane* near *Fleet-street,* 1681.

LUCIUS JUNIUS BRUTUS

Introduction

I Date and Stage History:

The stage history of LUCIUS JUNIUS BRUTUS is exceptionally brief. It was first produced at Dorset Garden in early December, 1680; and according to Giles Jacob, was received "with great applause."[1] But its success was short-lived: on December 11, after six days of performance, the play was banned by order of the Lord Chamberlain, because of "very Scandalous Expressions & Reflections upon ye Government." There is no record that it was ever presented again.

In 1703 Charles Gildon brought out an adaptation of Lee's play, which he entitled THE PATRIOT, OR THE ITALIAN CONSPIRACY. Gildon moved the scene from Rome to Florence, and substituted Cosmo di Medici for Brutus. He eliminated the mob scenes as being beneath the dignity of tragedy, and removed what he regarded as some rather offensive language. This adaptation was produced at the Theatre Royal, apparently with some success. Of its 1,770 lines, 1,060 are by Lee; thus the play is still largely Lee's, though a weakened version of the original.

II Sources:

Lee's chief sources for LUCIUS JUNIUS BRUTUS were Madeleine Scudéry's CLELIA (1655-1661),[2] and Livy's HISTORY OF ROME, with some details and suggestions from Plutarch's Life of Valerius Publicola and Machiavelli's DISCOURSES UPON THE FIRST DECADE OF TITUS LIVIUS.[3]

In Scudéry's CLELIA the story of Brutus and his sons is related with strong emphasis upon the love element. The father and brother of Brutus are slain by Tarquin. In order to protect himself and gain time for revenge, Brutus pretends stupidity and is regarded as a buffoon. He meets and falls in love with Lucrecia, but she is forced to marry Collatinus. Scudéry also portrays both the sons of Brutus as being in love with women of Tarquin's court: Titus with Ocrisia, and Tiberius with Teraminta. After the ravishment of Lucrecia, Brutus reveals his true nature, expels the Tarquins, and establishes the republic. Both his sons turn traitor because of their love for Ocrisia and Teraminta, and Brutus condemns them to death for their treachery.

Lee has obviously changed this story in several ways, to adapt it to his dramatic purposes. He ennobles the character of Brutus. He eliminates the love affair between Brutus and Lucrecia. Only one son, Titus, is in love, and Teraminta's affections are transferred from Tiberius to Titus. Tiberius is made into a villain who betrays his father purely out of his desire to ingratiate himself with the decadent Tarquin. Titus, on the other hand, is portrayed as a noble youth, attached to his father by close ties, and brought to betray him only by the imminent death of his sweetheart. All of these changes serve to strengthen the dramatic force of the play; they enable the dramatist to create scenes of fine tension; and they turn the story from a mere romance of love into a tragedy of depth and nobility.[4]

From Livy Lee drew such materials as the story of the wager among the nobles at the siege of Ardea as to what their wives were doing, and the consequent visit of them all to Collatia, where they found Lucrece working with her maidens; also from this source comes the speech of Tiberius (II, i, 9 ff.) contrasting the favor of monarchs with the impersonal justice of rule by law.[5]

The sacrificial scene in Act IV was suggested to Lee by a similar scene described by Plutarch in his Life of Valerius, where the two sons of Brutus pledge themselves with the Aquilians by drinking the blood of a man and "touching his entrails," the whole scene being watched secretly by Vinditius, as in Lee's play.[6]

From Machiavelli Lee drew the concept, expressed in the play by Brutus, that some signal punishment or piece of strict justice is necessary to cement the liberty of the newly founded republic: thus justifying the death of his sons.

One of the strongest elements in Lee's play -- the conflict in Titus between loyalty to his father and love for Teraminta -- is not found in any historical source or in **CLELIA**. Instead, as Professor Van Lennep has shown, it was apparently suggested by a similar situation in Otway's **CAIUS MARIUS** (1679), where Marius Junior is torn between loyalty to his father and love for Lavinia, the daughter of Metellus, his father's deadly enemy.[7] Lee's mob scenes may also owe something to Otway, though perhaps they owe even more to Shakespeare. The influence of the latter appears at various points throughout the play, and similarities of situation or wording are pointed out in the explanatory notes.

III Criticism:

Langbaine spoke enthusiastically of Lee's **BRUTUS**: "That he has shown a Master-piece in **LUCIUS JUNIUS BRUTUS**, which scarce one of his Contemporaries have equal'd, and none excel'd, can never be doubted."[8] This praise was repeated almost verbatim by Giles Jacob in **THE POETICAL REGISTER** (1719), and equal enthusiasm was shown by Theophilus Cibber, who called the play "certainly the finest of Lee's, and perhaps one of the most moving plays in our language."[9] An anonymous writer in the **RETROSPECTIVE REVIEW** (1823) said that Lee "has produced no play in which there is less to offend, or more to praise. The awful conflicts in the soul of the paternal judge [Lucius Junius Brutus] ; the earthquakes of heart ... are painted with a noble and generally a successful daring." He thinks also that the sons of Brutus are finely contrasted.[10]

Genest was somewhat more reserved in his judgment: " ... some parts of this T. are well written, but the subject is badly calculated for the stage -- the love scenes are a sad botch...."[11] R. Mosen thinks that, although it lacks true feeling and taste and is not always original, it is Lee's best. The scene between Brutus and Titus showing the struggle between patriotism and father's love is masterfully handled.[12] Ward was more critical of it: "This tragedy is devoid neither of bombast nor of pathos, but in the speeches of Brutus Lee proves unequal to his task, and the interval becomes apparent which even as to mere power of execution separates Elizabethan from Restoration tragedy."[13]

Most other critics, however, share Langbaine's enthusiasm rather than Ward's disdain. Allardyce Nicoll speaks of the play glowingly:

> The plot is well-arranged, and fine emotional situations are carried out with not a small touch of genius. Tiberius and Vitellius enter in one scene:
>
> TIBERIUS: Hark, are we not pursu'd?
> VITELLIUS: No; 'tis the Tread
>   Of our own Friends that follow in the dark....
>
> Such is a true touch of dramatic poetry, and it is merely one of a number of hints of a brighter fire, circling chiefly around the figures of Titus, Brutus and Teraminta. In spite of the fact that love sways the whole piece, in the hard, excessive person of Brutus, in the loyal and loving Titus, in the degenerate Tiberius and in the

clinging Teraminta, we are conveyed to a world that breathes of an inspiration far apart from Settle's heroes and from Howard's rants. We are there where poetry grips the sense, where the old Romans, even if in a seventeenth century dress, walk again the stony streets of a rock-built Capitol.[14]

Malcolm Elwin also praises it very highly. It is, he says, "a neglected master-piece of tragic drama," and claims that it is "one of the few tragedies of the Resto-ration, or of any other age, in the least comparable to the greater works of Shakes-peare."[15] Van Lennep admits that the long speeches tend to interrupt the action of the play, and that it shows structural weakness; yet he, too, praises it as "the finest creation" of Lee's pen, and contends that "there is not a tragedy of the Restoration or eighteenth century which surpasses it in loftiness of thought."[16]

This is high praise indeed, and perhaps it needs some qualification. The play is certainly not without defects, some of which have not been mentioned by the critics quoted above. Among these is the dubious motivation of the characters at certain points. Tiberius, for example, has hardly sufficient reason for wil-fully sacrificing his father's life to the revenge of the Tarquins; in doing so he becomes too black a villain to be plausible. Similarly, there is some question as to whether Brutus is really justified in insisting that Titus give up Teraminta on their very wedding night; and there is likewise question as to whether he is not being overly self-righteous in sacrificing Titus, when everyone else including all the Senate are willing to reprieve him. At times, it is true, the long speeches tend to interfere with the action of the plot; and the love scenes are not always well coordinated with the rest of the action. Yet, despite these weaknesses, the play probably has more strength than any other of Lee's works. Certainly it has greater nobility and greater virility than any other. No other play by Lee has the depth of thought or the greatness of ideas to be found in BRUTUS. Perhaps few readers would go so far as to agree with Malcolm Elwin that it is "comparable to the greater works of Shakespeare;" but most would agree with Van Lennep's concluding statement about it: "Without doubt, Lee's BRUTUS should be accorded a place along side of ALL FOR LOVE, THE ORPHAN and VENICE PRESERVED as one of the four outstanding tragedies of the Restoration."[17]

IV Text:

Editions compared:

Q_1	Richard Tonson and Jacob Tonson	1681
Q_2	R. Wellington	1708
C_1	R. Wellington	1713
C_2	M. P. & Sam Chapman	1722
C_3	W. Feales ...	1734

As copy-text for this edition, the first quarto, 1681, has been followed. Five copies of this quarto have been compared to determine what stop-press cor-rections were made. One of these copies is that of the University of Kentucky Li-brary, one is in the University of Texas Library, and three are in the Folger Shakespeare Library. Variants among these copies are recorded in the footnotes, the copies being designated as follows: Q_1(KU), Q_1(TxU), Q_1(DFo 1), Q_1(DFo 2), Q_1(DFo 3).[18]

The edition has the following collation:

4°; A-L^1, 41 leaves, pp. [8], 1-72, [2].

[A1^r]: <u>title-page</u>; [A1^v]: <u>blank</u>; A2^r: <u>(ornamental headpiece) Epistle</u>

<u>Dedicatory</u> To the Right Honourable / CHARLES, / Earl of DORSET and MIDDLE-SEX, / One of the Gentlemen of His / MAJESTIES / BED-CHAMBER, &c. / ; A2^V-3^V: <u>running-title</u> The Epistle Dedicatory. ; A4^r: Prologue; A4^V Dramatis Personae. Scene <u>ROME</u>; Bl^r: [<u>double rule</u>] <u>head-title</u> LUCIUS JUNIUS / BRU-TUS; / FATHER of his COUNTRY. / [<u>rule</u>] / ACT 1. SCE. I / [<u>rule</u>] <u>and text</u>; Bl^V-K4^V: <u>text</u>. <u>Running-title</u>: <u>Lucius Junius Brutus; Father of his Country</u>. ; Ll: Epilogue.

The first quarto was not especially well printed; there are more than the usual number of printer's errors, especially in the later signatures. But an examination of the five copies of this quarto reveals that, with one exception, the same errors appear in all. This exception is the "aside" on F4^V, lacking in DFo 3 and TxU, but corrected in other copies. This correction was made on outer forme F. Apparently no other changes were made when the forme was unlocked.

Q$_2$ was obviously printed directly from Q$_1$, the text of Q$_1$ up through I4 being followed line for line and page for page in Q$_2$. [19] In it a number of printer's errors have been corrected. The later collected editions, printed from Q$_2$, make a few other alterations, but introduce likewise a number of errors of their own. They also regularize many of the accidentals of the text. The present editors have followed closely the readings of Q$_1$, except for obvious printer's errors. Any deviations from Q$_1$ have been carefully recorded.

To the Right Honourable
CHARLES,
Earl of DORSET and MIDDLESEX,
One of the Gentlemen of His
MAJESTIES
BED-CHAMBER, &c.

My Lord,
With an Assurance I hope becoming the justice of my Cause I lay this
Tragedy at your Lordships Feet, not as a common persecution but as an
Offering suitable to your Virtue, and worthy of the Greatness of your Name.
There are some Subjects that require but half the strength of a great Poet,
but when Greece or old Rome come in play, the Nature Wit and Vigour of   5
foremost Shakespear, the Judgment and Force of Johnson, with all his
borrowed Mastery from the Ancients, will scarce suffice for so terrible
a Grapple. The Poet must elevate his Fancy with the mightiest Imagination,
he must run back so many hundred Years, take a just Prospect of the Spirit
of those Times without the least thought of ours; for if his Eye should   10
swerve so low, his Muse will grow giddy with the Vastness of the Distance,
fall at once, and for ever lose the Majesty of the first Design. He that
will pretend to be a Critick of such a Work must not have a Grain of Cecilius, he must be Longin throughout or nothing, where even the nicest
best Remarks must pass but for Allay to the Imperial Fury of this old   15
Roman Gold. There must be no Dross through the whole Mass, the Furnace
must be justly heated, and the Bullion stamp'd with an unerring hand.
In such a Writing there must be Greatness of Thought without Bombast,
Remoteness without Monstrousness, Virtue arm'd with Severity, not in Iron
Bodies, Solid Wit without modern Affectation, Smoothness without Gloss,   20
Speaking out without cracking the Voice or straining the Lungs. In short
my Lord he that will write as he ought on so Noble an Occasion must write
like you. But I fear there are few that know how to Coppy after so great
an Original as your Lordship, because there is scarce one genius Extant
of your own Size, that can follow you passibus aequis, that has the Felicity   25
and Mastery of the old Poets, or can half match the thoughtfulness of your
Soul. How far short I am cast of such inimitable Excellence, I must with
shame my Lord confess I am but too too sensible. Nature 'tis believed
(if I am not flattered and do not flatter my self) has not been niggardly
to me in the Portion of a Genius, tho I have been so far from improving   30
it, that I am half affraid I have lost of the Principle. It behoves me
then for the future to look about me to see whether I am a Lagg in the
Race, to look up to your Lordship and strain upon the track of so fair a
Glory. I must acknowledge however I have behav'd my self in drawing,
nothing ever presented it self to my Fancy with that solid pleasure as   35
Brutus did in sacrificing his Sons. Before I read Machivel's Notes upon
the place, I concluded it the greatest Action that was ever seen throughout
all Ages on the greatest Occasion. For my own Endeavour, I thought I never
painted any Man so to the Life before

---

1 become the justice Q_2.

Vis & Tarquinios reges animamq; superbam   40
Ultoris Bruti, fascesque videre receptos?
Infelix uctunque ferent ea facta Minores!

No doubt that divine Poet imagined it might be too great for any People
but his own, perhaps I have found it so, but Johnsons Catiline met no better fate as his Motto from Horace tells us.   45

--- His non plebecula gaudet &c.

Nay Shakespear's Brutus with much adoe beat himself into the heads
of a blockish Age, so knotty were the Oaks he had to deal with. For my
own Opinion, in spite of all the Obstacles my Modesty could raise, I could
not help inserting a Vaunt in the Title page, Coeloque, &c.   50

And having gain'd the List that he design'd,
Bold as the Billows driving with the Wind,
He loos'd the Muse that wing'd his free-born Mind.

On this I arm'd and resolv'd not to be stirr'd with the little Exceptions of a sparkish Generation, that have an Antipathy to Thought,   55
But alas how frail are our best resolves in our own Concerns. I show'd
no passion outward, but whether through an Over-Conceit of the Work, or
because perhaps there was indeed some Merit, the Fire burnt inward, and
I was troubled for my dumb Play, like a Father for his dead Child. 'Tis
enough that I have eas'd my heart by this Dedication to your Lordship.   60
I comfort my self too whatever our partial Youth alledge, your Lordship
will find something in it worth your Observation; which with my future
Diligence, Resolution to Study, Devotion to Vertue, and your Lordships
Service, may render me not altogether unworthy the Protection of your
Lordship.   65

My Lord,
Your Lordships most humble
and devoted Servant

NAT. LEE.

---

62 in it worth] Q$_{2+}$; in in worth Q$_1$.

Prologue to Brutus, written by Mr. Duke.

Long has the tribe of Poets on the Stage
Groan'd under persecuting Criticks rage,
But with the sound of railing and of rime,
Like Bees united by the tinkling Chime,
The little stinging Insects swarm the more   5
And buz is greater than it was before.
But oh! you leading Voters of the Pit,
That infect others with your too much Wit,
That well affected Members do seduce,
And with your malice poyson half the house,   10
Know your ill manag'd Arbitrary sway,
Shall be no more indur'd but ends this day.
Rulers of abler conduct we will choose,
And more indulgent to a trembling Muse;
Women for ends of Government more fit,   15
Women shall rule the Boxes and the Pit,
Give Laws to love and influence to Wit,
Find me one man of sence in all your roll,
Whom some one Woman has not made a fool.
Even business that intollerable load   20
Under which man does groan and yet is proud,
Much better they can manage wou'd they please,
'Tis not their want of Wit, but love of Ease.
For, spite of Art, more Wit in them appears
Tho we boast ours, and they dissemble theirs: 25
Witt once was ours, and shot up for a while
Set shallow in a hot, and barren Soyle;
But when transplanted to a richer Ground
Has in their Eden its perfection found.
And 'tis but Just they shou'd our Wit invade,   30
Whilst we set up their painting patching trade;
As for our Courage, to our shame 'tis known,
As they can raise it, they can pull it down.
At their own Weapons they our Bullies awe,
Faith let them make an Antisalick Law   35
Prescribe to all mankind, as well as playes,
And wear the breeches, as they wear the Bayes.

---

17 Wit. Q_{2+}.

DRAMATIS PERSONAE

Lucius Junius Brutus,	Mr. Betterton.	
Titus,	Mr. Smith.	
Tiberius,	Mr. Williams.	
Collatinus,	Mr. Wiltshire.	
Valerius,	Mr. Gillow.	5
Horatius,	Mr. Norris.	
Aquilius,		
Vitellius,		
Junius,		
Vinditius,	Mr. Nokes.	10
Fabritius,	Mr. Jeron.	
Lucretius,		
Lartius,		
Herminius,		
Mutius,		15
Flaminius,		
Fecialian Priests.	Mr. Percival, Mr. Freeman.	
A Flamen,		
Citizens, &c.		

WOMEN.

Sempronia,	Lady Slingsby.	20
Lucrece,	Mrs. Betterton.	
Teraminta,	Mrs. Barrey.	
Aquilia,		
Vitellia,		

Scene ROME.

---

10 Vinditius,]; Vindicius, Q_{1+}. Uniformly Vinditius in the text of the play.

12-16, 18 These names do not appear in the Dramatis Personae of any edition, although the persons appear in the play.

17 Fecialian]; Fecilian Q_{1+}. Uniformly Fecialian in the text of the play.

21 Lucrece]; Lucretia Q_{1+}. Uniformly Lucrece in the text of the play.

23-4 These names do not appear in the Dramatis Personae of any edition, although the persons appear in the play.

LUCIUS JUNIUS
BRUTUS;
FATHER of his COUNTRY.

Act I. Scene I.

Titus, Teraminta.

TIT. O Teraminta, why this face of tears?
Since first I saw thee, till this happy day,
Thus hast thou past thy melancholly hours,
Ev'n in the Court retir'd; stretch'd on a bed
In some dark room, with all the Cortins drawn;   5
Or in some Garden o're a Flowry bank
Melting thy sorrows in the murmuring Stream;
Or in some pathless Wilderness a musing,
Plucking the mossy bark of some old Tree,
Or poring, like a Sybil, on the Leaves: 10
What, now the Priest should joyn us! O, the Gods!
What can you proffer me in vast exchange
For this ensuing night? Not all the days
Of Crowning Kings, of Conquering Generals,
Not all the expectation of hereafter,   15
With what bright Fame can give in th' other World
Should purchase thee this night one minute from me.
    TER. O, Titus! if since first I saw the light,
Since I began to think on my misfortunes,
And take a prospect of my certain woes,   20
If my sad Soul has entertain'd a hope
Of pleasure here, or harbor'd any joy,
But what the presence of my Titus gave me;
Add, add, you cruel Gods, to what I bear,
And break my heart before him.   25
    TIT. Break first th' eternal Chain; for when thou'rt gone
The World to me is Chaos. Yes, Teraminta,
So close the everlasting Sisters wove us,
When e're we part, the Strings of both must crack:
Once more I do intreat thee give the Grave   30
Thy sadness; let me press thee in my arms,
My fairest Bride, my only lightness here,
Tune of my heart, and Charmer of my eyes;
Nay, thou shalt learn the extasie from me,
I'll make thee smile with my extravagant passion,   35
Drive thy pale fears away; and e're the morn
I swear, O Teraminta, O my Love,
Cold as thou art, I'll warm thee into blushes.
    TER. O, Titus! may I, ought I to believe you?

---

5 Curtains Q_{2+}.

Remember, Sir, I am the blood of Tarquin;   40
The basest too.
    TIT.   Thou art the blood of Heav'n,
The kindest influence of the teeming Stars;
No seed of Tarquin; no, 'tis forg'd t'abuse thee:
A God thy Father was, a Goddess was his Wife;
The Wood-Nymphs found thee on a bed of Roses,   45
Lapt in the sweets and beauties of the Spring,
Diana foster'd thee with Nectar dews,
Thus tender, blooming, chast, she gave thee me
To build a Temple sacred to her Name;
Which I will do, and wed thee there again.   50
    TER. Swear then, my Titus, swear you'l ne're upbraid me,
Swear that your Love shall last like mine for ever;
No turn of State or Empire, no misfortune,
Shall e're estrange you from me: Swear, I say;
That, if you should prove false, I may at least   55
Have something still to answer to my Fate;
Swear, swear, my Lord, that you will never hate me,
But to your death still cherish in your bosom
The poor, the fond, the wretched Teraminta.
    TIT. 'Till death! nay, after death if possible.   60
Dissolve me still with questions of this nature,
While I return my answer all in Oaths:
More than thou canst demand I swear to do.
This night, this night shall tell thee how I love thee:
When words are at a loss, and the mute Soul   65
Pours out her self in sighs and gasping joys,
Life grasps, the pangs of bliss, and murmuring pleasures,
Thou shalt confess all language then is vile,
And yet believe me most without my vowing.

            Enter Brutus with a Flamen.

But see, my Father with a Flamen here!   70
The Court comes on; let's slip the busie Croud.
And steal into the eternal knot of Love.   [Exeunt.
    BRUT. Did Sextus, say'st thou, ly at Collatia,
At Collatin's house last night?
    FLA.   My Lord, he did.
Where he, with Collatine and many others,   75
Had been some nights before.
    BRUT.   Ha! if before,
Why did he come again?
    FLA.   Because, as Rumor spreads,
He fell most passionately in love with her.
    BRUT. What then?
    FLA.   Why, is't not strange?
    BRUT.   Is she not handsom?
    FLA. O, very handsom.

BRUT.   Then 'tis not strange at all.   80
What, for a King's Son to love another man's Wife!
Why, Sir, I've known the King has done the same.
Faith, I my self, who am not us'd to caper,
Have sometimes had th' unlawful Itch upon me:
Nay, pr'ythee Priest, come thou and help the number.   85
Ha! my old Boy; the company is not scandalous:
Let's go to Hell together; confess the truth,
Did'st thou ne're steal from the Gods an hour, or so,
To mumble a new Prayer ---
With a young fleshy Whore in a baudy corner? ha!   90
    FLA. My Lord, your Servant. [Aside.] Is this the Fool? the Madman?
Let him be what he will, he spoke the truth:
If other Fools be thus, they're dangerous fellows.   [Exit.
    BRUT. solus. Occasion seems in view; something there is
In Tarquin's last abode at Collatine's: 95
Late entertain'd, and early gone this morning?
The Matron ruffled, wet, and dropping tears,
As if she had lost her wealth in some black Storm!
As in the Body, on some great surprise,
The heart still calls from the discolour'd face,   100
From every part the life and spirits down:
So Lucrece comes to Rome, and summons all her blood.
Lucrece is fair; but chast, as the fann'd Snow
Twice bolted o're by the bleak Northern blasts:
So lies this Starry cold and frozen Beauty,   105
Still watch'd and guarded by her waking Virtue,
A pattern, tho I fear inimitable,
For all succeeding Wives. O Brutus! Brutus!
When will the tedious Gods permit thy Soul
To walk abroad in her own Majesty,   110
And throw this Vizor of thy madness from thee?
O, what but infinite Spirit, propt by Fate,
For Empire's weight to turn on, could endure
As thou hast done, the labours of an Age,
All follies, scoffs, reproaches, pities, scorns,   115
Indignities almost to blows sustain'd,
For twenty pressing years, and by a Roman?
To act deformity in thousand shapes,
To please the greater Monster of the two,
That cries, bring forth the Beast, and let him tumble: 120
With all variety of Aping madness,
To bray, and bear more than the Asse's burden;
Sometimes to whoot and scream, like midnight Owls,

---

 90 fleshly Q$_{2+}$.
 91 [Aside.]; om. Q$_{1+}$.
 99 or some Q$_2$.
104 the black Northern Q$_2$.

Then screw my Limbs like a distorted Satyr,
The World's Grimace, th'eternal Laughing-stock,   125
Of Town and Court, the Block, the Jest of Rome;
Yet all the while not to my dearest Friend,
To my own Children, nor my bosome Wife,
Disclose the weighty Secret of my Soul.
O Rome, O Mother, be thou th'impartial Judge   130
If this be Virtue, which yet wants a name.
Which never any Age could parallel,
And worthy of the foremost of thy Sons.

           Enter Horatius, Mutius.

    MUT. Horatius, heard'st thou where Sextus was last night?
    HOR. Yes, at Collatia: 'tis the buz of Rome;   135
'Tis more than guess'd that there has been foul play,
Else, why should Lucrece come in this sad manner
To old Lucretius house, and summon thither
Her Father, Husband, each distinct Relation?

          Enter Fabritius, with Courtiers.

    MUT. Scatter it through the City, raise the People,   140
And find Valerius out: away, Horatius.   [Exeunt severally.
    FABR. Pr'ythee, let's talk no more on't. Look, here's Lord Brutus:
Come, come, we'll divert our selves; For 'tis but just, that we
who sit at the Helm, should now and then unruffle our State affairs with the impertinence of a Fool. Pr'ythee, Brutus, what's   145
a Clock?
    BRUT. Clotho, Lachesis, Atropos; the Fates are three: let
them but strike, and I'll lead you a Dance, my Masters.
    FAB. But hark you, Brutus, dost thou hear the news of
Lucrece?   150
    BRUT. Yes, yes; and I heard of the wager that was lay'd a-
mong you, among you whoring Lords at the Siege of Ardea;
Ha, Boy! about your handsome Wives:
    FAB. Well; and how, and how?
    BRUT. How you bounc'd from the Board, took Horse, and   155
rode like madmen, to find the gentle Lucrece at Collatia: but
how found her? why, working with her Maids at midnight.
Was not this monstrous, and quite out of the fashion? Fine stuff
indeed, for a Lady of Honor, when her Husband was out of the
way, to sit weaving, and pinking, and pricking of Arras? Now,   160
by this light, my Lord, your Wife made better use of her Pin-
cushion.
    FAB. My Wife, my Lord? By Mars, my Wife!
    BRUT. Why should she not, when all the Royal Nurses do the

---

131 name, C_{2+}.
159-160 for a Lady ... way, <u>om</u>. Q_2.

same? What? what, my Lord, did you not find 'em at it? when   165
you came from Collatia to Rome. Lartius, your Wife; and
yours Flaminius? with Tullia's Boys, turning the Cristals up,
dashing the Windows, and the Fates defying? Now, by the
Gods, I think 'twas Civil in you, discreetly done, Sirs, not to
interrupt 'em. But for your Wife, Fabritius, I'll be sworn for   170
her, she would not keep 'em company.

    FAB. No marry would she not; she hates Debauches: How
have I heard her rail at Terentia, and tell her next her heart
upon the qualms, that drinking Wine so late and tipling Spirits,
would be the death of her?   175

    BRUT. Hark you, Gentlemen, if you would but be secret now,
I could unfold such a business; my life on't, a very Plot upon the
Court.

    FAB. Out with it; we swear secresie.

    BRUT. Why thus then. To morrow Tullia goes to the Camp;   180
and I being Master of the Houshold, have command to sweep the
Court of all its Furniture, and send it packing to the Wars:
Pandars, Sycophants, upstart Rogues; fine Knaves and surly
Rascals; Flatterers, easie, supple, cringing, passing, smiling
Villains: all, all to the Wars.   185

    FAB. By Mars, I do not like this Plot.

    BRUT. Why, is it not a Plot? a Plot upon your Selves, your
Persons, Families, and your Relations; even to your Wives,
Mothers, Sisters, all your Kindred: For Whores too are included,
Setters too, and Whore-procurers; Bag and Baggage; all, all   190
to the Wars. All hence, all Rubbish, Lumber out; and not a
Baud be left behind, to put you in hope of hatching Whores
hereafter.

    FAB. Hark, Lartius, he'll run from fooling to direct mad-
ness, and beat our Brains out. The Devil take the hindmost: 195
your Servant, sweet Brutus; noble, honorable Brutus.   [Exeunt.

Enter Titus.

    TIT. 'Tis done, 'tis done, auspicious Heav'n has joyn'd us,
And I this night shall hold her in my arms.
Oh, Sir!

    BRUT. Oh, Sir! that exclamation was too high: 200
Such Raptures ill become the troubled times;
No more of 'em. And by the way, my Titus,
Renounce your Teraminta.

    TIT.   Ha, my Lord!

    BRUT. How now, my Boy?

    TIT.   Your counsel comes too late, Sir.

    BRUT. Your reply, Sir,   205

---

165 it, Q_2-C_2; it C_3.
166 Rome? C_{1+}.

Comes too ill-manner'd, pert and saucy, Sir.
    TIT. Sir, I am marry'd.
    BRUT.   What, without my knowledge?
    TIT. My Lord, I ask your pardon; but that Hymen ---
    BRUT. Thou ly'st: that honorable God would scorn it.
Some baudy Flamen shuffled you together;   210
Priapus lock'd you, while the Bachanals
Sung your detested Epithalamium.
Which of thy blood were the curs'd Witnesses?
Who would be there at such polluted Rites
But Goats, Baboons, some chatt'ring old Silenus;   215
Or Satyrs, grinning at your slimy joys?
    TIT. Oh, all the Gods! my Lord, your Son is marry'd
To Tarquin's ---
    BRUT.   Bastard.
    TIT.   No, his Daughter.
    BRUT.   No matter:
To any of his Blood; if it be his,
There is such natural Contagion in it,   220
Such a Congenial Devil in his Spirit,
Name, Liniage, Stock, that but to own a part
Of his Relation, is to profess thy self
Sworn Slave of Hell, and Bondman to the Furies.
Thou art not Marry'd.
    TIT.   O, is this possible?   225
This change that I behold? no part of him
The same; nor Eyes, nor Meen, nor Voice, nor Gesture!
    BRUT. Oh, that the Gods would give my Arm the vigor
To shake this soft, effeminate, lazy Soul
Forth from thy bosom. No, degenerate Boy,   230
Brutus is not the same; the Gods have wak'd him
From dead Stupidity, to be a Scourge,
A living Torment to thy disobedience.
Look on my face, view my eyes flame, and tell me
If ought thou seest but Glory and Revenge,   235
A blood-shot Anger, and a burst of Fury,
When I but think of Tarquin. Damn the Monster;
Fetch him, you Judges of th'eternal Deep,
Arraign him, Chain him, plunge him in double fires:
If after this thou seest a tenderness,   240
A Woman's tear come o're my resolution,
Think, Titus; think, my Son, 'tis Nature's fault,
Not Roman Brutus, but a Father now.
    TIT. Oh, let me fall low as the Earth permits me,
And thank the Gods for this most happy change,   245
That you are now, altho to my confusion,
That aw-ful, God-like, and Commanding Brutus

---

213 the blood C_{2+}.

Which I so oft have wish'd you, which sometimes
I thought imperfectly you were, or might be,
When I have taken unawares your Soul   250
At a broad glance, and forc'd her to retire.
Ah, my dear Lord, you need not add new threats,
New marks of Anger to compleat my Ruin,
Your Titus has enough to break his heart
When he remembers that you durst not trust him: 255
Yes, yes, my Lord, I have a thousand frailties;
The mould you cast me in, the breath, the blood,
And Spirit which you gave me are unlike
The God-like Author; yet you gave 'em, Sir:
And sure, if you had pleas'd to honor me,   260
T'immortalize my Name to after Ages
By imparting your high cares, I should have found
At least so much Hereditary Virtue
As not to have divulg'd them.
    BRUT.   Rise, my Son;
Be satisfy'd thou art the first that know'st me: 265
A thousand Accidents and Fated Causes
Rush against every Bulwark I can raise,
And half unhinge my Soul. For now's the time,
To shake the Building of the Tyrant down.
As from Night's Womb the glorious Day breaks forth.   270
And seems to kindle from the setting Stars:
So from the blackness of young Tarquin's Crime
And Fornace of his Lust, the virtuous Soul
Of Junius Brutus catches bright occasion.
I see the Pillars of his Kingdom totter: 275
The Rape of Lucrece is the midnight Lantorn
That lights my Genius down to the Foundation.
Leave me to work, my Titus; O, my Son;
For from this Spark a Lightning shall arise
That must e're Night purge all the Roman Air: 280
And then the Thunder of his ruin follows.
No more; but haste thee to Lucretius:
I hear the Multitude, and must among them.
Away, my Son.
    TIT.   Bound, and obedient ever.   [Exit.

    Enter Vinditius with Plebeians.

    1. CIT. Jupiter defend us! I think the Firmament is all on   285
a light fire. Now, Neighbour, as you were saying, as to the
Cause of Lightning and Thunder, and for the Nature of Prodiges.
    VIN. What! a Taylor, and talk of Lightning and Thunder?
why, thou walking Shred, thou moving Bottom, thou up-

---

270 forth, Q_{2+}.

right Needle, thou shaving edging Skirt, thou Flip-flap of   290
a Man, thou vaulting Flea, thou Nit, thou Nothing, dost
thou talk of Prodigies when I am by? O tempora, O mo-
res! But, Neighbours, as I was saying, what think you of
Valerius?
    ALL. Valerius, Valerius!   295
    VIN. I know you are piping hot for Sedition; you all gape for
Rebellion: but what's the near? For look you, Sirs, we the
People in the Body Politic are but the Guts of Government;
therefore we may rumble and grumble, and Croke our hearts
out, if we have never a Head: why, how shall we be nourish'd?   300
therefore I say, let us get us a Head, a Head my Masters.
    BRUT. Protect me, Jove, and guard me from the Fantom!
Can this so horrid Apparition be;
Or is it but the making of my Fancy?
    VIN. Ha, Brutus! what, where is this Apparition?   305
    1. CIT. This is the Tribune of the Celeres
A notable Head-piece, and the King's Jester.
    BRUT. By Jove, a Prodigy!
    VIN. Nay, like enough; the Gods are very angry:
I know they are, they told me so themselves;   310
For look you Neighbours, I for my own part
Have seen to day fourscore and nineteen Prodigies and a half.
    BRUT. But this is a whole one. O, most horrible!
Look, Vinditius, yonder, o're that part
O'the Capitol, just, just there man, yonder, look.   315
    VIN. Ha, my Lord!
    BRUT. I always took thee for a quick-sighted Fellow:
What, art thou blind? why, yonder, all o'fire;
It vomits Lightning; 'tis a monstrous Dragon.
    VIN. O, I see it: O Jupiter and Juno! By the Gods I see it: 320
O Neighbours, look, look, look, on his filthy Nostrils!
'T has eyes like flaming Saucers; and a Belly
Like a burning Caldron: with such a swinging Tail!
And O, a thing, a thing that's all o'fire!
    BRUT. Ha! now it fronts us with a Head that's mark'd   325
With Tarquin's name: and see, 'tis Thunder-strook!
Look yonder how it whizzes through the Air!
The Gods have strook it down; 'tis gone, 'tis vanish'd.
O, Neighbours, what, what should this Portent mean?
    VIN. Mean! why, it's plain; did we not see the Mark   330
Upon the Beast? Tarquin's the Dragon, Neighbours,
Tarquin's the Dragon, and the Gods shall swinge him.
    ALL. A Dragon! a Tarquin!
    1. CIT.   For my part, I saw nothing.
    VIN. How, Rogue? why, this is Prodigy on Prodigy!
Down with him, knock him down; what not see the Dragon?   335
    1. CIT. Mercy: I did, I did; a huge monstrous Dragon.
    BRUT. So; not a word of this, my Masters, not for your lives:
Meet me anon at the Forum; but not a word.

Vinditius, tell 'em the Tribune of the Celeres
Intends this night to give them an Oration.   [Exit Vindit. and Rabble.   340

     Enter Lucrece, Valerius, Lucretius, Mutius, Herminius,
        Horatius, Titus, Tiberius, Collatinus.

    BRUT. Ha! in the open Air? so near, you Gods?
So ripe your Judgments? nay, then let 'em break,
And burst the hearts of those that have deserv'd them.
    LUCR. O Collatine! art thou come?
Alas, my Husband! O my Love! my Lord!   345
    COLL. O Lucrece! see, I have obey'd thy Summons:
I have thee in my Arms; but speak, my Fair,
Say, is all well?
    LUCR.   Away, and do not touch me:
Stand near, but touch me not. My Father too!
Lucretius, art thou here?
    LUC.   Thou seest I am.   350
Haste, and relate thy lamentable Story.
    LUCR. If there be Gods, O, will they not revenge me?
Draw near, my Lord; for sure you have a share
In these strange woes. Ah, Sir, what have you done?
Why did you bring that Monster of Mankind   355
The other Night, to curse Collatia's walls?
Why did you blast me with that horrid Visage,
And blot my Honor with the Blood of Tarquin?
    COLL. O all the Gods!
    LUCR.   Alas, they are far off;
Or sure they would have help'd the wretched Lucrece.   360
Hear then, and tell it to the wondring World,
Last night the Lustful bloody Sextus came
Late, and benighted to Collatia.
Intending, as he said, for Rome next morning;
But in the dead of Night, just when soft sleep   365
Had seal'd my eyes, and quite becalm'd my Soul,
Methought a horrid voice thus thunder'd in my ear,
Lucrece, thou'rt mine, arise and meet my Arms:
When strait I wak'd, and found young Tarquin by me,
His Robe unbutton'd, red and sparkling eyes,   370
The flushing blood that mounted in his face,
The trembling eagerness that quite devour'd him,
With only one grim Slave that held a Taper,
At that dead stilness of the murd'ring Night
Sufficiently declar'd his horrid purpose.   375
    COLL. O, Lucrece, O!
    LUCR. How is it possible to speak the Passion
The fright, the throes, and labour of my Soul?
Ah, Collatine! half dead I turn'd away
To hide my shame, my anger, and my blushes,   380
While he at first with a dissembled mildness

Attempted on my Honor; ---
But hastily repuls'd, and with disdain,
He drew his Sword, and locking his left hand
Fast in my hair, he held it to my breast: 385
Protesting by the Gods, the Fiends and Furies,
If I refus'd him he would give me death;
And swear he found me with that swarthy Slave
Whom he would leave there murder'd by my side.
    BRUT. Villain! Damn'd Villain!   390
    LUCR. Ah Collatine! Oh Father! Junius Brutus!
All that are kin to this dishonor'd blood,
How will you view me now? Ah, how forgive me?
Yet think not, Collatine, with my last tears,
With these last sighs, these dying groans, I beg you   395
I do Conjure my Love, my Lord, my Husband,
Oh think me not consenting once in thought,
Tho he in act possess'd his furious pleasure:
For, oh, the name, the name of an Adultress! ---
But here I faint; Oh help me: 400
Imagine me, my Lord, but what I was,
And what I shortly shall be; cold and dead.
    COLL. Oh you avenging Gods! Lucrece; my Love,
I swear I do not think thy Soul consenting:
And therefore I forgive thee.
    LUCR.   Ah, my Lord!   405
Were I to live, how should I answer this?
All that I ask you now is to Revenge me;
Revenge me, Father, Husband, Oh revenge me:
Revenge me, Brutus; you his Sons revenge me;
Herminius, Mutius, thou Horatius too,   410
And thou Valerius; all; revenge me all:
Revenge the Honor of the Ravish'd Lucrece.
    ALL. We will Revenge thee.
    LUCR. I thank you all; I thank you, noble Romans:
And that my life, tho well I know you wish it,   415
May not hereafter ever give example
To any that, like me, shall be dishonor'd,
To live beneath so loath'd an Infamy;
Thus I for ever lose it, thus set free   [Stabs herself.*
My Soul, my Life and Honour all together: 420
Revenge me; Oh Revenge, Revenge, Revenge.   [Dyes.
    LUC. Strook to the heart, already motionless.
    COLL. O give me way t'Imbalm her with my tears;
For who has that propriety of Sorrow?
Who dares to claim an equal share with me?   425
    BRUT. That, Sir, dare I; and every Roman here.
What now? at your laments? your puling Sighs?

----

    * [Stabs herself.]; <u>om</u>. Q₁+.

And Womans drops? Shall these quit scores for blood?
For Chastity, for Rome, and violated Honor?
Now, by the Gods, my Soul disdains your tears: 430
There's not a common Harlot in the Shambles
But for a Drachma shall out-weep you all.
Advance the Body nearer: See, my Lords,
Behold, you dazled Romans, from the wound
Of this dead Beauty, thus I draw the Dagger,   435
All stain'd and reeking with her Sacred blood,
Thus to my lips I put the Hallow'd blade,
To yours Lucretius, Collatinus yours,
To yours Herminius, Mutius, and Horatius,
And yours, Valerius: kiss the Ponnyard round: 440
Now joyn your hands with mine, and swear, swear all,
By this chast Blood, chast ere the Royal Villain
Mixt his foul Spirits with the spotless Mass,
Swear, and let all the Gods be witnesses,
That you with me will drive proud Tarquin out,   445
His Wife, th'Imperial Fury, and her Sons,
With all the Race; drive 'em with Sword and Fire
To the World's limits, Profligate accurst:
Swear from this time never to suffer them,
Nor any other King to Reign in Rome.   450
    ALL. We Swear.
    BRUT. Well have you sworn: and Oh, methinks I see
The hovering Spirit of the Ravish'd Matron
Look down; She bows her Airy head to bless you,
And Crown th'auspicious Sacrament with smiles.   455
Thus with her Body high expos'd to view,
March to the Forum with this Pomp of Death.
Oh Lucrece! Oh!
When to the Clouds thy Pile of Fame is rais'd
While Rome is Free thy Memory shall be prais'd: 460
Senate and People, Wives and Virgins all,
Shall once a year before thy Statue fall;
Cursing the Tarquins, they thy Fate shall mourn:
But, when the thoughts of Liberty return,
Shall bless the happy hour when thou wert born.   [Exeunt.   465

      End of A C T I.

Act II. Scene I.
The Forum.

Tiberius, Fabritius, Lartius, Flaminius.

TIB. Fabritius, Lartius, and Flaminius,
As you are Romans, and oblig'd by Tarquin,
I dare confide in you; I say again,
Tho I could not refuse the Oath he gave us,
I disapprove my Father's undertaking: 5
I'm Loyal to the last, and so will stand.
I am in haste, and must to Tullia.
    FAB. Leave me, my Lord, to deal with the Multitude.
    TIB. Remember this in short. A King is one
To whom you may complain when you are wrong'd;   10
The Throne lies open in your way for Justice:
You may be angry, and may be forgiven.
There's room for favor, and for benefit,
Where Friends and Enemies may come together,
Have present hearing, present composition,   15
Without recourse to the Litigious Laws;
Laws that are cruel, deaf, inexorable,
That cast the Vile and Noble altogether;
Where, if you should exceed the bounds of Order,
There is no pardon: O, 'tis dangerous,   20
To have all Actions judg'd by rigorous Law.
What, to depend on Innocence alone,
Among so many Accidents and Errors
That wait on human life? Consider it;
Stand fast, be Loyal: I must to the Queen.   [Exit.   25
    FAB. A pretty Speech, by Mercury! Look you, Lartius,
when the words lye like a low Wrestler, round, close and short,
squat, pat and pithy.
    LAR. But what should we do here, Fabritius? the Multitude
will tear us in pieces.   30
    FAB. 'Tis true, Lartius, the Multitude is a mad thing; a
strange blunder-headed Monster, and very unruly: But eloquence
is such a thing, a fine, moving, florid, pathetical
Speech! But see, the Hydra comes: let me alone; fear not, I
say, fear not.   35

Enter Vinditius, with Plebeians.

VIN. Come, Neighbours, rank your selves, plant your selves,
set your selves in Order; the Gods are very angry, I'll say that
for 'em: pough, pough, I begin to sweat already; and they'l
find us work enough to day, I'll tell you that. And to say

truth, I never lik'd Tarquin, before I saw the Mark in his fore-   40
head: for look you, Sirs, I am a true Commonwealths-man,
and do not naturally love Kings, tho they be good; for why
should any one man have more power than the People? Is he
bigger, or wiser than the People? Has he more Guts, or more
Brains than the People? What can he do for the People, that   45
the People can't do for them selves? Can he make Corn
grow in a Famine? can he give us Rain in Drought? or make
our Pots boil, tho the Devil piss in the Fire?
    1. CIT. For my part, I hate all Courtiers; and I think I have
reason for't.   50
    VIN. Thou reason! Well, Taylor, and what's thy reason?
    1. CIT. Why, Sir, there was a Crew of 'em t'other Night
got drunk, broke my windows, and handled my wife.
    VIN. How Neighbours? Nay, now the Fellow has reason,
look you: his wife handled! why, this is a matter of moment.   55
    1. CIT. Nay, I know there were some of the Princes, for I
heard Sextus his name.
    VIN. I, I, the King's Sons, my life for't; some of the King's
Sons. Well, these roaring Lords never do any good among us
Citizens: they are ever breaking the Peace, running in our   60
Debts, and swindging our wives.
    FAB. How long at length, thou many-headed Monster,
You Bulls, and Bears, you roaring Beasts and Bandogs,
Porters and Coblers, Tinkers, Taylors, all
You Rascally Sons of Whores in a Civil Government,   65
How long, I say, dare you abuse our patience?
Does not the thought of Rods and Axes fright you?
Does not our presence, ha, these eyes, these faces
Strike you with trembling? Ha!
    VIN. Why, what have we here? a very Spit-fire, the   70
Crack-fart of the Court. Hold, let me see him nearer:
yes, Neighbours, this is one of 'em, one of your roaring
Squires that poke us in the night, beat the Watch, and deflowr
our Wives. I know him Neighbours, for all his bouncing and
his swearing; this is a Court-Pimp, a Baud, one of Tarquin's   75
Bauds.
    FAB. Peace thou obstreperous Rascal; I am a man of Honor.
One of the Equestrian Order; my name Fabritius.
    VIN. Fabritius! Your Servant, Fabritius. Down with
him. Neighbours; an upstart Rogue; this is he that was   80
the Queen's Coachman, and drove the Chariot over her Father's Body: Down with him, down with 'em all; Bauds,
Pimps, Pandars.
    FAB. O mercy, mercy, mercy!
    VIN. Hold, Neighbours, hold: as we are great, let us be   85
just. You, Sirrah; you of the Equestrian Order, Knight?
now, by Jove, he has the look of a Pimp; I find we can't
save him. Rise, Sir Knight; and tell me before the Majesty of the People, what have you to say, that you

should not have your neck broke down the Tarpeian   90
Rock, your Body burnt, and your Ashes thrown in the Tiber?
    FAB. Oh! oh! oh!
    VIN. A Courtier! a Sheep biter. Leave off your blubbering,
and confess.
    FAB. Oh! I will confess, I will confess.   95
    VIN. Answer me then. Was not you once the Queen's Coachman?
    FAB. I was, I was.
    VIN. Did you not drive her Chariot over the Body of her Father,
the dead King Tullus?
    FAB. I did, I did: tho it went against my Conscience.   100
    VIN. So much the worse. Have you not since abused the good
People, by seducing the Citizens Wives to Court, for the King's
Sons? have you not by your Bauds tricks, been the occasion of
their making assault on the Bodies of many a virtuous dispos'd
Gentlewoman?   105
    FAB. I have, I have.
    VIN. Have you not wickedly held the Door, while the
Daughters of the wise Citizens have had their Vessels broken up?
    FAB. Oh, I confess, many a time and often.
    VIN. For all which Services to your Princes, and so highly   110
deserving of the Commonwealth, you have receiv'd the Honor of
Knighthood?
    FAB. Mercy, mercy: I confess it all.
    VIN. Hitherto I have helpt you to spell; now pray put together
for your self: and confess the whole matter in three words.   115
    FAB. I was at first the Son of a Car-man, came to the honor
of being Tullia's Coachman, have been a Pimp, and remain a
Knight at the mercy of the People.
    VIN. Well, I am mov'd, my bowels are stir'd: take 'em away,
and let 'em only be hang'd: Away with 'em, away with 'em.   120
    FAB. Oh mercy! help, help.
    VIN. Hang 'em, Rogues, Pimps; hang 'em I say. Why,
look you, Neighbours, this is Law, Right, and Justice: this
is the Peoples Law; and I think that's better than the Arbitrary
power of Kings. Why, here was Trial, Condemnation, and   125
Execution, without more ado. Hark, hark; what have we here?
look, look, the Tribune of the Celeres! Bring forth the Pulpit,
the Pulpit.

Trumpets sound a dead March.

Enter Brutus, Valerius, Herminius, Mutius, Horatius, Lucretius,
Collatinus, Tiberius, Titus: with the Body of Lucrece.

    VAL. I charge you Fathers, Nobles, Romans, Friends,
Magistrates, all you People, hear Valerius.   130
This day, O Romans, is a day of wonders,
The villanies of Tarquin are compleat:
To lay whose Vices open to your view,

To give you Reasons for his Banishment,
With the Expulsion of his wicked Race;   135
The Gods have chosen Lucius Junius Brutus,
The stupid, sensless, and illiterate Brutus,
Their Orator in this prodigious Cause:
Let him ascend, and Silence be Proclaim'd.
    VIN. A Brutus, a Brutus, a Brutus! Silence there;   140
Silence, I say, Silence on pain of death.
    BRUT. Patricians, People, Friends, and Romans all,
Had not th'inspiring Gods by wonder brought me
From clouded Sence, to this full Day of Reason,
Whence, with a Prophets prospect, I behold   145
The State of Rome, and Danger of the World;
Yet in a Cause like this, methinks the weak,
Enervate, stupid Brutus might suffice:
O the eternal Gods! bring but the Statues
Of Romulus and Numa, plant 'em here   150
On either hand of this cold Roman Wife,
Only to stand and point that public wound;
O Romans, oh, what use would be of Tongues!
What Orator need speak while they were by?
Would not the Majesty of those dumb Forms   155
Inspire your Souls, and Arm you for the Cause?
Would you not curse the Author of the murder,
And drive him from the Earth with Sword and Fire?
But where, methinks I hear the People shout,
I hear the cry of Rome, where is the Monster?   160
Bring Tarquin forth, bring the Destroyer out,
By whose curs'd off-spring, Lustful Bloody Sextus,
This perfect mould of Roman Chastity,
This Star of spotless and immortal Fame,
This pattern for all Wives, the Roman Lucrece   165
Was fouly brought to a disastrous end.
    VIN. O, Neighbours, oh! I bury'd seven Wives without crying,
Nay, I never wept before in all my life.
    BRUT. O the Immortal Gods, and thou great Stayer
Of falling Rome, if to his own Relations,   170
(For Collatinus is a Tarquin too)
If wrongs so great to them, to his own blood;
What then to us, the Nobles and the Commons?
Not to remember you of his past Crimes,
The black Ambition of his furious Queen,   175
Who drove her Chariot through the Cyprian Street
On such a damn'd Design, as might have turn'd
The Steeds of Day, and shock'd the starting Gods,
Blest as they are, with an uneasie moment:
Add yet to this, oh! add the horrid slaughter   180
Of all the Princes of the Roman Senate,
Invading Fundamental Right and Justice,
Breaking the ancient Customs, Statutes, Laws,

With positive pow'r, and Arbitrary Lust;
And those Affairs which were before dispatch'd   185
In public by the Fathers, now are forc'd
To his own Palace, there to be determin'd
As he, and his Portentous Council please.
But then for you.
    VIN.   I, for the People, come;
And then, my Mirmydons, to pot with him.   190
    BRUT. I say, if thus the Nobles have been wrong'd,
What Tongue can speak the grievance of the People?
    VIN. Alas, poor People!
    BRUT. You that were once a free-born People, fam'd
In his Forefathers days for Wars abroad,   195
The Conquerors of the World; Oh Rome! Oh Glory!
What are you now? what has the Tyrant made you?
The Slaves, the Beasts, the Asses of the Earth,
The Soldiers of the Gods Mechanic Laborers,
Drawers of Water, Taskers, Timber-fellers,   200
Yok'd you like Bulls, his very Jades for luggage,
Drove you with Scourges down to dig in Quarries,
To cleanse his Sinks, the Scavengers o'th'Court:
While his lewd Sons, tho not on work so hard,
Employ'd your Daughters and your Wives at home.   205
    VIN. Yes marry did they.
    BRUT. O all the Gods! what are you Romans? ha!
If this be true, why have you been so backward?
Oh sluggish Souls! Oh fall of former Glory!
That would not rouze unless a Woman wak'd you!   210
Behold she comes, and calls you to revenge her;
Her Spirit hovers in the Air, and cries
To Arms, to Arms; drive, drive the Tarquins out.
Behold this Dagger, taken from her wound,
She bids you fix this Trophee on your Standard,   215
This Ponnyard which she stab'd into her heart,
And bear her Body in your Battels front:
Or will you stay till Tarquin does return,
To see your Wives and Children drag'd about,
Your Houses burnt, the Temples all profan'd,   220
The City fill'd with Rapes, Adulteries,
The Tiber choak'd with Bodies, all the Shores
And neighb'ring Rocks besmear'd with Roman blood?
    VIN. Away, away; lets burn his Palace first.
    BRUT. Hold, hold, my Friends. As I have been th'Inspirer 225
Of this most just Revenge; so I intreat you,
Oh worthy Romans, take me with you still:
Drive Tullia out, and all of Tarquin's Race;
Expel 'em without Damage to their persons,
Tho not without reproach. Vinditius, you   230
I trust in this. So prosper us the Gods,
Prosper our Cause, prosper the Commonwealth,

Guard and Defend the Liberty of Rome.
 VIN. Liberty, Liberty, Liberty.
 ALL. Liberty, &c.   [Exeunt.   235
 VAL. O Brutus, as a God, we all survey thee;
Let then the Gratitude we should express
Be lost in Admiration. Well we know
Virtue like thine, so fierce, so like the Gods,
That more than thou presents we could not bear,   240
Looks with disdain on Ceremonious honors;
Therefore accept in short the thanks of Rome:
First with our Bodies thus we worship thee,   [All kneel. *
Thou Guardian Genius of the Commonwealth,
Thou Father and Redeemer of thy Country;   245
Next we, as Friends, with equal Arms embrace thee,
That Brutus may remember, tho his vertue
Soar to the Gods, he is a Roman still.
 BRUT. And when I am not so, or once in thought
Conspire the Bondage of my Country-men,   250
Strike me, you Gods; tear me, O Romans, piece-meal,
And let your Brutus be more loath'd than Tarquin.
But now to those Affairs that want a view.
Imagine then the fame of what is done
Has reach'd to Ardea; whence the trembling King,   255
By Guilt and Nature quick and apprehensive,
With a bent brow comes post for his Revenge
To make examples of the Mutiniers:
Let him come on. Lucretius, to your care
The charge and custody of Rome is given;   260
While we, with all the Force that can be rais'd,
Waiting the Tarquins on the common Road,
Resolve to joyn the Army at the Camp.
What thinks Valerius of the consequence?
 VAL. As of a lucky hit. There is a number   265
Of Malecontents that wish for such a time:
I think that only speed is necessary
To Crown the whole event.
 BRUT.   Go then your self,
With these Assistants, and make instant head
Well as you can, numbers will not be wanting,   270
To Mars his Field: I have but some few Orders
To leave with Titus, that must be dispers't,
And Brutus shall attend you.
 VAL. The Gods direct you.   [Exeunt with the Body of Lucrece.

---

 * [All kneel.]; om. Q_{1+}.
 251 Strike me, you Gods;] C_{1+}; Strike me you, Gods; Q_1;
    Strike me you Gods; Q_2.
 262 Waiting] C_{2+}; Waving Q_1-C_1.

Manent Brutus, Titus.

BRUT. Titus, my Son?
TIT.   My ever honor'd Lord.   275
BRUT. I think, my Titus,
Nay, by the Gods, I dare protest it to thee,
I love thee more than any of my Children.
    TIT. How, Sir, oh how, my Lord, have I deserv'd it?
    BRUT. Therefore I love thee more, because, my Son,   280
Thou hast deserv'd it; for, to speak sincerely,
There's such a sweetness still in all thy manners,
An Air so open, and a brow so clear,
A temper so remov'd from Villany,
With such a manly plainness in thy dealing,   285
That not to love thee, O my Son, my Titus,
Were to be envious of so great a Vertue.
    TIT. O, all the Gods, where will this kindness end?
Why do you thus, O my too gracious Lord,
Dissolve at once the being that you gave me;   290
Unless you mean to screw me to performance
Beyond the reach of Man?
Ah why, my Lord, do you oblige me more
Than my humanity can e're return?
    BRUT. Yes, Titus, thou conceiv'st thy Father right,   295
I find our Genij know each other well;
And Minds, my Son, of our uncommon make
When once the Mark's in view, never shoot wide,
But in a Line come level to the White,
And hit the very heart of our Design: 300
Then, to the Shocking purpose. Once again
I say, I swear, I love thee, O my Son;
I like thy Frame, the Fingers of the Gods
I see have left their Mastery upon thee,
They have been tapering up thy Roman Form,   305
And the Majestick prints at large appear:
Yet something they have left for me to finish,
Which thus I press thee to, thus in my Arms
I fashion thee, I mould thee to my heart.
What? dost thou kneel? nay, stand up now a Roman,   310
Shake from thy Lids that dew that hangs upon 'em,
And answer to th'austerity of my Vertue.
    TIT. If I must dye, you Gods, I am prepar'd:
Let then my Fate suffice; but do not rack me
With something more.
    BRUT.   Titus, as I remember,   315
You told me you were Marry'd.
    TIT.   My Lord, I did.

---

293 more] Q$_{2+}$; more. Q$_1$.

BRUT. To Teraminta, Tarquin's natural Daughter.
TIT. Most true, my Lord, to that poor vertuous Maid,
Your Titus, Sir, your most unhappy Son,
Is joyn'd for ever.
    BRUT.   No, Titus, not for ever.   320
Not but I know the Virgin beautiful;
For I did oft converse her, when I seem'd
Not to converse at all: Yet more, my Son,
I think her chastly good, most sweetly fram'd,
Without the smallest Tincture of her Father;   325
Yet, Titus, --- Ha! what, man? what, all in tears?
Art thou so soft, that only saying yet
Has dash'd thee thus? nay, then I'll plunge thee down,
Down to the bottom of this foolish Stream
Whose brink thus makes thee tremble. No, my Son,   330
If thou art mine, thou art not Teraminta's;
Or, if thou art, I swear thou must not be,
Thou shalt not be hereafter.
    TIT.   O the Gods!
Forgive me, Blood and Duty, all respects
Due to a Father's name: not Teraminta's!   335
    BRUT. No, by the Gods I swear, not Teraminta's.
No, Titus, by th'eternal Fates, that hang
I hope auspicious o're the head of Rome,
I'll grapple with thee on this spot of Earth
About this Theam, till one of us fall dead: 340
I'll struggle with thee for this point of Honor,
And tug with Teraminta for thy heart
As I have done for Rome: yes, ere we part,
Fix'd as you are by Wedlock joyn'd and fast,
I'll set you far asunder: nay, on this,   345
This spotted blade, bath'd in the blood of Lucrece,
I'll make thee swear on this thy Wedding night
Thou wilt not touch thy Wife.
    TIT. Conscience, heart and bowels,
Am I a man? have I my flesh about me?   350
    BRUT. I know thou hast too much of Flesh about thee;
'Tis that, my Son, that and thy Blood I fear
More than thy Spirit, which is truly Roman:
But let the heated Chanels of thy Veins
Boil o're; I still am obstinate in this: 355
Thou shalt renounce thy Father or thy Love.
Either resolve to part with Teraminta,
To send her forth, with Tullia, to her Father,
Or shake hands with me, part, and be accurs'd;
Make me believe thy Mother play'd me false,   360
And, in my absence, stampt thee with a Tarquin.
    TIT. Hold, Sir, I do conjure you by the Gods,
Wrong not my Mother, tho you doom me dead;
Curse me not till you hear what I resolve,

Give me a little time to rouze my Spirits,   365
To muster all the Tyrant-man about me,
All that is fierce, austeer, and greatly cruel
To Titus and his Teraminta's ruin.
    BRUT. Remember me; look on thy Father's suff'rings,
What he has born for twenty rowling years;   370
If thou hast nature, worth, or honour in thee,
The contemplation of my cruel labours
Will stir thee up to this new act of glory:
Thou want'st the Image of thy Father's wrongs;
O take it then, reflected with the warmth   375
Of all the tenderness that I can give thee:
Perhaps it stood in a wrong light before;
I'll try all ways to place it to advantage.
Learn by my rigorous Roman Resolution
To stiffen thy unharrass'd Infant vertue: 380
I do allow thee fond, young, soft, and gentle,
Train'd by the Charms of one that is most lovely;
Yet, Titus, this must all be lost, when Honor,
When Rome, the World, and the Gods come to claim us:
Think then thou hear'st 'em cry, obey thy Father;   385
If thou art false, or perjur'd, there he stands
Accountable to us; but swear t'obey;
Implicitly believe him, that, if ought
Be sworn amiss, thou may'st have nought to answer.
    TIT. What is it, Sir, that you would have me swear,   390
That I may scape your Curse, and gain your blessing?
    BRUT. That thou this night will part with Teraminta.
For once again I swear, if here she stayes,
What for the hatred of the Multitude,
And my Resolves to drive out Tarquin's Race,   395
Her person is not safe.
    TIT.   Here, take me, Sir;
Take me before I cool: I swear this night
That I will part with (Oh!) my Teraminta.
    BRUT. Swear too, and by the Soul of Ravish'd Lucrece,
Tho on thy Bridal night, thou wilt not touch her.   400
    TIT. I swear, ev'n by the Soul of her you nam'd,
The Ravish'd Lucrece, Oh th' Immortal Gods!
I will not touch her.
    BRUT.   So; I trust thy Virtue:
And, by the Gods, I thank thee for the Conquest.
Once more, with all the blessings I can give thee,   405
I take thee to my arms; thus on my brest,
The hard and rugged Pillow of thy Honor,
I wean thee from thy Love: Farewel; be fast
To what thou'st sworn, and I am thine for ever.   [Exit.

---

394 Multitude,] C_{1+}; Multitude. Q_{1-2}.

TIT. <u>solus</u>. To what thou'st sworn! Oh Heaven and Earth what's that?   410
What have I sworn? to part with Teraminta?
To part with something dearer to my heart
Than my Life's drops? What! not this night enjoy her?
Renounce my Vows, the Rights, the Dues of Marriage,
Which now I gave her, and the Priest was witness,   415
Bless'd with a floud that stream'd from both our eyes,
And seal'd with sighs, and smiles, and deathless kisses;
Yet after this to swear thou wilt not touch her!
Oh, all the Gods, I did forswear my self
In swearing that, and will forswear again: 420
Not touch her! O thou perjur'd Braggard; where,
Where are thy Vaunts, thy Protestations now?

Enter Teraminta.

She comes to strike thy staggering Duty down:
'Tis fall'n, 'tis gone; Oh, Teraminta, come,
Come to my arms thou only joy of Titus,   425
Hush to my cares, thou mass of hoarded sweets,
Selected hour of all Life's happy moments;
What shall I say to thee?
        TER.   Say any thing;
For while you speak, methinks a sudden calm,
In spight of all the horror that surrounds me,   430
Falls upon every frighted faculty
And puts my Soul in Tune. O, Titus, oh!
Methinks my Spirit shivers in her house,
Shrugging, as if she long'd to be at rest;
With this foresight, to dye thus in your arms   435
Were to prevent a world of following ills.
        TIT. What ills, my Love? what power has Fortune now
But we can brave? 'Tis true, my Teraminta
The Body of the World is out of frame,
The vast distorted limbs are on the Rack   440
And all the Cable Sinews stretch'd to bursting,
The Blood ferments, and the Majestick Spirit,
Like Hercules in the invenom'd Shirt,
Lies in a Fever on the horrid Pile:
My Father, like an AEsculapius   445
Sent by the Gods, comes boldly to the Cure;
But how, my Love? by violent Remedies,
And saies that Rome, ere yet she can be well,
Must purge and cast, purge all th'infected humors
Through the whole mass; and vastly, vastly bleed,   450

---

437 TIT.] C_{1+}; TER. Q_{1-2}.
442 Spirits, C_{1+}.
444 Lye C_{1+}.

TER. Ah, Titus! I my self but now beheld
Th' expulsion of the Queen, driv'n from her Palace
By the inrag'd and madding Multitude;
And hardly scap'd my self to find you here.
    TIT. Why, yet, my Teraminta, we may smile.   455
Come then to bed, ere yet the night descends
With her black wings to brood o're all the World.
Why, what care we? let us enjoy those pleasures
The Gods have giv'n; lock'd in each others arms
We'll lye for ever thus, and laugh at Fate.   460
    TER. No, no, my Lord; there's more than you have nam'd,
There's something at your heart that I must find;
I claim it with the priviledge of a Wife:
Keep close your joys; but for your griefs, my Titus,
I must not, will not lose my share in them.   465
Ah, the good Gods, what is it stirs you thus?
Speak, speak, my Lord, or Teraminta dies.
Oh Heav'ns, he weeps! nay, then upon my knees
I thus conjure you speak, or give me death.
    TIT. Rise, Teraminta. Oh, if I should speak   470
What I have rashly sworn against my Love,
I fear that I should give thee death indeed.
    TER. Against your Love! No, that's impossible;
I know your God-like truth: nay, should you swear,
Swear to me now that you forswore your Love,   475
I would not credit it. No, no, my Lord,
I see, I know, I read it in your eyes,
You love the wretched Teraminta still:
The very manner of your hiding it,
The tears you shed, your backwardness to speak,   480
What you affirm you swore against your Love
Tell me, my Lord, you love me more than ever.
    TIT. By all the Gods, I do: Oh, Teraminta,
My heart's discerner, whether wilt thou drive me?
I'll tell thee then. My Father wrought me up   485
I know not how, to swear I know not what,
That I would send thee hence with Tullia,
Swear not to touch thee, though my Wife; yet, Oh,
Had'st thou been by thy self, and but beheld him,
Thou would'st have thought, such was his Majesty,   490
That the Gods Lightned from his awful eyes,
And Thunder'd from his tongue.
    TER.   No more, my Lord:
I do conjure you by all those Powers
Which we invok'd together at the Altar;
And beg you by the love I know you bear me,   495
To let this passion trouble you no farther;

_____

484 whither C$_{1+}$.

No, my dear Lord, my honor'd God-like Husband,
I am your Wife, and one that seeks your Honor:
By Heaven, I would have sworn you thus my self.
What, on the shock of Empire, on the turn   500
Of State, and universal change of things,
To lye at home and languish for a Woman!
No, Titus, he that makes himself thus vile,
Let him not dare pretend to ought that's Princely;
But be, as all the Warlike World shall judge him,   505
The Droll of th' People and the scorn of Kings.

                  Enter Horatius.

    HOR. My Lord, your Father gives you thus in Charge,
Remember what you swore: the Guard is ready;
And I am ordered to conduct your Bride,
While you attend your Father.
    TIT.   Oh, Teraminta!   510
Then we must part.
    TER.   We must, we must, my Lord:
Therefore be swift, and snatch your self away;
Or I shall dye with lingring.
    TIT.   Oh, a kiss.
Balmy as Cordials that recover Souls;
Chast as Maids sighs, and keen as longing Mothers.   515
Preserve thy self; look well to that, my Love;
Think on our Covenant: when either dyes,
The other is no more.
    TER.   I do remember;
But have no language left.
    TIT.   Yet we shall meet,
In spight of sighs we shall, at least in Heaven.   520
Oh, Teraminta, once more to my heart,
Once to my lips, and ever to my Soul.
Thus the soft Mother, tho her Babe is dead,
Will have the Darling on her bosom lay'd,
Will talk, and rave, and with the Nurses strive,   525
And fond it still, as if it were alive;
Knows it must go, yet struggles with the Croud,
And shrieks to see 'em wrap it in the Shroud.

               End of A C T II.

Act III.   Scene I.

Collatinus, Tiberius, Vitellius, Aquilius.

COLL. Th' expulsion of the Tarquins now must stand;
Their Camp to be surpris'd, while Tarquin here
Was scolded from our Walls! I blush to think
That such a Master in the art of War
Should so forget himself.
   VIT.   Triumphant Brutus,   5
Like Jove when follow'd by a Train of Gods,
To mingle with the Fates and Doom the World,
Ascends the Brasen steps o'th' Capitol,
With all the humming Senate at his heels;
Ev'n in that Capitol which the King built   10
With the expence of all the Royal Treasure:
Ingrateful Brutus there in pomp appears,
And sits the Purple Judge of Tarquin's downfal.
   AQUIL. But why, my Lord, why are not you there too?
Were you not chosen Consul by whole Rome?   15
Why are you not Saluted too like him?
Where are your Lictors? where your Rods and Axes?
Or are you but the Ape, the Mimic God
Of this new Thunderer, who appropriates
Those Bolts of Power which ought to be divided?   20
   TIB. Now, by the Gods, I hate his upstart pride,
His Rebel thoughts of the Imperial Race
His abject Soul that stoops to Court the Vulgar,
His scorn of Princes, and his lust to th' People,
O, Collatine, have you not eyes to find him?   25
Why are you rais'd, but to set off his honors?
A Taper by the Sun, whose sickly Beams
Are swallow'd in the blaze of his full Glory:
He, like a Meteor, wades th'Abyss of light,
While your faint luster adds but to the beard   30
That aws the World. When late through Rome he pass'd
Fixt on his Courser, mark'd you how he bow'd
On this, on that side, to the gazing heads
That pav'd the Streets and all imboss'd the Windows,
That gap'd with eagerness to speak, but could not,   35
So fast their Spirits flow'd to admiration,
And that to joy; which thus at last broke forth:
Brutus, God Brutus, Father of thy Country!
Hail Genius, hail! Deliverer of lost Rome!
Shield of the Common wealth, and Sword of Justice!   40
Hail, scourge of Tyrants, lash for Lawless Kings!
All hail they cry'd, while the long Peal of Praises

Tormented with a thousand Ecchoing cryes
Ran like the Volly of the Gods along.
    COLL. No more on't; I grow sick with the remembrance.   45
    TIB. But when you follow'd, how did their bellying Bodies
That ventur'd from the Casements more than half,
To look at Brutus, nay, that stuck like Snails
Upon the Walls, and from the Houses tops
Hung down like clustring Bees upon each other;   50
How did they all draw back at sight of you
To laze, and loll, and yawn, and rest from rapture!
Are you a man? have you the blood of Kings,
And suffer this?
    COLL.   Ha! is he not his Father?
    TIB. I grant he is.   55
Consider this, and rouz your self at home:
Commend my fire, and rail at your own slackness.
Yet more; remember but your last disgrace,
When you propos'd, with reverence to the Gods,
A King of Sacrifices should be chosen,   60
And from the Consuls; did he not oppose you?
Fearing, as well he might, your sure election,
Saying, It smelt too much of Royalty;
And that it might rub up the memory
Of those that lov'd the Tyrant? Nay, yet more;   65
That if the people chose you for the Place,
The name of King would light upon a Tarquin:
Of one that's doubly Royal, being descended
From two great Princes that were Kings of Rome?
    COLL. But, after all this, whether would'st thou drive?   70
    TIB. I would to Justice; for the Restauration
Of our most Lawful Prince: Yes, Collatine,
I look upon my Father as a Traytor;
I find, that neither you, nor brave Aquilius,
Nor young Vitellius, dare confide in me: 75
But that you may, and firmly, to the hazard
Of all the World holds precious; once again
I say, I look on Brutus as a Traytor,
No more my Father, by th'immortal Gods.
And to redeem the time, to fix the King   80
On his Imperial Throne, some means propos'd
That savor of a govern'd Policy,
Where there is strength and life to hope a Fortune,
Not to throw all upon one desperate chance;
I'll on as far as he that laughs at dying.   85
    COLL. Come to my armes: O thou so truly brave
Thou may'st redeem the errors of thy race!
Aquilius, and Vitellius, O embrace him,

---

70 whither C_{1+}.

And ask his pardon, that so long we fear'd
To trust so rich a Virtue. But behold,   90

    Enter Brutus and Valerius.

Brutus appears: Youngman, be satisfy'd,
I sound thy Politic Father to the bottom,
Plotting the assumption of Valerius,
He means to cast me from the Consulship:
But now, I heard how he Cajol'd the People   95
With his known industry, and my remissness,
That still in all our Votes, Proscriptions, Edicts,
Against the King, he found I acted faintly,
Still closing every Sentence, He's a Tarquin.
  BRUT. No, my Valerius, till thou art my mate,   100
Joynt master in this great Authority,
However calm the face of things appear,
Rome is not safe; by the Majestic Gods,
I swear, while Collatine sits at the helm,
A Universal wrack is to be fear'd: 105
I have intelligence of his Transactions,
He mingles with the young hot blood of Rome,
Gnaws himself inward, grudges my applause,
Promotes Cabals with highest Quality,
Such headlong youth as, spurning Laws and manners,   110
Shar'd in the late Debaucheries of Sextus,
And therefore wish the Tyrant here again:
As the inverted Seasons shock wise men,
And the most fixt Philosophy must start
At sultry Winters, and at frosty Summers;   115
So at this most unnatural stilness here,
This more than midnight silence through all Rome,
This deadness of discourse, and dreadful Calm
Upon so great a change, I more admire
Than if a hundred Politic heads were met,   120
And nodded Mutiny to one another;
More fear, than if a thousand lying Libels
Were spread abroad, nay, dropt among the Senate.
  VAL. I have my self employ'd a busy Slave,
His name Vinditius, given him Wealth and Freedom,   125
To watch the Motions of Vitellius,
And those of the Aquilian Family:
Vitellius has already entertain'd him;
And something thence important may be gather'd,
For these of all the youth of Quality   130
Are most inclin'd to Tarquin and his Race,
By Blood and Humor.
  BRUT.   O, Valerius!
That Boy, observ'st thou? O, I fear, my Friend,

He is a Weed, but rooted in my heart,
And grafted to my Stock; if he prove rank,   135
By Mars, no more but thus, away with him:
I'll tear him from me, though the blood should follow.
Tiberius.
    TIB. My Lord?
    BRUT.   Sirrah, no more of that Vitellius;
I warn'd you too of young Aquilius:
Are my words wind, that thus you let 'em pass?   140
Hast thou forgot thy Father?
    TIB.   No, my Lord.
  BRUT. Thou ly'st. But tho thou scape a Fathers Rod,
The Consul's Ax may reach thee: think on that.
I know thy Vanity, and blind Ambition;
Thou dost associate with my Enemies: 145
When I refus'd the Consul Collatine
To be the King of Sacrifices; strait,
As if thou had'st been sworn his bosom Fool,
He nam'd thee for the Office: And since that,
Since I refus'd thy madness that preferment,   150
Because I would have none of Brutus Blood
Pretend to be a King; thou hang'st thy head,
Contriv'st to give thy Father new displeasure,
As if Imperial Toyl were not enough
To break my heart without thy disobedience.   155
But by the Majesty of Rome I swear,
If after double warning thou despise me,
By all the Gods, I'll cast thee from my blood,
Doom thee to Forks and Whips as a Barbarian,
And leave thee to the lashes of the Lictor.   160
Tarquinius Collatinus, you are summon'd
To meet the Senate on the instant time.
    COLL. Lead on: my duty is to follow Brutus. [Ex. Brut., Val., Coll.*
    TIB. Now, by those Gods with which he menac'd me,
I Here put off all nature; since he turns me   165
Thus desperate to the World, I do renounce him:
And when we meet again he is my Fo.
All Blood, all Reverence, Fondness be forgot:
Like a grown Savage on the Common wild,
That runs at all, and cares not who begot him,   170
I'll meet my Lion Sire, and roar defiance,
As if he ne're had nurs'd me in his Den.

            Enter Vinditius, with the People, and two Fecialian
              Priests, Crown'nd with Laurel: two Spears in
                  their hands; one blody and half burnt.

---

134 tho' rooted C_{2+}.
150 thy preferment, C_{2+}.
  * Coll.]; <u>om</u>. Q_{1+}.

VIN. Make Way there, hey, news from the Tyrant, here
come Envoys, Heralds, Ambassadors; whether in the Gods
name or in the Divels I know not; but here they come, your   175
Fecialian Priests: well, good People, I like not these Priests;
why, what the Devil have they to do with State-affairs? what
side soever they are for, they'l have Heaven for their part, I'll
warrant you: they'l lug the Gods in whether they will or no.
    1. PRI. Hear, Jupiter; and thou, O Juno, hear;   180
Hear, O Quirinus; hear us all you Gods
Celestial, Terestrial, and Infernal.
    2. PRI. Be thou, O Rome, our Judge: hear all you People.
    VIN. Fine Canting Rogues! I told you how they'd be hook-
ing the Gods in at first dash: why, the Gods are their Tools   185
and Tackle; they work with Heaven and Hell; and let me
tell you, as things go, your Priests have a hopeful Trade on't.
    1. PRI. I come Ambassador to thee, O Rome,
Sacred and Just, the Legate of the King.
    2. PRI. If we demand, or purpose to require   190
A Stone from Rome that's contrary to Justice,
May we be ever banish'd from our Country,
And never hope to taste this vital Air.
    TIB. Vinditius, lead the Multitude away:
Aquilius, with Vitellius and my self,   195
Will strait conduct 'em to the Capitol.
    VIN. I go, my Lord; but have a care of 'em: sly Rogues
I warrant 'em. Mark that first Priest; do you see how he
leers? a lying Elder; the true cast of a holy Jugler. Come
my Masters, I would think well of a Priest, but that he has a   200
Commission to dissemble: a Pattent hypocrite, that takes pay
to forge; lyes by Law, and lives by the Sins of the People.
                                        [Exeunt with People.
    AQUIL. My life upon't, you may speak out, and freely;
Tiberius is the heart of our design.
    1. PRI. The Gods be prais'd. Thus then: the King commends   205
Your generous Resolves, longs to be with you,
And those you have ingag'd, Divides his heart
Amongst you; which more clearly will be seen
When you have read these Packets: as we go,
I'll spread the bosom of the King before you.   [Exeunt.   210

Scene II. The Senate.

BRUT. Patricians, that long stood, and scap'd the Tyrant,
The venerable moulds of your Forefathers,
That represent the wisdom of the Dead;

201-202 that takes Pay to forge Lies by law, Q_{2+}.

And you the Conscript chosen for the People,
Engines of Power, severest Counsellors,   5
Courts that examine Treasons to the Head:
All hail. The Consul begs th' auspicious Gods,
And binds Quirinus by his Tutelar Vow,
That Plenty, Peace, and lasting Liberty
May be your portion, and the Lot of Rome.   10
Laws, Rules, and Bounds, prescrib'd for raging Kings,
Like Banks and Bulwarks for the Mother Seas,
Tho 'tis impossible they should prevent
A thousand dayly wracks and nightly ruins,
Yet help to break those rowling inundations   15
Which else would overflow and drown the World.
Tarquin, to feed whose fathomless ambition
And Ocean Luxury, the noblest veins
Of all true Romans were like Rivers empty'd,
Is cut from Rome, and now he flows full on;   20
Yet, Fathers, ought we much to fear his ebb,
And strictly watch the Dams that we have rais'd.
Why should I go about? the Roman People
All, with one voice, accuse my fellow Consul.
    COLL. The People may; I hope the Nobles will not.   25
The People! Brutus does indulge the People.
    BRUT. Consul, in what is right, I will indulge 'em:
And much I think 'tis better so to do,
Than see 'em run in Tumults through the Streets,
Forming Cabals, Plotting against the Senate,   30
Shutting their Shops and flying from the Town,
As if the Gods had sent the Plague among 'em.
I know too well, you and your Royal Tribe
Scorn the good People, scorn the late Election,
Because we chose these Fathers for the People   35
To fill the place of those whom Tarquin murder'd:
And, tho you laugh at this, you and your Train,
The irreligious harebrain'd youth of Rome,
The Ignorant, the Slothful, and the Base;
Yet wise men know, 'tis very rarely seen,   40
That a free people should desire the hurt
Of Common Liberty. No, Collatine,
For those desires arise from their oppression,
Or from suspicion they are falling to it;
But put the case that those their fears were false,   45
Ways may be found to rectify their Errors;
For grant the People ignorant of themselves,
Yet they are capable of being told,
And will conceive a truth from worthy men:
From you they will not, nor from your adherents,   50
Rome's Infamous and Execrable Youth,
Foes to Religion and the Commonwealth,
To Virtue, Learning, and all sober Arts

That bring renown and profit to Mankind;
Such as had rather bleed beneath a Tyrant   55
To become dreadful to the Populace,
To spread their Lusts and Dissolutness round,
Tho at the daily hazard of their lives;
Than live at peace in a Free Government,
Where every man is Master of his own,   60
Sole Lord at home, and Monarch of his House,
Where Rancor and Ambition are extinguish'd,
Where Universal peace extends her wings,
As if the Golden Age return'd, where all
The People do agree, and live secure,   65
The Nobles and the Princes lov'd and Reverenc'd,
The World in Triumph, and the Gods Ador'd.
    COLL. The Consul, Conscript Fathers, saies the People,
For divers Reasons, grudge the Dignity,
Which I possess'd by general approbation,   70
I hear their murmurs, and would know of Brutus
What they would have me do, what's their desire.
    BRUT. Take hence the Royal name, resign thy Office;
Go as a Friend, and of thy own accord,
Lest thou be forc'd to what may seem thy will: 75
The City renders thee what is thy own
With vast increase, so thou resolve to go;
For till the name, the Race and Family
Of Tarquin Be remov'd, Rome is not free.
    COLL. Brutus, I yield my Office to Valerius,   80
Hoping, when Rome has try'd my faith by Exile,
She will recal me: So the Gods preserve you.   [Exit.
    BRUT. Welcome Publicola, true Son of Rome;
On such a Pilot in the roughest Storm
She may securely sleep and rest her cares.   85

    Enter Tiberius, Aquilius, Vitellius, and the Priests.

    1. PRI. Hear Jupiter, Quirinus, all you Gods,
Thou Father, Judge commission'd for the Message
Pater Patratus for the Embassy,
And Sacred Oaths which I must swear for truth,
Dost thou Commission me to seal the Peace,   90
If peace they choose; or hurl this bloody Spear
Half burnt in fire, if they inforce a War?
    2. PRI. Speak to the Senate, and the Alban People
The Words of Tarquin: this is your Commission.

---

71 and] Q_{2+}; an Q_1.

1. PRI. The King, to show he has more moderation   95
Than those that drove him from his lawful Empire,
Demands but restitution of his own,
His Royal Houshold-stuff, Imperial Treasure,
His Gold, his Jewels, and his proper State
To be transported where he now resides: 100
I swear that this is all the King requires;
Behold his Signet set upon the wax.
'Tis Seal'd and written in these Sacred Tables.
To this I swear; and as my Oath is Just,
Sincere and punctual, without all deceit,   105
May Jupiter and all the Gods reward me:
But if I act, or otherwise imagine,
Think, or design, than what I hear have sworn,
All you the Alban People being safe,
Safe in your Country, Temples, Sepulchers,   110
Safe in your Laws, and proper Houshold Gods;
Let me alone be strook, fall, perish, dye,
As now this Stone falls from my hand to Earth.
    BRUT. The things you ask being very controversial,
Require some time. Should we deny the Tyrant   115
What was his own, 'twould seem a strange injustice;
Tho he had never Reign'd in Rome; yet, Fathers,
If we consent to yield to his demand,
We give him then full power to make a War.
'Tis known to you, the Fecialian Priests,   120
No Act of Senate after Sun-set stands;
Therefore your offers being of great moment,
We shall defer your bus'ness till the morn:
With whose first dawn we summon all the Fathers,
To give th'affair dispatch. So Jove protect,   125
Guard, and Defend the Commonwealth of Rome.   [Exeunt.

Manet Tiberius, Aquilius, Vitellius, Priests.

    TIB. Now to the Garden, where I'll bring my Brother:
Fear not, my Lord; we have the means to work him;
It cannot fail.
    1. PRI.   And you, Vitellius, hast
With good Aquilius, spread the news through Rome,   130
To all of Royal Spirit; most to those
Young Noble men that us'd to range with Sextus!
Perswade a restitution of the King,
Give 'em the hint to let him in by night,
And joyn their Forces with th'Imperial Troops,   135
For 'tis a shove a push of Fate must bear it,
For you, the Hearts and Souls of enterprise,
I need not urge a reason after this:
What good can come of such a Government
Where tho two Consuls, wise and able persons,   140

As are throughout the World, sit at the helm,
A very trifle cannot be resolv'd;
A Trick, a Start, a Shaddow of a business,
That would receive dispatch in half a minute
Were the Authority but rightly plac'd,   145
In Rome's most lawful King? But now no more;
The Fecialian Garden is the place,
Where more of our sworn Function will be ready
To help the Royal Plot: disperse, and prosper.

Scene III.   The Fecialian Garden.

Titus solus.

TIT.   She's gone; and I shall never see her more:
Gone to the Camp, to the harsh trade of War,
Driven from thy bed, just warm within thy brest,
Torn from her harbor by thy Father's hand,
Perhaps to starve upon the barren plain,   5
Thy Virgin Wife, the very blush of Maids,
The softest bosom sweet, and not enjoy'd:
O the Immortal Gods! and as she went,
How er'e she seem'd to bear our parting well,
Methought she mixt her melting with disdain,   10
A cast of anger through her Shining tears:
So to abuse her hopes, and blast her wishes,
By making her my Bride, but not a Woman!

Enter Tiberius, Aquilius, Vitellius, and Priests,
with Teraminta.

TIB.   See where he stands, drown'd in his Melancholy.
1. PRI.   Madam, you know the pleasure of the Queen: 15
And what the Royal Tullia did command
I've sworn to execute.
TER.   I am instructed.
Since then my life's at stake, you need not doubt
But I will act with all the Force I can:
Let me intreat you leave me here alone   20
Some minutes, and I'll call you to the conquest.
                           [Exit. Tib., Aquil., Vit., and Priests.

TIT.   Choose then the gloomy'st place through all the Grove,
Throw thy abandon'd body on the ground,
With thy bare brest lye wedded to the Dew;
Then, as thou drink'st the tears that trickle from thee: 25
So stretch'd resolve to lye till death shall seize thee:

Thy sorrowful head hung or'e some tumbling Stream,
To rock thy griefs with melancholy sounds,
With broken murmers and redoubled groans,
To help the gurgling of the waters fall.   30
    TER. Oh, Titus, Oh, what Scene of Death is this! [aside.*
    TIT. Or if thy Passion will not be kept in,
As in that glass of nature thou shalt view
Thy swoln drown'd eyes with the inverted banks,
The tops of Willows and their blossoms turn'd,   35
With all the under Sky ten fathom down,
Wish that the shaddow of the swimming Globe
Were so indeed, that thou migh'st leap at Fate,
And hurl thy Fortune headlong at the Stars:
Nay, do not bear it, turn thy watry face   40
To yond' misguided Orb, and ask the Gods
For what bold Sin they doom the wretched Titus
To such a loss as that of Teraminta?
O Teraminta! I will groan thy name
Till the tir'd Eccho faint with repetition,   45
Till all the breathless Grove and quiet Myrtles
Shake with my sighs, as if a Tempest bow'd 'em.
Nothing but Teraminta: O Teraminta!
    TER. Nothing but Titus: Titus and Teraminta!
Thus let me rob the Fountains and the Groves,   50
Thus gird me to thee with the fastest knot
Of arms and Spirits that would clasp thee through;
Cold as thou art, and wet with night's faln dews,
Yet dearer so, thus richly dress'd with sorrows,
Than if the Gods had hung thee round with Kingdoms.   55
Oh, Titus, O!
    TIT.   I find thee Teraminta,
Wak'd from a fearful Dream, and hold thee fast:
'Tis real, and I give thee back thy joys,
Thy boundless Love with pleasures running o're;
Nay, as thou art, thus with thy trappings, come,   60
Leap to my heart, and ride upon the pants,
Triumphing thus, and now defie our Stars.
But, oh, why do we lose this precious moment!
The bliss may yet be bar'd if we delay,
As 'twas before. Come to thy Husband's bed;   65
I will not think this true till there I hold thee,
Lock'd in my Arms. Leave this Contagious Air;
There will be time for talk how thou cam'st hither
When we have been before hand with the Gods:
Till then ---

---

  * [aside. <u>om.</u> Q$_1$(DFo3, TxU).
38 might'st Q$_{2+}$.
64 barr'd Q$_{2+}$.

TER.   Oh, Titus, you must hear me first.   70
I bring a Message from the Furious Queen;
I promised nay, she Swore me not to touch you,
Till I had Charm'd you to the part of Tarquin.
     TIT. Ha, Teraminta! not to touch thy Husband,
Unless he prove a Villain?
     TER.   Titus, no;   75
I'm Sworn to tell you that you are a Traytor,
If you refuse to Fight the Royal Cause.
     TIT. Hold, Teraminta.
     TER.   No, my Lord; 'tis plain,
And I am sworn to lay my Reasons home.
Rouze then, awake, recal your sleeping Virtue;   80
Side with the King, and Arm against your Father,
Take part with those that Loyally have Sworn
To let him in by Night: Vitellius,
Aquilius, and your Brother wait without;
Therefore I charge you hast, subscribe your name,   85
And send your vow'd obedience to the King:
'Tis Teraminta that intreats you thus,
Charms, and Conjures you; tell the Royal Heralds
You'l head their Enterprise; and then, my Lord,
My Love, my noble Husband, I'll obey you,   90
And follow to your bed.
     TIT.   Never I swear.
O, Teraminta, thou hast broke my heart:
By all the Gods, from thee this was too much.
Farewel, and take this with thee. For thy sake,
I will not Fight against the King, nor for him: 95
I'll fly my Father, Brother, Friends for ever,
Forsake the haunts of Men; converse no more
With ought that's Human; dwell with endless darkness:
For, Since the sight of thee is now unwelcome,
What has the World besides that I can bear?   100
     TER. Come back, my Lord. By those immortal Pow'rs
You now invok'd, I'll fix you in this virtue.
Your Teraminta did but try how strong
Your Honour stood: and now she finds it lasting,
Will dye to root you in this solid Glory.   105
Yes, Titus, tho the Queen has Sworn to end me,
Tho both the Fecialians have Commission
To stab me in your presence, if not wrought
To serve the King; yet by the Gods I charge you
Keep to the point your constancy has gain'd.   110
Tarquin, altho my Father, is a Tyrant,
A bloody black Usurper; so I beg you
Ev'n in my death to view him.
     TIT.   Oh you Gods!
     TER. Yet guilty as he is, if you behold him
Hereafter with his Wounds upon the Earth,   115

Titus, for my sake, for poor Teraminta,
Who rather dy'd than you should lose your Honor,
Do not you strike him, do not dip your Sword
In Tarquin's blood, because he was my Father.
    TIT. No, Teraminta, no: by all the Gods,   120
I will defend him, ev'n against my Father.
See, see, my Love; behold the Flight I take:
What all the Charms of thy expected bed
Could not once move my Soul to think of Acting,
Thy tears and menac'd death, by which thou striv'st   125
To fix me to the Principles of Glory,
Have wrought me off. Yes, yes, you cruel Gods,
Let the eternal Bolts that bind this Frame
Start from their Order: since you push me thus
Ev'n to the Margin of this wide despair,   130
Behold I plunge at once in this dishonor,
Where there is neither Shore, nor hope of Haven,
No Floating mark through all the dismal Vast;
'Tis Rockless too, no Cliff to clamber up
To gaze about and pause upon the ruin.   135
    TER. Is then your purpos'd Honor come to this?
What now, my Lord?
    TIT.   Thy death, thy death, my Love:
I'll think on that, and laugh at all the Gods.
Glory, Blood, Nature, tyes of Reverence,
The dues of Birth, respect of Parents, all,   140
All are as this, the Air I drive before me.
What ho! Vitellius, and Aquilius, come,
And you the Fecialian Heralds, hast
I'm ready for the leap, I'll take it with you
Tho deep as to the Fiends.
    TER.   Thus hear me, Titus.   145
    TIT. Off from my knees, away.
What on this Theam, thy death? nay, stab'd before me!

       Enter Priests, with Tiberius, Aquilius, Vitellius.

Speak not; I will not know thee on this Subject,
But push thee from my heart, with all persuasions
That now are lost upon me. O, Tiberius,   150
Aquilius, and Vitellius, welcome, welcome;
I'll joyn you in the Conjuration, come:
I am as free as he that dares be formost.
    TER. My Lord, my Husband.
    TIT.   Take this woman from me.
Nay look you, Sirs, I am not yet so gon,   155
So headlong neither in this damn'd Design

---

156 his damn'd C_{1+}.

To quench this Horrid thirst with Brutus blood:
No, by th' eternal Gods, I bar you that;
My Father shall not bleed.
      TIB.   You could not think
Your Brother sure so Monstrous in his kind,   160
As not to make our Father's life his care.
      TIT. Thus then, my Lords, I List my self among you,
And with my Style in short Subscribe my self
The Servant to the King; my words are these.
Titus to the King,   165
Sir, you need only know my Brother's mind
To judge of me, who am resolv'd to serve you.
      1. PRI. 'Tis full enough.
      TIT.   Then leave me to the hire [Exeunt. Tib. Aquil.
Of this hard labor, to the dear bought prize,   Vit. and Priests.
Whose life I purchas'd with my loss of Honor: 170
Come to my brests, thou Tempest-beaten Flower,
Brim-full of Rain, and stick upon my heart.
O short liv'd Rose! yet I some hours will wear thee:
Yes, by the Gods, I'll smell thee till I languish,
Rifle thy sweets, and run thee o're and o're,   175
Fall like the Night upon thy folding beauties,
And clasp thee dead: Then, like the Morning Sun,
With a new heat kiss thee to life again,
And make the pleasure equal to the pain.

End of A C T III.

---

160 kind,] Q$_{2+}$; kind. Q$_1$.
175 thee] Q$_{2+}$; the Q$_1$.

Act IV. Scene I.

Tiberius, Vitellius, two men lying
at one side bound. *

TIB. Hark, are we not pursu'd?
VIT.   No; 'tis the tread
Of our own Friends, that follow in the dark.
TIB. What's now the time?
VIT.   Just dead of night.
And 'tis the blackest that e're mask'd a Murder.
TIB. It likes me better; for I love the Scoul,   5
The grimmest lowre of Fate on such a deed;
I would have all the Charnel Houses yawn,
The dusty Urns, and Monumental Bones
Remov'd, to make our Massacre a Tomb.
Hark! who was that that holloa'd fire?
VIT.   A Slave,   10
That snores i'th'Hall, he bellows in his Sleep,
And cries, The Capitol's o' fire.
TIB.   I would it were;
And Tarquin at the Gates: 'twould be a blaze,
A Beacon fit to light a King of Blood,
That vows at once the Slaughter of the World: 15
Down with their Temples, set 'em on a Flame?
What should they do with Houses for the Gods,
Fat Fools, the lazy Magistrates of Rome,
Wise Citizens, the Politick heads o'th'People,
That Preach Rebellion to the Multitude?   20
Why, let 'em off, and rowl into their Graves:
I long to be at work.

Enter Aquilius, Trebonius, Servilius, Minutius,
Pomponius. *

See, good Aquilius,
Trebonius too, Servilius and Minutius,
Pomponius hail: nay, now you may unmask,
Brow-beat the Fates, and say they are your Slaves.   25
AQUIL. What are those Bodyes for?
TIB.   A Sacrifice.

---

* two ... bound.]; <u>om.</u> Q₁₊. <u>See below</u>, <u>line 26 ff</u>.
16 Flame; Q₂₊.
* Enter ... Pomponius.]; <u>om.</u> Q₁₊.

These were two very busie Commonwealth's-men,
That, ere the King was banish'd by the Senate,
First set the Plot on foot in publick Meetings,
That would be holding forth 'Twas possible   30
That Kings themselves might err, and were but men,
The People were not Beasts for Sacrifice;
Then jogg'd his Brother, this cram'd Statesman here,
The bolder Rogue, whom ev'n with open mouth
I heard once bealch Sedition from a Stall: 35
Go, bear him to the Priests; he is a Victim
That comes as wish'd for them, the Cooks of Heav'n, [The two men
And they will Carve this Brawn of fat Rebellion,   are led off. *
As if he were a Dish the Gods might feed on.
    VIN. (From a Window.) Oh, the Gods! Oh the Gods! what   40
will they do with him? O these Priests, Rogues, Cutthroats! A
dish for the Gods, but the Devil's Cooks to dress him.
    TIB. Thus then. The Fecialians have set down
A platform, copy'd from the King's design:
The Pandane or the Romulide, the Roman,   45
Carmental and Janiculan Ports of Rome,
The Circ, the Capital, and Sublician Bridge
Must all be seiz'd by us that are within;
'Twill not be hard in the Surprise of night
By us, the Consuls Children and their Nephews,   50
To kill the drowsie Guards, and keep the Holds,
At least so long till Tarquin force his entrance
With all the Royalists that come to joyn us:
Therefore to make his broader Squadrons way,
Tarquinian is design'd to be the Entry   55
Of his most pompous and Resolv'd Revenge.
    AQUIL. The first decreed in this great Execution
Is here set down your Father and Valerius.
    TIB. That's as the King shall please; but for Valerius,
I'll take my self the honor of his Head   60
And wear it on my Spear. The Senate all
Without exception shall be Sacrific'd:
And those that are the mutinous Heads o'th' People
Whom I have mark'd to be the Soldier's Spoil,
For Plunder must be given, and who so fit   65
As those notorious limbs, your Commonwealth's men?
Their Daughters to be Ravish'd; and their Sons
Quarter'd like Brutes upon the Common Shambles.
    VIT. Now for the Letters, which the Fecialians
Require us all to Sign, and send to Tarquin,   70
Who will not else be apt to trust his Heralds
Without Credentials under every hand;

---

30 forth. Q_2; forth, C_{1+}.
  * [The...off.]; om. Q_{1+}.

The bus'ness being indeed of vast import,
On which the hazard of his Life and Empire,
As well as all our Fortunes, does depend.   75
    TIB. It were a break to the whole Enterprise
To make a Scruple in our great affair;
I will sign first: and for my Brother Titus,
Whom his new Wife detains, I have his hand
And Seal to show, as fast and firm as any.   80
    VIN. O Villany! Villany! What would they do with me, if
they should catch me peeping? knock out my brains at least;
another Dish for the Priests, who would make fine sauce of 'em
for the hanch of a fat Citizen!
    TIB. All hands have here Subscrib'd, and that your hearts   85
Prove Resolute to what your hands have giv'n,
Behold the Messengers of Heav'n to bind you,
Charms of Religion, sacred Conjurations,
With Sounds of Execration, words of horror
Not to disclose or make least signs or show,   90
Of what you have both heard, and seen, and sworn,
But bear your selves as if it ne'r had been:
Swear by the Gods Celestial and Infernal,
By Pluto, Mother Earth, and by the Furies,
Not to reveal, tho Racks were set before you,   95
A syllable of what is past and done.
Hark, how the Offer'd Brutes begin to roar!
O that the hearts of all the Traitor Senate,
And heads of that foul Hydra Multitude,
Were frying with their fat upon this Pile,   100
That we might make an Off'ring worth an Empire,
And Sacrifice Rebellion to the King.

        The Scene draws, showing the Sacrifice; One Burning,
        and another Crucify'd: the Priests coming forward
        with Goblets in their hands, fill'd with human blood.

    1. PRI. Kneel all you Heroes of this black Design,
Each take his Goblet fill'd with Blood & Wine;
Swear by the Thunderer, swear by Jove,   105
Swear by the hundred Gods above;
Swear by Dis, by Proserpine,
Swear by the Berecynthian Queen.
    2. PRI. To keep it close till Tarquin comes,
With Trumpets sound and beat of Drums: 110
But then to Thunder forth the Deed,
That Rome may blush, and Traytors bleed.
Swear all.
    ALL. We Swear.

———————

99 of all that foul Q$_{2+}$.

    1. PRI.   Now drink the Blood,
To make the Conjuration good.
    TIB. Methinks I feel the Slaves exalted blood   115
Warm at my heart: O that it were the Spirits
Of Rome's best life, drawn from her grizled Fathers!
That were a draught indeed to quench Ambition,
And give new fierceness to the King's Revenge.
    VIN. Oh the Gods! what, burn a man alive! O Canibals, Hell-   120
hounds! Eat one man, and drink another! Well, I'll to Valerius;
Brutus will not believe me, because his Sons and Nephews are in
the business. What, drink a man's blood! Roast him, and eat
him alive! A whole man roasted! would not an Ox serve the turn?
Priests to do this! Oh you immortal Gods! For my part, if this   125
be your worship, I renounce you. No; if a man can't go to Heaven,
unless your Priests eat him, and drink him, and roast him alive;
I'll be for the broad way, and the Devil shall have me at a
venture.   [Exit.

                Enter Titus.

    TIT. What hoa, Tiberius! give me back my hand.   130
What have you done? Horrors and midnight Murders!
The Gods, the Gods awake you to repentance,
As they have me. Would'st thou believe me Brother?
Since I deliver'd thee that fatal Scrole,
That Writing to the King, my heart rebell'd   135
Against it self; my thoughts were up in arms
All in a roar, like Seamen in a Storm,
My Reason and my Faculties were wrack'd
The Mast, the Rudder, and the Tackling gone;
My Body, like the Hull of some lost Vessel,   140
Beaten, and tumbled with my Rowling fears,
Therefore I charge thee give me back my Writing.
    TIB. What means my Brother?
    TIT.   O Tiberius, O!
Dark as it seems, I tell thee that the Gods
Look through a Day of Lightning on our City: 145
The Heav'n's on Fire; and from the flaming Vault
Portentous blood pours like a Torrent down.
There are a hundred Gods in Rome to night,
And every larger Spirit is abroad,
Monuments empty'd, every Urn is shaken   150
To fright the State, and put the World in Arms:
Just now I saw three Romans stand amaz'd
Before a Flaming Sword, then dropt down dead,
My self untouch'd: while through the blazing Air
A Fleeting head, like a full riding Moon,   155

---

149 every] Q$_{2+}$; ever Q$_1$.

Glanc'd by, and cry'd, Titus, I am Egeria;
Repent, repent, or certain death attends thee;
Treason and Tyranny shall not prevail:
Kingdom shall be no more; Egeria sayes it:
And that vast turn Imperial Fate design'd   160
I saw, O Titus, on th' eternal Loom,
'Tis Ripe, 'tis Perfect, and is doom'd to stand.
    1. PRI. Fumes, fumes; the Fantoms of an ill digestion;
The Gods are as good quiet Gods as may be,
They're fast asleep, and mean not to disturb us,   165
Unless your Frenzy wake 'em.
    TIT.   Peace fury, peace.
May the Gods Doom me to the pains of Hell
If I enjoy'd the beauties that I sav'd:
The horror of my Treason shock'd my joys,
Enervated my purpose, while I lay   170
Colder than Marble by her Virgin side,
As if I had drunk the blood of Elephants,
Drowsie Mandragora, or the Juice of Hemlock.
    1. PRI. I like him not; I think we had best dispatch him.
    TIT. Nothing but Images of horror round me,   175
Rome all in blood, the Ravish'd Vestals raving,
The Sacred fire put out; rob'd Mothers shrieks;
Deaf'ning the Gods with clamours for their Babes
That sprawl'd aloft upon the Soldiers Speares
The beard of Age pluck'd off by barbarous hands,   180
While from his piteous wounds and horrid gashes
The labouring life flow'd faster than the blood.

      Enter Valerius, Vinditius, with Guards, who seize all
      but the Priests, who slip away: Vinditius follows them.

    VAL. Horror upon me! what will this night bring forth?
Yes, you immortal Gods, strike, strike the Consul,
Since these are here, the crime will look less horrid   185
In me, than in his Sons. Titus, Tiberius!
O from this time let me be blind and dumb,
But hast there; Mutius, Fly; call hither Brutus,
Bid him for ever leave the down of rest,
And sleep no more: If Rome were all on Fire,   190
And Tarquin in the Streets bestriding Slaughter,
He would less wonder than at Titus here.
    TIT. Stop there, O stop that messenger of Fate;
Here, bind, Valerius, bind this Villan's hands,
Tear off my Robes put me upon the Forks,   195

---

178 from their C_{1+}.
191 Streets] C_{1+}; Srreets Q_1; Streats Q_2.
195 Robes, Q_{2+}.

And lash me like a Slave, till I shall howl
My Soul away; or hang me on a Cross,
Rack me a year within some horrid Dungeon,
So deep, so near the Hells that I must suffer,
That I may groan my Torments to the Damn'd: 200
I do submit, this Traitor, this curs'd Villain,
To all the Stings of most ingenious horror,
So thou dispatch me ere my Father comes.
But hark! I hear the tread of Fatal Brutus!
By all the Gods, and by the lowest Furies,   205
I cannot bear his face: away with me;
Or like a Whirlwind I will tear my way
I care not whither.   [Exit with Tiberius.
    VAL.   Take 'em hence together.

Enter Vinditius with the Priests.

    VIN. Here, here, my Lord, I have unkennel'd two:
Those there are Rascals made of Flesh and blood,   210
Those are but men, but these are the Gods Rogues.
    VAL. Go, good Vinditius, hast and stop the People,
Get 'em together to the Capitol:
Where all the Senate with the Consuls early,
Will see strict Justice done upon the Traytors.   215
For thee, the Senate shall decree rewards
Great as thy Service.
    VIN.   I humbly thank your Lordship.
Why, what, they'l make me a Senator at least,
And then a Consul; O th' Immortal Gods!
    My Lord, I go --- To have the Rods and Axes carry'd before   220
me, and a long purple Gown trailing behind my honorable heels:
well, I am made for ever!   [Exit.

Enter Brutus attended.

    BRUT. O, my Valerius, are these horrors true?
Hast thou, O Gods, this night embowel'd me?
Ransack'd thy Brutus Veins, thy Fellow Consul,   225
And found two Villains lurking in my blood?
    VAL. The blackest Treason that e're darkness brooded,
And who, to hatch these horrors for the World,
Who to seduce the Noble Youth of Rome,
To draw 'em to so damn'd a Conjuration,   230
To bind 'em too by new invented Oaths,
Religious Forms, and Devilish Sacrifices,
A Sacrament of blood, for which Rome suffer'd
In two the worthiest of her Martyr'd Sons;
Who to do this, but Messengers from Heav'n?   235
These Holy men that Swore so solemnly
Before the Senate, call'd the Gods to curse 'em,

If they intended ought against the State,
Or harbor'd Treason more than what they utter'd?
    BRUT. Now all the Fiends and Furies thank 'em for it.   240
You Sons of Murder, that get drunk with blood,
Then Stab at Princes, poyson Commonwealths,
Destroy whole Hecatombs of Innocent Souls,
Pile 'em like Bulls and Sheep upon your Altars,
As you would smoke the Gods from out their Dwelling: 245
You shame of Earth, and Scandal of the Heav'ns,
You deeper Fiends than any of the Furies,
That scorn to whisper Envy, Hate, Sedition:
But with a blast of Priviledge Proclaim it;
Priests that are Instruments design'd to Damn us,   250
Fit speaking Trumpets for the mouth of Hell.
Hence with 'em, Guards; secure 'em in the Prison
Of Ancus Martius. Read the Packets o're,
I'll bear it as I'm able, read 'em out.
    VAL. The sum of the Conspiracy to the King.   255
It shall begin with both the Consuls deaths;
And then the Senate; every man must bleed,
But those that have ingaged to serve the King.
Be ready therefore, Sir, to send your Troops
By twelve to morrow night, and come your self   260
In person, if you'll reascend the Throne:
All that have sworn to serve your Majesty
Subscribe themselves by name your faithful Subjects.
Tiberius, Aquilius, Vitellius,
Trebonius, Servilius, Minutius,   265
Pomponius, and your Fecialian Priests.
    BRUT. Ha! my Valerius, is not Titus there?
    VAL. He's here, my Lord; a paper by it self.
Titus to the King.
Sir, you need only know my Brother's mind   270
To judge of me, who am resolv'd to serve you.
What do you think, my Lord?
    BRUT.   Think my Valerius?
By my heart, I know not:
I'm at a loss of thought; and must acknowledge
The Councils of the Gods are fathomless;   275
Nay, 'tis the hardest task perhaps of life
To be assur'd of what is Vice or Virtue:
Whether when we raise up Temples to the Gods
We do not then Blaspheme 'em, O, behold me,
Behold the Game that laughing Fortune playes;   280
Fate, or the will of Heav'n, call't what you please,
That marrs the best designs that Prudence layes,
That brings events about perhaps to mock
At human reach, and sport with expectation.
Consider this, and wonder not at Brutus   285
If his Philosophy seems at a stand,

If thou behold'st him shed unmanly Tears
To see his Blood, his Children, his own Bowels
Conspire the death of him that gave 'em being.
    VAL. What heart, but yours, could bear it without breaking?   290
    BRUT. No, my Valerius, I were a beast indeed
Not to be mov'd with such Prodigious suffering;
Yet after all I justifie the Gods,
And will conclude Ther's Reason supernatural
That guides us through the World with vast discretion,   295
Altho we have not Souls to comprehend it:
Which makes by wondrous methods the same Causes
Produce effects tho of a different nature,
Since then, for Man's Instruction, and the Glory
Of the Immortal Gods, it is Decreed   300
There must be patterns drawn of fiercest Virtue;
Brutus submits to the eternal Doom.
    VAL. May I believe there can be such perfection,
Such a Resolve in Man?
    BRUT. First, as I am their Father,   305
I pardon both of 'em this black Design;
But, as I am Rome's Consul, I abhor 'em,
And cast 'em from my Soul with detestation:
The nearer to my blood, the deeper grain'd
The colour of their fault, and they shall bleed.   310
Yes, my Valerius, both my Sons shall dye:

Enter Teraminta.

Nay, I will stand unbowel'd by the Altar,
See something dearer to me than my entrails
Display'd before the Gods and Roman People;
The Sacrifice of Justice and Revenge.   315
    TER. What Sacrifice, what Victims, Sir, are these
Which you intend? O, you eternal Powers,
How shall I vent my Sorrows! Oh, my Lord,
Yet ere you Seal the death you have design'd,
The death of all that's lovely in the World,   320
Hear what the witness of his Soul can say,
The only Evidence that can, or dare
Appear for your unhappy guiltless Son;
The Gods command you, Virtue, Truth, and Justice,
Which you with so much rigor have Ador'd,   325
Beg you would hear the wretched Teraminta.
    BRUT. Cease thy laments: tho of the blood of Tarquin,
Yet more, the Wife of my forgotten Son,
Thou shalt be heard.
    TER.   Have you forgot him then?

---

319 Yet] Q_{2+}; Yer Q_1.

Have you forgot your self? the Image of you,   330
The very Picture of your excellence,
The Portraiture of all your manly Virtues,
Your visage stampt upon him; just those eyes,
The moving Greatness of 'em, all the mercy,
The shedding goodness; not so quite severe,   335
Yet still most like: and can you then forget him?
    BRUT. Will you proceed?
    TER.   My Lord, I will. Know then,
After your Son, your Son that loves you more
Than I love him, after our common Titus,
The wealth o'th' World unless you rob'em of it,   340
Had long endur'd th' Assaults of the Rebellious,
And still kept fix'd to what you had enjoyn'd him;
I, as Fate order'd it, was sent from Tullia,
With my death menac'd, ev'n before his eyes,
Doom'd to be stab'd before him by the Priests,   345
Unless he yielded not t'oppose the King,
Consider, Sir; Oh make it your own Case;
Just Wedded, just on the expected joys,
Warm for my bed, and rushing to my arms,
So loving too, alas, as we did love: 350
Granted in hast, in heat, in flame of passion
He knew not what himself, and so Subscrib'd.
But now, Sir, now, my Lord, behold a wonder,
Behold a Miracle to move your Soul!
Tho in my arms, just in the grasps of pleasure,   355
His noble heart strook with the thoughts of Brutus,
Of what he promis'd you, till then forgot,
Leapt in his brest and dash'd him from enjoyment;
He shriek'd, y'immortal Gods, what have I done!
No, Teraminta, let us rather perish,   360
Divide for ever with whole Seas betwixt us,
Rather than Sin against so good a Father.
Tho he before had barr'd your life and Fortune,
Yet would not trust the Traytors with the safety
Of him he call'd the Image of the Gods.   365
    VAL. O Saint-like Virtue of a Roman Wife!
O Eloquence Divine! now all the arts
Of Womens tongues, the Rhetoric of the Gods
Inspire thy soft and tender Soul to move him.
    TER. On this he rouz'd: Swore by the Powers Divine,   370
He would fetch back the Paper that he gave,
Or leave his life amongst 'em: kept his word,
And came to challenge it, but, oh! too late;
For, in the mid'st of all his Piety,
His strong perswasions to a swift repentance,   375
His vows to lay their horrid Treasons open,
His execration of the barbarous Priests,
How he abhor'd that bloody Sacrament

As much as you, and curs'd the conjuration;
Vinditius came that had before alarm'd   380
The wise Valerius, who with all the Guards
Found Titus here, believ'd him like the rest,
And seiz'd him too, as guilty of the Treason.
    VAL. But, by the Gods, my Soul does now acquit him.
Blest be thy tongue, blest the auspicious Gods   385
That sent thee, O true pattern of perfection!
To plead his bleeding Cause. There needs no more,
I see his Father's mov'd: Behold a joy,
A watry comfort rising in his eyes,
That sayes, 'Tis more than half a Heav'n to hear thee.   390
    BRUT. Hast, O Valerius, hast and send for Titus.
    TER. For Titus! Oh, that is a word too distant;
Say, for your Son, for your beloved Son,
The Darling of the World, the joy of Heav'n,
The hope of Earth, your eyes not dearer to you,   395
Your Soul's best wish, and comfort of your age.

Enter Titus, with Valerius.

    TIT. Ah, Sir! Oh whither shall I run to hide me?
Where shall I lower fall? how shall I lye
More groveling in your View, and howl for mercy?
Yet 'tis some comfort to my wild despair,   400
Some joy in death that I may kiss your feet,
And swear upon 'em by these streaming tears,
Black as I am with all my guilt upon me,
I never harbor'd ought against your person:
Ev'n in the height of my full fraught distraction,   405
Your life my Lord, was Sacred; ever dear,
And ever pretious, to unhappy Titus.
    BRUT. Rise, Titus: rise my Son.
    TIT.   Alas, I dare not;
I have not strength to see the Majesty
Which I have brav'd: if thus far I aspire,   410
If on your knees I hang and vent my groans,
It is too much, too much for thousand lives.
    BRUT. I pity thee, my Son, and I forgive thee:
And, that thou may'st believe my mercy true,
I take thee in my arms.
    TIT.   O all the Gods!   415
    BRUT. Now rise; I charge thee, on my blessing, rise.
    TER. Ah! See, Sir, see, against his will behold
He does obey, tho he would choose to kneel
An Age before you; see how he stands and trembles!
Now, by my hopes of mercy, he's so lost   420
His heart's so full, brimful of tenderness,
The Sence of what you've done has strook him Speechless:
Nor can he thank you now but with his tears.

BRUT. My dear Valerius, let me now intreat thee
Withdraw a while with gentle Teraminta,   425
And leave us to our selves.
    TER. Ah, Sir, I fear you now;
Nor can I leave you with the humble Titus,
Unless you promise me you will not chide,
Nor fall again to anger: Do not, Sir,   430
Do not upbraid his soft and melting temper
With what is past. Behold he sighs again!
Now by the Gods that hitherto have blest us,
My heart forebodes a storm, I know not why:
But say, my Lord; give me your God-like word   435
You'l not be cruel, and I'll not trust my heart,
How e're it leaps, and fills me with new horror.
    BRUT. I promise thee.
    TER.   Why, then I thank you, Sir;
Ev'n from my Soul I thank you, for this goodness:
The great, good, gracious Gods reward and bless you.   440
Ah Titus, ah my Soul's eternal treasure,
I fear I leave thee with a hard Usurer;
But I perforce must trust thee. Oh Farewell.   [Exit with Val.
    BRUT. Well Titus, speak; how is it with thee now?
I would attend awhile this mighty motion,   445
Wait till the Tempest were quite o'verblown,
That I might take thee in the Calm of Nature,
With all thy gentler Virtues brooding on thee,
So hush'd a stilness, as if all the Gods
Look'd down, and listn'd to what we were saying: 450
Speak then, and tell me, O my best belov'd,
My Son, my Titus, is all well again?
    TIT. So well, that saying how must make it nothing;
So well, that I could wish to dye this moment,
For so my heart with pow'erful throbs perswades me: 455
That were indeed to make you reparation,
That were, my Lord, to thank you home, to dye
And that for Titus too would be most happy.
    BRUT. How's that, my Son? would death for thee be happy?
    TIT. Most certain, Sir; For in my Grave I scape   460
All those affronts which I in life must look for,
All those reproaches which the eyes and fingers
And tongues of Rome will daily cast upon me;
From whom, to a Soul so sensible as mine,
Each single Scorn would be far worse than dying: 465
Besides, I scape the stings of my own Conscience,
Which will for ever Rack me with remembrance,
Haunt me by day, and torture me by night,
Casting my blotted honor in the way

    447 may take C$_3$.

Where e're my melancholy thoughts shall guide me.   470
   BRUT. But is not death a very dreadful thing?
   TIT. Not to a mind resolv'd. No, Sir, to me
It seems as natural as to be born:
Groans, and Convulsions, and discolour'd faces,
Friends weeping round us, blacks, and obsequies,   475
Make it a dreadful thing; the Pomp of death,
Is far more terrible, than Death it self.
Yes, Sir; I call the Powers of Heav'n to witness,
Titus dares dye, if so you have Decreed;
Nay, he shall dye with joy, to honor Brutus,   480
To make your Justice famous through the World
And fix the Liberty of Rome for ever:
Not but I must confess my weakness too;
Yet it is great thus to resolve against it,
To have the frailty of a mortal man,   485
But the Security of th' immortal Gods.
   BRUT. O Titus, Oh thou absolute young man!
Thou flatt'ring Mirror of thy Father's Image,
Where I behold my self at such advantage!
Thou perfect Glory of the Junian Race!   490
Let me indear thee once more to my bosom,
Groan an eternal Farewel to thy Soul;
Instead of tears weep blood, if possible,
Blood, the heart blood of Brutus, on his Child,
For thou must dye, my Titus, dye, my Son,   495
I swear the Gods have Doom'd thee to the grave,
The violated Genius of thy Country
Rears his sad head, and passes Sentence on thee:
This morning Sun, that lights my Sorrows on
To the Tribunal of this horrid vengeance,   500
Shall never see thee more.
   TIT.   Alas, my Lord!
Why are you mov'd thus? why am I worth your sorrow?
Why should the God-like Brutus shake to doom me?
Why all these Trappings for a Traytor's Hearse?
The Gods will have it so.
   BRUT.   They will, my Titus: 505
Nor Heav'n, nor Earth can have it otherwise.
Nay, Titus, mark; the deeper that I search,
My harrass'd Soul returns the more confirm'd:
Methinks I see the very hand of Jove
Moving the dreadful wheels of this affair   510
That whirl thee, like a Machine, to thy Fate.
It seems as if the Gods had preordain'd it
To fix the reeling Spirits of the People,
And settle the loose Liberty of Rome.
'Tis fix'd; O therefore let not Fancy fond thee: 515
So fix'd thy death, that 'tis not in the power
Of Gods or Men to save thee from the Ax.

TIT.   The Ax!   O Heav'n!   then must I fall so basely?
What shall I perish by the common Hangman?
    BRUT.   If thou deny me this, thou givest me nothing.   520
Yes, Titus, since the Gods have so Decreed,
That I must lose thee; I will take th' advantage
Of thy important Fate, Cement Rome's flaws,
And heal her wounded Freedom with thy blood:
I will ascend my self the sad Tribunal,   525
And sit upon my Sons; on thee, my Titus;
Behold thee suffer all the shame of death,
The Lictor's lashes, bleed before the People;
Then, with thy hopes and all thy youth upon thee,
See thy head taken by the Common Ax,   530
Without a groan, without one pittying tear,
If that the Gods can hold me to my purpose,
To make my Justice quite transcend example.
    TIT.   Scourg'd like a Bondman!   ha!   a beaten Slave!
But I deserve it all; yet here I fail: 535
The Image of this suff'ring quite unmans me;
Nor can I longer stop the gushing tears.
O Sir!   O Brutus!   must I call you Father,
Yet have no token of your tenderness?
No sign of mercy?   what, not bate me that!   540
Can you resolve, O all th' extremity
Of cruel rigor!   to behold me too?
To sit unmov'd, and see me whipt to death?
Where are your bowels now?   Is this a Father?
Ah, Sir, why should you make my heart suspect   545
That all your late compassion was dissembled?
How can I think that you did ever love me?
    BRUT.   Think that I love thee by my present passion,
By these unmanly tears, these Earthquakes here,
These sighs that twitch the very strings of life: 550
Think that no other cause on Earth could move me
To tremble thus, to sob, or shed a tear,
Nor shake my solid Virtue from her point
But Titus death: O do not call it shameful,
That thus shall fix the glory of the World.   555
I own thy suff'rings ought t'unman me thus,
To make me throw my Body on the ground,
To bellow like a Beast, to gnaw the Earth ,
To tear my hair, to curse the cruel Fates
That force a Father thus to drag his bowels.   560
    TIT.   O rise, thou violated Majesty,
Rise from the Earth; or I shall beg those Fates
Which you would curse, to bolt me to the Center.
I now submit to all your threatn'd vengeance:

---

528 before the People;] C_{2+}; before People; Q_1-C_1.

Come forth you Executioners of Justice,   565
Nay all you Lictors, Slaves, and common Hangmen,
Come, strip me bare, unrobe me in his sight,
And lash me till I bleed; whip me like Furies;
And when you have scourg'd me till I foam and fall,
For want of Spirits groveling in the dust,   570
Then take my head, and give it his Revenge:
By all the Gods I greedily resign it.
    BRUT. No more, Farewel, eternally Farewel:
If there be Gods, they will reserve a room,
A Throne for thee in Heav'n. One last embrace.   575
What is it makes thy eyes thus swim again?
    TIT. I had forgot: be good to Teraminta
When I am ashes.
    BRUT.   Leave her to my care.
See her thou must not; for thou canst not bear it.
O for one more, this Pull, this Tug of Heart-strings: 580
Farewel for ever.
    TIT.   O Brutus! O my Father!
    BRUT. Canst thou not say Farewel?
    TIT.   Farewel for ever.
    BRUT. For ever then; But Oh my tears run o're:
Groans choak my words; and I can speak no more.   [Exeunt.

End of A C T I V .

Act V. Scene I.

Valerius, Horatius, Herminius, Mutius.

HOR. His Sons condemn'd?
VAL.   Doom'd to the Rods and Axes.
HOR. What both of 'em?
VAL.   Both, Sir, both, both his Sons.
HOR. What, Titus too?
VAL.   Yes, Sir, his Darling Titus.
Nay, tho he knows him innocent as I am,
'Tis all one, Sir, his Sentence stands like Fate.   5
HOR. Yet I'll intreat him.
MUT.   So will I.
HER.   And I.
VAL. Intreat him! yes, you may, my Lords, and move him,
As I have done: why, he's no more a man;
He is not cast in the same Common mould,
His Spirit moves not with our Springs and wards.   10
He looks and talks, as if that Jove had sent him
To be the Judge of all the under World;
Tells me, this Palace of the Universe,
With that vast Moat, the Ocean, running round us,
Th'eternal Stars so fiercely rowling o're us,   15
With all that Circulation of Heav'ns Orbs,
Were so establish'd from before all Ages
To be the Dowry of Majestick Rome:
Then looks, as if he had a Patent for it
To take account of all this great expence,   20
And see the layings out of the round World.
HER. What shall be done then? for it grieves my Soul
To think of Titus loss.
VAL.   There is no help;
But thus to shake your head, and cross your arms,
And wonder what the Gods and he intend.   25
HER. There's scarce one man of this Conspiracy
But is some way Related if not nearly,
To Junius Brutus: some of the Aquilians
Are Nephews to him; and Vitellius Sister,
The grave Sempronia, is the Consul's Wife.   30
VAL. Therefore I have ingag'd that groaning Matron
To plead the Cause of her unhappy Sons.

Enter Titus, with Lictors.

But see, O Gods, behold the Gallant Titus,
The Mirror of all Sons, the white of Virtue;

Fill'd up with blots, and writ all o're with blood,   35
Bowing with shame his body to the ground;
Whipt out of breath by these Inhuman Slaves!
O, Titus! is this possible? this shame?
    TIT. O, my Valerius, call it not my shame;
By all the Gods, it is to Titus honor,   40
My constant suff'rings are my only glory:
What have I left besides? but ask Valerius,
Ask these good men that have perform'd their duty,
If all the while they whipt me like a Slave,
If when the blood from every part ran down   45
I gave one groan, or shed a Womans tear:
I think, I swear, I think, O my Valerius,
That I have born it well, and like a Roman.
But, O, far better shall I bear my death,
Which, as it brings less pain, has less dishonor.   50

             Enter Teraminta wounded.

    TER. Where is he? where, where is this God-like Son
Of an inhuman barbarous bloody Father?
O bear me to him.
    TIT.   Ha! my Teraminta!
Is't possible? the very top of Beauty,
This perfect face drawn by the Gods at Council,   55
Which they were long a making, as they had reason,
For they shall never hit the like again,
Defil'd and mangled thus! What barbarous wretch
Has thus blasphem'd this bright Original?
    TER. For me it matters not, nor my abuses;   60
But, Oh, for thee, why have they us'd thee thus?
Whipt, Titus, whipt! and could the Gods look on?
The glory of the World thus basely us'd?
Lash'd, whipt, and beaten by these upright Dogs?
Whose Souls, with all the Virtue of the Senate   65
Will be but Foyls, to any fault of thine,
Who hast a beauty ev'n in thy offending.
And did thy Father Doom thee thus? Oh Titus,
Forgive thy dying part, if she believes
A wretch so barbarous never could produce thee: 70
Some God, some God, my Titus, watch'd his absence,
Slipt to thy mothers bed and gave thee to the World.
    TIT. O this last wound, this stab to all my courage!
Had'st thou been well, I could have born more lashes:
And is it thus my Father does protect thee?   75
    TER. Ah Titus! what, thy murd'rer my Protector!
No, let me fall again among the People,

---

52 Inhumane Q$_2$.

Let me be whooted like a common strumpet,
Toss'd, as I was, and drag'd about the streets,
The Bastard of a Tarquin, foil'd in Dirt,   80
The cry of all those Bloodhounds that did hunt me
Thus to the Goal of death, this happy end
Of all my miseries, here to pant my last,
To wash thy gashes with my Farewel tears,
To murmur, sob, and lean my aking head   85
Upon thy breast, thus like a Cradle Babe
To suck thy wounds and bubble out my Soul.

    Enter Sempronia, Aquilia, Vitellia, Mourners &c.

    SEMP. Come Ladies, hast, and let us to the Senate;
If the Gods give us leave, we'll be to day
Part of the Council. Oh, my Son, my Titus!   90
See here the bloody Justice of a Father,
See how the Vengeance rains from his own bowels!
Is he not mad? If he refuse to hear us,
We'll bind his hands, as one bereft of reason.
Hast then: Oh Titus, I would stay to moan thee,   95
But that I fear his orders are gon out
For something worse, for death, to take the heads
Of all the Kindred of these wretched Women.
    TER. Come then: I think I have some Spirits left,
To joyn thee, o most pious, best of Mothers,   100
To melt this Rocky heart: give me your hand;
Thus let us march before this wretched Host,
And offer to that God of blood our vows:
If there be ought that's human left about him,
Perhaps my wounds and horrible abuses,   105
Helpt with the tears and groans of this sad Troop
May batter down the best of his resolves.
    TIT. Hark, Teraminta.
    TER.   No, my Lord, away.   [Exeunt.
    TIT. Oh, my Valerius! was there ever day
Through all the Legends of recorded time   110
So sad as this? But see, my Father comes!

    Enter Brutus, Tiberius, Lictors.

Tiberius too has undergone the Lash.
Give him the patience, Gods, of Martyr'd Titus,
And he will bless those hands that have chastis'd him.
    TIB. Enjoy the bloody Conquest of thy Pride,   115
Thou more Tyrannical than any Tarquin,
Thou fiercer Sire of these unhappy Sons,
Than impious Saturn or the gorg'd Thiestes:
This Cormorant sees, and owns us for his Children,
Yet preyes upon his entrails, tears his bowels   120

With thirst of blood, and hungar fetch'd from Hell,
Which Famish'd Tantalus would start to think on;
But end, Barbarian, end the horrid vengeance
Which thou so impiously hast begun,
Perfect thy Justice, as thou, Tyrant, call'st it,   125
Sit like a Fury on thy black Tribunal,
Grasp with thy monstrous hands these gory heads,
And let thy Flatt'ring Orators adore thee,
For Triumphs which shall make the smile at horror.
    BRUT. Lead to the Senate.
    TIB.   Go then to the Senate,   130
There make thy boast how thou hast doom'd thy Children
To Forks and Whips; for which, the Gods reward thee:
Away: my Spirit scorns more conference with thee.
The Ax will be as laughter; but the whips
That drew these stains, for this I beg the Gods   135
With my last breath, for every drop that falls
From these vile wounds, to Thunder curses on thee.   [Exit.
    BRUT. Valerius, hast; the Senate does attend us.   [Exit.
    TIT. Valerius, ere you go, let me conjure thee
By all the Earth holds great or honorable,   140
As thou art truly Roman, stampt a man,
Grant to thy dying Titus one request.
    VAL. I'll grant thee any thing, but do not talk
Of dying yet; for much I dare confide
In that sad company that's gone before: 145
I know they'l move him to preserve his Titus;
For, tho you mark'd him not, as hence he parted
I could perceive with joy a silent shower
Run down his silver beard: therefore have hope.
    TIT. Hope, say'st thou! O the Gods! what hope of life?   150
To live, to live! and after this dishonor!
No my Valerius, do not make me rave;
But if thou hast a Soul that's sensible
Let me conjure thee, when we reach the Senate,
To thrust me through the heart.
    VAL.   Not for the World.   155
    TIT. Do't; or I swear thou hast no Friendship for me.
First, thou wilt save me from the hated Ax,
The Hangman's hand; for by the Gods I tell thee
Thou may'st as well stop the eternal Sun,
And drive him back, as turn my Father's purpose: 160
Next, and what most my Soul intreats thee for,
I shall perhaps in death procure his pity;
For to dye thus, beneath his killing frown,
Is damning me before my execution.
    VAL. 'Tis granted; by the Gods, I swear to end thee   165

---

129 thee smile Q_{2+}.

For when I weigh with my more serious thought
Thy Father's conduct in this dreadful Justice
I find it is impossible to save thee.
Come then, I'll lead thee, O thou glorious Victim, 170
Thus to the Altar of untimely death,
Thus in thy trim, with all thy bloom of youth,
These Virtues on thee, whose eternal Spring
Shall blossom on thy Monumental Marble
With never fading glory.
  TIT.   Let me clasp thee,
Boyl out my thanks thus with my Farewel Spirits: 175
And now away, the Taper's almost out,
Never, Valerius, to be kindled more:
Or, if it be my friend, it shall continue,
Burn through all winds against the puff of Fortune,
To dazle still, and Shine like the fix'd Stars, 180
With beams of glory that shall last for ever. [Exeunt.

Scene II. Senate

 BRUT. Health to the Senate! To the Fathers hail!
Jupiter Horscius and Diespiter
Hospital and Feretrian, Jove the Stayer,
With all the hundred Gods and Goddesses,
Guard and defend the Liberty of Rome. 5
It has been found a famous truth in Story,
Left by the ancient Sages to their Sons,
That on the change of Empires or of Kingdoms,
Some sudden Execution, fierce and great,
Such as may draw the World to admiration, 10
Is necessary to be put in Act
Against the Enemies of the present State.
Had Hector, when the Greeks and Trojans met
Upon the Truce, and mingled with each other,
Brought to the Banquet of those Demy-Gods 15
The Fatal head of that illustrious Whore;
Troy might have stood till now; but that was wanting:

---

172 These] Q₂₊; This Q₁.
176-177 Between these two lines C₁₋₃ insert the line: "To lose the
 Light of this dear World for ever." This appears to be a printer's
 error. In Q₁ and Q₂ this line appears far more appropriately in
 Act V, Scene II, line 71.
177 more:] Q₂₊; more 1 Q₁.
178 be, Q₂₊.
 3 Teretrian C₃.

Jove having from eternity set down
Rome to be head of all the under-World,
Rais'd with this thought, and big with Prophesie   20
Of what vast good may grow by such examples,
Brutus stands forth to do a dreadful Justice:
I come, O Conscript Fathers, to a deed
Wholly Portentous, New, and Wonderful,
Such as, perhaps, has never yet been found   25
In all Memorials of Former Ages,
Nor ever will again. My Sons are Traytors,
Their Tongues and Hands are Witnesses confest;
Therefore I have already past their Sentence,
And wait with you to see their Execution.   30
     HOR. Consul, the Senate does not ask their deaths;
They are content with what's already done,
And all intreat you to remit the Ax.
     BRUT. I thank you, Fathers, but refuse the offer.
By the assaulted Majesty of Rome,   35
I swear there is no way to quit the Grace,
To right the Common-wealth, and thank the Gods,
But by the Sacrifycing of my Bowels:
Take then, you sad revengers of the Publick,
These Traytors hence; strike off their heads, and then   40
My Sons. No more: their Doom is past. Away.
Thus shall we stop the mouth of loud Sedition,
Thus show the difference betwixt the Sway
Of partial Tyrants, and of a Free-born People,
Where no man shall offend because he's great,   45
Where none need doubt his Wives or Daughter's honor,
Where all injoy their own without suspicion,
Where there's no innovation of Religion,
No change of Laws, nor breach of Priviledge,
No desperate Factions gaping for Rebellion,   50
No hopes of Pardon for Assassinates,
No rash advancements of the Base or stranger,
For Luxury, for Wit, or glorious Vice;
But on the contrary, a Balanc'd Trade,
Patriots incourag'd, Manufactors cherish'd,   55
Vagabonds, Walkers, Drones, and Swarming Braves,
The Froth of States, scum'd from the Common-wealth:
Idleness banish'd all excess repress'd,
And Riots check'd by Sumptuary Laws.
O, Conscript Fathers, 'tis on these Foundations   60
That Rome shall build her Empire to the Stars,
Send her Commanders with her Armies forth,
To Tame the World, and give the Nations Law,
Consuls, Proconsuls, who to the Capitol
Shall ride upon the Necks of Conquer'd Kings;   65
And when they dye, mount from the gorgeous Pile
In Flames of Spice, and mingle with the Gods.

HOR. Excellent Brutus! all the Senate thanks thee,
And says, that Thou thy self art half a God.

       Enter Sempronia, Teraminta, with the rest of the
           Mourners; Titus, Valerius, Junius.

SEMP. Gon, gon to death! already Sentenc'd! Doom'd!   70
To lose the light of this dear World for ever?
What, my Tiberius too! Ah, Barbarous! Brutus!
Send, hast, revoke the Order of their Fate.
By all the pledges of our Marriage bed,
If thou, Inhuman Judge, hast left me one   75
To put the yet in mind thou art a Father;
Speak to him, Oh you Mothers of sad Rome,
Sisters and Daughters, ere the Execution
Of all your blood, hast, hast, and run about him,
Groan, sob, howl out the terrors of your Souls,   80
Nay, fly upon him like rob'd Savages,
And tear him for your young.
    BRUT.   Away, and leave me.
    SEMP. Or if you think it better for your purpose,
Because he has the pow'r of Life and Death,
Intreat him thus: throw all your heartless brests   85
Low at his feet, and like a God Adore him;
Nay, make a Rampier round him with your Bodies
And block him up: I see he would be going;
Yet that's a Sign that our complaints have mov'd him,
Continu'd falls of ever streaming tears,   90
Such, and so many, and the chastest too
Of all the pious Matrons throughout Rome,
Perhaps may melt this Adamantine temper.
Not yet! nay, hang your Bodies then upon him,
Some on his arms, and some upon his knees,   95
And lay this Innocent about his neck,
This little smiling Image of his Father:
See how he bends, and stretches to his bosom!
Oh all you pittying pow'rs, the Darling weeps;
His pretty eyes ruddy and wet with tears,   100
Like two burst Cherries rowling in a storm,
Plead for our griefs more than a thousand Tongues.
    JUN. Yes, yes, my Father will be good to us,
And spare my Brothers; Oh, I know he will:
Why, do you think he ever was in earnest?   105
What, to cut off their heads? I warrant you
He will not; no, he only meant to fright 'em,

---

76 thee yet Q_{2+}.
82 from your young. C_{1+}.
99 pow'rs, the] C_{1+}; pow'rs of the Q_{1-2}.

As he will me, when I have done a fault:
Why, Mother, he has whipt 'em for't already,
And do you think he has the heart to kill 'em?   110
No, no, he would not cut their little fingers
For all the World; or if he should, I'm sure
The Gods would pay him for't.
    BRUT.   What hoa! without there!
Slaves, Villains, Ha! are not my Orders heard?
    HOR. Oh Brutus, see, they are too well perform'd!   115
See here the Bodies of the Roman youth
All headless by your Doom, and there Tiberius.
    TER. See, Sir, behold, is not this horrid Slaughter
This cutting off one limb from your own Body,
Is't not enough? Oh, will it not suffice   120
To stop the mouth of the most bloody Law?
Oh, it were highest Sin to make a doubt,
To ask you now to save the Innocent Titus,
The common wish, and general Petition
Of all the Roman Senate, Matrons, Wives,   125
Widdows, and Babes; nay, ev'n the madding People,
Cry out at last that Treason is reveng'd,
And ask no more: Oh, therefore spare him, Sir.
    BRUT. I must not hear you, Hark, Valerius.
    TER. By all these wounds upon my Virgin breast,   130
Which I have suffer'd by your cruelty,
Altho you promis'd Titus to defend me.
    SEMP. Yet hold thy bloody hand, Tyrannick Brutus,
And I'll forgive thee for that headless horror:
Grant me my Titus, Oh in death I ask thee,   135
Thou hast already broke Sempronia's heart;
Yet I will pardon that, so Titus live.
Ah, cruel Judge! thou pittyless avenger!
What art thou whisp'ring? Speak the horror out,
For in thy glaring eyes I read a Murder.   140
    BRUT. I charge thee, by thy Oath, Valerius,
As thou art here Deputed by the Gods,
And not a Subject for a Woman's folly,
Take him away, and drag him to the Ax.
    VAL. It shall be thus then; not the Hangman's hand.   145
                [Runs him through, the Women shriek.

    TIT. Oh bravely strook! thou hast hit me to the Earth
So nobly, that I shall rebound to Heav'n,
Where I will thank thee for this galiant wound. [Semp. swoons.
    BRUT. Take hence this Woman; hast, and bear her home.

_____

116-117 Apparently the scene draws at this point to reveal the bodies,
    but there is no stage direction to this effect in any edition.
140 glaring] Q2+; glaving Q1.

Why, my Valerius, did'st thou rob my Justice?   150
    TIT. I wrought him to it, Sir, that thus in death
I might have leave to pay my last obedience,
And beg your blessing for the other World.
    TER. Oh do not take it, Titus; what e're comes
From such a monstrous nature must be blasting.   155
Ah, thou inhuman Tyrant! but, alas,
I loiter here, when Titus stayes for me:
Look here, my Love; thou shalt not be before me.   [Stabs her self.
Thus, to thy arms then: Oh, make hast, my Titus,
I'm got already in the Grove of Death;   160
The Heav'n is all benighted, not one Star
To light us through the dark and pathless Maze:
I have lost thy Spirit; Oh, I grope about
But cannot find thee: now I sink in shaddows.   [Dyes.
    TIT. I come, thou matchless Virtue. Oh, my heart!   165
Farewel, my Love; we'll meet in Heav'n again.
My Lord, I hope your Justice is aton'd;
I hope the glorious Liberty of Rome,
Thus water'd by the blood of both your Sons,
Will get Imperial growth and flourish long.   170
    BRUT. Thou hast so nobly born thy self in dying,
That not to bless thee were to curse my self;
Therefore I give thee thus my last embrace,
Print this last kiss upon thy trembling lips:
And, ere thou goest, I beg thee to report me   175
To the great Shades of Romulus and Numa,
Just with that Majesty and rugged Virtue
Which they inspir'd, and which the World has seen.
So, for I see thou'rt gon, Farewel for ever:
Eternal Jove, the King of Gods and Men,   180
Reward and Crown thee in the other World.
    TIT. What happiness has Life to equal this?
By all the Gods I would not live again;
For what can Jove, or all the Gods give more:
To fall thus Crown'd with Virtu's fullest Charms,   185
And dye thus blest, in such a Father's arms?   [Dyes.
    VAL. He's gone; the gallant Spirit's fled for ever.
How fares this noble Vessel, that is rob'd
Of all its Wealth, spoil'd of its Top mast glory,
And now lyes floating in this World of ruin?   190
    BRUT. Peace, Consul, peace; let us not soil the pomp
Of this Majestick Fate with Womans brawls.
Kneel Fathers, Friends, kneel all you Roman People,
Hush'd as dead Calms, while I conceive a pray'r

---

150 Justice?] Q_{2+}; Justice: Q_1.
174 dying Lips: C_3.
189 topmost Q_{2+}.

That shall be worthy Rome, and worthy Jove.   195
   VAL. Inspire him, Gods; and thou, oh Rome, attend.
   BRUT. Let Heav'n and Earth for ever keep their bound,
The Stars unshaken go their constant Round;
In harmless labour be our steel employ'd,
And endless peace thro all the World enjoy'd,   200
Let every Bark the Waves in safety Plough,
No angry Tempest curl the Ocean's brow;
No darted flames from Heav'n make Mortals fear,
Nor Thunder fright the weeping Passenger;
Let not poor Swains for storms at Harvest mourn,   205
But smile to see their hoards of bladed Corn:
No dreadful Comets threaten from the Skies,
No venom fall, nor poys'nous Vapors rise.
Thou, Jove, who dost the Fates of Empires Doom,
Guard, and Defend the Liberty of Rome.   210

End of A C T   V.

EPILOGUE
Spoken by Mrs. Barrey. *

No cringing Sirs, the Poets Champion I,
Have sworn to stand, and ev'ry Judge defie;
But why each Bullying critick shou'd I name
A Judge, whose only business is to damne.
While you your Arbitrary fist advance   5
At Wit, and dust it like a boor of France
Who without show of reason or pretence
Condemn a man to dye for speaking sence.
How ere we term'd you once the wise the strong
Know we have born your impotence too long.   10
You that above your Sires presume to soare,
And are but copies dawb'd in Minuture.
You that have nothing right in heart nor tongue
But only to be resolute in wrong.
Who sence affect with such an Aukward Ayre   15
As if a Frenchman should become severe.
Or an Italian make his Wife a jest
Like Spaniards pleasant, or like Dutchmen drest.
That rank the noblest Poets with the vile
And look your selves in a Plebeian stile.   20
But with an Oath. ---
False as your Wit and Judgment now I swear
By the known Maiden heads of each Theater
Nay by my own; The Poets shall not stand,
Like Shrove-tide Cocks, the Palt of every hand.   25
Let not the purblind Critick's sentence pass
That shoots the Poet through an optick glass,
No peals of ill plac'd praise from galleries come
Nor punk below to clap or hiss presume
Let her not cackle at the fops that flout her   30
Nor clukk the Squires that use to pipp about her,
No full blown block head bloated like an Ox
Traverse the pit with-dam me, what a pox.
Know then for Ev'ry misdemeanor here
I'll be more stabbing, sharp, and more severe,   35
Then the Fell-she that on her Keeper comes
Who in his drink, last night laid wast her Roomes,
Thundred her China, damn'd her quality,
Her glasses broke, and tore her Point Venie;
That drag'd her by the hair, and broke her head,   40
A Chamber Lion, but a lamb in bed.

---

* Mrs.] C_{1+}; Mr. Q_{1-2}.
4 Judge,] Q_{2+}; Jugde, Q_1. damne? Q_{2+}.
30 as the C_{2+}.

Like her I'le teez you for your midnight storming
For your all talking, and your noe performing.
    You that with monstrous Judgment force the Stage
    You fribling, fumbling Keepers of the Age.   45

THE
DUKE
OF
GUISE.
A
TRAGEDY.

ACTED BY THEIR
Majesties Servants.

WRITTEN
By Mr. *DRYDEN*, and Mr. *LEE*.

Οὕτως ἢ φιλότιμοι φύσεις ἐν ταῖς πολιτείαις τὸ ἄγαν μὴ φυλαξάμϸϸαι,
τῶ ἀγαθῶ μεῖζον τὸ κακὸν ἔχυσι. Plutarch. in Agesilao.

LONDON,
Printed by *T. H.* for *R. Bentley* in *Russel-street*, near the *Piazza*
in *Covent-Garden* , and *J. Tonson* at the *Judge's Head* in
Chancery-lane. M.DC.LXXXIII.

THE DUKE OF GUISE

Introduction

I Date and Stage History:

Shortly after the publication of ABSALOM AND ACHITOPHEL, Lee asked Dryden to collaborate with him upon a play -- in return for Lee's aid in the composition of OEDIPUS. THE DUKE OF GUISE was the result. Dryden tells us in the VINDICATION OF THE DUKE OF GUISE (1683) that he had undertaken a play on the subject of the Guise, immediately after the Restoration, as a means for exposing the villainies of the "late rebellion." But, since it was his first effort at drama, the play died a-borning, though the scene of the Duke of Guise's return to Paris in the new play was taken from the early version. He explains further that he wrote the opening scene, the entire fourth act, and "the first half, or somewhat more, of the fifth," and that Lee wrote the rest of it. Thus we know somewhat more of the time and conditions of the composition than in most instances.

Being complained to, the Lord Chamberlain prohibited the performance of the play for several months -- in fact, from the time of its completion, 18 July, until (as Dryden says) it had been forgotten, the last day of November, 1682. [1] When it did appear at Drury Lane, however, it was supported by the Crown: the Queen attended on 1 December, 1682, and a box for her maids of honor was provided out of the Royal treasury. [2] In his VINDICATION Dryden says, "It succeeded beyond my very hopes, having been frequently Acted, and never without a considerable Audience." Yet, although it enjoyed success upon the stage during its first season, it is doubtful that it was ever revived. The manuscript which Genest followed recorded revivals on 9 August and 30 October, 1716; but as he observes, the play revived was not THE DUKE OF GUISE but THE MASSACRE OF PARIS. [3] Evidence of later revivals is not to be found.

II Sources:

The basic source of THE DUKE OF GUISE, as Dryden tells us, was Sir Charles Cottrell and William Aylesbury's translation of Davila's HISTORIA DELLE GUERRE CIVILI, the same work used as the basis for THE MASSACRE OF PARIS. In addition, certain scenes from the latter were transferred either in paraphrase or verbatim to THE DUKE OF GUISE, as Lee tells us in his Dedication to THE PRINCESS OF CLEVE. To these two sources must be added François de Rosset's LES HISTOIRES TRAGIQUES DE NOSTRE TEMPS (a collection of historical and semi-historical novella), certain passages from Pulci's MORGANTE MAGGIORE (as Dryden tells us), elements from Marlowe's FAUSTUS, and a few passages from Shakespeare, especially from THE TEMPEST.

The chief borrowings from Davila are the details at the opening of the play, certain passages in Act III, the scene between Guise and Charles at the opening of Act IV (a simple dramatization of Davila's very words done by Dryden), the last scene of Act IV, the opening scene of Act V between Henry and the deputies of the Three Estates (written by Dryden), and the last scene of Act V (written by Lee), in which the assassination of the Guise takes place and the reaction of the King to the assassination is given.

From THE MASSACRE OF PARIS Lee adapts or takes over verbatim somewhat more than he admits in the dedicatory epistle to THE PRINCESS OF CLEVE. There he confesses to having borrowed two scenes. [4] Actually a considerable portion of Act I, scene i, is taken over into the later play, as well as most of Act I, scene ii; a few lines from Act III, scene ii, are paraphrased; and almost all of the last scene of Act IV.[5] The adaptation is on the whole quite ingenious. For instance, the lines spoken by the Admiral in Act IV of THE MASSACRE OF PARIS are frequently put into the mouth of the Duke in THE DUKE OF GUISE: the situations in the plot have been completely reversed, just as Lee's politics have been.

From Rosset's HISTOIRES TRAGIQUES Dryden and Lee seem to have got a suggestion of the Malicorne-Melanax material. This came from the story of CANOPE GENTIL-HOMME, RENOMMÉ DE PERSE, AYANT FAICT DONATION DE SON CORPS & DE SON AME AUX DEMONS, etc., a rather full treatment of which is given in Montague Summers' edition of Dryden's plays.[6] Dryden also borrows (as he tells us) for the Malicorne story certain materials from Pulci's Il MORGANTE MAGGIORE, to be exact, from Canto XXVI, stanzas lxxxii, lxxxviii, and from Canto XXV, stanza cciii.[7] More important, however, than either of these elements in the Malicorne story is the Faust material here. The compact with a devil as a dramatic theme was common; it need not come directly from any one place. Yet the lines in Act V, scene ii, resemble in many ways the final scene in Marlowe's DOCTOR FAUSTUS, especially such lines as 77, in which Malicorne asks for more time: "Add but a day, but half a day, an hour." Though echoes from Shakespeare are cited in the explanatory notes, attention may be called especially to Malicorne's threat to shut Melanax up in an oak (Act V, ii, 46 ff.) as being similar to the fate from which Prospero freed Ariel (TEMPEST, I, ii, 274-293), who was shut up in a pine by Sycorax. Prospero's having constantly to threaten Ariel is likewise similar to Malicorne's threats.

These, then, seem to be the chief sources of the play. Though Langbaine would have us believe that the writers owed something to Mezeray and P. Mathieu, there seems little if any indebtedness to them.

III Criticism:

THE DUKE OF GUISE has received considerable comment from the historians and critics, not so much because of its interest as a work of dramatic art as because of its political implications. Following its production Dryden was drawn into a minor pamphlet war in which he defended it from the Whig critics, who attacked the piece (not without good reason) as a Tory document. In answer to THE TRUE HISTORY OF THE DUKE OF GUISE (1683) and SOME REFLECTIONS ON THE PRETENDED PARALLEL IN THE PLAY THE DUKE OF GUISE (written perhaps by Hunt and Settle in 1683) Dryden wrote his VINDICATION: OR, THE PARALLEL OF THE FRENCH HOLY LEAGUE, AND THE ENGLISH LEAGUE AND COVENANT, TURN'D INTO A SEDITIOUS LIBELL AGAINST THE KING AND HIS ROYAL HIGHNESS, BY THOMAS HUNT AND THE AUTHORS OF THE REFLECTIONS UPON THE PRETENDED PARALLEL IN THE PLAY CALL'D THE DUKE OF GUISE (1683). Here in answer to his critics, he maintains that the play is merely a parallel of factions, not a parallel of persons at all. He protests that any resemblance of the Duke of Guise in the play to the Duke of Monmouth in real life is read into the character by his Whiggish enemies, and that any resemblance of Henry III in the play to Charles II is entirely imagined. He holds that

Our intention therefore was to make the play a Parallel, betwixt the Holy League plotted by the House of Guise and its Adhaerents, with the Covenant plotted by the Rebels in the time of King Charles the First, and those of the new Association, which was the Spawn of the old Covenant.

In spite of this disclaimer, however, it is impossible to make such a distinction: the characters produce the factions, and one who reads or sees cannot easily blink the parallel of persons. The Council of Sixteen in the play recalls the sixteen Whig peers who petitioned Charles in February 1680/1 not to hold a Parliament at Oxford. The Duke of Guise, though not the son of Henry III, takes the role, nevertheless, of the Duke of Monmouth; Henry III, that of Charles II; and Navarre, that of the Duke of York. The plot to seize Henry parallels the plot the Tories claimed to have discovered when they found the paper of Association among Shaftesbury's belongings. Guise's joyful return to Paris and Henry's subsequent displeasure parallel Monmouth's return to London on 27 November, 1679, against the King's will. Henry's calling the States General at Blois parallels Charles's calling the Parliament at Oxford in March 1680/1. The demand that Henry exclude Navarre from the throne and appoint Guise Lieutenant-General parallels Commons' demand that Charles approve the Exclusion Bill and place the militia under the command of Monmouth, making it accountable only to Parliament. Finally, Guise's assassination may well have served as a warning to Monmouth that continued rebellion would bring him to the scaffold. It was this parallel with the Monmouth situation that kept the play off the stage for so long a time. When it was finally presented late in November of 1682, London was safe in Tory hands and favorable to Charles; Shaftesbury had fled; Monmouth was in disgrace, having been arrested for promoting insurrection; and the Whigs were thoroughly discredited. [8] With all these immediate and obvious political connections, the play has quite naturally stimulated more historical than critical comment.

Yet there have been a few, if casual, critical evaluations. Genest (I, 393) remarks that "this is not a bad play, but is sadly disgraced by a story similar to that of Dr. Faustus." The BIOGRAPHIA DRAMATICA (II, 178) carries the statement that several parts of it are "very fine." Scott remarks that "The last scene betwixt the necromancer and the fiend [probably written by Lee, not by Dryden] is horribly fine", and comments upon the powerful interest produced by such appeal to superstition, though he does not altogether approve of such appeal. He further comments that "Lee's part of this play is, in general, very well written, and contains less rant than he usually puts in the mouths of his characters." [9] Sir Augustus Ward thought that the play "arouses no interest corresponding to the occasion which produced it," but admits that Lee's parts were freer of rant than usual. [10] Professor Ham says that the parts of the play written by Dryden are vigorous, but that those done by Lee show a decided falling off in powers, with his verse failing and his powers of imagination declining. He thinks the love scenes, for instance, are "bloodless adaptations" from VENICE PRESERVED. [11] On the other hand, Professor Van Lennep holds that the Marmoutier-Henry Guise love plot is well contrived out of THE MASSACRE OF PARIS and re-handled with a certain freshness, that the styles of Lee and Dryden are well blended, and that while Dryden made of the play a party weapon, Lee made it a dramatic piece for the stage. [12]

By and large, these opinions of the worth of THE DUKE OF GUISE are brief and in some instances casually given. This is not the place for an exhaustive critical analysis; yet attention may be called to certain particular qualities which afford a fairer judgment of the play.

It is indeed something of shreds and patches, pieced together from Davila, THE MASSACRE OF PARIS, FAUSTUS, Rosset, and Shakespeare, the pieces not being too carefully matched or seamed. Yet there are effective scenes. The opening, with the Council of Sixteen, even though it is versified out of Davila, none

the less moves ahead easily and constitutes an effective means for getting the
action going. Act II, ii, in which the Guise and Grillon very nearly come to blows,
though it is based on a similar scene between Guise and the Admiral in THE MASS-
ACRE OF PARIS, is well prepared for and comes to an effective climax. Moreover, if one doesn't remember too well the final scene in Marlowe's FAUSTUS,
one will be moved by Scene ii of Act V, in which Melanax carries Malicorne off
to hell. The character of Grillon, the bluff old soldier-courtier type, compares
favorably with Clytus in THE RIVAL QUEENS and even with the Admiral in THE
MASSACRE OF PARIS. Though the Queen-Mother is not so well realized here as
she was in THE MASSACRE OF PARIS, nor Henry so well as Charles IX, yet the
one is a quiet, determined force and the other more nearly a genuine monarch --
not a vacillating, irresolute boy, as was his brother in THE MASSACRE OF PARIS.
The dialogue, divested mostly of rant, often moves swiftly, surely, and powerful-
ly, as in Act V, i, when the Deputies report to the King. And it should be noted
that the frequently-mentioned scene of Malicorne's taking off is not merely a
means for raising goose flesh, but is quite consciously designed, and quite effectively used, as an ironic foreshadowing of Guise's assassination. The famous
song "Tell Me, Thirsis", the music for which is included at the end, is of course
one of Dryden's best. The music for it was done by Captain Henry Pack, who was
popular at setting songs. Some of his compositions appeared in Playford's CHOICE
AYRES, among them this one in the 1683 edition.[13] It is true that the parts of the
play written by Lee are not his best (and there may be passages that indicate the
mental break to come); but with the help of Dryden's scenes, with the songs and
the Malicorne material, and with two or three well-drawn characters, one can
easily believe that Dryden's claims for the success of the play were wholly justified -- and not merely on the grounds of the political parallel.

IV The Text:
    Texts Compared:

Q_1	R. Bentley and J. Tonson,	1683.
Q_2	R. Bentley and J. Tonson,	1687.
Q_3	Jacob Tonson,	1699.[14]
F	THE COMEDIES, TRAGEDIES, AND OPERAS WRITTEN BY JOHN DRYDEN, ESQ. etc. Printed for Jacob Tonson,	1701.
C_1	R. Wellington,	1713.
C_2	M.P. & Sam. Chapman,	1722.
C_3	W. Feales...,	1734.

    Scott and Saintsbury. THE WORKS OF JOHN DRYDEN,
        Vol. VII,   1883.
    Summers. DRYDEN: THE DRAMATIC WORKS, Vol. V, 1932.

As copy-text for this edition the first quarto, 1683, has been followed. Five
copies of this quarto have been compared for stop-press corrections made by the
authors or the printers. One of these copies is in the Library of the University of
Kentucky; the four others are in the Folger Shakespeare Library. The copies are
designated as follows: Q_1(KU), Q_1(DFo 1), Q_1(DFo 2), Q_1(DFo 3), Q_1(DFo 4).[15]
    The edition has the following collation:
4°; A-K^{4}L^2[M]^2; 44 leaves, pp [8] 1-76, pp [4].
    [A1^r]: title-page; [A1^v] blank; A2^r: Epistle Dedicatory To the Right Hon-
ourable / LAWRENCE, / EARL of ROCHESTER, &c. / A2^v-3^r: running title

EPISTLE DEDICATORY. ; A3^V-A4^V: PROLOGUE. /, followed by EPILOGUE and
Dramatis Personae. SCENE, PARIS. ; B1^r: [double rule] THE / DUKE of GUISE.
/ [rule] / ACT. I. SCEN. I. and text; B1^V-[L2^V] : text, followed by [rule] AD-
VERTISEMENT. [rule] . Running title The Duke of GUISE; [L3^r-L4^V] : A SONG
in the Fifth ACT of the DUKE of GUISE.

   A comparison of the five copies reveals a few variations, apparent corrections on the part of the printer. For instance, in Q$_1$(DFo 3) D2^r is numbered
"91" instead of "19," an error that was corrected in the other copies. "A Song
in the Fifth Act of the Duke of Guise" is inserted between K4^V and L1^r in Q$_1$
(DFo 4), whereas it should go (if inserted at all) between I4^V and K1^r, since the
direction "After a Song and Dance," etc., appears on K1^r. (It is bound up in
other copies at the end of the play.) The catchword at the bottom of G3^V reads
"You" in Q$_1$(KU), Q$_1$(DFo 2 and 3), but in Q$_1$(DFo 1 and 4) the word has been
set in from the margin so as to allow for the printing of the whole word "Your";
and on F2^r, line 18, in both Q$_1$(KU) and Q$_1$(DFo 3) "Guise" is printed "Guis e,"
the e having slipped, whereas in the other copies examined it appears in the proper place. Apparently only inner forme D and outer forme G were corrected.
These variations among the copies indicate a few printer's, but no authors',
changes as the play went through the press.

   The text of the first quarto is, nevertheless, generally sound, though perhaps not quite so free from error as Summers would have us believe.[16] Not
only does one find such an error as "Sripling" for "Stripling", but one is occasionally irritated by the faulty lining of the poetry, usually found in the parts
written by Dryden; by the lack of clarifying stage directions or by faulty directions
(for instance, I, i, 147); by the omission of words from lines (such as that in IV,
ii, 54); by verbal transpositions (such as that in II, ii, 74); by confusing punctuation (such as that in II, i, 92); and by faulty scene markings (such as that for III,
ii). Some few of these lapses are corrected in the later printings, especially
those having to do with the sense of the line; but many of them appear in the later
texts, even in the modern ones. The sequence of editions is as follows: Q$_2$ was
printed from Q$_1$, Q$_3$ from Q$_2$, F from Q$_1$, C$_1$ from Q$_2$, C$_2$ from C$_1$, and C$_3$ is
a page-by-page reprint of C$_2$.

   Summers gives little evidence of having really compared Q$_2$ and Q$_3$ with
Q$_1$ (though he says that he did) or of having compared any of these with C$_1$, C$_2$,
or C$_3$. His record of variant readings included only eight from Q$_2$ and only one
from Q$_3$, and these are variants in accidentals, hardly worth recording. On the
other hand, he gives 55 variants taken from F, only three of which involve a real
change of meaning. Some of his emendations, moreover, he would have found
already made for him if he had consulted the later editions. Seemingly he took
as authoritative in some instances F (a bad edition generally, having little if any
evidence in it of the author's supervision).[17] Moreover, he fails altogether to take
into account the faulty scene divisions, printing the quarto as he found it without
regard to the meaning as it stands. Thus the Summers edition has been of little
help.

   The present editors have tried to follow Q$_1$ prudently, making only such
changes as are required to clarify misleading directions and scene markings,
to regularize the lining of the poetry where possible, and to emend obvious errors
in the text. In every case, any change from the reading of Q$_1$ has been recorded
in the notes.

To the Right Honourable
LAWRENCE,
EARL of ROCHESTER, &c.

My Lord,

The Authors of this Poem, present it humbly to your Lordships Patronage,
if you shall think it worthy of that honour. It has already been a Confessor,
and was almost made a Martyr for the Royal Cause. But having stood two
Tryals from its Enemies, one before it was Acted, another in the Repre-
sentation, and having been in both acquitted, 'tis now to stand the Publick   5
Censure in the reading: Where since, of necessity, it must have the same
Enemies, we hope it may also find the same Friends; and therein we are
secure not only of the greater Number, but of the more Honest and Loyal
Party. We only expected bare Justice in the Permission to have it Acted;
and that we had, after a severe and long Examination, from an Upright   10
and knowing Judge, who having heard both sides, and examin'd the Merits
of the Cause in a strict perusal of the Play, gave Sentence for us, that it
was neither a Libel, nor a Parallel of particular Persons. In the Repre-
sentation it self, it was persecuted with so notorious Malice by one side,
that it procur'd us the Partiality of the other; so that the Favour more than   15
recompenc'd the Prejudice: And 'tis happier to have been sav'd (if so we
were) by the Indulgence of our good and faithful Fellow-Subjects, than by
our own Deserts; because thereby the weakness of the Faction is discover'd, which in us, at that time, attack'd the Government; and stood combin'd, like the Members of the Rebellious League, against the Lawful Sov-   20
eraign Authority. To what Topique will they have recourse, when they are
manifestly beaten from their chief Post, which has always been Popularity,
and Majority of Voices? They will tell us, That the Voices of a People are
not to be gather'd in a Play-House; and yet even there, the Enemies as well
as Friends have free Admission; but while our Argument was serviceable   25
to their Interests, they cou'd boast that the Theaters were True Protestant,
and came insulting to the Plays, where their own Triumphs were represented. But let them now assure themselves, that they can make the major
part of no Assembly, except it be a Meeting-House. Their Tyde of Popularity is spent, and the natural Current of Obedience is in spight of them,   30
at last prevalent. In which, my Lord, after the merciful Providence of
God, the unshaken Resolution, and prudent Carriage of the King, and the
inviolable Duty, and manifest Innocence of his Royal Highness, the prudent
Management of the Ministers is also most conspicuous. I am not particular
in this Commendation, because I am unwilling to raise Envy to your Lord-   35
ship, who are too just not to desire that Praise shou'd be communicated to
others, which was the common Endeavor and Co-operation of all. 'Tis
enough, my Lord, that your own Part was neither obscure in it, nor unhaz-
ardous. And if ever this excellent Government so well establish'd by the
Wisdom of our Forefathers, and so much shaken by the Folly of this Age,   40
shall recover its ancient Splendor, Posterity cannot be so ungrateful, as
to forget those, who in the worst of Times, have stood undaunted by their
King and Countrey, and for the Safeguard of both, have expos'd themselves
to the malice of false Patriots, and the madness of an headstrong Rabble.
But since this glorious Work is yet unfinish'd, and though we have reason   45
to hope well of the success, yet the Event depends on the unsearchable

Providence of Almighty God, 'tis no time to raise Trophees, while the Victory is in dispute: but every man by your example, to contribute what is in his power, to maintain so just a Cause, on which depends the future Settlement and Prosperity of Three Nations. The Pilot's Prayer to Neptune was   50
not amiss, in the middle of the Storm: Thou may'st do with me, O Neptune, what thou pleasest, but I will be sure to hold fast the Rudder. We are to trust firmly in the Deity, but so as not to forget, that he commonly works by second Causes, and admits of our Endeavors with his concurrence. For our own parts, we are sensible as we ought, how little we can contribute   55
with our weak assistance. The most we can boast of, is, that we are not so inconsiderable as to want Enemies, whom we have rais'd to our selves on no other account, than that we are not of their number: and since that's their Quarrel, they shall have daily occasion to hate us more. 'Tis not, my Lord, that any man delights to see himself pasquin'd and affronted by their   60
inveterate Scriblers, but on the other side it ought to be our glory, that themselves believe not of us what they write. Reasonable men are well satisfi'd for whose sakes the venom of their Party is shed on us, because they see that at the same time, our Adversaries spare not those to whom they owe Allegiance and Veneration. Their Despair has push'd them to   65
break those Bonds; and 'tis observable, that the lower they are driven, the more violently they write: As Lucifer and his Companions were only proud when Angels, but grew malicious when Devils. Let them rail, since 'tis the only solace of their miseries, and the only revenge, which we hope they now can take. The greatest and the best of men are above their reach, and   70
for our meanness, though they assault us like Foot-padders in the dark, their Blows have done us little harm; we yet live, to justifie our selves in open day, to vindicate our Loyalty to the Government, and to assure your Lordship, with all Submission and Sincerity, that we are

Your LORDSHIPS

Most Obedient, Faithful Servants,

JOHN   DRYDEN,   NAT.   LEE.

PROLOGUE.

Written by Mr. Dryden: Spoken by Mr. Smith.

Our Play's a Parallel: The Holy League
Begot our Cov'nant: Guisards got the Whigg:
Whate'er our hot-brain'd Sheriffs did advance,
Was, like our Fashions, first produc'd in France:
And, when worn out, well scourg'd, and banish'd there,   5
Sent over, like their godly Beggars here.
Cou'd the same Trick, twice play'd, our Nation gull?
It looks as if the Devil were grown dull;
Or serv'd us up, in scorn, his broken Meat,
And thought we were not worth a better Cheat.   10
The fulsome Cov'nant, one wou'd think in reason,
Had giv'n us all our Bellys-full of Treason:
And yet, the Name but chang'd, our nasty Nation
Chaws its own Excrement, th' Association.
'Tis true, we have not learn'd their pois'ning way,   15
For that's a mode but newly come in play;
Besides, Your Drug's uncertain to prevail;
But your True Protestant can never fail,
With that compendious Instrument, a Flail.
Go on; and bite, ev'n though the Hook lies bare;   20
Twice in one Age expel the lawful Heir:
Once more decide Religion by the Sword;
And purchase for us a new Tyrant Lord.
Pray for your King; but yet your Purses spare;
Make Him not Two-Pence richer by your Prayer.   25
To show you love Him much, chastise Him more;
And make Him very Great, and very Poor.
Push Him to Wars, but still no Pence advance;
Let Him lose England, to recover France.
Cry Freedom up with Popular noisie Votes: 30
And get enough to cut each others Throats,
Lop all the Rights that fence your Monarch's Throne;
For fear of too much Pow'r, pray leave Him none.
A noise was made of Arbitrary Sway;
But in Revenge, you Whiggs, have found a way,   35
An Arbitrary Duty now to pay.
Let His own Servants turn, to save their stake;
Glean from His Plenty, and His Wants forsake.
But let some Judas near His Person stay,
To swallow the last Sop, and then betray.   40
Make London independant of the Crown:
A Realm apart; the Kingdom of the Town.
Let Ignoramus Juries find no Traytors:
And Ignoramus Poets scribble Satyrs.

And, that your meaning none may fail to scan,
Do, what in Coffee-houses you began;
Pull down the Master, and Set up the Man.

DRAMATIS PERSONAE.

The King	Mr. Kynaston.
Duke of Guise	Mr. Betterton.
Duke of Mayenne	Mr. Jevon.
Grillon	Mr. Smith.
The Cardinal of Guise	Mr. Wiltshyre. 5
Archbishop of Lyons	Mr. Perin.
Alphonso Corso	Mr. Monfert.
Polin	Mr. Bowman.
Aumale	Mr. Carlile.
Bussy	Mr. Saunders. 10
The Curate of St. Eustace	Mr. Underhill.
Malicorne	Mr. Percival.
Melanax, a Spirit	Mr. Gillo.
Two Sheriffs	Bright and Samford.
Abbot Delbene	15
Revol	
Devil	
Bellieure	
Larchant	

Citizens and Rabble, &c. 20

WOMEN.

Queen-Mother	Lady Slingsby.
Marmoutier	Mrs. Barry.

SCENE, PARIS.

---

5 Wiltshire. C_{1+}.
7 Monfort. F, Scott and Saintsbury; Mountfort. C_3.
14 Samford. Q_{1+}. <u>Doubtless intended for</u> Sanford.
15-19 Abbot Delbene, Revol, Devil, Bellieure, Larchant] <u>om.</u> Q_{1+}.

THE
DUKE of GUISE.

Act I. Scene I.

The Council of Sixteen Seated: An Empty Chair
prepar'd for the Duke of Guise.

Bussy and Polin two of the Sixteen.

BUSS. Lights there! more Lights: what burn the Tapers dim,
When glorious Guise, the Moses, Gideon, David,
The Saviour of the Nation, makes approach?
POL. And therefore are we met; the whole Sixteen
That sway the Crowd of Paris, guide their Votes,   5
Manage their Purses, Persons, Fortunes, Lives,
To mount the Guise, where merit calls him, high;
And give him a whole Heaven, for room to shine.

Enter Curate of St. Eustace.

BUSS. The Curate of S. Eustace comes at last;
But, Father, why so late?   10
CUR. I have been taking godly pains, to satisfie some Scruples
rais'd amongst weak Brothers of our Party, that were staggering in the Cause.
POL. What cou'd they find t' Object?
CUR. They thought, to Arm against the King was Treason.
BUSS. I hope you set 'em right?   15
CUR. Yes; and for answer, I produc'd this Book.
A Calvinist Minister of Orleans
Writ this, to justifie the Admiral
For taking Arms against the King deceas'd:
Wherein he proves that irreligious Kings   20
May justly be depos'd, and put to death.
BUSS. To borrow Arguments from Heretick Books
Methinks was not so prudent.
CUR. Yes; from the Devil, if it would help our Cause.
The Author was indeed a Heretick;   25
The Matter of the Book is good and pious.
POL. But one prime Article of our Holy League,
Is to preserve the King, his Pow'r and Person.
CUR. That must be said, you know, for decency;
A pretty Blind to make the Shoot secure.   30
BUSS. But did the Primitive Christians e're rebell,
When under Heathen Lords? I hope they did.
CUR. No sure, they did not; for they had not Pow'r;
The Conscience of a People is their Power.
POL. Well; the next Article in our Solemn Covenant   35
Has clear'd the Point again.

BUSS. What is't? I shou'd be glad to find the King
No safer than needs must?
POL. That in case of Opposition from any person whatsoever ---
CUR. That's well, that's well; then the King is not excepted,   40
if he oppose us ---
POL. We are oblig'd to join as one, to punish
All, who attempt to hinder or disturb us.
BUSS. 'Tis a plain Case; the King's included in the Punishment,
In case he rebell against the People.   45
POL. But how can he rebell?
CUR. I'll make it out: Rebellion is an Insurrection against
the Government; but they that have the Power are actually the
Government: Therefore if the People have the Power, the Rebellion
is in the King.   50
BUSS. A most convincing Argument for Faction.
CUR. For Arming, if you please; but not for Faction.
For still the Faction is the fewest number;
So, what they call the Lawful Government,
Is now the Faction; for the most are ours.   55
POL. Since we are prov'd to be above the King; I wou'd gladly
understand whom we are to obey; or whether we are to be all Kings
together?
CUR. Are you a Member of the League, and ask that Question?
There's an Article, that, I may say, is as necessary as any   60
In the Creed: Namely, that we, the said Associates, are
Sworn to yield ready Obedience, and Faithful Service, to that
Head which shall be deputed.
BUSS. 'Tis most manifest, that by Virtue of our Oath
We are all Subjects to the Duke of Guise. The King's   65
An Officer that has betray'd his Trust; and therefore we
have turn'd him out of Service.
OMNES. Agreed, agreed.

Enter the Duke of Guise; Cardinal of Guise, Aumale:
Torches before them. The Duke takes the Chair.

BUSS. Your Highness enters in a lucky hour;
Th' unanimous Vote you heard, confirms your Choice,   70
As Head of Paris, and the Holy League.
CARD. I say Amen to that.
POL. You are our Champion; Buckler of our Faith.
CARD. The King, like Saul, is Heaven's repented Choice;
You his Anointed one, on better thought.   75
GUISE. I'm what you please to call me; Any thing,
Lieutenant General, Chief, or Constable,

44-5 Printed as prose in Q_{1+}.
62-3 Service/ To that... C_3.
68 F prints as part of line 67.

Good Decent Names, that only mean your Slave.
    BUSS. You chas'd the Germans hence, Exil'd Navarre;
And rescu'd France from Hereticks and Strangers.   80
    AUM. What he and all of us have done, is known.
What's our Reward? Our Offices are lost,
Turn'd out like Labour'd Oxen, after Harvest,
To the bare Commons of the wither'd Field.
    BUSS. Our Charters will go next: Because we Sheriffs   85
Permit no Justice to be done on those
The Court calls Rebels, but we call them Saints.
    GUISE. Yes; we are all involv'd, as Heads, or Parties:
Dipt in the noisy Crime of State, call'd Treason:
And Traitours we must be, to King, or Country.   90
    BUSS. Why then my Choice is made.
    POL.   And mine.
    OMN.   And all.
    CARD. Heav'n is it self Head of the Holy League;
And all the Saints are Cov'nanters, and Guisards.
    GUISE. What say you, Curate?
    CUR.   I hope well, my Lord.
    CARD. That is, he hopes you mean to make him Abbot,   95
And he deserves your care of his Preferment.
For all his Prayers are Curses on the Government;
And all his Sermons Libels on the King.
In short, a Pious, Hearty, Factious Priest.
    GUISE. All that are here my Friends, shall share my Fortunes;   100
There's Spoil, Preferments, Wealth enough in France,
'Tis but deserve and have: The Spanish King
Consigns me fifty thousand Crowns a Week
To raise and to foment a Civil-War.
'Tis true, a Pension from a Foreign Prince   105
Sounds Treason in the Letter of the Law,
But good intentions justify the deed.
    CUR. Heaven's good; the Cause is good; the Money's good;
No matter whence it comes.
    BUSS. Our City Bands, are twenty thousand strong;   110
Well Disciplin'd, well Arm'd, well season'd Traitors;
Thick rinded heads, that leave no room for Kernel;
Shop Consciences, of proof against an Oath,
Preach'd up, and ready tin'd for a Rebellion.
    GUISE. Why then the Noble Plot is fit for birth;   115
And Labouring France cries out for Midwife-hands.
We miss'd surprizing of the King at Blois,
When last the States were held; 'twas over-sight:
Beware we make not such another Blot.
    CARD. This Holy time of Lent we have him sure;   120
He goes unguarded, mix'd with whipping Fryars,

------

93 And all that are Cov'nanters and Guisards. Q_3.

In that Procession, he's more fit for Heav'n:
What hinders us to seize the Royal Penitent,
And close him in a Cloyster?
    CUR.   Or dispatch him:
I love to make all sure.
    GUISE.   No; guard him safe;   125
Thin Diet will do well; 'twill starve him into Reason,
Till he exclude his Brother of Navarre,
And graft Succession on a worthier Choice:
To favour this, five hundred Men in Arms,
Shall stand prepar'd to enter at your call;   130
And speed the Work: St. Martins Gate was nam'd:
But the Sheriff Conty, who Commands that Ward,
Refus'd me passage there.
    BUSS.   I know that Conty:
A Sniveling, Conscientious, Loyal Rogue:
He'll Peach, and Ruine all.   135
    CARD. Give out he's Arbitrary; a Navarrist;
A Heretick; discredit him betimes;
And make his Witness void.
    CUR.   I'll swear him Guilty.
I swallow Oaths as easie as Snap-dragon,
Mock-Fire that never burns.   140
    GUISE. Then Bussy, be't your care t'admit my Troops,
At Porte St. Honore: (rises) Night wears apace,
And Day-light must not peep on Dark Designs.
I will my self to Court: Pay Formal Duty;
Take leave; and to my Government retire: 145
Impatient to be soon recall'd; to see
The King Imprison'd, and the Nation free.   [Exeunt. *

Enter Malicorne solus.

MAL. Each dismal Minute when I call to Mind
The Promise that I made the Prince of Hell,
In one and twenty years to be his Slave,   150
Of which near twelve are gone, my Soul runs back,
The Wards of reason rowl into their Spring.
O horrid thought! but one and twenty years,
And twelve near past, then to be steep'd in Fire,
Dash'd against Rocks, or snatcht from molten Lead,   155

124-25 Divided thus in Q_{1+}:
    And close him in a Cloyster?
        CUR. Or dispatch him: I love to make all sure.
        GUISE. No; guard him safe;
  * [Exeunt.] C_3, Scott and Saintsbury; [Exeunt all but Guise.
    Q_1-F, Summers; [Ex. C_2. Since he enters following 173 below,
    Guise must have made his exit at this point.

Reeking, and dropping, piece-meal born by Winds,
And quench'd ten thousand fathom in the deep!
But hark! he comes, see there, my Blood stands still, [Knocking at
My Spirits start an end for Guise's Fate.   the Door.

A Devil rises.

MAL.   What Counsel does the Fate of Guise require?   160
DEV.   Remember with his Prince there's no delay,
But, the Sword drawn, to fling the Sheath away;
Let not the fear of Hell his Spirit grieve,
The Tomb is still, whatever Fools believe;
Laugh at the Tales which wither'd Sages bring,   165
Proverbs and Morals, let the Waxen King
That rules the Hive, be born without a Sting;
Let Guise by Blood resolve to mount to Pow'r,
And he is Great as Mecha's Emperour;
He comes, bid him not stand on Altar Vows,   170
But then strike deepest, when he lowest bows;
Tell him Fate's aw'd when an Usurper Springs,
And joyns to crow'd out Just Indulgent Kings.   [Vanishes. *

Enter the Duke of Guise, and Duke of Mayenne.

MAY.   All Offices and Dignities he gives
To your profest and most inveterate Foes;   175
But if he were inclin'd, as we could wish him,
There is a Lady Regent at his Ear,
That never Pardons.
GUISE.   Poyson on her Name,
Take my hand on't, that Cormorant Dowager
Will never rest, till she has all our Heads   180
In her lap. I was at Bayon with her,
When She, the King, and Grisly d'Alva met;
Methinks I see her listening now before me,
Marking the very motion of his Beard,
His Op'ning Nostrils and his Dropping Lids,   185
I hear him Croak too to the Gaping Council;

---

* The Scott and Saintsbury edition marks a change of scene here.
173-174 Between these lines Van Lennep would insert the following
two lines as part of the Devil's speech:
      For Conscience, and Heav'ns Fear, Religion's Rules,
      They're all State-Bells, to toll in pious Fools.

These are the last lines of Act II of THE MASSACRE OF PARIS,
inserted into the DUKE OF GUISE by Lee, but suppressed because
of Hunt's objection. Dryden says they came in Act II or III, but,
as Van Lennep says (p. 568), they fit best here. See Dryden's
VINDICATION, Scott and Saintsbury edition, VII, 170.

Fish for the great Fish, take no care for Frogs,
Cut off the Poppy-Heads, Sir; Madam, charm
The Winds but fast, the Billows will be still.
    MAY. But Sir, how comes it you should be thus warm   190
Still pushing Councils when among your Friends;
Yet at the Court Cautious and cold as Age,
Your Voice, your Eyes, your Meen so different,
You seem to me two Men.
    GUISE.   The Reason's plain,
Hot with my Friends, because the Question giv'n,   195
I start the Judgment right where others drag.
This is the Effect of Equal Elements,
And Atoms justly pois'd; nor should you wonder
More at the strength of Body than of Mind;
'Tis equally the same to see me plunge   200
Headlong into the Seine all over Arm'd,
And Plow against the Torrent to my point,
As 'twas to hear my Judgment on the Germans;
This to another Man wou'd be a brag,
Or at the Court among my Enemies,   205
To be as I am here quite off my Guard,
Would make me such another thing as Grillon,
A blunt, hot, honest, downright, valiant Fool.
    MAY. Yet this you must allow a failure in you,
You love his Neece, and to a Politician,   210
All Passion's bane, but Love directly death.
    GUISE. False, false, my Mayenne, thou'rt but half Guise agen,
Were she not such a wondrous Composition;
A Soul so flush'd as mine is with Ambition,
Sagacious and so nice, must have disdain'd her;   215
But she was made when Nature was in humour,
As if a Grillon got her on the Queen,
Where all the honest Atoms fought their way;
Took a full Tincture of the Mother's Wit,
But left the dregs of Wickedness behind.   220
    MAY. Have you not told her what we have in hand?
    GUISE. My utmost aim has been to hide it from her,
But there I'm short, by the long Chain of Causes
She has scan'd it, just as if she were my Soul,
And though I flew about with Circumstances,   225
Denials, Oaths, Improbabilities;
Yet through the Histories of our Lives, she look'd,
She saw, she overcame.
    MAY. Why then, we're all undone.
    GUISE.   Agen you err.
Chast as she is, she wou'd as soon give up   230

187-89 Placed in quotation marks in C$_3$.
189 The] Q$_{3+}$; the Q$_{1-2}$.

Her Honour, as betray me to the King;
I tell thee, she's the Character of Heaven;
Such an habitual over-Womanly Goodness,
She dazles, walks meer Angel upon Earth.
But see, she comes, call the Cardinal Guise,   235
While Malicorn attends for some Dispatches,
Before I take my farewell of the Court.

       Enter Marmoutier

    MAR. Ah Guise, you are undone.
    GUISE.   How, Madam?
    MAR.   Lost,
Beyond the possibility of hope,
Despair, and die.
    GUISE.   You menace deeply Madam,   240
And should this come from any Mouth but yours,
My smile should answer how the ruine touch'd me.
    MAR. Why do you leave the Court?
    GUISE.   The Court leaves me.
    MAR. Were there no more but weariness of State,
Or cou'd you like great Scipio retire,   245
Call Rome ungrateful, and sit down with that;
Such inward Gallantry would gain you more
Than all the sullied Conquests you can boast;
But Oh, you want that Roman Masterie;
You have too much of the tumultuous times.   250
And I must mourn the Fate of your Ambition.
    GUISE. Because the King disdains my Services,
Must I not let him know I dare begon?
What when I feel his Council on my Neck,
Shall I not cast 'em backward if I can;   255
And at his Feet make known their villany?
    MAR. No Guise, not at his Feet, but on his Head;
For there you strike.
    GUISE.   Madam, you wrong me now;
For still what-e're shall come in Fortunes whirle,
His Person must be safe.
    MAR.   I cannot think it.   260
However, your last words confess too much.
Confess, what need I urge that Evidence,
When every hour I see you Court the Crowd,
When with the shouts of the Rebellious Rabble,
I see you born on shoulders to Cabals;   265
Where with the Traiterous Council of Sixteen,
You sit and Plot the Royal Henry's Death.
Cloud the Majestick Name with Fumes of Wine,
Infamous Scrowls, and Treasonable Verse;
While, on the other side, the Name of Guise,   270
By the whole Kennel of the Slaves, is rung,

Pamphleteers, Balladmongers sing your Ruine,
While all the Vermin of the vile Parisians
Toss up their greasie Caps where e're you pass,
And hurl your dirty Glories in your Face.   275
    GUISE. Can I help this?
    MAR.   By Heaven, I'd Earth my self,
Rather than live to act such black Ambition:
But, Sir, you seek it with your Smiles and Bows,
This Side and that Side congeing to the Crowd;
You have your Writers too, that cant your Battels,   280
That stile you the New David, Second Moses,
Prop of the Church, Deliverer of the People.
Thus from the City, as from the Heart they spread
Thro all the Provinces, alarm the Countries,
Where they run forth in Heaps, bellowing your Wonders,   285
Then cry, The King, the King's a Hugonot,
And, spight of us, will have Navarre succeed,
Spight of the Laws, and spight of our Religion:
But we will pull 'em down, down with 'em, down.   [Kneels.
    GUISE. Ha, Madam! Why this Posture?
    MAR.   Hear me, Sir: 290
For, if 'tis possible, my Lord, I'll move you.
Look back, return, implore the Royal Mercy,
E're 'tis too late, I beg you by these Tears,
These Sighs, and by th' ambitious Love you bear me;
By all the Wounds of your poor groaning Country,   295
That bleeds to death, O seek the Best of Kings,
Kneel, fling your stubborn Body at his Feet:
Your Pardon shall be sign'd, your Country sav'd,
Virgins and Matrons all shall sing your Fame,
And every Babe shall bless the Guise's Name.   300
    GUISE. O rise, thou Image of the Deity;
You shall prevail, I will do any thing;
You have broke the very Gall of my Ambition,
And all my Powers now float in Peace agen:
Be satisfi'd that I will see the King,   305
Kneel to him, e're I Journey to Champagn,
And beg a kind Farewell.
    MAR.   No, no, my Lord;
I see, thro that, you but withdraw a while,
To muster all the Forces that you can,
And then rejoyn the Council of Sixteen.   310
You must not go.
    GUISE.   All the Heads of the League
Expect me, and I have engag'd my Honour.
    MAR. Would all those Heads were off, so yours were sav'd.
Once more, O Guise, the weeping Marmoutier
Entreats you do not go.
    GUISE.   Is't possible   315
That Guise should say, in this he must refuse you?

MAR. Go then, my Lord. I late receiv'd a Letter
From one at Court, who tells me the King loves me:
Read it, there is no more than what you hear.
I have Jewels offer'd too, perhaps may take 'em: 320
And if you go from Paris, I'll to Court.
    GUISE. But, Madam, I have often heard you say,
You lov'd not Courts.
    MAR.   Perhaps I have chang'd my Mind:
Nothing as yet could draw me, but a King,
And such a King, so Good, so Just, so Great,   325
That at his Birth the Heavenly Council paus'd,
And then at last cry'd out, This is a Man.
    GUISE. Come, 'tis but Counterfeit; you dare not go.
    MAR. Go to your Government, and try.
    GUISE.   I will.
    MAR. Then I'll to Court, nay, to the King.
    GUISE.   By Heaven   330
I swear, you cannot, shall not, dare not see him.
    MAR. By Heaven I can, I dare, nay, and I will:
And nothing but your Stay shall hinder me;
For now, methinks, I long for't.
    GUISE.   Possible!
    MAR. I'll give you yet a little time to think: 335
But if I hear you go to take your leave,
I'll meet you there, before the Throne I'll stand,
Nay, you shall see me kneel, and kiss his Hand.   [Exit.
    GUISE. Furies and Hell! She does but try me: Ha!
This is the Mother-Queen and Espernon,   340
Abbot Delbene, Alphonso Corso too,
All packt to plot, and turn me into Madness.   [Reading the Letter.

    Enter Cardinal Guise, Duke of Mayenne, Malicorne, &c.

Ha! can it be! Madam, the King loves you.   [Reads.
But Vengeance I will have; to pieces, thus,
To pieces with 'em all.   [Tears the Letter.
    CARD.   Speak lower.
    GUISE.   No;   345
By all the Torments of this galling Passion,
I'll hollow the Revenge I vow, so loud,
My Father's Ghost shall hear me up to Heaven.
    CARD. Contain your self; this Outrage will undo us.
    GUISE. All things are ripe, and Love new points their Ruine.   350
Ha! my good Lords, what if the murd'ring Council
Were in our Power, should they escape our Justice?
I see by each Mans laying of his Hand
Upon his Sword, you swear the like Revenge.
For me, I wish that mine may both rot off ---   355
    CARD. No more.
    MAY.   The Council of Sixteen attend you.

GUISE. I go --- That Vermin may devour my Limbs,
That I may die like the late puling Francis,
Under the Barbers Hands, Imposthumes choak me,
If while alive I cease to chew their Ruine;   360
Alphonso Corso, Grillon, Priest, together,
To hang 'em in Effigie, nay, to tread,
Drag, stamp, and grind 'em, after they are dead.   [Exeunt.

End of ACT I.

Act II.   Scene I.

Enter Queen-Mother, Abbot Delbene, Polin.

Q. M.   Pray mark the Form of the Conspiracy;
Guise gives it out he Journeys to Champagn,
But lurks indeed at Lagny, hard by Paris,
Where every Hour he hears, and gives Instructions.
Mean time the Council of Sixteen assure him   5
They have Twenty thousand Citizens in Arms.
Is it not so, Polin?
    POL.   True, on my Life;
And if the King doubts the Discovery,
Send me to the Bastile till all be prov'd.
    Q. M.   Call Colonel Grillon, the King would speak with him. [Exit Polin.   10
    ABB.   Was ever Age like this?
    Q. M.   Polin is honest:
Beside, the whole Proceeding is so like
The hair-brain'd Rout, I guess'd as much before.
Know then, it is resolv'd to seize the King,
When next he goes in Penitential Weeds,   15
Among the Friars, without his usual Guards;
Then, under shew of Popular Sedition,
For Safety, shut him in a Monastery,
And sacrifice his Favourites to their Rage.
    ABB.   When is this Council to be held again?   20
    Q. M.   Immediately upon the Duke's departure.
    ABB.   Why sends not then the King sufficient Guards,
To seise the Fiends, and hew 'em into pieces?
    Q. M.   'Tis in appearance easie, but th' Effect
Most hazardous; for straight, upon th' Alarm,   25
The City would be sure to be in Arms:
Therefore to undertake, and not to compass,
Were to come off with Ruine and Dishonour.
You know th' Italian Proverb, Bisogna Copriersi:
He that will venture on a Hornets Nest,   30
Should Arm his Head, and Buckler well his Breast.
    ABB.   But wherefore seems the King so unresolv'd?
    Q. M.   I brought Polin, and made the Demonstration,
Told him Necessity cry'd out to take
A Resolution to preserve his Life,   35
And look on Guise as a reclaimless Rebel.
But thro the Natural Sweetness of his Temper,
And dangerous Mercy, coldly he reply'd,
Madam, I will consider what you say.
    ABB.   Yet after all, could we but fix him.
    Q. M.   Right,   40

The Business were more firm for this Delay;
For Noblest Natures, tho they suffer long,
When once provok'd, they turn the Face to Danger.
But see, he comes, Alphonso Corso with him;
Let us withdraw, and when 'tis fit, rejoyn him.   [Exeunt.   45

   Enter King, Alphonso Corso.

  KING. Alphonso Corso.
  ALPH.   Sir.
  KING.   I think thou lov'st me.
  ALPH. More than my Life.
  KING.   That's much; yet I believe thee.
My Mother has the Judgment of the World;
And all things move by That? but, my Alphonso,
She has a Cruel Wit.   50
  ALPH. The Provocation, Sir.
  KING.   I know it well:
But if thou'dst have my Heart within thy Hand,
All Conjurations blot the Name of Kings.
What Honours, Interest, were the World to buy him,
Shall make a Brave Man smile, and do a Murder?   55
Therefore I hate the Memory of Brutus,
I mean the latter, so cry'd up in Story.
Caesar did ill, but did it in the Sun,
And foremost in the Field; but sneaking Brutus,
Whom none but Cowards and white-liver'd Knaves   60
Would dare commend, lagging behind his Fellows,
His Dagger in his Bosom, stabb'd his Father.
This is a Blot which Tully's Eloquence
Could ne're wipe off, tho the mistaken Man
Makes Bold to call those Traytors, Men Divine.   65
  ALPH. Tully was wise, but wanted Constancy.

   Enter Queen-Mother, Abbot Delbene.

  Q. M. Good-even, Sir; 'tis just the time you order'd
To wait on your Decrees.
  KING.   Oh, Madam.
  Q. M.   Sir.
  KING. Oh Mother, but I cannot make it way;
Chaos and Shades, 'tis huddl'd up in Night.   70
  Q. M. Speak then, for Speech is morning to the Mind,
It spreads the Beautious Images abroad,
Which else lie furl'd and clouded in the Soul.
  KING. You would Embark me in a Sea of Blood.
  Q. M. You see the Plot directly on your Person;   75

---

 49 that: C_{1-3}; that; Scott and Saintsbury.

But give it ore, I did but state the Case.
Take Guise into your Heart, and drive your Friends,
Let Knaves in Shops prescribe you how to sway,
And when they read your Acts with their vile Breath,
Proclaim aloud, they like not this or that,   80
Then in a drove come Lowing to the Louvre,
And cry they'l have it mended, that they will;
Or you shall be no King.
    KING.   'Tis true, the People
Ne're know a Mean, when once they get the Power;
But O, if the Design we lay should fail,   85
Better the Traytors never should be touch'd,
If Execution cries not out 'tis done.
    Q. M. No Sir; you cannot fear the sure Design;
But I have liv'd too long, since my own Blood
Dares not Confide in her that gave him Being.   90
    KING. Stay Madam, stay, come back, forgive my fears;
Where all our thoughts should creep like deepest streams,
Know then I hate aspiring Guise to Death,
Whor'd Margerite, Plots upon my life,
And shall I not Revenge?
    Q. M.   Why this is Harry;   95
Harry at Moncontour, when in his Bloom
He saw the Admiral Colligny's Back.
    KING. O this Whale Guise, with all the Lorain Fry,
Might I but view him after his Plots and Plunges,
Strook on those Cowring Shallows that await him.   100
This were a Florence Master-piece indeed.
    Q. M. He comes to take his leave.
    KING.   Then for Champagn;
But lies in wait till Paris is in Arms.
Call Grillon in, all that I beg you now,
Is to be hush'd upon the Consultation,   105
As Urns that never blab.
    Q. M.   Doubt not your Friends;
Love 'em, and then you need not fear your Foes.

          Enter Grillon.

    KING. Welcome my Honest-Man, my old try'd Friend.
Why dost thou flye me Grillon, and Retire?
    GRILL. Rather let me demand your Majesty,   110
Why fly you from your self? I've heard you say,
You'd Arm against the League, why do you not?
The Thoughts of such as you, are Starts Divine,
And when you mould with second Cast the Spirit,
The Air, the Life, the Golden Vapour's gone.   115

----

93 aspiring Guise] Q$_2$-Scott and Saintsbury; aspiring, Guise Q$_1$, Summers.

KING. Soft, my Old Friend, Guise Plots upon my life,
Polin shall tell thee more; hast thou not heard
Th'unsufferable Affronts he daily offers,
War without Treasure on the Hugonots,
While I am forc'd against my bent of Soul,   120
Against all Laws, all Custom, Right, Succession,
To cast Navarre from the Imperial Line.
  GRILL. Why do you Sir? Death, let me tell the Traytor?
  KING. Peace, Guise is going to his Government;
You are his Foe of Old: Go to him Grillon;   125
Visit him as from me, to be Employ'd
In this great War against the Hugonots;
And prethee tell him roundly of his Faults;
No farther, Honest Grillon.
  GRILL.   Shall I fight him?
  KING. I charge thee not.
  GRILL.   If he provokes me, strike him?   130
You'l Grant me that?
  KING.   Not so, my Honest Souldier.
Yet speak to him.
  GRILL. I will by Heav'n to th' purpose,
And if he force a beating, who can help it? [Exit. Grill.
  KING. Follow Alphonso, when the storm is up,
Call me to part 'em.
  Q. M.   Grillon, to ask him Pardon,   135
Will let Guise know, we are not in the Dark.
  KING. You hit the Judgment; yet, O yet, there's more,
Something upon my heart, after these Counsels,
So soft, and so unworthy to be nam'd.
  Q. M. They say that Grillon's Niece is come to Court,   140
And means to kiss Your Hand. [Exit. Q. Mother.
  KING.   Could I but hope it.
O my Dear Father pardon me in this,
And then enjoyn me all that Man can suffer;
But sure the Powers above will take our Tears
For such a fault, Love is so like themselves. [Exeunt.   145

Scene II. The Louvre.

Enter Guise attended with his Family, Marmoutier meeting him New
Drest, attended, &c.

  GUISE. Furies, she keeps her Word, and I am lost;
Yet let not thy Ambition shew it to her,

---

133 it?] Q$_{2-3}$, C$_{1-3}$, Scott and Saintsbury; it. Q$_1$, F, Summers.

For after all she does it but to try me,
And foil my vow'd Design: Madam, I see
You're come to Court; the Robes you wear become you,   5
Your Air, your Meen, your Charms, your every Grace,
Will Kill at least your thousand in a day.
   MAR. What, a whole day, and kill but one poor thousand?
An hour you mean, and in that hour ten thousand?
Yes, I wou'd make with every Glance a Murder.   10
Mend me this Curle.
   GUISE.   Woman!
   MAR.   You see, my Lord,
I have my Followers, like you: I swear
The Court's a Heav'nly Place; but O my Heart,
I know not why that sigh should come uncall'd;
Perhaps 'twas for your going, yet I swear   15
I never was so mov'd, O Guise, as now;
Just as you enter'd, when from yonder Window
I saw the King.
   GUISE.   Woman, all over Woman.
The World confesses, Madam, Henry's Form
Is Noble and Majestick.
   MAR.   O you grudge   20
The extorted Praise, and speak him but by halfs.
   GUISE. Priest, Corso, Devils! how she carries it!
   MAR. I see, my Lord, you are come to take your leave;
And were it not to give the Court Suspicion,
I would oblige you, Sir, before you go,   25
To lead me to the King.
   GUISE.   Death and the Devil!
   MAR. But since that cannot be, I'le take my leave
Of you, my Lord, Heav'n grant your Journey safe.
Farwell once more. Not stir? Does this become you?
Does your Ambition swell into your Eyes?   30
Jealousie by this Light: Nay then, proud Guise,
I tell you, you're not worthy of the Grace,
But I will carry't, Sir, to those that are,
And leave you to the Curse of Bosom-War.   [Exit.
   MAY. Is this the Heavenly?
   GUISE.   Devil, Devil, as they are all;   35
'Tis true, at first she caught the Heav'nly Form,
But now Ambition sets her on her Head,
By Hell, I see the Cloven Mark upon her:
Ha! Grillon here! some New Court-Trick upon me.

            Enter Grillon.

   GRILL. Sir, I have business for your Ear.
   GUISE.   Retire. [Exeunt his   40
                                      Followers.
   GRILL. The King, my Lord, commanded me to wait you,

And bid you welcome to the Court.
      GUISE.   The King
Still loads me with New Honours, but none greater
Than this, the last.
      GRILL.   There is one greater yet,
Your High Commission against the Hugonots;   45
I and my Family shall shortly wait you,
And 'twill be Glorious Work.
      GUISE.   If you are there,
There must be Action.
      GRILL.   O, your Pardon, Sir,
I'm but a Stripling in the Trade of War;
But you, whose Life is one continued Broyl,   50
What will not your triumphant Arms accomplish!
You, that were form'd for Mastery in War,
That, with a start, cry'd to your Brother Mayenne,
To Horse, and slaughter'd forty thousand Germans.
      GUISE. Let me beseech you, Colonel, no more.   55
      GRILL. But, Sir, since I must make at least a Figure
In this great Business, let me understand
What 'tis you mean, and why you force the King
Upon so dangerous an Expedition.
      GUISE. Sir, I intend the Greatness of the King,   60
The Greatness of all France, whom it imports
To make their Arms their Business, Aim, and Glory,
And where so proper, as upon those Rebels
That covered all the State with Blood and Death?
      GRILL. Stor'd Arsenals and Armories, Fields of Horse,   65
Ordnance, Munition, and the Nerve of War,
Sound Infantry, not Harrass'd and Diseas'd,
To meet the fierce Navarre, should first be thought on.
      GUISE. I find, my Lord, the Argument grows warm,
Therefore, thus much, and I have done: I go   70
To join the Holy League in this great War,
In which no place of Office, or Command,
Not of the Greatest, shall be bought or sold;
Whereas too often Honours are Conferr'd
On Souldiers, and no Souldiers: This Man Knighted   75
Because he Charg'd a Troop before his Dinner,
And sculk'd behind a Hedg i'th' Afternoon:
I will have strict Examination made
Betwixt the Meritorious and the Base.
      GRILL. You have Mouth'd it bravely, and there is no doubt,   80
Your Deeds would answer well your haughty Words;
Yet let me tell you, Sir, there is a Man,
Curse on the Hearts that hate him, that wou'd better,

---

49 Stripling] Q_{2+}; Sripling Q_1.
74 too often Honours] Q_{2+}; too Honours often Q_1.

Better than you, or all your puffy Race,
That better would become the Great Battalion;   85
That when he Shines in Arms, and Suns the Field,
Moves, Speaks, and Fights, and is himself a War.
    GUISE. Your Idol, Sir, you mean the Great Navarre;
But yet, ---
    GRILL. No Yet, my Lord of Guise, no Yet;
By Arms, I bar you that; I swear, No Yet: 90
For never was his like, nor shall again,
Tho' voted from his Right by your Curs'd League.
    GUISE. Judge not too rashly of the Holy League,
But look at home.
    GRILL.   Ha! dar'st thou justifie
Those Villains?
    GUISE.   I'le not justify a Villain   95
More than your self; but if you thus proceed,
If every heated Breath can puff away,
On each surmise, the Lives of Free-born People,
What need that Awful General Convocation,
The Assembly of the States? Nay let me urge,   100
If thus they villifie the Holy League,
What may their Heads expect?
    GRILL.   What, if I cou'd,
They should be certain of, whole Piles of Fire.
    GUISE. Collonel, 'tis very well I know your Mind,
Which, without fear, or flattery to your Person,   105
I'le tell the King, and then, with his permission,
Proclaim it for a warning to our People.
    GRILL. Come, you're a Murderer your self within,
A Traytor.
    GUISE. Thou a -- hot old Hair-brain'd Fool.
    GRILL. You were Complotter with the Cursed League,   110
The black Abettor of our Harry's Death.
    GUISE. 'Tis false.
    GRILL.   'Tis true, as thou art double-hearted:
Thou double Traytor, to Conspire so basely,
And when found out, more basely to deny't.
    GUISE. O Gracious Harry, let me sound thy Name,   115
Lest this old rust of War, this knotty Trifler,
Should raise me to extreames.
    GRILL.   If thou'rt a Man,
That did'st refuse the Challenge of Navarre,
Come forth.
    GUISE. Go on, since thou'rt resolv'd on Death,
I'le follow thee, and rid thy shaking Soul.   120

       Enter King, Queen-Mother, Alphonso, Abbot, &c.

But see, the King: I scorn to ruin thee,
Therefore go tell him, tell him thy own Story.

KING. Ha, Colonel, is this your Friendly visit?
Tell me the truth, how happen'd this disorder?
Those ruffl'd Hands, red Looks, and port of Fury?   125
    GRILL. I told him, Sir, since you will have it so,
He was the Author of the Rebel League,
Therefore a Traytor, and a Murderer.
    KING. Is't possible?
    GUISE.   No matter, Sir, no matter;
A few hot words, no more upon my Life;   130
The old Man rowz'd, and shook himself a little:
So if your Majesty will do me Honour,
I do beseech you let the business die.
    KING. Grillon, submit your self, and ask his pardon.
    GRILL. Pardon me, I cannot do't.
    KING.   Where are the Guards?   135
    GUISE. Hold, Sir; come Colonel, I'le ask Pardon for you:
This Souldierly Embrace makes up the breach;
We will be sorry, Sir, for one another.
    GRILL. My Lord, I know not what to answer you,
I'm friends, and I am not, and so farewell.   [Exit.   140
    KING. You have your Orders; yet before you go,
Take this Embrace: I court you for my Friend,
Tho' Grillon wou'd not.
    GUISE.   I thank you on my Knees.
And still while Life shall last, will take strict care
To justify my Loyalty to your Person.   [Exit.   145
    Q. M. Excellent Loyalty, to lock you up!
    KING. I see even to the bottom of his Soul:
And, Madam, I must say the Guise has Beauties,
But they are set in Night, and foul Design:
He was my Friend when young, and might be still.   150
    ABB. Mark'd you his hollow accents at the parting?
    Q. M. Graves in his Smiles.
    KING.   Death in his bloodless Hands.
O Marmoutier! now I will haste to meet thee;
The Face of Beauty, on this rising Horrour,
Looks like the midnight-Moon upon a Murder;   155
It gilds the dark design that stays for Fate,
And drives the Shades that thicken from the State. [Exeunt.

End of A C T II.

Act III.   Scene I.

Enter Grillon and Polin.

GRILL. Have then this Pious Council of Sixteen
Scented your late Discovery of the Plot?
POL. Not as from me, for still I kennel with them,
And bark as loud as the most deep-mouth'd Traytor,
Against the King, his Government and Laws;   5
Whereon immediately there runs a Cry
Of, Seize him on the next Procession, seise him,
And clap the Chilperick in a Monastry;
Thus it was fixt, as I before discover'd:
But when, against his Custom, they perceiv'd   10
The King absented, streight the Rebels met,
And roar'd, they were undone.
GRILL.   O, 'tis like 'em,
'Tis like their Mungrel Souls; flesh 'em with Fortune,
And they will worry Royalty to Death:
But if some crabbed Virtue turn and pinch 'em,   15
Mark me, they'l run, and yelp, and clap their Tails,
Like Curs, betwixt their Legs, and howl for Mercy.
POL. But Malicorne, sagacious on the point,
Cry'd, Call the Sheriffs, and bid 'em arm their Bands;
Add yet to this, to raise you above hope,   20
The Guise my Master will be here to day,
For, on bare guess of what has been revealed,
He wing'd a Messenger to give him notice;
Yet spight of all this Factor of the Fiends
Cou'd urge, they slunk their Heads like Hinds in Storms: 25
But see, they come.

Enter Sheriffs with the Populace.

GRILL.   Away, I'le have amongst 'em;
Fly to the King, warn him of Guises coming,
That he may straight dispatch his strict Commands
To stop him.
1st SHER. Nay, this is Colonel Grillon,
The Blunderbuss o'th' Court, away, away,   30
He carries Ammunition in his Face.
GRILL. Hark you my Friends, if you are not in haste,
Because you are the Pillars of the City,
I wou'd inform you of a General Ruine.
2nd. SHER. Ruine to the City! marry, Heaven forbid!   35
GRILL. Amen, I say; for look you, I'm your Friend:
'Tis blown about you've plotted on the King,

To seize him, if not kill him; for who knows,
When once your Conscience yields, how far 'twill stretch;
Next, quite to dash your firmest hopes in pieces,   40
The Duke of Guise is dead.
    1st. SHER.   Dead, Colonel!
    2nd. SHER. Undone, undone!
    GRILL.   The World cannot redeem you;
For what, Sirs, if the King, provok'd at last,
Should joyn the Spaniard, and shou'd fire your City,
Paris your Head, but a most Venemous one,   45
Which must be blooded?
    1st. SHER.   Blooded, Colonel!
    GRILL. Ay, blooded, thou most Infamous Magistrate,
Or you will blood the King, and burn the Louvre;
But 'ere that be, fall million miscreant Souls,
Such Earth-born minds as yours; for, mark me, Slaves,   50
Did you not Ages past consign your Lives,
Liberties, Fortunes, to Imperial hands,
Made 'em the Guardians of your sickly Years,
And now your grown up to a Boobies Greatness,
What, wou'd you wrest the Scepter from his Hand?   55
Now, by the Majestie of Kings I swear,
You shall as soon be sav'd for packing Juries.
    1st. SHER. Why, Sir, mayn't Citizens be sav'd?
    GRILL.   Yes, Sir,
From drowning, to be hangd, burnt, broke o'th' Wheel.
    1st SHER. Colonel, you speak us plain.
    GRILL.   A Plague confound you,   60
Why should I not? what is there in such Raskals
Should make me hide my Thought, or hold my tongue?
Now, in the Devils name, what make you here,
Dawbing the inside of the Court like Snails,
Sliming our Walls, and pricking out your Horns?   65
To hear, I warrant, what the King's a doing,
And what the Cabinet-Council, then to th'City
To spread your monstrous Lyes, and sow Sedition?
Wild-fire choak you.
    1st. SHER.   Well, we'll think of this,
And so we take our leaves?
    GRILL.   Nay, stay, my Masters;   70
For I'm a thinking now just whereabouts
Grow the two tallest Trees in Arden Forest.
    1st. SHER. For what, pray Colonel, if we may be so bold?
    GRILL. Why to hang you upon the highest Branches;
Fore-God it will be so; and I shall laugh   75
To see you dangling to and fro i'th'Air,

---

54 you are Q$_3$; you're F-Scott and Saintsbury.
70 our leaves. Q$_{2-3}$, C$_1$-Scott and Saintsbury.

With the honest Crows pecking your Traytors Limbs.
   ALL. Good Colonel!
   GRILL.   Good Rats, my precious Vermin,
You moving Dirt, you rank stark Muck o'th' World,
You Oven-Bats, you things so far from Souls,   80
Like Dogs, you're out of Providence's reach,
And only fit for hanging; but be gone,
And think of Plunder --- You right Elder Sheriff,
Who Carv'd our Henry's Image on a Table,
At your Club-Feast, and after stabb'd it through?   85
   1st. SHER. Mercy, good Colonel.
   GRILL.   Run with your Nose to Earth,
Run Blood-hound, run, and scent out Royal Murder.
You second Rogue, but equal to the first,
Plunder, Go hang, nay take your tackling with you,
For these shall hold you fast, your Slaves shall hang you 90
To the mid Region in the Sun:
Plunder, be gone Vipers, Asps, and Adders.   [Exeunt Sheriffs
                                     and People.

         Enter Malicorne.

Ha, but here comes a Fiend that soars above,
A Prince o'th'Air, that sets the Mud a moving.
   MAL. Collonel, a word.
   GRILL.   I hold no speech with Villains.   95
   MAL. But, Sir, it may concern your Fame and Safety.
   GRILL. No matter, I had rather die traduc'd,
Than live by such a Villains help as thine.
   MAL. Hate then the Traytor, but yet love the Treason.
   GRILL. Why, are not you a Villain?
   MAL.   'Tis Confess'd.   100
   GRILL. Then in the Name of all thy Brother Devils,
What wou'dst thou have with me?
   MAL.   I know you're honest,
Therefore it is my business to disturb you.
   GRILL. Fore God I'le beat thee, if thou urge me farther.
   MAL. Why tho' you shou'd, yet if you hear me after,   105
The pleasure I shall take in your vexation,
Will heal my Bruises.
   GRILL.   Wert thou definite Rogue,
I'faith, I think that I should give thee hearing;
But such a boundless Villany as thine,
Admits no Patience.
   MAL.   Your Niece is come to Court,   110
And yields her Honour to our Henry's Bed.
   GRILL. Thou ly'st, damn'd Villain.   [Strikes him.
   MAL.   So, why this I look'd for:

---

107 thou a definite Rogue, Q_3; thou definite, Rogue, C_{2-3}.
112 So, this I Q_3.

But yet I swear by Hell, and my Revenge,
'Tis true as you have wrong'd me.
    GRILL.   Wrong'd thee, Villain!
And name Revenge! O wer't thou Grillon's Match,   115
And worthy of my Sword, I swear by this
One had been past an Oath; but thou'rt a Worm,
And if I tread thee dar'st not turn again.
    MAL. 'Tis false, I dare like you, but cannot act;
There is no force in this Enervate Arm.   120
Blasted I was e're born, Curse on my Stars,
Got by some dotard in his pithless Years,
And sent a wither'd Saplin to the world.
Yet I've Brain, and there is my Revenge;
Therefore I say agen these Eyes have seen   125
Thy Blood at Court bright as a Summers Morn,
When all the Heaven is streak'd with dappl'd Fires,
And fleck'd with Blushes like a rifl'd Maid;
Nay, by the Gleamy Fires that melted from her
Fast Sighs and Smiles, swoln Lips and heaving Breasts,   130
My Soul presages Henry has enjoy'd her.
    GRILL. Again thou ly'st; and I will crumble thee,
Thou bottl'd Spider, into thy Primitive Earth,
Unless thou swear thy very Thought's a Lye.
    MAL. I stand in Adamant, and thus defie thee;   135
Nay draw, and with the edge betwixt my Lips,
Even while thou rak'st it through my Teeth, I'le swear
All I have said is true, as thou art honest,
Or I a Villain.
    GRILL.   Damn'd infamous Wretch,
So much below my scorn, I dare not kill thee: 140
And yet so much my hate, that I must fear thee.
For should it be as thou hast said, not all
The Trophies of my Lawrell'd Honesty
Shou'd bar me from forsaking this bad World,
And never draw my Sword for Henry more.   145
    MAL. Ha, 'tis well, and now I am Reveng'd.
I was in hopes thou would'st have utter'd Treason,
And forfeited thy Head to pay me fully.
    GRILL. Hast thou Compacted for a Lease of Years
With Hell, that thus thou ventur'st to provoke me?   150
    MAL. Perhaps I have: (How right the Blockhead hits.)
Yet more to rack thy Heart, and break thy Brain,
Thy Niece has been before the Guise's Mistress.
    GRILL. Hell-hound, avant.
    MAL.   Forgive my honest meaning. [Exit.
    GRILL. 'Tis hatch'd beneath, a Plot upon mine honour,   155
And thus he lays his Baits to Catch my Soul:

---

147 utter'd] Q_{2+}; utter' Q_1.

Ha! but the Presence Opens, who comes here!
By Heaven my Niece, led by Alphonso Corso!

       Enter Alphonso, Marmoutier.*

Ha, Malicorne is't possible, Truth from thee!
Tis plain, and I in Justifying Woman   160
Have done the Devil wrong.
    ALPH.   Madam, the King,
Please you to sit, will instantly attend you.
    GRILL. Death, Hell, and Furies! ha, she comes to seek him,
O Prostitute, and on her prodigal Flesh
She has lavish'd all the Diamonds of the Guise   165
To set her off, and sell her to the King.
    MAR. O Heavens! did ever Virgin yet attempt
An Enterprise like mine? I that resolv'd
Never to leave those dear delightful Shades,
But act the little part that Nature gave me,   170
On the Green Carpets of some guiltless Grove,
And having finish'd it forsake the World,
Unless sometimes my Heart might entertain
Some small remembrance of the taking Guise:
But that far, far from any dark'ning Thought,   175
To Cloud my Honour, or Eclipse my Virtue.
    GRILL. Thou ly'st, and if thou hadst not glanc'd aside,
And spy'd me coming, I had had it all.
    MAR. By Heav'n, by all that's good ---
    GRILL.   Thou hast lost thy Honour,
Give me thy Hand, this Hand by which I caught thee   180
From the bold Ruffian in the Massacre,
That would have stain'd thy almost Infant Honour,
With Lust, and Blood, dost thou remember it?
    MAR. I do, and bless the Godlike Arm that sav'd me.
    GRILL. 'Tis false, thou hast forgot my generous Action;   185
And now thou laugh'st to think how thou hast cheated,
For all his kindness, this old grisl'd Fool.
    MAR. Forbid it Heaven!
    GRILL.   But oh that thou hadst dy'd
Ten thousand Deaths, e're blasted Grillon's Glory,
Grillon that sav'd thee from a barbarous World,   190
Where thou hadst starv'd, or sold thy self for Bread,
Took thee into his Bosom, foster'd thee
As his own Soul, and lap'd thee in his Heart-strings;
And now, for all my Cares, to serve me thus!
O 'tis too much ye Powers! double Confusion   195

---

    * Enter Alphonso, Marmoutier] C2-3; om. Q1-C2, Summers;
   Scott and Saintsbury place the direction following on line 161.

On all my Wars; and oh, out, shame upon thee,
It wrings the Tears from Grillon's Iron Heart,
And melts me to a Babe.
   MAR.   Sir, Father, hear me;
I come to Court, to save the Life of Guise.
   GRILL. And prostitute thy Honour to the King.   200
   MAR. I have look'd, perhaps, too nicely for my Sex,
Into the dark Affairs of fatal State;
And to advance this dangerous Inquisition,
I listn'd to the Love of daring Guise.
   GRILL. By Arms, by Honesty, I swear thou lov'st him. 205
   MAR. By Heav'n, that gave those Arms success, I swear
I do not, as you think, but take it all.
I've heard the Guise, not with an Angels temper,
Something beyond the tenderness of pity,
And yet, not Love.   210
Now, by the Powers that fram'd me, this is all;
Nor should the World have wrought this close Confession,
But to rebate your Jealousie of Honour.
   GRILL. I know not what to say, nor what to think;
There's Heaven still in thy Voice, but that's a Sign   215
Virtue's departing, for thy better Angel
S ill makes the Womans Tongue his rising Ground,
Wags there a while, and takes his flight for ever.
   MAR. You must not go.
   GRILL.   Tho' I have Reason plain
As day, to judge thee false, I think thee true: 220
By Heaven, methinks I see a Glory round thee;
There's something says thou wilt not lose thy Honour:
Death, and the Devil, that's my own Honesty:
My foolish open Nature, that would have
All like my self; but off; I'le hence and Curse thee. 225
   MAR. O stay!
   GRILL.   I wo'n not.
   MAR.   Hark, the King's a coming.
Let me conjure you, for your own Souls quiet,
And for the everlasting rest of mine,
Stir not till you have heard my Hearts design.
   GRILL. Angel, or Devil, I will --- nay, at this rate 230
She'll make me shortly bring him to her Bed,
Bawd for him? No, he shall make me run my Head
Into a Cannon, when 'tis Firing, first.
That's honourable sport, but I'll retire.
And if she plays me false, here's that shall mend her. [Retires to rear 235
                    of Stage. *
       [Marmoutier Sits. Song and Dance.

---

  * [Retires to rear of Stage.]; om. Q₁₊; [Touching his dagger, exit.
  Scott and Saintsbury. But see line 271.

Enter the King.

KING. After the breathing of a Love-sick Heart,
Upon your Hand, once more, nay twice, forgive me.
MAR. I discompose you, Sir.
KING.   Thou dost, by Heaven;
But with such Charming pleasure,
I love, and tremble, as at Angels view.   240
MAR. Love me, my Lord?
KING.   Who shou'd be lov'd, but you?
So lov'd, that even my Crown, and self are vile,
While you are by, try me upon despair;
My Kingdom at the stake, Ambition starv'd;
Revenge forgot, and all great Appetites   245
That whet uncommon Spirits to aspire,
So once a day I may have leave ---
Nay, Madam, then you fear me.
MAR. Fear you, Sir, what is there dreadful in you?
You've all the Graces that can Crown Mankind: 250
Yet wear 'em so, as if you did not know 'em:
So stainless, fearless, free in all your actions,
As if Heaven lent you to the World to Pattern.
KING. Madam, I find you're no Petitioner;
My People would not treat me in this sort;   255
Tho' 'twere to gain a part of their Design:
But to the Guise they deal their faithless Praise
As fast, as you your flattery to me;
Tho' for what end I cannot guess, except
You come, like them, to mock at my Misfortunes.   260
MAR. Forgive you, Heaven! that thought: no, mighty Monarch,
The Love of all the Good, and wonder of the Great;
I swear, by Heaven, my Heart adores, and loves you.
KING. O, Madam, rise.
MAR.   Nay, were you, Sir, unthron'd
By this Seditious Rout that dare despise you;   265
Blast all my days, ye Powers, torment my Nights;
Nay, let the Misery invade my Sex,
That cou'd not for the Royal Cause like me,
Throw all their Luxury before your Feet,
And follow you like Pilgrims through the World.   270
GRILL. Sound Wind, and Limb, fore-God a gallant Girl.   [Aside.
KING. What shall I answer to thee, O thou Balm
To heal a broken, yet a Kingly Heart;
For, so I swear I will be to my Last:
Come to my Arms, and be thy Harry's Angel,   275
Shine through my Cares, and make my Crown sit easie.
MAR. O never, Sir.
KING.   What said you, Marmoutier?
Why dost thou turn thy Beauties into Frowns?
MAR. You know, Sir, 'tis impossible, no more.

KING. No more --- and with that stern resolv'd behaviour: 280
By Heaven, were I a dying, and the Priest
Shou'd urge my last Confession, I'd cry out,
Oh Marmoutier, and yet thou say'st, no more.
MAR. 'Tis well, Sir, I have lost my aim, farewell.
KING. Come back, O stay, my Life flows after you.   285
MAR. No, Sir, I find I am a trouble to you,
You will not hear my Suit.
KING.   You Cannot go,
You shannot --- O your suit, I kneel to grant it,
I beg you take whatever you demand.
MAR. Then, Sir, thus low, or prostrate, if you please,   290
Let me intreat for Guise.
KING.   Ha, Madam, what!
For Guise; for Guise! that stubborn arrogant Rebel,
That laughs at proffer'd Mercy, slights his Pardon,
Mocks Royal Grace, and plots upon my Life:
Ha! and do you protect him? then the World   295
Is sworn to Henry's Death: does Beauty too,
And Innocence it self, conspire against me;
Then let me tamely yield my Glories up,
Which once I vow'd with my drawn Sword to wear
To my last drop of Blood? Come, Guise, come Cardinal,   300
All you lov'd Traytors, come --- I strip to meet you;
Sheath all your Daggers in Curst Henry's Heart.
MAR. This I expected, but when you have heard
How far I would intreat your Majesty,
Perhaps you'll be more Calm.
KING.   See, I'm hush'd;   305
Speak then, how far, Madam, wou'd you Command?
MAR. Not to proceed to last Extremities,
Before the Wound is desperate, think alone,
For no Man Judges like your Majesty;
Take your own Methods, all the heads of France   310
Cannot so well advise you, as your self:
Therefore resume, my Lord, your Godlike temper,
Yet do not bear more than a Monarch should:
Believe it, Sir, the more your Majesty
Draws back your Arm, the more of Fate it Carries.   315
KING. Thou Genius of my State, thou perfect Model
Of Heaven it self, and abstract of the Angels,
Forgive the late disturbance of my Soul,
I'm clear by Nature, as a Rockless Stream,
But they dig through the Gravel of my Heart;   320

320-21 Between these two lines in F is inserted this line:
        And raise the Mud of Passions up to cloud me,
        Scott and Saintsbury and Summers follow F in including
        the line in the text.

Therefore let me conjure you do not go;
'Tis said the Guise will come in spight of me;
Suppose it possible, and stay to advise me.
    MAR. I will, but on your Royal word, no more.
    KING. I will be easie   325
To my last gasp, as your own Virgin Thoughts,
And never dare to breathe my Passion more;
Yet you'll allow me now and then to Sigh
As we discourse, and Court you with my Eyes.

              Enter Alphonso.

Why do you wave your Hand, and warn me hence?   330
So looks the poor Condemn'd,
When Justice beck'ns, there's no hope of Pardon.
Sternly, like you, the Judge his Victim eyes,
And thus, like me, the Wretch despairing dies.   [Exit with Alph.
    Grill. [Coming forward] O Rare, rare Creature, by the Power
that made me: 335
Wer't possible we cou'd be damn'd again:
By some new Eve, such Virtue might relieve us;
O I cou'd clasp thee, but that my Arms are rough,
Till all thy Sweets were broke with my Embraces,
And kiss thy Beauties to a dissolution.   340
    MAR. Ah Father, Uncle, Brother, all the Kin,
The precious Blood that's left me in the World,
Believe, dear Sir, what-e're my actions seem,
I will not lose my Virtue for a Throne.
    GRILL. Why, I will Carve thee out a Throne my self;   345
I'le hew down all the Common-wealths in Christendom,
And seat thee on their Necks, as high as Heaven.

           Enter Abbot Delbene.

    ABB. Colonel, your Ear.
    MAR.   By these whispering Councils,
My Soul presages that the Guise is coming:
If he dares come, were I a Man, a King,   350
I'd sacrifice him in the City's sight.
O Heavens! what was't I said? Were I a Man,
I know not that, but, as I am a Virgin,
If I wou'd offer thee, too lovely Guise,
It shou'd be kneeling to the Throne for Mercy.   355
Ha! then thou lov'st, that thou art thus concern'd,

---

330 Printed as two lines in Q_{1+}.
335 [Coming forward]; Enter Grillon. Q_{1+}; but see lines 235, 271.
337 redeem us; F, Scott and Saintsbury.
355 of Mercy. F, C_1, Scott and Saintsbury.

Down, rising mischief, down, or I will kill thee,
Even in thy Cause, and strangle new born pity:
Yet, if he were not married! ha, what then?
His Charms prevail, no, let the Rebel dye.   360
I faint beneath this strong oppression here,
Reason and Love rend my divided Soul,
Heav'n be the Judg, and still let Virtue Conquer;
Love to his Tune my jarring Heart wou'd bring,
But Reason over-winds and Cracks the String.   [Exit.   365
    ABB.   The King dispatches Order upon Order,
With positive Command to stop his coming.
Yet there is notice given to the City;
Besides Belleure brought but a half account,
How that the Guise reply'd he would obey   370
His Majesty in all, yet if he might
Have leave to justify himself before him,
He doubted not his Cause.
    GRILL.   The Ax, the Ax,
Rebellion's pamper'd to a Plurisie,
And it must bleed.   [Shout within.
    ABB.   Hark, what a shout was there!   375
I'le to the King, it may be 'tis reported
On purpose thus. Let there be Truth or Lies
In this mad Fame, I'le bring you instant word.   [Exit. Abbot.

> Manet Grillon: Enter Guise, Cardinal, Mayenne,
> Malicorne, Attendants, &c. Shouts again.

    GRILL. Death, and thou Devil, Malicorne, is that
Thy Master?
    GUISE. Yes, Grillon. 'tis the Guise,   380
One that wou'd Court you for a Friend.
    GRILL.   A Friend,
Traytor, thou mean'st, and so I bid thee welcome;
But since thou art so insolent thy blood
Be on thy Head, and fall by me unpitied.   [Exit.
    GUISE. The bruises of his Loyalty have craz'd him. [Shouts louder.   385

> Spirit within Sings.

> Malicorne, Malicorne, Malicorne, ho!
> If the Guise resolves to go,
> I charge, I warn thee let him know,
> Perhaps his head may lye too low.

    GUISE. Why, Malicorne?
    MAL.   [starting.] Sir, do not see the King.   390

---

377 Printed as two lines Q$_{1-3}$.

GUISE. I will.
MAL.   'Tis dangerous.
GUISE.   Therefore I will see him,
And so report my danger to the People.
Halt to your Judgment, let him, if he dare;
But more, more, more, why, Malicorne, again?
I thought a look with us had been a Language;   395
I'le talk my mind on any point but this
By Glances; ha, not yet, thou makest me blush
At thy delay; why, Man, 'tis more than Life,
Ambition, or a Crown.
MAL.   What, Marmoutier!
GUISE. Ay, there a Generals Heart beat like a Drum,   400
Quick, quick, my Reins, my Back, and Head, and Breast,
Ake, as I'de been a Horse-back forty hours.
MAL. She has seen the King.
GUISE. I thought she might. A trick upon me, well.
MAL. Passion o'both sides.
GUISE.   His thou meanest.
MAL.   On hers.   405
Down on her Knees.
GUISE.   And up again, no matter.
MAL. Now all in Tears, now smiling, sad at parting.
GUISE. Dissembl'd, for she told me this before,
'Twas all put on that I might hear and rave.
MAL. And so, to make sure work on't, by Consent   410
Of Grillon, who is made their Bawd.
GUISE.   Away.
MAL. She's lodg'd at Court.
GUISE.   'Tis false, they do belye her.
MAL. But, Sir, I saw the Apartment.
GUISE.   What, at Court?
MAL. At Court, and near the King, 'tis true by Heaven,
I never play'd you foul, why should you doubt me?   415
GUISE. I wou'd thou hadst, e're thus unmann'd me, Heart,
Blood, Battles, Fire, and Death, I run, I run.
With this last blow, he drives me like a Coward;
Nay, let me never win a Field again,
If with the thought of these irregular Vapours,   420
The blood han't burst my Lips.
CARD.   Peace, Brother.
GUISE. By Heaven, I took thee for my Souls Physitian,
And dost thou vomit me with this loath'd peace?
'Tis contradiction; no, my peaceful Brother,
I'le meet him now, tho' Fire, arm'd Cherubins   425
Shou'd cross my way. O Jealousie of Love!

---

416 my Heart, Q_{3+}.
425 Fire-arm'd C_1-Scott and Saintsbury.

Greater than Fame: Thou eldest of the Passions,
Or rather, all in one, I here invoke thee,
Where-e're thou'rt Thron'd in Air, in Earth, or Hell,
Wing me to my Revenge, to Blood, and Ruin.   430
    CARD. Have you no temper?
    GUISE.   Pray, Sir, give me leave,
A moments thought; ha, but I sweat and tremble,
My Brain runs this and that way, 'twill not fix
On ought but vengeance, Malicorne; call the People,   [Shouts within.
But hark, they shout again, I'le on and meet 'em,   435
Nay, head 'em to his Palace as my Guards;
Yet more, on such exalted Causes born,
I'le wait him in his Cabinet alone,
And look him pale, while in his Courts without,
The People shout him dead with their alarms,   440
And make his Mistress tremble in his Arms.   [Exeunt.

Scene II.*

Enter King and Council.

[Shouts without.

    KING. What mean these Shouts?
    ABB.   I told your Majesty,
The Sheriffs have puff'd the Populace with hopes
Of their Deliverer.   [Shouts again.
    KING.   Hark, there rung a Peal
Like Thunder; see, Alphonso, what's the Cause.

Enter Grillon.

    GRILL. My Lord, the Guise is come.   5
    KING. Is't possible! ha, Grillon, said'st thou, come?
    GRILL. Why droops the Royal Majesty? O Sir ---
    KING. O Villain, Slave, wert thou my late born Heir,
Giv'n me by Heav'n, ev'n when I lay a dying;
But peace, thou festring thought, and hide thy Wound;   10
Where is he?
    GRILL. With her Majesty, your Mother;
She has tak'n Chair, and he walks bowing by her,
With thirty thousand Rebels at his heels.
    KING. What's to be done? No pall upon my Spirit;

---

   * Scene II.] Scott and Saintsbury; SCENE the Third. Q$_{1-3}$, Summers;
    Scence the third. F; SCENE III. C$_{1-3}$.

But he that loves me best, and dares the most   15
On this nice point of Empire, let him speak.
    ALPH. I would advise you, Sir, to call him in,
And kill him instantly upon the Spot.
    ABB. I like Alphonso's Counsel, short, sure Work,
Cut off the Head, and let the Body walk.   20

        Enter Queen-Mother.

    Q. M. Sir, the Guise waits.
    KING.   He enters on his Fate.
    Q. M. Not so, forbear, the City's up in Arms;
Nor doubt, if in their heat you cut him off,
That they will spare the Royal Majesty.
Once, Sir, let me advise, and rule your Fury.   25
    KING. You shall, I'le see him, and I'le spare him now.
    Q. M. What will you say?
    KING.   I know not;
Colonel Grillon, call the Archers in,
Double your Guard, and strictly charge the Swits
Stand to their Arms, receive him as a Traytor.   [Exit Grill.   30
My Heart has set thee down, O Guise, in Blood,
Blood, Mother, Blood, ne're to be blotted out.
    Q. M. Yet you'l relent when this hot fit is over.
    KING. If I forgive him, may I ne're be forgiv'n;
No, if I tamely bear such Insolence,   35
What act of Treason will the Villains stop at?
Seize me, they've sworn, Imprison me's the next,
Perhaps Arraign me, and then doom me dead;
But e're I suffer that, fall all together,
Or rather, on their slaughter'd Heaps erect   40
Thy Throne, and then proclaim it for Example,
I'm born a Monarch; which implies, alone
To weild the Scepter, and depend on none.   [Exeunt.

        End of A C T III.

Act IV. Scene I.
The Louvre.

A Chair of State plac'd; the King appears sitting in it; a Table by him, on which he leans; Attendants on each side of them: amongst the rest, Abbot, Grillon, and Bellieure. The Queen-Mother enters led by the Duke of Guise, who makes his approach with three Reverences to the King's Chair; after the third, the King rises, and coming forward, speaks.

KING. I Sent you word you should not come.
GUISE. Sir, that I came---
KING.   Why, that you came, I see.
Once more, I sent you word, you should not come.
    GUISE. Not come to throw my self, with all submission,
Beneath your Royal Feet: to put my Cause   5
And Person in the Hands of Soveraign Justice!
    KING. Now 'tis with all submission, that's the Preface,
Yet still you came against my strict Command,
You disobey'd me, Duke, with all submission.
    GUISE. Sir, it was the last necessity that drove me   10
To clear my self of Calumnies, and Slanders,
Much urg'd, but never prov'd, against my Innocence;
Yet had I known it was your express Command,
I should not have approach'd.
    KING. 'Twas as express, as words could signifie;   15
Stand forth Bellieure, it shall be prov'd you knew it,
Stand forth, and to this false Mans Face declare
Your Message, word for Word.
    BELL. Sir, thus it was, I met him on the way,
And plain as I could speak, I gave your Orders,   20
Just in these following Words---
    KING. Enough, I know you told him;
But he has us'd me long to be contemn'd,
And I can still be patient, and forgive.
    GUISE. And I can ask forgiveness, when I err;   25
But let my Gracious Master, please to know
The true intent of my mis-constru'd Faith.
Should I not come to vindicate my Fame,
From wrong Constructions? And---
    KING. Come, Duke, you were not wrong'd your Conscience knows,   30
You were not wrong'd, were you not plainly told,
That if you dar'd to set your Foot in Paris,
You shou'd be held the cause of all Commotions,
That shou'd from thence ensue, and yet you came.
    GUISE. Sir, will you please with patience but to hear me?   35
    KING. I will, and wou'd be glad, my Lord of Guise,
To clear you to my self.

GUISE.   I had been told
There were in agitation here at Court,
Things of the highest note against Religion,
Against the common Properties of Subjects,   40
And Lives of honest well affected men;
I therefore judg'd---
   KING.   Then you, it seems, are Judge
Betwixt the Prince and People, Judge for them,
And Champion against me?
   GUISE.   I fear'd it might be represented so,   45
And came Resolv'd---
   KING.   To head the Factious Crowd.
   GUISE.   To clear my Innocence.
   KING.   The means for that,
Had been your absence from this hot-brain'd Town---
Where you, not I, are King---
I feel my Blood kindling within my Veins,   50
The Genius of the Throne knocks at my Heart,
Come what may come, he dies.
   Q.M. stopping the King. What mean you Sir,
You tremble and look pale, for Heavens sake think,
'Tis your own Life you venture, if you kill him.
   KING.   Had I ten thousand Lives, I'le venture all.   55
Give me way, Madam.
   Q.M.   Not to your destruction.
The whole Parisian Herd is at your Gates;
A Crowd's a Name too small, they are a Nation,
Numberless, arm'd, enrag'd, one Soul informs 'em.
   KING.   And that one Soul's the Guise, I'le rend it out,   60
And damn the Rabble all at once in him.
   GUISE.   (aside.) My Fate is now i'th' Ballance, Fool within,
I thank thee for thy foresight.
   Q.M.   Your Guards oppose 'em.
   KING.   Why not? a Multitude's a Bulky Coward.
   Q.M.   By Heaven there are not Limbs in all your Guards,   65
For every one a Morsel.
   KING.   Caesar quell'd 'em,
But with a Look and Word.
   Q.M.   So Galba thought.
   KING.   But Galba was not Caesar.
   GUISE.   I must not give 'em time for Resolution.   [Aside.
My Journey, Sir, has discompos'd my Health,   [To the King.   70
I humbly beg your leave I may retire,
Till your Commands re-call me to your Service.   [Exit Guise.

---

55 I'd venture C_{1-3}.

Manet King, Queen-Mother, Grillon, Abbot.

KING. So you have counsell'd well, the Traytors gone.
To mock the meekness of an injur'd King,   [To Queen-Mother.
Why did not you, who gave me part of Life,   75
Infuse my Father stronger in my Veins?
But when you kept me coop'd within your Womb,
You pall'd his generous Blood with the dull mixture
Of your Italian Food, and milk'd slow Arts
Of Womanish tameness in my Infant Mouth,   80
Why stood I stupid else, and miss'd a blow,
Which Heaven and daring folly made so fair.
    Q. M. I still maintain, 'twas wisely done to spare him.
    GRILL. A pox o'this unseasonable Wisdom;
He was a Fool to come; if so, then they   85
Who let him go, were somewhat.
    KING. The event, th' event will shew us what we were,
For like a blazing Meteor hence he shot,
And drew a sweeping Fiery Train along.
O Paris, Paris, once my Seat of Triumph;   90
But now the Scene of all thy King's misfortunes,
Ungrateful, perjur'd, and Disloyal Town,
Which by my Royal Presence I have warm'd
So long, that now the Serpent hisses out,
And shakes his forked Tongue at Majesty,   95
While I---
    Q. M. While you lose time in idle talk.
And use no means for safety and prevention.
    KING. What can I do! O Mother, Abbot, Grillon!
All dumb! nay, then 'tis plain, my Cause is desperate.
Such an o're-whelming ill makes Grief a Fool,   100
As if Redress were past.
    GRILL.   I'le go to the next Sheriff,
And beg the first Reversion of a Rope;
Dispatch is all my business, I'le hang for you.
    ABB. 'Tis not so bad, as vainly you surmise;
Some space there is, some little space, some steps   105
Betwixt our Fate and us; our Foes are powerful,
But yet not Arm'd, nor Martiall'd into Order;
Believe it, Sir, the Guise will not attempt,
'Till he have rowl'd his Snow-ball to a heap.
    KING. So, then, my Lord, we are a day off from Death,   110
What shall to morrow do?
    ABB.   To morrow, Sir.
If hours between slide not too idle by,
You may be Master of their Destiny,
Who now dispose so loftily of yours.

_____

108 attempt,] Q_{2+}; artempt, Q_1.

Not far without the Suburbs there are Quarter'd   115
Three thousand Swisse, and two French Regiments.
   KING. Wou'd they were here, and I were at their head.
   Q.M. Send Mareschal Byron to lead 'em up.
   KING. It shall be so, by Heaven there's Life in this,
The wrack of Clouds is driving on the Winds,   120
And shows a break of Sun-shine.
Go, Grillon, give my Orders to Byron,
And see your Souldiers well dispos'd within,
For Safeguard of the Louvre.
   Q.M.   One thing more,
The Guise (his bus'ness yet not fully ripe,)   125
Will treat at least for show of Loyalty:
Let him be met with the same Arts he brings.
   KING. I know, he'll make exorbitant Demands,
But here your part of me will come in play;
Th' Italian Soul shall teach me how to sooth: 130
Even Jove must flatter with an empty hand,
'Tis time to thunder, when he gripes the Brand.   [Ex. Omnes.

Scene II A Night-Scene*.

Enter Malicorne solus.

   MAL. Thus far the Cause of God: but God's or Devils,
I mean my Master's Cause, and mine succeed:
What shall the Guise do next?   [A flash of lightning.

Enter the Spirit Melanax.

   MEL. First seize the King, and after murder him.
   MAL. Officious Fiend, thou com'st uncall'd to Night.   5
   MEL. Always uncall'd, and still at hand for mischief.
   MAL. ---But why in this Fanatick Habit, Devil?
Thou look'st like one that preaches to the Crowd,
Gospel is in thy Face, and outward Garb,
And Treason on thy Tongue.
   MEL.   Thou hast me right,   10
Ten thousand Devils more are in this Habit,
Saintship and Zeal are still our best disguise:
We mix unknown with the hot thoughtless Crowd,
And quoting Scriptures, which too well we know,
With impious Glosses ban the holy Text,   15
And make it speak Rebellion, Schism and Murder,

---

    * Scene II] Scott and Saintsbury; <u>om</u>. Q₁-C₃, Summers.

So turn the Arms of Heaven against it self.
    MAL. What makes the Curate of St. Eustace here?
    MEL. Thou art mistaken Master, 'tis not he,
But 'tis a zealous, godly, canting Devil,   20
Who has assum'd the Churchman's lucky shape,
To talk the Crowd to Madness and Rebellion.
    MAL. O true Enthusiastick Devil, true;
For Lying is thy Nature, even to me:
Didst thou not tell me, If my Lord the Guise   25
Enter'd the Court, his Head should then lie low?
That was a Lye; he went, and is return'd.
    MEL. 'Tis false; I said, Perhaps it should lie low.
And, but I chill'd the blood in Henry's veins,
And cram'd a thousand ghastly, frightful Thoughts,   30
Nay, thrust 'em foremost in his lab'ring Brain,
Even so it would have been.
    MAL.   Thou hast deserv'd me,
And I am thine, dear Devil; What do we next?
    MEL. I said, First seize the King.
    MAL.   Suppose it done:
He's clapt within a Convent, shorn a Saint,   35
My Master mounts the Throne.
    MEL.   Not so fast, Malicorne;
Thy Master mounts not, till the King be slain.
    MAL. Not when depos'd?
    MEL.   He cannot be depos'd:
He may be kill'd, a violent Fate attends him;
But at his Birth there shone a Regal Star.   40
    MAL. My Master had a stronger.
    MEL. No, not a stronger, but more popular.
Their Births were full oppos'd, the Guise now strongest;
But if th' ill Influence pass o'r Harry's Head,
As in a year it will, France ne're shall boast   45
A greater King than he, now cut him off
While yet his Stars are weak.
    MAL.   Thou talk'st of Stars:
Canst thou not see more deep into Events,
And by a surer way?
    MEL.   No, Malicorne,
The ways of Heaven are brok'n since our Fall,   50
Gulph, beyond Gulph, and never to be shot:
Once we cou'd read our mighty Maker's mind,
As in a Chrystal Mirror, see th' Idea's
Of things that always are, as He is always.

---

  23 MAL.] Q2+; MEL. Q1.
  35 Convent,] Q2-3, C1-Scott and Saintsbury; Covent, Q1, F, Summers.
  46 than he; Q2-3, C1-Scott and Saintsbury.

Now shut below in this dark Sphere,   55
By Second causes dimly we may guess,
And peep far off on Heavens revolving Orbs,
Which cast obscure Reflections from the Throne.
   MAL. Then tell me thy Surmises of the future.
   MEL. I took the Revolution of the Year,   60
Just when the Sun was entering in the Ram:
Th' ascending Scorpion poyson'd all the Sky,
A sign of deep deceit and treachery.
Full on his Cusp his angry Master sate,
Conjoyn'd with Saturn, baleful both to Man: 65
Of secret Slaughters, Empires overturn'd,
Strife, Blood, and Massacres expect to hear,
And all th' Events of an ill omen'd Year.
   MAL. Then flourish Hell, and mighty Mischief reign,
Mischief to some, to others must be good;   70
But hark, for now, tho' 'tis the dead of Night,
When silence broods upon our darkned world,
Methinks I hear a murmuring hollow sound,
Like the deaf Chimes of Bells in Steeples touch'd.
   MEL. 'Tis truly ghess'd: 75
But know, 'tis from no nightly Sexton's hand,
There's not a damned Ghost, nor hell-born Fiend,
That can from Limbo scape, but hither flies,
With leathern wings they beat the dusky Skies.
To sacred Churches all in Swarms repair,   80
Some crowd the Spires, but most the hallow'd Bells,
And softly Toll for Souls departing Knells,
Each Chime thou hear'st, a future death foretells.
Now there they perch to have 'em in their Eyes,
Till all go loaded to the Neather Skies.   85
   MAL. To morrow then.
   MEL.   To morrow let it be:
Or thou deceiv'st those hungry, gaping Fiends,
And Beelzebub will rage.
   MAL. Why Beelzebub? Hast thou not often said,
That Lucifer's your King?
   MEL.   I told thee true: 90
But Lucifer, as he who foremost fell,
So now lies lowest in th' Abyss of Hell.
Chain'd till the dreadful Doom, in place of whom
Sits Beelzebub, Vicegerent of the damn'd,
Who listning downward hears his roaring Lord,   95
And executes his purpose, but no more

---

55 Q$_1$, F, and Summers leave a blank space between "dark" and
    "Sphere," as though the authors had left such a space in their
    manuscript, intending to fill it in later and thus make the line
    a regular pentameter.

The morning creeps behind yon Eastern hill,
And now the Guard is mine, to drive the Elves
And foolish Fairies from their Moon-light Play,
And lash the Laggers from the sight of day.   [Descends.   100

Enter Guise, Mayenne, Cardinal, and Archbishop.

MAY. Sullen, methinks, and slow the Morning breaks,
As if the Sun were listless to appear,
And dark designs hung heavy on the day.
     GUISE. Y'are an old Man too soon, y'are superstitious,
I'le trust my Stars, I know 'em now by proof,   105
The Genius of the King bends under mine,
Inviron'd with his Guards he durst not touch me;
But aw'd and craven'd as he had been spell'd,
Would have pronounc'd, Go kill the Guise, and durst not.
     CARD. We have him in our power, coopt in his Court,   110
Who leads the first Attack? Now by yond Heaven---
That blushes at my Scarlet Robes, I'll d'off
This womanish Attire of godly peace,
And cry, Lie there Lord Cardinal of Guise.
     GUISE. As much too hot, as Mayenne too cool,   115
But 'tis the manlier fault o'th' two.
     ARCHB. Have you not heard the King, preventing day,
Receiv'd the Guards into the City Gates,
The jolly Swisses marching to their Fifes.
The Crowd stood gaping heartless, and amaz'd,   120
Shrunk to their shops, and left the passage free.
     GUISE. I would it should be so, 'twas a good horror,
First let 'em fear for Rapes, and ransackt Houses;
That very fright when I appear to head 'em,
Will harden their soft City Courages: 125
Cold Burghers must be struck, and struck like Flints,
Ere their hid Fire will sparkle.
     ARCHB. I am glad the King has introduc'd these Guards.
     CARD. Your Reason.
     ARCHB.   They are too few for us to fear,
Our numbers in old martial Men are more,   130
The City not cast in, but the pretence
That hither they are brought to bridle Paris,
Will make this Rising pass for just defence.
     MAY. Suppose the City should not rise.
     GUISE. Suppose as well the Sun should never rise: 135
He may not rise, for Heaven may play a trick;
But he has risen from Adam's time to ours.
Is nothing to be left to Noble Hazard?

---

117 [ARCHB.] C_{1-3}, Scott and Saintsbury; BISHOP. Q_{1-3}, F, Summers.
The same correction is made for lines 128, 129.

No Venture made, but all dull Certainty;
By Heav'n I'le tug with Harry for a Crown,   140
Rather than have it on tame terms of yielding,
I scorn to poach for Power.

       Enter a Servant, who whispers Guise.

A Lady, say'st thou, Young, and Beautiful,
Brought in a Chair?
Condust her in---   [Exit Serv.
    CARD.   You wou'd be left alone---   145
    GUISE. I wou'd, Retire.   [Exeunt May. Card. , etc. *

     Re-enter Servant with Marmoutier, and Exit.

Starting back. Is't possible I dare not trust my Eyes,
You are not Marmoutier.
    MAR. What am I then?
    GUISE.   Why any thing but she:
What should the Mistress of a King do here?   150
    MAR. Find him, who wou'd be Master of a King.
    GUISE. I sent not for you, Madam.
    MAR. I think my Lord the King sent not for you.
    GUISE. Do you not fear your Visit will be known?
    MAR. Fear is for guilty Men, Rebels, and Traytors;   155
Where e're I go, my Virtue is my Guard.
    GUISE. What devil has sent thee here to plague my Soul?
O that I could detest thee now as much
As ever I have lov'd, nay even as much
As yet in spite of all thy Crimes I love: 160
But 'tis a Love so mixt with dark Despair,
The Smoke and Soot smother the rising flame,
And make my Soul a Furnace: Woman, Woman,
What can I call thee more, if Devil 'twere less,
Sure thine's a Race was never got by Adam,   165
But Eve play'd false engendring with the Serpent,
Her own part worse than his.
    MAR.   Then they got Traytors.
    GUISE. Yes, Angel Traytors fit to shine in Palaces,
Fork'd into Ills, and split into Deceits;
Two in their very frame: 'twas well, 'twas well,   170
I saw not thee at Court, thou Basilisk;
For if I had, those Eyes, without his Guards,

---

  * [Exeunt May. Card. , etc.] Scott and Saintsbury; om. Q$_1$-C$_3$, Summers.
172 had,] Q$_{2-3}$, C$_{1+}$; had' Q$_1$, F. The apostrophe with "had" is obviously
  a comma slipped out of place in Q$_1$ and followed by the printer in F.

Had done the Tyrant's work.
    MAR.   Why then, it seems,
I was not false in all; I told you, Guise,
If you left Paris, I would go to Court: 175
You see I kept my Promise.
    GUISE.   Still thy Sex:
Once true in all thy Life, and that for Mischief.
    MAR. Have I said I lov'd you?
    GUISE.   Stab on, Stab,
'Tis plain you love the King.
    MAR.   Nor him, nor you,
In that unlawful way you seem to mean.   180
My Eyes had once so far betray'd my Heart,
As to distinguish you from Common Men,
What e're you said, or did, was Charming all.
    GUISE. But yet, it seems, you found a King more Charming.
    MAR. I do not say more Charming, but more Noble,   185
More truly Royal, more a King in Soul,
Than you are now in wishes.
    GUISE.   May be so:
But Love has oyl'd your tongue to run so glib,
Curse on your Eloquence.
    MAR. Curse not that Eloquence, that sav'd your Life: 190
For when your wild Ambition, which defy'd
A Royal Mandat, hurried you to Town;
When over-weening pride of Popular Power,
Had thrust you headlong in the Louvre Toyls,
Then had you dy'd: For know, my haughty Lord,   195
Had I not been, offended Majesty
Had doom'd you to the death you well deserv'd.
    GUISE. Then was't not Henry's fear preserv'd my Life?
    MAR. You know him better, or you ought to know him;
He's born to give you fear, not to receive it.   200
    GUISE. Say this again, but add you gave not up
Your Honour as the Ransom of my Life;
For if you did, 'twere better I had dy'd.
    MAR. And so it were.
    GUISE.   Why said you, So it were?
For tho 'tis true, methinks 'tis much unkind.   205
    MAR. My Lord, we are not now to talk of kindness,
If you acknowledge I have sav'd your Life.
Be grateful in return, and do an Act
Your Honour, though unaskt by me, requires.
    GUISE. By Heav'n and you, whom next to Heaven I love,   210
(If I said more, I fear I should not lie,)
I'le do what e're my Honour will permit.

---

207 your Life; Q_{2-3}; your Life, C_1-Scott and Saintsbury.
211 (If] Q_{2-3}, C_{1+}; (if Q_1, F.

MAR. Go throw your self at Henry's Royal Feet,
And rise not, till approv'd a Loyal Subject.
   GUISE. A Dutious Loyal Subject I was ever.   215
   MAR. I'le put it short, my Lord, depart from Paris.
   GUISE. I cannot leave
My Countrey, Friends, Religion, all at stake;
Be wise, and be before-hand with your Fortune;
Prevent the turn, forsake the ruin'd Court;   220
Stay here, and make a merit of your Love.
   MAR. No, I'le return, and perish in those Ruines;
I find thee now ambitious, faithless Guise,
Farewel the basest, and the last of Men.
   GUISE. Stay, or -- O Heav'n! I'le force you: Stay ---   225
   MAR. I do believe
So ill of you, so villainously ill,
That if you durst, you wou'd:
Honour you've little, Honesty you've less;
But Conscience you have none.   230
Yet there's a thing call'd Fame, and Mens Esteem,
Preserves me from your force, once more farewel:
Look on me Guise, thou seest me now the last;
Tho Treason urge not Thunder on thy head,
This one departing Glance shall flash thee dead.   [Exit.   235
   GUISE. Ha said she true? Have I so little Honour.
Why then a Prize so easie, and so fair,
Had never scap'd my Gripe; but mine she is,
For that's set down as sure as Harry's Fall:
But my Ambition, that she calls my Crime: 240
False, false by Fate, my Right was born with me,
And Heaven confest it in my very frame;
The Fires that would have form'd ten thousand Angels,
Were cram'd together for my single Soul.

Enter Malicorne.

   MAL. My Lord, you trifle precious hours away,   245
The Heavens look gaudily upon your greatness,
And the crown'd moments court you as they fly;
Brisac and fierce Aumale have pent the Swisse,
And folded 'em like sheep in holy ground,
Where now with order'd Pikes, and Colours furl'd,   250
They wait the word that dooms 'em all to dye:
Come forth and bless the Triumph of the day.
   GUISE. So slight a Victory requir'd not me:
I but sate still, and Nodded like a God
My World into Creation, now 'tis time   255

---

224 the worst of Men. C_{2-3}.
236 little Honour? Q_{2-3}, C_{1-3}, Scott and Saintsbury.

To walk abroad, and carelesly survey
How the dull Matter does the Form obey.   [Exit with Malicorne.

Enter Citizens, and Melanax in his Fanatick Habit,
at the head of 'em.

MEL.   Hold, hold a little, Fellow Citizens, and you Gentlemen
of the Rabble, a word of Godly Exhortation to strengthen your
hands, ere you give the Onset.   260
1st CIT.   Is this a time to make Sermons? I wou'd not hear the
Devil now, tho he should come in God's Name, to preach Peace to us.
2nd CIT.   Look you, Gentlemen, Sermons are not to be despis'd,
We have all profited by godly Sermons that promote Sedition,
Let the precious man Hold-forth.   265
OMNES.   Let him Hold forth, let him Hold-forth.
MEL.   To promote Sedition is my business: It has been so before any
of you were born, and will be so when you are all dead and damn'd; I
have led on the Rabble in all Ages.
1st CIT.   That's a Lye, and a loud one.   270
2nd CIT.   He has led the Rabble both Old and Young, that's all Ages. A
heavenly sweet Man, I warrant him, I have seen him somewhere in a Pulpit.
MEL.   I have sown Rebellion everywhere.
1st CIT.   How every where? That's another Lye: How far have you
Travel'd Friend?   275
MEL.   Over all the World.
1st CIT.   Now that's a Rapper.
2nd CIT.   I say, No: For, look you Gentlemen, if he has been a
Traveller, he certainly says true, for he may lye by Authority.
MEL.   That the Rabble may depose their Prince,   280
Has in all Times, and in all Countries, been accounted lawful.
1st CIT.   That's the first true Syllable he has utter'd: But as how,
and whereby, and when may they depose him?
MEL.   When ever they have more power to Depose, than he has to
Oppose, and this they may do upon the least Occasion.   285
1st CIT.   Sirra, you mince the Matter; you should say, we may
do it upon no Occasion, for the less the better.
MEL.   aside.   Here's a Rogue now will out-shoot the Devil in his
own Bow.
2nd CIT.   Some Occasion, in my mind, were not amiss; For, look   290
you Gentlemen, if we have no Occasion, then whereby we have no
Occasion to depose him; and therefore either Religion or Liberty, I
stick to those Occasions: for when they are gone, Goodnight to
Godliness and Freedom.
MEL.   When the most are of one side, as that's our case, we are   295

---

271   2nd CIT.] C_2-Scott and Saintsbury; <u>om</u>. Q_1-C_1, Summers.
273   I have sown] F, Scott and Saintsbury, Summers; I sown Q_{1-3};
          I've sown C_{1-3}.
291   then we have no occasion whereby to depose him; C_{2-3}.

always in the right; for they that are in power, will ever be the
Judges: So that if we say White is Black, poor White must lose
the Cause, and put on Mourning, for White is but a single Syllable,
and we are a whole Sentence: Therefore go on boldly, and lay on
resolutely for your Solemn League and Covenant, and if here be any   300
squeamish Conscience who fears to fight against the King, tho I that
have known you Citizens these thousand years, suspect not any, let such
understand, That his Majesties Politick Capacity is to be distinguish'd
from his Natural; and though you murder him in one, you may preserve him
in the other, and so much for this time, because the Enemy is at hand.   305
   2nd CIT. looking out. Look you, Gentlemen, 'tis Grillon the fierce Colonel,
He that devours our Wives, and ravishes our Children.
   1st. CIT. He looks so Grum, I don't care to have to do with him,
Wou'd I were safe in my Shop behind the Counter.
   2nd CIT. And wou'd I were under my Wives Petticoats,   310
Look you, Gentlemen.
   MEL. You, Neighbour, behind your Compter yesterday, paid a Bill
of Exchange in Glass Louisdors, and you Friend, that cry, Look you
Gentlemen, this very morning was under another Womans Petticoats, and
not your Wives.   315
   2nd CIT. How the Devil does he know this?
   MEL. Therefore fight lustily for the Cause of Heaven, and to
make even Tallies for your Sins, which that you may do with a better
Conscience, I absolve you both, and all the rest of you: Now go on
merrily, for those that escape shall avoid killing; and those who do   320
not escape, I will provide for in another world.
           [Cry within on the other side of the Stage,
               Vive le Roy, Vive le Roy.

          Enter Grillon, and his Party.

   GRILL. Come on, Fellow Soldiers, Commilitones, that's my word,
as 'twas Julius Caesar's of Pagan memory; 'fore God I am no Speech-
maker, but there are the Rogues, and here's Bilbo, that's a word and
a blow; we must either cut their Throats, or they cut ours, that's pure   325
necessity for your comfort: Now if any man can be so unkind to his
own Body, for I meddle not with your Souls, as to stand still like a
good Christian, and offer his Weeson to a Butcher's Whittle, I say
no more but that he may be sav'd, and that's the best can come on
him.   330
           [Cry on both sides, Vive le Roy, Vive Guise.
               They Fight. *

---

313 Glass Louisdors,] Q_2 ; Glass, Louisdors, Q_1, F, Summers;
     Glass Louisdors; Q_3; Glass Louis d'ors; C_{1-3}; glass louis d'ors;
     Scott and Saintsbury. Scott and Saintsbury suggest "glass" is an
     error for "brass".
  * They Fight.] C_1-Scott and Saintsbury; The Fight. Q_1-F, Summers.

MEL. Hey for the Duke of Guise and Property, Up with Religion
and the Cause, and down with those Arbitrary Rogues there:
Stand to't you Associated Cuckolds.   [Citizens go back.
O Rogues, O Cowards, Damn these Half-strain'd Shop-keepers, Got
between Gentlemen and City-Wives, how Naturally they quake, and   335
run away from their own Fathers, Twenty Souls a Penny were a dear
Bargain of 'em.   [They all run off, Melanax with them, the
                                   1st and 2nd Citizens taken.

GRILL. Possess your selves of the place Maubert,
And hang me up those two Rogues for an example.
1st CIT. O spare me sweet Colonel, I am but a young Beginner, and   340
new set up.
GRILL. I'le be your Customer, and set you up a little better, Sirrah,
Go hang him at the next Sign post:
What have you to say for your self, Scoundrel?
Why were you a Rebel?   345
2nd CIT. Look you, Colonel, 'twas out of no ill meaning to the
Government, all that I did, was pure Obedience to my Wife.
GRILL. Nay, if thou hast a Wife that wears the Breeches,
Thou shalt be condemn'd to live:
Get thee home for a Hen-peckt Traytor---   350
What, Are we encompass'd? Nay then, Faces this way;
Wee'l sell our Skins to the fairest Chapmen.

        Enter Aumale and Soldiers on the one side, Citizens on the other,
                Grillon and his Party are disarm'd.

1st CIT. Bear away that bloody-minded Colonel,
And hang him up at the next Sign-post:
Nay, when I am in power, I can make examples too.   355
OMNES. Tear him piece-meal, tear him piece-meal. [Pull and hale him.
GRILL. Rogues, Villains, Rebels, Traytors, Cuckolds,
'Swounds, What do you make of a Man? Do you think
Legs and Arms are strung upon a Wire, like a Jointed Baby?
Carry me off quickly, you were best, and hang me decently,   360
according to my first Sentence.
2nd CIT. Look you, Colonel, you are too bulky· to be carried off
all at once, a Leg or an Arm is one Man's Burden:
Give me a little Finger for a Sample of him, whereby
I'le carry it for a Token to my Soveraign Lady.   365
GRILL. 'Tis too little, in all Conscience, for her,
Take a bigger Token, Cuckold. Et tu Brute whom I sav'd,
O the Conscience of a Shop-keeper!
2nd CIT. Look you, Colonel, for your saving me, I thank you
heartily, whereby that Debt's paid; but for speaking Treason   370
against my anointed Wife, that's a new Reck'ning between us.

----

351 Nay, then face C_{1-3}.
352 We'll Q_2-Scott and Saintsbury.

Enter Guise with a General's Staff in his hand, Mayenne,
Cardinal, Archbishop, Malicorne, and Attendants.

OMNES. Vive Guise.
GUISE. bowing, and Bare-headed. I thank you Countrey-men, the
hand of Heaven
In all our Safeties has appear'd this day,
Stand on your Guard, and double every Watch,   375
But stain your Triumph with no Christian blood,
French we are all, and Brothers of a Land.
CARD. What mean you, Brother, by this Godly talk?
Of sparing Christian Blood, why these are Dogs;
Now by the Sword that cut off Malchus Ear,   380
Meer Dogs that neither can be sav'd nor damn'd.
ARCHB. Where have you learnt to spare inveterate Foes?
GUISE. You know the Book.
ARCHB.   And can expound it too:
But Christian Faith was in the Nonage then,
And Roman Heathens lorded o're the World,   385
What madness were it for the weak and few,
To fight against the many and the strong;
Grillon must dye, so must the Tyrant's Guards,
Least gathering head again, they make more work.
MAL. My Lord, the People must be flesh'd in Blood,   390
To teach 'em the true Relish, dip 'em with you---
Or they'l perhaps repent.
GUISE. You are Fools, to kill 'em were to shew I fear'd 'em;
The Court disarm'd, disheartned, and besieg'd,
Are all as much within my power, as if   395
I grip'd 'em in my Fist.
MAY.   'Tis rightly judg'd:
And let me add, who heads a Popular Cause,
Must prosecute that Cause by Popular Ways:
So whether you are merciful or no,
You must affect to be.   400
GUISE. Dismiss those Prisoners, Grillon, you are free,
I do not ask your Love, be still my Foe.
GRILL. I will be so: But let me tell you, Guise,
As this was greatly done, 'twas proudly too;
I'le give you back your life when next we meet,   405
Till then I am your Debtor.
GUISE.   That's till Dooms-day. [Grillon and his Exeunt
                                        one way, Rabble the other.
Haste Brother, draw out Fifteen thousand Men,
Surround the Louvre, least the Prey should scape,
I know the King will send to treat,
We'll set the Dice on him in high demands,   410
No less than all his Offices of Trust,
He shall be par'd, and canton'd out, and clipt,
So long he shall not pass.
CARD.   What do we talk

Of paring, clipping, and such tedious work,
Like those that hang their Noses o're a Potion,   415
And Qualm, and keck, and take it down by Sipps.
    ARCHB.   Best make advantage of this Popular Rage,
Let in th' orewhelming Tyde on Harry's head,
In that promiscuous Fury who shall know
Among a thousand Swords who kill'd the King.   420
    MAL.   O my dear Lord, upon this onely day
Depends the series of your following Fate:
Think your good Genius has assum'd my shape
In this Prophetick doom.
    GUISE.   Peace croaking Raven,
I'le seize him first, then make him a led Monarch;   425
I'le be declar'd Lieutenant General
Amidst the Three Estates that represent
The glorious, full, majestick Face of France,
Which in his own despight the King shall call:
So let him reign my Tenant during life,   430
His Brother of Navarre shut out for ever,
Branded with Heresie, and barr'd from Sway,
That when Valois consum'd in Ashes lies,
The Phoenix Race of Charlemain may rise.   [Exeunt.

Scene III. The Louvre.

Enter King, Queen-Mother, Abbot, Grillon.

    KING.   Dismist with such Contempt?
    GRILL.   Yes, Faith, we past
Like beaten Romans underneath the Fork.
    KING.   Give me my Arms.
    GRILL.   For what?
    KING.   I'le lead you on.
    GRILL.   You are a true Lyon, but my Men are Sheep;
If you run first, I'le swear they'l follow you.   5
    KING.   What, all turn'd Cowards? Not a Man in France
Dares set his Foot by mine, and perish by me.
    GRILL.   Troth I can't find 'em much inclin'd to perishing.
    KING.   What can be left in danger, but to dare?

415-16 Printed as prose in Q_1-F, Summers.
  1-2 Divided as follows Q_1-C_3, Summers:
    KING. Dismist with such Contempt?
    GRILL. Yes, Faith, we past like beaten Romans underneath the Fork.
    The division followed in the present text is that of Scott and Saintsbury.

No matter for my Arms, I'le go Bare-fac'd,   10
And seize the first bold Rebel that I meet.
  ABB. There's something of Divinity in Kings
That sits between their Eyes, and guards their Life.
  GRILL. True, Abbot, but the mischief is, you Churchmen
Can see that something further than the Crowd;   15
These Musket Bullets have not read much Logick,
Nor are they given to make your nice distinctions:

  One enters, and gives the Queen a Note, she reads---

One of 'em possibly may hit the King
In some one part of him that's not Divine,
And so the mortal part of his Majesty wou'd draw   20
The Divinity of it into another world, sweet Abbot.
  Q. M. 'Tis equal madness to go out or stay,
The Reverence due to Kings is all transfer'd
To haughty Guise, and when new Gods are made,
The old must quit the Temple, you must fly.   25
  KING. Death, Had I wings, yet I would scorn to fly.
  GRILL. Wings, or no wings, is not the Question:
If you won't fly for't, you must ride for't,
And that comes much to one.
  KING. Forsake my Regal Town.
  Q. M.   Forsake a Bedlam: 30
This Note informs me, Fifteen thousand Men
Are marching to inclose the Louvre round.
  ABB. The business then admits no more dispute,
You, Madam, must be pleas'd to find the Guise,
Seem easie, fearful, yielding, what you will,   35
But still prolong the Treaty all you can,
To gain the King more time for his Escape.
  Q. M. I'le undertake it---Nay, no thanks my Son,
My blessing shall be given in your deliverance;
That once perform'd, their Web is all unravel'd,   40
And Guise is to begin his work again. [Exit Q. Mother.
  KING. I go this minute.

    Enter Marmoutier.

Nay then, another minute must be given.
O how I blush, that thou shouldst see thy King
Do this low Act that lessens all his Fame: 45
Death must a Rebel force me from my Love!
If it must be---
  MAR. It must not, cannot be.
  GRILL. No, nor shall not Wench, as long as my Soul wears a Body.

---

48 not, C_3, Scott and Saintsbury.

KING. Secure in that, I'le trust thee; Shall I trust thee?
For Conquerors have Charms, and Women Frailty: 50
Farewel, Thou may'st behold me King agen,
My Soul's not yet depos'd, why then farewel,
I'le say't as comfortably as I can:
But O curs'd Guise, for pressing on my time,
And cutting off Ten thousand more Adieus.   55
    MAR. The moments that retard your Flight are Traytors,
Make haste my Royal Master to be safe,
And save me with you, for I'le share your Fate.
    KING. Wilt thou go too?
Then I am reconcil'd to Heaven again: 60
O welcome thou good Angel of my way,
Thou Pledge and Omen of my safe Return;
Not Greece, nor hostile Juno cou'd destroy
The Hero that abandon'd burning Troy,
He scap'd the dangers of the dreadful Night,   65
When loaded with his Gods he took his Flight.

                              [Exeunt King, leading her.

                    End of ACT IV

Act V. Scene I.

The Castle of Blois.

Enter Grillon, Alphonso Corso.

GRILL. Welcome Colonel, welcome to Blois.
ALPH. Since last we parted at the Barricadoes,
The World's turn'd upside down.
GRILL. No, Faith, 'tis better, now 'tis downside up,
Our part o'th' wheel is rising, tho but slowly.   5
ALPH. Who lookt for an Assembly of the States?
GRILL. When the King was escap'd from Paris, and got out
of the Toyles, 'twas time for the Guise to take 'em down, and
pitch others: That is, to treat for the Calling of a Parliament,
where being sure of the major part, he might get by Law, what   10
he had miss'd by Force.
ALPH. But why should the King assemble the States, to
satisfie the Guise after so many Affronts?
GRILL. For the same reason that a Man in a Duel says, he
has received satisfaction when he is first wounded, and after-   15
wards disarm'd.
ALPH. But why this Parliament at Blois, and not at Paris?
GRILL. Because no Barricado's have been made at Blois:
This Blois is a very little Town, and the King can draw it after
him. But Paris is a damn'd, unweildy Bulk, and when the   20
Preachers draw against the King, a Parson in a Pulpit is a
devilish Fore-horse. Besides, I found in that Insurrection,
what dangerous Beasts these Townsmen are; I tell you, Colonel, a Man had better deal with ten of their Wives, than with
one zealous Citizen: O your inspir'd Cuckold is most implacable. 25
ALPH. Is there any seeming kindness between the King, and
the Duke of Guise?
GRILL. Yes, most wonderful: They are as dear to one another, as an old Usurer, and a rich young Heir upon a Mortgage.
The King is very Loyal to the Guise, and the Guise is very gra-   30
cious to the King: Then the Cardinal of Guise, and the Archbishop of Lyons, are the two Pendants, that are always hanging
at the Royal Ear; They ease His Majesty of all the Spiritual
business, and the Guise of all the Temporal, so that the King is
certainly the happiest Prince in Christendom, without any care   35
upon him: so yielding up every thing to his Loyal Subjects that
he's infallibly in the way of being the greatest, and most glorious
King in all the world.
ALPH. Yet I have heard, he made a sharp reflecting Speech
upon their Party at the opening of the Parliament, admonish'd   40
Men of their Duties, pardon'd what was past, but seem'd to
threaten Vengeance, if they persisted for the future.

GRILL. Yes, and then they all took the Sacrament together:
He promising to unite himself to them, and they to obey him
according to the Laws; yet the very next morning they went on,   45
in pursuance of their old Commonwealth designs, as violently
as ever.

ALPH. Now am I dull enough to think they have broken their
Oath.

GRILL. Ay but you are but one private Man, and they are the   50
three States; And if they Vote that they have not broken their
Oaths, Who is to be Judge?

ALPH. There's One above.

GRILL. I hope you mean in Heaven, or else you are a bolder
Man than I am in Parliament-time; but here comes the Master   55
and my Neece.

ALPH. Heaven preserve him, if a Man may pray for him without Treason.

GRILL. O Yes, You may pray for him, the Preachers of the
Guises side, do that most formally: Nay, You may be suffer'd   60
Civilly to drink his Health, be of the Court, and keep a place of
Profit under him: For, in short, 'tis a judg'd Case of Conscience,
to make your best of the King, and to side against him.

Enter King and Marmoutier.

KING. Grillon, Be near me,
There's something for my service to be done,   65
Your Orders will be sudden, now withdraw.

GRILL. aside.] Well, I dare trust my Neece, even tho' she
comes of my own Family; but if she Cuckolds my good Opinion
of her Honesty, there's a whole Sex fall'n under a General Rule
without one Exception.   [Exeunt Grillon and Alphonso.   70

MAR. You bid my Uncle wait you.

KING.   Yes.

MAR.   This hour.

KING. I think it was.

MAR. Something of moment hangs upon this hour.

KING. Not more on this, than on the next and next,
My time is all ta'ne up on Usury;   75
I never am before hand with my hours,
But every one has work before it comes.

MAR. There's something for my service to be done,
Those were your words.

KING.   And you desire their meaning.

MAR. I dare not ask, and yet perhaps may ghess.   80

KING. 'Tis searching there where Heaven can only pry,

---

48 Now I am dull Q$_{2-3}$, C$_{1-3}$, Scott and Saintsbury.
50 Ay] Q$_3$, C$_1$-Scott and Saintsbury; I Q$_{1-2}$, F, Summers.

Not Man, who knows not Man but by surmise;
Nor Devils, nor Angels of a purer Mould,
Can trace the winding Labyrinths of Thought,
I tell thee, Marmoutier, I never speak   85
Not when alone, for fear some Fiend should hear,
And blab my Secrets out.
    MAR.   You hate the Guise.
    KING. True, I did hate him.
    MAR.   And you hate him still.
    KING. I am reconcil'd.
    MAR.   Your Spirit is too high,
Great Souls forgive not injuries, till time   90
Has put their Enemies into their power,
That they may shew Forgiveness is their own;
For else 'tis fear to punish that forgives:
The Coward, not the King.
    KING.   He has submitted.
    MAR. In show, for in effect he still insults.   95
    KING. Well, Kings must bear sometimes.
    MAR. They must, till they can shake their burden off,
And that's, I think, your aim.
    KING.   Mistaken still:
All Favours, all Preferments, pass through them,
I'm pliant, and they mould me as they please.   100
    MAR. These are your Arts to make 'em more secure,
Just so your Brother us'd the Admiral,
Brothers may think, and act like Brothers too.
    KING. What said you, ha! what mean you Marmoutier?
    MAR. Nay, what mean you? That Start betray'd you, Sir.   105
    KING. This is no Vigil of St. Bartholmew,
Nor is Blois Paris.
    MAR.   'Tis an open Town.
    KING. What then!
    MAR.   Where you are strongest.
    KING.   Well, what then?
    MAR. No more, but you have Power, and are provok'd.
    KING. O! Thou hast set thy Foot upon a Snake,   110
Get quickly off, or it will sting thee dead.
    MAR. Can I unknow it?
    KING.   No, but keep it secret.
    MAR. Think, Sir, your Thoughts are still as much your own,
As when you kept the Key of your own Breast:
But since you let me in, I find it fill'd   115
With Death and Horror; you would murder Guise.
    KING. Murder! what Murder! use a softer word,
And call it Soveraign Justice.
    MAR.   Wou'd I cou'd:
But Justice bears the Godlike shape of Law,
And Law requires Defence, and equal Plea   120
Betwixt th' Offender, and the righteous Judge.

KING. Yes, when th' Offender can be judg'd by Laws,
But when his Greatness overturns the Scales,
Then Kings are Justice in the last Appeal:
And forc'd by strong Necessity may strike,   125
In which indeed th'y assert the Publick Good,
And, like sworn Surgeons, lop the gangren'd Limb:
Unpleasant wholsom work.
    MAR.   If this be needful.
    KING. Ha, didst not thou thy self in fathoming
The depth of my designs, drop there the Plummet?   130
Didst thou not say Affronts, so Great, so Publick,
I never could forgive?
    MAR.   I did but yet ---
    KING. What means, But yet? 'Tis Evidence so full,
If the last Trumpet sounded in my Ears,
Undaunted I should meet the Saints half way: 135
And in the Face of Heaven maintain the Fact.
    MAR. Maintain it then to Heaven, but not to me:
Do you love me?
    KING.   Can you doubt it?
    MAR. Yes, I can doubt it, if you can deny:
Love begs once more this great Offender's life,   140
Can you forgive the man you justly hate,
That hazards both your Life and Crown to spare him?
One whom you may suspect I more than pity,
(For I would have you see that what I ask,
I know is wond'rous difficult to grant)   145
Can you be thus extravagantly Good?
    KING. What then? For I begin to fear my firmness:
And doubt the soft destruction of your tongue.
    MAR. Then in Return, I swear to Heaven, and you,
To give you all the Preference of my Soul: 150
No Rebel Rival to disturb you there,
Let him but live, that he may be my Convert.
        [King walks awhile, then wipes his eyes, and speaks.

    KING. You've Conquer'd, all that's past shall be forgiv'n,
My lavish Love has made a lavish Grant:
But know this Act of Grace shall be my last.   155
Let him repent, yes, let him well repent,
Let him desist, and tempt Revenge no further:
For by yond Heaven that's Conscious of his Crimes,
I will no more by Mercy be betray'd.

    Deputies appearing at the Door.

The Deputies are entring, You must leave me: 160
Thus Tyrant Business all my hours usurps,
And makes me live for others.
    MAR. Now Heav'n reward you with a prosperous Reign,
And grant you never may be good in vain.   [Exit.

Enter Deputies of the Three States,
Cardinal of Guise, and Archbishop of Lyons,
        at the Head of 'em.

KING. Well, my good Lords, what matters of importance   165
Employ'd the States this Morning?
    ARCHB.   One high Point
Was warmly canvass'd in the Commons House,
And will be soon Resolv'd.
    KING.   What was't?
    CARD.   Succession.
    KING. That's one high Point indeed, but not to be
So warmly canvass'd, or so soon Resolv'd.   170
    CARD. Things necessary must sometimes be sudden.
    KING. No sudden danger threatens you, my Lord.
    ARCHB. What may be sudden, must be counted so;
We hope, and wish Your Life: But Yours, and Ours,
Are in the hand of Heaven.
    KING.   My Lord, They are: 175
Yet in a Natural way I may live long,
If Heaven and You my Loyal Subjects please.
    ARCHB. But since good Princes, like Your Majesty,
Take care of dangers meerly possible,
Which may concern their Subjects whose they are,   180
And for whom Kings are made.
    KING.   Yes, we for them,
And they for us, the Benefits are mutual,
And so the Tyes are too.
    CARD.   To cut things short,
The Commons will decree to exclude Navarre
From the Succession of the Realm of France.   185
    KING. Decree, my Lord! What one Estate decree,
Where then are the other two, and what am I?
The Government is cast up somewhat short,
The Clergy and Nobility casheer'd,
Five hundred popular Figures on a Row,   190
And I my Self that am, or should be King,
An o'regrown Cypher set before the Sum:
What Reasons urge our Soveraigns for th'Exclusion?
    ARCHB. He stands suspected, Sir, of Heresie.
    KING. Has he been call'd to make his just defence?   195
    CARD. That needs not, for 'tis known.
    KING.   To whom?
    CARD.   The Commons.
    KING. What is't those Gods the Commons do not know?
But Heresie you Church-men teach us Vulgar,
Supposes obstinate and stiff persisting

---

199 still persisting Q_3, C_{1-3}.

In Errors prov'd, long Admonitions made,   200
And all rejected, has this Course been us'd?
    ARCHB. We grant it has not, but ---
    KING.   Nay, give me leave,
I urge from your own Grant, it has not been:
If then in process of a petty Sum,
Both Parties having not been fully heard,   205
No Sentence can be giv'n:
Much less in the Succession of a Crown,
Which after my decease, by Right Inherent,
Devolves upon my Brother of Navarre.
    CARD. The Right of Souls is still to be preferr'd,   210
Religion must not suffer for a Claim.
    KING. If Kings may be excluded, or depos'd,
When e're you cry Religion to the Crowd,
That Doctrine makes Rebellion Orthodox,
And Subjects must be Traytors to be sav'd.   215
    ARCHB. Then Heresy's entail'd upon the Throne.
    KING. You would entail Confusion, Wars and Slaughters:
Those ills are Certain, what you name Contingent.
I know my Brother's nature, 'tis sincere,
Above deceit, no crookedness of thought,   220
Says what he means, and what he says, performs:
Brave, but not rash; successful, but not proud.
So much acknowledging that he's uneasie,
Till every petty service be o're paid.
    ARCHB. Some say revengeful.
    KING.   Some then libel him: 225
But that's what both of us have learn't to bear.
He can forgive, but you disdain Forgiveness:
Your Chiefs are they no Libel must profane:
Honour's a Sacred Thing in all but Kings;
But when your Rhimes assassinate our Fame,   230
You hug your nauseous, blund'ring Ballad-wits,
And pay 'em as if Nonsense were a merit,
If it can mean but Treason.
    ARCHB. Sir, we have many Arguments to urge ---
    KING. And I have more to answer, let 'em know   235
My Royal Brother of Navarre shall stand
Secure by Right, by Merit, and my Love.
God, and good men will never fail his Cause,
And all the bad shall be constrain'd by Laws.
    ARCHB. Since gentle means t' exclude Navarre are vain,   240
To morrow in the States 'twill be propos'd,
To make the Duke of Guise Lieutenant-General,
Which Power most graciously confirm'd by you,

---

221 Says what] C$_{1-3}$, Scott and Saintsbury; Says, what Q$_{1-3}$, F.,
    Summers.

Will stop this headlong Torrent of Succession,
That bears Religion, Laws, and all before it,   245
In hope you'll not oppose what must be done,
We wish you, Sir, a long and prosp'rous Reign. [Exeunt Omnes, but the King.
    KING. To morrow Guise is made Lieutenant-General,
Why then to morrow I no more am King;
'Tis time to push my slack'nd vengeance home,   250
To be a King, or not to be at all;
The Vow that manacled my Rage is loos'd,
Even Heaven is wearied with repeated Crimes,
Till lightning flashes round to guard the Throne,
And the curb'd Thunder grumbles to be gone.   255

       Enter Grillon to him.

    GRILL. 'Tis just the pointed hour you bid me wait.
    KING. So just, as if thou wert inspir'd to come;
As if the Guardian Angel of my Throne,
Who had o'reslept himself so many Years,
Just now was rouz'd, and brought thee to my rescue.   260
    GRILL. I hear the Guise will be Lieutenant-General.
    KING. And canst thou suffer it?
    GRILL. Nay, if you will suffer it, then well may I.
If Kings will be so civil to their Subjects, to give up all things
tamely, they first turn Rebels to themselves, and that's a fair   265
example for their Friends; 'Slife, Sir, 'tis a dangerous matter
to be Loyal on the wrong side, to serve my Prince in spight of
him; if you'l be a Royalist your self, there are Millions of honest
Men will fight for you; but if you wo'n not, there are few will hang for you.
    KING. No more: I am resolv'd,   270
The course of things can be with-held no longer
From breaking forth to their appointed end:
My vengeance, ripen'd in the womb of time,
Presses for birth, and longs to be disclos'd.
Grillon, the Guise is doom'd --- to sudden death: 275
The Sword must end him; Has not thine an Edge?
    GRILL. Yes, and a Point too; I'le challenge him.
    KING. --- I bid thee kill him.   [Walking. *
    GRILL.   --- So I mean to do.
    KING. --- Without thy hazard.
    GRILL. Now I understand you, I shou'd murder him: 280
I am your Soldier, Sir, but not your Hangman.
    KING. --- Dost thou not hate him?
    GRILL.   --- Yes.
    KING.   Hast thou not said,
That he deserves it?
    GRILL.   Yes, but how have I
Deserv'd to do a Murder?

---

  *[Walking.] Q_{2+}; [Walping. Q_1.

KING.   'Tis no Murder:
'Tis Soveraign Justice urg'd from Self Defence.   285
    GRILL. 'Tis all confest, and yet I dare not do't.
    KING. Go, Thou art a Coward.
    GRILL.   You are my King.
    KING. Thou say'st thou dar'st not kill him.
    GRILL. Were I a Coward, I had been a Villain,
And then I durst ha' don't.   290
    KING. Thou hast done worse in thy long course of Arms,
Hast thou ne're kill'd a Man?
    GRILL. Yes, when a Man wou'd have kill'd me.
    KING. Hast thou not plunder'd from the helpless Poor?
Snatch'd from the sweating Labourer his Food?   295
    GRILL. Sir, I have eaten and drunk in my own defence,
When I was hungry and thirsty.
I have plunder'd,
When you have not paid me ---
I have been content with a Farmer's Daughter,   300
When a better Whore was not to be had.
As for Cutting off a Traytor, I'le execute him lawfully
In my own Function, when I meet him in the Field:
But for your Chamber-practice, that's not my Talent.
    KING. Is my Revenge Unjust, or Tyrannous?   305
Heaven knows, I love not Blood.
    GRILL. No, for your Mercy is your onely Vice.
You may dispatch a Rebel lawfully,
But the mischief is, that Rebel
Has given me my Life at the Barricadoes,   310
And till I have returned his Bribe,
I am not upon even terms with him.
    KING. Give me thy hand, I love thee not the worse;
Make much of Honour, 'tis a Soldier's Conscience,
Thou shalt not do this Act, thou'rt ee'n too good;   315
But keep my Secret, for that's Conscience too.
    GRILL. When I disclose it, think I am a Coward.
    KING. No more of that, I know thou art not one:
Call Lognac hither straight, and St. Malin;
Bid Larchant find some unsuspected means   320
To keep Guards doubled at the Council door,
That none pass in or out, but those I call:
The rest I'le think on further, so farewel.
    GRILL. Heaven bless your Majesty!
Tho I'le not kill him for you, I'de defend you when he's kill'd,   325
For the honest part of the Jobb let me alone.   [Exeunt severally.

Scene II.

The Scene opens, and discovers Men and Women at a Banquet, Malicorne
standing by.

MAL. This is the Solemn Annual Feast I keep,
As this day Twelve Year on this very hour
I sign'd the Contract for my Soul with Hell;
I barter'd it for Honours, Wealth, and Pleasure,
Three things which mortal Men do covet most.   5
And, Faith, I over-sold it to the Fiend:
What, One and twenty Years, Nine yet to come,
How can a Soul be worth so much to Devils?
O how I hug my self, to out-wit these Fools of Hell!
And yet a sudden damp, I know not why,   10
Has seiz'd my spirits, and like a heavy weight
Hangs on their active springs, I want a Song
To rouze me, my blood freezes: Musick there?

A SONG and Dance. *

Shepherdess. Tell me Thirsis, tell your Anguish,
              Why you Sigh, and why you Languish;   15
              When the Nymph whom you Adore,
              Grants the Blessing of Possessing,
              What can Love and I do more?
Shepherd.   Think it's Love beyond all measure,
              Makes me faint away with Pleasure;   20
              Strength of Cordial may destroy,
              And the Blessing of Possessing
              Kills me with excess of Joy.
Shepherdess. Thirsis, how can I believe you?
              But confess, and I'le forgive you;   25
              Men are false, and so are you;
              Never Nature fram'd a Creature
              To enjoy, and yet be true.
Shepherd.   Mine's a Flame beyond expiring,
              Still possessing, still desiring.   30
              Fit for Love's Imperial Crown;
              Ever shining, and refining,
              Still the more 'tis melted down.
                        [Loud knocking at the door.

---

2 Twelve Years Q_{2-3}, C_{1-3}.
* Q_1 omits the song here, but includes it with the music
   (written by Captain Pack) at the end of the play.

                    Enter Servant.

What Noise is that?
        SERV.   An ill-look'd surly Man,
With a hoarse voice, says he must speak with you.   35
        MAL. Tell him I dedicate this day to pleasure,
I neither have, nor will have Business with him.   [Exit Serv.
What louder yet, what sawcy Slave is this?   [Knock louder.

                    Re-enter Servant.

        SERV. He says you have, and must have Business with him,
Come out, or hee'l come in, and spoil your Mirth.   40
        MAL. I wo'n not.
        SERV.   Sir, I dare not tell him so,   [Knock again more fiercely.
My hair stands up in bristles when I see him:
The Dogs run into Corners; the Spade Bitch
Bayes at his back, and howls.
        MAL. Bid him enter, and go off thy self.   [Exit Serv.   45

            Scene closes upon the Company.

    Enter Melanax, an Hour-glass in his hand almost empty.

How dar'st thou interrupt my softer hours?
By Heaven I'le ramm thee in some knotted Oak,
Where thou shalt sigh and groan to whistling winds,
Upon the lonely Plain: Or I'le confine thee
Deep in the Red Sea grov'ling on the Sands,   50
Ten thousand Billows rowling o're thy head.
        MEL. Hoh, hoh, hoh.
        MAL.   Laugh'st, thou malicious Fiend?
I'le ope my Book of bloody Characters,
Shall rumple up thy tender airy Limbs,
Like Parchment on a flame.
        MEL.   Thou canst not do't,   55
Behold this Hour-glass.
        MAL.   Well, and what of that?
        MEL. See'st thou these ebbing Sands?
They run for thee, and when their Race is run,
Thy Lungs the Bellows of thy mortal breath,
Shall sink for ever down, and heave no more.   60

49-50 Divided as follows Q_1-C_2, Summers:

    Upon the lonely Plain:
    Or I'le confine thee deep in the Red Sea grov'ling on the Sands,

    The division of the present text follows that of C_3 and Scott and
    Saintsbury.

MAL. What, resty Fiend?
Nine Years thou hast to serve.
    MEL.   Not full Nine Minutes.
    MAL. Thou ly'st, look on thy Bond, and view the date.
    MEL. Then wilt thou stand to that without Appeal?
    MAL. I will, so help me Heav'n.
    MEL.   So take thee Hell. [Gives him the Bond. 65
There, Fool, behold, who lyes, the Devil or thou?
    MAL. Ha! One and twenty Years are shrunk to twelve,
Do my Eyes dazle?
    MEL.   No, they see too true:
They dazl'd once, I cast a Mist before 'em,
So what was figur'd Twelve, to thy dull sight   70
Appear'd full Twenty one.
    MAL. There's Equity in Heaven for this, a Cheat.
    MEL. Fool, thou hast quitted thy Appeal to Heaven,
To stand to this.
    MAL.   Then I am lost for ever.
    MEL. Thou art.
    MAL.   O why was I not warn'd before?   75
    MEL. Yes, to repent then thou hadst cheated me.
    MAL. Add but a day, but half a day, an hour:
For sixty Minutes I'le forgive nine Years.
    MEL. No not a Moments thought beyond my time:
Dispatch, 'tis much below me to attend   80
For one poor single Fare.
    MAL.   So pitiless?
But yet I may command thee, and I will:
I love the Guise even with my latest breath
Beyond my Soul, and my lost hopes of Heav'n;
I charge thee by my short-liv'd power, disclose   85
What Fate attends my Master.
    MEL.   If he goes
To Council when he next is call'd, he dyes.
    MAL. Who waits?

                Enter Servant.

             Go, give my Lord my last adieu,
Say I shall never see his Eyes agen:
But if he goes when next he's call'd to Council,   90
Bid him believe my latest breath, he dyes.   [Exit Serv.
The Sands run yet, O do not shake the Glass: [Devil shakes the Glass.
I shall be thine too soon, cou'd I repent,
Heaven's not confin'd to Moments, Mercy, Mercy.
    MEL. I see thy Prayers disperst into the winds,   95
And Heaven has puft 'em by:
I was an Angel once of foremost Rank,

---

65 I will, so help] C$_1$-Scott and Saintsbury; I will so, Q$_1$-C$_2$, Summers.

Stood next the shining Throne, and wink'd but half,
So almost gaz'd I glory in the Face
That I could bear it, and star'd farther in,   100
'Twas but a Moments pride, and yet I fell,
For ever fell, but Man, base Earth-born Man,
Sins past a Sum, and might be pardon'd more,
And yet 'tis just; for we were perfect Light,
And saw our Crimes, Man in his Body's mire,   105
Half-soul, Half-clod, sinks blindfold into sin,
Betray'd by Frauds without, and Lusts within.
    MAL.   Then I have hope.
    MEL.   Not so, I preach'd on purpose
To make thee lose this Moment of thy Prayer,
Thy Sand creeps low, Despair, Despair, Despair.   110
    MAL.   Where am I now? Upon the brink of Life,
The Gulph before me, Devils to push me on,
And Heaven behind me closing all its doors.
A thousand Years for ev'ry Hour I've past,
O cou'd I scape so cheap! But Ever, Ever,   115
Still to begin an endless round of Woes,
To be renew'd for Pains, and last for Hell?
Yet can Pains last, when Bodies cannot last?
Can earthy Substance endless Flames endure?
Or when one Body wears, and flits away,   120
Do Souls thrust forth another Crust of Clay?
To fence and guard their tender forms from fire ---
I feel my heart-strings rend, I'm here, I'm gone:
Thus Men too careless of their future State,
Dispute, know nothing, and believe too late.   125
       [A flash of Lightning, they sink together.

    Duke of Guise, Cardinal, Aumale.

    CARD.   A dreadful Message from a dying Man,
A Prophesie indeed!
For Souls just quitting Earth, peep into Heaven,
Make swift Acquaintance, with their Kindred forms,
And Partners of Immortal Secrets grow.   130
    AUM.   'Tis good to lean on the securer side:
When Life depends, the mighty Stake is such,
Fools fear too little, and they dare too much.

    Enter Archbishop.

    GUISE.   You have prevail'd, I will not go to Council,
I have provok'd my Soveraign past a Pardon,   135
It but remains to doubt if he dare kill me:
Then if he dares but to be just, I dye,
'Tis too much odds against me, I'le depart,
And finish Greatness at some safer time.

ARCHB. By Heaven 'tis Harry's Plot to fright you hence,   140
That, Coward-like, you might forsake your Friends.
  GUISE. The Devil foretold it dying Malicorne.
  ARCHB. Yes, some Court-Devil, no doubt:
If you depart, consider, good my Lord,
You are the Master-spring that move our Fabrick,   145
Which once remov'd, our Motion is no more.
Without your Presence, which buoys up our hearts,
The League will sink beneath a Royal Name:
Th' inevitable Yoke prepar'd for Kings,
Will soon be shaken off; Things done, repeal'd;   150
And Things undone, past future Means to do.
  CARD. I know not, I begin to taste his Reasons.
  ARCHB. Nay, were the danger certain of your stay,
An Act so mean would lose you all your Friends,
And leave you single to the Tyrant's Rage: 155
Then better 'tis to hazard Life alone,
Than Life, and Friends, and Reputation too.
  GUISE. Since more I am confirm'd, I'le stand the shock: .
Where e're he dares to call, I dare to go.
My Friends are many, faithful and united,   160
He will not venture on so rash a deed:
And now I wonder I should fear that Force,
Which I have us'd to Conquer and Contemn.

Enter Marmoutier.

  ARCHB. Your Tempter comes, perhaps, to turn the Scale,
And warn you not to go.
  GUISE.   O fear her not,   165
I will be there. What can she mean, Repent?   [Exeunt Archbishop and
Or is it cast betwixt the King and her   Cardinal.
To sound me; Come what will, it warms my heart
With secret joy, which these my ominous Statesmen
Left dead within me, ha! she turns away.   170
  MAR. Do you not wonder at this Visit, Sir?
  GUISE. No, Madam, I at last have gain'd the Point
Of mightiest Minds to wonder now at nothing.
  MAR. --- Believe me, Guise, 'twere gallantly resolv'd,
If you cou'd carry't on the inside too,   175
Why came that Sigh uncall'd? For Love of me
Partly perhaps, but more for thirst of Glory,
Which now agen dilates it self in Smiles,
As if you scorn'd that I should know your purpose.
  GUISE. I change 'tis true, because I love you still,   180
Love you, O Heav'n, ev'n in my own despight,
I tell you all even at that very Moment,

_____

166 <u>Printed</u> <u>as</u> <u>two</u> <u>lines</u> Q_{1+}.

I know you straight betray me to the King.

  MAR. O Guise, I never did, but, Sir, I come
To tell you, I must never see you more.   185

  GUISE. The King's at Blois, and you have reason for't,
Therefore what am I to expect from pity?
From yours, I mean, when you behold me slain.

  MAR. First answer me, and then I'le speak my heart,
Have you, O Guise, since your last Solemn Oaths,   190
Stood firm to what you swore? Be plain, my Lord,
Or run it o're awhile, because agen
I tell you I must never see you more.

  GUISE. Never! She's set on by the King to sift me,
Why by that Never then, all I have sworn   195
Is true, as that the King designs to end me.

  MAR. Keep your Obedience, by the Saints you live.

  GUISE. Then mark, 'tis judg'd by heads grown white in Council,
This very day he means to cut me off.

  MAR. --- By Heaven then you'r forsworn, you've broke your Vows. 200

  GUISE. --- By you the Justice of the Earth I have not.

  MAR. --- By you Dissembler of the world you have,
I know the King.

  GUISE.   --- I do believe you, Madam.

  MAR. --- I have try'd you both.

  GUISE.   --- Not me, the King you mean.

  MAR. --- Do these o'reboyling Answers suit the Guise, 205
But go to Council, Sir, there shew your truth,
If you are innocent you're safe, but O
If I shou'd chance to see you stretcht along,
Your Love, O Guise, and your Ambition gone,
That venerable Aspect pale with death,   210
I must conclude you merited your end.

  GUISE. --- You must, you will, and smile upon my Murder.

  MAR. Therefore if you are conscious of a Breach,
Confess it to me: Lead me to the King,
He has promis'd me to conquer his Revenge,   215
And place you next him; therefore if you're right,
Make me not fear it by Asseverations:
But speak your heart, and O resolve me truly.

  GUISE. --- Madam, I ha' thought, and trust you with my Soul;
You saw but now my parting with my Brother,   220
The Prelate too of Lyons, 'twas debated
Warmly against me that I should go on.

  MAR. --- Did I not tell you, Sir?

  GUISE.   --- True, but in spight
Of those Imperial Arguments they urg'd,
I was not to be work'd from second thought,   225
There we broke off; And, mark me, if I live,
You are the Saint that makes a Convert of me.

  MAR. Go then, O Heaven! Why must I still suspect you?
Why heaves my Heart? And why o'reflow my Eyes?

Yet if you live, O Guise, there, there's the Cause,   230
I never shall converse, nor see you more.
    GUISE. O say not so, for Once again I'le see you,
Were you this very Night to lodge with Angels,
Yet say not Never; for I hope by Virtue
To merit Heaven, and wed you late in Glory.   235
    MAR. This Night, my Lord, I'm a Recluse for ever.
    GUISE. Ha! Stay till Morning Tapers are too dim;
Stay till the Sun rises to salute you;
Stay till I lead you to that dismal Den
Of Virgins, buried quick, and stay for Ever.   240
    MAR. Alas! Your Suit is vain, for I have vow'd it:
Nor was there any other way to clear
Th' imputed stains of my suspected Honour.
    GUISE. Hear me a word, one Sigh, one Tear, at parting,
And one last Look; for, O my earthly Saint,   245
I see your Face pale, as the Cherubins
At Adam's Fall.
    MAR.   O Heaven I now confess,
My heart bleeds for thee Guise.
    GUISE. Why Madam, why?
    MAR.   Because by this Disorder,
And that sad Fate that bodes upon your Brow,   250
I do believe you love me more than Glory.
    GUISE. Without an Oath I do, therefore have Mercy,
And think not Death cou'd make me tremble thus:
Be pitiful to those Infirmities
Which thus Unman me, stay till the Council's o're;   255
If you are pleas'd to grant an hour or two
To my last Pray'r, I'le thank you as my Saint;
If you refuse me, Madam, I'le not murmur.
    MAR. Alas, my Guise! O Heav'n, what did I say?
But take it, take it, if it be too kind,   260
Honour may pard'n it, since it is my last.
    GUISE. O let me crawl, Vile as I am, and kiss [She gives him her Hand.
Your Sacred Robe. Is't possible, Your Hand!
O that it were my last expiring Moment,
For I shall never taste the like again.   265
    MAR. Farewell my Proselyte, your better Genius
Watch your Ambition.
    GUISE.   I have none but you,
Must I ne're see you more?
    MAR.   I have sworn you must not:
Which Thought thus roots me here, melts my Resolves,   [Weeps.
And makes me loyter when the Angels call me.   270
    GUISE. O ye Celestial Dewes! O Paradise!
O Heav'n! O Joys! Ne're to be tasted more.
    MAR. Nay take a little more, cold Marmoutier,
The temperate, devoted Marmoutier
Is gone, a last Embrace I must bequeath you.   275

GUISE. And O let me return it with another.
MAR. Farewell for ever; Ah, Guise, tho now we part
In the bright Orbs prepar'd us by our Fates,
Our Souls shall meet --- Farewell --- and Io's sing above,
Where no Ambition, nor State-Crime, the happier spirits prove,   280
But all are blest, and all enjoy an everlasting Love.   [Exit Mar.

Guise solus.

GUISE. Glory, where art thou? Fame, Revenge, Ambition,
Where are you fled? there's Ice upon my Nerves:
My Salt, my Mettal, and my Spirits gone,
Pall'd as a Slave that's Bed-rid with an Ague,   285
I wish my flesh were off: What now! Thou bleed'st
Three, and no more! What then? And why what then?
But just three drops! And why not just three drops,
As well as four or five, or five and twenty?

Enter a Page.

PAGE. My Lord, your Brother and the Archbishop wait you.   290
GUISE. I come, down Devil, ha! Must I stumble too?
Away ye Dreams, What if it thunder'd Now?
Or if a Raven cross'd me in my way:
Or now it comes, because last Night I dreamt
The Council-Hall was hung with Crimson round,   295
And all the Cieling plaister'd o're with black.
No more, blue Fires, and ye dull rowling Lakes,
Fathomless Caves, ye Dungeons of old Night,
Fantoms be gone, if I must dye, I'le fall
True Polititian, and defie you all.   300

Scene III. The Court before the Council-Hall.

Grillon, Larchant, Soldiers plac'd, People crowding.

GRILL. Are your Guards doubl'd, Captain?
LARCH.   Sir, They are.
GRILL. When the Guise comes, remember your Petition,
Make way there for his Eminence; Give back,
Your Eminence comes late.

Enter two Cardinals, Counsellors, the Cardinal of Guise,
Archbishop of Lyons, last the Guise.

GUISE. Well, Colonel, Are we Friends?
GRILL.   Faith, I think not.   5

GUISE. Give me your Hand.
GRILL.   No, for that gives a Heart.
GUISE. Yet we shall clasp in Heaven.
GRILL.   By Heaven we shall not,
Unless it be with Gripes.
GUISE.   True Grillon still.
LARCH. My Lord.
GUISE.   Ha Captain, you are well attended,
If I mistake not, Sir, your Number's doubl'd.   10
LARCH. All these have serv'd against the Hereticks,
And therefore beg your Grace you would remember
Their Wounds, and lost Arrears.
GUISE.   It shall be done.
Agen my heart, there is a weight upon thee,
But I will sigh it off, Captain Farewell. [Exeunt Cardinal, Guise, &c. 15
GRILL. Shut the Hall-door, and bar the Castle-Gates:
March, March there Closer yet, Captain to the door.   [Ex.

Scene IV. Council-Hall.

Guise, Archbishop, Cardinal.*

GUISE. I do not like my self to day.
ARCHB.   --- A Qualm, he dares not.
CARD. --- That's one Man's thought, he dares, and that's anothers.

Enter Grillon.

GUISE. O Marmoutier, Ha never see thee more,
Peace my tumultuous heart, why jolt my spirits
In this unequal Circling of my Blood,   5
I'le stand it while I may, O Mighty Nature!
Why this Alarm, why dost thou call me on
To fight, yet rob my Limbs of all their use.   [Swoons.
CARD. Ha! He's fall'n, chafe him: He comes agen.
GUISE. I beg your Pardons, Vapours no more.
GRILL.   Th' Effect   10
Of last Nights Lechery with some working Whore.

Enter Revol.

REVOL. My Lord of Guise, the King would speak with you.
GUISE. O Cardinal, O Lyons, but no more,
Yes, one word more, thou hast a Priviledge   [To the Cardinal.

---

*Guise, Archbishop, Cardinal.]; <u>om.</u> Q_{1+}.

To speak with a Recluse, O therefore tell her,   15
If never thou behold'st me breathe again,
Tell her I sigh'd it last --- O Marmoutier.   [Exit bowing.
    CARD. You will have all things your own way, my Lord,
By Heav'n, I have strange horror on my Soul.
    ARCHB. I say agen, that Henry dares not do't.   20
    CARD. Beware your Grace of Minds that bear like him,
I know he scorns to stoop to mean Revenge;
But when some mightier Mischief shocks his Toure,
He shoots at once with thunder on his wings,
And makes it Air, but hark, my Lord, 'tis doing.   25
    GUISE. within.] Murderers, Villains!
    ARCHB. I hear your Brother's voice, run to the door.
    CARD. Help, help, the Guise is murder'd.
    ARCHB.   Help, help.
    GRILL. Cease your vain Cryes, you are the King's Prisoners,
Take 'em Dugast into your Custody.   30
    CARD. We must obey, my Lord, for Heaven calls us.   [Exeunt.

The Scene draws behind it a Traverse.

The Guise is assaulted by Eight, They stab him
in all parts, but most in the head.

    GUISE. O Villains! Hell-hounds! Hold: [Half draws, his Sword, is held.
Murder'd, O basely, and not draw my Sword,
Dog, Logniac, but my own blood choaks me, [Flings himself upon   35
Down, Villain, Down, I'm gone, O Marmoutier.   him --- Dies.

The Traverse is drawn.

The King rises from his Chair, comes forward with his
Cabinet Council.

    KING. Open the Closet, and let in the Council;
Bid Dugast execute the Cardinal,
Seize all the Factious Leaders, as I order'd,
And every one be answer'd on your Lives.

Enter Queen-Mother, followed by the Counsellors.

O, Madam, you are welcome, how goes your health?   40
    Q. M. A little mended, Sir, what have you done?
    KING. That which has made me King of France, for there
The King of Paris at your Feet lies dead.
    Q. M. You have cut out dangerous work, but make it up
With speed and resolution.
    KING.   Yes, I'le wear   45
The Fox no longer, but put on the Lyon;
And since I could resolve to take the Heads
Of this great Insurrection, you the Members

Look to't, Beware, turn from your stubbornness,
And learn to know me, for I will be King.   50
    GRILL. 'Sdeath, how the Traytors lowre and quake, and droop,
And gather to the wing of his protection,
As if they were his Friends, and fought his Cause.
    KING. looking ⎫ Be witness, Heaven, I gave him treble warning,
    upon Guise. ⎭ He's gone, no more disperse, and think upon't,   55
Beware my Sword, which if I once unsheath,
By all the Reverence due to Thrones and Crowns,
Nought shall atone the Vows of speedy Justice,
Till Fate to Ruine every Traytor brings,
That dares the Vengeance of indulgent Kings.   60

---

56 for if Q₃.

ADVERTISEMENT.

There was a Preface intended to this Play, in Vindication of it, against
two scurrilous Libels lately printed: But it was judg'd, that a Defence
of this nature wou'd require more room, than a Preface reasonably could
allow: For this Cause, and for the Importunity of the Stationers, who
hasten'd their Impression, 'tis deferr'd for some little time, and will   5
be printed by it self. Most men are already of Opinion, that neither of
the Pamphlets deserve an Answer, because they are stuff'd with open
Falsities, and sometimes contradict each other; but, for once, they shall
have a day or two thrown away upon them, though I break an old Custom
for their sakes, which was to scorn them.   10

FINIS.

EPILOGUE.

Written by the same Author*: Spoken by Mrs. Cooke.

Much Time and Trouble this poor Play has cost;
And, Faith, I doubted once the Cause was lost.
Yet no one Man was meant; nor Great, nor Small;
Our Poets, like frank Gamesters, threw at All.
They took no single Aim:---   5
But, like bold Boys, true to their Prince and hearty,
Huzza'd, and fir'd Broad-sides at the whole Party.
Duels are Crimes; but when the Cause is right,
In Battel, every Man is bound to fight.
For what shou'd hinder Me to sell my Skin   10
Dear as I cou'd, if once my hand were in?
Se Defendendo never was a Sin.
'Tis a fine World, my Masters, right or wrong,
The Whiggs must talk, and Tories hold their Tongue.
They must do all they can---   15
But We, Forsooth, must bear a Christian mind;
And fight, like Boys, with One Hand ty'd behind;
Nay, and when one Boy's down, 'twere wond'rous wise,
To cry, Box fair, and give him time to rise.
When Fortune favours, none but Fools will dally: 20
Wou'd any of you Sparks, if Nan or Mally
Tipt you th' inviting Wink, stand shall I, shall I?
A Trimmer cry'd, (that heard me tell this Story)
Fie, Mistress Cooke! Faith you're too rank a Tory!
Wish not Whiggs hang'd, but pity their hard Cases;   25
You Women love to see Men make wry Faces.
Pray, Sir, said I, don't think me such a Jew;
I say no more, but give the Dev'l his due.
Lenitives, says he, suit best with our Condition.
Jack Ketch, says I, 's an excellent Physician.   30
I love no Bloud --- Nor I, Sir, as I breath;
But hanging is a fine dry kind of Death.
We Trimmers are for holding all things even:
Yes --- just like him that hung 'twixt Hell and Heaven.
Have we not had Mens Lives enow already?   35
Yes sure: --- but you're for holding all things steddy:
Now since the Weight hangs all on one side, Brother,
You Trimmers shou'd, to poize it, hang on t'other.
Damn'd Neuters, in their middle way of steering,
Are neither Fish, nor Flesh, nor good Red-Herring: 40
Not Whiggs, nor Tories they; nor this, nor that;

---

* That is, Dryden, the author of the Prologue.
22 shill I, shall I? C_{1-3}.
31 breathe; C_2-Scott and Saintsbury.

Not Birds, nor Beasts; but just a kind of Bat:
A Twilight Animal; true to neither Cause,
With Tory Wings, but Whiggish Teeth and Claws.

Another
EPILOGUE*
Intended to have been Spoken to the
PLAY, before it was forbidden,
last Summer.

Written by Mr. Dryden

Two Houses joyn'd, two Poets to a Play?
You noisy Whiggs will sure be pleas'd to day;
It looks so like two Shrieves the City way.
But since our Discords and Divisions cease,
You, Bilbo Gallants, learn to keep the Peace: 5
Make here no Tilts: let our Poor Stage alone;
Or if a decent Murther must be done,
Pray take a Civil turn to Marybone.
If not, I swear we'll pull up all our Benches;
Not for your sakes, but for our Orange-Wenches: 10
For you thrust wide sometimes; and many a Spark,
That misses one, can hit the other Mark.
This makes our Boxes full; for Men of Sense
Pay their four Shillings in their own defence:
That safe behind the Ladies they may stay;   15
Peep o'er the Fan, and Judg the bloudy Fray.
But other Foes give Beauty worse alarms;
The Posse Poetarum's up in Arms:
No Womans Fame their Libells has escap'd;
Their Ink runs Venome, and their Pens are Clap'd.   20
When Sighs and Pray'rs their Ladies cannot move,
They Rail, write Treason, and turn Whiggs to Love.
Nay, and I fear they worse Designs advance,
There's a damn'd Love-trick new brought o'er from France,
We charm in vain, and dress, and keep a Pother,   25
While those false Rogues are Ogling one another.
All Sins besides, admit some expiation;
But this against our Sex is plain Damnation.
They joyn for Libells too, these Women-haters;
And as they club for Love, they club for Satyrs: 30
The best on't is they hurt not: for they wear

---

* This Epilogue is based on the text of the 1683 edition printed with
the Prologue to the Duke of Guise and the Epilogue "for Jacob
Tonson, at the Judge's Head in Chancery Lane." See MacDonald,
item 101, for collation. The copy-text is that of the Folger Shakespeare Library, printed with permission. It is easily identified
by the number "D 2338" on the upper right-hand margin of B2^V.
29 They oyn Summers.
29 woman haters; Scott and Saintsbury; Women haters; Summers.

Stings in their Tayls; their onely Venom's there.
'Tis true, some Shot at first the Ladies hit,
Which able Marksmen made and Men of Wit:
But now the Fools give fire, whose Bounce is louder;   35
And yet, like mere Train-bands, they shoot but Powder.
Libells, like Plots, sweep all in their first Fury;
Then dwindle like an Ignoramus Jury:
Thus Age begins with Towzing and with Tumbling;
But Grunts, and Groans, and ends at last in Fumbling.   40

FINIS

A Song in the Fifth ACT of the DUKE of GUISE.

Shepherdeß.

TELL me *Thirsis*, tell your Anguish,

why you Sigh, and why you Languish; when the Nymph whom

you A—dore, grants the Bles—sing of Pos—ses—sing,

what can Love and I do more? what can Love, what can Love and

Shepherd.

I do more?   Think it's Love be-yond all measure,

A Song in the *Duke* of **Guise**.

makes me faint a--way with Pleafure; ftrength of Cor--dial

may deftroy, and the Bleffing of Poffeffing kills me with ex-

Shepherdeß.

cefs of Joy.   *Thir--fis,* how can I believe you?

but con--fefs, and I'le forgive you; Men are falfe, and

fo are you; ne—ver Nature fram'd a Creature to en-

A Song in the Duke of Guise.

joy, and yet be true; ne—ver Nature fram'd a Creature

to en—joy, and yet be true; to en—joy, and yet be

Soft. true, and yet be true. *Shepherd.* Mine's a Flame be-

yond ex——pi——ring, still pof—fef—fing, still de——fi——ring,

fit for Love's Im————pe——rial Crown; e—ver fhi—ning,

A Song in the Duke of Guise.

and re——fi——ning, ftill the more 'tis mel——ted down.

Chorus together.

Mine's a Flame beyond ex-pi-ring, ftill pof-fef-fing, ftill de-

Mine's a Flame beyond ex-pi-ring, ftill pof-fef-fing, ftill de-

firing, fit for Love's Im-pe-rial Crown; e-ver fhining, and re-

firing, fit for Love's Im-pe-rial Crown; e-ver fhining, and re-

fining, ftill the more 'tis   mel————ted down.

fining, ftill the more 'tis, ftill the more 'tis melted down.

FINIS.

Conſtantine

THE

GREAT;

A

TRAGEDY.

ACTED at the

Theatre-Royal,

By their Majeſties Servants.

Written by *NAT. LEE*, Gent.

LONDON,

Printed by *H. Hills* Jun. for *R. Bently*, in *Ruſſel-Street*, *Covent-Garden*, and *J. Tonſon*, at the *Judges-Head* in *Chancery-Lane* near *Fleet-ſtreet*. 1684.

CONSTANTINE THE GREAT

Introduction

I Date and Stage History:

Although Professor Ham argues that CONSTANTINE THE GREAT was written during Lee's earlier career, his period of heroic drama, there seems to be little evidence to support such belief.[1] The political implications of the play provide evidence sufficient to make untenable his opinion that Lee was too near a mental collapse in 1683 to write a play, however poor; for these implications rather unmistakably refer to events that took place in that year.[2] And there is no evidence either external or internal that Lee was mentally incapacitated at the time. It was assuredly written in the summer and autumn of 1683 and was brought to the Drury Lane stage on or before 12 November of that year.[3] It was the last play, so far as we know, that Lee completed, and the last but one that he brought upon the stage. Furthermore, since its initial season it has not again been produced.

II Sources:

Langbaine says that many authors have written upon the subject of Constantine's illustrious actions, and that he thinks Ammiamus Marcellinus told the story of Fausta and Crispus. Though he mentions them as having handled the story, he does not say that "Socrates, Sozomen, Eusebius, Zonaras" and the rest were used as sources.[4] It has been shown by Genest and all later commentators that the story does not appear in Marcellinus,[5] and indeed that there is very little that is historical in the play. The best accounts of its sources are found in Häfele's introduction to his edition of the play and in Van Lennep's work. Both agree that the dependence upon the historians is slight, so slight indeed that Van Lennep thinks Lee must have had as an intermediary plot-source a romance on the subject of Constantine, such, for instance, as he used in THE PRINCESS OF CLEVE.[6] It is possible that Lee used Zosimus and Zonares, whose work was available to him in the Latin and in the French,[6a] though his account of the Fausta-Crispus story differs greatly from theirs. They both say, for instance, that Fausta was the wife of Constantine, that Crispus was the son of Constantine by an earlier wife, and that upon suspicion of intimacy between them Constantine put both to death, Fausta being killed in a poisoned bath.

In addition to the hints that he may have had either directly or indirectly from the historians, Lee makes use of plot situations and devices that were to be found in the English and French drama of his own and the preceding ages. For instance, as Van Lennep demonstrates at some length, the plot situation of a father and son in love with the same woman was almost commonplace in the drama of the Restoration: Lee himself had used it in MITHRIDATES; Racine, in MITHRIDATE (1673); Dryden, in AURENG-ZEBE; and Otway, in DON CARLOS (1676). It is quite probable that Lee took from Racine the scene of the King's tricking Monime into betraying her lover. Even the dialogue of Lee's scene is similar to that of Racine. Perhaps, as Ward mentions and as Van Lennep is at some pains to show,[7] Lee owes an even greater debt to Otway's DON CARLOS: in both CONSTANTINE and DON CARLOS a picture and a poisoned bath are used; like Serena in the one, Eboli in the other is hopelessly in love with the hero and like her secures his portrait; the villain, Rui Gomez in DON CARLOS, prepares the poisoned bath for one of the antagonists (though he is not in the end thrown into it, but is stabbed); Don John, the King's brother in DON CARLOS, is the firm friend of Don Carlos, the King's son; and, finally, each play has a scene in which the brother tries to prevent the King from killing his son. Lee would appear to be consciously following Otway in DON CARLOS, a fact which accounts for the heroic manner of CONSTANTINE and easily invalidates Ham's suggestion of an earlier date for the play. Thus the poet is perhaps more deeply indebted to the recent drama than he is to any ancient story.

III Criticism:

The criticism of CONSTANTINE THE GREAT, as is frequently the case with Lee's plays, has been casual, lacking in detail, and generally impression-istic. Langbaine makes no mention of the quality of this play, and Downes ignores it entirely. Charles Dibden (1800) thinks the play "not without merit, but it has not enough to entitle it to permanent success."[8] An anonymous article in the RETROSPECTIVE REVIEW (1821) maintains that CONSTANTINE THE GREAT "is the most utterly worthless of all his compositions,"[9] but Genest thinks that, though Lee in this play deviated grossly from history, he has written "a tolera-bly good Tragedy."[10] R. Mosen (1879) thinks the plot is most objectionable, its parts being confused and disordered;[11] but Sanders, in his survey of Lee's plays, says, charitably, that CONSTANTINE shows Lee's "great power over the emo-tions," that it has something of THE ORPHAN and MITHRIDATES in it, that it has an excellent villain in Arius, and that it has "many touches of Lee's old power; but it is not one of his best plays," for his powers were too far gone by the time he wrote it.[12] Lee's power to portray emotions is evident here, especially his ability to present pity.

The later historians of the drama say little. Ward remarks that it "becomes a mere drama of erotic passion;"[13] Dobrée, that it has in it reminiscences of Webster;[14] William Archer, that "THEODOSIUS and CONSTANTINE THE GREAT, do, indeed, contain striking scenes handled with a certain force; but there is no sustained constructive power in either play;"[15] Elwin, that it "compares credi-tably with the conventional heroic drama of the day;"[16] and Montague Summers, that it is "an interesting and powerful drama."[17] Häfele, in his edition, though he assembles most of what has been said critically of the play, himself ventures no judgment. Finally, Van Lennep thinks CONSTANTINE a dull play, showing without a doubt that Lee's dramatic powers were upon the wane by 1683.[18] Al-together it has received little critical attention.

And perhaps it has not merited much attention. It is certainly true, as Mosen says, that the plot is confused, and it is also true that certain characters lack motivation. Why, for instance, if Constantine believes that Arius is a traitor (as he says he does), does he allow Arius to go free and continue his evil doings? It is true also that the play lacks a dedication and that the author trusted others to give it an epilogue if not a prologue. Generally its production and publication seem to have been accomplished in some haste. This haste is easily explained on the basis that the author and producers wanted it to get before the public while it was yet politically exciting. It might have been a better play if the author had taken more time to write it. Its weaknesses are as easily attributed to his lack of time as to his waning powers. A political play, as this one undoubtedly is, is most exciting and most successful when presented while the events which brought it into being are yet fresh in the minds of the theatre-goers. They recognized

Arius undoubtedly as Shaftesbury, Dalmatius as the Duke of York, perhaps Lycinius as Algernon Sidney, and Crispus as Monmouth; and the sensational events
of the Rye-House Plot here presented, albeit by suggestion and political parallel,
were so fresh in the public mind as to make exciting their immediate presentation.

In spite of its obvious weaknesses, CONSTANTINE, nevertheless, has some
merits. Lee was a practiced popular dramatist by the time he wrote it, and he
knew pretty well what would go on the London stage. As an acting piece, then,
it was not unsuccessful. Like the heroic plays (to which it has often been compared), it does not end in the death of the principals, but with that of the villain --
a conclusion calculated to please the audience, especially since the political implications were to be satisfied. It opens dramatically with an excellent song set to
the music of Farmer, [19] and sung by angels who descend with banners in their
hands. At the conclusion of the song they ascend, and the sleeping Constantine
wakes. This opening is based on the opening scene of THEODOSIUS. Quite as
dramatic is the use of the poisoned bath at the close, wherein the evil Arius is
(unhistorically) ironically destroyed by the device he had planned for others.
There are also rapid-moving scenes in which the dialogue is effective. In the
first scene, for example, the dialogue between Constantine and Sylvester moves
well, accomplishing the exposition necessary and yet carrying forward the action.
Likewise in Scene ii of the first act, the dialogue between Crispus and Annibal is
broken and sharp. And toward the end of Act II Crispus' discovery that his father
is apparently betrothed to Fausta makes good "theatre." Occasionally, too, there
are good lines; and one must agree with Sanders that Arius is a good villain. Lee
could still write effective scenes for the stage, though no one will claim for CON-
STANTINE THE GREAT a place among his best works.

IV Text:

    Texts compared:

Q_1	R. Bentley and J. Tonson,	1684
C_1	R. Wellington,	1713
C_2	M. P. & Sam. Chapman,	1722
C_3	W. Feales ...,	1734
Häfele	Walter Häfele (ENGLISCHE TEXTBIBLIOTHEK)	
	Heidelberg,	1933

As copy-text for this edition, the first quarto, 1684, has been followed.
Five copies of this quarto have been compared for possible stop-press corrections. One of these five copies is in the Library of the University of Kentucky;
the other four are in the Folger Shakespeare Library. Variants among these
copies are recorded in the textual notes. The copies are designated as follows:
Q_1(KU), Q_1(DFo 1), Q_1(DFo 2), Q_1(DFo 3), and Q_1(DFo 4). [20]

The edition has the following collation:

4°; A-H^4 I^2, 34 leaves, pp. [8], 1-60.

[A1^r] : title-page; [A1^V] : blank; A2^r: [double rule] Dramatis Personae. ;
A2^V: A Catalogue of PLAYS, Printed for / R. Bentley. / A3: PROLOGUE. ; A4:
EPILOGUE. ; B1^r: [double rule] Constantine / THE / GREAT. / [rule] / The
First Act. Scene 1st. / [rule] , and text; B1^V-I2^V: text. Running title: CON-
STANTINE The GREAT.

A comparison of these five copies reveals no stop-press corrections among
them. There appear to be only a few failures in inking. Thus, the end of line
55, Act III, i, Q_1(KU), reads "Secr", whereas all copies of the Folger Q_1 read

"Secrets." Similarly, the end of line 188 of Act III, i, failed to ink, or had lost the type, in Q_1(KU) and Q_1(DFo 1), and thus reads "To wh," whereas in Q_1(DFo 2-4) the line inked perfectly, or the type was in place, and we get the correct reading "To whom?" Another instance of the sort is found in Act IV, i, 132. Otherwise the copies are virtually identical. There is no indication in the copies examined that the author or the printer made any changes in the text, once it was set.

Indeed, there is little evidence, as Häfele suggests, that Lee had anything to do with the preparation of this play for the press or with the printing of it. It has no dedication; the epilogue was not done by the author; and there are passages in the text which the author would surely have corrected had he prepared them for a printer or seen them in proof. Further evidence of the laxity in publication may be seen in that the play was printed from a prompter's copy. That it was from a prompter's copy is best illustrated by the directions left in the text: the compositor retained them in inner and outer formes C and inner forme D. Thus, we have opposite line 43 of Act II, i, "Ready Trumpets, a March at distance," and a few lines later we find "Call Serena." The trumpets that are called sound off at a distance, according to a direction opposite line 63, and Serena's entry is marked between lines 79-80. At least three other instances of this sort occur, plainly indicating the prompter's copy as source for the text.

In spite of the lack of careful supervision of the printing, however, the text is not a bad one. Generally the meaning is clear. Later editors did not find many unintelligible passages, nor did they offer a great many corrections of their own. Such as they did make were mostly corrections of obvious errors; a few were simply rationalizations. Thus, the 1722 edition corrects "This Son" (Act II, i, 411) to "Thy Son.", and the 1713 edition correctly prints as one line what appears as two lines in Q_1 (line 11, Act III, i). Such correction is common. The fact that there were no quartos after 1684, moreover, perhaps saved the text from the customary deterioration brought about by reprintings. C_1 was printed from Q_1, as was to be expected; C_2 from C_1; and C_3 from C_2.

The modern text of Häfele, 1933, is carefully prepared. It follows Q_1 as copy-text; it attempts to record, not only the substantive variations of the later editions, but also a great many of the accidentals, most of which have no bearing upon the meaning. The line numbering of Häfele is based on the line divisions of the text of Q_1; hence partial lines are treated as complete lines and receive numbers accordingly. Since there is a question as to the authorship of the Prologue and the Epilogue, Häfele is at pains to compare other editions of these found in broadsides and in the works of Otway and of Dryden. Actually he finds no substantive variations among the various texts; nor does he throw any further light upon the authorship of the two. [21] It has not been considered necessary to reprint here Häfele's textual notes.

PROLOGUE.

Spoken by Mr. Goodman.

What think ye meant wise Providence, when first
Poets were made? I'd tell you, if I durst,
That 'twas in Contradiction to Heaven's Word,
That when its Spirit o're the Waters stir'd,
When it saw All, and said That All was good,   5
The Creature Poet was not understood.
For, were it worth the Pains of six long Days,
To mould Retailers of dull Third-Day-Plays,
That starve out threescore Years in hopes of Bays.
'Tis plain they ne're were of the first Creation,   10
But came by meer Equiv'cal Generation.
Like Rats in Ships, without Coition bred;
As hated too as they are, and unfed.
Nature their Species sure must needs disown,
Scarce knowing Poets, less by Poets known.   15
Yet this poor Thing, so scorn'd, and set at nought,
Ye all pretend to, and would fain be thought.
Disabl'd wasting Whore-Masters are not
Prouder to own the Brats they never got,
Than Fumbling, Itching Rhimers of the Town,   20
T' adopt some base-born Song that's not their own.
Spite of his State, My Lord sometimes descends,
To please the Importunity of Friends.
The dullest he thought most for Business fit,
'Twill venture his bought Place, to aim at Wit.   25
And though he sinks with his Imploys of State,
Till Common Sense forsake him, he'll Translate.
The Poet and the Whore alike complains,
Of trading Quality, that spoils their Gains;
The Lords will Write, and Ladies will have Swains.   30
Therefore, all you who have Male Issue born,
Under the Starving Sign of Capricorn;
Prevent the Malice of their Stars in time,
And warn them early from the Sin of Rhime:
Tell 'em how Spencer starv'd, how Cowley mourn'd,   35
How Butler's Faith and Service was return'd;
And if such Warning they refuse to take,
This last Experiment, O Parents, make!
With Hands behind them see the Offender ty'd,
The Parish Whip, and Beadle by his side.   40
Then lead him to some Stall that does expose
The Authors he loves most, there rub his Nose;

---

9 Bays? C_{1+}.
11 of mere equiv'cal Generation: C_{2+}.

Till like a Spaniel lash'd, to know Command,
He by the due Correction understand,
To keep his Brains clean, and not foul the Land.   45
Till he against his Nature learn to strive,
And get the Knack of Dullness how to thrive.

DRAMATIS PERSONAE

Constantine	Mr. Smith.	
Dalmatius	Mr. Griffin.	
Crispus	Mr. Betterton.	
Annibal	Mr. Goodman.	
Lycinius	Mr. Wiltshire.	5
Arius	Mr. Gillo.	
Labienus	Mr. Perin.	
Eubulus	Mr. Saunders.	
Sylvester	Mr. Bowman.	

WOMEN

Fausta	Mrs. Barrey.	10
Serena	Mrs. Cook.	

Angels, Priests, Guards, and Attendants.

---

8 Eubulus] C$_{2+}$, and in the text of the play; Eubolus Q$_1$-C$_1$.
10 Mrs. Barry. C$_{2-3}$.

Act I. Scene I.

Constantine sleeping in a Pavillion, Sylvester standing at distance,
two Angels descend with Banners in their hands.

This Motto, In hoc signo vince, Writ in Gold.

I Angel sings. *

    1. ANG. Awake: O Constantine! awake;
Or in thy sleep the Prospect take!
Here in this hallow'd streaming Gold,
The Prospect of thy Life behold:
This Emblem of a bleeding Love,   5
Shall both thy Cross and Triumph prove.
For, alas! 'tis decreed by the Heavenly Doom,
To purge thy past Crimes, there's a Torment to come.
    2. ANG. Yet, after the Storm, believe in me,
No more disturb'd thy thoughts shall be,   10
But all Serene as a breathless Sea.
    CHOR. And still thy Handmaid Victory,
Where er'e thou go'st, shall wait on thee;
And all shall end in Harmony.
    3. ANG. speaks. Awake, and ponder the Celestial Song;   15
Thy vow'd Conversion is delay'd too long.
Awake; remember the Celestial Doom,
That threatned Torments, and a Cross to come.
Yet after all the Menaces of Fate,
Be wash'd: And Calms shall on those Tempests wait,   20
For true Repentance never comes too late.   [Angels ascend.

#

Constantine awakes.

CONST. Stay! I adjure you, by the Holy Name,
That bows your Airy Heads; I charge you stay:
They're gone: Those Beauteous Legates of the Skies;
And left me puzling here to die in doubt,   25
Unless Sylvester guide me with a Clew,
Through the dark Mazes of this folding Dream.
    SYLV. To purge your past Crimes, there's a Torment to come.
Ay, there the Torment too repeated thrice.
    CONST. But say, what Torment?   30
    SYLV. A dangerous Torment, govern'd by ill Stars:

---

* I Angel sings.] C_{2+}; Sing. Q_1; 1 Ang. Sing. C_1.

Which were I Emperour should be soon prevented.
    CONST. By Heaven it shall by me.
    SYLV.   You must not Swear,
Lest you shou'd be forsworn.
    CONST.   If Heaven require
My Life as an Atonement for my Sins: 35
Lead to the Altar, Saint, and I will bleed.
    SYLV. I dare believe you would: But this is more.
    CONST. More then my Life: Why, then 'tis Reputation.
But I have learnt in Christian Schools to lay
My Honour down. And own my self a Worm.   40
To wash the Pilgrims Feet, to bid the Saints
Tread on this Earth: This trash, this heap of Sin.
    SYLV. But there's a Bosom Foe to Conquer yet,
And there's my fear.
    CONST. Your fear, my Saint, after what I have said?   45
    SYLV. My fear, my Emperour, though you had sworn.
    CONST. Had I a Race of Sons like Crispus dear,
Hope of my vows, my Souldier and my Love
Early Renown'd, and Pious from the Womb:
Yet were my Bowels Foes to that Religion,   50
Whose Infant growth I water'd with my Blood,
I Swear by Heav'n, they should be mine no more.
    SYLV. Your Son's the Angels care, and when he dies,
The foremost of the Quire shall meet him with a Crown.
But have you not a Wife?
    CONST.   You know I had   55
A dear one, and by much my better part.
    SYLV. But have you not another?
    CONST.   When she dy'd,
All Beauty fled with her.
    SYLV.   This Beauty lives:
Can you deny a Truth?
    CONST.   Sylvester, why?
Why dost thou press me thus, to my Confusion?   60
    SYLV. Because this Beauty, Sir, may bring confusion.
    CONST. Large as an Angels knowledg, be your own,
And at one View, receive whole Nature in,
Yet if you tax my Choice, with least dishonour,
I must declare you wrong her.   65
    SYLV. Then you are at least contracted to Maximinus Daughter:
A Heathen born?
    CONST.   But bred a Cherubin,
She has all the Beauties, of her Sex below;
And equal Virtues, with the blest above.
    SYLV. Dares Constantine, the Christian so Renownd,   70
Say this to me?

---

40 down, C_{1+}. Worm; C_{2+}.

CONST.   Dares any Saint deny't?
SYLV. That Fausta is not Guilty!
CONST.   Ha! of what?
SYLV. Of all the ills, that shall attend your Life.
Of all ---
CONST. Hold, hold -- lest I fall out with Heaven.
SYLV. Of all the Blots, that shall in after times   75
Stain your white Character, and blast your Fame:
While weeping Readers shall lament your Story.
Therefore away with her.
CONST.   First, let me die.
Penurious Heaven; and Oh! thou Niggard Saint,
Did I not Offer you my Darling Son,   80
With all my Race, as Victims to your Shrines
If they were Guilty in a point of Faith,
To wash their Heresies with Royal Blood?
And do you grudge me one, but one poor Pleasure,
For all the Pains of my Unwearied Wars?   85
Then take my Life, take Empire, Glory, all,
Take all I offer'd this Ungrateful Priest,
Who in requital, will allow me nothing.
SYLV. Forgive me Heaven! my too officious Care,
For interposing, in thy dark Decrees: 90
In Christian patience, he is yet but young.
Chastise him now: And make the Tryal strong.
CONST. What have I said, that I am past forgiveness?
Your Silence argues me undone for ever:
Yet think me not, so lost in desperate Love,   95
But while offending I can kneel for Pardon.
SYLV. What I have offer'd to your Choice,
Was not Commission'd me to say from Heaven;
Therefore the pardon must be mutual.
All I have urg'd was but a thoughtful boding: 100
No more of that; be happy in your Love.
CONST. Oh! you have Charm'd me into Life agen;
And fear not but she shall become a Christian;
I must confess, that yet she is a Heathen,
As such I Lov'd Her, in Her Fathers Court,   105
Where first we Plighted vows in Arius hands.
But the dark Contract was so close Contriv'd,
I wonder how you reach'd the Truth so soon:
But Heaven reveal'd it, or you cou'd not know it;
Since I may swear, She is not yet enjoy'd.   110
SYLV. By you!
CONST.   By me? Your answer's short and home:
Who shou'd possess her else?
SYLV.   Young and a Heathen?

---

106 hands: C_{1+}.

Left in the Sensual Maximians Court?

   CONST. No, Sir; She's Guarded, and secure at Rome,
Crispus, not yet acquainted with our Contract,   115
Is sent in show, for I had other purpose,
To make his Judgment of my Fausta's Person,
Whether to be preserv'd, or like Her Father,
To hinder Insurrections, be destroy'd,
But hark! What March is this? Perhaps 'tis he!   120
And these his Trumpets, with the Legions Rais'd.   [Trumpets without.

        Enter Arius, and Eubulus.

   BOTH. Long live the Emperour.
   CONST.   Is Crispus come,
With those Auxiliar Legions we requir'd;
And Money sent to pay the last Arrears?
   ARI. Nothing obey'd: When first your Orders came,   125
Which by your Brother were in the Forum Read;
I never saw so sudden a Revolt.
At once they Cry'd, our Liberty's betray'd,
Our Courts of Justice Rob'd; Old Rights Infring'd;
Our Gods must down, our Shrines and Temples burn: 130
And all for a phantastick, Old Wives Tale;
A Cross they Cry'd, one of Sylvesters Lies:
Which never yet was seen by waking Eyes;
But either feign'd, or Dreamt of in the Skies.
   CONST. Is this their Answer to my strict Commands?   135
   ARI. Crispus by this return'd, to join your Brother;
When straight some Devil whisper'd in their Ears,
Your Son already had begun the Change,
The Statue of Apollo was pull'd down,
To make his Fathers Place: Whereon they cry'd   140
Your Image should be Burnt, and with a breath
The Cockle, and the Corn, bow'd all that way.
   EUB. But were reversed by a more Powerful Gale,
Your Brother and your Son, appear'd like Gods,
And stopt the Madmen in their full Career.   145
   ARI. At close of day, in Dark Cabals they met,
And in the Morning gave their Final Answer;
Lycinius, who that Night was brought a Captive,
To grace the Triumph of your first appearance,
Was first propos'd, to share th' Imperial Power: 150
Next they demand a general Persecution
Of all the Christians, and Sylvesters head.
   CONST. Tell 'em their City shall be Ashes first,
Have I for this, with hazard of my Life,

----

114 Rome. C_{1+}.

So oft Redeem'd 'em from their Tyrants Racks,   155
When all their Streets, were but one Hideous Grave;
There Wives, and Daughters Ravisht in their View?
When Age was drain'd of its last Ebbing drop,
When Babes were snatch'd their Earliest breath to give,
And dy'd ere knowing what it was to live.   160

                Trumpets --- Enter Dalmatius.

More Treason --- Arius, or do the Slaves Repent?
My Brother here. Still to my Arms, and heart,
Thou Nerve of all my Wars: How fares my Friend,
And my beloved?
        DALM.   Crispus, our care is well.
And the late Tempest which must reach your Ear,   165
By Skilful Pilots, Rockt into a Calm;
Believe me Sir, your presence gains the Cause.
Therefore upon the Instant march to Rome;
Vanquisht Lycinius waits to Grace your Triumph.
Bless me! Is't possible? Arius with you Sir?   170
Arius the Traitor?
        CONST.   Have you found him so?
        DALM. The Subtlest Snake, the softest Civil Villain
That ever warm'd himself in Princes --- Bosom;
Diseases, Blasts, Plagues, Death and Hell are in him:
What e're his outside seems: This shameless Traitor   175
Was the foul Spring of all these poison'd Waters,
That late had like to overflow the Empire;
Yet while his Emissaries Fired the People;
This Judas on my side, appear'd an Angell:
For after the first Mutiny was quel'd;   180
Though he had Sworn to Justifie your Cause,
He warn'd the Slaves, I have his hand to show,
Next day to make those Impudent demands.
        ARI. Plots on my Innocence; as I am a Christian,
If ere I set my hand to such a Treason,   185
May these rot off, which thus I hold to Heaven:
As I am of Priestly Order.
        DALM.   A Devil Ordain'd ---
Sir, if I do not prove him.
        CONST.   I believe you,
I know him Heretick, a Seditious Traitor,
But yet have Reasons to defer his Ruin,   190
Therefore no more at present. Arius hence;

---

155 the Tyrants C3.
157 Their Wives C_{1+}.
161 More Treason, Arius --- or C_{2+}.
173 Prince's Bosom; C_{1+}.

And let me hear no further of these Mischiefs.
I have pardon'd you; be gone, you Eubulus, and tell the Rebels,
I come Embattel'd now for my Revenge;
My Standard, and my Banners, bear the Cross.   195
Tell 'em Lycinius, whom once before
I took to Grace, and Marry'd to my Sister,
Their new Petition'd Caesar soon shall bleed.
    SYLV. Forgive your Enemies.
    CONST.   But not my Friends:
Lycinius was my Friend, and has betray'd me;   200
Therefore I'le Execute him in their View.
Away and warn him, for the Doom that's given.   [Ex. Arius, Eubulus.
'Tis not by halfs, that we will worship Heaven:
No; my Dalmatius, I have made a vow,
The Romans, or their Emperour shall bow.   205
They're Subjects, and 'tis fit: Nay, bow they shall:
Or Caesar in th'attempt, their Victim fall;
Bow to the Man, whom Heaven Ordain'd for Sway,
And in his great Vicegerent learn their Maker to Obey ---   [Exeunt.

Scene II. ROME. Constantines Palace.

Enter Lycinius, Labienus.

    LABI. The mischief's Ripe, and ready for our wish:
Confusion to the House of Constantine,
And Fortune points their Fate. For mark the Method
The Father sends the Son to see the Prisoner;
The Son, not knowing of his Fathers Contract,   5
Appears a God to Fausta's Charming Eyes,
And Marry'd her.
    LYCIN.   How came you by the Secret?
    LABI. Arius told me; he who Betrothed the Father Weds the Son,
And stands for ever bound to serve Lycinius.
    LYCIN. He's Voted Heretick among the Christians.   10
    LABI. No matter what they Vote him, Sir; He's yours,
And Foe too all Religion, but his Friends.
    LYCIN. By Mars, he falls the Righter to my purpose.
I was my self bred up in Blood and Wars,
Untaught, and Scoft at by these Civil Cowards,   15
Wherefore I hate Religion, Arts, and Learning;
And if I ever Mount the Caesars Throne,

---

195 Cross.] C_{1+}; Cross Q_1.
198 Caesar, C_{1+}.
  3 Method: C_{1+}.

I'le Raise another General Persecution,
Like Nero; Bait these Christian Dogs to Death;
And Build the Temples of the Old Gods again.   20
    LABI. And be a God your Self: In the mean time,
Let your Wife's tears prevail upon your Temper.
Supple your Haughty Spirit, bow your Body,
Low as the Earth, before the Emperours Feet.
    LYCIN. I had rather dye: If he thinks fit to save me,   25
'Tis well; if not; why let him take my Head.
    LABI. Yet for the sake of those, whom you must Govern,
Rebate this Martial Fire, and hear your Wife:
Hear what return our long'd for Arius brings.

        Enter Crispus, with Annibal.

But soft! the Bridegroom, Crispus and his Friend: 30
Constantia with impatience waits your coming;
Constantia, who has Power to save your Head;
Though Caesar with an Oath had Doom'd you Dead.
                     [Ex. Lycinius, Labienus.

    CRISP. How Annibal: What! out of temper now?
When Crowns are offer'd, and the Caesars Purple?   35
What, though not born in the immediate way?
Yet thou art Collaterally Great as I.
And if I ever Heir this Spacious Empire,
By Heaven, thou shalt not share, but guide, engross
My hearts best Love, and all the World beside.   40
    ANNI. Your Heart? Ay there you Eccho'd my desires,
Enrich me there, and trowle your empty Globe
To those Crown'd Slaves, that know no other Greatness:
But tel! me, O my Crispus! All Mens Joy;
Tell me, and truly from thy Generous Soul,   45
Hast thou a Friend, whom more thou Lov'st then me?
    CRISP. Not more belov'd, more Fonded then my self,
But more ---
    ANNI. Nay add not, to that broken Truth,
There's more in that, no more, then thou had'st Sworn.
    CRISP. Wilt thou not hear me out?
    ANNI.   There needs no more;   50
Thou art no Friend, that Lov'st another more:
Nay half so much: But now I find that all
The former Flatteries of thy Glozing Friendship,
Were Courtiers promises, and Womens Vows,
But let me know his Name.   55
    CRISP. Thy Father Annibal my Godlike Friend,
Dalmatius, who before thou could'st Write Man,

---

  22 Wife's] C$_{1+}$; Wives Q$_1$.

Hugg'd Crispus to his Heart: Like Lambs in Peace
Together we lay down, together rose,
In War like Lyons, Coupled on a side;   60
Ere yet thy Infant Arms, a Sword could Wield,
And drove like Herds, the Nations from the Field.
    ANNI. Why then we're Friends agen, more fast then ever,
Yet since we have happen'd into this disorder,
To make a Tryal of renew'd affection,   65
I'le put thee to the Test.
    CRISP.   Name the Danger,
Though Kin to Death, my Arm, Young-man, shall Right thee.
    ANNI. 'Tis death indeed: Most certain Death to me,
Unless thy Softning Charms, have power to save me.
    CRISP. Speak this close grief: That wrings thee with the Anguish,   70
If I am not Eloquent in such a Cause,
Cut out my Tongue.
    ANNI.   My life is in the hands
Of one that hates me; or what wounds me more,
Of one, my Crispus, that can never love me.
    CRISP. Not love thee? O ye Powers! what heart is that?   75
    ANNI. Hast thou not seen the Beauteous Prisoners?
    CRISP.   Ha!
What, Fausta meanst thou?
    ANNI.   Fausta and Serena.
    CRISP. Say which of 'em? Which Beauty has Inflam'd thee?
    ANNI. Which shou'd, but the most soft and Artless melter?
The Languishing ---
    CRISP.   The killing Beauteous -- Come ---   80
    ANNI. Ha! Crispus thou art Concern'd!
    CRISP.   I am to help thee ---
Her Name?
    ANNI. Why take it then, the Fair Serena.
    CRISP. O She's the softest sweetest, killing Fair
By Heaven -- I am glad -- I'm ravisht that 'tis She!
By this Embrace I promise thee success,   85
I know her temper well --- No more but leave me,
I was upon the Instant when I met thee,
Going to their Appartment; --- Nay look up ---
And trust thy Friend.
    ANNI.   Plead then for my Life,
I beg thee as a God to plead my Cause;   90
Thou canst not know o'th' sudden, how 'tis with me:
How Great, how Mortal, and how deep the wound.
May all the Saints, and Powers that pitty Love,
Inspire thy Brest, as if 'twere possible
That Annibals Soul cou'd actuate thy body,   95
So sigh, weep, languish, and for Mercy sue,

---

83 Fair. C$_{1+}$.

As were I Crispus, I my self wou'd do ---   [Ex. Annibal.
    CRISP. The Youth is Haughty, Martial, Hot and Brave;
Right for the Field, unhappy parts for Love:
Therefore perhaps, the Virgin likes him not.   100
But thou hast luckier Stars: No sooner seen
But lik'd --- Lov'd, Marry'd --- Ha! --- but where's the Transport?
Without thy Fathers knowledge thou wert Marry'd:
'Tis the first Fault of my unhappy youth,
Yet 'tis a Fault --- but 'tis the fault of Love.   105
Had he not lov'd, Crispus had not been here;
Away, you Damps, and darkning Images.
Be gone I say --- Behold she comes to meet me;

        Enter Fausta.

Lag as I am, in this great Race of Love ---
O Fausta, Fausta!
    FAUST.   O my Constantine!   110
    CRISP. Ha!
    FAUST.   A mistake; my fear out-went my Love.
    CRISP. My Constantine! Thy fear --- by Heaven 'twas Ominous:
What cause hast thou to fear?
    FAUST.   Bondage and Death.
Are not those Reasons for a Virgins fear?
    CRISP. Yes for another, Fausta, not for thine.   115
For Oh! when he has seen and heard like me,
The Abstracted Charms of all this Beauteous World,
Expect not death, but offers of a Throne.
    FAUST. 'Tis possible: Yet by thy self I swear,
By dear lov'd thee, my Crispus in a Cottage   120
Shall be prefer'd to all the Thrones on Earth.
    CRISP. And thou, forgive me Heaven! I had almost said
To Heaven it self: No Fausta, that's the Jar,
Religion makes this discord in my Soul.
I find it now. Hence come my Starts and fears,   125
Even in the height of my expected joys
But Time, the Saints and Miracles must win thee.
    FAUST. No Time, no Miracle, no Saint but thou:
Why, thou art all the Wonders of the Earth,
My Saint, my hearts Religion, and my Heaven;   130
With thee I am imbarkt to live or Perish,
Not only here but in the World hereafter.
    CRISP. Oh Extacy! Oh pattern for thy Sex:
Yet shalt thou Master me by this Subjection.
Give me thy hand. Thy Lip --- the sweets are Richer,   135
The tast Enobled. Oh! my ravisht Love

---

106 lov'd,] C_{1+}; lov'd Q_1.
134 Subjection.] C_{1+}; Subjection Q_1.

Glows with the pointed Charms. The Heavens are open'd
And I behold thee Crown'd a Saint already.
But I will hold thee fast, lest that the Angels snatch thee:
Ere we have mingled Souls ---
    FAUST.   Oh not to Night!   140
    CRISP. Ha! not to night? Not on this Lov'd Confession?
Not when thou hast set my Spirits all on fire?
Not now enjoy thee? Thou mak'st my fears return,
Far more Extravagant then they were before.
Lest e're we join an Apoplex shou'd seize me,   145
The Palace fall, and thousand other Chances,
That awe th' Imagination of my Love.
Oh Come ---
    FAUST. I will, and with these longing arms
Hold thee till Morn: And from that Morn till Evening:
From Evening to Mid-day: From day to Night: 150
From Night to Death --- I'le clap thee thus for ever.
    CRISP. Let's haste then, while the beckoning Minute smiles.
    FAUST. But I must swear thee first.
    CRISP.   Take Oath on Oath:
I swear to obey thee without asking why.
    FAUST. Swear thou wilt never leave thy Wedded Fausta;   155
What ever dreadful Chance, or strange Misfortune,
Shou'd start to undo me, almost to a Crime.
    CRISP. No Crime: But want of Love: Nor that, by Heaven,
Shall make me hate thee, though it bring me Death.
Oh thou soft Dear! if ever I forsake thee,   160
At my last hour, may I despair of Mercy,
And may those Saints, that knew the wrong I did thee,
When at Heavens Gate, I beg for Entrance, answer,
Remember what thou did'st to Fausta swear,
Be gone, for ever leave this happy Sphere;   165
For perjur'd Lovers have no Mansion here.   [Ex. Ambo.

End of ACT I.

---

151 clasp C_{1+}.

Act II. Scene I.
Scene ROME.

Enter Arius, Labienus, and Eubulus. *

ARI. We have done our Work by halfs; follow'd by the Scent,
Trac'd to our Holes! Oh I could play the Mad-man!
Men of our Make so poorly hide a Murder,
That Dogs can Rake it up. Spies, Spies by Hell!
The Course of former Councils was too slow,   5
I am proclaim'd a Traitor, Heretick,
And Poniards must proclaim my Accuser nothing.
    LABI. Were it not better to comply?
    ARI.   Impossible!
The Genius of the proud imperial Brothers
And mine, by Nature Mortally oppos'd,   10
Hate strongly at first sight, which hate improv'd,
By the late flaw I found in their Religion:
They hear too how I tainted Infant Julian:
Yet being made the Emperours Confident,
In the late Contract, all might have been retreiv'd;   15
And I at Helm, had not his hated Brother
Thus interpos'd to my eternal Ruine ---
Poison and Ponyard ---
    EUB.   Is it come to that?
    ARI. It is: without dispatch, we are all undone.
Oh for a Slave to mould, some Malecontent;   20
His blood adust, and blackned with the blows
Of adverse Fortune: yet of Soul elate,
And to be flush'd for Fame, or hire
To any kind of daring!
    LABI.   Why?
    ARI. I would work the Melancholy brave   25
To stab Dalmatius.
    EUB.   Why not Constantine?
    ARI. Because ten Constantines live at least in him;
The one's not half so open to Destruction,
As t'other close: and on the Guard to save him;
He has unravell'd our close Webb of Thought,   30
And from the bottom of our dark Design
Drawn Treason forth, perhaps to hang us all.
    LABI. 'Tis justly thought; this Lett must be remov'd;
And who so fit to hew it into pieces

---

  * Labienus and Eubulus.] C_{1+}; and Labienus, Eubolus. Q_1.
10 mine,] C_{1+}; mine Q_1. oppos'd,] C_{1+}; oppos'd. Q_1.

As that ambitious, brawny Fool, Lycinius?   35
    ARI. Thou hast hit the Man my busie Brain had lost.
The Emperour dooms him dead; by whose Advice?
Tell me; I hear the dull Lycinius cry,
That e're I fall the Victim of the War,
I may at once destroy his Life and Name.   40

           Enter Lycinius. Guards.

But see he comes! I bring you News.
    LYCIN. Ha! of my Death! I read it in thy Face.
    ARI. The Emperour, as at first I told your Story, [Ready Trumpets, a
Inclin'd to Mercy: but fierce Dalmatius   March at distance.
Repeal'd the hint of your half granted Pardon,   45
And forc'd him to your Death.   [Call Serina.
    LYCIN.   By Mars I'll fight him.
    ARI. 'Tis not in your Power;
You're Pris'ner of War.
    LYCIN.   Yet I may curse:
My Tongue is not their Prisoner; therefore I'll curse,
Bitterly curse Dalmatius: curse 'em all.   50
    ARI. Curse for the loss of Empire, and of Life!
Bitterly curse! Why Whores will there out-do you.
I blush to think the great Lycinius
Should e're be brought in such Comparison!
Would it not seem more worthy your past Honour   55
To strike than say? Strike, if I may advise,
And e're you suffer. ---
    LYCIN.   Kill Dalmatius,
Constantine, Crispus, Annibal, nay all, ---
Quite root up all the Imperial Stock at once.
    ARI. This Dagger then be yours: the Legacy   60
Of an old Prophetess: who dying, told me,
He that had Courage to employ it well,
And where it ought, should make himself the Greatest. ---
                    [Trumpet at distance.
    LYCIN. It shall be well employ'd, and where it ought.
But hark! th' Emperour comes!
    ARI.   Rather Dalmatius,   65
Perhaps commission'd for your Execution!
    LYCIN. Why then I'll forth and meet him. By the Fates,
If I must fall, he shall not live to laugh:
And in remembrance of this solemn Oath,
I kiss the ominous Gift thou hast bequeath'd me;   70
I'll treasure it next my Heart; where it shall rest,
Till sheath'd by Vengeance in Dalmatius Brest.   [Exit.
    ARI. Or live or dye, thou art contriv'd for Mischief!

---

55 past] C_{1+}; pact Q_1.

Next I must mend the Heresies I've broach'd,
And reconcile my self by some bold Offer,   75
With Constantine; which while I undertake,
Be it your Care to spread the old poisonous Doctrine:
Sow it in all Habits, Persons, Forms, and Places;
Grow with the Times, and cultivate Sedition.

Enter Serina.

My fair Devotess: --- but hence, as I have order'd,   80
And meet me at the Tryal of Lycinius.   [Ex. Labi. & Eub.
   SEREN. The Morning's come, and fain I would have rest,
Who all the Night have wak'd upon my Pillow,
And made it wet with Tears: my solitary Groans
That pierc'd Heav'ns Vaults: tho Heav'n was deaf the while;   85
Deaf to redress, have made my Brest so sore
That I can sigh no longer.
Crispus and Fausta! Oh you happy Lovers!
Not so with you the gladsome Minutes past:
For, e're 'twas day, I left my tedious Bed,   90
And listen'd to your Joys.
   ARI.   Her Sorrows lull me,
And I grow good, I know not how, o'th' sudden.
   SEREN. Such soft Expressions flow'd from the charming Crispus,
As did but aggravate my Passion more;
Yet hide it, O Serena! though thou diest,   95
Tell it to none, but to the midnight Groves,
The Flocks and Streams, and those unhappy Stars,
Whose merciless Fires thus fated thy undoing.
   ARI. What! not to Arius! to thy Confessor;
To him who has a Priviledge from Heav'n?   100
   SEREN. Oh Arius! would I had the Power to hide it;
But you have heard it all;
And will, perhaps, proclaim a Virgins Frailty.
But, Sir, I shall not long survive my shame:
And since 'tis known, confess it to the World;   105
Confess, that Passion has dethron'd my Reason,
That unbelov'd, I love the best of Men.
And sigh unheard, and without Witness mourn,
And dote to Death, without the least Return.
   ARI. 'Tis said, young Annibal is vow'd your Servant.   110
   SEREN. O Arius! mark the malice of our Fates!
That Prince loves me, as Crispus is belov'd,
And failing in his Suit, employ'd his Friend
To plead his Cause! Oh had it been his own! ---
But all my Pray'rs, alas! are now in vain,   [Ready Trumpets   115
And wanting Crispus, I must wed my Grave.   for a Call.
Therefore I beg you, Sir, procure his Picture
To entertain my melancholy Thoughts,
Since him himself I ne're must see again.

ARI. That, and all Helps which Arius can command.   120
   SEREN. I thank you Sir, by the blest Saints I do;
I thank you for this Favour, from my Heart.
But hark! they come: Crispus and Fausta come!
Oh Heart! why dost thou leap against my Bosom
Like a cag'd Bird, and beat thy self to Death   125
For an impossible Freedom?
   ARI.   Stay to salute 'em.
   SEREN. No Arius, no: I cannot, dare not stand 'em:
But see, they come, wreath'd in each others Arms,
And mingling Kisses. Has not then the Night
Been long enough, but you must love by Day?   130
Do Fausta, do, be stifled with the Joy.
Follow him from thy Chamber to the Grove,
To Garden haunts, and clasp him in the Bowers,
Thence to your golden Beds again, while I
Sink to my Grave, and there forgotten, lye.   [Exit. Serena.   135
   ARI. Crispus to court Serena for his Friend,
His Picture she shall have it --- Mischief, Hell!
And if it be thy Will thy Slave obeys.
Crispus and Annibal, that late were Friends ---
Shall strait be foes. But hush, the Lovers come. ---   140
This Closet hides me to discover more.

            Enter Crispus and Fausta.

This Closet be my School, to learn their Language.
   FAUST. Your Fathers Trumpets call you. Let 'em call,
You shall not go. Oh are there any Sounds
To charm, more powerful than your Fausta's Cries?   145
   CRISP. No, not the Tongues of Angels! O best Joy
Of my abounding Soul! What shall I call thee?
By Heav'n, thou art all Heav'n, all Paradise.
Talk not then of going from thee: for, I'll stay till Age
Has snow'd a hundred Winters on my Head,   150
Yet give and take Enjoyments then, as now.
   FAUST. And oh, for thee, thou dearest of the World,
My Souls best Life, and my Hearts grasp'd Desire,
Oh what Return! The Mother on her throws,
After the Rack when hanging o're her Babe,   155
With bleeding Joys, wild Looks, and earning Smiles,
Loves not her Darling more than I love Crispus.
Thou shalt not leave me, Crispus.
   CRISP.   Yes, to meet again;
Our Loves approv'd, by him that gave me Being,
And then ---
   FAUST. What then? He dooms me to that place;   160

---

137 His picture! C_{1+}.

Where in his Shrowd the poor Maximian lies,
Where I shall lye as I had never been,
Nor think of Crispus more ---
    CRISP.   Canst thou fear Death,
While I have Life?
    FAUST.   Oh do not trust thy Father!
Trust not the Passions of a Conquerour;   165
For in his fatal Look, when last he left me,
Something I saw, that bid me fly his Presence.
Fly to the Verge of Earth, and leap the bounds,
Rather than ever meet his Eyes again.
    CRISP. Thy Father's Fate makes thee mistrust thy own.   170
    FAUST. No Crispus, not Mistrust, but certain Danger;
Which like a moulding Promontory hangs,
Bursting above our Heads; and threatens Death,
Unless we House betimes, and scape the fall.
    CRISP. What danger? Death? What fall?
    FAUST.   Thy Father.
    CRISP.   Ha!   175
    FAUST. Thy Father, Crispus.
    CRISP.   Knows not we are marry'd,
But shall, and will I hope forgive my passion.
    FAUST. I dream't last night, thy Father was in love;
In love with me, my Crispus; catch'd us clasp'd,
And with his Dagger, stabb'd us in the fold.   180
    CRISP. Is't possible?
    FAUST.   Most true.
    CRISP.   And catch't thee with me?
    FAUST. Catch't us in bed.
    CRISP.   There?
    FAUST.   Here. Why dost thou wonder?
'Twas but a dream.
    CRISP.   Yet there is wonder in't.
Because, by Heav'n, I dreamt the very same.
Is it not strange?
    FAUST.   If it should happen true!   185
    CRISP. That would be strange indeed.
    FAUST. Therefore let's fear the worst: and Arm against it;
For oh, Why should I hide a secret from thee?
When I beheld him last, He languished,
And wrung my hand at parting.
    CRISP.   But what said he?   190
    FAUST. I will not tell you Crispus, till you answer
What you would do with me, my dearest Joy,
If it were true indeed, your Father lov'd me.
    CRISP. What, at your parting? ha!
    FAUST.   Why if 't were true,

---

176 Crispus --- C_{1+}.

Would you forsake me?
    CRISP.   Be my own murderer!   195
I know not what, but speak your parting. Oh!
    FAUST. Why are you so enrag'd? I dare not tell you.
    CRISP. If ought thou hid'st, by Heav'n thou dost not love me.
    FAUST. By Heav'n! I hope no other Heav'n, but thee.
What if he talkt a little? Age will talk,   200
And think of it no more.   [Trumpets ready for a Call.
    CRISP.   What was your talk?
I'le know each syllable.
    FAUST.   Why so you shall:
But then be calm; What if he talk't of love?
And what? Oh be not angry, and I'll tell you,
What if to save my life I promis'd him ---   205
    CRISP. Ha! promis'd Fausta?
Promise the Father and engage the Son?
But speak, I stand upon a Precipice;
For if 'tis true, that e're so little past
Of love before ---
    FAUST.   What then?
    CRISP.   And thou hast promis'd?   210
    FAUST. Suppose I have Sworn.
    CRISP.   Suppose then thy dishonour:
Suppose me never to behold thee more;
Suppose my death; both Soul and Bodies ruin.
    FAUST. Suppose no more, but what my Soul hath Sworn,
To love his Son, none but the lovely Crispus;   215
O therefore clear thy brow, and take me to thee,
Be still my love, forgive this little fault,
And jealousie shall ne're offend thee more.
    CRISP. O Charmer! Beauty, What! where was the need?
Why hast thou kept me on the Rack so long?   220
Tho taken down, I feel the strains upon me,
And shall, I fear, too long. But hark, they call,   [Trumpets.
And I must go.
    FAUST.   But will you then return?
    CRISP. Quick as thy wishes, or my own desires;
But make no more such Tryal. Hark again.   [Trumpets again. 225
    FAUST. I cannot part with you, tho for a moment.
    CRISP. I'll but enquire whether my Father's come.
    FAUST. Swear to come back then, Swear before you see him,
To give me one look more.
    CRISP.   What needs an Oath?
Before I speak with him ---
    FAUST.   You'l speak with me,   230
For I have much to say of mighty moment;
Swear therefore to return.

---

200 a little?] C_{1+}; alittle? Q_1.

CRISP.   Swear on thy Lips;
Thus with my Heart I seal my Vows for ever.   [Ex. Crispus.
    FAUST. Heart and the Holiest Vows deep writ in Blood;
Blood and dishonor: Take then, take my cause;   235
Thou, that hast made me sin, O mighty love!
And let thy Mother plead it with her Tears,
He sees his Father, and my crime at once;
And then resolves never to see me more.

                Enter Arius.   [Call Dalmatius, Cris-
                                                 pus, all Attendants.
    ARI. What then?
    FAUST.   What then! O Arius, Dost thou know me?   240
And ask what then, when he ne're sees me more?
I'll tell the then, I'll never see the day:
Shades, Night and Death, Despair and Dungeons hold me,
When those dear Eyes shall never light me more.
    ARI. Since you enjoy'd him, let the Tides of love   245
Be swallow'd in the Ocean of Ambition.
    FAUST. Ambition, Pomp, and greatness of the World,
All empty sounds to love! But thine's a downward sense,
Thou hast no tast of these sublimer joys.
But haste! look out; Why comes he not again?   250
He swore, he would; but he has seen his Father!
Who stops him, with my first unhappy Contract.
    ARI. I see him yonder.
    FAUST.   Blessings on thy Tongue;
But I'll run forth to meet him, and no longer,
Conceal the Innocent deceit of Love.   255
    ARI. Hold Madam, stay, Dalmatius comes; retire.
    FAUST. Dalmatius! Let me see my self.
    ARI.   They come.
    FAUST. Dalmatius! Gods, 'tis He, He tells him all;
Th' Emperor told it him. Nay it must out,
I am lost, undone: But gentle Arius, wait,   260
And watch, and bring me word, how Crispus bears it.
Oh that I were a Spirit to stand unseen!
To mark his passions how they rise and fall,
With every Glance of those dear, dreadful Eyes:
But see they come, and yet I cannot stir,   265
I grow distracted with my hope and fear,
Compell'd to go; yet long to tarry here.   [Ex. Fausta.

        Enter Dalmatius and Crispus to Arius.

    DALM. I have much against you, Crispus; and you know it;
Therefore with all the freedom of a friend,

----

242 thee then, C_{1+}. day:] C_{1+}; day Q_1.

Tell me what is the cause, you have not been   270
So free as formerly.
    CRISP.   You know I am.
    DALM. I'll press you Sir, no more, only remember,
There stands a Villain, whom I have seen you whisper.   [Ex. Arius.
    CRISP. I'll tell you all.
    DALM. You dare not: Come there is a guilt at bottom,   275
You blush to own, a Crime of such a nature,
As will admit no Pardon. Thou hast sin'd
Against the great Divinity of friendship;
Which my Soul takes to death.
    CRISP.   Can it be
Ever too late to gain a Pardon here?   280
    DALM. I cannot tell; Yet I can tell thee this,
There was a time, not many days are past,
Since I preferr'd thy friendship to the World;
When I cou'd say; Why yonder goes the Man,
Whom my Soul worships more then Constantine,   285
And Loves beyond my Son. By Heav'n thy fault
Is ominous, and grinds my temper through.
    CRISP. That Son you nam'd unhappily 's in Love.
    DALM. Then He's a Fool. With whom?
    CRISP.   Maximians Daughter;
The younger Beauty.
    DALM.   Ha! And you Love the Elder: 290
My life on't some such masterly design;
This makes you shun the Camp, to lurk beneath
The Eeves of Palaces, and droop in Corners.
But Sir your Pardon. I almost forgot
To urge your swiftest speed, to wait your Father.   295
    CRISP. I will but take my leave.
    DALM.   I fear there is
Too much already taken; but no more ---
If you have ought to say, I'll visit for you. ---
    CRISP. Be all as you would have it! Oh your hand!
Nay, I will force my Entrance to your Heart,   300
By opening all my own; and so farewell.   [Ex. Crispus.
    DALM. I blame my friend for walking in the Dark,
Yet hide my self, who when I seem most strange
Am fondest of his Love. So Sir, What now?

               Enter Annibal.

    ANNI. The fair Constantia with condemn'd Lycinius,   305
Drest in the saddest Glass of dying sorrow,
Was coming to entreat you for his Pardon;
But soon as she had heard from weeping Arius,
Her Husbands doom, she in our Arms Expir'd.
    DALM. I mourn her Fate; But for Lycinius,   310
I urg'd at first, and still resolve, his Death

Is necessary to the Emperors life
Nor should a few weak drops by Women shed,
Stop a Decree so Absolute and Royal.
    ANNI. He comes attended with a mournful crowd,   315
To sue for life.
    DALM. I'll have him Executed in their view;
Yes Annibal, and shew thy Youth a pattern
Of the old Romans, for thy imitation:
Who hast but poorly Copy'd from thy Father.   320
    ANNI. Why Sir? What Villain has traduc'd my Vertue?
    DALM. No Villain, but thy Prince has own'd thy weakness;
And says thou Lov'st a Captive Foe of Rome.
    ANNI. The Virgin's beautiful, and greatly born.
    DALM. Perhaps the Virgin may as greatly die,   325
And yield her Beauties to the Fatal stroke.
    ANNI. To the Fatal stroke! Oh all ye Powers!
No Sir: The fair Serena shall not die
While I wear this.
    DALM.   Ha Rebel! Traytor! How!
Not at the Emperors Doom?
    ANNI.   No nor at yours,   330
That gave me Sir my being; take it again,
Unless you give me leave to lay it there,
Where I have plac'd my Love.
    DALM.   The Emperor
Decrees thee Cappadocia: Wilt thou forfeit
The noble Heritage of such Ambition   335
For Infamous Love?
    ANNI.   Wrong not a Passion,
That equals your own Virtue. For could Caesar
Give with a Daughter of his own the World,
I would prefer my Love in this Condition,
To all the proffers of his Blood and Empire.   340
    DALM. Hence from my sight; And till thou break'st this passion,
See me no more.
    ANNI.   Then I must never see you.
For when I cease to Love, where I have vow'd,
I am no more: Therefore upon my Knees,
I beg you to recall this dreadful sentence.   345
Repeal my Banishment, and give me leave,
To win the Heart of this unhappy Maid,
Or bid me die before you.
    DALM.   Rise my Boy:
Thou Lov'st indeed, who canst refuse a Kingdom.

       Enter Arius, Lycinius, Labienus, Eubulus, with
              the Populace.

But see Lycinius with his followers here,   350

---

312 life: C_{1+}.

Take to the habit of thy former Wars;
And soften not my Justice by thy sorrows.
    ANNI. I have heard Lycinius lately threatned you,
Therefore your Guardians Eye be watchful o're you.
    DALM. Fear not, I'm Arm'd against 'em. Know, Lycinius,   355
The Emperor has decreed to shew his Subjects,
What weary'd Mercy dares resolve to do.
Cleanthes; you the Captain of the Guard:
Lead to the Forum, and in the Peoples view
Strike off his Head.   360
    LYCIN. --- I bear the sentence as becomes my Honour:
And all the favour which I beg in Death,
Is to reveal a secret to your Ear,
Which may import the Emperors life, and Yours.
    DALM. What would you Sir?
    LYCIN.   My Lord, Are you in earnest?   365
Or is there room for hope?
    DALM.   Sir, be not flatter'd:
Hope is the fawning Traytor of the mind,
Which while it cozen's with a colour'd friendship,
Robs us of our last Vertue, Resolution.
    LYCIN. Speak then the force of Resolution --- Thus.   370
    ANNI. No Villain --- Thus.   [Annibal disarms and offers to
    DALM.   Hold, Annibal! Hold thy Hand.   Stab him.
An executioner in the best of Causes,
Is a vile trade for Honourable men;
Therefore let slaves dispatch him.
    ANNI.   Rack him First,
To know who counsel'd him to this damn'd deed?   375
    DALM. No: To Sylvester let him own his fault,
And die a Christian, I am satisfy'd.
    LYCIN. Ha ha! --- A Christian! What and fall a Sheep?
Confess! No, as he urg'd, bring forth the Rack:
Wire-draw my Limbs, Spin all my Nerves like Hairs,   380
And work my tortured Flesh as thin as Flame,
You shall not know a title more then this;
I was set on to stab Dalmatius;
And would the Emperor, were he in my reach.
Who were the Gods that prompted thus my Arm,   385
You Christian Curs shall never know from me;
Therefore go learn the Mystery in Hell.
Thus much I may acquaint you; They are living,
Warm in your Bosoms, and I hope will sting you;
Sting you to Death. Plagues, Famine, Sword, and Fire;   390
Fire from the Gods on your proud City fall;

---

372 An Execution C_3.
375 Deed. C_{1+}.
382 Tittle C_{1+}.

And with that dying Curse I leave you all.   [Ex. Guarded.
    DALM. His Fate was just; now Romans to the Triumph;
Go forth and meet your Emperor, whose mercy
Extends her peaceful Wings to all that seek him;   395
And is the Darling attribute of his Soul.
But hark! He comes! The Saviour of your Empire;
Bring forth his Statues; Crown his Images;
Meet him with Garlands, Songs and Shouts of Triumph.
But see his entrance is already made,   400
And there He comes, with Crispus in his Arms.

    Enter Constantine, Crispus, &c. To the Triumph.

    CONST. Dalmatius, I must thank thee for the Fate,
Of that too stubborn troubler of our Reign;
Sylvester to his Hermitage retires,
And says the Saints are sad at my delay: 405
Tell him, e're long, and urge him to return,
The Emperor and the Court shall be Baptiz'd.
    DALM. Take to your former freedom, Mirth and Humor,
For 'tis observ'd, you are not as you were.
    CONST. Oh Brother! Friend! In all my hazards try'd,   410
Thy Son shall share the Heart and Empire too,
Of my lov'd Crispus, whom for some few minutes,
I would discourse alone.
    DALM.   Your wishes on you;
Peace to your thoughts, and Heaven still guide your Councils. [Exeunt.
                         [Manent Constantine, Crispus.

    CONST. Hast thou perform'd thy Embassy, my Crispus?   415
And seen the Daughter of Maximian?
    CRISP. I have seen Her Sir; And seen Her Beauteous Sister.
    CONST. How lik'st thou? Ha! Are they not charming both?
Both Beautiful?
    CRISP.   They are. But why Sir both?
    CONST. Because the latter only Catch'd thy praise,   420
When Fausta in the Pride of blooming Nature,
As much transcends her as the Summers Rose
The little Beauties of a backward Spring.
    CRISP. 'Tis true, She is the Elder.
    CONST.   And the fairer,
In all comparisons to be prefer'd,   425
Not only to her Sister, but the World.
    CRISP. Is't possible?
    CONST.   That thou should'st be so dull,
To ask the Question, having seen the wonder!
    CRISP. But Sir, when I was sent you talk't of Death.

---

411 Thy] C_{2-3}; This Q_1-C_1.

CONST. Death to my self, and thee, and all mankind,   430
Rather then wound a part of my Lov'd Fausta.
    CRISP. Oh Heav'n! What said you? Do you Love her then?
    CONST. Love her my Son! In Age I Love her more,
Then in my Youth I Lov'd the chace of Glory.
    CRISP. And does she know you Love her?
    CONST.   Know? Approves;   435
Approving joyn'd, and Seal'd the Contract sure.
    CRISP. Death and Despair! Approv'd, Joyn'd, Seal'd, Contracted!
How Seal'd? And how Contracted?
    CONST.   Why our Lips
Have Sign'd and Seal'd an Everlasting Love.
    CRISP. What, kiss'd her? Ha! But I'm too Credulous: 440
All you have said is but to try my temper,
How much your Son can bear.
    CONST.   I must confess,
Thy fears were just, had'st thou another Father;
But as I am, I swear what ever Issue
I have by Fausta, Thou shalt Heir my Power.   445
    CRISP. Talk not of Power, but tell me of your Love;
Distract me not with these Ambiguous Answers,
But tell me; Swear to save my loss of reason,
If as you Love, you are by Fausta Lov'd.
    CONST. That I Love Fausta; is as true by Heav'n,   450
As I Love thee; But whether I am Lov'd,
With just return, is hard indeed to swear:
Yet as I said before, our Hands have joyn'd,
Our Lips have seal'd, and binding Oaths have past.
    CRISP. What Oaths?
    CONST.   Betrothing Oaths.
    CRISP.   Oh, All ye Saints!   455
Are you contracted too?
    CONST.   Ay Crispus, we're contracted;
Weep not my Son; I swear by this Embrace,
Thou shalt not less be Lov'd then heretofore.
    CRISP. Betroth'd! Oh Heav'n! And have you Sir enjoy'd her?
    CONST. No Crispus; That's a Heav'n I have to come.   460
    CRISP. A Hell! All Hell! And if not yet enjoy'd,
Let me conjure you by my Mothers ashes,
Touch her not for the World.
    CONST.   What means my Son?
I have decreed to marry her this Night;
And tast the sweets of long expected joys.   465
    CRISP. By Heav'n I swear those sweets have poison in 'em,
Bane to your Soul, your Empire, Life and Glory.
    CONST. Take heed my Crispus, that thou do not wrong her;
I know the hazard of Succession frights thee.
    CRISP. No: By your sacred life; nothing but Honour   470
Provokes me in the point: She's false, forsworn,
And to my certain knowledg loves another.

Oh! Therefore touch her not; and to convince you,
That Empire could not work me thus: This night
I'll turn a Hermit, and renounce the World.   475
    CONST. If she be false: I know his temper well;
And nature cannot make such faults o'th' sudden,
If she be false! By Heav'n, thou hast moved me Crispus:
But speak the Traitors name, who thus has wrong'd me.
    CRISP. Pardon me, Sir, his name; He could not wrong you,   480
Because he knew not.
    CONST.   What?
    CRISP.   Your Love.
    CONST.   His name,
There's more in this; His name, again I charge thee,
Not only name him, but produce his person;
Or I shall think all forgery thou hast sworn.
    CRISP. O let me beg you, wed her not to night,   485
And when I see you next, I'll tell you more;
Perhaps betray the Innocent to Death.
    CONST. Let that be prov'd; I swear he shall not die,
Thou art it seems his friend as well as mine;
But look you calm the Tempest you have rais'd,   490
Or I will make thee stranger to my Soul.   [Ex. Constantine.
    CRISP. <u>Solus</u>. I am content; if that some pittying Power,
Would make me too a stranger to my self:
But hold my Heart a while, till I have found her.
Yet there's a lucid joy in these distractions;   495
To know he has not bedded her; then had follow'd,
Her death and mine, and consequent Damnation:
Yet lest she should consent, I'll haste, and warn her;
When warn'd I'll watch, and if she after Yield,
Through Love or Fear, to his Incestuous charms,   500
I'll rush through all and stabb her in his Arms.   [Exit.

                End of ACT II.

---

493 make me] C$_{1+}$; make make me Q$_1$.

Act III. Scene I.

Enter Annibal and Serena.

ANNI. Is this your Answer then, You cannot love me?
This the Reward for Offers of my Blood?
And braving a stern Father to preserve you?
This the Effect of Crispus Eloquence!
To make his Friend a most untimely Grave?   5
For, bear it as you please, or laugh or grieve,
I will not be a Trouble to you long.
    SEREN. What shall I say? Alas! I might delude you, Annibal,
Like other faithless Beauties of the Age;
But the Gods fram'd me of so plain a Temper,   10
I cannot hide my Thoughts, though to my undoing.
But something more there is, if you could bear it,
To turn your desp'rate Love for ever from me.
    ANNI. Produce it then; for, what can Nature shew me
Than Death more dreadful, wilder than Despair,   15
Which now are my Familiars?
    SEREN.   Take it, Sir,
The only Secret of my wounded Soul.
I love, I languish, and despair like you.
    ANNI. What, do you love another?
    SEREN. Love him to death, nor does he know I love him;   20
Or if he did, he would not make Return.
    ANNI. Can this be possible! But where, where is he?
That I may rush with all my Rage upon him,
And bear him with me, to the other World.
    SEREN. Not for a thousand Worlds you must not hate him ---   25
    ANNI. Plagues! Curses on his Head, Rage and Despair.
Is this then the Return of all my Vows,
To make my setting yet more deep in Blood?
But give me quick his Quality and Name.
    SEREN. His Name! what, after such Resolves of Vengeance!   30
Your Fate and mine should not compell it now.
    ANNI. What, not to save my Life!
    SEREN. No: for what Life can stand in Competition,
When his is threaten'd? Better you, and I,
And all the rest of humane Kind, should perish,   35
Than he, the Master-piece of Nature, suffer.
And should you know him, spite of your Resolves,
Sir, you would kneel and worship too like me.

---

8 Annibal, om. C_{1+}.
11 Divided into two lines Q_1; as one C_{1+}.

ANNI. Show me the God then, if I must adore.
SEREN. No, since you have sworn, I should do ill to trust you: 40
Yet, for his Preservation, I must tell you,
When e're he dies Serena too shall bleed.
From the same hand, the same Dispatch I crave,
And, if at last one Monument we have,
What Joys can Life compare with such a Grave!   [Exit.   45

Enter Arius with Crispus Picture.

ANNI. Death, Hell, and Furies; if my Sword have Charms,
Which never fail'd me yet, I'll find him out;
This Rival God ---
And drive him from the World.
ARI.   Ha! Goes it there?
Then to my Task!
ANNI.   Arius in Contemplation!   50
'Twere worth my while to spy; Crispus Picture!
Forgive me Arius, if I rob your Hand
Of what's so deep ingraven in my Heart.
For whom this pretty Present?
ARI. Your Pardon --- The Mystery is one of Loves great Secrets.   55
ANNI. Crispus in Love, and hide it from his Friend!
From Annibal, that open'd all to him!
'Twas much unkind: Arius I am concern'd:
And you must tell me where his Heart's engag'd,
E're I return the Picture.
ARI.   Sir, I am in haste;   60
And dare not tell her Name; therefore I beg you:
She waits my coming --- Good my Lord, --- she loves
To that degree, each Moments Stay is Death:
Therefore, let me conjure you.
ANNI. Thou dost but raise my Admiration more: 65
Therefore, your Business, or farewel. ---
ARI.   Stay, Stay!
My Lord, you are his Friend! yet 'tis a Breach
Of Trust: but since there is no other help,
And the fair Mistress of his Heart may pine
To death upon the loss; restore the Picture,   70
And take the Secret, Sir: her Name's Serena.
ANNI. Traitor, thou ly'st: and, but thy Robe protects thee,
Should'st feel, even now, th' Effects of my Revenge.
ARI. To clear th' Aspersion, bear it Sir, your self,
And to Serena's Face, I'll justifie   75
The Secret of her Love; tho Crispus kill me.
ANNI. By Heav'n, thou dost recall a dreadful Image:
Of late I met him e're I made my Visit

---

55 Secr Q_1(KU); Secrets. Q_1(DFo1-4).

To Her thou hast nam'd, and ask'd him of my Love!
He seem'd in haste! his Answers were abrupt;   80
His Count'nance sad: and thus in short return'd;
Hunt not the Bubble Beauty, like a Boy;
Fall like a Man: and let your Rest be Fame.
And so it shall: If what thou say'st be true,
I'll level him with Earth.
    ARI.   What said you, Sir?   85
    ANNI.   Yet I will have more Proof; she shall, her self,
Be witness to the Fall of this high Virtue:
Then Friendship to the Winds, like meeting Tides,
We'll fight the Tempest out, nor give it o're,
Till one lies dash't, and broken on the Shore.   [Exit.   90
    ARI.   Thus far the Devil is the best mounted yet,
And Heresie at last shall win the Race.

Enter Labienus and Eubulus.

Ha! Labienus here,
And my Eubulus; We shall shortly govern.
    LABI.   I met the Emperour of late, alone;   95
Who ask'd for you.
    ARI.   I'll instantly attend him.
Where is his Son?
    EUB.   I left him with Dalmatius.
    ARI.   Unloading his sick Heart upon his Friend.

Enter Dalmatius and Crispus.

But see, the Master Enemy's at hand;
Sculk to your Posts, and dive in Mists away.   [Ex. Ari. Lab. Eub.   100
    CRISP.   Now my Dalmatius, now thou hast my Heart,
And make good use on't, if I ne're see thee more.
By Heav'n, my Friend, I have not hid a Point
Of that sad Story that must make my Ruine.
    DALM.   Would thou hadst told me half of it before!   105
I might have sav'd thee many a Sigh and Tear:
Pray Heav'n no worse come on't; but 'tis no time
T' upbraid thee now; What wou'dst thou have me do?
    CRISP.   Perswade my Father from enjoying her,
For if that be to night, as once he vow'd,   110
Thou shalt behold thy Crispus dead to morrow.
    DALM.   And what of Fausta?
    CRISP.   I know not what.
That subtle, false one, that has thus deceiv'd me,
And with her charms ensnar'd my innocent Soul:
But I will hence.
    DALM.   For what?
    CRISP.   To execute   115
The Vows I made.

DALM.   Go then and kill her.
CRISP.   Ha!
DALM.   Kill th' Adulteress: This incestuous Charmer:
And have her born in Triumph to thy Father:
Then tell thy Tragick story like a Man;
And greatly thus Atone for both your Crimes.   120
CRISP.   Farewell: I'll find another way to end her.
DALM.   Tongue --- kill her, go: or swear and be forsworn,
Thou ne're wilt see her more.   Heav'n! That a Man
Born to the Empire of the World, should dote
On such slight stuff as Woman!
CRISP.   See my Father,   125
Look thou to Him, as I'll be guard on Her.
Incest! Dishonour! To all future Ages ---
Think, --- Think on that --- and push him from his ruine.   [Ex. Crispus.

Enter Constantine and Sylvester. *

CONST.   What say the People to the rumour spred
Of my new Contract?
SYLV.   All the Christians mourn,   130
And sicken in their Souls, as if Heav'n warned
The Earth, of some unheard Calamity:
The Heathens on the other side rejoice,
And cry, a Persecution is at hand.
CONST.   No matter to the point; Knowst thou the man,   135
Whom Fausta Loves?
SYLV.   I told you Sir before,
I would be dumb for ever on this Theam.
CONST.   Yet this implies thou knowst, but wilt not show him:
All know him, all, all but he that shou'd;
For Crispus has confess'd,   140
Yet hides the name; --- But I'll find out one,
Less meriting respect, whom Racks shall force.
DALM.   If you intend your Empires safety, Sir,
Cast Fausta from your Bosom; Turn her out;
Away with her --- far let her be Exil'd,   145
With all her race; For Death is in her Beauty.
CONST.   My Brother offer this!
Death in her Beauty?
DALM.   Violent, sudden Death;
Death to your Health, and Ruine to your Glory.
CONST.   Perhaps he is the man. Her Lover! Yes: 150
And thus conceals his flame with Covert rage,
For else what Cause could thus provoke his Passion?

---

122 Tongue-kill C$_{1+}$.
  * and Sylvester.] C$_{1+}$; Sylvester, Dalmatius. Q$_1$. Q$_1$ is in error,
     since Dalmatius is already on stage.

What is the Publick Interest here concern'd?
Their murmurings, or their joys; which with a nod,
My Power can hush. By Heav'n there's more at bottom,   155
And I will find it out; Their looks betray 'em:
Priest: Princes: all engag'd; and for some great one.

Enter Arius.

But hold --- here comes my Man! Brother I've thought
And will consider further what you urg'd,
Against my Wife.
     DALM.   We leave you to Heav'ns care,   160
And wish you to beware that waiting Fiend.   [Ex. Dalm. Sylv.
     CONST. So, now your business, Arius!
     ARI.   Sir.
     CONST.   Your business?
The Coast is clear; be your Confession so;
And speak what all the Court have sworn to hide.
     ARI. Sir, Labienus gave me your Commands,   165
That I shou'd wait.
     CONST.   Dost thou dally with me?
Thou knowst the least of thy Enormous Crimes
Deserve a lengthen'd death: Think on thy Treason,
Atheism, Blasphemies against the Highest;
Think on the purpos'd murther of my Brother,   170
Wrought by thy Charms, thou damn'd one; after this,
Let thy affrighted Soul despise my wrath,
And if she dares be dumb to my demands.
     ARI. What must I Answer?
     CONST.   Give me Truth for Truth.
Once more then; And this warning be thy last,   175
Show me the robber of my hearts repose,
Friend to my Crispus, but his Fathers Foe;
The Conquering Rival of my ravish't Love.
     ARI. What, has your Son reveal'd?
     CONST. He says she's false; but tells me not to whom;   180
Swears she's foresworn: And when I see him next,
I shall know more.
     ARI.   What if you never see him?
     CONST. Why dost thou start a Question so unlikely?
     ARI. I cannot think he will betray his Friend;
He who betrays his friend, betrays himself;   185
And rather than do that, I judge he'll leave
Your sight, The Empire, and his Love for ever.
     CONST. Love, Arius! Ha! His Love! What Love? To whom?
     ARI. Why Love to you:
What other Love shou'd Crispus entertain?   190

----

188 To wh Q$_1$(KU), Q$_1$(DFo 1); To whom? Q$_1$(DFo 2-4).

He has no Mistress sure!
    CONST.   Thou seem'st to hint,
As if he had: Mark thy foregoing words:
He who betrays his friend, betrays himself:
By Heav'n! Thou hast set my anxious Soul a'work.
For when thou saidst; he has no Mistress, sure ---   195
Thy meaning was, to make me think he had;
And that this Mistress could be none but Fausta.
    ARI. I hope, dread Sir, you will not wrest my words,
And Innocent thoughts to any evil purpose.
    CONST. What! at your tricks agen? Be quick my Traitor,   200
And spread at once thy double Heart before me;
Dost thou not judge my Son, his Father's Rival?
    ARI. If you would know my Heart, indeed, I do.
    CONST. Why, what a Devil wert thou then to deny't?
So pittifully play the Hypocrite;   205
And scrue that lying Face into a show
Of Innocence,
When nature stampt thee for a Villain!
    ARI. Forgive me, Sir, if I avow 'twas fear,
Not Villany that made me hide my thought.   210
    CONST. All fear, but fear of Heav'n, betray's a guilt;
And guilt is Villany. But let thy fear
Produce what past betwixt the wicked pair;
Show me th' Adulteress and Adulterer;
Where, how and when, this Incest was Committed,   215
Who was the Instrument and Cursed Bawd,
And damn'd contriver of their horrid joys.
    ARI. Oh Heav'n!
    CONST.   O Hell! For there shalt thou be hurl'd,
And rost in Sulphur, if Thou not tell me all;
Thou, who perhaps thy self wer't the Contriver,   220
The Bawd I nam'd, and Instrument of their lust.
    ARI. Hold Sir! And I'll confess: I've seen your Son
Oftner then I have wish'd, attend your Fausta,
And seen him late from her Apartment come;
I've heard him praise her long, and when the praise   225
Was finish'd, sigh, that he durst praise no longer:
At least I thought so, but my thought's no proof.
    CONST. No Arius, not enough for Crispus Death,
But there's enough to turn my Spirit from him,
To make me loath his form: When next we meet,   230
From Head to Foot to measure him with my Eye,
Both as an Object of my scorn and hate.
    ARI. That Love has past betwixt 'em is past doubt,
But for enjoying ---
    CONST.   Knowst thou ought of that?
    ARI. Not I, by Heav'n!

207-08 Printed as one line by Häfele.

CONST.   Why didst thou start it then?   235
ARI. Sir to be satisfi'd, what you wou'd do,
Upon the demonstration.
     CONST.   Both shou'd bleed,
Both dye, as sure as we are living, Arius;
For him, 'twere sacriledge to think to save him,
If thus he has transgress't; not then my vows,   240
Not all the Conquests of his blooming Years,
With my whole Empires Knees and lifted Hands:
Not the remembrance of his Mothers Tears,
When on her death-bed, she bequeathed his safety
To my best Care and Love, shall once redeem him.   245
     ARI. What shall be done to him that finds the truth?
     CONST. Reward and Honour. He shall be my friend.
     ARI. I ask no more; henceforth I'm yours;
To search, tho at the Peril of my life
The bottom of this business.
     CONST.   Say and do ---   250
But send my Wardrobe now, to Fausta's side,
Bear her the Diadem, with stile of Empress:
And say this night I bed Her.
     ARI.   That will prove her ---
If she refuse; You know Sir what to judge.
Nor would it be amiss to break discourse,   255
About your Son, and sift her subtle Soul. ---
     CONST. I apprehend thee: But as I commanded ---
Away --- Oh Constantine! Yet e're this search,   [Ex. Ari. *
Whatever comes, Remember he's thy Son;
Son of thy Love, and once was next thy Soul.   260
But as the best are worst, when once corrupted,
If he has sinn'd at all, he has sinn'd to Death;
The Thought distracts me; Heav'n remove this Trouble,
Or I shall run to my old Gods again.
But hush awhile: I'll bear my Passion cold,   265
I'll curb it while the Reins of Reason hold;
But if they break, then Nature, where's thy Call?
Be deaf to Reason, Nature, Judgment, All ---
The Precipice is Fate; and if we roul,
The Fault is theirs that fool'd us with a Soul.   [Exit.   270

Scene II.

Enter Crispus with a Dagger, and Fausta.

FAUST. Hold, hold thy hand ---
CRISP.   Think not I meant to kill Thee ---

---

* [Ex. Ari.] C$_{1+}$; <u>om</u>. Q$_1$.

No, thou seducer, were thy Stains more deep
Think not Despair, and Rage cou'd so unman me
To hurt a Woman. Yet thou shalt hear me Fausta:
And if the Story of thy Crimes can kill thee,   5
I'll lay thy Wounds wide open to the Air;
Display the Perjuries of thy bleeding Heart,
And to thy Incest, add at last a Murder.
    FAUST. Stab with thy Dagger then; but let thy Tongue
Destroy no more.   10
    CRISP. Oh all ye Powers, who that had known last Night,
The Joys which I have known, could once have thought it!
Who that had heard her Vows, when on my Breast,
Weary'd with Oaths, and out of Breath with Kisses
She panting swore! And wish'd Destruction seize her,   15
If she were not content, so one night more
Her ravish'd Soul like that might entertain,
To live her Miseries and past Life again.
    FAUST. By all those Powers you name, and by your own,
I wish so still.
    CRISP.   Yet at that very Minute   20
When thus she swore, to know she was forsworn,
Conscious her Faith was plighted to another!
And who that other pick'd from all Mankind,
To make her more abhor'd, but my own Father?
    FAUST. What, Load on Load?
    CRISP.   Her violated Hands   25
Were plighted fast with his; and Kisses past. ---
    FAUST. Hold, hold, and let my Tears atone, my Lord,
Or sink upon the Earth.
    CRISP.   The Center, Fausta,
The Center cannot hide thee from the Horrors
Of thy own Conscience, which are my Avengers: 30
And wheresoe're thou fly'st, shall follow thee
With inward Hells, for the base Wrong thou hast done me.
    FAUST. O Crispus! never, never, wilt thou end?
    CRISP. By Heav'n! I know thy damnable Design:
Thou hast this Night contriv'd to ruine Nature,   35
To make the Angels sick with such a Crime,
As equals hers that first betray'd the World.
    FAUST. I'll stop thee with my Kisses!
    CRISP.   Off Crocodile!
    FAUST. Why use thy Ponyard then.
    CRISP.   Nor that, nor this.
I had design'd, 'tis true, to stab my self;   40
But second Thoughts instruct me thus to haunt thee;
Like an eternal Fiend to follow thee:
To hollow still Damnation in thy Ear,

---

3 Think not Despair,] C_{1+}; Think not too, Despair, Q_1.

And hinder thee from Incest with my Father.
Oh horrid Thought!
  FAUST.   Oh horrid Thought indeed!   45
  CRISP. Why does it not possess thee!
Thou fair insinuating Snake! wouldst thou then guild thy Poison?
Swear on my Ponyard, swear, and damn thy self;
Thou hast not plotted, as this Night, to twist
Thy incestuous Arms about my Father's Neck!   50
  FAUST. Yes, I will swear. But let me lean my Head
Against thy Breast, while I recover Breath:
For I am faint with Groans.
  CRISP.   Oh Heart! Oh Love!
She grasps so hard, and locks so with her Charms,
I cannot put her from me! Fausta! is't possible!   55
Is it then possible! Thou canst be good?
So good at least, as being thus gone in Sin,
To go no further?
  FAUST.   Let me swear;
For I will face the Gods in such a Cause;
And standing on the Guard of Innocence,   60
Swear, all I've done was but th' Effect of Love.
  CRISP. Again thou'rt fallen; for thou art guilty, Fausta,
Of Impious Treasons, and incestuous Love.
  FAUST. I am not, Crispus.
  CRISP.   Ha! not guilty, Fausta?
Then farewel all.
  FAUST. Hold, hold, not guilty to my Crispus. 65
Fall not to Rage again, and I'll confess
I was compell'd to be contracted to him:
Not wedded, nor possest.
  CRISP.   Why didst thou hide thy Contract?
  FAUST. Because 'twas forc'd by Fear; nor did I dare
Reveal it to thee, e're I had thee sure.   70
So much I lov'd thee, Crispus.
  CRISP. But what hadst thou decreed to do to night,
This fatal Night, if that the Emperour
Had sworn to enjoy thee?
  FAUST.   Stop him with my Tears;
Or if they fail'd, to dam his Passion thus,   75
And sheath this hidden Ponyard in my Heart.
  CRISP. Is't possible, Thou should'st so greatly dare?
  FAUST. Yes Crispus. Thou shalt see by what's to come.
Oh! therefore take me to thy Breast, and swear ---
  CRISP. Swear first thy self, he never shall possess thee. 80
  FAUST. What needs an Oath after possessing Thee?
  CRISP. Yet, for the Satisfaction of my Soul,
And Cement of our everlasting Loves,
Swear thou wilt never.

70-71 Printed as one line in Q₁, C₁.

FAUST.   Never Crispus, never.
By Heav'n and Earth, by all that's great, and holy,   85
I swear thy Father never shall embrace me.
  CRISP.   What never! Oh yet closer! Never Fausta?
  FAUST.   By all this Dearness, never Crispus, never.

                Enter Arius.

  ARI.   What Faults are gone and past, it matters not:
But you had best beware of what's to come ---   90
Haste Sir away. --- See there the Beds prepar'd ---   [Scene draws.
The Diadem; and Name of Empress given ---
Your Father's at my Heels! hark! you are warn'd.   [Soft Musick.
I hear him come, and wish you Sir away.   [Ex. Arius.
  CRISP.   Oh Fausta!
  FAUST.   Take no Thought.
  CRISP.   If he should charm thee,   95
Or scare thee to Compliance ---
  FAUST.   That distrust
Again! by Heav'n I'll dye before he enters.
  CRISP.   Hold thee, my Heart! my Life, my Love, my Soul,
I'll stay --- and hazard all --- but hark! he comes.
I would advise --- Live, if thou canst with Honour ---   100
If not --- he's here, fall, and I'll follow thee.   [Ex. Crispus.

        Re-enter Arius with Constantine.

  CONST.   Ha Arius! see'st thou there?
  ARI.   Crispus, I think.
  CONST.   Did'st thou not see him?
  ARI.   Yes.
  CONST.   Why dost thou then suppose it but thy Thought?
  ARI.   Because I do not like his being here.   105
  CONST.   Nor I, by Heav'n! Withdraw; and wait my Call. [Ari. retires.
What now, my Fausta! Ha! in Tears my Fair!
What, on thy Wedding Night? Why dost thou fly me?
Am I a Ravisher? Howe're reputed
Bloody in Fields, in Chambers I am gentle   110
As thy own Thoughts.
Therefore let our Vows be seal'd, and then to bed.
  FAUST.   What said you, Sir?
  CONST.   Why, to Bed my Love;
And hide thy Virgin Fears. Thou wilt be bolder there ---
  FAUST.   Alas! I dare not.
  CONST.   Why?
  FAUST.   I've sworn, my Lord.   115
  CONST.   What, and to whom?
  FAUST.   To Heav'n I've sworn,

---

104 by Thought? C_{2+}.

Howe're contracted, that I will not wed you.
    CONST. When?
    FAUST.   Not to night.
    CONST.   When then?
    FAUST.   Press me no further,
For I can only answer with my Tears.
    CONST. Speak, for I'll know th' Extremity to night ---   120
Why then to morrow; but by Heav'n no longer;
For now I've sworn too.
    FAUST.   But I vow'd first:
And swear again to keep that Vow till Death.
To morrow and to morrow, add to those
Ten Millions more. You never shall embrace me ---   125
    CONST. Is't possible! after thy Faith was given!
    FAUST. Not given, but by a Conquerour compell'd.
    CONST. And hast thou rightly scan'd the Conquerour's Rage!
Ha! Fausta! hast thou plac'd thy Fathers Fate
Before thy Eyes? And thought upon thy own?   130
    FAUST. Just to your purpose: I'm prepar'd for Death,
Rather than entertain you in my Bed:
Therefore if you set down t'enjoy me, Sir,
Or doom me dead, upon the Earth I beg you
To speak your Will. And Fausta shall revenge you.   135
This Ponyard strait shall act your vow'd Revenge,
And take her from the World. ---
    CONST.   Rise, Fausta! rise ---
By Heav'n I find 'tis vain to strive against thee!
Take then what more thou valu'st than the World,
And what, in spite of me, the Fates ordain thee ---   140
My Crispus for thy Love ---
    FAUST.   Ah, Sir, what mean you?
    CONST. Why would'st thou strive to hide what Nature shows?
Dalmatius, Arius, and Sylvester, know it:
And over-wrought me for my Empires Safety,
To this great Act to yield thee to my Son.   145
    FAUST. Did Arius too? No sure, they rather wrought you
To yield me to my Grave ---
    CONST.   No. To my Throne:
Already 'tis decreed: my Caesar weds thee.
Not but I own I came to work thee from him.
But since not Death it self can daunt thy Love,   150
Forbid it Heav'n, that I should break such Union.
Haste Arius! Call my Son. I'll give him now;
Now while my Reason lets me see my Dotage.
How ill such Autumn suits thy Beauties Spring!
But haste and bring him, while the heat is on me;   155
For I will have you wedded in my presence:
And if thy Heart consent to make a Turn,
As strange as kind; this Night he shall enjoy thee.
    FAUST. Oh Heav'n, instruct my Frailty what to answer!

Can this be real Sir! is't possible? 160
    CONST. My Council know it, and confirm the Order.
    FAUST. That I shall wed your Son?
    CONST.   Why thus repeated?
    FAUST. And you approve it?
    CONST.   Canst thou doubt me still?
    FAUST. No. I will own Sir, since you approve it:
Own it to Death, I love him more than Life. 165
    CONST. O Fausta!
    FAUST.   Ha! what now? He turns away.
He blushes! Gods --- I'm lost, betray'd, undone!
Undone for ever. Crispus is betray'd:
The innocent Crispus. ---
    CONST.   Guilty, guilty Crispus ---
And guilty Fausta! Guilty both to death; 170
But most my Son who wrought thee to this ruin.
    FAUST. O say not so. 'Twas Fausta wrought your Son ---
And over Lov'd him, to his own destruction,
Therefore as you're powerful be just,
And let the stroak of Vengeance light on me. 175
But Sir for him ---
    CONST.   For him each Syllable
Thou plead'st in his behalf but wings his death.
    FAUST. By the just Heav'ns! And by the Saint that bore you,
By your Religion Sir, I do conjure you,
Spair, spair his Innocence ---
    CONST.   If thou consent, 180
That I this night shall wed thee. ---
    FAUST.   Wed me Constantine!
    CONST. Fausta, Why not?
Art thou enjoy'd already, married? Speak, confess ---
That I may pardon thee ---
    FAUST.   What you know, you know;
You have betray'd me once, but shall no more: 185
More! There's no more, but that I Love your Son,
And whether he Loves me, the Gods can tell:
I know the natural goodness of your temper,
How e're transported will not let you kill him.
Therefore I leave you ---
    CONST.   Stay and tell me when; 190
When I may hope Loves Consummation sure?
    FAUST. When you behold me Wedded to your Son,
As you engag'd, and past your Royal word,
When after many rowling years I bring you
A race of smiling Boys to bless your Age, 195
To play about your Throne, and be your Caesars:
Then may your happiness compleated be,
Then may your Eyes the Consummation see,
But never hope for other joys from me.   [Ex. Fausta.
    CONST. What Arius! help and free me from this plunge 200

Of Love and Nature. She Loves; She Loves to Death;
And tho she hides it, is belov'd agen.
  ARI. What's your resolve? To give her to your Son?
  CONST. No Arius; first I'll give her to the Grave ---
Resign my Empire: All ---
  ARI.   Then Crispus dies ---   205
  CONST. If he has not enjoy'd her, he shall live,
For that I Lov'd him once is full as true
As that, tho now he has sin'd, I cannot hate him,
But if enjoy'd! How shall I find it out?
I'll seise and Rack him.
  ARI.   How Sir, Rack your Son!   210
  CONST. By Heav'n 'twas well remember'd by a Villain:
Therefore I swear thou shalt be Rack't thy self.
  ARI. Who I, my Lord?
  CONST.   Ay Villain: Traitor, Thou!
I'll Rack the Racker, till I find it out;
For my misgiving Heart says thou know'st more: 215
Therefore, when next I see thee, bring me proof,
She's not enjoy'd, her vows and vertue clear;
Do't, or thy Death shall teach succeeding Kings ---
No more by false reports to be abus'd ---
But strait confront th' Accuser with the Accus'd ---   220
To prove the Treasons urg'd against the Throne; ---
Or show the Sycophants that set 'em on:
So shall the Soveraign pow'r unclouded sway,
When such Court Devils, shun the glorious Ray,
And drive like Foggs, before the rising Day.   [Exeunt. 225

     End of A C T III.

---

223 sway,] C_{2+}; sway. Q_1-C_1.

Act IV. Scene I.

Enter Annibal and Serena.

ANNI. Then you confess you did bespeak the Picture?
Gods! and you own you Love him! Love the Traitor?
    SEREN. Call him not Traitor, Annibal, he who spoke
The kindest things of you.
    ANNI.   Wondrous kind!
Accurst dissembler! That could speak for me,   5
But acted for himself.
    SEREN.   Just contrary.
For when by signs, which passion could not hide,
I let him know my Love; he turn'd away,
Shaking his head as loth to understand me,
Anger and pitty combating in his Face,   10
And with his blushes taught Serena shame.
    ANNI. Shameless himself, and Traitor to my friendship!
For all I have heard, your Love has forg'd to save him.
    SEREN. Heav'n knows 'tis true! Nothing was left unsaid,
To his own disgrace and your Immortal Honour: 15
In the most melting Terms and sweetest words
That Heart could think, or Friendship could invent:
Therefore forgo my Lord, this fruitless passion,
And speak for Crispus as he spoke for you.
    ANNI. I will; and speak so loud the Gods shall hear me: 20
There! Take his Picture, feed your hungry passion,
Till with my Sword I carve another feast,
To glut your fatal Eyes ---
    SEREN.   Hold; Whither go you?
And what fierce purpose has your Heart in hand?
    ANNI. I'll tell thee: And if possible force a warmth   25
In that cold Breast; kindle a dying spark,
In that inhospitable Land of Love;
And never see thee more --- I go to die,
To blot my youth and glory from the World;
Tho Conquest waits my Sword, I swear to die,   30
And make thee sport with my untimely fall.
    SEREN. To die! By whom? For what?
    ANNI.   For Love of thee.
But if I suffer by the Hand of Crispus,
And perjury should prosper in my ruine,
Then you may revel in each others Arms,   35
And laugh indeed at my ridiculous fortune.
Yet, if revenging Ghosts have power to rise,
Expect me at the Riot of your joys:
With hollow Eyes, to stare you in the Face,

At midnight, look to have your Curtains drawn; 40
Expect me in your Bed, a Coarse of clay,
To clasp your trembling Limbs with cold embraces,
And print my gelid kisses on your Lips,
So to revenge my death upon your scorn,
And groan about you till the dawning morn --- [Exit. 45
  SEREN. Stay --- and I'll tell thee; 'tis impossible ---
Crispus already is in Love with Fausta ---
He's gone to the execution of his purpose ---
And Crispus must be slain: Why then my Hour
Of Fate is come: What's that to Crispus murder? 50
He's gone to fight; perhaps not give him leave,
But take the Innocent at unawares;
Haste after him, and by thy own destruction,
Prevent both ruins, follow the fate that wafts thee,
And let no interrupter cross thy passage. [Exit. 55

   Enter Constantine, Sylvester, Dalmatius.

  CONST. Were you both Fathers, and in Love like me;
I no more doubt, what you would put in Act,
Than now I doubt my self, who am resolv'd.
  DALM. On what?
  CONST.   On Death.
  SYLV.   Of whom?
  CONST.   Of any man
That knows, yet hides this secret Treason from me. 60
  DALM. Has Crispus own'd he Lov's her?
  CONST.   Yes, in effect;
For when I first reveal'd this contract to him,
He stopt me from enjoying her with Oaths.
He knew her false, forsworn: To whom? To him;
To him himself: For this last night I prov'd; 65
Drawing the secret from her by a wile,
Which she before as craftily conceal'd.
  DALM. But have you married and enjoy'd her, Sir?
  CONST. O no; the Ceremonies and the dues,
Without a blush were frontlesly deny'd: 70
In all the Heat of boyling Love deny'd:
Not only from possessing her that night,
But, matchless impudence! deny'd for ever:
Now judge if 'tis not fit I should let go
The strugling Thunder, and destroy 'em both. 75
  DALM. Not both --- for yet you have not heard your Son;
Hear him but plead ---
  CONST.   Then let him plead in time. [Ex. Dalm.
The Bolts are brandish't, and 'twill be too late,

  54 Ruins. C_{1+}.

To lift his blasted hands, when I have hurl'd.
    SYLV. How far Sir, would your utmost search extend?   80
    CONST. To know if Actually they have embrac'd
Each other, as in will th'have done already.
    SYLV. Be not too hasty in your Answer Sir,
If I should ask what then; What then must follow?
    CONST. Death certain, on the instant; imminent Death;   85
Death; And I swear not all the Gods shall save him.
    SYLV. Ruin of piety! Not all the Gods!
That your Religion?
    CONST.   Oh forgive me, Saint,
I am eaten up with passion: So o're-wrought,
With racking Love I knew not what I said.   90
But if he has enjoy'd her: By that power
Whom thou remember'st well, I now adore,
His Death must wash th' incestuous Guilt away.
    SYLV. Not Incest, Sir.
    CONST.   Not if he has enjoy'd her?
    SYLV. No: for to prove the Guilt compleated Incest,   95
You must have married and enjoy'd her first.
    CONST. True; but what makes his Crime deserving Death
More than imputed Treason, Incest, all;
All Faults by Art and Nature joyn'd in one.
If he has touch'd her, she must ne're be mine;   100
And that's a Cause so pointing to his Fate,
That Death's their due that offer to excuse him.
    SYLV. He comes. --- I'm silenc'd. Nature, now or never.

Enter Crispus and Dalmatius.

    CRISP. O Emperour! for I dare not call you Father,
Behold me at your Feet prepar'd for Death.   105
    CONST. O Crispus! for I must not call thee Son,
Justice surveys thee as a Criminal.
But rise then and speak; plead like a Man for Life.
Come on, and look thy Father in the Face;
I call thee Traitor, and I'll prove thee one,   110
Who impiously, for all my former Love,
Hast dar'd to violate my sacred Bed.
Now answer Criminal. What canst thou say
That Sentence should not pass upon thy Treason?
    CRISP. Most aweful Emperor, my Judge and Father!   115
Father, alas! I would have offer'd first.
But since you are not pleas'd it should be so,
I'll do as Criminals use, and you command:

---

  92 adore,] C_{1+}; adore. Q_1.
  94 Sir.] C_{1+}; Sir? Q_1.
 108 But rise and speak; C_{1+}.

Thus plead my Innocence at your Judgment-Bar;
If either, Sir, I saw or lov'd the Princess,   120
You were the only Cause, 'twas you that sent me:
So far from once but hinting this your Contract,
You told me Sir, her Fate was yet in doubt;
Which made me wonder when I saw the Virgin,
So innocent, so beautiful, so young: 125
Which Charms did more my Admiration move;
Wonder begot my Pity; that my Love.
    CONST. But if I told you that her Fate was doubtful,
I told you too, she was a Foe to Rome;
Therefore, to think of loving her was Treason.   130
    CRISP. If Love be Treason, Sir, I own I am guilty;
Guilty indeed; because it was a fault,
In any Case to wed without your Knowledge:
But yet I hop'd, in time you might forgive me;
And so my Conscience tells me still you would,   135
Had you not been engag'd your self before.
    CONST. Rebellion, not thy Pardon, was thy Thought:
If otherwise, how canst thou answer Traitor,
For not confessing all when first I met thee?
    CRISP. Pardon me Sir, for that I had done too,   140
Had you not told me first you were betroth'd;
But conscious then, how closely I was link'd,
I durst not tempt your Wrath.
    CONST. How closely, Traitor! Hast thou then enjoy'd her?
    CRISP. Can you forgive me?
    CONST.   No. By this shaking Flesh   145
Tho there thy Mother kneelt too by thy side.
If thou hast touch'd her, Death and Curses on thee.
    CRISP. Oh by those Knees and Hands which I must hold,
Racks, Racks, and Death; but not your Curses, Sir.
    CONST. If thou would'st have my Blessing, swear then, swear   150
Thou hast not enjoy'd her.
    CRISP.   Swear then to forgive me.
    CONST. Forgive thee, Villain! if thou hast possest her,
Speak, or be curst.
    CRISP.   I will: but give me time.
    CONST. Let go. What time? Thou hast confess'd already
By that Demand; I swear thou hast enjoy'd her.   155
    CRISP. Swear not, and I'll confess this Moment.
    CONST.   What!
    CRISP. O Heav'n,
What if your Son has plighted holy Vows?
    CONST. Why then I make that Vow and Marriage vain.
Therefore, if thou hast not embrac'd her yet,   160

---

122 thus your C$_{1+}$.
132 fault, Q$_1$(DFo 1-4), C$_{1+}$; <u>in</u> Q$_1$(KU) <u>illegible</u>.

I charge thee, on my Blessing, never hope it,
Nor ever think of loving her again.
    CRISP. Impossibilities! Were you a God,
And doom'd me thus, I could not, Sir, obey you:
For I have sworn to love her while I have Life;   165
And if I love her I must hope Enjoyment.
    CONST. Death then and Curses on thy Disobedience!
Off Villain! Traitor! grovel there on Earth.
What, are you Plotters too? nay, then 'tis time
To haste his Ruine. Ruine is thy doom;   170
And wing'd with all my Curses it shall come.   [Ex. with Dalm. & Sylvester.
    CRISP. Dalmatius and Sylvester! Call him back,
And I'll renounce my Love: Heav'n 'tis too much!
But hark! I hear a Voice cry, Crispus come,
Come to the thoughtless Grave where all is still.   175
It shall be so: up then, and fall a Man.
Come forth, thou Minister of others Fates,   [Draws his Sword. *
And be thy Masters now! Where art thou, Fausta?
Where is my Love to close my dying Eyes?

            Enter Annibal.

    ANNI. Ha, Traitor! Art thou then prepar'd for Death?   180
    CRISP. Yes Annibal, I will receive it calmly,
From any Hand but thine. What have I done
That he should call me Traitor?
    ANNI.   Guard thy self,
Or else by Heav'n thou dy'st.
    CRISP. Hold. Is't possible! so quickly?   185
Can the desire of Empire lose a Friend!
My Father I offended, but not Thee;
Execute then the Ruine which he dooms,
Ungrateful Man. I will not make Defence,
But spread my Arms t'embrace the Death he sends me.   190
    ANNI. What thou deserv'st from him I neither know
Nor care, resolv'd upon my own Revenge;
Not but I think the Man who did his Friend
So horrible a Wrong as thou hast done,
Is fit for any Mischief. Therefore guard thee.   195
    CRISP. Never to fight with thee; not tho my Father
Should grant my Love. Therefore I sheath my Sword.
    ANNI. Traytor, Coward.
    CRISP. Oh Annibal, I know I am no Traytor.
And thou whose Life I have so oft preserv'd,   200
Know'st but too well I am no Coward.
    ANNI.   Draw.
Draw then, or perish. By the Gods I'll kill thee: [Strikes him with his
                                                Sword.

---

    * [Draws his Sword.]; <u>om</u>. Q₁₊.

Be what thou wilt: and take this to provoke thee.
    CRISP. Well Annibal. 'Tis well. Thou hast done well.
Yet thus much Villany am I content to bear;   205
No longer, oh ungrateful for thy sake.
Who injur'st me, yet will not tell the Cause.
But for thy noble Father I will spare thee,
Spare thee thus far; so thou resolve to leave me.
    ANNI. Not yet? Why then another?   [Strikes him again. *
    CRISP.   But the next   210
Be mine: Humanity can bear no further.   [Anni. falls. **
    ANNI. I have my Death: and now my Heart relents ---
    CRISP. Cut off my Hand.
    ANNI.   Crispus, thou hast wrong'd me.
    CRISP. Speak how, and where?

Enter Serena.

    ANNI.   See, she comes to tell thee.
Serena, Oh Serena!   [Dies.
    CRISP.   Gone for ever!   215
    SEREN. Oh, never to return! and I, alas,
Who could not love again, the wretched Cause!
    CRISP. The Cursed Cause.
    SEREN.   Call me not Cursed, Crispus,
Who think no Blessing equal to thy Love.
    CRISP. Wert thou a Man, by Heav'n such Love I bear thee,   220
I think that I should seek thee through the World;
To give thee Death ---
    SEREN.   Take then the Death you threaten,
Prepare to suffer by a Virgins hand.
    CRISP. Kill me, and I'll forgive thee Annibal's Death:
But take this Sword, yet reeking with his Blood,   225
And thrust it through my Heart.
    SEREN.   Yet hold Serena:
What will become of him when thou art slain?
Kill himself last, and that I would prevent.
    CRISP. Why dost thou stay?

Enter Sylvester.

    SYLV. Crispus, I come to tell thee, Thy Father will not hear us.   230
    SEREN. Take these Swords, Sylvester; bear 'em hence,
Without Reply, --- or Crispus kills himself. --- Away.
    SYLV. Crispus Death!
I thank thee Heav'n! that sent me to preserve him.   [Exit.
    CRISP. Why hast thou thus delay'd my Ruine?   235

---

  206 sake, C_{1+}.
    * [Strikes him again.]; om. Q_{1+}.
  ** Actually Annibal runs upon Crispus' sword; see 1.266 below.

SEREN. To make thy Torments lasting,
Live, that my Ghost and Annibal's may haunt thee;
Yet when I come, believe, for all my Threatnings,
My Soul shall seek thee in a gentle form:
Court thee to Cells, and to the Garden shade,   240
And tell thee there, what Love with us is made;
What Fires the Fiends for willfull Murder make;
And what my Spirit suffers for thy sake.
But hark! I'm call'd --- behold the Dead awake.
They waft me, Crispus, to the sleepy Shore,   245
And I shall never, never see thee more.   ⌊Ex. Seren.
    CRISP. She's gone: and takes the means of Death too from me.
So what's the next? What have the Fates to add
To my past Sufferings? Lightning blast me,
Mountains fall on me, gape to the Center Earth,   250
To hide me from my friend.

                Enter Dalmatius.

    DALM. Why my dearest Crispus! but alas ---
In vain I urg'd thy Father, deaf to all,
Our prayers, remorsless, rocky and unmov'd,
Yet think not but I press'd with all my Love.   255
    CRISP. Therefore in great requital for thy Love
Look there, and let thy Blood congeal to Stone,
Behold thy Annibal butcher'd by this Hand.
    DALM. Cold, cold my Boy. Crispus. Have I --- have I?
But I waste time by such unmanly wailing.   260
Take to thy Sword.
    CRISP.   Thou seest I've none: but strike ---
    DALM. What could provoke thee to this horrid deed?
    CRISP. His jealousie, and Anger of the Heav'ns:
Jealous I robb'd him of Serena's Love.
He call'd me Traitor, Coward, strook me twice,   265
Before I drew, then ran upon my Sword.
    DALM. Whatever happen'd -- I'm a wretched Father,
And thou hast robb'd me of an only Child.
Therefore hereafter we no more are one,
Where e're I go I'll ask before I enter   270
If Crispus be not there? that I may shun thee.
Therefore if thou hast any Gratitude
For those kind offices, which I have done thee,
Fly these sad Eyes, as I will run from thine,
To moan my Son, and howl my life away.   ⌊Ex. Dalmatius.   275

----

249 vast Sufferings? C_{2+}.
264 Love, C_{1+}.
266 then] C_{1+}; than Q_1.

CRISP. <u>Sol.</u> And whither thou? Thou heap of walking woe!
Thou that hast pull'd thy Father's Curse upon thee;
Kill'd thy best friend, and ruin'd all that Lov'd thee ---
Where will at last thy Cruel fortune drive thee?
Hence tear thy Robes: And naked fly the World;   280
Unmantled to the Weather, wander on
To some dark wild, where Sun-beam never shone.   [Ex. Crispus.

Scene II.

Enter Constantine, Arius, Fausta, Sylvester.

FAUST. Consider Sir his Youth ---
CONST.   I have consider'd all ---
But find thy Love so rooted in my heart
I must forgo my life, or lose my Claim.
Yet mark how deep thy tears have wrought my temper,
If thou wilt swear to null thy marriage with him,   5
By wedding me in publick, and, this night,
By making me thy Lord ---
FAUST. No Sir, 'tis impossible, yet if you'll swear,
To save your Son if I should prove him guiltless:
I'll tell you wonders Sir, which otherwise   10
Not Racks shall e're compel.
CONST. Forbid it Heav'n! I should destroy the guiltless,
Tho strangers to my blood, much less my Son:
Therefore I swear by Heav'n and all the Saints,
Prove Crispus innocent he shall not die.   15
FAUST. Be witnesses, Oh Arius and Sylvester!
What he has sworn: Let Crispus strait be call'd,
And quitted of his Crime: Run, Arius, haste,
That I may see the Royal friendship made.   [Ex. Arius.
CONST. By an entire surrender of thy self,   20
To me.
FAUST. To Crispus!
CONST. By all thy former Oaths I swear to me.
FAUST. I told you, 'twas impossible before,
And now confirm it.
CONST.   How?
FAUST.   I am married.
CONST. Curses and Vengeance. Married! say to whom?   25
FAUST. To Crispus.
CONST.   When? Thou false one; When? And where?

---

5 thy] C$_{1+}$; my Q$_1$.
25 to] C$_{2+}$; by Q$_1$-C$_1$.

FAUST. Here in your Palace, on that happy night,
Before you made your dreadful triumph.
    CONST. Dreadful indeed: For now the wretch shall die,
Tho Angels pleaded ---
    SYLV.   Emperor, you have sworn.   30
    CONST. I know it Sir, to spare the innocent blood;
But I will prove him now.
    FAUST.   White as the Saints;
By all the powers of Heav'n and Earth I swear,
'Twas I that push'd the marriage: Conscious before,
What I had sworn to you; nay cast the Veil   35
Of Modesty aside to make him sure,
And after Marriage, you may ghess the rest.
    CONST. Oh Curses! Vengeance! Curses yet unthought!
Such Curses as thou wilt let fly at me,
When thou shalt see his Head beneath the Ax,   40
Even Womans Curses on thee.
    SYLV.   How Sir, the Ax!

Enter Arius with Crispus.

    CONST. Dost thou not find the Traitor?
But see he comes. Oh thou dissembler, answer,
Didst thou not tell me, when thy life was stak'd,
This marriage was not yet comsummate, speak.   45
    CRISP. 'Tis true dread Sir.
    CONST.   Mark all he has confess'd!
His own mouth has condemn'd him --- he shall die.
    CRISP. I own'd Sir, I was marry'd --- but confess'd
No further.
    CONST. How Traitor!
Did I not force the Question often?
    CRISP.   True;   50
Which I as often wav'd with low submissions ---
    CONST. Yet those thy low submissions all were lies.
For well thou know'st thy subtle working wrought me
To a satisfaction that thou hadst not possest her.
    CRISP. That was alas my Crime.
    CONST.   That Crime was Treason: 55
Purpos'd abuse. A Plot upon thy Father.
Nay the whole Cozenage shows thee rank in sin,
Or Ha! --- How know I yet she is enjoy'd?
I have but thy word and her's, and both are Traitors,
But see my Brother comes to joyn my Justice.   60

Enter Dalmatius.

    DALM. What, Crispus here?

---

58 enjoy'd?] C_{1+}; enjoy'd. Q_1.

CONST.   Stay, my Dalmatius, stay.
DALM. Your pardon Sir,
There's one among you, whom I cannot suffer,
And Crispus knows the Cause.   [Exit. Dalm.
CRISP.   Come back, and hear it then,
Hear thou unhappy Father, hear me own   65
The murder which this Cursed hand committed,
That hand that slew the wretched Annibal.
CONST. Annibal slain! O Traitor! And by thee!
Is murder added to thy Treason too?
CRISP. It shall not stand me Sir instead to say,   70
Mistaken Annibal forc'd me to his ruin.
For see I lay my Body at your Feet,
And plead for Death, as others begg for Life.
CONST. Cleanthes take him --- Crispus thou shalt die,
Therefore be this our fatal last farewell ---   75
One struggle more. His Mother's in his Eyes.
FAUST. And where's his Father; but in all his form?
His every grace; his smiles --- All but his frowns:
So exact in Body, Qualities of Mind,
That if you kill your Son, you kill your self.   80
Oh therefore listen to the call of Nature,
And once more view him with an Eye of Mercy.
CONST. I have lookt my last, and now am Judg agen.
Cleanthes! Take 'em both: They're both your Prisoners,
Crispus and Fausta. Arius --- look you to 'em!   85
Keep 'em apart; and wait me in my Closet ---
What yet agen? 'Tis the last tugg of Nature ---
And yet another --- Why that sigh uncall'd? ---
And these wet Eyes? Oh --- if I longer stay!
My vows of Justice will dissolve away ---   [Ex. with Sylvester.   90
                              [Manent Crispus, Fausta, Arius, Guard.

FAUST. Ruin on ruin, let destruction come,
With all the wings of the most violent death,
Yet arm'd with Innocence, I'll face the Gorgon,
And brave his bloodiest Terrors: But thy death,
My Crispus death, my spirit cannot bear ---   95
Therefore I have resolv'd, and think not Crispus,
Think not thy tears shall move me from my purpose.
CRISP. Speak Fausta; speak, how come these Earthquakes here?
And these o'reflowings? Why do thy sighs redouble?
FAUST. Because my dearest life; my all; my Crispus,   100
Soul of my Soul, that's martyr'd for thy Love ---
I am resolv'd rather then see thy death,
To wed thy Father. ---
CRISP.   Ha! Do I hear thee truly?

---

99 those o'reflowings? C_{1+}. thy] C_{1+}; the Q_1.

But speak agen, for I'll not trust my senses.
 FAUST. To wed him Crispus.
 CRISP.   Sorrow sure distracts thee. ---   105
 FAUST. No --- tis th' effect of reason ---
That makes me desp'rate in this last resolve ---
 CRISP. No more of this. Haste, cast the poison up,
Tis Hell that tempts thee to Eternal ruin.
Therefore if thou desir'st my spirit shou'd part   110
In peace, and leave my Love and blessing with thee;
Repent this last result of thy despair,
Lest I conclude thee false. ---
 FAUST.   How false, my Crispus?
 CRISP. False to thy Vows, unconstant to thy Love,
And that thy Soul unable for a ruin,   115
Chose rather to sustain an infamous life,
Then die with honor.
 FAUST.   Oh I cannot bear it!
 CRISP. Not when I begg thee with my latest breath ---
 FAUST. Thy death my Dear! And I the hated Cause?
 CRISP. Therefore I Love thee: And wou'd die agen 120
For such another proof of thy affection.
 FAUST. As wrought thy death? ---
 CRISP.   Thy purpose was to save me,
And die thy self. Therefore let's fall together ---
Be not cast down, my Fair: But raise the Eyes,
Those watry setting Suns, shine forth, my Fausta, 125
And make our Love look beautiful in ruin. ---

      Enter Souldier.

 ARI. The Emperor sends agen to have you parted.
 FAUST. Oh Crispus! Whither now?
 CRISP.   To our long Home,
Where purer Spirits drink immortal Air:
And thin clad Souls in flying Chariots move,   130
And give, and take, an everlasting Love.
 FAUST. Such Love grant Heav'n, our meeting Souls betide,
Which no inhumane Father may divide:
Where at first sight, our minds enlarg'd may spread;
Thro' all the space, and know the mighty Dead. 135
Such is my hope: But, Crispus, What my fear?
If I should seek: But never find you there. ---
 CRISP. One last Embrace! Oh Fausta! do not stain,
Our bliss with fears, we ne're shall meet again.
Through all the Heav'n in all their Mansions blest, 140
To ev'ry Saint my Prayers shall be addrest
Nor shall the happy tast a moments rest:

---

128 Home,] C_{1+}; name, Q_1.

Till some kind Angel guides my wandring Eyes,
And shews me where thy charming spirit flies.
Then Crown'd with joys, we never knew before,   145
We'l waste the stock of Loves immortal store,
And cruel fate shall never part us more.   [Exeunt.

End of A C T IV.

Act V. Scene I.

Enter Dalmatius and Serena.

SEREN. Now Sir, you have it all, the whole sad story
Of your unhappy Son, his Love and mine:
Serena's Guilt, and Crispus Innocence;
Therefore if you ask blood, and would revenge him;
Here waits his Murdress, for the stroak of death.   5
But hate not Crispus: Hate not the Innocent:
Much less proceed to the Murder of your friend,
Your faultless, guiltless, too deserving friend;
The gentlest, best, of all the Imperial Race.
DALM. No more: There needs no more; my Son is dead: 10
Eternal peace attend him: A few sad drops,
And now no more; Serena, I believe thee.
My Heart avows th' Innocence of my friend:
Which I had own'd before, had not the wounds
Of Annibal, lain green upon my Soul;   15
But that I now forgive him be thou witness,
Be witness Heav'n, and this last resolution,
I now put on to save my Crispus life,
Or lose my own.
SEREN. O let me kneel to such exalted Virtue.   20
But Sir, be quick to save him, or this goodness
Will come too late.
DALM.   Where is the Emperor?
SEREN. Lockt in his Closet, deaf to the Peoples cries:
Fly Sir, I saw him pass in fury by,
With Arius in discourse.
DALM.   I fear that Traitor.   25
SEREN. Your fears my Lord, are mine. I never lik'd him,
The Picture which he gave your Son, has shown him:
He has all the marks, we Virgins reckon Ominous,
A pale, down look, red Hair, and leering Eyes,
Mischief is in him: He's with th' Emperor now,   30
Perhaps solliciting the fate we fear.
I met 'em Sir, and interrupted Caesar;
Who first receiv'd me kindly; but at the name
Of Crispus frown'd, and shook me from his arm.
DALM. Fear not, as thou hast counsel'd, I will join   35
Sylvester on the instant.
SEREN.   Force the door,
If he refuse to let you in, do all
That pity, love, and friendship can inspire,
Do all that I would do, were I Dalmatius.   [Ex. Severally.

Scene II.

The Scene a Bedchamber.
A Bowl and a Dagger on the Table.

Enter Constantine and Arius.

CONST.   Arius!
ARI.   Sir.
CONST.   I am resolv'd to be at rest,
Thou art my friend, Physician, I am sick,
Sick even to death: Reach me that goblet hither:
The Dagger too.
ARI.   Sir.
CONST.   What an easie matter   5
It were for any man, in any Case,
Tho Rack't with th'Gout, Stone, any kind of torture,
With one of these to sleep?
ARI.   For ever Sir?
CONST. Right Arius.
ARI.   Then there is Poison in the Bowl.
CONST. There is most deadly.
ARI.   May I, Sir, presume
To ask for what?
CONST.   Arius, thou art my friend,   10
I think too, thou would'st venture life. Why yes! ---
'Tis Poison, and I'll tell thee too for what:
To see how long a Dog will be a dying.
Or say, what if we try'd it on a man;
Some Enemy that Laws will not take hold of?   15
ARI. Sir, I understand you.
CONST. Look then you do: How dost thou understand me?
ARI. Why thus, you past your Oath, your Son shou'd live,
If Fausta prov'd him Innocent.
CONST.   'Tis true:
And spite of my revenge, my Heart must clear him.   20
ARI. Right Sir, I find it, you are grip'd in Conscience,
Now if a Friend should help you: So: or fate
Not always answering most mens Expectations,
Should call your Son to Heav'n.
CONST.   To Heav'n Arius!
ARI. To Heav'n, or Hell, it matters not for that,   25
So he be out o'th' way, and you not know't.

---

8 Bowl? C_{1+}.
21 find you are, C_3.

CONST.   And I not know't?
ARI.   No Sir, nor I.   What then?
How then!   you never see him more.
And so farewell --- I'll take this Poison with me.
  CONST.   Stay stay!   Come back.   30
How strange a guilt is mine, who dare not speak,
But indirectly, what my Soul desires
Directly done.   Why shou'd I hide my thoughts
From thee?
  ARI.   Why Sir indeed?
  CONST.   When no Eye sees.
  ARI.   None.
  CONST.   None but the Eye of Heav'n.   35
But Walls they say have Ears: Therefore we'll whisper
This Horrid, Barbarous; and Unnatural Murder!
Give him his Choice.   Tell him I cannot live,
Unless he dies: Tell him I strove to save him,
And nature pleaded wonders in his Cause.   40
  ARI.   I'll stabb him first, and tell him after. ---
  CONST.   No, Poison's the gentler Fate.   Thou art too lowd ---
O Conscience how it heaves, within my bosom ---
  ARI.   Conscience!   The Souls rising of the Lights.   Drink Blood. ---
  CONST.   Blood say'st thou!   What the Blood of Crispus?   Hark!   45
Who's there?   Run to the Door!   Say I am not well,
I'll not be seen to night.
  ARI.   Your fancy Sir.
  CONST.   I thought I heard my Mothers Voice.
But she's long dead: 'Twas as thou say'st, my fancy,
My fear, my guilt that haunts me: But begone,   50
If he must fall there is no hiding it:
Call it no longer Murder, but a Justice,
Survey him as a Thief that robb'd thy Soul
Of all its wealth: Arius --- how am I now?
  ARI.   All Emperor.   And Sir I'll haste to obey you.   55
  CONST.   Thou shalt: But go not Arius, till I send thee ---
All Emperor, and Judge.   But where's the Father?
Work me there Nature, save him if thou canst;
Remember him as once thy bosom-love.
  ARI.   I like not this Remembrance.   60
  CONST.   Remember the whole Progress of his Life;
Obedient all, ev'n in his Infant Years:
When every Morning to my Bed-side he came,
And as I blest him, thank'd me with his Tears.
                            [Serena knocking without.
  SEREN.   My Lord, the Emperour.
  CONST.   Arius, hark.   Who's there?   65
Hark, 'tis my Wife.   Run to the door.   My Wife!

---

37 barbarous, C_{1+}.
63 **Morn** C_{2+}.

She's risen from the dead to save my Son.
    SEREN.   I will have Audience.
    ARI.   Madam, you must not enter.
    CONST.   Arius, Let her in.

                      Enter Serena.

    SEREN.   Caesar, Save thy Son;
Save him in time; the People are in Arms.   70
Dalmatius, with the Guards, is gone to quell 'em.
    CONST.   How! mutiny? And in my Sons behalf?
Is this the course to save him? Arius hence ---
And execute my Orders.
    SEREN.   May I think it?
A Bowl of Poison, Sir: Is that your Order?   75
    CONST.   There is no Mystery now to be conceal'd ---
'Tis as you said: And Crispus dies this Minute.
Arius away.
    SEREN.   He sha'n't, till you hear me.
Think Sir, oh think!
    CONST.   I've thought too much already:
But with this last Revolt my Heart is steel'd;   80
Though as you enter'd I was fooling Time
With Thoughts of Mercy.
    SEREN.   And has this cursed Wretch prevented you?
    CONST.   Dalmatius and Sylvester will be here
To hinder Justice: Break her Hold. Away.   85
    SEREN.   Fall then Serena first. And stay that fury. [Stabs her self.
    CONST.   Arius, come back. What hast thou done Serena?
    SEREN.   I've paid the Debt of Nature e're my Time.
    CONST.   'Twas a too honest Part. What was the Cause?
    SEREN.   The Love of Crispus: Love of him you hate.   90
But let this Victim to Despair suffice.

           Enter Dalmatius and Sylvester.

Your Brother here! Dalmatius pardon me.
Your Son is now reveng'd. Restrain the Emperour ---
And look to Arius. Oh!   [She dies.
    DALM.   The Joys of Heav'n,   [Exit Arius. *
And an eternal Requiem waft thy Soul.   95
    CONST.   Brother, How are the People?
    DALM.   All hush'd again.
Why will you harbour, Sir, that Snake about you,
That puts you on these fatal Resolutions?

---

    * [Exit Arius.]; om. Q1+. It is possible that Arius leaves the stage
      at line 87.
   95 waft] C_{1+}; waste Q_1.

For, else could it be possible a Prince
So good, so full of every Kingly Grace, 100
Should once conceive a Thought to put his Son,
His guiltless Son, to an untimely Death,
Without the Instigation of a Devil?
    SYLV. Consider, Caesar, you that have had the Glory
By Miracles from Heav'n to be converted: 105
We know your Passion manacles your Reason;
But here are Hands to help you.
    CONST. Is that then the Result of all your Reason?
To hope for sober Actions from a Mad-man?
    DALM. Not till the Frenzy leaves him. But we know 110
You are not so far gone, to lose all Temper.
Your Hopes, and Fears, your broken Resolutions,
Are Symptoms all of a most noble Nature,
Where Judgment seems half sunk, but not quite drown'd.
    CONST. Why this I can alledge as well as you; 115
I know the Lawrels which I've worn so long
Must wither: If my Son should find a Grave,
My present Fame, and Glory too hereafter,
Is all upon the hazard: But what then?
I see the Storm before me threatning Wrack, 120
I see the Shelves, but who can point the Shore?
    SYLV. Cast over-board the Casket of your Love.
I know 'tis precious; but 'twill sink you, Sir.
Divorce her, Sir; and give her to your Son.
    CONST. Forgo my Fausta! 'tis impossible. 125
    DALM. Nothing's Impossible to a Mind resolv'd:
But pass beyond Sylvester's mild Remonstrance,
And ease your Love by Death, by Fausta's Death.
When she is past Recall you'll love no more;
Envy no more.
    CONST. If that could be resolv'd --- 130
The Conquest were a great one.
    DALM. The more you think, the more the Thought will strike you.
See but the difference of Counsellors;
What Colours good and bad can give to Reason.
Had Arius stay'd, by this time you had doom'd 135
Your Son to Death; who now have gain'd the Conquest.
    CONST. Would half were gain'd: yet, since the Start was noble,
I'll try to win in this Olympick Race.
Tho hilly all the way, and at the Gole
The Summit touches Heav'n. 140
    DALM. Urge the Necessity; she or Crispus dies:
Th' innocent Crispus, or the guilty Fausta
That after all her Vows, could thus deceive you.
Deceive you both. Who if your Son were dead,

---

143 you, C_{1+}.

No doubt, as quick would practise with another.   145
    CONST. By Heav'n, why not? She that could swear, and was
Forsworn, may swear and be forsworn again:
Oh! I remember now with what a Look,
An Angel-look, she vow'd.
    DALM.   Yet with that Look,
This Angel, like a Devil, drew in your Son: 150
Methinks the very grossness of the Cheat
Should make you loath her.
    CONST.   Ha!
    DALM.   Detest and scorn her.
    CONST. Scorn on her Scorn, and Death Disdain succeed;
By Majesty, by Empire, she shall bleed.
    SYLV. Banish her, Caesar. ---
    DALM.   No Sir; Death, or nothing.   155
Banish her to day, and she'll be here to morrow:
Down with her, down; dwell on her perjur'd Vows,
When the same Breath that swore her yours for ever
Dam'd her anothers.

               Enter Arius. *

    CONST.   Arius, bring her forth.
She dies! I'll sweat and bleed, but I will conquer ---   160
Call, call my Son. --- Henceforth but name a Woman,
'Tis Treason to my Ear: Why, what a Plague
Might she have here engender'd! Forc'd a Father
To put his guiltless Son to horrid Death.
    DALM. Royally urg'd. By Heav'n 'twas ever thus   165
Where Women had to do. Therefore behold her
As a Gangreen to the State.
    CONST.   And cut her off.
    DALM. The Bane of Empire ---
    CONST.   And the Rott of Power!
Yet there I'll stay and fix my Imagination,
On all their Mischiefs, Murders, Massacres.   170
And Seas of Blood they have spilt in former Ages.
Woman, no more. And when my Heart is going,
Sound but that Name, the pow'rful spell shall bind
Beyond Circean and AEgyptian Charms,
'Twill raise the lowest Devils up in swarms,   175
Unhinge the Globe, and put the World in Arms.
Woman that dooms us all to one sure Grave,
And faster damns than Providence can save.   [Exit.

       Enter Constantine and Fausta.

    CONST. Fausta, thou art false, forsworn.

---

159 Doom'd C_{1+}.
  * Enter Arius.]; <u>om.</u> Q_{1+}.
178 [Exeunt. C_{2+}.

FAUST.   I say so too.
CONST.   Therefore shalt dye.
FAUST.   I have no other Wish.   180
CONST.   What, not to live, if I should pardon thee?
FAUST.   That were Life indeed;
To gain your Pardon, and to live for Crispus.
CONST.   No, Wretch! remember as you swore to me,
I now return; it is impossible.   185
Yet thou shalt dye for Crispus.
FAUST.   And not with him, Sir?
CONST.   No; I've decreed that thou shalt dye to save him.
FAUST.   But have you, Sir, decreed to love him too
On Fausta's Death?
CONST.   I have.
FAUST.   Oh! then the Gods   190
Have heard my Pray'rs, which, next to living for him,
Was, still to dye to save him.
Yet grant me Sir in Death one last Farewel.
CONST.   No; thou hast look'd thy last.
FAUST.   Yet you may let 'em bear me by his Window;   195
If it be possible to snatch a Glance,
And not delay my Execution, Sir.
CONST.   She weeps; and there is Magick in her Tears.
I shall weep too. Bring forth the Poison. Haste ---
She shall not stay the making of a Bath.   200
What Arius!
ARI.   Sir.
CONST.   Give her the Poison. Haste and see her dye.
FAUST.   Stay Sir, come back. I have no load upon me ---
But what you all may know: give me the Bowl;
I'll drink it for my Love. Alas my Lord,   205
Methinks one last farewel, had not been much;
But since you judge it Sir unfit --- I'll die,
Without complaining. Therefore tell my Love ---
That my last Pray'r was for his life and yours.
CONST.   Hold Fausta: Arius, take the Poison from her,   210
And bring the Bath. My Son shall see her die,
Call Crispus hither, since her Fates decreed,
'Twere just he shou'd be harden'd with the view.   [Exit Arius. *
She weeps agen. And with the trick unmans me,
Spite of my vows, she works my Lyon Heart   215
And melts me into Love. How fares my Fausta?
FAUST.   Sir.

---

181 Printed as two lines in Q_1-C_2; as one in C_3.
188 Printed as two lines in Q_1-C_2; as one in C_3.
193 Printed as two lines in Q_1-C_1; as one in C_{2+}.
212 Fate's C_{1+}.
  * [Exit Arius.]; om. Q_{1+}.

CONST. Thy hand before we part for ever. Fausta ---
I am lost --- I'm vanquish't. With a touch o'recome ---
   DALM. Wake Sir. Where are you?
   CONST.   Ha!
   DALM.   Sylvester's here: 220
And Crispus waits.
   CONST.   Why then she dies agen.
Haste, Bring him in, bring him to my relief.
The yerning of a Father comes upon me,
And my Soul longs to meet him. Fausta, turn;
Turn thy bright Eyes on death: And carry fires   225
To scorch new Worlds; but warm the old no more.
For here's the rising Sun, to eclipse thy beams.

       Enter Crispus with Sylvester.

O Crispus! Who that has beheld our distance?
That infinite space that passion cast betwixt us,
Would e're have thought we thus should meet agen?   230
   CRISP. What can be added, Heav'n, to such a kindness!
   CONST. What Crispus! What indeed to make it lasting?
See'st thou that fair one?
   CRISP. Sir, you give me hopes; Tho dash't with fears.
But hold, perhaps I have to death offended,   235
For sinning but in wish: A dawning joy,
Shines in her Eyes, and revels in her smiles,
Which seem to tell me, we shall both be happy.
   CONST. Would'st thou be happy in thy Fathers Love?
   CRISP. Judge me you Powers, if that be not my thought: 240
The utmost reach of my extended Soul,
Which knows no other wish, but Fausta's Love ---
   CONST. And that's the Love, which you, by my example
Must learn to hate.
   CRISP.   To hate Sir! What?
   CONST.   Hate thy Love:
Or what's all one, to bear the effect of hate,   245
Her execution here before thy Eyes.
   CRISP. My Fausta's death?

      Scene draws. Arius, Labienus, Eubulus, with a Bath.

   CONST.   Behold the Poison'd Bath.
   CRISP. For me -- I am ready Sir. Haste, Launch my Veins:
You that are destin'd here for my Destruction,
Unrobe me --- haste ---
   CONST.   None touch him, on your lives.   250
They may as safely Launch their Emperor,

---

223 yerning] C_2; earning Q_1-C_1.
228 distance, C_{1+}.

As wound his Son. But Fausta must prepare,
There is no other way to reconcile us.
    CRISP. Then hold me Sir, at everlasting distance,
Cast me agen for ever from your sight.   255
Banish me; Curse me, as you did before ---
But make not Fausta's death the Cursed cause,
To save this Villains life. This hangman Traitor,
Nay Coward that can live and hear her threatned!
    FAUST. My Love, my Lord, Blame not thy noble Father,   260
Nor Curse thy self, for this was all my seeking. ---
    CRISP. Thy seeking. Ha! And seekest thou my embraces ---
After the base dishonor thou hast done me?
Hence from my Arms ---
    FAUST.   I will not, I will hold thee
To my last gasp, and grasp thee after death,   265
Why push me yet agen: Nay, strike me Crispus,
I will not leave thy Bosom.
    CRISP.   See he's going ---
By my blest Mothers Soul, let me come at him ---
    CONST. Arius, see it done.
All Prayers are vain; some of you, break his hold.   270
    CRISP. Dalmatius and Sylvester will not sure,
And for the rest, let me but see who dares.
    CONST. Their Emperor commands 'em --- help to force him,
I charge thee Crispus, leave me,
And dare not by this willfulness provoke me.   275
    CRISP. I have no willfulness: But these stubborn Tears:
Hear my last sighs. For groans quite choak my words,
My Fausta's life: Or break my heart before you.
    FAUST. Sir, do not hear him, snatch your self away,
And leave us here --- I'll hush him e're I die;   280
And send him weeping to you for his Pardon.
    CONST. He sees 'tis vain. And has let go his hold.
Withdraw --- yet Brother, we'll observe unseen ---
I do not like this sudden sullenness ---
Fausta farewel, Arius dispatch. No more.   [Exeunt.   285

Crispus, Arius, Fausta. Executioners.

    FAUST. Now Crispus: Now my Dear, wilt thou forgive me
This glorious Conquest of Triumphing Love?
    CRISP. No: By my Soul, and by my hopes of Heav'n,
Not at thy parting groan, will I forgive thee.
But rather Curse the hour, when first I saw thee,   290
Curse our first Kisses, Marriage and Embraces,
Unless thou joyn me --- Ha --- come forwarder:

---

262 seeking? C_3.
276 Tears:] C_1; Tears Q_1; Tears; C_{2+}.

With Arius, joyn me, to provide some means,
That I may bear thee company in Death.
If this thou dost deny me, by the Saints,   295
By all our Loves --- I swear thou never Lov'st me ---
    ARI. By Heav'n my Lord I pitty you; and if ---
    FAUST. If Arius! What? Thou wilt not joyn his madness?
    CRISP. Hark Arius: By our friendship --- I conjure thee,
For I have sworn I will not eat nor drink: 300
Tho I survive this hour ---
    ARI.   I have the means.
    CRISP. A Dagger. Blessings on thee --- Give't me I say ---
    FAUST. Arius, thou art a Villain!
    CRISP. I'll tell my Father, that I forc'd it from thee.
    FAUST. Keep, Keep it from him, or I'll tell the Emperor,   305
'Twas you that first betray'd him to my Love;
And Marry'd us.
    ARI.   Hold Madam! Let me begg you ---
    CRISP. Now Love, I am for thee.
    FAUST.   No! I'll call the Emperor.
Oh that damn'd Villain, Traitor, Devil, Arius.
Help there without. Crispus is Murder'd. Help ---   310
    ARI. Nay then 'tis time to fly ---   [Constantine meets him with
    CONST.   Yes Fiend, to Hell,   the rest.
Where thou shalt make thy Damn'd account. --- In with him ---
Cast the unblooded Villain in the Bath,
Which he prepar'd for others: Throw him in.
    ARI. Hold Sir, the Bath's not Poison'd.
    CONST.   How!   315
    ARI. Compassion, for your Empress,
Made me contrive this only way to save her.
    CONST. Thou hast done well. Yet in with him, to try.
    ARI. Hold Sir! And I'll confess, it is, it is,
'Tis Poison'd --- Pardon.
    CONST.   Down with him, keep him down   320
Till he be dead. Then give him to his Slaves. ---
                          [The Bath sinks with him.

O Crispus --- Why? Why dost thou Eye me thus
With snatch'd regards? Why dost thou Eye thy Father?
Now looking on thy Dagger, now on Fausta ---
As if 'twere possible to deny her still?   325
    CRISP. Deny her? Why Sir? Mean you then to give her?
    CONST. Or let me stand a Curse to after Ages.
It is the hand of Heav'n, not mine that gives her:
The Treasons of the perjur'd Arius
So turn my Soul, and quite reduce my reason,   330
That I will give her thee without a Pang.
Take her my Son, And with her all the blessings,
And all the Love, my loaded Bosom bears;
The Dews of Heav'n, and these thy Fathers Tears.

CRISP. Oh Joys!
FAUST.   Oh Heav'n!
CRISP.   Fausta!
FAUST.   Crispus! Caesar!   335
CRISP. Father!
But let us prostrate --- as a God, approach him ----
Thou glorious Image of the Deity!
What shall we answer?
CONST.   Crispus! Fausta --- Nothing;
Nothing but rise, and take me in your Arms.   340
Thus brooding o're you with a fruitful Joy,
I prophecy by my example led;
Such Love and peace, thro' all the World shall spread,
And Roman Arts that British Isle adorn,
Where Helena Deceas'd, and I was Born.   345
      While Crispus thus, to Fausta's Love, I give:
      And both for ever, in my Bosom live.   [Ex. Omnes.

FINIS

EPILOGUE,

Spoken by Mrs. COOK.

Our Hero's happy in the Plays Conclusion,
The holy Rogue at last has met Confusion:
Though Arius all along appear'd a Saint,
The last Act shew'd him a true Protestant.
Eusebius, (for you know I read Greek Authors)   5
Reports, that after all these Plots and Slaughters,
The Court of Constantine was full of Glory,
And every Trimmer turn'd Addressing Tory;
They follow'd him in Herds as they were mad:
When Clause was King, then all the World was glad.   10
Whiggs kept the Places they possest before,
And most were in a way of getting more;
Which was as much as saying, Gentlemen,
Here's Power and Money to be Rogues again.
Indeed there were a sort of peaking Tools,   15
Some call them Modest, but I call 'em Fools,
Men much more Loyal, tho not half so loud;
But these poor Devils were cast behind the Croud.
For bold Knaves thrive without one Grain of Sense,
But good Men starve for want of Impudence.   20
Besides all these, there were a sort of Wights,
(I think my Author calls them Teckelites;)
Such hearty Rogues against the King and Laws,
They favour'd even a Foreign Rebel's Cause.
When their own damn'd Design was quash'd and aw'd,   25
At least they gave it their good Word abroad.
As many a Man, who, for a quiet Life,
Breeds out his Bastard, not to nose his Wife.
Thus o're their Darling Plot these Trimmers cry;
And though they cannot keep it in their Eye,   30
They bind it Prentice to Count Teckely.
They believe not the last Plot, may I be curst,
If I believe they e're believ'd the first.
No wonder their own Plot, no Plot they think;
The Man that makes it, never smells the Stink.   35
And, now it comes into my Head, I'll tell
Why these damn'd Trimmers lov'd the Turks so well.
The Original Trimmer, though a Friend to no Man,
Yet in his Heart ador'd a pretty Woman:
He knew that Mahomet laid up for ever,   40
Kind Black-ey'd Rogues, for every true Believer:
And, which was more than mortal Man e're tasted,
One Pleasure that for threescore Twelve-months lasted:
To turn for this, may surely be forgiven:
Who'd not be circumcis'd for such a Heav'n!   45

LEE'S OCCASIONAL POEMS

Introduction

In addition to his plays Lee wrote a few occasional and incidental poems. From the first, written while he was yet at Cambridge, to the last they are distinguished neither by their wit nor their elegance.   Included among them are an extravagant eulogy upon the death of General Monck, the Duke of Albemarle, an epithalamium of questionable taste for the marriage of William of Orange to Mary, a fulsome ode upon Dryden's publication of his "Poem of Paradice," another upon the appearance of ABSALOM AND ACHITOPHEL (1681), a fairly effective obituum for Mrs. Aphra Behn, his benefactor and friend, and a bawdy song. THE CHARACTER OF AN ENGLISH-MAN, a broadside which Lee recommended for publication, is not thought to be his own work.   Taken altogether, there is little among his poems to commend the author.

In the explanatory notes to the several poems the facts of publication are given, insofar as they are known.   Only in the case of the poem TO THE PRINCE AND PRINCESS OF ORANGE is there any textual problem.   Variants are recorded in footnotes.

On the Death of the Duke of Albemarle

1

Arise ye Ghosts of anceint Heroes fled
        To shades below,
Where all things hush'd in silence gently flow,
Forsake awhile the mansions of the dead:
        In all your honours mantled,   5
        With all your glories garnished,
        With lawrels crown'd, draw near,
        Approach with Panick fear
Come all, with jealous wonder, come,
And kneeling bow your heads before our Gen'ral's tomb.   10

2

Bow: lest his pow'rful Manes should start forth,
        And lightning all around
        Your formal pomp confound;
And totally eclipse your glimm'ring worth.
        Your urns decay, your honours die,   15
        Nor can your memory
        Flourish eternally;
In you these were immoderate desires:
        But He this mighty HE
        Shall shine beyond posterity,   20
Encircl'd all about with loyal fires.

3

That which we real vertue call
        Did onely rest,
Within the bulwark of his gen'rous breast;
        For you are fictions all,   25
        He the true General.
Cesar and Pompey could not bear the hate
O'th' Gods, but sunk beneath the weight,
        Murm'ring at fate:
But this the Man so worthily admir'd,   30
Smil'd at the shock of death, and peacefully retir'd.

4

Sorrow in purple clad,
        With Royal gravity array'd,
        To's mighty Herse did come
Attended by the beauties of the Court   35
In solemn form, and melancholy sort.
        All sate and sigh'd their wo,
        Stunn'd by this fatal blow.

---

* Title assigned by editors.

Greatness and goodness wept about the Room.
Princes with terrour did behold his fall,   40
Stagg'ring beneath so great a funerall.

                        5

                      But oh!
              What Pen, what tongue can show
                    Infinite wo?
      The Earth, which lately was o'respread   45
              With a vast icy coverlet,
          Which nature had a while obdurate kept,
    At such, so great a loss did seem concern'd;
              She thaw'd o'th' sudden, wept:
      And her great bowels with compassion yearn'd.   50

                        6

              Farewel Great Conquerour,
      Our better Genius, and our morning Star;
        Who having chac'd with happy war
                Usurping fires away,
                Did usher to his throne   55
                Our long expected Sun,
      With golden beams to crown and bless the day;
          Then with the kindest aspect hurl'd
              O're England's ev'ry part,
              On ev'ry English heart,   60
          He shot away to gild the other world.

                        Nathaniel Lee, A. B. Trin. Coll.

To the Prince and Princess of Orange, upon Their
Marriage.

Written by Mr. Nat. Lee.

Hail, happy Warriour! hail! whose Arms have won
The fairest Jewel in the English Crown.
Happy in famous Dangers in the Field,
Happy in Courts which brightest Beauties yield.
Oh Prince! whose Soul is known so justly great,   5
As if that Heav'n took leisure to create;
First, the rich Oar refin'd, then did allay,
Stampt thee his own, not shuffl'd thee away.
With wonder thus we all thy temper prize,
Not but th' art bold and brave, as thou art wise.   10
Like the cool English, who approach their Fate
With awe, and gravely first with Death debate.
They kindle slowly, but when once on Fire,
Burn on, and in the blaze of Fame expire.

Hail Princess! hail! thou fairest of thy Kind!   15
Thou shape of Angels, with an Angel's Mind!
Whose Vertues shine, but so as to be born,
Clear as the Sun, and gentle as the Morn.
Whose brighter Eyes like lambent Glories move,
And ev'ry glance wounds like a Dart of Love.   20
How well, oh Prince, how nobly hast thou fought,
Since to thy Arms the Fates such Beauty brought!
Methinks I hear thee in thy Nuptial Bed,
When o're the Royal Maid thy Arms were spread.

Enough, kind Heav'n, well was my Sword employ'd,   25
Since all the Bliss Earth holds shall be enjoy'd.
Pains I remember now with vast delight,
Well have I brav'd the thund'ring French in fight,
My hazards now are Gains, and if my Blood
In Battel mix and raise the vulgar Flood,   30
Her Tears (for sure she'll be so good to mourn)
Like Balm shall heal the Wounds when I return.

But heark, 'tis rumour'd that this happy pair
Must go, the Prince for Holland does declare,
Call'd to the Business of Important War.   35
Go then, if thy Departure be agreed,
Your Friends must weep, your Enemies shall bleed.
And if in Poets minds, those vaster Souls,
Where all at once the vast Creation rouls,
To whom the Warriour is as much oblig'd,   40
As to Relievers Towns that are besieg'd.
(For Death would to their Acts an end afford,

Did not Immortal Verse out-do the Sword)
If ought of Prophesie their Souls inspire,
And if their fury gives a solid Fire,   45
Soft shall the Waftage be, the Seas and Wind,
Calm as the Prince, and as the Princess kind.
The World, why should not Dreams of Poets take,
As well as Prophets who but dream awake?
I saw them launch, the Prince the Princess bore,   50
While the sad Court stood crowding on the Shore.
The Prince still bowing on the Deck did stand,
And held his weeping Princess by the hand.
Which waving oft, she bid them all farewell,
And wept as if she wou'd the Ocean swell.   55

Farewel! thou best of Fathers, best of Friends!
While the mov'd Duke, with a heav'd Sigh, commends
To Heav'n the Care; in Tears his Eyes wou'd swim,
But Manly Vertue binds them to the brim.
Farewel (she cry'd) my Sister, thou dear part,   60
Thou sweetest part, of my divided Heart.
To whom I all my Secrets did unfold,
Dear Casket! who did all my Treasures hold.
My little Love! her Sighs she did renew,
Once more (oh Heavens) a long and last adieu!   65
Part! must I ever lose those pretty Charms?
Then swoons, and sinks into the Prince's Arms.
The Court beheld, and wept.

Streight from their Griefs the pompous Navy fled
So fast, as if our Sighs increas'd their speed.   70
When of a sudden, from the Reedy Court,
The Trytons all with their griev'd God resort;
In Troops upon the wandring Waves they glide,
And round their lifted Lord in Triumph ride.
At their first call the singing Mermaids come,   75
While the crown'd Dolphins lash the Silver Foam.

Thus waited, the glad Prince beheld from far
The Belgick Shore, and heard the sound of War.
Some Hand unseen Heav'ns Azure Curtains drew
To make his Mighty Triumph Great and New,   80
A thousand Golden Heads peep'd forth to view.
Cries, Shouts, and clapping Hands, all Extasie,
A hundred Cannons thundred to the Skie.
The Thunder answering did my Dream destroy,
And wak'd me from the Visionary Joy.   85

On the Marriage of the Prince and Princess
of Orange*

Hail happy Warrior! whose Arms have won
The fairest Jewel in the English Crown.
Happy in th' horrid Dangers of the Field;
Happy in Courts, which brightest Beauties yield.
O Prince, whose Soul is known so truly great!   5
Whom Heav'n did seem to take time to create:
First the rich Ore refin'd, then did allay,
Stamp'd thee his own, not shuffled thee away.
With wonder thus we thy cool Temper prize,
Not but thou art as brave and bold as wise.   10
Like the true English, who approach their Fate
With Awe, and gravely first with Death debate:
They kindle slowly, but when once on fire,
Burn on, and in the blaze of Fame expire.
    Hail Princess! Hail thou fairest of thy kind!   15
Thou shape of Angels with an Angel's Mind!
Whose Virtues shine, but so as to be born;
Clear as the Sun, and gentle as the Morn.
Whose radiant Eyes like lambent Glory move;
And ev'ry Glance wounds like a Dart of Love.   20
How well, O Prince, how nobly hast thou fought,
Since to thy Arms such Charms the Fates have brought!
Methinks I hear thee in the Nuptial Bed,
When o'er the Royal Maid thy Arms were spread.
    Enough, kind Heav'n! well was my Sword employ'd,   25
Since all the Bliss Earth holds shall be enjoy'd.
Pains I remember now with vast Delight,
Well have I brav'd the thundring French in Fight:
My Hazards now are Gains; and if my Blood
In Battel mix, and swell the vulgar Flood,   30
Her Tears, for sure she'll be so good to mourn,
Like Balm, shall heal the Wounds when I return.
    But hark! 'tis rumour'd that this happy Pair
Must go: the Prince for Holland does declare,
Call'd to the dreadful Business of the War.   35
Go then: if thy Departure is decreed,
Thy Friends must weep, thy enemies shall bleed.
And if in Poets Minds, their vaster Souls,
Where all at once the whole Creation rouls;
To whom the Warrior is as much oblig'd,   40
As to Relievers, Towns that are besieg'd:

---

* This shorter and considerably altered version of the preceding poem
appeared in volume III of POEMS ON AFFAIRS OF STATE. FROM 1640.
TO THIS PRESENT YEAR 1704. This collection was published in four
volumes: I (1697), II (1703), III (1704), IV (1707). The text reprinted
here is taken from the copy of volume III in the Folger Library.

For Death would to their Acts an end afford,
Did not immortal Verse out-do the Sword.
If ought of Prophecy their Thoughts inspire;
And if their Fury give a solid Fire;   45
Soft shall your Waftage be; the Seas and Wind
Calm as the Prince, and as the Princess kind:
The World why should not Dreams of Poets take
As well as Prophets, who but dream awake?
I saw the Ship the Prince and Princess bore,   50
While the sad Court stood crowding on the Shore:
The Prince still bowing on the Deck did stand,
And held his weeping Princess by the Hand:
Which waving oft she bid them all farewel,
And wept as if she would the Ocean swell.   55
Farewel the best of Fathers, best of Friends,
While the mov'd Duke with a hurl'd Sigh commends
To Heav'n his Care; in Tears his Eyes would swim,
But manly Virtue binds 'em in the brim.
Farewel she cry'd, my Sister, thou dear Part,   60
Thou sweetest part of my divided Heart:
To whom I all my Secrets did unfold;
Dear Casket, who dost all my Treasure hold.
My Sister O! her Sighs did then renew,
Once more, O Heav'n, a long and last Adieu!   65

To Mr. Dryden, on his Poem of
Paradice

Forgive me, awful Poet, if a Muse,
Whom artless Nature did for plainness chuse,
In loose attire presents her humble thought,
Of this best POEM, that you ever wrought.
This fairest labor of your teeming brain   5
I wou'd embrace, but not with flatt'ry stain;
Something I wou'd to your vast Virtue raise,
But scorn to dawb it with a fulsome praise;
That wou'd but blot the Work I wou'd commend,
And shew a Court-Admirer, not a Friend.   10
To the dead Bard, your fame a little owes,
For Milton did the Wealthy Mine disclose,
And rudely cast what you cou'd well dispose:
He roughly drew, on an old fashion'd ground,
A Chaos, for no perfect World was found,   15
Till through the heap, your mighty Genius shin'd;
His was the Golden Ore which you refin'd.
He first beheld the beauteous rustic Maid,
And to a place of strength the prize convey'd;
You took her thence: to Court this Virgin brought   20
Drest her with gemms, new weav'd her hard spun thought
And softest language, sweetest manners taught.
Till from a Comet she a star did rise,
Not to affright, but please our wondring eyes.
Betwixt ye both is fram'd a nobler peice,   25
Than ere was drawn in Italie or Greece.
Thou from his source of thoughts ev'n Souls dost bring
As smileing gods, from sullen Saturn spring.
When nights dull Mask the face of Heav'n does wear,
'Tis doubtful light, but here and there a Star,   30
Which serves the dreadful shadowes to display,
That vanish at the rising of the day;
But then bright robes the Meadows all adorn,
And the World looks as it were newly born.
So when your Sense his mystic reason clear'd,   35
The melancholy Scene all gay appear'd;
New light leapt up, and a new glory smil'd,
And all throughout was mighty, all was mild.
Before this Palace which thy wit did build
Which various fancy did so gawdy gild   40
And judgment has with solid riches fill'd.
My humbler Muse begs she may centry stand,
Amongst the rest that guard this Eden Land.
But there's no need, for ev'n thy foes conspire
Thy praise, and hating thee, thy Work admire.   45
On then O mightiest of the inspir'd men,
Monarch of Verse; new Theams employ thy Pen.

The troubles of Majestick CHARLES set down,
Not David vanquish'd more to reach a Crown,
Praise him, as Cowly did that Hebrew King,   50
Thy Theam's as great, do thou as greatly sing.
Then thou mayst boldly to his favor rise
Look down and the base serpent's hiss despise,
From thund'ring envy safe in Lawrel sit,
While clam'rous Critiques their vile heads submit   55
Condemn'd for Treason at the bar of Wit.

                    N A T .   L E E .

To the Unknown Authour of this Excellent Poem[1]

Take it as Earnest of a Faith renew'd,
Your Theme is vast, your Verse divinely good:
Where, tho the Nine their beauteous stroaks repeat,
And the turn'd Lines on Golden Anvils beat,
It looks as if they strook 'em at a heat.   5
So all Serenely Great, so Just, refin'd,
Like Angels love to Humane Seed enclin'd,
It starts a Giant, and exalts the Kind.
'Tis Spirit seen, whose fiery Atoms roul,
So brightly fierce, each Syllable's a Soul.   10
'Tis minuture of Man, but he's all heart;
'Tis what the World woud be, but wants the Art:
To whom ev'n the Phanaticks Altars raise,
Bow in their own despite, and grin your praise.
As if a Milton from the dead arose,   15
Fil'd off the Rust, and the right Party chose.
Nor, Sir, be shock't at what the Gloomy say,
Turn not your feet too inward, nor too splay.
'Tis Gracious all, and Great: Push on your Theme,
Lean your griev'd head on David's Diadem.   20
David that rebel Israels envy mov'd,
David by God and all Good Men belov'd.

The beauties of your Absalom excell:
But more the Charms of Charming Annabel;
Of Annabel, than May's first Morn more bright,   25
Chearfull as Summer's Noon, and chast as Winter's Night.
Of Annabel the Muses dearest Theme,
Of Annabel the Angel of my dream.
Thus let a broken Eloquence attend,
And to your Master-piece these Shadows send.   30

---

[1] Dryden's ABSALOM AND ACHITOPHEL.

To the DUKE
On His RETURN.

Written by NAT. LEE.

Come then at last, while anxious Nations weep,
Three Kingdoms stak't! too pretious for the deep.
Too pretious sure, for when the Trump of fame
Did with a direfull sound your Wrack proclaim,
Your danger and your doubtfull safety shown,   5
It dampt the Genius, and it Shook the Throne,
Your Helm may now the Sea-born Goddess take,
And soft Favonius safe your passage make.
Strong, and auspicious, bee the Stars that reign,
The day you launch, and Nereus sweep the Main.   10
Neptune aloft, scowr all the Storms before,
And following Tritons, wind you to the Shore;
While on the Beach, like Billows of the Land,
In bending Crowds the Loyal English stand:
Come then, thô late, your right receive at last;   15
Which Heaven preserv'd, in spite of Fortunes blast,
Accept those hearts, that Offer on the Strand;
The better half of this divided Land.
Venting their honest Souls in tears of Joy,
They rave, and beg you wou'd their lives employ,   20
Shouting your sacred name, they drive the air,
And fill your Canvas Wings with gales of prayer.
Come then I hear three Nations shout agen,
And, next our Charles, in every bosome reign;
Heaven's darling Charge, the care of regal stars,   25
Pledge of our Peace, and Triumph of our Wars.
Heav'n eccho's Come, but come not Sir alone,
Bring the bright pregnant Blessing of the Throne.
And if in Poets charms be force or skill,
We charge you, O ye Waves, and Winds be still,   30
Soft as a sailing Goddess bring her home,
With the expected Prince that loads her Womb,
Joy of this Age and Heir of that to come.
Next her the Virgin Princess shines from far,
Aurora that, and this the Morning Star.   35
Hail then, all hail, They land in Charle's Armes,
While his large Breast, the Nation's Angel warms.
Tears from his Cheeks with manly mildness roul,
Then dearly grasps the treasure of his Soul:
Hangs on his Neck, and feeds upon his form,   40
Calls him his Calm, after a tedious Storm.
O Brother! He cou'd say no more, and then,
With heaving Passion clasp'd him close again.
How oft he cry'd have I thy absence mourn'd,
But 'tis enough Thou art at last return'd: 45

Said I return'd! O never more to part,
Now draw the vital warmth from Charles his heart.
Once more, O Heav'n, I shall his Vertue prove,
His Council, Conduct, and unshaken Love.
My People too at last their Errour see,   50
And make their Sovereign blest in loving Thee.
Not but there is a stiff-neck'd-harden'd Crew
That give not Caesar, no nor God his due.
Reprobate Traytors, Tyrants of their Own,
Yet Grudge to see their Monarch in his Throne.   55
Their stubborn Souls with brass Rebellion barr'd,
Desert the Laws, and Crimes with Treason guard.
    Whom I -- but there he stop'd, and cry'd 'tis past,
Pity's no more, this warning be their last;
Then sighing said, my Soul's dear purchas'd rest,   60
Welcome, Oh welcome, to my longing Brest:
Why should I waste a tear while thou art by,
To all extreams of Friendship let us fly,
Disdain the factious Crowd that wou'd rebell
And mourn the Men that durst in death excell,   65
Their Fates were Glorious since for thee they fell.
And as a Prince has right his Arms to weil'd,
When stubborn Rebels force him to the Field;
So for the Loyal, who their Lives lay down,
He dares to Hazard both his Life and Crown.   70

FINIS.

Printed for J. Tonson, at the Judge's Head in Chancery-lane, 1682.

On Their Majesties Coronation.

By Nat. Lee Gent.

To the KING,

Monarch and Prince and mightiest of thy Line,
Where all the praises of the publick joyn;
Auspicious Lord, and the most Sovereign Good,
Whom poor Conspirators, in vain withstood
By subterfuge, and little daring Arts,   5
And brainless Heads oppos'd to English Hearts.
Whose truth by honour and by love was prov'd,
When last extreams by dreadful causes mov'd.
Such black designs the Muses blush to name,
That turn the Blood and blow it to a flame.   10
But generous Monarchs easily forgive,
And tis your condescention that they live.
Heav'n has rewards, and Heav'n remits the care,
To a Mild King, that makes their Arts despair.
No scorn, no hate, but all Majestick Grace,   15
The stamp of God upon a Royal Face.
You shall be Blest, in spite of their design,
And Crown'd the Monarch of a Monarch's Line;
To whom the Blest in their bright Liveries run,
Like Morning Clouds upon a rising Sun.   20
The mildest Greatness, and serenest Love,
As if the Nations by their Shepherd drove.
This mounts your Royal Power, tis this alarms
Astrea's rest, and binds you to her Arms.
That happy beauty where the World's amazed,   25
As if the Stars on their own Goddess gaz'd.
That Heav'nly Nature, and Imperial Grace,
Those Eyes of Triumph, and that Conquering Face.
Where all the pleasures of the Earth refine
Like waters forc'd, that in a Diamond mine.   30
The Luxury of Heav'n, that cou'd unload
It self, to joyn a Heroine with a God.
Peace to your Days, Peace to your Nights and Years,
Forget the Dangers, and forgive the Fears.
Where all our Spirits tremble to your Crown,   35
Like cautious Guardians when the Furies frown.
Be yours the safety, and be ours the care,
That will be watchful on the Foes despair.
So when the Serpent to his Covert ran,
The Guardian Angel took the charge of Man.   40
We'll grow more wise by our first Monarch's fall,

---

13 care,]; cure, 1689.

And keep the second stand or perish All.
Accept this humble Paper from a Hand,
That owns obedience to the last Command.
That looks with joy upon your rising Power,   45
If Poets minutes make a pleasant Hour.
That poor unhappy Tribe whom Nature sent,
For foils to Power and Heav'n for beauty lent.
But charg'd and fate consented to the Law,
To veil the greatness which they cou'd not draw.   50
Then let the Acclamations of the croud,
And all the Hearts that to your entrance bow'd,
Joyn in Eternal Prayer to bless your Crown,
And London's shouts the Cannon's ecchoes down.

London, Printed for Abel Roper at the Bell in Fleetstreet, 1689.

ON THE DEATH
of
Mrs. BEHN

By Nat. Lee, Gent.

The Sadness of thy Death extends my Muse,
To rail at Nature, and the Fates abuse:
That doom'd such Wit and Goodness to the Grave,
To grieve the Wise, and make the Temperate rave.
Why art thou dead? Or wherefore didst thou live?   5
Such Pangs for Pleasure after Death to give.
I lov'd thee inward, and my Thoughts were true;
And after Death thy Vertue I pursue.
Thou hadst my Soul in secret, and I swear
I found it not, till thou resolv'dst to Air.   10
To Air, to Flame, to Beauty, and that Light,
Where Heav'ns perpetual blushing, and more bright.
Melpomene the stateliest of the Nine;
And more Majestick where thy Numbers shine;
Commands my Thoughts a mightier Urn to raise,   15
And Crown thy Verse with an Immortal Praise.
I mourn thy Death like Nightingales their Young:
My Grief's like thee, too precious for the Throng.
I'll bury it in Smiles, and force my Tears
Back to those Fountains where no Spring appears.   20
Flatman thy Mate, and that dear part of me;
But I'll expect till all the blest agree
To mount me in their Arms, and draw me near,
Where I shall never shed another Tear.

---

18 "precious fot" is the reading of the text, an obvious misprint.
London, Printed for Abel Roper at the Bell in Fleetstreet, 1689.

Love's Opportunity Neglected

By Mr. Nat. Lee

Oh! the time that is past,
   When she held me so fast,
And declar'd that her Honour no longer cou'd last!
No Light, but her languishing Eyes did appear,
To prevent all Excuses of Blushing, and Fear.   5

How she sigh'd, and unlac'd,
   With such trembling, and haste,
As if she had long'd to be closer embrac'd!
My Lips the sweet Pleasure of Kisses enjoy'd,
While my Hands were in search of hid Treasure employ'd.   10

With my Heart all on Fire
   In the Flames of Desire,
When I boldly pursu'd what she seem'd to require,
She cry'd, Oh! for Pity's sake change your ill Mind,
Pray, Amyntas be civil, or I'll be unkind.   15

All your Bliss you destroy,
   Like a naked young Boy,
Who fears the kind River he came to enjoy:
Let's in, my dear Chloris, I'll save thee from harm,
And make the cold Element pleasant and warm.   20

Dear Amyntas! she cries;
   Then she cast down her Eyes,
And with Kisses confest what she faintly denies.
Too sure of my Conquest, I purpos'd to stay
'Till her freer Consent did more sweeten the Prey.   25

But too late I begun;
   For her Passion was done:
Now Amyntas, she cry'd, I will never be won;
Thy Tears and thy Courtship no Pity can move,
Thou hast slighted the Critical Minute of Love.   30

A SONG.

Writ by the Famous Mr. Nat. Lee.

Philander and Sylvia, a gentle soft Pair,
Whose business was loving, and kissing their Care;
In a sweet smelling Grove went smiling along,
'Till the Youth gave a vent to his Heart with his Tongue:
Ah Sylvia! said he, (and sigh'd when he spoke)   5
Your cruel resolves will you never revoke?
No never, she said, how never, he cry'd,
'Tis the Damn'd that shall only that Sentence abide.

She turn'd her about to look all around,
Then blush'd, and her pretty Eyes cast on the Ground;   10
She kiss'd his warm Cheeks, then play'd with his Neck,
And urg'd that his Reason his Passion would check:
Ah Philander! she said, 'tis a dangerous Bliss,
Ah! never ask more and I'll give thee a Kiss;
How never? he cry'd, then shiver'd all o'er,   15
No never, she said, then tripp'd to a Bower.

She stopp'd at the Wicket, he cry'd let me in,
She answer'd, I wou'd if it were not a sin;
Heav'n sees, and the Gods will chastise the poor Head
Of Philander for this; straight Trembling he said,   20
Heav'n sees, I confess, but no Tell-tales are there,
She kiss'd him and cry'd, you're an Atheist my Dear;
And shou'd you prove false I should never endure:
How never? he cry'd, and straight down he threw her.

Her delicate Body he clasp'd in his Arms,   25
He kiss'd her, he press'd her, heap'd charms upon charms;
He cry'd shall I now? no never, she said,
Your Will you shall never enjoy till I'm dead:
Then as if she were dead, she slept and lay still,
Yet even in Death bequeath'd him a smile: 30
Which embolden'd the Youth his Charms to apply,
Which he bore still about him to cure those that die.

To the Author & Translatour of the following Book*

As Esdras once did into Order draw,
And, to the new-freed Tribes, revive the Law;
So you, from Chains of Darkness which they wore,
The Captived ORACLES themselves Restore.
Hail, inspired Father, who couldst force thy Way   5
Through Night's vast Empire to the Realm of Day.
Your self creates the Sun that gives you Light,
And forms the History by which you write:
One Age dissolves (such Force your Judgment bears)
The settling clouds of many Thousand years.   10
To Vindicate the Sacred Books, a New,
But onely Certain Method, you pursue.
And shewing Th'are corrupted, prove 'em True.
This Work's first Fame is Thine that cou'd Create;
The second, His that cou'd so well Translate: 15
From whose join'd Beams a perfect Light we draw,
The URIM & the THUMMIM of the Law.

N. L.

---

* CRITICAL HISTORY OF THE OLD TESTAMENT.
1 Esdras]; Eldras 1682.

NOTES TO VOLUME II

NOTES

INTRODUCTION TO THE MASSACRE OF PARIS

1 THE WORKS OF JOHN DRYDEN, ed. by Scott and Saintsbury (Edinburgh, 1883, 18 volumes), VII, 201.

2 See R. G. Ham, OTWAY AND LEE, BIOGRAPHY FROM A BAROQUE AGE (New Haven, 1931), pp. 165-67, and William Van Lennep, THE LIFE AND WORKS OF NATHANIEL LEE: A STUDY OF THE SOURCES (unpublished diss., Harvard, 1933), I, 265.

3 Ham, p. 167, and Van Lennep, I, 269, ft. n. 3, cite THE REASONS FOR MR. JOSEPH HAINS CONVERSION (1690), Part III, p. 24, as indicative of the sentimental reception of the play: "There were more weeping eyes in the church than there were at the first acting of Mr. Lee's Protestant Play."

4 John Genest, SOME ACCOUNT OF THE ENGLISH STAGE, 10 volumes (Bath, 1832), II, 580. Genest notes that there is a mistake in the MS from which he draws. The play is called THE DUKE OF GUISE; evidently it was THE MASSACRE OF PARIS.

5 Genest, IV, 188. Genest comments that the play was "Not acted 30 years," and that on 1 November it was acted with the original prologue, but a new epilogue. The comment upon the last acting is accurate, if we accept the revival of 1716 as the last.

6 Oldys, in his manuscript notes to Langbaine's ACCOUNT OF THE ENGLISH DRAMATICK POETS, says that the last production was at the time of the rebellion of 1745, "But there being too much murder in the Play even for our stage to endure, it lasted but a night or two."

7 Van Lennep, I, 264-327, passim.

8 W. Geiersbach, NATHANIEL LEE'S ZEITTRAGÖDIEN UND IHRE VORLÄUFER IM DRAMA ENGLANDS (Rostock, 1907).

9 Van Lennep, I, 320-21.

10 Ibid., I, 282.

11 Ibid., I, 323.

12 Ibid., I, 324.

13 David Erskine Baker and Isaac Reed, BIOGRAPHIA DRAMATICA (1812), III, 29.

14 A. W. Ward, A HISTORY OF ENGLISH DRAMATIC LITERATURE TO THE DEATH OF QUEEN ANNE, New and Revised Edition, 3 volumes (London, 1899), III, 412. Ward says it is "one of the best of Lee's plays."

15 PLAYGOER'S HANDBOOK TO RESTORATION DRAMA (New York, n.d.), p. 94.

16 CBEL lists an edition for 1689. Here as elsewhere the compilers of that bibliography were apparently depending upon the term catalogues for their information, rather than printed copy. The present editors have discovered no edition for that year.

17 Q_1(KU 1), at present unbound, has been trimmed several times for binding; immediately following the scene marking on E1^r appear illegible markings in an eighteenth-century hand, and similar markings in the same hand appear on E3^V; on E2^V, line 17, the letter t in but is illegible because of a flaw in the paper; and on F2^V, line 18, the last two words have partially failed to ink. Q_1(KU 2) is bound up in what appears to have been a nonce collection of Lee's plays, but only OEDIPUS (1701), THE DUKE OF GUISE (1699), and THE PRINCESS OF CLEVE (1697) now remain together with it;

on E2^r, line 2, the letter c in the word courts has slipped up into line 1 above. Q$_1$(DFo 1) is identified by the bookplate of Clifford Lefferts and a brown leather binding with gold lines on the border.   Q$_1$(DFo 2) is the John Genest copy of the play. Q$_1$(DFo 3) has in it the bookplate of R. Todd and is bound up with Settle's FEMALE PRELATE and other plays.

18 See especially Act I, scene ii, lines 35, 37. In these two the printer follows copy which had been corrected from THE DUKE OF GUISE.

THE MASSACRE OF PARIS

Prologue, 27. "And his Allies by Sacred Union joyn'd:" The reference is to the Grand Alliance completed in the spring of 1689 between England, Spain, Austria, and the Germanic and Batavian Federation against France. War came in 1690.

Dramatis Personae, 1. "King Charles IX." of France (1560-1574) was the melancholy, neurotic son of the powerful and astute Catherine de' Medici. He was of a restless and impulsive nature, given to excessive physical exercise. For a time he came under the sway of the brilliant Admiral of France, Gaspard de Coligny, but the clever mind of Catherine intervened to disrupt this relation.

Dramatis Personae, 2. "Duke of Guise." Henry I of Lorraine, also known as Balafré, was Henry, Duke of Guise, son of Francis Lorraine, Duke of Guise. He brilliantly defended Poitiers against the Admiral in 1569. Next to Catherine de' Medici he was the leading spirit behind the Massacre of St. Bartholomew's Day, 1572. He was instrumental in the formation of the Holy League (1576) against the Bourbons. In defiance of King Henry III's orders he came to Paris and was assassinated by the Royal Guard, December, 1588.

Dramatis Personae, 3. "Cardinal of Lorrain." Louis II of Lorraine, 1555-1588, was the younger brother of Henry I of Lorraine (Duke of Guise). He became Archbishop of Reims; then, Cardinal, 1578. He was assassinated at Blois the day after his brother Henry's death.

Dramatis Personae, 4. "Duke of Anjou." François, Duc d'Alençon (1554-1584), was later (1574) made Duc d'Anjou. He was the son of Henry II and Catherine de' Medici. At one time he was the leading suitor for the hand of Elizabeth of England.

Dramatis Personae, 5. "Alberto Gondi." He was Count of Retz, one of the Italians among the conspirators against the Protestants.

Dramatis Personae, 6. "Ligneroles." A hanger-on of Anjou, the young Ligneroles was killed by the King's command and by an assassin of the Duke of Guise because he had learned from Anjou of the plot against the Huguenots. Davila is Lee's source for this digressive story.

Dramatis Personae, 7. "Admiral of France." Gaspard (II) de Coligny, 1519-1572, of the noble house of Châtillon-sur-Loing, was the second son of Gaspard (I) de Coligny. He became Colonel of Infantry in 1547 and Admiral of France in 1552. While prisoner of war in the Netherlands (1557-59), he came to assert his Protestantism. He then became joint leader with Louis I, Prince of Condé, of the Huguenots. He aided them by sending some as colonists to the New World. He was opposed by the Guises, lost the siege of Poitiers to the Duke of Guise, 1569, and joined Henry of Navarre as leader of the Huguenots in the same year. His influence over King Charles IX aroused the Catholics, who under the Guise and Catherine planned and carried out the Massacre of St. Bartholomew's Day, in which the Admiral was murdered.

Dramatis Personae, 8. "Cavagnes." Armaud de Cavagnes (or Cavaignes), supporter and ambassador of the Huguenots and de Coligny, was proposed as emissary to the court of Queen Elizabeth to gain funds for the Protestant cause. See A. W. Whitehead, GASPARD DE COLIGNY, ADMIRAL

OF FRANCE (London, n. d.), pp. 366–367.

Dramatis Personae, 9. "Langoiran." Another of Coligny's supporters, Langoiran is reported to have feared the treachery of Charles and Catherine when the Admiral went to Paris. Hence he left the city before the Massacre.

Dramatis Personae, 10. "Queen Mother." Catherine de' Medici, 1519–1589, was born in Florence, daughter of Lorenzo de' Medici; she married Henry, son of Francis I of France, and became queen of France (1547). Three of her four sons became kings of France. She began to assert herself in the government during the reign of her eldest son Francis II; she was regent during the minority of Charles IX and virtual ruler during most of his reign. A Machiavellian ruler, she sided with the party or person whom she could use, playing off one faction against another so as to get and maintain power. Thus she was suspected of having Francis, Duke of Guise, murdered and of placing the blame upon the Admiral of France. At one time she favored the Protestants; at another, the Catholics. She is responsible for planning the Massacre of St. Bartholomew's Day.

Dramatis Personae, 11. "Marguerite." Margaret of Valois, daughter of Catherine de' Medici and Henry II of France, was married to Henry of Navarre just before the Massacre of St. Bartholomew's Day. She was known for her beauty, learning, and loose living. Her marriage with Henry was dissolved by the Pope after Henry's accession to the French throne.

Dramatis Personae, 12. "Queen of Navarre." Jeanne d'Albret, 1528–1572, was queen of Navarre, 1562–1572, daughter of Henry II of Navarre, wife of Anthony of Bourbon, mother of Henry III of Navarre, who became Henry IV of France. She was one of the most powerful supporters of Protestantism in France, a woman of deep conviction in religion and keen intelligence.

Dramatis Personae, 13. "Antramont Wife to the Admiral." Jacqueline d' Entremonts of Savoy, second wife of the Admiral, was fired so much by the heroism of de Coligny that she offered him her hand and made the dangerous journey to La Rochelle to find and marry him. The wedding took place in March, 1571.

Dramatis Personae, 15. "Columbier." Sieur de Columbiere, soldier and member of the Admiral's Staff.

Dramatis Personae, 16. "Morvele." Maurevel was an adherent of the Duke of Guise and almost certainly the person who attempted the assassination of the Admiral on 22 August. (See Whitehead, op. cit., p. 259.)

Dramatis Personae, 17–20. "Aumale." Apparently Claude II of Lorraine, Duke of Aumale, adherent of the Guise and the Catholic party, was killed (1573) at the siege of Rochelle. "Elbeuf." Rene of Lorraine, Marquis of Elboeuf, youngest son of François de Lorraine (Duke of Guise) and brother to Henri I of Lorraine (Duke of Guise). "Angolesme." Henri d'Angoulême, the Bastard, took active part in the murder of de Coligny. "Provost de Marchand." Le Charron, president of the board of taxation (Board of Excise) and provost of the merchants, was called in to the Louvre, told of a conspiracy against the King's life and ordered to call out the militia and close the gates of the city.

Dramatis Personae, 21–22. "Sartabons." This is obviously a corrupt spelling of Sarlabos, one of the assassins of de Coligny. (See Whitehead, p. 267.)

"Besnie." Again we have a slight corruption in the spelling. It is Bême, another of the assassins.

Dramatis Personae, 23. These were all noblemen and leaders of the Admiral's Protestant party. The first was Francis III, La Rochefoucauld, the Admiral's nephew; Piles was Armand de Clermont de Pilles, heroic defender of St. Jean d' Angely.

I, i, 89-92. These lines echo Bacon's essay OF LOVE: "You may observe, that amongst all the great and worthy persons, whereof the memory remaineth, either ancient or recent, there is not one that hath been transported to the mad degree of love.... You must except nevertheless, Marcus Antonius, the half-partner of the empire of Rome, and Appius Claudius, the decemvir...."

I, i, 96-98. In these lines Catherine de' Medici is compared to the constellation of Cassiopeia's Chair, as well as to the wife of Cepheus and mother of Andromeda.

I, i, 112 ff. "D'Alva." Don Fernando Alvarez de Toledo, Duke of Alva, was the great Spanish leader in the Netherlands. Catherine had connived with him on various occasions, especially in 1565.

I, i, 122. "Chastillon." Gaspard d'Coligny, the Admiral of France was Seigneur of Châtillon, his ducal castle.

I, i, 129. "upon my Father's Death!" Guise's father was killed by John Poltrot, a petty nobleman, who was thought to be an assassin in the pay of the Admiral, though such would seem to be highly doubtful. Lee follows his source, Davila, in this as in other matters. (See Van Lennep, I, 304.)

I, i, 144. "That I may add Damnation to the rest." Cf. HAMLET, III, iii, 89-95.

I, i, 156. "That I may dy like the late puling King." Guise is speaking of the sickly young Francis II, whose queen was Mary of Scotland, and who died at Rambouillet in March, 1560. His surgeon, a follower of Coligny later, was one of the best surgeons of the day, Ambroise Paré.

I, ii, 12. "Like Nero, tho' at Agrippina's Ruin." Nero had his mother Agrippina murdered because she criticized him, or watched too carefully over his doings. (See Lee's NERO, passim.)

I, ii, 35. "His dagger in his Bosom, Stab'd his Father." Plutarch says there was a story that Caesar was intimate with Servilia, Mother of Brutus, and that she was passionately in love with him. This intimacy came at such an interval before the birth of Brutus as to make Caesar believe Brutus was his own son. Such belief explains why Caesar ordered that, if Brutus was captured by his army (Brutus supported Pompey), he should be allowed to escape if he would not come peaceably to Caesar.

I, ii, 40. "Tully was wise, but wanted constancy." Though the line is Baconian, Lee is here (perhaps unconsciously) echoing Lyly's EUPHUES: "Tully, eloquent in his gloses, yet vainglorious. Solomon wise, yet too too wanton."

I, ii, 136. "Like a She Wolf, in Jane of Albret's Shape." The reference is apparently to Joan of Albret, Queen of Navarre, the great Huguenot leader.

II, i. The scene is set at Rochelle, whence the Admiral was invited to Paris.

II, i, 36. "Who blew the coals of Calvin's kindled Doctrine." Coligny received his first letter from Calvin in September, 1558. Calvin, an astute leader, hearing of the Admiral's defection from Catholicism, himself blew upon the spark that spread the fire of Protestantism.

II, i, 37. "And earth'd the little Sect at Hugo's Gate." According to Henri Es-
tienne, APOLOGIE D'HERODOTE (1566), the Protestants at Tours used to
gather by night at the gate of King Hugo, whom they held to be a spirit.
Hence a Monk declared in a sermon that the Lutherans should be called
Huguenots, since they were in a sense kinsmen of King Hugo, like him going abroad only at night. The nickname stuck, and the French Protestants
after 1650 were so called. It was for a long time explained as coming
from the German "Eidgenossen," the name given the Genevans when they
were admitted into the Swiss confederation. Lee was familiar with the
other, and apparently correct, explanation of the origin.

II, i, 54. "And, though we lost the fight at Moncontour." The fight took place
on 3 October, 1569. The Admiral lost the battle and was himself wounded,
though he killed with his own hand John Philip, Count of Salm, the Rhinegrave mentioned in line 59 below.

II, i, 71 ff. So far as we know, this letter was not sent by the king to the Queen
of Navarre. The text is corrupt.

II, i, 80 ff. The entrance of the Prince of Navarre and the Prince of Condé
brings to the stage Henry of Navarre, later Henry IV of France, and Louis
of Bourbon, Prince of Condé, husband of Coligny's niece, Eleanor of Roye.

II, i, 118. "Say, that her Cato's bound for Utica." The comparison of Coligny
with Cato Uticensis is made in the source, Davila.

II, i, 182 ff. The comparison of Coligny with Cato and Antramont (Jacqueline
d'Entremonts) with Cato's wife Martia is continued here by Lee quite effectively.

II, i, 204. "Calphurnia's bloody Dream, and Scent of Slaughter." On the night
before his assassination, Caesar, according to Plutarch, being awakened
by the doors and windows flying open, sat up in bed and heard his wife
Calphurnia utter inarticulate groans in her sleep. From them he could
make out that she fancied herself holding the butchered Caesar in her
arms. See also Shakespeare's JULIUS CAESAR, II, ii, 1-4.

III, i, 38. "What, he that keeps the Tye, the sacred Contract." The Cardinal
of Lorraine apparently held the marriage contract between Marguerite and
the Guise. See III, ii, 130-140.

IV, ii, 111. "Chastillon will not steal a Victory." According to Bacon's "Of
the True Greatnesse of Kingdomes and Estates", the line is from Alexander's speech at Arbela.

IV, ii, 153-155. "Were I in Heav'n," etc. The reference is to the parable of
Lazarus and the rich man. See Luke 16:19-24.

IV, ii, 155-156. "For Beza too,/That set him on." Poltrot, the assassin of
the elder Duke of Guise, said that he had been incited to the murder by
Theodore of Beza, author of HISTOIRE ECCLÉSIASTIQUE and a leading
Huguenot.

V, i, 17 ff. The speech of Genius here is a song. The music for it was done by
Purcell. See Day and Murrie, #3361, p. 354. The music was printed in
three songbooks: #145, #166, #210. Westrup says, without citing his authority, that the music was twice set by Purcell for this song.

V, i, 31. "He has of late been troubled with such Faintings." It seems that
Lee here has in mind, not Charles IX, but his weakling brother Francis
II, who was subject to fainting fits.

V, i, 129. "I think I saw some of his Fingers fly." Maurevel, here describing his attempted assassination of Coligny, speaks as from Davila, Lee's source. Davila says Maurevel shot the Admiral with a brace of bullets, "one of which took off the fore-finger of his right hand, and the other wounded him grievously near the left elbow." See Van Lennep, I, 288.

V, ii, 15 ff. Here Lee continues the comparison of Coligny to Cato and his wife d'Entremonts to Martia, Cato's wife. Cato died at Utica. See II, i, 118; II, i, 182 ff.

V, iii, 11. "Wear a Shirt-sleeve, and a white Cross in's Hat." This is an accurate description of the insignia of those who massacred the Huguenots. The insignia were worn at Royal command. See Whitehead, op. cit., p. 265.

V, iv, 1 ff. The scene here is left confused. Though it is marked "The City. Lights in the window, etc.", we know from the sources that the Admiral was killed in his bedchamber. Lee assuredly has that in mind shortly after the opening, when Cavagnes enters and reports that "Death is in the Court," meaning that the assassins have attacked in the courtyard below. Still later, line 53, the Guise orders the body to be thrown below. It seems that the scene should be marked: The Admiral's Bedchamber. Here is what appears to be a case of editing in the composing room, rather than in the author's study.

V, v. The scene here is puzzling, and the directions confusing. Apparently the Queen Mother is standing with the Cardinal et al. in a window of the Louvre at the side of the stage and above. A pair of flats are then pulled revealing the Huguenot leaders and the firing squad. Then another pair of flats are pulled at the back of the stage to reveal the body of the Admiral.

V, v, 19 ff. This final speech of the King is developed by Lee from Bacon's "Of Unity in Religion," wherein Bacon mentions the Massacre of Paris directly: "What would he [Lucretius] have said if he had knowne of the Massacre in France, or the Powder Treason of England? He would have beene Seven Times more Epicure and Atheist, then he was...."

Epilogue. "By Mr. Powell." Since Powell did not appear in the dramatis personae, it is unlikely that he spoke these lines. It is more likely, as Van Lennep suggests (I, 267), that they were spoken by Betterton. This epilogue is a shortened form of "A Prologue, To the Massacre of Paris: For Mr. Betterton" which appeared in Thomas D'Urfey's SONGS COMPLETE, PLEASANT AND DIVERTIVE; SET TO MUSIC BY DR. JOHN BLOW, MR. HENRY PURCELL, AND OTHER EXCELLENT MASTERS OF THE TOWN, 1719, pp. 351-52. Indeed, the two versions are quite dissimilar, as is indicated in the textual notes.

Epilogue, 9. "Is just come out by th'Habeas Corpus Act." The act was passed 26 May, 1679.

Epilogue, 22-25. William and Mary had quite altered the government. The Catholics were on the run.

Epilogue, 30-31. "as to behold once more, / An English Army on the Gallick Shore." This is an expression of the hope that war against France will come. Indeed, preparations for it were well under way.

NOTES

INTRODUCTION TO CAESAR BORGIA

1 The anonymous author remarks in his Dedication that his play "would be far more difficult to get play'd than CAESAR BORGIA."

2 John Downes, ROSCIUS ANGLICANUS, ed. Montague Summers, p. 41.

3 For a full discussion of these sources, see Van Lennep, THE LIFE AND WORKS OF NATHANIEL LEE. A STUDY OF THE SOURCES (unpublished diss., Harvard, 1933), II, 330 ff.

4 A. W. Ward, HISTORY OF ENGLISH DRAMATIC LITERATURE, III, 410.

5 R. G. Ham, OTWAY AND LEE, p. 124.

6 G. H. Nettleton, ENGLISH DRAMA OF THE RESTORATION AND EIGHTEENTH CENTURY (New York, 1914), p. 98.

7 John Genest, SOME ACCOUNT OF THE ENGLISH STAGE, I, 278.

8 Allardyce Nicoll, RESTORATION DRAMA, p. 136.

9 Bonamy Dobrée, RESTORATION TRAGEDY, p. 119.

10 Van Lennep, op. cit., II, 378.

11 Ibid., II, 381.

12 These copies may be identified as follows:

Q_1(KU) is bound in brown paper, and has slight perforation on the title page between the "G" and "E" of TRAGEDY.

Q_1(DFo 1) is bound in 3/4 leather, with board of variegated colors. On B1^V, line 5, the word "Cherubin" is printed in full, whereas in Q_1(KU) and Q_1(DFo 2) the "i" is missing; identified by case 174.

Q_1(DFo 2) is listed in the Folger catalogue as "another issue." It contains the variant form of the Epistle Dedicatory, as given in the textual footnote, involving A1^V and A2^r. This copy is bound up with other plays of Lee in a red leather binding. The volume is No. 205 of the Kean Collection, case 193.

Q_1(TxU 1) has the call number Aj/L514/680c.

Q_1(TxU 2) has this same call number, but on K2^V, 1. 15, it has "shali" in place of "shall".

CAESAR BORGIA

Dedication. "PHILIP, Earl of PEMBROKE and MONTGOMERY." Philip Herbert (1653-1683), seventh Earl of Pembroke, was notorious for his dissolute life; in 1678 he had killed a man named Nathaniel Cony in a drunken scuffle; he was tried and convicted of manslaughter by the House of Lords, but was pardoned by the king. He was married to Henrietta de Querouaille, sister of the Duchess of Portsmouth, one of the king's favorite mistresses. He does not seem to have shared that interest in literature which had characterized his ancestors.

Dedication, 1. "an Universal Consternation." Lee here refers to the Popish Plot, which had caused great furor in England for over a year. Titus Oates had made his notorious accusations in the summer of 1678; Sir Edmund Bury Godfrey had been murdered in October of that same year. Over twenty men, including Coleman, the secretary of the Duke of York, had been executed for treason. The first exclusion bill had been introduced into Parliament in May of 1679, and Charles had prevented its passing only by proroguing Parliament.

Dedication, 13. "the whole world censures." Cf. Lee's similar complaints of criticism and hard usage in the Prologue and Dedication to GLORIANA, where he speaks of himself as being "blasted in my hopes."

Dedication, 15. "the Almanack Hero, all over wounds." Lee is referring to the figure of a man, printed on the cover of many almanacs, and used to illustrate anatomy.

Dedication, 25. "he refus'd to be a King." In 1577 Sidney engaged in a mysterious correspondence with a man named Languet. It was rumored that this concerned his being proposed as a candidate for the crown of Poland. Fuller says that Sidney declined the honor, preferring to be "a subject to Queen Elizabeth than a sovereign beyond the seas." The story, however, has little basis.

Dedication, 45. "a Jesuit's Powder." Powdered Cinchona bark or Peruvian bark (quinine); so called because first introduced into Europe by the Jesuits.

Dedication, 50-51. "as your Lordships Great Uncle shone upon the mighty Ben." The Great Uncle of the seventh Earl of Pembroke was William Herbert, the third Earl of Pembroke (1580-1630); he was a patron of Ben Jonson, and used to present him with £20 yearly for the purchase of books. Jonson dedicated his collection of epigrams to him, and wrote one of these epigrams about him.

Prologue, 13-15. During the excitement of the Popish Plot, interest in the drama had fallen to a very low ebb. In 1680 the two dramatic companies initiated plans to unite because of this lack of interest. The union took place in 1682 and lasted until 1695.

Prologue, 19. Scott and Saintsbury were unable to identify these particular wonders, but pointed out that the period was a time when many such wonders were reported. For instance, there was "The wonderful blazing star; with the dreadful apparition of two armies in the air ... seen on the 17th December, 1680, betwixt four and five o'clock in the evening, at Ottery;" and another wonder was a "monstrous child with two heads, four arms, four legs, and all things thereunto belonging...."

Prologue, 23. "Which whilome of Requests was call'd the Court." The Court of Requests was a chief rendezvous for all newsmongers and politicians. Titus Oates was said to resort there very frequently.

Prologue, 40. "Infalliable as is the Chair." I.e., the Pope; the Chair of St. Peter denotes the Papal office or see.

Dramatis Personae, 2. "Palante, Duke of Gandia." It is not known where Lee got the name "Palante"; Tomasi gives the duke's name as "Jean".

I, i, Opening stage direction. "little American Boys." The action of the play occurs in 1502, just after the discovery of America; Guicciardini has frequent references to Columbus and the discovery of America in his HISTORIA D'ITALIA (1561), one of Lee's chief sources.

I, i, 5. "Duke Valentinois." I.e., Caesar Borgia.

I, i, 11. "Twelve Cardinals at once created." It is historically true that Alexander VI created twelve cardinals at once, but Ascanio Sforza was not one of these.

I, i, 102. "Perhaps in the Embraces of a Nun." Tomasi says that Borgia's mother was a mistress of Alexander VI named Vanosse, not a nun.

I, i, 156. "Forms of Zemes." A Zemi is a carved image or idol, in human or animal form, supposed to represent the tutelary god of a tribe or clan among the West Indian natives.

I, i, 261-269. Both Guicciardini and Tomasi refer to the incest among the Borgias; in Tomasi it is the real cause for the murder of Gandia, whom Lucretia preferred to Caesar Borgia. See below, II, 314-317; III, i, 72-74.

I, i, 272. "When all the wandering Atoms hit at last." Cf. Lucretius, DE RERUM NATURA, Bk. V, 416 ff.

I, i, 299. "the poor Venetian Lady." This woman was a high-born attendant of Elizabeth Gonsague, Duchess of Urbin, and fiancée of Jean-Baptiste Caracciolo, Colonel-General of the Venetian infantry. The incident is related by Tomasi, VITA DEL DUCA VALENTINO.

I, i, 305. "truss'd at least 40 the pretty'st Rogues." This incident is related by both Tomasi and Guicciardini.

I, i, 357. "Neapolitan Pox." I.e., syphilis; Guicciardini gives an account of the "Neapolitan pox" being brought to Naples from Spain.

I, i, 412. "Receives the Rose before the Consistory." The giving of the Rose, or "Golden Rose", was one of the highest honors of the papacy. Tomasi gives an account of the bestowal of the Rose upon Borgia, but he states that the ceremony took place in St. Peter's, not before the Consistory.

I, i, 488. "this Child, my Son!" Stephano is a fictitious character; he does not appear in any of the histories of the time.

I, i, 516. "Charlotta's scorn." Charlotta was the daughter of Frederick of Naples; she was trained up in the French Court. The Pope tried to arrange a marriage between her and Caesar Borgia, but the young lady, persuaded either by her parents or by the French king, refused the match. Cf. I, i, 591 ff.

II, i, 54. "Rage resume me." The NED gives no use of the word resume in this sense of consume or possibly inspire.

II, i, 55. "seest thou this?" I.e., a dagger; see l. 59.

II, i, 69 ff. Orsino's curse on Bellamira is somewhat similar to Lear's curse on Goneril: KING LEAR, I, iv, 299-313.

II, i, 126 ff.   The parting of Bellamira and Gandia here is very similar to that of Varanes and Athenais in THEODOSIUS, Act IV.

II, i, 324.   "To follow Nature." Lee here reflects the influence of Hobbes and Lucretius, so widespread during the Restoration.

II, i, 383.   Cf. PARADISE LOST, V, 124.

III, i, 17-21.   Alonzo here is similar to Bosolo in THE DUCHESS OF MALFI and other Jacobean assassins.

III, i, 180.   "the brave Gonsalvo." Gonsalvo was a famous Spanish warrior in Italy. Guicciardini and Tomasi both mention him, but neither speaks of this particular episode in his life.

III, i, 245-246.   "Who does not love himself? /Self-love's the Universal Beam of Nature." Here again, Lee reflects the current influence of Lucretius and Hobbes. The doctrine of self-love as man's chief motivating force is also seen later in Pope's ESSAY ON MAN and Mandeville's FABLE OF THE BEES.

III, i, 333.   "When the great Cato gave his Friend his Wife." Cato the Younger, known as Cato Uticensis, gave his wife, Marcia, to his friend Hortensius to bear him an heir. Cato himself officiated at the marriage. See Plutarch, "Cato the Younger", LIVES (Mod. Library ed.), pp. 931-932.

III, i, 428.   "No more; 'tis gone: O Marriage! now I find thee." Cf. OTHELLO, III, iii, 446-447:
> All my fond love thus do I blow to heaven:
> 'Tis gone.

III, i, 616-623.   Cf. Iago's speech on jealousy: OTHELLO, III, iii, 165-175.

IV, i, 1 ff.   "Blush not redder than the Morning." Day and Murrie, #386; music by Farmer: Songbooks 55 (pp. 10-11), 210A (p. 312), 242 (p. 195).

IV, i, 9-12.   Lee here echoes the thought of Herrick's famous lines,

> "To the Virgins, to Make Much of Time":
> Gather ye rosebuds while ye may,
> Old time is still a-flying:
> And this same flower that smiles to-day
> To-morrow will be dying.

IV, i, 144.   "the fearful Plant." Mimosa pudica, often called the "sensitive plant". See Shelley's poem "The Sensitive Plant."

IV, i, 166.   "'Tis mountainous to Faith." Apparently in the sense of "monstrous"; cf. CORIOLANUS, II, iii, 127: "And mountainous Error be too highly heapt."

IV, i, 206.   "As Pyrrhus, daub'd in Murder at the Altar." Pyrrhus, the son of Achilles, slew Priam and his son Polites at an altar in Priam's palace during the sacking of Troy. See AENEID, Bk. II.

IV, i, 207.   "As Tullia, driving through her Fathers Bowels." According to legend, Tullia caused her husband, Lucius Tarquinius, to murder her father, Servius Tullius, and afterwards she drove her chariot over his body as it lay in the street.

IV, i, 209.   "As Nero bathing in his Mothers Womb." Nero had incestuous relations with his mother and later had her executed; see Suetonius, NERO, XXVIII, XXXIV. But Lee's exact meaning in this line is not clear.

IV, i, 242-243.   Cf. OTHELLO, V, ii, 141-144:

> Nay, had she been true,
> If heaven would make me such another world
> Of one entire and perfect chrysolite,
> I'd not have sold her for it.

IV, i, 253. "the Sinigallian Victors." Sinigallia was a city on the shore of the Adriatic. After their supposed reconciliation with Borgia, the Orsini and Vitelli, acting as his allies, besieged and took the town, except for the fortress, which the castellan would not surrender to anyone but Borgia himself.

IV, i, 263 ff. This whole scene of Machiavel and Borgia cursing Gandia and Bellamira is just a paraphrase of the scene in HENRY VI, Part II (Act III, ii, 307 ff.) between Queen Margaret and Suffolk.

IV, i, 292-294. Cf. OTHELLO, III, iii, 477-479:

> Come, go with me apart; I will withdraw
> To furnish me with some swift means of death
> For the fair devil. Now art thou my lieutenant.

IV, i, 304 ff. The idea for Adorna's death by poisoned gloves comes from Davila's HISTORY OF THE CIVIL WARS OF FRANCE, which was the source for THE MASSACRE OF PARIS. According to Davila, the Queen of Navarre was murdered in 1572 "by poison administered ... in the perfume or trimming of a pair of gloves."

V, i, 35. "Tarquins Poppies." When the son of Lucius Tarquinius had gained the confidence of the leaders of the Gabii, and sent to ask his father what he should do with them, Tarquin made no reply but walked up and down the garden striking off the heads of the tallest poppies.

V, i, 120 ff. Bellamira's denunciation of Borgia is very similar to Emilia's diatribe against Othello and Iago in OTHELLO, V, ii, 160 ff.

V, i, 199 ff. Cf. THE DUCHESS OF MALFI, IV, ii, 274 ff.

V, i, 254. "see you Crown'd Rome's Emperour." This historically was Machiavelli's real aim.

V, i, 262 ff. These lines describing the lunatic were prophetic of Lee's own coming insanity.

V, i, 267-268. These two lines were quoted in "A Satire upon the Modern Poets", to describe Lee himself in Bedlam.

V, ii. This whole scene is based on the account given in Tomasi, Part I.

V, iii, 17 ff. For Machiavelli's own expression of these policies, see THE PRINCE, Ch. III.

V, iii, 31 ff. Machiavel's vision of the death of Borgia and the Pope is based on a similar vision seen by Borgia's servant, Carassa, as related by Tomasi.

V, iii, 66-75. This passage is a mere paraphrase of a passage in THE PRINCE, Chapter XXV, "What Fortune Can Effect in Human Affairs, and How to Withstand Her."

V, iii, 110 ff. Ascanio's account of how the common people received the news of Gandia's death is based on KING JOHN, IV, ii, where Hubert tells the king how the common people received the news of Arthur's death.

V, iii, 200. "I am caught my self." According to Guicciardini, Borgia did drink from the same poisoned wine as his father, but he recovered and lived some years afterwards.

V, iii, 286. "Hercules in the Nemean-skin." The first of the twelve labors of Hercules was to slay the lion of Nemea, whose skin he afterwards wore as his robe. Here Lee seems to confuse it with the shirt of Nessus, which burnt into and poisoned the flesh of Hercules, causing his death.

V, iii, 320-332. This passage is a close paraphrase of PARADISE LOST, III, 487-497. Either intentionally or unintentionally, Lee misquotes, and also makes the line division irregular; possibly he was quoting from memory. For instance, Milton's version of the last three lines is as follows:

Fly o'er the backside of the World far off
Into a Limbo large and broad, since called
The Paradise of Fools; to few unknown....

V, iii, 342 ff. Here Lee refers again to the Popish Plot, and the supposed plan of the Catholics to murder Charles II in order to put the Catholic James upon the throne.

V, iii, 371-372. These last two lines are a direct refutation of the lines spoken by Machiavelli in the Prologue to THE JEW OF MALTA:

Might first made Kings and Lawes were then most sure
When like the Dracos they were writ in blood.

Cf. KING JOHN, IV, ii, 104-105:

There is no sure foundation set on blood,
No certain life achiev'd by others' death.

Epilogue, 18. "Yet more, the horrid Chair the Mid-night show" -- Lee here refers to the circumstances of the murder of Sir Edmund Bury Godfrey. Cf. the Prologue to VENICE PRESERVED:

Here's not one murdered magistrate at least,
Kept rank like ven'son for a city feast,
Grown four days stiff, the better to prepare
And fit his pliant limbs to ride in chair.

Epilogue, 37-38. The reference here is to Barbara Villiers, Countess of Castlemaine and Duchess of Cleveland, one of the king's oldest mistresses. She had declared her conversion to Catholicism as far back as 1663; but the words "turn true Catholicks at last" refer to the fact that in 1677, after quarreling with Charles, she retired to Paris, where she gave £1,000 to the English Nuns of the Immaculate Conception, and placed her youngest daughter in that nunnery.

NOTES

INTRODUCTION TO THE PRINCESS OF CLEVE

1 See THE WORKS OF JOHN DRYDEN, ed. Scott and Saintsbury, X, 401-404; Hugh Macdonald, JOHN DRYDEN. A BIBLIOGRAPHY OF EARLY EDITIONS (1939), 42a. This prologue and epilogue were first printed in Dryden's MIS-CELLANY POEMS, 1684.

2 ROSCIUS ANGLICANUS, ed. Montague Summers, p. 38.

3 John Genest, SOME ACCOUNT OF THE ENGLISH STAGE, I, 319.

4 A. W. Ward, HISTORY OF ENGLISH DRAMATIC LITERATURE, III, 410. H. M. Sanders ("The Plays of Nat. Lee, Gent," TEMPLE BAR, CXXIV, 502) says it is a poor play.

5 G. H. Nettleton, ENGLISH DRAMA OF THE RESTORATION AND EIGHT-EENTH CENTURY, p. 98.

6 R. G. Ham, OTWAY AND LEE, p. 169.

7 Allardyce Nicoll, RESTORATION DRAMA, p. 137.

8 Van Lennep, II, 400.

9 Ibid., II, 401.

10 See Thomas B. Stroup, "The Princess of Cleve and Sentimental Comedy," RES, XI (1935).

11 These copies can be identified as follows:

Q$_1$(KU) has the figure "50" written in ink in the lower right-hand corner of the title-page; it has a dark water stain in the upper right-hand corner of leaves A1-4.

Q$_1$(DFo) has the cancelled D1, lacking in Q$_1$(KU). It has the number "10" in dark brown ink written on the title-page under the e in "Printed," and is further identified by the accession number, cs. 2005.

Q$_1$(ICN) has the cancelled D1; on the title-page is written in pencil "Ist edit."; on A2^r at the top of the page above the rules is written "G 4978".

Q$_1$(ICU) lacks the cancelled D1; on the title-page it has written "#3" above the SS of "PRINCESS"; and after the "Nat." is written "haniel".

Q$_1$(TxU) is bound in dark red boards, with dark red leather back; it has the cancelled D1, and its call number is Aj/L514/689p.

THE PRINCESS OF CLEVE

Dedication. "Charles Earl of Dorset and Middlesex." Charles Sackville (1638-1706), Lord Buckhurst, and sixth Earl of Dorset. In his youth he was a member of the wild and witty circle of Rochester, Sedley, and Etherege; as he grew older he became more staid. He was the patron of Dryden, and Lee had dedicated his LUCIUS JUNIUS BRUTUS to him in 1681. Dorset had aided in the Glorious Revolution of 1688, and hence was in the favor of William and Mary. It was for this reason that Lee turned again to this former patron in hope that through his influence the favor of the new monarchs might be secured, despite Lee's own former Tory sympathies.

Dedication, 5. "What was borrowed in the Action is left out in the Print." It seems likely that the excerpted scenes were in the beginning of Act II, i, and the end of Act V, iii: both concern meetings of Marguerite and Nemours, and both have obviously been cut or altered.

Dedication, 6-7. "But the Duke of Guise...has wrested two whole Scenes from the Original." I.e., the scenes Act II, i and ii.

Dedication, 15. "Whetstone's-Park". According to Genest (I, 322), "Whetstone's Park was on the Holborn side of L.I.F. -- it is mentioned in several old plays, and seems to have been much frequented by women of the town."

Dedication, 16-17. THE CHANCES, originally by Fletcher (1613) had been reshaped for the Restoration stage by Buckingham in 1667. Dryden's MARRIAGE A LA MODE (1673) hardly deserves Lee's condemnation. THE LIBERTINE (1676) and EPSOM WELLS (1672) were both by Shadwell, the new poet laureate and favorite of the Whigs.

Dedication, 18. "like the Gladiator in the Park." See Genest (I, 322, n.): "The Gladiator is mentioned in the Fools Preferment -- In Sir Harry Wildair, it is said 'as impudent as the naked statue was in the Park.'"

Dedication, 20-21. "'tis all to introduce the Massacre of Paris to your Favour, and approve it to be play'd in its first Figure." This play was produced in the following year, both the King and Queen being present at its performance.

Prologue, 18. "the Hag that rides 'em all the night." The nightmare, according to one tradition, was a "mare" or hag who rode up and down on the chest of the sleeper, causing him to suffocate or have bad dreams.

Prologue, 19. "The little Mob, the City Wastcoateer." Both were vulgar terms for prostitutes. The NED cites this line as an example of this use of "mob"; for the second term cf. Beaumont and Fletcher, WIT WITHOUT MONEY, IV, iv: "your wastcoateers, your base Wenches."

Prologue, 24. "A Monarch on a Throne sublime." William III, whose favor Lee is here trying to gain.

Dramatis Personae, 7. "Poltrot." This name Lee took, not from Mme. de la Fayette, but from Davila's HISTORY OF THE CIVIL WARS OF FRANCE, the source of THE MASSACRE OF PARIS.

I, i, 4 ff. "Song." Day and Murrie #124; music by Turner; Songbook #59 (134), p. 35.

I, i, 51-57. In THE MASSACRE OF PARIS, Marguerite is in love with the Duke of Guise, and the Queen wants her to marry Henry of Navarre, not the Dauphin, as in this passage.

I, ii, 90. "Count Rosidore is dead." Rosidore is Rochester, who had died July 26, 1680. Lee had dedicated his first play, NERO, to Rochester, but the latter had satirized Lee in "An Allusion to the Tenth Satire of the First Book of Horace" (1680), and relations between the two had apparently been very cold. Lee here pays glowing tribute to the brilliance of his former patron; but this praise of the greatest of the Restoration rakes seems somewhat out of place in a play which is a trenchant satire of Restoration immorality.

I, ii, 98-100. Cf. HAMLET, V, i, 235-236:

> Imperious Caesar, dead and turn'd to clay,
> Might stop a hole to keep the wind away:

I, ii, 160. "as wanton as any little Bartholomew Bore-Pig." Cf. HENRY IV, Pt. II, Act II, iv, 250: "Thou whorson little tidy Bartholomew boar-pig...."

I, ii, 165 ff. "Phillis is soft, Phillis is plump." This song is not listed in Day and Murrie.

I, iii, 1 ff. "Song." This song is not listed in Day and Murrie.

I, iii, 19. "Then you must own it on occasion." In the novel, this letter actually does belong to the Vidam, and not to Nemours, although the latter is suspected of being the real owner.

II, ii, 20. "leave trising your Curls." Pulling or plucking at his wig.

II, ii, 190-195. In this passage Tournon is vying in politeness with Celia and Elianor as to who shall go out of the door last. Celia remarks that since it is their home, Tournon must go out first.

II, iii. This scene presumably takes place in the Bower or Musick-Bower mentioned later, IV, i, 245; IV, iii, 11; IV, iii, 21 ff. It is here that the Princess makes her confession in the novel.

III, i, 14. "the Man fork'd in the Book of Fate." I.e., doomed to be horned or cuckolded.

III, i, 133. "Thus sung Rosidore in the Urn." The reference is apparently to Rochester's poem "Upon Drinking in a Bowl;" but the preceding lines of Nemours' speech are not a very accurate paraphrase of the thought of this poem. Lee probably had in mind the general idea of the last stanza, though he enlarges and distorts it:

> Cupid and Bacchus my saints are;
> May drink and love still reign:
> With wine I wash away my cares,
> And then to love again.

III, i, 230. "Why, what is the Breeze in your Tails?" The "breeze" was a term for a gadfly. Cf. Pope's ODYSSEY, XXII, 335: "Like oxen maddened by the breeze's sting." See also OEDIPUS, I, i, 102: "As if the Breeze had stung 'em."

III, i, 273. "the Dumb Man, the Highlander that made such a noise." See, later, Act IV, i, 65 ff. The man referred to here must have been similar to Duncan Campbell, the deaf and dumb Highlander who claimed powers of second sight and whose life was written up by Defoe. But Campbell did not come to London until 1694.

IV, i, 76. "the Chriss cross-row." I.e., the alphabet in a horn book, so called because of the "Christ's cross" at the head of it.

IV, i, 104-105. "I will have my Eunuchs fling her from the Window." The reference here is to the death of Jezebel as related in II Kings, ix, 30-37.

IV, i, 122. "the Beetle to drive him." "Beetle" was a term used for a large, heavy, wooden mallet.

IV, i, 232. "the new found Lock." Lee implies here and in line 235 that the padlock was a newly invented device. The NED, however, gives uses of the word as far back as the fifteenth century. Possibly the reference is to some new type of padlock.

IV, i, 255-56. "like her that gave Acteon Horns." Artemis changed Acteon into a stag because he had seen her and her nymphs bathing. He was then torn to pieces by his own dogs.

IV, ii, 17-18. Tournon here is playing upon the meaning of legal terms: "Satis"--enough, or satisfactory (used in regard to evidence in a case); "Non Satis"--not enough, insufficient or unsatisfactory; "Nunquam Satis"--at no time, never, or by no means enough or satisfactory; "Ignoramus"--literally, we ignore it, the term used when a jury dismisses a case for insufficient evidence.

IV, ii, 35-36. "I have as many Bobs as Democritus when he cry'd Poor Jack." The exact meaning of this expression is not clear. Apparently Lee is using the term "Bobs" in the sense either of tricks, taunts, jests (see NED) or possibly of blows or raps: cf. Cibber, THE RIVAL FOOLS, III: "I only find Bobs, Blows, and Noise in my poor wooing." Democritus was the so-called "laughing philosopher" of the fifth century B.C., who was known for his taunting and deriding of mankind, but Lee's reference to an occasion when he "cry'd Poor Jack" is obscure. Note that Lee used this phrase again V, iii, 291 ff., where the word "Bobs" seems to be used specifically for blows.

IV, ii, 39. "look to 'em, they'll do 'em, look to 'em, they'll do 'em." Cf. THE REHEARSAL, I, ii, 284-285: "Look to't, look to't; we'll do't, we'll do't; look to't, we'll do't."

IV, iii, 20. "I'll face him till he enters the Bower." The NED records no use of the word "face" in this sense of follow or trail; it is just possible that this is a printer's error, and that the word in the author's manuscript was "trace."

IV, iii, 22 ff. "Song." Day and Murrie #2131; music by Blow; Songbooks #59 (134), pp. 28-29; #65, pp. 3-5.

V, i, 9. "Cuckolding Trojan Race." I.e., the English; according to legend Britain was first colonized by Brutus of Troy.

V, i, 34-39. This passage denouncing women is taken from a romance, THE FRENCH ROGUE (1672), p. 132.

V, i, 60-61. "hunch'd him on the side like a full Acorn'd Boar, cry'd Oh! and mounted." Cf. CYMBELINE, II, v, 16-17:
> "Like a full-acorn'd boar, a German one,
> Cried 'O!' and mounted."

V, i, 64. "a Carted Bawd." Cf. HUDIBRAS, II, i, 81-82:
> "Democritus ne'er laugh'd so loud,
> To see bawds carted through the crowd."

Bawds and prostitutes were often punished by being publicly carried through the streets in a cart, and usually whipped during this exhibition.

V, i, 132. "like the Man in the Almanack." I.e., the figure of a man, often printed on the cover of almanacs, used to illustrate anatomy. Cf. CAESAR BORGIA, Dedication, "like the Almanack Hero, all over Wounds."

V, ii, 31. "Go thy ways Petronius." Petronius Arbiter was famous for his elegance in pleasures and debaucheries at the court of Nero. Lee had used the character in his own NERO.

V, iii, 1 ff. "Weep all ye Nymphs, your Floods unbind." Day and Murrie #3589; music by Blow; Songbooks #78 (134), pp. 46-47; #182 (208, 213, 227) pp. 212-213; #233 (238) pp. 200-201.

V, iii, 118. "That I shou'd wear these Rags of Life away." Cf. ALL FOR LOVE, V, i, 293-294:

> "The life I bear is worn to such a rag,
> 'Tis scarce worth giving."

V, iii, 275 ff. This is probably one of the scenes where Lee cut out a passage he had used from THE MASSACRE OF PARIS. Obviously the audience has been prepared for a scene of some length and importance between Marguerite and Nemours, but the quarrel between the two is limited to two lines. Apparently Lee cut the scene out and put nothing in to replace it.

V, iii, 290. "though I haule Cats at Sea." Cervantes uses this expression in the sense of something insuperable or very difficult, DON QUIXOTE, Part I, ch. 8: "Quien ha de llevar el gato al agua." Lee, however, seems to use it to mean something menial, a low type of activity in the same class as "crying" or selling "Small-coal." According to Harrison Weir, OUR CATS (London, 1889), the term "cat" was applied to a small vessel of the Norwegian type used to haul coal, and it was applied also to a type of tackle used to haul up an anchor. These uses of the word might possibly have some bearing upon this particular expression.

Epilogue, 1. "What is this Wit which Cowley cou'd not name?" Lee is referring to Cowley's famous ode "Of Wit."

Epilogue, 4. "Is it a Whig, a Trimmer, or a Tory." These terms had just recently come into use during the furor over the Popish Plot and the Exclusion Bill. A Trimmer was one who tried to trim his sails so as to steer between the two extremes of Whigs and Tories.

Epilogue, 11. "The Danaid's filling of a Leakey Sieve." The daughters of Danaos, because they murdered their husbands on their wedding night, were condemned in Hades to the endless task of trying to fill a bottomless jar with water drawn up in a sieve.

NOTES

INTRODUCTION TO THEODOSIUS

1 John Downes, ROSCIUS ANGLICANUS, ed. Montague Summers, p. 38.
2 Charles Gildon, THE LAWS OF POETRY (1721), pp. 37-38.
3 George C. D. Odell, ANNALS OF THE NEW YORK STAGE, I, 88, 164.
3a Robert L. Sherman, DRAMA CYCLOPEDIA (Chicago, 1944), p. 538.
THEODOSIUS, rightly assigned to Lee, is wrongly listed as THEODORUS.
3b Eola Willis, THE CHARLESTON STAGE IN THE XVIII CENTURY (Columbia, S.C., 1924), pp. 44, 73.
4 Parts I-VII of the romance were by La Calprenède; it was continued by Vaumoriere, Parts VIII-XII, 1665-1670. See Fritz Resa's edition of THEODOSIUS (1904) for an extended, though somewhat indiscriminate, treatment of the sources of the play, pp. 33-64.
5 John Genest, SOME ACCOUNT OF THE ENGLISH STAGE (1832), I, 289.
6 BIOGRAPHIA DRAMATICA, III, 330.
7 "The Plays of Nat. Lee, Gent.," TEMPLE BAR, CXXIV (1901), 501.
8 Van Lennep, II, 425, 451.
9 Malcolm Elwin, THE PLAYGOER'S HANDBOOK TO RESTORATION DRAMA, pp. 129-30.
10 Allardyce Nicoll, RESTORATION DRAMA (1928), pp. 136-37.
11 Van Lennep, op. cit., II, 449.
12 SPECTATOR, No. 39.
13 These copies of Q_1 may be identified as follows:
Q_1(KU) is bound in blue paper; on the title-page under the word ACTS is written "by Purcell".
Q_1(CLUC): on the title-page, following the date, is written in an old hand: "31st Year of Charles y 2^d."
Q_1(CSmH) has pencilled on the title-page, above the first "S" of THEODOSIUS, the figure "138"; it has no list of plays on $I4^v$.
Q_1(DFo 1) is bound in calf and bears the case number 224.
Q_1(DFo 2) is bound in green paper and has in it the bookplate of Godfrey E. P. Arkwright.
14 This advertisement is lacking in some copies.

THEODOSIUS

Dedication. "The DUTCHESS of RICHMOND." Frances Stewart, "La belle Stewart" (1647-1702); having resisted the advances of Charles II for some years, she eloped with the Duke of Richmond in 1667. After her marriage she became one of the king's favorite mistresses. Lee's flattery of her beauty and charm was justified; but his flattery of her "Greatness of Mind" was not. Hamilton remarked: "It is hardly possible for a woman to have less wit and more beauty."

Dedication, 6-12. This quotation is from Donne's "An Anatomy of the World. The First Anniversary", 112-114, and 117-120. Lee omits ls. 115-116.

Dedication, 14. "the best Writer of the Age." John Dryden, Lee's friend and collaborator.

Dedication, 47 ff. Donne's "An Anatomy of the World. The Second Anniversary", l. 244 ff.

Dedication, 53. "Ziphares and Semandra." These are the two lovers in Lee's MITHRIDATES.

Prologue, 21. "small blue Band." Blue was the color of the Whig party, to which most of the Dissenters belonged.

Prologue, 36. "Spencer starv'd." There was a popular belief in the seventeenth century that Spenser actually starved to death. See note on Prologue to CONSTANTINE THE GREAT.

I, i, stage direction. "In hoc signo vinces." Lee took this motto from Eusebius' life of Constantine. It is given also at the opening of Act I of Lee's CONSTANTINE.

I, i, 1-5. Song listed in Day and Murrie, #2744.

I, i, 6. "O Leontine! was ever Morn like this." Cf. Fielding's ridicule of such lines as this in TOM THUMB, I, i, 1.

I, i, 10. "Chrysostom." The famous Patriarch of Constantinople 398-404; called "golden-mouthed" because of his great eloquence.

I, i, 28. "Marina and Flavilla." In PHARAMOND and in the historical accounts of the time, it was Flaccilla who joined Marina in forsaking the world.

I, i, 47. "Who, when his father sent him into Persia." This is Lee's own invention. It is not according to PHARAMOND or the histories of the time.

I, i, 85. "Orosmasdes." Or Ormazd, the good spirit of Zoroaster's philosophy, opposed to Ahriman, the evil spirit.

I, i, 247 ff. Lee here gives a loose paraphrase of A MIDSUMMER-NIGHT'S DREAM, IV, i, 125 ff.

I, i, 256-260. The reference here is to Seneca's THE MAD HERCULES.

I, i, 321 ff. This song is listed in Day and Murrie, #476.

I, i, 381. "my dar'd Soul." I.e., frightened, dazed; cf. Shakespeare, HENRY VIII, Act III, ii, 282: "Let his Grace go forward, And dare us with his Cap, like Larkes." Cf. II, i, 340, in the present play.

I, "Song after the First ACT." Listed in Day and Murrie, #2416; found also in Songbook #55, "Choice Ayres and Songs" (1681).

II, i, 1. "the Emperour Honorius." Flavius Honorius (384-423 A.D.) was Emperor of the West; he was the second son of Theodosius I, and therefore the uncle of the Theodosius who appears in this play.

II, i, 116. "Pharamond." This fabulous hero is first mentioned in the GESTA

FRANCORUM (c. 720); he was supposed to have ruled over France c. 420-428; he was the subject of La Calprenède's romance PHARAMOND, which was the source of THEODOSIUS.

II, i, 128. "Rome's Clelia, and the fam'd Semiramis." Clelia was a legendary young Roman girl who was given as hostage to Porsenna, King of the Etruscans; she escaped by swimming the Tiber, was sent back to Porsenna by the Romans, but was released by that king on account of her bravery and returned to Rome laden with gifts. Semiramis was the fabulous queen, wife of Nimes, founder of Nineveh. She is said to have built Babylon with its famous hanging gardens.

II, i, 135. "their late Salique Law." Lee's concept of the Salique law is an erroneous one, drawn from Davila's HISTORY OF THE CIVIL WARS OF FRANCE. The law is really a civil law, not a political one, and prevents women from inheriting private property.

II, i, 183. "Your Grand Father, whose Frown could awe the World." I.e., Theodosius I, called the Great (c. 346-395); his son Arcadius was father of Theodosius II and Pulcheria.

II, i, 300. "Isdigerdes." The father of Varanes.

II, "Song after the Second ACT." Listed by Day and Murrie, #2843; also found in Songbook #65.

III, i, 54. "the Hypodrome." The arena for horse and chariot races, similar to the Circus Maximus in Rome.

III, ii, 1 ff. Not listed in Day and Murrie.

III, ii, 206-207. Cf. THE WAY OF THE WORLD, II, i, 361-363: "Here she comes, i'faith, full sail, with her fan spread and her streamers out...."; cf. also SAMSON AGONISTES, 710-719.

III, end of Act. "SONG." "Hail to the Mirtle Shade." Listed in Day and Murrie, #1227; also found in Songbooks #55, 182, and 233.

IV, i, 130. "He is a Boy, and as a Boy you'l use him." Theodosius had come to the throne as a child, and he was still very young at this time.

IV, ii. "Song." Listed in Day and Murrie, #1236, p. 233, the music not having been printed.

IV, ii, 32. "Germanicus." Roman general (15 B.C. -19 A.D.), son of Nero Claudius Drusus, and nephew of Tiberius. He led three expeditions against the Germans, 14-16 A.D.; was said to have been poisoned by the emperor through jealousy of his military success and popularity.

IV, ii, 82-124. The various details here referred to regarding Nero are drawn from Suetonius, NERO, XX-XXXI.

IV, ii, 153. "the former Brutus." I.e.. Lucius Junius Brutus, the subject of Lee's following play.

IV, ii, 446-457. This parting of Varanes and Athenais is very similar to the parting of Gandia and Bellamira in CAESAR BORGIA.

V, i, 31 ff. "SONG." Listed in Day and Murrie, #35; appears also in Songbooks #55, 188, and 234.

Epilogue, 4. "Finsbury." A district north of the City. In Finsbury Field the city train bands used to drill, and the place was frequented as a resort by the citizens of London.

Epilogue, 8. "his Crequi and his Conde too." Charles duc de Crequi (1623-1687) was a leading French general; he was ambassador to England in 1671. The Prince de Condé (Louis II de Bourbon) (1621-1686), known as "the Great Condé" was perhaps the most celebrated French general of the time.

NOTES

INTRODUCTION TO LUCIUS JUNIUS BRUTUS

1 Giles Jacob, THE POETICAL REGISTER (London, 1719), I, 162.
2 Translated by John Davies, 1656-1661.
3 For a few minor details Lee was also indebted to Dionysius Halicarnasensis. For a full discussion of the sources, see Van Lennep, THE LIFE AND WORKS OF NATHANIEL LEE: A STUDY OF THE SOURCES.
4 In certain scenes, however, Lee has followed the romance especially closely: (1) the scene in which Brutus makes his speech over Lucrece's body; (2) the opening of Act III, where Brutus forces Collatinus to resign; (3) the scene in Act III, where Brutus receives the envoys from Tarquin.
5 See Livy, II, lvii; II, iii.
6 Plutarch's LIVES (Mod. Library ed.) p. 119. Cf. also Jonson's CATILINE, I, i, where Catiline and his followers sacrifice a slave and vow in his blood to overthrow Rome.
7 In return, Otway borrowed from Lee the idea of having Jaffeir stab Pierre in VENICE PRESERVED, as Valerius stabs Titus in BRUTUS.
8 Langbaine, ACCOUNT OF THE ENGLISH DRAMATICK POETS (1699), p. 85.
9 Theophilus Cibber, LIVES OF THE POETS (1753), II, 230-231.
10 RETROSPECTIVE REVIEW, III (1823), 261.
11 John Genest, SOME ACCOUNT OF THE ENGLISH STAGE (1832), I, 311.
12 "Über Nathaniel Lee's Leben und Werke," ENGLISCHE STUDIEN, II (1879), 435.
13 A. W. Ward, HISTORY OF ENGLISH DRAMATIC LITERATURE (1899), III, 411.
14 Allardyce Nicoll, RESTORATION DRAMA (1928), p. 137.
15 Malcolm Elwin, PLAYGOER'S HANDBOOK TO RESTORATION DRAMA (n.d.), pp. 130-131.
16 Van Lennep, op. cit., II, 520.
17 Ibid., II, 523.
18 These copies may be identified as follows:
    Q_1(KU) unbound; has written on title-page under COUNTRY, the figures "2/10/"; stain mark above the "and" in the second line from the foot of the page.
    Q_1(TxU) has call no. Wj/L514/681; on F2^V the catch-word "I" is missing at the foot of the page.
    Q_1(DFo 1) is bound in three-fourths black leather and blue-and-red mottled binding; cs 174.
    Q_1(DFo 2) is bound up with SOPHONISBA and other plays of Lee; cs 193; Kean collection 205; inscribed "To Edmund Kean...from...Wm Henry Halpim."
    Q_1(DFo 3) is bound in three-fourths black paper, and red, blue, yellow mottled binding, with "Shakespeare Library" device inside cover; the Warwick copy; it does not have L1 with the Epilogue.
19 K1-4 adds an extra line to each page so as to obviate the addition of L1, as found in Q_1.

LUCIUS JUNIUS BRUTUS

Dedication. "CHARLES, Earl of Dorset and Middlesex." See an account of this patron in the explanatory notes to the Dedication of THE PRINCESS OF CLEVE.

Dedication, 13-14. "Cecilius." Caecilius Statius, a Gaul who came to Rome in the second century B. C., and wrote a number of comedies. Cicero condemned him for his bad Latin.

Dedication, 36-37. "Machivel's Notes upon the place." I. e., Machiavelli's DISCORSI SOPRA LA PRIMA DECA DE T. LIVIO, 1512-1517.

Dedication, 40-42. These lines are quoted from the AENEID, VI, 817-818, 822.

Prologue. "Mr. Duke." Richard Duke (1658-1711), of Trinity College, Cambridge; he was a clergyman and minor poet, a close friend of Dryden and Otway; he was appointed tutor to a son of the king by the Duchess of Portsmouth. See Johnson's LIVES OF THE POETS, where he merits one page.

Prologue, 35. "Antisalick Law." The Salic Law originated among the German tribes and was originally designed to prevent women from holding property; in France it was generally conceived as a law preventing women from inheriting the crown.

I, i, 26. "Break first th'eternal Chain." This is another of Lee's frequent references to the concept of the great chain of being, so prevalent in the philosophy of the seventeenth and eighteenth centuries.

I, i, 73. "Collatia." A Sabine town in Latium, near the right bank of the Anio. It was the home of Collatine and Lucrece.

I, i, 152. "Ardea." Chief town of the Rutuli in Latium, about three miles from the sea; it was the capital of Turnus; conquered by the Romans c. 442 B. C.

I, i, 167. "Tullia's Boys." Tullia had three sons: Sextus, Titus, and Arruns.

I, i, 177-178. "a very Plot upon the Court." Here, as in many other places, Lee is obliquely referring to the notorious Popish Plot of 1678-9.

I, i, 190. "Setters." A setter was a confederate of sharpers or swindlers. According to Greene's DISCOVERY OF COSENAGE, the setter worked in collaboration with two other swindlers: the verser and the barnacle.

I, i, 282. "Lucretius." The father of Lucrece.

I, i, 306. "The Tribune of the Celeres." The Celeres were a bodyguard of 300 cavalry chosen originally by Romulus to attend him in peace or war; the tribune of the Celeres was the commander of these men.

II, i, 41. "I am a true Commonwealths-man." This and the following speeches reflect extreme Whig sentiments, of the kind which brought a ban upon the play after its sixth day.

II, i, 59. "these roaring Lords." Cf. the so-called "roaring boys" of the Restoration, forerunners of the Mohocks in the time of Swift.

II, i, 81-82. "drove the Chariot over her Father's Body." Cf. lines 180-183. Tullia, wife of Tarquinus Superbus, persuaded her husband to seize the throne and murder her father Servius Tullius. As his body lay in the street, she drove her chariot over it on her triumphant way to the Senate.

II, i, 142 ff. There is an obvious similarity between the opening of Brutus's speech and that of Antony in JULIUS CAESAR.

II, i, 169. "thou great Stayer." I. e., Jupiter. Cf. V, ii, 3: "Jove the Stayer."

II, i, 180-181. "add the horrid slaughter / Of all the Princes of the Roman Senate." When he murdered Servius Tullius and seized the throne, Tarquin put to death all those senators and patricians whom he mistrusted. Cf. III, ii, 35-36.

III, i. Act III opens some considerable time after the close of Act II, probably some weeks later. There is no direction to this effect in any text, but the lapse of time is apparent from the context.

III, i, 176. "Fecialian Priests." The Feciales or Fetiales were a collegium of Roman priests who acted as guardians of the public faith, and were especially commissioned to undertake missions of peace or war. Lee purposely misrepresents them in order to satirize the Catholic priesthood and the Popish Plot.

III, ii, 1 ff. Note how Lee has followed the classic form of the oration in this speech of Brutus: the exordium, proposition, arguments, etc.

III, ii, 83. "Publicola." This was the name given to Valerius in recognition of his services to the people. See Plutarch's life of Valerius.

III, ii, 90-92. For these practices of the Fecialian or Fetialian priests, including the hurling of the half-burnt spear, see Livy, XXXVI, 3.

III, ii, 93. "the Alban People." According to legend, Rome was first colonized by Alba Longa, the most ancient town in Latium; hence the Romans were referred to as the "Alban People."

IV, i, 1-12. Note the resemblance between this scene and that in MACBETH, II, ii, between Macbeth and Lady Macbeth just after the murder of Duncan. Notice also that Macbeth mentions "Tarquin's ravishing strides" in the preceding scene: II, i, 55.

IV, i, 45-47. The names of the particular places mentioned here are all taken from CLELIA, Bk. II, parts ii, iii. The Sublician Bridge, which derived its name from the wooden beams (sublicae) of which it was built, was the only bridge in Rome until the 2nd century B.C.

IV, i, 103 ff. This scene of human sacrifice is an obvious satire on the supposed methods of the Spanish Inquisition, portrayed by Lee in an effort to arouse the English against the Catholics, and remind them that such methods might again be adopted if the Catholics gained supremacy in England.

IV, i, 108. "the Berecynthian Queen." I.e., Cybele, who was worshipped at Berecyntus; her other name was Rhea; she was goddess of earth, daughter of Uranus, and wife of Chronos.

IV, i, 156. "Egeria." a Roman goddess, legendary consort of King Numa, and goddess of fountains and prophecy.

IV, i, 172. "As if I had drunk the blood of Elephants." There was a popular belief that this would induce impotence; cf. Beaumont and Fletcher, THIERRY AND THEODORET, IV, iii:

> Sure I have drunk the blood of elephants!
> The tears of mandrakes and the marble dew,
> Mix'd in my draught, have quench'd my natural heat,
> And left no spark of fire, but in mine eyes.

IV, i, 191. "And Tarquin in the Streets bestriding Slaughter." Cf. MACBETH, II, i, 55: "Tarquin's ravishing strides."

IV, i, 250. "Priests that are Instruments design'd to Damn us." Here again, Lee is satirizing the Jesuits, who were so feared during the Popish Plot.

IV, i, 253. "Ancus Martius." Fourth king of Rome, c. 640-616 B.C.; grand-
son of Numa; he was succeeded by Tarquinius Priscus, whom Martius's
sons murdered.

IV, i, 471 ff. This passage of death is taken almost verbatim from Bacon's essay "Of Death":
> And by him that spake onely as a Philosopher and Natural Man,
> it is well said, <u>Pompa</u> <u>Mortis</u> magis <u>terret</u> <u>quam</u> <u>Mors</u> <u>ipsa</u>.
> Groans and Convulsions and a discoloured Face, and Friends
> weeping, and Blackes, and Obsequies, and the like, shew
> Death Terrible.... It is as Natural to die as to be borne."
> BACON'S ESSAYS, ed. A. S. West (Cambridge, 1920) pp. 4-5.

V, i, 118. "Than impious Saturn or the gorg'd Thiestes." Saturn or Chronos
devoured all his children except Zeus, because it was foretold that he
would be dethroned by one of them. Thyestes, brother of Atreus, seduced
his brother's wife; and in punishment, Atreus invited him to a feast where
he served up to him the flesh of his two sons. When Thyestes discovered
the truth, he fled in horror, and the gods cursed the house of Atreus.

Epilogue, 39. "Point Venie." Lace made wholly with the needle in imitation of
that made at Venice; Flanders and Venice were the most famous producers of fine lace during the time.

INTRODUCTION TO THE DUKE OF GUISE

1 THE WORKS OF JOHN DRYDEN, ed. by Scott and Saintsbury, VII, 148.
2 Nicoll, RESTORATION DRAMA, p. 311. See Scott and Saintsbury, VII, 150, also.
3 Rev. John Genest, SOME ACCOUNT OF THE ENGLISH STAGE, II, 580.
4 See the Dedicatory Letter to THE PRINCESS OF CLEVE, "To the Right Honourable Earl of Dorset and Middlesex."
5 A complete and more exact statement of the borrowings from the earlier play is as follows:

> Act I, scene i, lines 200-203 are derived from THE MASSACRE OF PARIS, Act I, scene i, lines 68-71; I, i, 352-363 from I, i, 150-160; II, i, 46-106 generally from I, ii, 15-19, 25-40, 76-78, 79, 83-96, 108-111, 115, 116-117, 155-156, I, i, 123-25; II, i, 126-128 from IV, i, 50-52; II, ii, 41-140 generally from IV, ii, 63-74, 87-94, 97-100, 105-108, 113-123, 137-148, 168-183, 193-215; II, ii, 151-157 from IV, ii, 244-250; III, i, 125-128 from III, ii, 25-28.

6 DRYDEN, THE DRAMATIC WORKS, ed. by Montague Summers, V, 209-211.
7 Ibid., V, 211, 477.
8 See Van Lennep, II, 531, for a brief summary of the political parallel.
9 Scott and Saintsbury, DRYDEN, DRAMATIC WORKS, VII, 8-9.
10 A HISTORY OF DRAMATIC LITERATURE, III, 379-80.
11 Ham, OTWAY AND LEE, p. 173.
12 Van Lennep, II, 555, 616-617.
13 See THE SONGS OF JOHN DRYDEN, ed. by Lawrence Day (Cambridge, Mass., 1932), pp. 61-64.
14 Another issue of this edition was printed for R. Wellington and E. Rombull, 1699. It differs only in the title-page, a cancel which has the lower portion of the title reset; the two lines mentioning the VINDICATION are removed; for the original imprint the following is inserted: "London, Printed for R. Wellington, and E. Rombull, 1699." With this is a ten-line advertisement of Lee's works. See Macdonald, #87d.
15 These copies may be identified as follows:

> Q_1(KU), bound in three-quarter brown leather with gold tooling and lettering, has brown ink-stain on all the pages of music. On A2^r in the left-hand margin is written in pencil: "Simons 4/29/ 49 35.00."
> Q_1(DFo 1) is an uncut copy in contemporary (1683) binding from the Herschel V. Jones Library. It is marked cs. 1267, and the Wing number is D2264.
> Q_1(DFo 2) is bound up in a nonce collection of DRYDEN'S PLAYS, 1672-1682, volume 3. Plays are separately dated, and the volume is marked cs. 159; the Wing number is D2394. Volume 3 has eleven plays in it, the tenth being THE DUKE OF GUISE.
> Q_1(DFo 3) is likewise bound up in a nonce collection called DRYDEN'S PLAYS. It appears in volume 3 of this collection, a volume marked from Dobell as "First Edition." Page 19 is marked in error "91". This copy came from the Malone col-

lection, with Edmund Malone's initials engraved on the front
cover. The signature "Jo: Fitzherbert" in brown ink slightly
smeared appears on the title page of THE DUKE OF GUISE, to
the right of the imprint. Inserted between A4 and B1 is "Another / Epilogue / Intended to have been spoken to the / Duke
of Guise, / before it was forbidden last Summer. / Written by
Mr. Dryden." This is written in Malone's hand and has at the
bottom of the verso page: "London; Printed for Jacob Tonson,
at the Judge's head in Chancery Lane. 1683."
Q_1 (DFo 4) is bound up in a MISCELLANY OF OLD PLAYS, volume 1. It is marked cs. 968 and has the Wing number D2393.
A worm hole beginning on the title-page in the lower left-hand
corner continues through each sheet to K4. In this copy "A
Song..." is inserted between K4 and L1, awkwardly glued in.

16 In his edition of the play Summers remarks (DRYDEN: THE DRAMATIC
   WORKS, V, 392) that the text of the 1683 edition is good and the variants in
   the later editions comparatively few and unimportant.

17 DRYDEN: THE DRAMATIC WORKS, V. See pages 393-95 for Summers'
   textual notes.

THE DUKE OF GUISE

Dedication. "LAWRENCE, EARL of ROCHESTER." Lawrence Hyde (1641-1711), second son of Edward Hyde, first Earl of Clarendon, was created Earl of Rochester in 1682, following the death (1680) of the notorious John Wilmot, second Earl of Rochester. He was noted for his opposition to the Exclusion Bill, a fact which makes appropriate this dedication. At the time of the play he was Commissioner of the Treasury; later under James, he became Lord High Treasurer. Following the succession of William and Mary he was for a time out of Royal favor, but he regained his place on the Privy Council in 1692. He was a regular patron of Dryden, who also dedicated CLEOMENES to him.

Dedication, 3-15. See the Introduction to THE DUKE OF GUISE for a discussion of the controversy over the production and the delay in production. The "Judge" was not the Lord Chamberlain, as Scott and Summers say, but rather Charles II himself, who Dryden says in the VINDICATION was the best judge and was responsible for allowing the play to be produced.

Dedication, 26. "Theatres were True Protestant." The reference is to such plays as Shadwell's LANCASHIRE WITCHES (1681) and Settle's notorious FEMALE PRELATE (1679), both strongly Whig in sentiment.

Dedication, 50. "The Pilot's Prayer to Neptune." As Summers says, Dryden's immediate source for this passage is Montaigne's ESSAYS, II, xvi. Ultimately the passage may have come from Seneca or Cicero.

Prologue, 1-2. "The Holy League / Begot our Cov'nant." The "Solemn League and Covenant" was proposed at Leith between the English and Scotch 7 August, 1643, was adopted by the Scotch ten days later, and finally by the English on 25 September, 1643. It was designed to establish uniformity in religion in England, Ireland, and Scotland. It abolished episcopacy and adopted the Presbyterian form of church government. Here Dryden sees the French Holy League as a forerunner of the Covenant.

Prologue, 3. "hot-brain'd Sheriffs." The reference is to Pilkington and Shute, who were elected sheriffs in June, 1681. They were remembered for fomenting riots and other disorders, stuffing the ballot, and a year later causing trouble at the election of North and Rich as sheriffs. Sheriff trouble in London was in large measure responsible for Charles's revocation of the City's charter in 1683.

Prologue, 6. "like their godly Beggars here." Huguenots were coming to England in numbers because of their repression under Louis XIV prior to the revocation of the Edict of Nantes, 1685.

Prologue, 14. "th' Association." The Paper of Association found when Shaftesbury was arrested at Thanet House, Aldersgate Street (1681), was considered by the Tories as a plot to exclude the Duke of York from the succession, capture the King, and gain control of the Army, Navy, and Parliament.

Prologue, 19. "a Flail." The Protestant flail, a deadly sort of bludgeon said to have been invented by Stephen College to be carried in one's pocket and used as a protection against sudden assaults of Papists.

Prologue, 21. "Twice in one Age expel the lawful Heir." The first was Charles I; the second was to be James II.

Prologue, 43. "Let Ignoramus Juries." The London grand jury, packed by the
Whigs, on 24 November, 1681, refused to find a bill against Shaftesbury.
The foreman of the jury wrote "ignoramus" on the back of the bill, which
"stately word", as Roger Worth said, "became the appellative of the
whole corrupt practice."

Dramatis Personae, 1. "The King." Henry III of France, who reigned from
1574 to 1589, was Duke of Anjou before becoming king, the son of Catherine de' Medici, the Queen-Mother of the play.

Dramatis Personae, 2. "Duke of Guise." Henry of Lorraine. See Explanatory Notes, THE MASSACRE OF PARIS.

Dramatis Personae, 3. "The Duke of Mayenne." Charles of Lorraine (1554-
1611) was a strong military leader in the religious wars of France. He
acquitted himself especially well at the battle of Moncontour.

Dramatis Personae, 4. "Grillon." The name is from Davila: Monsignor di
Griglione. Actually the name was Crillon.

Dramatis Personae, 5. "The Cardinal of Guise." See Explanatory Notes,
THE MASSACRE OF PARIS.

Dramatis Personae, 6. "Archbishop of Lyons." Peter d'Espinac, a member
of Guise's faction, spared by Henry when Guise was murdered, though he
was at Blois at the time.

Dramatis Personae, 7. "Alphonso Corso." Colonel Alphonso Ornano of the
Isle of Corsica.

Dramatis Personae, 8. "Polin." Apparently Nicholas Poulain, Lieutenant of
the Provost Marshal of the Ile-de-France. He was a member of the
Council of Sixteen but in the pay of Henry. He delivered secrets of the
Council to the King.

Dramatis Personae, 9. "Aumale." Claude of Lorraine, Duke of Aumale.

Dramatis Personae, 10. "Bussy." Bussy d'Amboise (Louis de Clermont
d'Amboise, Sieur de Bussy, 1549-1579), the brilliant gentleman, soldier,
and courtier, who was said to be the lover of Margaret of Valois. Hero
of Chapman's BUSSY D'AMBOIS.

Dramatis Personae, 12. "Malicorne." The name is from Davila.

Dramatis Personae, 21. "Queen-Mother." Catherine de' Medici. See Explanatory Notes, MASSACRE OF PARIS.

Dramatis Personae, 22. "Marmoutier." Davila says she was Marquise de
Noirmoutiers. If so, then her character was suggested by the beautiful
and brilliant Charlotte de Sauve, whose second husband was the Marquis
de Noirmoutiers and for whom Henry, Duke of Guise, was said to have
had a fatal passion.

Act I, i. "The Council of Sixteen." The plotters against the life and government of the spoiled Henry III, parallel to the sixteen Whig peers who petitioned Charles II not to call the Parliament at Oxford. The Sixteen of the
Council represented the sixteen districts of the League in Paris and related themselves to the Duke of Guise; thus Guise completely controlled
Paris.

I, i, 17-18. "a Calvinist Minister"...etc. These two lines, not in Davila, the
source of the passage, were inserted, as Van Lennep observes, to satirize the Whigs. The Admiral was Gaspard de Coligny, great Huguenot
leader. See Explanatory Notes, THE MASSACRE OF PARIS.

I, i, 85-87. "Because we Sheriffs"... etc. The parallel is to the perfidious
London Sheriffs, who stuffed the ballot and incited riots. Charles did

later revoke the charter of the city.

I, i, 93. "And all the Saints are Cov'nanters, and Guisards." The parallel is to the English-Scottish Covenant of 1643. See note on lines 1-2 of the Prologue.

I, i, 105-106. "a Pension from a Foreign Prince"...etc. Here the satire is intended against Shaftesbury, who was supposed to be receiving foreign aid; actually Charles II was, ironically, receiving money from Louis XIV, though Dryden and Lee did not know it.

I, i, 110. "Our City Bands, are twenty thousand strong." Shaftesbury's reputed boast was that he could raise 10,000 Londoners in revolt at a moment's notice.

I, i, 121. "whipping Fryars." The Flagellants were very active in France in the sixteenth century. At Avignon in 1574, for instance, Catherine de' Medici herself led a procession of Black Penitents, and in 1583 Henry III organized a great procession of the Augustinians in which he took part himself, together with all the other dignitaries. Davila is the direct source for the plan here presented to capture the king while unguarded among the friars.

I, i, 127. "Till he exclude his Brother of Navarre." Dryden here deviates from Davila, making the exclusion and succession fit the demands of the Council of Sixteen, that is, Shaftesbury and his faction.

I, i, 182. "and Grisly d'Alva met." The account of this meeting is given in Davila. It took place at Bayonne in 1565: Catherine, Charles IX, and the queen of Spain met with d'Alva.

I, i, 210. "You love his Neece"...etc. The love story emphasized here does not appear in the source. Lee is responsible for it.

I, i, 245. "like great Scipio retire." Scipio Africanus was brought to trial on trumped up charges by his political enemies in 185 A.D., on the anniversary of the battle of Zama. His speech roused the public in his behalf, and he was not prosecuted. Nevertheless, he was so embittered by his country's ingratitude that he retired from public life and secluded himself in his home at Liternum.

I, i, 263. "I see you Court the Crowd." A handsome, affable, gracious young man, the Duke of Monmouth made himself most popular with the people. Guise is here his counterpart.

I, i, 280. "You have your Writers too." In the parallel the English writers were Settle, Shadwell, and Hunt.

I, i, 327. "This is a Man." Cf. Shakespeare's JULIUS CAESAR, V, v, 75. The whole speech is based on Antony's famous last speech.

I, i, 358. "the late puling Francis." Francis II of France. See Explanatory Notes, THE MASSACRE OF PARIS. This passage is excerpted from that play.

II, i, 1. This speech and those immediately following are based directly on Davila.

II, i, 29. "Bisogna coprierse." According to Davila, when the intentions of the Council of Sixteen were discovered and reported to the king, there was much debate as to what was to be done. But the number of adherents to the Council was so great as to make direct attack inadvisable. In the deliberations Catherine de' Medici is said to have quoted the proverb: Bisogna copriersi bene il viso inani che struzzicare il vespaio. It is translated in the lines of the play immediately following.

II, i, 62. "stabbed his Father." See Explanatory Notes, MASSACRE OF PARIS. Brutus was thought by some to have been the son of Caesar.

II, i, 94. "Whor'd Margerite." Princess Marguerite, said to have been mistress to Henry of Guise.

II, i, 96. "Harry at Moncontour." Henry III, at the time Henry of Anjou, on 3 October, 1569, routed the Huguenot forces under Admiral de Coligny.

II, i, 122. "To cast Navarre from the Imperial line." Navarre in the parallel corresponds to James, Duke of York.

II, ii, 54. "and slaughter'd forty thousand Germans." The reference is to Guise's bold defeat of a superior force of Germans near Montagis in 1587.

II, ii, 118. "refuse the Challenge of Navarre." Davila reports that Henry of Navarre challenged Guise to mortal combat in 1585.

II, ii, 134. "and ask his pardon." The whole passage is from THE MASSACRE OF PARIS, wherein Guise refuses to ask pardon of the Admiral, and the Admiral magnanimously asks pardon of Guise.

III, i, 37. "you've plotted on the King." This parallels Shaftesbury's reputed plot in the "Association". The whole passage is a satire on the sheriffs of London.

III, i, 51-55. "Did you not Ages past consign your Lives"...etc. The author is here apparently making use of Hobbes's theory of the social contract.

III, i, 84-85. "Who carv'd our Henry's Image on a Table"...etc. This is an allusion to the defacing of the Duke of York's portrait in the Guildhall in January, 1681/2.

III, i, 367. "to stop his coming." Guise came to Paris against Henry's command; Monmouth returned to London without Charles's permission.

III, ii, 22-24. "the City's up in Arms"...etc. Monmouth was very popular in London upon his return, as was Guise in Paris.

IV, i, 66. "Caesar quell'd 'em." Caesar appeared before the men of the Tenth Legion, who were crying for a discharge and threatening revolt, and with the word "citizens" rather than "soldiers" quieted them; for they replied at once that they were his soldiers and insisted upon following him. (See Suetonius, LIVES OF THE CAESARS, Book I, "The Deified Julius," LXX.)

IV, i, 67. "So Galba thought." Dryden suggests that the situation is similar to that of Galba on the day of his death. (See Tacitus, HISTORY, I, xxxii-xxxv)

IV, ii, 8. "one that preaches to the Crowd." Melanax appears in the guise of a non-conformist preacher, the new version of Satan in a friar's frock.

IV, ii, 40. "there shone a Regal Star." At the birth of Charles II, according to the EIKON BASILIKE, a new star appeared and shone at noon.

IV, ii, 85. "the Neather Skies." Cf. MORGANTE MAGGIORE, xxvi, 82, 89, speech of Ashtoreth on taking leave of Rinaldo. See Scott's note.

IV, ii, 97. "behind yon Eastern hill." Cf. HAMLET, I, i, 166.

IV, ii, 313. "Glass Louisdors." Summers suggests "Brass Louisdors", and notes that the coin was unknown in France at the time of Henry III. Whether it should read "Brass" or "Glass", the point is made: the money is counterfeit.

IV, ii, 322. "Commilitones." Suetonius says that Caesar kept up the morale of his soldiers by addressing them not as _milites_ (soldiers), but as _commilitones_ (comrades). (See THE LIVES OF THE CAESARS, Book I, "The Deified Julius," LXVII)

IV, ii, 359. "Jointed Baby?" A puppet or doll.

IV, ii, 380. "Malchus Ear." Cf. John 18:10: "Then Simon Peter, having a sword, drew it and smote the high priest's servant, and cut off his ear. The servant's name was Malchus."

IV, iii, 2. "Like beaten Roman's underneath the Fork." As Summers notes, Grillon is here thinking of the Roman custom of making vanquished enemies pass under the iugum, a spear laid across two upright spears.

IV, iii, 66. "When loaded with his Gods he took his flight." Henry compares himself to Aeneas, as Aeneas, carrying Anchises and the household gods and leading his son Ascanius, leaves burning Troy. (See AENEID, II, 707 ff.)

V, i, 12. "assemble the States." The Estates General were hardly the equivalent of Parliament, but Dryden treats them as if they were. He is making Charles's Parliament at Oxford, March, 1681, parallel the Assembly at Blois in 1588.

V, i, 39. "he made a sharp reflecting Speech." So did Charles at Oxford.

V, i, 102. "your Brother us'd the Admiral." See THE MASSACRE OF PARIS, wherein Charles IX allowed Guise to assassinate Admiral de Coligny. Dryden and Lee are aware of the irony of Guise receiving the same fate he had previously meted out.

V, i, 122. "when th' Offender can be judg'd by Laws." According to Hobbes, the King is not subject to the laws that he governs by.

V, i, 132. "I never could forgive?" The parallel here breaks down. Charles never planned to have Monmouth assassinated. Indeed he was quite solicitous of the Duke's personal welfare.

V, i, 190. "Five hundred popular figures on a Row." It is said that Charles, in passing from his throne to the dressing room immediately following his dissolution of the Parliament at Oxford, remarked that "It is better to have one King than five hundred." Here is joined the conflict over supremacy of the crown and supremacy of Parliament.

V, i, 231. "your nauseous, blund'ring Ballad-wits." The Whig writers, such as Shadwell and Settle.

V, ii, 35. "says he must speak with you." Here the plot appears to follow in some detail Rosset's HISTOIRES TRAGIQUES. (See Summers' note, V, 482.)

V, ii, 47. "I'le ramm thee in some knotted Oak"...etc. Cf. Shakespeare's TEMPEST, I, ii, 274-293.

V, ii, 77. "but half a day, an hour"... Cf. Marlowe's DR. FAUSTUS, Scene xiv, 88 et passim.

V, iv, 12. This speech of Revol's (one of the King's secretaries) follows Davila exactly.

V, iv, 35. "Dies." The stage direction here seems to go further than either Dryden or Lee intended in the parallel. They would hardly suggest that Monmouth should be assassinated as Guise was.

Epilogue. "Spoken by Mrs. Cooke." Mrs. Sarah Cooke was prominent on the London stage from 1677 until her death in 1688--especially as a speaker of prologues and epilogues.

Epilogue, 3. "Yet no one Man was meant." Thus Guise may possibly represent Shaftesbury as well as Monmouth. Certainly such a disclaimer was necessary to clear the poets from suggestion that Monmouth be assassinated.

Epilogue, 30. "Jack Ketch." The common executioner. He became hangman in 1663. Among others, he is said to have executed such notables as Monmouth and Lord Russel.

Epilogue, 33. "We Trimmers." The small party of political moderates who tried to effect a compromise between Whigs and Tories. They met with little success, for they seemed always to be merely vacillating. Among them was Lord Halifax.

Another Epilogue, 1. "Two Houses joyn'd." The Theatre Royal was compelled to close in April, 1682. A union was effected between the two houses in May, but the United Companies did not begin joint production until November. Possibly this play was the first they brought upon the stage.

Another Epilogue, 5. "Bilbo Gallants." Young dandies who stand ready to draw a sword at the slightest provocation.

Another Epilogue, 8. "turn to Marybone." Marylebone Fields, well-known as dueling grounds.

Another Epilogue, 14. "their four Shillings." The price of admission to a box.

NOTES

INTRODUCTION TO CONSTANTINE THE GREAT

1 R. G. Ham, OTWAY AND LEE, BIOGRAPHY FROM A BAROQUE AGE (1931), pp. 206-208.

2 A. L. Cooke and Thomas B. Stroup, "The Political Implications in Lee's CONSTANTINE THE GREAT," JEGP, XLIX (Oct., 1950), 506.

3 The dating of the first production of the play is determined by a note written by Malone in his copy of the first edition of CONSTANTINE. Under the prologue he wrote: "Published first in folio 12 November, 1683.... In Mr. Bindley's collection." The note refers to the single half-sheet folio edition of the prologue and epilogue of the play which was published just as it came on the stage or immediately after. Hence the date given is c. 12 November, 1683. Langbaine merely gives the date of the first quarto and the BIO-GRAPHIA DRAMATICA follows him. Genest assigns 1684 as the date of first performance. It probably did stay upon the stage for the season, 1683-84.

4 Langbaine, p. 322.

5 Genest, I, 418.

6 Van Lennep, II, 622.

6a Zonares, Joannes, and Zosimus, HISTOIRE ROMAINE, ÉCRITE PAR XI-PHILIN, PAR ZONARE, ET PAR ZOSIME, transl. par Louis Cousin (Paris, 1678).

7 A. W. Ward, A HISTORY OF ENGLISH DRAMATIC LITERATURE TO THE DEATH OF QUEEN ANNE, III, 410; Van Lennep, II, 625.

8 Charles Dibden, COMPLETE HISTORY OF THE ENGLISH STAGE, IV, 187.

9 "Plays Written by Mr. Nathaniel Lee," THE RETROSPECTIVE REVIEW, III, (1821), 266.

10 Genest, I, 413.

11 R. Mosen, "Über Nathaniel Lee's Leben und Werke," ENGLISCHE STUD-IEN, II (1879), 437.

12 H. M. Sanders, "The Plays of Nat. Lee Gent.," TEMPLE BAR, CXXIV (1901), 504.

13 Ward, III, 411.

14 Bonamy Dobrée, RESTORATION TRAGEDY, p. 123.

15 William Archer, THE OLD DRAMA AND THE NEW (Boston, 1923), p. 152.

16 Malcolm Elwin, THE PLAYGOER'S HANDBOOK TO RESTORATION DRAMA, p. 131.

17 Montague Summers, THE COMPLETE WORKS OF THOMAS OTWAY, 3 volumes (Nonesuch Press), III, 327.

18 Van Lennep, II, 629.

19 See Day and Murrie #284. It is listed as appearing in Songbook #78 (134) p. 14, the music by Farmer.

20 These copies are identified as follows:
   Q_1(KU), loosely bound in stiff brown paper, has an incompletely printed line on E1^V, one on E3^V, and one at the bottom of G1^r. On [A1^V] in the right lower corner in brown or faded black ink is the word "at", encircled.
   Q_1(DFo 1) is bound in the Kean collection #1, with SOPHONISBA and others of Lee's plays.
   Q_1(DFo 2) is the "Genest" copy, unbound, with "1st Edition" written in ink on the title-page.

Q_1(DFo 3) is bound in ORIGINAL EDITIONS OF 17TH CEN-
TURY DRAMATISTS, with R. Gould, TO THE SOCIETY OF
BEAUX ESPRITS, 1687. It lacks a title-page.
Q1(DFo 4) is bound in volume II of MISCELLANY OF OLD
PLAYS, together with LUCIUS JUNIUS BRUTUS and other
plays. This copy lacks B2-3.

21 See J. C. Ghosh, THE WORKS OF THOMAS OTWAY (1932), I, 65-66, for a
discussion of the authorship of the prologue and of the epilogue of the play.
They both appeared together (according to Malone's note in his copy of the
first quarto now in the Bodleian, on 12 November, 1683) on the two sides of
a single half-sheet folio printed for C. Tebroc, without mention of authorship; hence they were at first supposed to have been written by the author of
the play, Lee himself. But in the following year, on one side of a similar
half-sheet appeared "A True Copy of the Epilogue to Constantine the Great.
That which was first published being surreptitious and false printed. Written by Mr. Dryden." The publisher was Jacob Tonson. Tonson also attributed the epilogue to Dryden in his edition of the MISCELLANY POEMS, Part
I, 3rd edition, 1702. In his collected edition of Otway in 1712 Tonson attributed the prologue to Otway. On the other hand, it may be noted that R.
Wellington failed to mark either the epilogue or the prologue as being the
work of Otway or Dryden, suggesting, at least, that he had no reason for
regarding them as from any other pen than that of the author of the play.
Häfele accepts Tonson's attribution. Although the present editors do not regard Wellington's failure to attribute these to other poets than Lee as conclusive evidence that he knew they were Lee's, the editors do not, on the
other hand, see at all conclusive Tonson's attribution of the prologue to Otway. The appearance of the broadside would seem fairly conclusive evidence that Tonson knew what he was doing in saying that the epilogue was
Dryden's, but his inclusion without comment of the prologue in Otway's collected works seems not sufficient proof that it belonged there.

It seems all the more doubtful that the latter attribution is valid when one
looks at the internal evidence. The prologue to THEODOSIUS has for its
subject matter the neglect of poets, their mistreatment and their penury,
essentially the same theme as the prologue for CONSTANTINE. Now, ad-
mittedly this is not an uncommon subject for prologues and epilogues. Yet
here the prologue for CONSTANTINE echoes that of THEODOSIUS, a prologue unquestioned as Lee's. The couplet in the first,

> Think what penurious Masters you have serv'd:
> Tasso run mad, and noble Spencer starv'd:

is obviously developed in the latter:

> Tell 'em how Spencer starv'd, how Cowley mourn'd,
> How Butler's Faith and Service was return'd.

Now it is just possible that Otway, bitterly feeling his mistreatment, might
echo Lee's lines; but it seems more probable that Lee was here rephrasing
his own earlier lines, perhaps not altogether unwittingly. This would seem
to be doubly reasonable because of the obvious affinity between the opening
scenes of the two plays in question. The opening spectacular scene of CON-
STANTINE is connected with the opening spectacle of THEODOSIUS, Constantine himself appearing in both and the sign from heaven being employed
in both.

In view of this positive internal evidence to support Lee's authorship and the lack of any contrary evidence other than Tonson's casual inclusion of the piece among Otway's works, the present editors assign the prologue to Lee and include it among his works.

CONSTANTINE THE GREAT

Prologue. For a discussion of the authorship see the preceding note. The speaker, Mr. Goodman, played the role of Annibal. He was one of the most colorful actors of the time, being notable for his duels and his improvidence, as well as his tragic roles. He achieved a reputation as Alexander in THE RIVAL QUEENS and as Pharnaces in MITHRIDATES.

Prologue, 4-5. "That when its Spirit"...etc. See Genesis, 1, passim.

Prologue, 35. "how Spencer starv'd, how Cowley mourn'd." Lee sets forth the popular error that Spenser died in poverty, if not indeed of starvation. Jonson had said that he perished from lack of bread, and Camden, John Weever, Phineas Fletcher, and many another popularized the idea. Abraham Cowley in "The Complaint" (1683) spoke of himself as the melancholy poet, much lamenting his neglect. He did fail to gain patronage. Cf. Prologue to THEODOSIUS, line 36. Here Lee refers to Spenser's starving.

Prologue, 36. "How Butler's Faith".... Samuel Butler (1612-1680), writer of HUDIBRAS, began and continued his career as a supporter of the crown. His neglect by the crown became almost the literary scandal of the age. Though Charles was lavish of his praises and promises, he did nothing to relieve the poverty of his most excellent defender.

Dramatis Personae, 1. "Constantine" (288 ?--337). Called "The Great" because of his activities in behalf of the Roman Empire and his recognition of Christianity as the official religion of the Empire. Through an alliance with Licinius he made himself secure as a joint ruler of the Empire; then, with Licinius' growing indolence and his persecutions of the Christians, Constantine turned upon him, defeated him and ultimately put him to death. Constantine's second wife was Fausta. He is said to have banished and executed Crispus, his son, because of accusations brought against him by Fausta. Later he put her to death, when he found out that her accusations were false. Legend also has it that for these deeds Constantine was stricken with leprosy, but that he repented of his crimes, received absolution from Sylvester I, and was baptized. Lee shows familiarity with these stories, making use especially of the father-son-mistress triangle so popular in the heroic plays, though he is by no means interested in adhering closely either to history or legend.

Dramatis Personae, 6. "Arius." A Greek theologian who died in 336. He was responsible for the Arian heresy, which was settled, in so far as the Western Church was concerned, against Arius at the Council of Nicaea in 325. Constantine presided over this Council. Hence the bad reputation of Arius among Western Christians. The chief dispute was over the nature of the God-head, Arius maintaining that the three persons were not co-equal or co-eternal, that Christ is not of the same substance with the Father nor his equal.

I, i. "Constantine sleeping in a Pavilion"...etc. This description of the setting and the ensuing action is based on the well-known story, deriving originally from Eusebius' life of Constantine, in which Constantine in 312 moved directly upon Rome following his defeat of Manentius' generals. This bold stroke came as the result of a miracle in which Constantine had a vision of the cross aflame at midday and with it in the sky the famous

motto "In hoc signo vince." It was said that this miracle brought about
the conversion of Constantine. This scene and setting is to be compared
with the opening scene of THEODOSIUS.

I, i, 66. "contracted to Maximinus daughter." Fausta, who became Constantine's wife, according to history. She was the daughter of Maximianus,
with the spelling of whose name Lee was apparently not familiar.

I, i, 123-24. "With those Auxiliar Legions"...etc. The situation is roughly
parallel to the political situation in England in 1678. At the time Charles
had 20,000 men under the command of Monmouth in Scotland. A dispute
between Charles and Parliament developed over whether such force was
necessary and whether Parliament should provide money to pay their
wages, which were in arrears. See Cooke and Stroup, "Political Implications in Lee's CONSTANTINE THE GREAT," JEGP, XLIX (1950), 514.

I, i, 126. "Which by your Brother were in Forum Read." In the political parallel the brother would be the Duke of York.

I, i, 128-30. "Our Courts of Justice Rob'd; Old Rights"...etc. The situation
described here was, from the Whig point of view, parallel to the situation
in England at the time. Arius represents satirically the Whig position.

I, i, 146. "in Dark Cabals they met." The phrase is characteristic of the political intrigues of the time at which the play was written.

I, i, 148-150. "Lycinius, who that Night"...etc. Licinius was at first consul
with Constantine; later Constantine wrested power from him, partly on
account of his persecution of Christians.

I, i, 153. "Tell 'em their City shall be Ashes first." Charles had much trouble with Whiggish London, wherein were packed juries, corrupt sheriffs,
and the headquarters of Shaftesbury. He threatened the revocation of the
charter.

I, i, 162. "My Brother here." In the political allegory Dalmatius, brother of
Constantine, would represent the Duke of York, brother of Charles.

I, i, 166. "Rockt into a Calm." The political allusion is to the triumph of the
Tories in 1681-82.

I, i, 172. "The Subtlest Snake, the softest Civil Villain." This line and the
entire speech of Dalmatius is a characterization of Shaftesbury. He was
considered the source of all opposition to the crown, and the reference in
line 182 to his hand would seem to be to the "Association paper."

I, i, 200. "Lycinius was my Friend." Historically, Licinius was consul with
Constantine; together Licinius and Constantine ruled the Empire until Licinius became ruthless and violent, particularly in his persecutions.

I, ii, 14. "I was myself bred up in Blood and Wars." It is possible that Lycinius represents Algernon Sidney, who was referred to by the Royalists
as rash, uncouth, and scornful of the arts. The wars in the allegory
were, of course, the Puritan revolts. The mention of Nero in line 19 is
perhaps a reference to Cromwell.

II, i, 3. "Men of our Make so poorly hide a Murder"...etc. This is perhaps
a reference in the allegory to the discovery of the body of Sir Edmund Bury
Godfrey in a field near London. He was supposedly murdered by the
Catholics, though Lee here suggests that the Whigs committed the crime.

II, i, 13. "I tainted Infant Julian." Julian the Apostate (Flavius Claudius Juli-
anus, 331-363), the Roman emperor, nephew of Constantine, though
reared a Christian, was early attracted to the ancient religion and philosophy and rejected Christianity. His definite conversion to paganism is

attributed to the neoplatonist Maximus of Ephesus, not to Arius as is here
suggested.

II, i, 26. "To stab Dalmatius." Possible reference to the Rye-House Plot and
the plans to kill the King and the Duke of York.

II, i, 117. "procure his Picture." The device of the picture is evidently drawn
from Otway's DON CARLOS (1676).

II, i, 149-50. "I'll stay till Age / Has snow'd a hundred Winters on my Head."
The passage is an echo from Donne's Song, "Go and Catch a Falling Star."
The line is "Till Age snow white hairs on thee."

II, i, 200. "Age will talk." Cf. RIVAL QUEENS, I, i, 59. "Yet the Old man
must talk."

II, i, 317. "I'll have him Executed in their view." This could be a reference in
the parallel to the execution of Lord Russell in front of his father's home
in Lincoln's Inn Fields, 21 July, 1683.

III, i, 82. "Hunt not the Bubble Beauty." Cf. AS YOU LIKE IT, II, vii, 152.
"Seeking the bubble reputation, etc."

III, i, 122. "Tongue---kill her, go: or swear and be forsworn." It is possible
that here is veiled reference to the notorious Dr. Tonge, Titus Oates' collaborator, so frequently forsworn in the Popish Plot case.

III, i, 123-25. "Heav'n That a Man"...etc. Cf. RIVAL QUEENS, I, i, 57.
Clytus, speaking of Alexander's infatuation and his weakness for women
exclaims, "O that a Face should thus bewitch a Soul!"

III, i, 170. "the purpos'd murther of my Brother." Paralleled in the Rye-
House Plot to kill James, Duke of York.

III, i, 259. "Whatever comes, Remember he's thy Son." Charles might well
have said this of Monmouth. The statement well represents his attitude.

III, ii, 144-45. "And over-wrought me for my Empires Safety"...etc. Constantine here tricks Fausta into a confession, a device that comes directly
from Racine's MITHRIDATE. See Van Lennep, II, 622.

III, ii, 219-25. "No more by false reports to be abus'd"--- etc. The lines are
particularly applicable to the outcome of the Popish Plot.

IV, i, 106-09. "for I must not call thee Son"...etc. The lines might well be
recognized by the audience as referring to Charles in his upbraidings of
Monmouth.

IV, ii, 56. "A plot upon thy Father." The passage might well apply to
Charles' consideration of the acts of Monmouth.

V, i, 28-30. "He has all the marks, we Virgins reckon Ominous..." etc. The
description of Arius does not quite fit Shaftesbury, as Van Lennep suggests, though it might well be taken as referring to him. Apparently
Shaftesbury did not have red hair, but he was sickly, emaciated, and
lecherous.

V, ii, 37. "This Horrid, Barbarous, and Unnatural Murder." Cf. HAMLET,
I, v, 25 ff.

V, ii, 105. "By Miracles from Heav'n to be converted." See the opening scene
of the play. Constantine was said to have been converted by the vision
from heaven.

V, ii, 247. "Behold the poison'd Bath." The poisoned bath, like the device of
the picture, is to be found in Otway's DON CARLOS.

V, ii, 315. "the Bath's not Poison'd." Arius' last-minute trick here reminds
one of the trick of the Cardinal in THE DUCHESS OF MALFI or of that of
the Cardinal in Shirley's THE CARDINAL.

V, ii, 328. "It is the hand of Heav'n, not mine that gives her." Here Lee
twists history in order to give the play a happy conclusion. Fausta was
Constantine's wife.

Epilogue, 8. "And every Trimmer"...etc. The word derives from the seaman's vocabulary, to trim a ship, that is, to set in order or to adjust sail
to the direction of wind and course. The "Trimmers" were those who
refused to take sides politically, trying to maintain a nice balance between
the two parties. See THE CHARACTER AND HUMOUR OF A TRIMMER,
printed in Roger L'Estrange's OBSERVATOR, 1684, and the Marquis of
Halifax's celebrated reply to it in his CHARACTER OF A TRIMMER,
which circulated in manuscript before it was published in 1688.

Epilogue, 10. "When Clause was King." King of the Beggars in Fletcher and
Massinger's BEGGAR'S BUSH. His real name was Gerrard.

Epilogue, 22. "calls them Teckelites." "Teckelites" was a nickname given to
the Whigs in 1683, for they were alleged to sympathize with the followers
of Count Teckely (Imre Tökölyi, 1656-1705), the Lutheran Hungarian patriot who revolted against the Catholic government and joined the Turks
against Austria.

Epilogue, 32-33. "They believe not the last Plot"...etc. Apparently the
meaning is that the Trimmers believed in neither the Rye-House nor the
Popish Plot.

OCCASIONAL POEMS

ON THE DEATH OF THE DUKE OF ALBEMARLE.
This poem was published without title on X4^r-Y1^r of MUSARUM CANTA-
BRIGIENSIUM, 1670. The title-page of this book appears on page 4 and runs as
follows: Musarum Cantabrigiensium/T H R E N O DI A /IN / O BI T U M /Incom-
parabilis Herois ac D u c i s/Illustrissimi/G E O R G I I /DUCIS ALBAEMARLAE,/
Regiarum Copiarum/ARCHISTRATEGI,/Regis, & Regnorum Magnæ Britanniæ/
Felicissimi Restauratoris./[double rule] /CANTABRIGIAE,/Ex Officina Joann.
Hayes, celeberrimæ Academiæ/Typographi, 1670. The particular copy from
which this text is taken is in the University of Texas Library. This copy may
be identified by what appears to be the numeral 3 in ink above the letter C in
Cantabrigiensium. Also, to the right of I N in the third line appear in ink these
words: Vol 4 Num 3. The book is a quarto.
    The text is clear and well printed.
    George Monck (or Monk), Duke of Albemarle, was born in 1608 and died
"like a Roman general and soldier, standing almost up in his chair..." 3 January, 1670. His funeral, of great pomp and circumstance, was not held until
April, 1670. In addition to the volume of verses from Cambridge that was
brought out in his honor, there was one from Oxford, a folio, appearing under
the title: EPICEDA UNIVERSITATIS OXONIENSIS IN OBITUM GEORGII DUCIS
ALBEMARLIAE, 1670.

TO THE PRINCE AND PRINCESS OF ORANGE, UPON THEIR MARRIAGE.
    The text of this poem is taken from EXAMEN POETICUM: BEING THE
THIRD PART OF MISCELLANY POEMS (London: Jacob Tonson, 1693), pp.
168-174; the copy used, by permission, is that in the Folger Shakespeare Library. Presumably the poem would have first appeared as a broadside at the
time of the marriage in 1677; but no copy of such a broadside has been located.
A shorter and much altered version of this poem appeared under the title "On
the Marriage of the Prince and Princess of Orange" in volume III of POEMS ON
AFFAIRS OF STATE. FROM 1640. TO THIS PRESENT YEAR 1704 (London,
1704); this version is printed in the present edition following the 1693 text. It
does not seem to be a revision of the 1693 version, but possibly represents an
earlier draft of the poem, as found in a manuscript or early broadside.
    Negotiations for the marriage of William and Mary were begun by Sir Wil-
liam Temple, then Ambassador at the Hague, in 1676. In October, 1677, en-
couraged by Danby, William came to England to press his suit for Mary's hand.
The marriage was solemnized on November 4, 1677. William and his bride returned to the Hague in December, 1677.

TO MR. DRYDEN, ON HIS POEM OF PARADICE.
    This tribute to Dryden was first printed on A4^{rv} of the first edition of
Dryden's THE STATE OF INNOCENCE, AND FALL OF MAN (London: Henry
Herringman, 1677). The fulsome praise which Lee gives Dryden for his tagged
version of Milton's PARADISE LOST shows little critical judgment, and his low
estimate of Milton justly merits condemnation. Lee was obviously swept away
by his over-enthusiastic admiration for his friend. Dryden returned the compli-
ment later in this same year in his poem TO MR. LEE, ON HIS ALEXANDER,
prefixed to the first edition of THE RIVAL QUEENS (1677).

48-51. These lines seem to forecast Dryden's ABSALOM AND ACHITO-
PHEL, which Dryden did not begin to write until 1680, according to Tate's ac-
count. The reference in line 50 is to Cowley's unfinished religious epic DAVID-
EIS (1656).

TO THE UNKNOWN AUTHOUR OF THIS EXCELLENT POEM.

This poem first appeared on an extra, unsigned leaf inserted in the second
London edition of ABSALOM AND ACHITOPHEL (London: W. Davis, 1681). The
text here printed is that which appears in Jacob Tonson's MISCELLANY POEMS
(London, 1684), where the poem is first attributed to Lee.

24. "Charming Annabel." Lee is referring to Anne, Duchess of Buccleuch
and Monmouth, wife of the Duke of Monmouth, and a former patroness of Dryden.

TO THE DUKE ON HIS RETURN.

This poem was first printed as a broadside by Jacob Tonson in 1682. The
text here reproduced is that of this broadside. The copy used is that of the Huntington Library. On the front page in the upper right-hand corner is the number
128, and under the word "RETURN" in the title is written in ink the date 29. May.
1682.

James, Duke of York, under orders from Charles II, had left the Kingdom
in May, 1679. Since 1680 he had been in Scotland, whence he was allowed to return to London in March, 1682. On this occasion he did not bring the Duchess
back with him, but went to Scotland in May to fetch her. He came back to England with her by the end of the month. The date written on the Huntington copy
is probably that of James's arrival in London.

4. "your Wrack proclaim." The reference is to the wreck of the frigate
Gloucester off the Yorkshire coast, when the Duke was returning to Scotland to
bring back the Duchess. It is said that on this occasion he did not conduct himself as became the great seaman he was reputed to be.

34. "the Virgin Princess." The reference is to the Princess Anne, who
was not married until the following year. She had gone twice in 1681 to Scotland
to visit her parents.

ON THEIR MAJESTIES CORONATION.

This poem first appeared as a broadside printed by Abel Roper in 1689.
The text of this edition follows that of the broadside.

The Coronation of William and Mary took place on 11 April, 1689, Bishop
Compton of London performing the ceremony and Bishop Burnet (who had come
over from the Hague with them) preaching the coronation sermon.

Lee had already courted the favor of these monarchs with a poem on their
marriage (1677). In the year of the coronation he also published THE PRIN-
CESS OF CLEVE with a special prologue praising William. Even though Lee
had been for a time an ardent Tory, with the coming of William and Mary he returned to his old politics and apparently succeeded in gaining the good will of the
sovereigns in that they attended the performance of THE MASSACRE OF PARIS
later this same year.

ON THE DEATH OF MRS. BEHN.

This poem first appeared as a broadside printed in 1689 for Abel Roper.
The text followed here is from a copy of this broadside in the University of
Texas Library.

Mrs. Aphra Behn (1640-89), traveler, dramatist, government agent, novelist, poet and pamphleteer, was one of the first professional women writers in England. Indeed, she has been called the George Sand of the Restoration. She is remembered for such plays as THE FORC'D MARRIAGE (1671), and ABDEL-AZAR (1676), and for such novels as OROONOKO, based in part upon her experiences as a child and young woman in the West Indies. She was especially remembered for her kindnesses to the younger dramatists such as Otway and Lee. A warm-hearted, industrious, witty, emancipated woman, her death deserved the notice it here received.

21. "Flatman thy mate." The reference may be to Thomas Flatman (1637-1688), but so far as is known, except for this strange reference by Lee, Mrs. Behn had no connection with him.

LOVE'S OPPORTUNITY NEGLECTED.

The text of this poem is taken from volume four of MISCELLANY POEMS, Tonson, 1716, where it is attributed to Lee. For full bibliographical description, see Macdonald #49. The actual copy followed, by permission, is that of the Folger Shakespeare Library. The date of composition is not known. Assuredly the poem adds nothing to Lee's reputation.

A SONG. WRIT BY THE FAMOUS MR. NAT. LEE.

The text of this poem is taken from Thomas D'Urfey's WIT AND MIRTH; OR PILLS TO PURGE MELANCHOLY (London: J. Tonson, 1719) volume V, pages 140-41. We are indebted for this text to Mr. Alan L. McLeod of Sidney, Australia.

TO THE AUTHOR & TRANSLATOUR OF THE FOLLOWING BOOK. *

This poem, signed "N. L.," appeared with two other commendatory poems, signed "R. D." and "N. T.," at the front of Henry Dickinson's translation of Father Richard Simon's HISTOIRE CRITIQUE DU VIEUX TESTAMENT, published by Jacob Tonson in 1682. The three poems did not appear in a second edition of this same translation published the same year by Walter Davis in Amen Corner. Father Simon's HISTOIRE was the famous work which called forth Dryden's RELIGIO LAICI. The editors are indebted to Mr. Alan McLeod of Sidney, Australia, for the text of this poem.

1. The Jews having been freed from their captivity by Darius, returned to Jerusalem, where Esdras, the scribe, priest, and reader of the Law of Moses, was commissioned by Artaxerxes to re-establish the Law. See I Esdras, Chapter VIII, of THE APOCRYPHA.

17. "URIM & the THUMMIM." That is, "the manifestation and the truth." See I Esdras, Chapter V. Upon the return of the Jews from captivity to Jerusalem, certain of the priests were considered usurpers of the priesthood. It was therefore decreed that they should be excluded from their offices until "there arose up a high priest wearing Urim and Thummim." This high priest was Esdras.